CW01368949

Explorations in Transactional Analysis:
The Meech Lake Papers

To Celia —

Many of these papers were written from both mind & heart. I hope you find moments in these pages that both stimulate & touch your mind & heart.

Enjoy!

Bill
1/09

Explorations in Transactional Analysis: The Meech Lake Papers

William F. Cornell

TA Press
Pleasanton, California

© 2008 William F. Cornell and the
International Transactional Analysis Association, Inc.

All rights reserved. No part of this publication may be reproduced,
stored in a retrieval system, or transmitted in any form or by any means,
electronic, mechanical, photocopying, recording, or otherwise,
without the prior permission of the publisher.

Photos © Tim Fabian 2006/2008.
All Rights Reserved, www.timfabian.com

Printed in the United States of America
ISBN 978-0-89489-007-9

Published by TA Press
2186 Rheem Dr., #B-1
Pleasanton, California 94588-2775, U.S.A.
Phone: 925-600-8110
Fax: 925-600-9112
E-mail: itaa@itaa-net.org
Web site: www.itaa-net.org

To Seth, Noah, and Caleb
with my love
and with much pride for the men you have become

———————————

And to Robin Fryer and Suzanne Robinson,
without whom this book would not exist

Contents

Preface xi

Section I: The Experience of Psychotherapy

Introduction 3

1. What Am I Getting Myself Into?
   William F. Cornell 5

2. Setting the Therapeutic Stage: The Initial Sessions
   William F. Cornell 16

3. Impasse and Intimacy: Applying Berne's Concept of Script Protocol
   William F. Cornell and N. Michel Landaiche, III 23

4. The Intricate Intimacies of Psychotherapy and Questions of Self-Disclosure
   William F. Cornell 40

Section II: Questions of Theory

Introduction 51

5. Life Script Theory: A Critical Review from a Developmental Perspective
   William F. Cornell 53

6. Therapeutic Relatedness in Transactional Analysis: The Truth of Love or the Love of Truth
   William F. Cornell and Frances Bonds-White 66

7. In the Terrain of the Unconscious: The Evolution of a Transactional Analysis Therapist
   William F. Cornell 78

8. What Do You Say If You Don't Say "Unconscious"?: Dilemmas Created for Transactional Analysts by Berne's Shift Away from the Language of Unconscious Experience
   William F. Cornell 90

9. Nonconscious Processes and Self-Development: Key Concepts from Eric Berne and Christopher Bollas
   William F. Cornell and N. Michel Landaiche, III 97

10. Cognitive and Social Functions of Emotions: A Model for Transactional Analysis Counselor Training
   William F. Cornell and Jenni Hine 114

11. If Berne Met Winnicott: Transactional Analysis and Relational Analysis
   William F. Cornell 125

Section III: The Body in Psychotherapy

Introduction 133

12. Why Body Psychotherapy?: A Conversation
   William F. Cornell and N. Michel Landaiche, III 135

13. Babies, Brains, and Bodies: Somatic Foundations of the Child Ego State
   William F. Cornell 141

14. "My Body Is Unhappy": Somatic Foundations of Script and Script Protocol
   William F. Cornell 159

15. Solitude, Self, and Subjectivity: Discussant Paper to Lewis Aron's "Relational Psychoanalysis: The Evolution of a Tradition"
   William F. Cornell 171

16. Body-Centered Psychotherapy
   William F. Cornell 176

17. Consequences of Childhood Bodily Abuse: A Clinical Model for Affective Interventions
   William F. Cornell and Karen A. Olio 199

Section IV: Supervision in Practice

Introduction 215

18. Live and in Limbo: A Case Study of an In-Person Transactional Analysis Consultation
   William F. Cornell, Carole Shadbolt, and Robert Norton 217

19. Teaching Transactional Analysts to Think Theoretically
   William F. Cornell and Marilyn J. Zalcman 229

20. Dual Relationships in Transactional Analysis: Training, Supervision, and Therapy
   William F. Cornell 238

Section V: Perspectives in Ethics

Introduction 251

21. Teaching People What Matters
    William F. Cornell 253

22. The Inevitability of Uncertainty, the Necessity of Doubt, and the Development of Trust
    William F. Cornell 257

23. A Community for Thinking
    William F. Cornell 265

24. On Learning, Knowing, and Telling: Reflections on Clinical Research and Writing
    William F. Cornell 268

25. Touch and Boundaries in Transactional Analysis: Ethical and Transferential Considerations
    William F. Cornell 275

26. Boundaries or Barriers: Who Is Protecting Whom? A Personal Essay/Book Review
    William F. Cornell 283

27. Thinking about Suicide: Standing in the Face of Despair
    William F. Cornell 290

28. Reflections on Violence
    William F. Cornell and Caleb Cornell 295

Epilogue

Looking Back/Looking Ahead
    William F. Cornell 303

Additional Publications by William F. Cornell 305

About the Author and Coauthors 307

About the International Transactional Analysis Association 308

Index 309

Preface

Nearly every therapist likes to think that the patient chose him and his profession because in this choice at least he was rational, intelligent, and discriminating, no matter how confused he might be about everything else. This feeling of being chosen on merit—the merit of one's profession and personal merit as well—is a healthy one, and is one of the rewards of our vocation. Every therapist, therefore, is entitled to bask in it and to enjoy it to the utmost—for about five or seven minutes. After that, he should put it on the shelf with his other trophies and diplomas, and forget it permanently if he wants the patient to get well. (Berne, 1972, pp. 303-304)

From its beginning with Eric Berne's humanism and his challenge to the authoritarianism of the psychoanalysis of his day, transactional analysis has sought to add rapid and practical value to people's lives—not only in clinical offices and hospitals but also in the places where people work, live, and love. Early in my career, I had the good fortune to be the director of a large community mental health center. This was back in the day when our professions were known as "the mental health fields," in contrast to the contemporary cast of "behavioral health." Nearly everyone on the staff was trained in transactional analysis. The center offered long-term, dynamic psychotherapy; short-term counseling; group treatment; and a coffee house for adolescents that they ran using transactional analysis principles for problem solving. We taught transactional analysis groups and classes in the schools, local churches, and in programs for young mothers. It was an extraordinary time. While I practice and train now primarily as a psychotherapist, many of the papers in this book will reflect that perspective and the practice of transactional analysis in diverse settings.

The subtitle of this book, "The Meech Lake Papers," reflects the context for the writing of many of the chapters in this book. Twenty years ago I received an unexpected phone call from Suzanne Robinson, a transactional analysis consultant and trainer in Ottawa, Canada. I barely knew Suzanne, but she had read one of my *Transactional Analysis Journal* articles, in which I critiqued the theory of script formation (Chapter 1 in this volume). She said she was impressed with the article and that she imagined I had much more to say. I agreed that I did, and she asked how I found the time to do so much reading and writing. I told her it was not easy. Then Suzanne made a proposal: She had a cottage on Meech Lake outside of Ottawa and offered to fly me up for a week by myself to work uninterrupted on my writing. I accepted. Suzanne's cottage is on the far side of the lake, accessible only by boat, and it has no electricity, a perfect place for creative reflection and focused attention.

That was the beginning of a wonderful tradition. For 2 decades now I have gone to Meech Lake every summer for a writing retreat. The basic routine never varies. I arrive laden with books and journal articles to read. Every morning I get up early and make a really good pot of coffee. I read and write in a small cottage separate from the main house. When the sun begins to go down, I go down to the main house, cook dinner for Suzanne (unless Suzanne's husband, Vince Gilpin, is there and he cooks), and we go to the boat house roof to eat, drink, and talk about what I am working on far into the dark. Having this special time for reading and writing has been an extraordinary gift.

In the beginning, I usually wrote by hand, outlining material for two or three articles that I would then finish during subsequent years. Now, of course, I have my laptop and can work directly on the computer. Most of the articles in this volume had their start at Meech Lake.

The subtitle of this book also reflects another aspect of these papers. Meech Lake was the location for a major Canadian conference in the late 1980s to address issues related to the sovereignty of the province of Quebec. French speaking and deeply identified with French rather than British culture, Quebec had been seeking more independence, some people even arguing for secession from Canada. The Meech Lake Accord, drawn up in 1987, was the first official document (although it ultimately failed) to bridge the cultural gap, to recognize Quebec's status as a distinct society, and to offer some autonomy within the Canadian provincial structure. I have quite identified with that task in my writing as so many of my papers strive to bridge the gap between seemingly distinct, irreconcilable, and often competitive frames of reference.

In looking back over the course of one's writings, there are endless numbers of people who could be acknowledged for their influence. Many are people I have read but never met. However, three people within the transactional analysis community stand out for me. Suzanne Robinson, for obvious reasons, is one. Rebecca Trautmann is another. While editor of the *Transactional Analysis Journal*, Rebecca invited me to write for the *TAJ*. Initially I declined, but she persisted, coaching my through my first article. Then I was hooked. The third person is someone I can never thank enough: Robin Fryer. She and I have now collaborated on *The Script* newsletter and the *Transactional Analysis Journal* for many years. It has been a deeply satisfying partnership. More than any other person, Robin has skills that have contributed to my evolution as a writer. Her careful attention and critical eye is in the background of every paper in this book. Finally, many of the articles presented here are coauthored. There is a particular challenge and satisfaction in coauthorship. My coauthors (with the exception of my son, Caleb) are colleagues with whom I have worked closely, often training and teaching together. Our wrestling with some technical or theoretical issue has produced many of the chapters of this volume.

I read somewhere that Michel Foucault (or perhaps it was Jacques Derrida) said that he wrote in order to find out what he thought. I remember thinking to myself at the time, "Well, I'm glad it helped him, but his writing sure doesn't help me to understand what he thinks." And it raised the question for me, why do I write? I realized that I write when I am not satisfied with my work. Almost without exception, every article in this volume began as an effort to grapple with some area of dissatisfaction in my work and my thinking—carrying me off first to the library, then to discussion or arguments with colleagues, and finally to writing a paper. That is why I write (and why I read, for that matter). It is my deepest hope that some of these papers will inform, challenge, and change how you work and how you understand the work we do.

REFERENCE
Berne, E. (1972). *What do you say after you say hello?: The psychology of human destiny.* New York: Grove Press.

Section I:
The Experience of Psychotherapy

Ultimately, it must be the client's Adult who determines what it is he/she no longer needs or wants, or, rather, what it is he/she now *wants* in order to drop an unwelcome pattern of behavior. There may still be some short-lived discomfort for so doing, with an old threat and survival conclusion still coming up in a nightmare, for instance, the way an amputee continues to "feel" the amputated limb for a while, until adjusting to its absence.

English, 2003, p.71

Section I

Introduction

It is not easy to write in a way that conveys, even evokes, the experience of psychotherapy. In the early years of my writing, I tended to emphasize theory, seeking to expand or critique existing theoretical frames or to bridge among differing theoretical stances. There is certainly value in doing so, but I began to realize that I was also hiding behind theory.

Two men, Christopher Bollas and Jim McLaughlin, have been particularly important influences in my evolution as an author. Both are superb writers. Much of Bollas's work reads more like literary essays than psychoanalytic treatises. His writings are evocative—often paradoxical—investigations written as a kind of sorting out, a questioning, rather than to provide answers. One gets a vivid sense of what it might be like to lie on the couch as his analysand. McLaughlin, raised in the traditions of his Irish ancestry and steeped in Irish literature and music, writes in elegant, poetic prose. Both authors invite the reader into their thinking processes. Both have the skill to convey the experience of being deeply, often unconsciously, engaged in the analytic/therapeutic process.

I have had the benefit of supervision with Bollas and a rich collaboration with McLaughlin. Both challenged me to be more personal, more revealing in my writing and to make far greater use of case material. I had read Jim's work for years before I we had personal contact, but once we met, he took an abiding interest in my writing. He pushed me hard. Having met me once, he pronounced, "I have the distinct impression that the closer something is to your heart, the quieter you become. Now why that's so is your personal business, but I must say that it weakens your writing. You must learn to write from your heart." He had a point. He soon made a second point:

> When I listen to you, I have two conflicting reactions. I get excited and I get scared. You're not afraid to be provocative or to go your own way, and I find that exciting. But you think and work very differently than I do, so there are these huge gaps in my understanding. I have no question that you know what you are doing, but I don't know what you're doing, and then I get scared. When there are gaps and I get scared, I fill in the gaps and calm my scare by thinking about what I would do. That then makes what you are doing wrong. You must write with more clinical detail so that I can bridge the gaps and articulate your thinking in more detail so that I don't get scared. I'm sure I'm not alone in these reactions. (J. McLaughlin, personal communication, 8 November 2000)

Since this encounter, my writing has become far more personal and detailed. I make greater use of case material to invite the reader into the process and ideas that I am exploring. The articles of recent years thus have a distinctly different tone and style from my earlier work.

Each of the chapters in this first section were intended to evoke the experience of being in psychotherapy. The opening chapter was written for a special issue of the *Transactional Analysis Journal* edited by Carol Solomon, who had the idea of an issue of the *Journal* written for clients rather than colleagues. I was asked to write about the process and experience of psychotherapy. The change of audience was a real challenge and the result quite satisfying. I told the story of one particularly determined client, our struggles together, and what it demonstrated about psychotherapy.

The second chapter, a very early article of mine, is also focused on how to convey experientially the nature of the psychotherapeutic process to the client in the early stages of treatment, while affording diagnostic clues to the therapist. It is an early article that has held up well over time.

The third chapter, coauthored with Mick Landaiche, grew out of a stimulating workshop we taught in Rome. The level of participation and the questions of the group were exceptional and stimulated many hours of conversation afterward, finally resulting in this article, which was first published in Italian in *Rivista Italiana di Analisi Transazionale e Metodologie Psicoterapeutiche* and later in English in the *Transactional Analysis Journal*. It is an article that both brings a deeper understanding of the body to script theory—with our emphasis on Berne's concept of protocol—and seeks to vividly portray the mutual vulnerabilities of therapist and client alike, which reflects the influence of Jim McLaughlin.

The closing chapter is one of the most personal I have ever written, and it truly conveys the intimate experience of psychotherapy. It was originally written for the *European Journal of Psychotherapy and Counselling;* it is a pleasure to republish it here within a transactional analysis context.

REFERENCE

English, F. (2003). How are you? And how am I? Scripts, ego states, and inner motivators. In C. Sills & H. Hargaden (Eds.), *Ego states* (Key concepts in transactional analysis: Contemporary views) (pp. 55-72). London: Worth Publishing.

What Am I Getting Myself Into?

William F. Cornell

"So, what am I getting myself into here?" Suzanne asked me this question toward the end of our initial session. She had led quite a life up to the point at which she decided to enter therapy. As she approached retirement from her post as a university professor and campus minister, her life, at least from the outside, seemed full of accomplishment and—one would imagine—personal satisfaction. Suzanne was one of a handful of women to gain admission to a certain theological seminary and eventually to become ordained, although only after a valiant struggle. Ultimately, she rose to a position of leadership within her denomination.

Suzanne was the only one of her siblings to leave the area where she grew up, the only one to go to college, the only one to win any visible acclaim. And yet she was the black sheep of the family. Now, as she approached retirement, she was alienated from her family and did not experience much pride or satisfaction in her professional accomplishments. Throughout a lifetime of professional struggle and gain, she lived alone, could not sustain close personal relationships, and suffered recurrent bouts of depression. She was terrified of a retirement marked by loneliness and depression. Suzanne decided to enter psychotherapy to see if she could understand and change her depressive and isolating tendencies and thus anticipate a different sort of retirement. Suzanne, like many people who enter psychotherapy, was extremely successful in some realms of her life and lost and ineffective in others. Psychotherapy works to deepen self-understanding so as to increase the range of personal autonomy and effectiveness in a person's life.

Suzanne consciously chose transactional analysis psychotherapy because she had read a number of transactional analysis books and found them sensible and somewhat helpful. She had done enough reading and talking with colleagues to know that many transactional analysis authors and organizational leaders were women. Some had even made contributions to the feminist literature. She said she understood herself better from the reading but still could not significantly change her way of living. She chose me as her therapist because she knew I practiced transactional analysis and because she knew a couple of colleagues who had seen me for treatment. They considered their work with me successful and had recommended me to her.

After Suzanne asked what she was getting into, I responded that I did not really understand the intent of her question. She explained that she wanted to know what she could expect to accomplish and how psychotherapy might help. She wanted to be reasonably sure that she was spending her limited time and money well. She said she knew people who had really changed in therapy, "but I don't understand what psychotherapy is or how it works." The answer did not roll out of my brain and off my tongue. I took up her question seriously and answered as best I could. At that point in my practice, I routinely asked my clients what they needed to know about me, but it had never occurred to me that clients might have the same question about therapy itself. How does it work? What am I getting myself into? I have since learned that many clients enter therapy with this question in mind but do not feel free to ask it.

This essay is my answer to the questions of how transactional analysis therapy works and what you, as a client, might be getting yourself into. Your therapist—even if she or he has a transactional analysis frame of reference—may have a different perspective. Ask. Push past the standard theoretical explanations to talk more openly with your therapist about what you each know and expect of psychotherapy, what you each know and believe about how people change. That initial discussion can lay an important foundation for the work you will do together.

Psychotherapy is a hard and exciting endeavor. It is work, rewarding work. Transactional analysis psychotherapy is a collaborative effort ("collaborate" comes from the Latin word *collaborare,* which means "labor together"). You and your therapist will have a *working* relationship, one that may be gentle and supportive at times but challenging, conflictual, and even disorganizing at others. Your therapist's primary job is to provide you with a respectful and reliable space within which the two of you (or perhaps a group of you) can reflect, explore, and experiment with feelings, beliefs, and interpersonal behavior. Things that you may have taken for granted about yourself, life, and others will be opened to question. You will have the opportunity to examine how you relate to yourself internally and with others interpersonally. You will work with your present-day relationships, on the one hand, and look at the lingering influences of childhood relationships on the formation of your beliefs, feelings, and behavior, on the other. Your willingness to question, be questioned, reflect, challenge your beliefs, and experiment with new possibilities is at the heart of your job as a client.

In the remainder of this essay I will consider how transactional analysis psychotherapy works by addressing four areas of the psychotherapeutic process: script formation and insight, new possibilities for feeling and thinking, skill development, and changes in neural pathways. I will return occasionally to Suzanne's life and the therapeutic work she and I did together to offer some concrete examples of how the process works.

Why I Was Drawn to Transactional Analysis

Transactional analysis was created during the 1950s and 1960s by Eric Berne, a psychoanalyst who wanted to develop of model of psychotherapy that was more humanistic and user-friendly than the psychoanalytic model in which he had trained. He wrote several important books about psychotherapy for psychotherapists. He also wrote *Games People Play* (1964), which became a huge best seller and a model for the many self-help books that have been published since. Berne developed terms—"games," "rackets," "scripts," and "strokes"—that he hoped clients would find practical, easy to grasp, and a bit humorous. In fact, much of the early terminology of transactional analysis has by now become part of our ordinary language.

Berne called his model *transactional* analysis to distinguish it from psychoanalysis and to emphasize that this new approach looked actively at the meaning of what goes on between people as well as what goes on within our own minds. In fact, in transactional analysis we look at both transactions (interactions) between people *and* transactions with ourselves, within our own minds. Berne recognized that we all have states of mind within ourselves, which he called "ego states." These can be quite varied and even contradictory because they are formed at different ages and within the context of different relationships. Berne studied the transactional dynamics between people and within groups, but he also recognized that often the most compelling and challenging interactions are the ones we have within ourselves! Therefore, Berne taught therapists to pay attention to the conversations people have with others and the conversations that they have with themselves.

I was drawn to transactional analysis more than 30 years ago for two reasons. As a psychology undergraduate student, I read a paper by Berne in which he described leading supervision groups in a clinic where the clients who were being discussed by their therapists were invited to attend the consultation group. Both therapist and client thus had the opportunity to discuss what was working and what was not, to examine their patterns of transactions, and to look together at ways to improve their work. I was enormously impressed by the act of respect that Berne extended to clients in this learning structure. He presumed that whatever the difficulties a client was struggling with, he or she wanted to get well and would become seriously engaged in the therapeutic process.

Transactional analysis also offered an approach that supported both cognitive/behavioral interventions and affective/psychodynamic work, in contrast to most models of psychotherapy, which choose one side or the other of that therapeutic divide. The dual focus in transactional analysis offers an important flexibility to clients in terms of the models of therapy that can be used.

For example, there is tremendous pressure these days from insurance companies and health delivery systems for short-term counseling and psychotherapy, which almost always takes the form of some version of a cognitive/behavioral therapy. For many people entering treatment that uses a cognitive/behavioral model, the question is, "Please help me understand what I'm doing and how to do this more effectively." For a number of therapeutic issues, this level of intervention is sufficient. And for many people, it is a familiar way of seeking help. You may have conversations like this with trusted friends, family members, or a minister, colleague, or teacher who might respond, "Hey, this is how I think about that. Try it this way. This works for me, maybe it'll work for you."

Of course, friends, family members, ministers, and others may have some investment in your making a particular choice. One of the advantages of seeing a therapist is the offer of more objectivity. A therapist will help you look at *how* you think and *how* those thoughts influence your behavior. A therapist will not (unless you are in emergency circumstances) tell you *what* to think or do. Sometimes a cognitive/behavioral level of intervention relieves symptoms for a while, but usually the quality of a person's life and his or her emotional/psychological structures do not change significantly. People realize there is more that needs to be done, that a different level of self-assessment is needed. This points to longer-term psychotherapy. Here transactional analysis offers a strong advantage for clients who decide to make this shift in focus: They do not need to change the therapeutic model or therapist to deepen and extend their therapy.

Getting back to Suzanne, at the time she entered therapy with me, she knew she would be in longer-term, psychodynamic therapy. That was what her question, "What am I getting myself into?" was about. The nature of long-term psychotherapy is more of a mystery to many people. It is not a normal and familiar way of relating to someone else. Images of "shrinks," "mind readers," and "gurus" often come to mind. Perhaps the following sections of this essay will begin to help you understand how the experience and process of long-term transactional analysis therapy works.

Script, Ruts, and Transference

It is part of human nature to try to make sense of life, others, and ourselves. We constantly create and tell stories: We listen to them, read them, watch them on television and in the movies. Stories can excite, soothe, disturb, explain, or entertain, thus serving many important psychological and emotional functions. We all have favorite stories from and about childhood; we grow up with family stories and have our own recollections of important childhood events. Stories help us make sense of life, providing not only a chronicle of history but tales of meaning and emotion as well. Life stories can be lived like a historical novel, a great adventure, a fairy tale, science fiction, a romance, a whodunit, a thriller, a tragedy, or even a bad joke. In Eric Berne's words, we have an innate hunger for structure, by which he meant familiar and predictable ways of making sense of ourselves internally and of life outside of us. This need for psychological structure fosters a tendency to create accounts of our lives, or stories, that can provide psychological stability but can also limit how we see the possibilities for ourselves and others. The power of childhood stories can be such that we turn a new experience into the same old thing, not even seeing the new experience. The power of "the same old thing" can create patterns that make the outcomes of life seem inevitable and change seem impossible.

For example, seen from the outside, Suzanne was typically praised as intelligent, independent, and highly principled. As her therapist, I would not quarrel with these characterizations. At the same time, however, I knew that the story of Suzanne's life, as she experienced it, was considerably more complicated. Remember, she saw herself as the black sheep of the family, the misfit, the unwanted daughter and sibling. She was the youngest (and unexpected) child, a burden to her mother, and was turned over to the care of older siblings. Little Suzanne's sisters and brother were already adolescents, and they did not welcome a new baby. They did not want to be bothered with serving as babysitters or substitute parents. Suzanne gradually came to conclude that depending on anyone was bad news, that being a girl left a good deal to be desired, and that she simply did not fit in among others.

Suzanne did not leave home because she wanted to but because she was not wanted. Recall that her siblings all stayed in the area and remained involved in each other's lives and families. For Suzanne, leaving home for college was more of a failure (a banishment) than a success. No one from her family came to visit. In fact, they found her whole life at an urban college threatening.

As a girl, Suzanne had found church comforting, the privacy of prayer and religious fantasy soothing. She found some kindness from the parish minister; she identified with him and eventually set off for a theological college in a major city. However, there she found herself ripped from her family and the comfort of a small country parish. She landed in an academic community that feared women and was dominated by arrogant men. These were not the gentle, sensible parish ministers with whom she had grown up. She found herself, again, a black sheep. Given Suzanne's experience of life to this point, being a black sheep once more seemed to her to be inevitable and somehow deserved.

Transactional analysis therapists often refer to such stories about oneself and the world as "life scripts." Berne used the term "script," rather than story, because it captured the sense that we often feel as though these stories have been written for us within our families and then imposed on us. Although we, in part, create these stories (often unconsciously) ourselves, we may feel as though we are following someone else's wishes, speaking lines handed to us as in a script. As children, we create scripts that seek to adapt to our families and cultures so as to have a sense of belonging and to avoid disapproval. As transactional analysis therapists, we often speak of childhood "script decisions," which can make it seem as though Suzanne (or you) sat down as a child and decided, "So this is what my life is about." It does not happen quite that way. It is more like gradually but repeatedly feeling as though our life and family are teaching us certain inevitable lessons about who we are and what life is going to be like. Some parts of our personal stories can be exciting, unpredictable, and open-ended. But the script aspects of the life story feel like the ruts in a well-worn road.

Most of us experience a contradiction between areas of life in which we feel reasonably autonomous and effective and other areas in which we feel trapped and ineffective, leading a life that is not really of our own choosing. Are we the author of a story or a character in someone else's design for us? One of the important ways that transactional analysis therapy works is that therapist and client work together to identify the enduring stories of one's life, that is, to identify the recurrent patterns of life script. This is the process of pattern recognition and the development of insight—the capacity to see inside yourself from an outside perspective. Your therapist may never use the word "script," but he or she will help you notice the patterns in your life that seem inevitable, those things that you keep doing even though you know they do not work.

Scripts often emerge during the therapeutic process and are lived out with the therapist. In the transactional analysis language of Eric Berne, this living out of script is called a "game." If you read about psychotherapy these days, this phenomenon is usually called "transference." For example, Suzanne, as the designated black sheep of her family, was extremely sensitive to any signs of my not liking her or "wanting to be rid of her." She anticipated from the beginning (even before meeting me) that as a psychotherapist I would be biased against her religious orientation, regarding it as childish or dumb. Suzanne expected me to want to get rid of her. If I forgot something from a previous session, she viewed this as evidence that "as soon as I'm out of sight, I'm out of your mind." Our work together almost collapsed when I double booked her session after a vacation. Even though I owned the mistake as mine and the other client agreed to come back at another time, Suzanne felt that I had humiliated her and that this was clear evidence that I did not care and wanted to be rid of her. In Suzanne's mind it seemed perfectly obvious that she had somehow become a bore or a burden to me. It seemed better to leave than be angry with me.

This mistake on my part and Suzanne's reaction to it became a pivotal moment in her therapy. It was clear to her that we were both extremely uncomfortable in the face of my error, but I did not get rid of her. She could see that I could tolerate my own discomfort and maintain an investment in her well-being. This provided her with an emotional space within which we could examine all of her various reactions. She was able to begin to see that the only way she could understand my mistake was as a desire to be rid of her, that this habitual explanation was an expression of her script that imposed a particular meaning on what had happened. If this meaning were accurate, it made sense that she (as usual) should prepare to leave yet another important place of hope in her life and yet again to go it alone.

As she was able to see the power of her script expectations—those well-worn psychological ruts—with me, Suzanne was increasingly able to gain insight into herself. She began standing apart from the power of the stories of her past and saw how those assumptions also played out in other relationships. She realized that there were other times when she presumed she had become undesirable or a burden to someone and left the relationship. She began to see that there could be other reasons for difficulties in relationships and that solutions could be found to allow her to stay rather than leave.

This story of Suzanne's transference reactions to me underscores one of the most important jobs of the psychotherapist and a crucial piece of how psychotherapy works through the transference. In this instance, her transference reaction (or psychological game) reflected her early childhood experience and decision that she was unwanted. When transference is not examined and understood, it has the power to reduce a new relationship into the same old and predictable story. The analysis of transference is an invaluable means of insight and pattern recognition, a crucial mechanism in how psychotherapy works. Often in work relationships, friendships, and intimacy, we live out elements of our script stories without ever being aware of them, feeling instead resigned to predictable ways of relating, inevitable disappointments, and little that seems new or creative. Therapy allows us to engage in a mutual, respectful scrutiny of how and why we do what we do. Part of the therapist's job—a skill that requires a great deal of training and practice—is to stand simultaneously inside and outside this working relationship. The therapist provides a space in which to reflect together and experiment with new meanings and possible ways of relating.

When Suzanne first asked me what she was getting into, part of my reply was along these lines: We'll be working actively with what emerges between us as our relationship develops. Either of us, at any time, can address our relationship directly—conflicts, appreciations, surprises, mistakes, deceptions, impatience, excitement, misunderstandings—whatever may affect the quality and effectiveness of our relationship. People tend to create in the therapy whatever they tend to exclude or distort in daily life. We need to identify, understand, and change those patterns. It's not always comfortable to do this, but this is a place to practice.

Insight is another essential element in how psychotherapy works. The development of insight is a learned skill. Like most learning, insight requires a teacher and practice. With practice, insight fosters a mind that becomes stronger and more flexible, just as exercise can foster a body that is both stronger and more flexible. It is not always a pleasant process to undertake this kind of self-examination and to see the traps we set for ourselves. Such insight can be very difficult to accomplish without the eyes, ears, and mind of another, which are an important part of what a therapist supplies. Often when a client begins to examine the well-worn tracks of script there can be a deep sense of failure, depression, hopelessness, or shame. The therapist needs to sustain an attitude of curiosity and respect, which will help to make the experience of insight more palatable. Stories, when they are not script bound, often express our wishes, desires, strengths, and creativity. The curiosity, respect, and insight afforded in psychotherapy can go a long way toward restoring the vitality of our life stories and overcoming the deadness of life scripts.

New Possibilities

Suzanne reported to me in her first session that she had gained insight by reading transactional analysis books, but she could not yet turn the insight into action. Insight, in and of itself, does not necessarily lead to change. However, new possibilities emerge within the therapeutic process through insight ("I never thought of it that way before"), emotions that emerge in therapy ("I didn't know these feelings could be acceptable to someone"), and the therapeutic relationship ("I don't know what to expect of you").

Insight is primarily a cognitive process. It is a necessary, although often not sufficient, condition for change. Suzanne's experience of gaining insight through reading but being unable to actualize her insights is not uncommon. For example, she was afraid to retire and afraid not to retire. Her wishes for a life with less depression and more intimacy were accompanied by fear, anger, and shame. As an adult, she was able to channel her anger into professional causes: the rights of women in her church, the responsibility of the church to the disadvantaged, the role of academic and religious freedom in campus life. There her anger accomplished a great deal. But she could not bring her anger to bear on the loneliness of her personal life: to solve problems with friends rather than leave them, to make effective demands on those she wanted more from, to move toward people she desired. In her personal relationships her anger took her away from people, not toward them. Even in sessions with me, revealing her desire to be closer to friends felt frightening and shameful. All that she could imagine was that she would be exposing herself to the disinterest of others and thus to further rejection and humiliation. The depression created by her loneliness seemed preferable to the humiliation of rejection. She could be alone and understand herself better through her reading, but she could not be alone and figure out how to change herself.

Over the course of therapy, clients typically find themselves returning to childhood experiences as they explore new possibilities in the present. Suzanne needed to look back at her familiar memories and stories of childhood, to view them now with an adult's mind rather than only through a child's eyes. Through a child's eye, she was an unloved and unlovable burden. The life she saw around her was hard on everyone. She hated being the castaway child but dreaded becoming an adult. She admired her father for his hard work and pride, but she rarely saw him happy. Her mother seemed happier, but Suzanne saw her as self-indulgent and irresponsible, felt disgusted by her, and hated herself for hating her mother. She was consumed with envy and jealousy toward her siblings. As a young girl, she was convinced that her family somehow knew she had these horrible feelings, so they made her the black sheep. As an adult, she felt as a Christian she should rise above these feelings. In her heart Suzanne felt sinful and filled with shame. Her feelings, perhaps, could be forgiven, but they did not deserve interest or compassion.

In therapy, Suzanne found space for all of her feelings. She began to understand how her anger and hatred were a defense against her loving feelings and the helplessness she felt to make a place for herself in her family. She began to feel that therapy was a place for her. It often surprised her that I did not render judgment about her hatred and jealousy, that I did not reassure her that her family really did desire her or had done the best they could. Instead, I remained steadfast that she could create a different environment for herself. Perhaps the biggest surprise was that when something went wrong between us, we mostly managed to learn something from it. We did not distance from one another. Gradually, she could understand and then feel that bad feelings were indications of desires that remained unacknowledged and of problems that needed to be solved.

Transactional analysis therapists often make use of contracts—clearly stated, mutually negotiated therapeutic goals—to explore new possibilities for behavioral and emotional change. New experiences, however much desired, can be enormously threatening. Letting go of a familiar emotional or relational way of being (Berne's structure hunger) is a complex and often anxiety-provoking undertaking. The end result of something new is something unpredictable. Therapeutic contracts are a means of managing the rate of experimentation, the size of the risk, and the degree of anxiety involved in trying something new. Gradually, new experiences accumulate to buffer the old, familiar pains and failures and create the ground for new, more vigorous stories. We slowly internalize new models for ourselves and about how relationships can work.

Skill Development

When we are reasonably fortunate, childhood and adolescence are years of tremendous learning and skill development. A satisfying life is a skilled life, the product of a lot of learning. We need skills at forming and keeping social/loving bonds, skills for separation and differentiation, skills for healthy aggression and conflict resolution, skills for work, skills for play, skills to think and create meaning in life, and skills to deal with frustration, failure, and personal misdeeds. Most of us are fortunate enough in our family and school environments to arrive at adulthood with a reasonable range of skills. And most of us have significant gaps or downright gaping holes. Most of us try to rely on our familiar skills to cover or compensate for the gaps. But it is a gap that brings most people into psychotherapy, which is a rich means by which to mind and mend the gaps in our range of skills. Part of the reason it helps is that skill development requires opportunities and practice.

Far more often than not, people come into psychotherapy with a deeply held belief that there is something wrong with them (or with someone else). An important part of the assessment that a therapist undertakes is to evaluate developmental gaps and skill acquisition. Clients are often plagued by self-perceptions of character flaws, sinfulness, stupidity, failure, shame, or unlovableness (or the projection and blame of such qualities onto others), all of which intensify feelings of hopelessness and helplessness. It is a powerful therapeutic experience to have a therapist translate self-blame or projective blaming into areas of needed skills.

To return to Suzanne, if you compare the list of developmental skills listed at the start of this section with the skills evidenced in her family as Suzanne was growing up, the gaps are glaring. Suzanne could not learn what was absent in the environment, could not learn what the people around her did not know how to do (or, in her eyes as a child, did not want to do for her). One of my jobs as Suzanne's therapist was to help her see the limits of her childhood environment as often just that: limits in the people who were raising her rather than judgments about or reactions to her worth and lovability. She had, indeed, used the available family skills of separation and hard work to strong advantage in her life. But she knew little of how to give love, receive love, sustain emotional relationships, play, or express feelings and desires in ways that helped those around her know her better. To understand the limited skills in her family (and their limited quality of life) provided Suzanne with a very different and more compassionate perspective on herself and her family. This allowed a gradual reconciliation with her siblings. It allowed her to feel far less flawed and ashamed because she knew she could learn, even as hurt and unsure of herself as she was in the world of relationships.

At times, usually when she was scared or disappointed, Suzanne would become angry at how "unreal" therapy was, attacking it as "a weird kind of bubble that has nothing to do with real life." "Maybe," she would say derisively, "if *everyone* at the university were in psychotherapy, then this would all seem more real." This was one of Suzanne's ways to "leave the scene," to escape the uncertainty or vulnerability of being more engaged with me. Part of my job was to speak to the realities of her uncertainty and her vulnerability while gently persisting in (and if need be insisting on) the exploration of new skills in her life outside the therapy room. She began to discover that some of the people around her had a far greater range of skills in life than her family members had. She began to realize that a few people would welcome her tentative (and sometimes awkward) efforts at trying new skills. It is not easy, for example, to give up sarcasm and say "I'm scared." However, she found a few people in her daily life who actually seemed to prefer a rather scared and tentative Suzanne to a distant and sarcastic one, even in an academic environment!

The initial opportunities for skill development typically occur in the therapy office with a therapist and/or a therapy group. But a therapist and treatment group can only provide so much. Then it is the job of the client to carry the work with the new skills outside of the therapeutic setting into daily life. Usually, there is a period of time when you may carry your therapist around in your mind ("in your hip pocket," Berne used to say). When a colleague of mine, who had been in therapy with Eric Berne, read the first draft of this essay, she wrote to me about an experience with Berne:

When I was a kid, I was prettier than my older sister. When anyone complimented me, my mother would whisper to them, "Please, stop it," as it would hurt my sister's feelings. Needless to say, I felt guilty about being attractive. When I was in therapy with Berne, I was overweight, bought no new clothes, and so on. One day he told me, "You should fix yourself up." He pulled out his prescription pad and wrote on it, "License to be beautiful." I carried that prescription around in my wallet for *years*. That was 35 years ago, and I know I still have that piece of paper somewhere. Soon after that I lost weight, learned how to use makeup, bought new clothes, and voilà!

For a period of time, what is new seems possible only because of the therapist. The emerging possibilities seem to belong more to the therapist than the client, in a kind of psychological dependency. This dependency (the hip-pocket cure) is changed only when the client practices these new skills in his or her everyday world. Learning gradually becomes internalized as belonging to the client, not a product of the therapist. Just as the power of the disappointments of childhood need to be broken for insight to occur, so too must the power of attribution to the therapist be broken for learning to be internalized.

Changes in Neural Pathways

These days advertisements and the popular press suggest a pandemic of mood and mental disorders —depression, anxiety, social anxiety, obsessive-compulsive disorder, attention deficit disorder, bipolar disorder—affecting adults and children alike. Medication is all too often suggested as the magic solution. Although medication can sometimes enhance the effectiveness of psychotherapy and at other times is a necessary component of psychotherapy, it is rarely sufficient to achieve lasting change. Many of the life problems that bring people into psychotherapy—loss of a loved one, low self-esteem, confusion about meaning and purpose in life, difficulties in separation and autonomy with loved ones, intimate and sexual dissatisfactions, problems with anger and control—may not be significantly helped by medication and certainly are not cured by a pill.

To appreciate why, it is helpful to understand a little about the workings of the brain. The 1990s were known as the "Decade of the Brain" in recognition of the tremendous strides that new technologies made in the study of that organ. Today our understandings of mental and emotional functioning continue to unfold at a rapid rate. New research has, among other things, facilitated the development of many new drugs as we better understand the structure and neurochemistry of the brain. These are exciting developments, and it is easy to imagine how medication can be helpful to those who seek psychotherapy. After all, while most of us have not taken an antidepressant, almost everyone has taken an aspirin to chase away a headache. In the same way, it is not hard to imagine the effects of medications on the brain. In contrast, it is a bit more difficult to grasp how talking to someone, as in psychotherapy, can also have an effect on our functioning as well.

One of the outcomes of the Decade of the Brain is an understanding of how the brain creates a mind, that is to say, how the experience of the mind is created in the brain. For a long time, it seemed like the mind and its invisible, subjective realms of experience were the territory of philosophers, psychotherapists, and poets. The brain, as an objective, neurochemically based organ of the mind, was the territory of scientific researchers. There was little dialogue, and often great suspicion, between the two fields of study. Contemporary brain research now demonstrates the myriad of links between brain and mind, and the clinical and research disciplines are in ever closer dialogue.

Why is it that medications alone are often not sufficient for many of the issues that bring people into psychotherapy? At the heart of the answer to this question is the fact that most psychotropic drugs do not significantly impact the cerebral cortex, which is a part of the brain crucial to many of the cognitive/emotional difficulties that bring people into psychotherapy. What is it that the talking work of psychotherapy can accomplish that medication cannot? In a highly readable book, *The Talking Cure: The Science Behind Psychotherapy,* Vaughan (1997) described the relationship between medication and psychotherapy this way:

> Even though sometimes taking medication and feeling better can help people feel quite different and can allow them to make impressive strides on their own to change themselves and their lives, often such change is either totally terrifying to patients and results in their stopping the medication, or not enough for them to really change their lives. *For most people, medication changes how they feel, but psychotherapy is what changes what their lives are like.* (p. 140, italics added)

Medication does not create self-reflection and self-understanding. Medication, when properly prescribed, can shift mood and enhance the capacity for thinking. Chronic, unrelenting depression and/or anxiety do not facilitate clear thinking or hope for the future. Medication in such cases can be invaluable. It can make it easier to think and help restore a fuller range of emotions. Psychotherapy provides a setting in which we learn to think with someone and a means through which we can learn to think about our thinking. Psychotherapy, in an important way, shifts the locus of control in the experience of one's life from external events as causal factors to internal awareness and the development of life skills (one of which may be knowing the importance of your medication). There is increasing evidence from brain research that the brain, from the moment of birth, is a profoundly social organ, that is, it grows and changes through relational experiences. Knowing this helps us to understand how the intense emotional and cognitive interchanges of ongoing psychotherapy literally open and alter neural pathways in the brain.

The life situations that can create the lasting disruptions and inhibitions that bring most people into psychotherapy impact the brain in two fundamental areas: the deep, affective regions of the brain (the cortico-limbic pathways) and the cognitive capacities of the cerebral cortex. Most of the new antidepressant and antianxiety medications improve the availability of essential neurotransmitters in the central, limbic regions of the brain, rather like adjusting the neurochemical bathwater that saturates the deep, affective regions of the brain. These are the areas directly affected and disturbed by early childhood loss, trauma, neglect, deprivation, or violent intrusion, although they can also be profoundly disturbed at any time in the course of life when events overwhelm our personal, emotional capacities and our interpersonal world does not respond with adequate structure and relief.

These deep disturbances of affect are carried in the deep limbic structures and right hemisphere of the brain, the regions that are prelinguistic and precognitive. When these areas are disturbed, we feel disturbed, although we may not know how or why. These regions of the brain profoundly affect our sense of being, but the meaning of these disturbances comes from a different region of the brain: the left hemisphere of the cerebral cortex.

We looked earlier in this chapter at the human importance of making sense of things, of creating stories and meaning. It is not until the third year of life that these neural circuits in the left hemisphere of the brain—with their capacity for language development and reflective cognition—begin to develop. These circuits are the story-creating, script-forming mechanisms of the brain. Needless to say, for many people the early years of life, before these cognitive circuits develop, have already left their emotional marks. Thus, we have deep, emotionally colored representations of ourselves and the world around us before we have any capacity to make sense of the world in which we live. These primary emotional representations precede our capacities to think and provide the unconscious shape and tone of emotional and relational worlds. The stories we tell ourselves, the scripts we develop, are a later developmental effort to make sense of deep inner feeling states and relational patterns and to gain some sense of mastery over them.

In addressing the question of what psychotherapy can provide that is different and distinct from what medication can offer, it is important to realize that the neural structure of the upper brain network—the portion of the brain that makes sense of things—is not affected directly by our current repertoire of psychotropic drugs. Medication primarily affects the deeper regions of the brain, but not so much the cognitive, linguistic areas of the brain. Psychotherapy affects both. Perhaps the most important thing, as we ask the questions of how transactional analysis psychotherapy works, is to understand how psychotherapy works in this upper region of the brain through its careful, persistent examination of thinking patterns and story/script formation.

For example, Suzanne felt in the core of her being that she was unwanted. We might say that soon after birth she came to "know" in the limbic regions of her brain that something was seriously amiss. She felt something wrong within herself. Being unwanted was all that she "knew" of herself. From her earliest months we can imagine that she felt the distance, impatience, neglect, and hostility of her older siblings. She rarely felt the comfort of another person's warm and welcoming body. Being alone was her most deeply held sense of self. We might say that being alone was the place she "knew" best in the limbic regions of her brain. By the time she reached adulthood, Suzanne had accepted her aloneness, often with pride and defiance (script), but she hated and feared her tendency to become depressed.

Suzanne was not depressed when she entered treatment with me. She had tried medication in the past, was troubled by the side effects, and found it accomplished no lasting change. From her script-bound perspective, she saw medication as a "crutch"; from a more objective perspective, she found it to be insufficient. She had concluded that her depressions were not biologically based but an outcome of her isolation. She was coming into psychotherapy to address her isolation, not her depression. She was not on medication and made it clear from the start that she did not want to use any. In fact, she threatened that if I suggested medication she would presume that I found her too much of a burden and wanted to be rid of her so she would end the treatment. At the start of therapy, I simply accepted and respected her position about medication. Later, as Suzanne gained more insight into her script beliefs and defenses, we were able to return to her position about medication and her threat to terminate (one of many) as an expression of her script and a cover for her fear of relying on anyone, including her therapist. Eventually, she could imagine that if I brought up medication it would not be because I was trying to find relief from experiencing her as a burden. As she learned more about her beliefs about relationships and learned to expect more of people around her, she was able to take up a discussion about medication as a responsible expression of concern for her well-being.

Room for More

Suzanne did not use medication over the course of her therapy with me, so we will never know if it might have facilitated her work. But we worked hard with the left hemisphere, sense-making, script-forming part of her cerebral cortex. An important emotional relationship developed between the two of us, one that not only tolerated but welcomed a range of deep, and sometimes difficult, emotions. Her feelings enriched and enlivened her thinking. Her thinking helped her explore new possibilities within herself and among others. Through psychotherapy, Suzanne learned to experience and use her mind differently, and I think her brain changed as a result. Her thinking patterns opened up to novel possibilities. Her mood and affects became more fluid and varied. Suzanne's emotional sense of self opened to a richer range of affect. Desire, longing, and excitement became as much a part of her as depression, anger, and blackness. As she developed more skills for intimacy, she began to feel the pleasure of others' company and the pleasure of her company to others. Suzanne attempted reconciliation with her siblings, but only one brother was willing to invite her back, rather tentatively, into his life. At the end of treatment, she remained easily bruised, a bit too quick to move into argument (now tempered by a capacity to apologize and reengage), but now able to imagine a retirement rich with possibilities rather than laden with anxiety and loss.

Conclusion

By the time most of us reach adulthood, life has come to feel rather fixed and predictable. The predictability of life serves both as a comfort and a constraint. Psychotherapy is a means by which we can examine the constraints of our lives, both in terms of how we live within the actual confines of our daily lives and with those emotional and psychological constraints we impose on ourselves. Good psychotherapy creates more room for fuller living within our minds and in our relationships.

Epilogue

Shortly after Suzanne finished therapy she was diagnosed with an untreatable immunological disease that attacked her nervous system. The progress of the disease was horrifyingly rapid, and within 2 years she had very little voluntary movement and was confined to a wheelchair in a nursing home. But her mind never weakened. I saw her often at her home and in the nursing home until she died. I did not see her as a therapist. Her therapy was done. I saw her as someone who had come to respect and care deeply for her and as someone who felt a moral responsibility to be with her through that tragic process.

One day I asked Suzanne if she was bitter to have made such an effort in her psychotherapy only to have her life cut so short. "No," she replied, "I am bitter that I am dying. But I will never regret the therapy. Without the therapy, I would have died without ever knowing what it was like to be alive." As she got closer to death, she gave me many books from her library, all decidedly left wing. She asked that I do something to preserve the meaning of her therapy, to find an occasion to publish her case, so that others might learn from the effort she had made. This article is the fulfillment of the commitment I made to her.

She also asked that I attend her funeral and speak with any of her siblings who might want to speak with me to understand her better. She had asked that her memorial service be secular, officiated by a dear friend of hers, a lesbian minister. One last time, her siblings split. I walked into the funeral home to find literally two funerals being carried out for Suzanne. One wake was with her body and the minister she requested with no religious overtones. The other wake was without her body but with a "proper" minister and prayers. Two siblings were in one room, two were in the other, with no one but me going from one room to the other. Up to her death and beyond, the family script that Suzanne had worked so hard to overturn was still operating in full force. Rarely have I seen such concrete evidence of a family script in action. Rarely have I felt such regard and appreciation for the therapeutic work that a client accomplished.

REFERENCES
Berne, E. (1964). *Games people play: The psychology of human relationships.* New York: Grove Press.
Vaughan, S. C. (1997). *The talking cure: The science behind psychotherapy.* New York: Grosset/Putnam.

The original version of this chapter was published in the Transactional Analysis Journal, *Volume 33, Number 1, pp. 4-14, January 2003.*

Setting the Therapeutic Stage: The Initial Sessions

William F. Cornell

Traditionally, the initial interview in psychotherapy serves primarily to gather and assess relevant diagnostic information. It is the therapist's job to structure this initial contact, focus questions, develop rapport, possibly administer tests, and arrive at an evaluation of the client's functioning. Such a professional evaluation will form the basis for a treatment plan, initial therapeutic contracts, and possibly a written report.

The diagnostic phase of treatment is sometimes viewed as separate from the therapeutic process. In mental health clinics, for example, initial interviews are often carried out by a specialist who does not see the client in therapy. Over the years, I have developed an understanding of, and approach to, the initial interview that includes much more than a diagnostic effort.

In my work, I approach the "initial interview"—which may actually involve several sessions—as the first and a crucial phase of introducing a client to the nature of therapeutic work and engaging him or her immediately in that work. By the time a client leaves the first session, I want to have established the beginning of a relationship with that person, to have provided a "taste" of what therapy will be like, and to have mutually defined a purpose for our working together.

This chapter will discuss three primary functions of the initial interview: engagement and collaboration, establishment of the therapeutic canon, and the assessment of strengths and difficulties.

Prior to my involvement with transactional analysis, there were several strong influences on my understanding of the nature of therapeutic work. Reich and his followers (Bellis, 1981) placed a unique emphasis on the person's capacities for contact, love, play, and pleasure. Sullivan (1954) placed great emphasis on the interpersonal aspects of the therapeutic relationship and wrote a rich and detailed book on interview technique.

In developing the approach described here, phenomenological psychology offered me an important critique of and alternative to traditional psychology thinking, quite consistent with Berne's challenges to the traditional psychoanalytic approach. Fischer (1978a) wrote that all traditional methodologies in psychology

> assume an external viewpoint, looking for explanation in conditions, events, or constructs that are seen as more basic or essential (if not linearly causal) than the person's own experience and behavior. In contrast to this natural science approach, existential phenomenology grounds what I prefer to call a "human-science" approach that attempts to preserve the unity of a person's life while still being an empirical rigorous discipline. (p. 211)

Fischer's (1978b) approach to collaborative psychological assessment

> recognizes that the professional's understandings are no more real, valid, or influential within the client's life than are the client's. Collaborative assessment, then, is one in which client and professional *labor together* (from the Latin, *collaborare*) toward mutually set goals, sharing their respective background information and emerging impressions. They develop and try out alternative approaches for the client as they explore the particular circumstances and ways in which he or she has wound up in some sort of difficulty. (p. 42)

If the assessment is to result in a written report, Fischer invites the client to participate in the formulation of the report and to review and sign the finished product.

With this background, my interest in transactional analysis—with its emphasis on a client's strengths, mutual respect, and mutually defined treatment contracts (James & Contributors, 1968/1977)—was immediate.

Engagement and Collaboration

The idea of a mutual collaboration between therapist and client in the diagnostic effort is not new to transactional analysts. Berne's respect for the intelligence and integrity of his clients is evident throughout his work and has become a cornerstone in transactional analysis as a treatment philosophy (James & Contributors, 1968/1977; Steiner, 1968).

Berne's high regard for mutual collaboration was probably nowhere more evident than in his utilization of "staff-patient-staff" conferences (Berne, 1977), in which clients were invited to sit in on their therapists' consultations and treatment planning. Berne wrote that "the 'staff-patient-staff' conference first attacks the comfortable and well-established sociological roles of 'therapist' and 'patient' and substitutes a 'bilateral contract' with rational exceptions" (p. 159). Steiner's emphasis on the involvement of a client in his or her own diagnosis is even stronger and more direct than Berne's. Steiner states that the client's reaction to the diagnosis is of utmost importance. For Steiner (1974), "No matter how convinced the diagnostician is of her diagnosis, the final test of any diagnosis is the extent to which the subject of it finds it to be accurate, to feel right, to sit well, and to make sense" (p. 82). My own emphasis in diagnostic collaboration is not so much on the agreement and acceptance of the client as it is on mutual respect and involvement, with an openness to disagreement, conflict, and discussion between therapist and client.

Emphasis on mutual collaboration in diagnosis has gained significant attention in the psychological and psychiatric literature. Fischer (1979, 1985) presented a comprehensive approach in theory and practice to collaborative diagnosis. Shectman and Smith (1984) similarly challenged the "expert," unilateral approach to diagnosis, in which "the diagnostician is the knower, the patient is an ignoramus" (Pruyser, 1984, p. 8), favoring instead a bilateral process.

In viewing the initial sessions as "setting the therapeutic stage," I seek from the start to engage the client in an active sense of a mutual working relationship. I do not use any formal interview procedure because I want to facilitate a relaxed but directed conversational mode that promotes questioning, exploring, and learning.

I screen potential clients carefully in the initial telephone contact to ascertain whether what I have to offer is likely to be useful to the caller. I find it extremely important in the first phone call to get a clear statement of the presenting problem and to deal explicitly with questions of schedules and fees. This minimizes later distractions from the real work of the initial interview, that of beginning a relationship, starting to understand the client, and defining the purpose of the therapeutic work. A valuable discussion of the initial phone contact and pattern of resistance to therapy can be found in *Mastering Resistance: A Practical Guide to Family Therapy* (Anderson & Stewart, 1983). From the first telephone contact, I want to be reasonably sure that when I meet face-to-face with a client for the first time, we have an expectation of continuing to work together. In this way, I feel free to be quite vigorous in the initial interview.

While I do not have a standard interview procedure, I do have a standard opening question: "What do you need to know about me?" I find this question to be useful both in helping to establish the mutuality of our working relationship and in providing diagnostic information. This kind of opening for the interview serves as a form of "consumer education." Many clients are unaware they have a right to ask questions of the therapist. This opening question lets clients know that the initial session does not require them to continue with me and that they can evaluate me and may choose to consider another therapist. It demonstrates to the client that he or she has the right to question as well as to be questioned. A person need not commit blindly to doing important life work with a total stranger, even if the stranger appears to be a well-qualified professional. I find that the invitation to question me facilitates the development of mutual interaction.

There are, of course, times when a client comes to the initial session in such distress that he or she needs simply to talk, and I save my usual opening question for a later interview.

More often than not, a new client looks uneasy and surprised by the question and mumbles something like, "Oh, no, not really I guess . . . I mean I've heard a lot of good things about you. I mean, ya know, I guess, I really wouldn't know what to ask." But even with these awkward starts, at some point during the session, questions often arise for the client. Some of them are quite surprising and lead to areas of discussion that would not emerge if I were left to my own questions. Recently, for example, a woman struggling with depression and an unsatisfying marriage asked me abruptly in the midst of the session if I believed in reincarnation. I replied that I did not accept reincarnation as a matter of belief but thought of it as an interesting question. I then asked her why she wanted to know. (People do not typically bring up reincarnation in an initial session, so I was quite curious.) She was referred to me through a "New Age" church that she had recently joined. She took from the church permission to learn, to grow, to change her life, and to enter therapy. She also took an interpretation of reincarnation that led her to conclude that she was "fated" to be in this unhappy marriage to "work out" something from a past life with her husband. She was stuck with a dual message to grow and change, but only if her growth did not threaten her marriage. This conflict added to her confusion and depression. Further exploration demonstrated that her misinterpretation of the church's teachings on reincarnation was rooted in her punitive parental background, including the strong message, "You've made your bed, now lie in it."

From a diagnostic perspective, I find out what people want to know about me, what they think they should not want to know about me, what they already know, what they think they already know, or what somebody else wants them to know about me or about therapy. I gain insight into their fears and their hopes for what therapy can offer. I get initial impressions of what they feel entitled to look for and expect in a relationship.

Throughout the initial sessions, I purposely maintain a conversational style in order to engage the client in active self-exploration. I want to demonstrate at the start that our effort is to understand the client's experience, not to explain it or criticize the person for difficulties in life. I probe, hypothesize, challenge, and offer more statements and observations than questions.

Fischer (1978b) wrote with exceptional clarity about this collaborative mode:

My role is to guide him, through my specialized training, to engage actively in delineating the ways and occasions in which he gets into difficulty as well as the pivot points already available for trying out alternatives. . . . We both experience ourselves as working progressively toward useful comprehensions rather than as looking for causal explanations or precise truth. The goal here is for the client to leave the opening session having learned something new about himself, having identified concrete possibilities for change, and knowing that I'll respect and invite his self-understanding and personal responsibility. (p. 49)

Establishing the Therapeutic Canon

In his discussion of group authority, Berne (1963) noted that "the object of the canon is to regulate the group work, and particularly the internal group process" (p. 109). He stressed the importance of the canon in establishing the underlying, typically covert fabric of the therapeutic relationship. The canon is established through what actually happens rather than by what is said. Masterson in his presentation at the 1985 ITAA Winter Congress, discussed the concept of the "therapeutic frame," emphasizing that initial errors in the frame become rapidly institutionalized and are difficult to change.

The collaborative nature of therapy described earlier is a key element in the therapeutic canon I seek to establish. The unspoken statement here, as Fischer (1978b) described it, is that "as the client engages in this sort of exploration, he discovers in a powerful way that his life is indeed in his own hands, that things don't have to be the way they have been, and that change can be self-initiated" (pp. 51-52).

Over the course of the sessions(s), I intentionally provide samples of various therapeutic encounters. It is likely that within the first hour, the client will experience me offering strokes, confrontations, observations, interpretations, and the opportunity to define the initial treatment contract. From the start, my style is typically inquisitive, direct, and quite confrontational. In this way, the client gets a direct sample of what is to come if we continue working together. At the same time, I have a diagnostic opportunity to observe and likely comment on the client's reaction to various types of intervention.

I recently concluded an initial interview by asking a client if there was anything else she needed to ask before we finished the session. She said, "Yeah, I know people who've really changed in therapy, but I don't have the slightest idea what actually happens in this room. I feel good about what happened here today; I'm excited. But I don't understand what psychotherapy is or how it works." I considered her comment carefully and decided to answer her directly and in some detail. I explained that I think of psychotherapy as involving careful attention to three interwoven tracks: her effectiveness and ineffectiveness in managing her day-to-day life and relationships outside of the therapy room, the quality and effectiveness of our working relationship within the therapy room, and the influence of her life history in shaping her success and satisfaction in the two previous tracks.

Previous to my client's comment, I had always looked for opportunities in the initial session to embed and illustrate these themes through the style I use and through exploring the expectations and fantasies the client holds regarding me and the nature of therapy. More recently, I have been experimenting with telling people, as part of the initial interview, about my understanding of and values in therapy and inviting them to respond. I summarize and paraphrase below how I describe these three "tracks" (i.e., the therapeutic canons) to new clients:

1. "I'm going to be asking you and asking myself throughout the course of our work how effective you are in your life. I'll expect you to carry out into your life the things we discuss here. I'm interested in people leading quality lives that are socially useful and emotionally satisfying. In our work, I'll treat you with integrity and respect, and I'll expect the same from you. In relationships, I want people to treat others with high regard and to get themselves treated with high regard. I am demanding. It's not my job to make you comfortable or to simply support you. It's my job to facilitate your effectiveness in living a full life."

2. "We'll be working actively with what emerges between us as our relationship develops. Either of us, at any time, can address our relationship directly—conflicts, appreciations, mistakes, deceptions, impatience, excitement, misunderstandings—whatever may affect the quality and effectiveness of our relationship. One of the primary functions of the therapeutic relationship is to identify and resolve differences between what we typically communicate through our overt social behavior and what we desire and feel at a covert, psychological level. People tend to exclude from the therapeutic relationship what they exclude or distort in daily life. We need to identify, understand, and change those patterns. It is not always comfortable learning to make the covert overt, but this is a place to practice."

3. "When it's relevant, I'll ask about historical information, attitudes, and beliefs that may support you seeing your present life and choices as being like the past and difficult to change. Our history can contaminate how we define problems, how we solve problems, and what goals we set. We'll be working to challenge and open up the historical frame of reference."

I am still experimenting with making statements such as these in the initial stage of treatment. What I have seen so far is that it helps to disrupt the "ideal parent" fantasies and the "you fix me" expectations people often bring to therapy. It seems to function as a form of informed consent about the nature of the therapeutic effort. It is, of course, useless to say these things if the therapist does not believe and demonstrate them. At the end of the session, I often use these three themes to help the client summarize the session and define the initial focus of attention in our treatment goals and contracts.

The paper on which this chapter is based was written nearly 20 years before Chapter 1 of this volume. My experimenting continues. Both chapters illustrate the importance of the initial sessions and the direct involvement of the client in negotiating the nature of the work right from the start. My work with Suzanne, as described in Chapter 1, further illustrates the evolution of my understanding of the process and goals of psychotherapy and human relations work.

Assessment

The initial contact is rarely easy for new clients. Given the stress and anxiety—and quite possibly the denial and blaming—clients may bring to the first session, they will likely present a severely limited, problem-centered portrayal of themselves and their lives. It is, of course, important to undertake a careful exploration of clients' difficulties and their explanations of those difficulties. Much can be learned quickly about clients' coping strategies and interpersonal defenses by attending to their style of self-presentation in this first contact. I do not think a problem-centered orientation is sufficient for the initial session. I seek to move beyond the initial problem presentation to a discussion of life skills and successes in addition to life problems. While not wanting to minimize a client's distress, I do not want to foster a crisis orientation or a sense of helplessness and victimization. I want to develop a comprehensive understanding of the client, one in which I value and attend to competencies as well as disturbances.

I have found an article by Strayhorn (1983) and the developmental schemes presented by Maslow (1954, 1962), Vaillant (1977), and Kegan (1982) to be especially useful in this regard. While it is beyond the scope of this chapter to discuss the work of these authors, the reader is referred to their work for exciting perspectives on healthy personal and interpersonal development.

Strayhorn's (1983) article presented a critique of the problem-centered "symptom-cluster" scheme of diagnosis presented in the *DSM-III* (American Psychiatric Association, 1980). Strayhorn (1983, pp. 677-678) attempted to step past the technical and theoretical biases of particular treatment modalitites to develop a common language of skills and abilities in diagnosis. He defined skills as "proficiency in thought, feeling or behavior patterns that are enacted repetitively in dealing with a certain type of circumstance" (pp. 677-678). He continued, "Within the broadened definition of the word *skill,* psychotherapy is seen as an intervention wherein the learning of psychological health skills is promoted. All the skills listed here are thought to be amenable to the learning promoted by psychotherapy and other interpersonal influences" (p. 679).

Within the framework of psychological and interpersonal development, Strayhorn (1983) described life skills axes in six fundamental arenas: skills that form social bonds—of giving and receiving love; skills that deal successfully with the forces that may weaken or threaten social bonds—separation and interpersonal conflict; skills to deal with frustration, failure, and personal misdeeds as well as skills to enhance and enjoy success, favorable events, and prosocial deeds; skills for working and playing; skills of allowing thought to influence action; and skills to utilize guiding principles and meaning in life. I have found Strayhorn's attention to developmental skill and mastery an important balance to the concern for developmental gaps and impasses that often dominate the initial assessment.

I do not emphasize personal or family history in the initial interviews unless there are indications of physical or sexual abuse, addictive disorders, or patterns of recurrent depression. Otherwise, I inquire only about history relevant to the discussion at hand because I do not wish to foster the notion that the past is either the sole or primary "cause" of current difficulties or a necessary focus of our attention.

If collateral material from a referring professional or relative is available, I do not look at it until the client has had the opportunity to present himself or herself to me in his or her own way. Such an approach is consistent with the advice of Berne (1966, p. 33) and Sullivan (1954, p. 63). I consider the assessment and diagnostic phase complete when the client and I have had enough discussion to provide information about and an understanding of the following questions:

- What is bothering the client and how does he or she define the problem?
- How is it that the client has chosen this particular time to enter therapy?
- Has the client had previous therapeutic experience and how has that experience been utilized?
- What responsibility does the client take for his or her current difficulties?
- What role does he or she define for himself or herself in solving these problems?
- How does the client see me and my job as therapist? What do I anticipate about how our working relationship will need to be structured in order to be effective in promoting change?

- What are the client's primary intrapersonal and interpersonal defensive maneuvers (i.e., games, psychological rackets, life script)?
- What evidence is there of significant developmental gaps or trauma?
- In presenting the problem, does the client tend to primarily exclude awareness and consideration of self, others, or the environment?
- What effective life skills does the client demonstrate and readily utilize?
- What are the client's sources of play and pleasure (Bellis, 1981)?
- What is the client's experience of loving, intimate, and sexual relationships?
- How varied are the client's life experiences and social relationships (Bellis, 1981)?
- What life problems has the client already been able to resolve through the course of normal maturation and development?

While additional questions will likely emerge in the course of therapy, with the completion of a thorough, collaborative assessment, we have set the stage for a highly interactive, confrontive, health-oriented approach to psychotherapy.

Supervisory Notes

Marilyn Zalcman and I identified the particular significance for ongoing clinical supervision of case consultations following the initial interviews. The initial contact can establish patterns of an active, mutual treatment relationship that can enhance therapy or establish expectations and obstacles that burden and confuse the therapeutic project.

I include here a brief list of questions I have found useful in supervising the initial interview and "setting the stage" for continuing case consultation:

- How did the therapist invite and reinforce the client's participation and clear thinking in the interview?
- Is as much attention paid to what works and why as to what does not work and why not?
- Does the therapist demonstrate concern for and interest in the client's quality of life and relationships?
- How much attention is given to personal and family history? Is this history used to foster understanding rather than to "explain" the client?
- Does the therapist establish an avenue to actively discuss the therapist/client relationship?
- Can the therapist predict the structure of the therapeutic relationship and the nature of the therapeutic project from the interview material?
- Does the therapist offer a preliminary theoretical understanding of the client's functioning?
- Can the therapist envision more than one approach to treatment?
- Has the client left the session having learned something new about himself or herself?
- What did the session teach the client about the therapist and his or her role?
- What did the session teach the client about the nature of therapy?
- Are there areas that need to be pursued more thoroughly?
- What treatment goals were established overtly? What goals were established covertly?

Supervision at this point in the therapy can be especially effective because it occurs before either the client or therapist becomes too strongly entrenched in particular behaviors and expectations.

Conclusion

People, often under duress and with considerable anxiety and reluctance, seek professional guidance when they feel out of control within themselves, in their relationships, or in the course of their lives. These are times that may be filled with resistance, blame, vulnerability, avoidance, fantasy, and hope, all present at the same time in a chaotic blend. The structure and process of the initial meeting provides powerful tools in setting the stage for the work that lies ahead. The initial sessions demonstrate, consciously and unconsciously, the frame of reference for the nature of the working relationship. I view it as crucial that these initial sessions create room not only for the problems and distress that have precipitated turning to professional involvement but also for the experience of collaboration, confrontation, exploration, and competence.

REFERENCES

American Psychiatric Association. (1980). *Diagnostic and statistical manual of mental disorders* (3rd ed.). Washington, DC: Author.

Anderson, C. M., & Stewart, C. (1983). *Mastering resistance: A practical guide to family therapy.* New York: Guilford Press.

Bellis, J. (1981). On the initial interview in bioenergetic analysis. *Energy & Character: The Journal of Bioenergetic Research, 12*(1), 67-72.

Berne, E. (1963). *The structure and dynamics of organizations and groups.* New York: Grove Press.

Berne, E. (1966). *Principles of group treatment.* New York: Oxford University Press.

Berne, E. (1977). Staff-patient-staff conferences. In M. James & Contributors, *Techniques in transactional analysis for psychotherapists and counselors* (pp. 153-165). Reading, MA: Addison-Wesley. (Original work published 1968)

Fischer, C. (1978a). Personality and assessment. In R. Valle & M. King (Eds.), *Existential-phenomenological alternatives for psychology.* New York: Oxford University Press.

Fischer, C. (1978b). Collaborative psychological assessment. In C. Fischer & S. Brodsky (Eds.), *Informed participation by clients in the human services: The Prometheus principle.* New Brunswick, NJ: Transaction Press.

Fischer, C. (1979). Individualized assessment and phenomenological psychology. *Journal of Personality Assessment, 42*(2), 115-122.

Fischer, C. (1985). *Individualizing psychological assessment.* Monterey, CA: Brooks-Cole.

James, M., & Contributors. (1977). *Techniques in transactional analysis for psychotherapists and counselors.* Reading, MA: Addison-Wesley.

Kegan, R. (1982). *The evolving self: Problem and process in human development.* Cambridge, MA: Harvard University Press.

Maslow, A. H. (1954). *Motivation and personality.* New York: Harper & Row.

Maslow, A. H. (1962). *Toward a psychology of being.* Princeton, NJ: Van Nostrand.

Pruyser, P. (1984). The diagnostic process: Touchstone of medicine's values. In F. Shectman & W. Smith (Eds.), *Diagnostic understanding and treatment planning: The elusive connection* (pp. 5-17). New York: Wiley.

Shectman, F., & Smith, W. (1984). *Diagnostic understanding and treatment planning: The elusive connection.* New York: Wiley.

Steiner, C. (1968). Transactional analysis as a treatment philosophy. *Transactional Analysis Bulletin, 7*(27), 61-64.

Steiner, C. (1974). *Scripts people live: Transactional analysis of life scripts.* New York: Grove Press.

Strayhorn, J. (1983). A diagnostic axis relevant to psychotherapy and preventative mental health. *American Journal of Orthopsychiatry, 53,* 677-696.

Sullivan, H. S. (1954). *The psychiatric interview.* New York: Norton.

Vaillant, G. E. (1977). *Adaptation to life.* Boston: Little, Brown.

The original version of this chapter was published in the Transactional Analysis Journal, *Volume 16, Number 1, pp. 4-10, January 1986.*

3

Impasse and Intimacy: Applying Berne's Concept of Script Protocol

William F. Cornell and N. Michel Landaiche, III

The word "impasse"... is an unfortunate and daunting term: "an impassable road or way; a blind alley, cul-de-sac; hence, a position or predicament allowing no escape."... Still, it has usually been possible to back out or muddle our way to an escape route. (McLaughlin, 1994, p. 1)

The closest relationships are the ones that we know the least about. (Berne, 1970, pp. 114-115)

Eric Berne drew inspiration from his original psychoanalytic training to create a new model of psychotherapy that was both more efficient and more user-friendly than the psychoanalysis of his time. His model—transactional analysis—also proved more comprehensive. It could be used to analyze intrapsychic transactions within the client's mind as well as interpersonal transactions in the client's life. It could be used to treat individuals suffering from problems in addition to helping those seeking personal learning and growth. Transactional analysis could also be applied to understanding the dynamics and difficulties of groups and organizations. These broad traditions continue to underlie the many forms of transactional analysis being practiced and taught today. They also continue to make transactional analysis a powerful tool for social learning and change.

Yet there are times when the model functions poorly. In spite of our best efforts, certain interactions with some clients become intractably stuck. What can transactional analysis teach us about resolving such impasses in our therapeutic, educational, and consulting work? How could transactional analysis be modified to increase its usefulness in these difficult encounters?

Looking back, we can see that—along with the many useful traditions inherited by transactional analysis practitioners and trainees—there are also some that seem counterproductive. For example, in spite of Berne's sincere efforts to develop a treatment model that was more accessible to clients and based on a mutual, contractual working relationship, he also held himself carefully apart from his clients and his therapeutic engagement with them, much as his psychoanalytic contemporaries did. Berne maintained the role of the external observer, examining and analyzing patterns of intrapsychic and interpersonal interaction in his diagnosis of each client's ego states, transactions, games, and script phenomena. Berne's emphasis on making change through conscious, intentional choice has also fostered a professional culture that can be intolerant of what cannot be changed through insight alone.

We in transactional analysis can trace some of our technical failures to this legacy of disengagement on the part of the therapist and an overemphasis on the cognitive. However, this legacy also continues to exert its influence because of the considerable difficulties that arise when working in a more engaged manner. When it comes to making contact with states of self and affect that do not readily lend themselves to words or diagrams, many of us are reluctant to experience the disturbances our clients bring to and evoke in us. Yet such disturbances seem an inevitable consequence of the intimacy that develops in every therapeutic and consulting relationship. The very nature of such close contact between any two or more human beings is bound to affect us at levels that operate outside of consciousness and that inform our most fundamental patterns of relating. As a result, we may discover ourselves and our working relationships stalled in habitual ways of being, often accompanied by feelings of frustration, anger, and a sense of inadequacy. Once our work has become so maddeningly stuck, how do we find our way back to productive engagement?

Theoretical Perspectives on the Nature of Impasses

In the early transactional analysis literature, the term "impasse" was used by Goulding and Goulding (1978, 1979), Erskine (1978/1997), Johnson (1978), Mellor (1980), and others to refer to a conflict or stalemate between ego states within the client. The term did not refer to a breakdown in the therapeutic process per se. Therefore, interventions to address impasses were designed to facilitate a resolution and were focused on intrapsychic redecisions, not on understanding the relationship dynamics between the professional and client. Gradually, however, the term "impasse" was used to describe the experience of being stuck in the working relationship, as impasses were initially being explored by Novellino (1984), Moiso (1985), and others. Even Bob Goulding, 10 years later, was discussing impasses in terms of the therapist's countertransference contribution (Hoyt & Goulding, 1989).

This shift was consistent with growing interest in the transactional analysis community in understanding the dynamics of the working relationship through such concepts as parallel process, transference and countertransference, and projective identification and the contributions these phenomena make to difficulties in treatment. Today, discussions of transference and countertransference are as common in transactional analysis as they are in other schools of psychotherapy. We, therefore, believe it is important for transactional analysts to be familiar with these and related terms, if only to access the rich literature and ongoing debates pertaining to these complex dynamics in psychotherapy, counseling, teaching, and supervision. While most of the literature addressing these issues has been written from a clinical perspective, we see these dynamics operating across the range of psychotherapeutic, counseling, training, supervisory, and educational fields. Thus, throughout this chapter we will refer to professionals and practitioners so as not to isolate this discussion to clinical fields.

An impasse typically impoverishes the therapeutic or consultative experience. Impasses situated within the client's intrapsychic dynamics (i.e., within script and counterscript) will limit the client's Adult capacities, and autonomous functioning may be severely compromised by childhood influences. In the face of actual client-centered impasses, the professional will most likely be able to observe, think, and relate effectively, and these abilities can then function as significant resources for the client who is trying to get out of his or her own bind. However, sometimes the client's professional resource is disabled when conflicts and inhibitions within the professional's functioning restrict his or her capacity to observe, think, and relate flexibly. In such situations, professional-centered supervision is necessary to prevent the work from becoming repetitive, superficial, cognitively dominated, and ultimately ineffective or harmful. Once the therapist or consultant has resolved his or her own impasse, the client can return to making use of the professional as a source of help.

Intrapsychic Impasse. One means of understanding a point of impasse within the therapeutic/educational process is to focus on a potential impasse within the mind (between the ego states) of the client. The theory of impasses was first developed in transactional analysis by Goulding and Goulding (1978, 1979) and further elaborated by Mellor (1980).

According to Mellor (1980), first-degree impasses are the internalization of verbalized and demonstrated parental counterinjunctions and accordingly are carried in language. Second-degree impasses are a result of script-level injunctions originating much earlier in development and are encoded and communicated through emotions. Mellor posits third-degree impasses as being related to "primal protocols" (p. 214) that originate in "very early experience, perhaps even prenatal" (p. 214). In keeping with the redecision model developed by the Gouldings, Mellor goes on to suggest that treatment interventions focus on remembering/recreating with the client the scenes in which the original parental injunctions were taken in by the child, which led the child to make a script decision that becomes evident in later life through areas of intrapsychic impasse. In this model, resolution of first-degree impasses between P_2 and C_2 occurs through redecisions from A_2, and resolution of second-degree impasses occurs between P_1 and C_1 by redecision in A_1. Third-degree impasses are understood to occur between P_0 and C_0 with the redecision by A_0, but we find it hard to conceive of a "redecision" being made at a level of psychic experience and organization that has no real capacity to observe or think. We suggest, and will elaborate later, that third-degree impasses are rooted in the level of experience Berne called "protocol" and that they are enacted within the working relationship and change as they are reorganized (rather than redecided) within the therapeutic relationship. When the understanding of impasses moves from the intrapsychic realm of the client to include the interpersonal realm between client and practitioner (therapist, educator, consultant, etc.), then various forms of transference/countertransference come into play as described in the following section.

Transference and Countertransference. The essence of theories of transference and countertransference is that there is unconscious communication and interpersonal pressure from the client to the therapist arising from the client's emotional (Child ego state) confusion of the therapist with an early parental figure that causes the therapist to seem to the client to feel and behave like that historical figure. Berne's game theory provides one avenue for analyzing and intervening in the interpersonal communication patterns that sustain transference/countertransference dynamics. Seen from the perspective of script theory, the client's script is enacted within the transference/countertransference matrix with the unconscious cooperation of the therapist, who has been drawn into participating as a character in the client's script. Seen from the perspective of classical transactional analysis, the therapist is hooked into a game that maintains the client's script, and neither is able to think clearly about what is occurring. The inability of the therapist and client to step outside of what is happening and think about it creates the conditions for an impasse in which the interpersonal behavior becomes repetitive and thus reinforced rather than changed.

In our view, script-centered, historical interpretations that focus primarily on the intrapsychic conflicts and distortions within the client can serve to keep the professional's own intrapsychic experience out of view, thus shielding the professional and client from the intimacies and uncertainties of their working relationship. As Rosenfeld (1987/1995) observed, "If the analyst has many areas which can be described as 'private: no entry' . . . then the analyst and patient may collude unconsciously to keep those areas out of the analysis and so create a therapeutic impasse" (p. 39).

The literature on transference and countertransference is immense, and detailed consideration of it is outside the scope of this chapter. Within the transactional analytic literature, readers are referred to thorough discussions of these dynamics in two special issues of the *Transactional Analysis Journal* (Friedlander, 1991a, 1991b), as well as in Clarkson (1992) and Hargaden and Sills (2002). Over time, these terms have come to refer to unconscious emotional and psychological patterns between therapist and client in which the therapist may be drawn into the client's script or vice versa. Script-level interpretations and interventions with one or both members of the pair are needed to dislodge the impasse.

Parallel Process. Parallel process is a form of transference in which the practitioner enacts with a third party (typically a supervisor) dynamics that originally arose with a client. Discussions of parallel process tend to posit the origins of a therapeutic impasse within the functioning of the therapist rather than the client. The central supervisory intervention is to identify an element of the therapist's script that has been evoked in the work, because once "in script," the therapist can no longer be effective. Supervisory attention is then shifted to the therapist's intrapsychic experience and away from that of the client. Although little has actually been written in the transactional analysis literature about parallel process, use of the concept has become commonplace within the supervisory models used in transactional analysis training throughout Europe and North America. However, in our experience, it seems that the concept of parallel process has been taken up in supervisory contexts without sufficient explication and examination in the published transactional analysis literature.

The concept of parallel process emerged in the psychoanalytic literature within discussions of the supervisory process as first put forth by Searles (1955), Ekstein and Wallerstein (1958), and Arlow (1963). Each of these explorations of the supervisory process makes rich reading, quite apart from the specific issues we are addressing here. For example, Searles described the process through which a therapist would unconsciously show (we would now say "enact") rather than tell the patient about those aspects of their interactions with which the therapist had great difficulty.

Ekstein and Wallerstein were perhaps the first to use the term "parallel process," by which they meant that the therapist's problems of understanding and learning in supervision are related to the patient's problems in therapy. They emphasized that the supervisor and the therapist can also create a parallel process that is then conveyed back to the patient because supervision is also an emotionally charged process devoted to learning and change in which both parties can experience personal vulnerability and stuck points.

Arlow emphasized that elements of parallel process are inevitable and educative for all (supervisor, therapist, and client). For him, parallel process is a result of the therapist's identification with the conflicts and struggles of the patient. Parallel process is a result of an overidentification in which the therapist cannot clearly observe and think about what is going on and so transmits the problem in supervision through actions rather than words. Arlow stresses that parallel process does not mean that the therapist is stuck in a pathological countertransference (i.e., "hooked in script") but is engaged in a level of experience with the client that is not yet available through words. He emphasized that supervision is a kind of psychoanalysis of a psychoanalysis. It is not a psychoanalysis of the psychoanalyst. We strongly concur that the function of supervision, especially when working with points of impasse in treatment and/or parallel process, is to reach an understanding and opening up of the therapeutic process—it is not a form of treatment of the professional.

Projective Identification. Projective identification, an aspect of transference (Goldstein, 1991; Ogden, 1982), was first articulated within the Kleinian tradition (Klein, 1946). It involves a deep, unconscious pattern of emotional communication, usually from the client to the practitioner but also potentially from the practitioner to the client or the supervisor. Kleinians offer a particular understanding of projective identification as "that aspect of the transference that involves the therapist's being enlisted in an interpersonal actualization (an actual enactment between patient and therapist) of a segment of the patient's internal world" (Ogden, 1982, p. 69).

We understand projective identification as an unconscious effort at affect regulation in which the client experiences an emotional, intrapsychic disturbance, usually a state of intense affect, that he or she cannot tolerate. This affective disturbance is understood to be projected by the client into the professional, who then feels what the client cannot tolerate. In these situations the professional's feelings, while often intense and uncomfortable, are not a result of his or her own unresolved conflicts (as is understood in parallel process) but are a consequence of the projection of the client's disowned feelings. If the practitioner is able to tolerate and observe these states of projected affect, she or he can contain the disturbance and use those affective states to understand the client's internal world. Gradually the feelings can then become tolerable to the client and can be used for self-understanding and conscious communication. When the professional is unable to tolerate these deep states of affective disturbance, an impasse is likely to occur in which there will be a defensive splitting of good and bad—tolerable and intolerable—that renders understanding and conscious communication virtually impossible.

These conceptualizations of intrapsychic impasse, parallel process, transference/countertransference, and projective identification are each a description of the defensive dynamics of script and tend to suggest that impasses reflect the psychopathology of the client, the mental health professional, or both. We have found, over years of training and supervision, that these terms are often useful, but not always sufficient, for understanding and changing points of interpersonal impasse. Moreover, these ideas are often accompanied by both attributions of immaturity to all unconscious and unworded phenomena and a mystification of ordinary modes of nonverbal communication. We wish to emphasize that such mystification and judgmental attributions to the unconscious and the nonverbal do not help professionals or clients understand that we continually live large sectors of our lives outside of conscious awareness and that we conduct many of our most essential, nonproblematic, and often intimate transactions without using words.

We have also found that often at exactly those points of breakthrough from script (that of the client or the practitioner)—that is, just when one might expect an impasse to be resolved—a stalemate may nonetheless occur. At such times in treatment and change, intense anxiety may emerge within the working dyad (in contrast to an intrapsychic disturbance in one or the other of the pair). This anxiety seems to be generated by the simultaneous breaking of the familiarity and predictability of script combined with movement into unfamiliar, unmapped modes of relating. These moments are more a matter of falling into health and novelty rather than into pathology and history.

In addition to our understanding of impasses from the perspectives just described—intrapsychic impasse, transference/countertransference, parallel process, and projective identification—we have gained significant insight from the use of Berne's original concept of protocol (Berne, 1961, p. 117; 1963/1975, p. 228). At moments of potential therapeutic transformation, there are no templates for the future, which creates both excitement and anxiety. We have observed that at these times there is often a heightened vulnerability to the reemergence of our earliest relational patterns, which Berne called "protocols," as a means of managing the anxiety of the unknown. When early protocols emerge within the working dyad, impasse is much more likely to occur than transformation and growth.

Before discussing Berne's theory of protocol, we will elaborate the idea of the "working couple" in the context of education, treatment, and consultation.

The Working Couple

To understand the dynamics of impasse that arise in the course of psychotherapy, education, supervision, and consultation, we have found it useful to frame them in terms of a working therapeutic or consultative couple.

Obviously, the term "couple" can be highly evocative. It is often associated with sexuality, romance, and the parental dyad along with images of sexual, romantic, and partnering failure. All of these emotional features and fantasies can arise in professional relationships that form for the purpose of promoting self-understanding and development. Human relationships always operate within erotic fields of varying intensities. In any new relationship, there is frequently a sense of hope and romance associated with what the other might bring to make one's life richer. And once any two of us begin working together, we typically develop a sense of familiarity that can move between trust and mistrust and comfort and irritation, not to mention autonomy and dependence. All of these conditions can stimulate our most fundamental sense of what it means to be in relationship with our intimates.

For these reasons, we believe the word "couple" aptly describes the intimacy characteristic of therapy, consultation, and mentoring. Although a couple usually refers to a dyadic relationship, the emotional characteristics associated with the word apply as well in settings in which there are more than two people working together. And while the terms "group" and "family" also can be emotionally charged, they fail to convey the degree of proximity that develops in group contexts and within which all individuals working together must come to some recognition of their own bodily responses and unspoken patterns of interaction. Simply put, the term "couple" points to our most intense, primary, and challenging modes of relating.

Furthermore, the image of the couple underscores a fundamental human process of interaction to which certain professional skills and contractual obligations are brought to bear. The contract in a professional setting may be to address what is not working in the client's life, what is insufficiently developed, or what new personal or professional skills need to be learned. Any of these may be the reason a working therapeutic or consultative couple comes into being. Yet the inherent relational asymmetry is also counterbalanced by the fact that neither party is necessarily healthier, smarter, or better educated. Both can contribute as full partners to the task at hand.

As this couple begins to work, the development of intimacy or closeness is unavoidable, even in situations in which there appears to be substantial professional distance. In recognition of this fact of relational life, we use the term "intimacy"—as we do "couple"—for its evocative associations of physical and emotional proximity and for its precision. We are not suggesting a therapeutic goal or ideal.

Intimacy sometimes connotes tenderness and quiet. But for some it can evoke crowding, suffocation, and noise. Perhaps at its most productive, intimacy is a bodily capacity for sustaining affect, thinking, and working to put experiences into language within an ongoing relationship. Even without physical contact, intimacy describes the way we get into and under the skin of the other person and the way the other gets into and under our skin, too. It is not always pleasurable, although it sometimes can be.

In some situations, intimacy may encourage the capacity for experimentation, exploration, self-reflection, and recognition of differences as well as the capacity for those involved to think together about the functioning of the couple or the group. It may also encourage the reverse: the avoidance of differences, the collapse of thinking and reflection, and the prohibition of dynamic interplay. Indeed, the intimacy that develops within therapeutic and consultative couples may be characterized by many of the same gratifications, satisfactions, irritations, and blinds spots that attend any of our closest relationships. Such intimacy often touches and disturbs us where we least expect it and, particularly, where we are least prepared to understand what is going on. Even when interactions within the working couple are apparently going well, we are always deeply immersed in modes of being that have been typical throughout our lives with other intimates, both past and present. At the same time, regardless of how things are going, the ground is being laid for the unique interplay and character that develops within each therapeutic or consultative couple. And it is on that rich and unwitting basis—in that complex, often turbulent interpersonal field—that intimacy can so easily lead to impasse.

In a consultative, learning, or therapeutic setting, impasse describes the experience of the work being stuck—unable to move forward or step out of its repetitive loop. An impasse for the therapeutic or consultative couple is characterized by the loss of reflective or free-thinking capacities. It is an induction into an automatic or predictable way of being with self and others, an arrested form of development. In essence, the relationship of the couple stops evolving and maturing. Both members of the couple become stuck in a region of the mind and body that neither can think about. This is typically due to the intensity of affect that resides in our closeness with one another and the passions we inevitably experience in that proximity.

Many impasses take the form of covert contracts or collusions that are negotiated outside awareness of the working couple. These take innumerable forms, as diverse as the quality of the intimacy that can develop between any two people. And although impasses are often seen as a kind of catastrophic or overtly destructive stuckness, there are also impasses of the blissfully stuck kind in which there is an agreement, again made outside awareness, to remain in a state of immovable complementarity.

Whatever the emotional valence of the impasse, it is typically the result of an overload or threat of affect that gets out of hand and mind. However, impasses can also occur in the apparent absence of any affect, within a working relationship that looks and feels utterly dead, especially if an unconscious agreement has been reached within the couple not to stir things up too much. As Hinshelwood (1994) asked, "What is going on when it seems nothing is going on? The stilling of lively contact by the patient—perhaps with the analyst's collusion—can be understood as a protective endeavor to remain afloat among flooding anxieties" (p. 193). The threat of affective intensity can be sufficient to sustain a stillness that is at once reassuring and deadening.

In an intimate impasse, both people are trapped in a mode of relating and both experience it as the only available option. Impasse is a kind of emotional activation that occurs "under the skin" and that is responded to in highly repetitive, sometimes nonproductive ways, as if each party only knows one thing to do under the circumstances. With any luck, some intervention can be made to address this process (often input from a third party) while there is still time to discover what is going on, before the illusion of permanence has a chance to kill the life of the couple. For instance, in a therapist-client couple, hopefully the impasse can be brought to supervision before the desperate professional escalates the diagnosis of his or her own pathology or that of the client.

Impasses within the professional couple, however, can threaten the very existence of the work as well as the viability of the relationship. These are the relational impasses in which it is not uncommon for the psychotherapist or consultant to terminate the work prematurely (sometimes under the guise of making a more appropriate referral) or in which clients feel deeply damaged and may themselves abruptly quit, personally attack the therapist, or bring ethics charges. We find it helpful to think of these intimate, seemingly intractable impasses as arising out of the mutual evocation of each person's unconscious, relational protocols, as Berne defined the concept.

Protocol: The Relational Template for Intimate Contact and Disturbance

Before proposing his idea of protocol, Berne was deeply interested in what he called "intuition," which today we might see as the unconscious organization of sensory, nonverbal experiences. Berne's early writings on this topic were collected posthumously in *Intuition and Ego States* (Berne, 1977a).

In one of these papers, "Intuition IV: Primal Images and Primal Judgments," Berne (1955/1977b) discussed the relationship between the infant's early, primal image of a significant other and the infant's primal judgment based on that image. He defined the primal image as the infant's "presymbolic, non-verbal representation of interpersonal transactions" (p. 67). In essence, a primal image is an impression made on the child's body by a significant other's "mode of relating" (p. 68). It is a cluster of sensations, organized outside awareness by the child, one that reflects his or her experience of another before the child has access to words or symbols. Berne considered the child's organizing role to be an act of primal judgment, similar to the judgments we make about our worlds throughout life and, in particular, about others we see as significant allies or enemies. Berne defined this kind of judgment as "an image of reality which affects behavior and feelings toward reality. An image is formed by integrating sensory and other impressions with each other and with inner tensions based on present needs and past experiences" (p. 72).

In Berne's conception, the formation of the image and the action of judging are nearly simultaneous processes. They describe what occurs when we have a flash of intuition about a person or situation we have encountered, an assessment that may or may not be accurate. Berne essentially combined his early ideas about primal images and primal judgments into his later concept of the protocol. With characteristic humor, Berne (1963/1975) conveyed his sense of the simultaneously creative and defensive functions of the protocol:

> Each person has an unconscious life plan, formulated in his earliest years, which he takes every opportunity to further as much as he dares in a given situation. This plan calls for other people to respond in a desired way.... The original set of experiences which forms *the pattern for the plan* is called the protocol..... Partly because of the advantages of being an infant, even under bad conditions, every human being is left with some nostalgia for his infancy and often for his childhood as well; therefore, in later years he strives to bring about as close as possible a reproduction of the original protocol situation, either to live it through again if it was enjoyable, or to try to re-experience it in a more benevolent form if it was unpleasant. (pp. 218-219, italics added)

As Berne (1963/1975) went on to describe, these unconscious patterns of relating then become the basis for later script decisions:

> The original drama, the protocol, is usually completed in the early years of childhood, often by the age of 5, occasionally earlier. This drama may be played out again in more elaborate form, in accordance with the growing child's changing abilities, needs and social situation, in the next few years. Such a later version is called the palimpsest. A protocol or palimpsest is of such a

crude nature that it is quite unsuitable as a program for grown-up relationships. It becomes largely forgotten (unconscious) and is replaced by a more civilized version, the script proper: a plan of which the individual is not actively aware (preconscious), but which can be brought into consciousness by appropriate procedures. (p. 228)

In essence, Berne suggested that the protocol is a latent level of somatic and relational organization that precedes the formation of script and operates outside of conscious awareness. Contemporary infant observation research suggests that relational protocols are established well before the age of five. In his groundbreaking observations, Stern (1985) wrote:

Our concern . . . is with preverbal infants and with different happenings such as what happens when you are hungry and at breast, or what happens when you and mom play an exciting game. Moreover, our interest concerns not only the actions but also the sensations and affects. What we are concerned with, then, are episodes that involve interpersonal interactions of different types. Further, we are concerned with the interactive experience, not just the interactive events. I am suggesting these episodes are also averaged and represented preverbally. (p. 97)

What Berne accounted for initially in his speculations about intuition and subsequently in his observations of the protocol would today be accounted for in the contemporary language of implicit relational knowing (Lyons-Ruth, 1999) or the coconstruction of intersubjectivity (Beebe & Lachmann, 2000).

Protocol-based behavior is not a game-like, ulterior form of communication but a deeply compelling, implicit (wordless) memory of primary relational patterns lived through the immediacy of bodily experience. Protocols function as ongoing, unconscious templates for making judgments about the significant figures and encounters in our lives. Yet protocols are not necessarily pathological; they embody an innate human capacity for making unconscious sense of life with others. They only become problematic when they interfere with the ability to generate new bodily and relational possibilities.

According to Steere (1985), one of the few transactional analysis practitioners and researchers to substantively address the concept of protocol,

the best explanation for the phenomenon of protocol is that the Child ego state preserves in particular psychomotor patterns an often repeated sequence of events from formative years. Our earliest way of thinking, from birth to 18 month according to Piaget (Piaget & Inhelder, 1954), is in the form of sensorimotor schemes. . . . The sensorimotor constructs contain all the cognitive substructures that will serve as a point of departure for later perceptual and intellectual development, as well as the elementary affect reactions that shape emotional life. (p. 254)

Given how little Berne actually wrote about protocol, it is not surprising that not much else has been written about this key concept in his theory. The term "protocol" has typically been used only in passing by most transactional analysis theorists. As an exception, Greve (1976) proposed a form of intervention for protocol based on the gestalt redecision models prevalent at the time. Steere (1985), as just noted, explored in greater depth the way protocol elements appear in bodily postures as clients live out their scripts. Hostie (1984) and Müller (2000) discussed protocol in the context of the evolution of Berne's thinking, and Cornell (2003) has elaborated Berne's original concept more explicitly in terms of contemporary interest in somatic process, unconscious communication, and creative interplay in therapy.

Woods (2003) is among the contemporary transactional analysts who believe it is important to focus attention on here-and-now communications between the client and professional, on communications that are occurring outside awareness, and on the unconscious content of games. From that perspective, exclusively historical interpretations of client protocol material can be experienced as distancing from the immediate encounter with that client's active, if unconscious, sense of self in the world and in interaction with the professional today. Caravella and Marone (2003) wrote of this balanced attention in regard to working with psychotic patients, which they do by listening "freely to the patient's pain" and by establishing "an intimate Child-Child communication and a therapeutic alliance with the Adult . . . even during the psychotic phase" (p. 252).

Protocol is not a set of adaptive or defensive decisions like a script. It is not remembered in a narrative fashion but felt/lived in the immediacy of one's body. Protocol is the literal embodiment of the repetitive, often affectively intense, patterns of relatedness preceding the infant's capacity of ego function. Script, in contrast, is—as Berne emphasized—preconscious, that is, potentially available to conscious awareness. Script can be recognized as an adaptation of the ego, often to the underlying protocol. The situations in which script decisions are made can often be remembered in the context of some sort of story or narrative. Protocol, on the other hand, precedes and underlies the subsequent, narrative-based script.

We are suggesting that with his concept of protocol, Berne was trying to capture the sense of the most fundamental, nonverbal aspects of what it means to relate to someone. He was describing an unconscious, fundamental relational experience that underlies many transferential experiences, be they expressed as impasses, enactments, parallel process, or projective identification. Protocol is a kernel of nonverbal, somatic experience that may be touched or triggered in intimate relationships. Such moments are often impregnated with both hope and dread. When the experience of a therapeutic relationship evokes protocol, the Child ego state is deeply opened, and the transference dynamics that may then be played out become more anxiety provoking and more difficult to tolerate, understand, and resolve for both client and practitioner. Protocol does not exist separate from a person's sense of self but is the very matrix from which we each organize our relational experiences. It is inextricable from our bodies and selves. The most salient aspect of protocol, as distinct from script, is that it cannot be cognitively changed, redecided, or rescripted. Protocol can only be brought into awareness, understood, and lived within. We can only alter how we behave as a consequence of our protocols. In short, we can decide not to act on the sense made with our bodies at one time in life if that sense does not serve us well at this time in life. But we cannot change what the sense feels like because it operates "under our skin." Protocols are with us for life, never fully analyzed or understood, like our experiences of unconscious realms in general. We can never diffuse their intensity, but we can open them to new experience and action. In contrast to script, which can be changed through cognitive processes, protocol changes gradually through new, lived experiences that teach us new possibilities for being alive in our bodies and with others.

The dictionary definition of protocol is "an original draft, copy, minute, or record of a document or transaction; a body of official formulas," a term not easily translated into other languages. This sense of "how things are done," a feeling of procedures bred in the bone, seems to be what Berne was trying to evoke in choosing this particular word. While we suspect that the "shadow" of the protocol always remains, it does change, and it is often at points of impasse that the opportunity for change presents itself. The possibilities that emerge within the struggles and intimacies of the working couple can breathe a sense of new life and possibility (for client and professional alike), expanding parameters at the protocol level of organization.

The deepening intimacy within a therapeutic or consultative relationship brings us in contact with our passions about others and the world, and that growing contact and intensity can lead us to become stuck. In that sense, an impasse at the level of the protocol is a defense against deepening affect and intimacy within the therapeutic couple.

For example, a therapist in supervision described his disgust with a certain client's lack of hygiene and his frustration in their work together. However, once he explored the situation further, he realized he was actually troubled by sitting with a woman who was living her life in madness. It was the pervasive impact of her deep emotional disturbance, not her actual body odor, that he could not bear to name or take into his physical being. This insight shook his conception of himself as a therapist who believed he could, with skilled interpretations and careful emotional reserve, cure the troubled people who came his way. In fact, that particular client was in a psychotic state and desperately needed emotional engagement and containment from her therapist, not interpretation or detachment.

This therapist, through his transactional analysis training and personal therapy, had come to understand that much of his motivation and style as a therapist was script based. His had been a chaotic family system, one from which he protected himself by increasing layers of emotional distance and finely tuned critical thinking. He remembered his decision as an adolescent to become a psychiatrist, feeling if he could not cure the suffering and chaos within his own family, he could at least relieve it in the lives of others not so close to him. As he addressed his impasse with this unkempt, psychotic woman, he began to realize that he felt invaded by her. With her smell and her madness, he could not maintain his script-based distancing. He felt moved by her, touched as well as invaded, and he realized how disorganized he felt in her presence. He remembered that he had often felt this way in his mother's presence, though he could not recall specific instances. He also realized that this psychotic client had, for some reason, come to trust him and was committed in her own peculiar way to a real relationship with him. Neither knew quite what to do with themselves or each other. This characterized their impasse.

When given the idea of protocol as a tool with which to think about his experience, in addition to what he knew of his script, the therapist began to feel his fear of the invasiveness of his mother's anxiety and disorganization. He then felt less afraid of his client and her madness and began to feel, to his surprise, a kind of tenderness toward her. Though he did not share any of this with her, he could see that she felt the difference in his way of being with her. He gained confidence that he could accept and contain her deep disturbances. They recovered their capacity to feel, think, and work together.

So, although their coupling began with two separate histories and two sets of unconscious, relational protocols, this therapist and his client were together developing a discomfiting history and protocol mix of their own. Together, they also needed to find a way of being with one another that allowed a gradual closeness and understanding—an emotional sanity and compassion—in the face of madness and habitual recoiling from closeness.

In moments of therapeutic intimacy, professional and client both show one another what it means and how it feels to be close. Their encounter starts with a way of being, each with the other. Words may follow, but they do not lead. As Bollas (1999) reflects, "Each patient creates an environment in which both participants are meant to live a psychoanalytic lifetime together. The therapist must be willing to suffer the illness of such a place" (p. 142). As we conceive of the work in therapy, education, and consultation, the word "illness" does not suggest pathology as much as it does a feeling of being deeply ill at ease in a way of being, as if we were feeling sick. Nor is suffering meant to suggest victimization or masochism. As Bollas uses the term, he means the act of being with and informed by a client's way of living such that we know it keenly from inside our own bodies.

With each client, we live a unique encounter in time. Moreover, our openness to understanding our clients' modes of being means that we will develop an intimacy with them that will affect or infect us with many of our strongest feelings and protocols. We, in turn, convey those experiences back to our clients, in a reciprocal and often unspoken dialogue about what it means to be in the world with others. The often subtle interaction of those relational cues and countercues can be traced in the following case illustration.

Getting "Under the Skin": A Case of Protocol at Work

Anna, a therapist in her mid-forties with considerable clinical experience, had been presenting a troubling case for several months in supervision. The work with her client, Catherine, a successful advertising writer in her late thirties, had apparently proceeded well for the first 3 years. Catherine had entered treatment after a devastating breakup with a lover. She described herself as the one who broke men's hearts by leaving them when the relationship peaked in its excitement. This gave her a great sense of desirability and power. She told Catherine that for years she had fucked men, not loved them. This most recent lover, however, she had begun to love, and his leaving left her furious, humiliated, and bereft. Although Catherine spent many of the early sessions raging about what a "pig" this man was, she knew she had actually entered therapy to give up what she saw as her perverse sexual behavior and learn to love someone. She wanted children and a family and feared she was not capable of such attachments.

Anna felt a deep respect for Catherine's commitment to therapy and found herself growing quite fond of her client. She did not want Catherine to get hurt again and at the same time felt silently judgmental of Catherine's risky sexual exploits. Catherine, on the other hand, had begun to complain of feeling too vulnerable and dependent on Anna. In some way, Anna's respect and affection had begun to register in Catherine's experience, but she felt disoriented with it and could not recognize it for what it was—one woman (who happened to be a therapist) coming to respect and care for another woman (who happened to be a client). Catherine grew increasingly anxious in her relationship with Anna and started to become silently suspicious of Anna's motives. At the same time, Catherine acknowledged that she was gaining a good deal of insight, had stopped leaping from one relationship to another, and—with Anna's active insistence—was spending a period of time alone in her life without a lover to stimulate and distract her.

Catherine told Anna that she felt her interest and investment but did not understand her motives. What she did not tell Anna was that she had begun to project onto Anna many romantic and sexual fantasies to explain Anna's deepening interest in her. Catherine could only understand experiencing their deepening intimacy in the familiar terms of sexual usage. She pressed Anna to explain how she really felt about her. Unable to tolerate or explore Catherine's deepening anxiety and confusion, Anna finally gave in to the pressure and explained to Catherine that she was not treating her any differently than any other client, that she was invested in the quality of Catherine's life, and that she did not want to foster a dependent relationship. Catherine was profoundly shocked and humiliated by this explanation, though she could not risk telling Anna how she felt.

Up to this point, the treatment relationship had been productive, but it had also stayed within the essential elements of both Anna's and Catherine's scripts. Anna, due to her own therapy, had subtly begun to change her way of relating to her clients, including Catherine. She had started to discover that being less habitually nurturing to her clients left her feeling more open and deeply engaged with them. The closeness, she found, could also be quite unnerving. The therapeutic relationship between Anna and Catherine, although still influenced by script constraints, was productive enough to begin opening levels of intimacy, shifting each of the women from predictable, script-level styles of relating into more unpredictable realms. Neither was conscious of the shift, but each felt increasingly disorganized and anxious. Neither could tolerate and reflect on the anxiety, and both shifted into escalated script behavior to ward off anxiety and the uncertainty of what was emerging between them.

In retrospect, we can speculate about the script and protocol levels of interaction for both Anna and Catherine. Anna was born to a very young mother who had not finished high school and who greeted the birth of her daughter with overwhelming anxiety. Anna "knew" through her body, from her earliest days, that she was a profound source of anxiety to her mother, which her mother enacted with massively intrusive behavior. Her father, immature and frightened of the world (and of his wife), withdrew from his endlessly distressed and inconsolable wife and from the baby. Anna quickly discovered that if she calmed herself down, Mom was more at ease and available. Infant Anna probably scanned the environment constantly for signs of anxiety. Anxiety was the defining state of affect at the level of protocol, and separation of one sort or another among family members was the relational means of reducing anxiety. As she grew older, Anna learned to soothe her mother and entertain her father, in a severe and chronic reversal of roles—and the beginning of her script. Anna's earlier protocol was dominated by anxiety and distancing, while her caretaking and entertaining script provided a more satisfying (if defensive) experience of relationship. When other siblings were born, Anna became the caretaker and buffer for all anxieties—more script. We could say that, by age 3, a "therapist" was already hard at work.

Catherine, in contrast, was an only child, born out of wedlock. Her father did not want the baby and threatened to leave his girlfriend if she did not have an abortion. Due to pressures from both families, the young couple married and had the baby, or "the little brat," as Catherine's father typically referred to her. Catherine's mother, terrified of losing her reluctant husband, often left "the brat" in the care of grandparents or girlfriends and renewed a vigorous sexual relationship with her husband, serving at his beck and call. Catherine never had a chance of breaking into this fused and immature couple. Life in the house was saturated with sexual energy. Her body knew little of tenderness or constancy but a great deal about anxiety, loneliness, and hostility; this was her protocol. Her script was centered in hatred and in living up to her nickname, "the brat." She insisted that her earliest memory was of wishing her father dead. No one could tell her what to do. She was smoking at 10, drinking at 12, having sex and using drugs by 13. She was raped for the first time at 15. In a later adolescent evolution of her script, she became the rapist, and then as an advertising writer she obtained great satisfaction in writing "bullshit," "getting over on everybody," and making a good deal of money.

The deepening involvement and intimacy between Anna and Catherine carried each of them beyond the safety of their scripts. The closeness threatened them both, and the resulting anxieties pushed each into affective and bodily experiences at the level of protocol, which for these two women would become bad news. Neither was able to tolerate either the intimacy or the anxiety, and no one in the treatment system was aware of the idea of protocol so as to help them understand what was happening. Each reacted to the pain and anxiety of the protocol level of experience by moving back into script defenses with unconscious urgency.

In what seemed to Anna to be an abrupt change, treatment took a turn for the worse. In session after session, Catherine accused Anna of having lied to her, of having seduced her sexually, and of causing her depression and suicidality to worsen. Outside the sessions, Catherine began photographing Anna and her car and home. Anna's efforts to explore what had gone wrong were increasingly derailed by Catherine's escalating behavior both during and outside their sessions. Catherine began sending long, rambling letters and cards in which she included passionate poems and spoke of the friendship the two would have once the therapy relationship was over. At the same time, Catherine initiated several calls to the agency where Anna worked, citing ethics violations and incompetence.

Anna tried to absorb these shocks as she attempted to repair what had seemed a positive and productive relationship. Her script-level interpretations to Catherine about her projections and her behavior—when she could hold on to her mind long enough to formulate them—were met with fury. Anna's efforts in her personal therapy to understand past relationship troubles seemed to go in unhelpful, discouraging circles. She was also becoming increasingly confused, anxious, and paranoid in a way that she felt was affecting her work with other clients, many of whom had histories of trauma and numerous failed treatments.

Anna's supervisor, Paul, a seasoned clinician in his late fifties, responded to her case first by listening and asking questions, then by offering more script-level interpretations and advice in the face of her increasing anxiety, and finally by distancing himself from her developing depression. He found himself angered by Anna's presentation of herself as a victim and by her apparent inability to stem what to him was a clear need to interpret her client's behavior and to set professional limits. He thought she ought to refer her client for medication—which Anna had done many times before but to no avail—and if Catherine refused to be evaluated psychiatrically, Paul strongly believed Anna should terminate the relationship by offering Catherine an appropriate referral to another psychotherapist.

As the months of this supervisory process wore on, Paul became increasingly rigid emotionally, physically, and intellectually. He began to suspect that some of the accusations made by Anna's client might, in fact, be true. He questioned Anna's competence. He began documenting his interventions with Anna to protect himself in case Catherine's threatened legal actions against Anna grew to involve him. Additionally, he felt guilty and angry about the fact that, over the years of supervising Anna, he had enjoyed her attractiveness and had always looked forward to their sessions together. This was now replaced by a feeling of being burdened and angry that she could not make use of his advice. Curiously, he also avoided discussion of this case with the woman he saw for his own monthly consultation.

Quite understandably, the affective intensity and impasse developing within these interlocking relationships made thinking extremely difficult. What remained was primarily a suffocating mix of anxiety and contempt for all parties, including others being dragged into the situation: friends, partners, professional colleagues, attorneys, and advocates at a local women's sexual assault center.

This was not the kind of situation that was likely to turn out well. Indeed, it was eerily reminiscent for all of prior catastrophic situations in school, at work, in families, and among friends. But those reminiscences were operating outside of conscious awareness. They were present more in the form of forebodings and compulsions to escape from something that had turned so bad.

The resolution of this complicated impasse began in an unexpected way. Catherine—who sought help and healing from a variety of people—was at that time also consulting a nutritionist named Sarah. Sarah lived on a small farm, outside the city, where she grew vegetables and fruit, some of which she gave to clients as a way of supporting better eating habits. Catherine had been telling Sarah about her unethical therapist, as she had been telling everyone. Sarah, in turn, had been lending a sympathetic and empathetic ear, as she was inclined to do with her clients. One day, Catherine was at Sarah's picking up her nutritional supplements as well as a small bag of tomatoes and peppers from Sarah's garden. Sarah, in response to Catherine's latest report on Anna, made a casual remark to the effect that perhaps Catherine also had a role to play in what was happening with Anna. Without missing a beat, Catherine's face froze; she dropped the bag of vegetables to the ground, and with one move placed her foot squarely on the vegetables. She leaned toward Sarah, saying with quiet fury, "You better stick to what you know about. I don't need you poisoning me, too."

Sarah's response was to step back in shock and fear. Then, although she nearly began to cry, she chose instead to recover by breathing deeply, alternately looking Catherine in the eye and turning away to collect herself. Finally, after what seemed an eternity to both of them, Sarah looked directly at Catherine and said, "I'm not interested in a phony, abusive relationship, Catherine." Sarah was still shaking. "I don't think it's good for either of us. When you are ready to apologize for ruining what I gave you, you are welcome to come back here again." Then she stood facing Catherine, trembling and waiting for her to leave, which Catherine did in a state of bewilderment and anger.

Catherine spent a week feeling utterly depressed and pained. She could not even function at work, which had not been a problem during the conflict with Anna. Yet Catherine did not join in with her friends when they suggested that Sarah was just another treacherous witch. Instead, she found herself with little enthusiasm for her campaign against Anna. She became terrified of the idea that maybe the whole thing had been a terrible misunderstanding. She made one trip out to Sarah's, with the intention of both hurting her and apologizing, yet when she got out of her car and saw Sarah looking at her from the garden, Catherine began sobbing without knowing why. She fled. She then called Anna the next day to ask for a special appointment, which Anna later said she must have been crazy to accommodate given everything that had been happening.

Yet a corner had been turned. Catherine's encounter with Sarah—to whom Catherine eventually apologized after some months of working with Anna—had precipitated a sequence of painful realizations for Catherine, Anna, and Paul. When Paul first heard what had happened with Sarah and Catherine, for example, he also felt close to tears, then went blank and found himself thinking of an experience he had had recently with a young male client who had been acting out and missing sessions. For the first time, Paul began talking about his impasse with Anna, both with his consultant and a close friend. Anna, too, shifted how she presented her experience with Catherine and began to recognize how Paul's responses had not been helpful. She ventured some timid suggestions to that effect, which Paul was able to explore with her without either blaming himself or distancing, although he continued to feel uncomfortable with the new intimacy in their relationship. His prior feelings of attraction and disdain for her were being replaced by a new sense of her as a person and as a colleague, feelings that he found even more disconcerting.

Anna and Catherine worked together for another year and a half, trying to sort out what had happened, and eventually deciding together that it would be helpful for Catherine to see another therapist. Catherine felt sadness at this decision but believed it was the right one. She found it too difficult to think with Anna about what had happened. She left grateful for what Anna had given her. Anna, for her part, just felt relief when Catherine was gone. She began to consider taking an administrative position at her agency, believing that she could no longer emotionally handle her work as a therapist.

Discussion: Applying the Concept of Protocol in Order to Move through an Impasse

After conducting the interviews from which we assembled this case illustration, we were struck by how the resolution of the impasse was simultaneously productive and saddening. Both of us could identify with the story based on our own clinical experience, and it resonated with the impasses to which we each have been a party. It also left us with the sense that it is impossible to emerge from an intimate encounter without being deeply affected. In particular, it seems impossible to grow within a therapeutic or consultative couple without feeling a sense of both accomplishment and loss.

In hindsight, the crisis or disruptive impasse that occurred for these three individuals likely arose from the disruption of a more confluent, script-level impasse that had been operating for some time between the client and therapist and between the therapist and supervisor. As a therapist, Anna had behaved with Catherine in ways that she typically did with others in her life, repeating a script-based, relational role of being supportive, nonconfronting, and overly responsible. This had suited Catherine just fine. Anna's therapeutic style was a welcome respite from the hopeless neglect that Catherine experienced in the midst of her parents' intensely fused and rejecting relationship, and so the first 3 years of treatment seemed to have gone quite well. In fact, there was little room for individuality, surprise, or robust intimacy. Yet Anna had, over those years, continued her own work in personal therapy, supervision, and training and had begun to mature to the point that she was less inclined to follow some of her old script patterns. She had begun to change gradually, and many of her clients had adjusted productively to the change in her style of engagement. Catherine, however, experienced Anna's change as a threat and a betrayal and so had retaliated in kind, feeling as if her most fundamental trust had been violated.

In this case, the resolution of the impasse did not occur because the therapist and supervisor came to their senses, were able to think again, and helped the client think. Rather, the turning point occurred outside the therapeutic context and was then brought by the client back into the therapeutic setting, whereupon it was relayed into the supervisory situation.

That sequence usefully illustrates two principles. The first is that an intimate, protocol-level impasse cannot be resolved until someone in the relationship is willing to sit with the extreme discomfort of the activated affect, feel it, and gradually find words to think about and communicate it to the other. This brings to mind Bion's (1963/1977) concept of containing, whereby the therapist or consultant willingly receives the client's affect-drenched experience and demonstrates that it is possible to experience the impact of it and find meaning in it rather than immediately defend against it by acting out of script. We see an example of containment in the response of Sarah, the nutritionist, to Catherine. Once Sarah had demonstrated that she could withstand the strength of her own intense reactions to her client without acting in a rejecting or retaliatory way, her way of being began to have an effect on Catherine's experience. It destabilized a fundamental and unconscious worldview—that is, protocol—that Catherine had been living out in every other area of her life. Sarah's protocol in this case was not hooked—shocked, yes, but permitting of enough perspective to recognize that her relationship with Catherine might yet be salvaged and that her anger and limit setting were appropriate. She did not blame Catherine or turn her into an overwhelmingly fearful monster. Sarah set a personal boundary and spoke of the relationship in terms that she believed might function more effectively in the future.

Work in a therapeutic or consultative relationship can begin to move again once the therapeutic or consultative couple's history and feeling tones have been contained. As McLaughlin (1994) writes in regard to impasses in the analytic setting,

> I do not wish to assert that growth of personal insight in the analyst invariably disposes of all stalemates, nor that his bettered involvement can heal all woundings. But I feel confident that seeking to restore one's optimal competence is the best, and sometimes the only, recourse in times of analytic impasse. Without this personal investment in self-scrutiny by the analyst, he is very likely to keep inflicting hurts and abandonment. These can become chronic strain traumata which will erode beyond restoration the aliveness and hope essential for both members of the dyad if they are to sustain their investment in reaching for analytic engagement.

Thus, the professional may be the one to recognize the need for self-analysis.

The second principle that this case illustrates is that the resolution of an impasse can begin with the initiative of either partner in the therapeutic or consultative couple. Things can begin moving when at least one partner can begin to reflect on the affect that both are living within. In this particular case, the client initiated the process of thinking within the therapeutic relationship, which in turn was carried into the supervisory relationship in an instance of what might be called "productive parallel process."

What most characterizes the clinical situation involving Anna, Catherine, and Paul as a protocol-based impasse is the intensity with which certain emotional patterns were activated in what had been long-term working relationships. The intimacy within them had come to be taken for granted, as habitual and familiar as the ways each person negotiated that intimacy. However, when the impasse occurred, the capacity to think while remaining engaged had simply collapsed and was most likely on the road to fulfilling the highly negative fantasies each person had about his or her significant relationships.

It is important to note, however, that Catherine's initial response to Sarah was not appreciative or even insightful. She instead felt her interior world and certainties being shaken. She experienced a collapse. She entertained intense fantasies of revenge, nearly leading to action. Yet instead of reacting out of force of habit by attacking Sarah further, which would have been a continuing enactment of script, Catherine chose to take Sarah's goodwill toward her on faith, a goodwill grounded both in their history as nutritionist and client and in Sarah's demonstration of courage in the moment. Catherine could feel the possibility of a new way of relating.

Anna, for her part, could have also chosen to take Catherine's rapprochement as an opportunity simply to cover over the ugliness of the preceding months. She could have pacified Catherine and appeared to be engaged in a process of reconciliation. But she decided, instead, to look at herself and her other relationships. We do not know whether her idea of changing careers was the result of reflection, her typical habit of retreat, or being burned out. But there is reason to believe that whatever decision she finally came to would be made with considerably more thoughtfulness than if she had not chosen to reflect in depth on what had happened in her work with Catherine.

Paul also took the opportunity to look at some of his usual ways of relating, especially to the women in his life. He showed a bit more emotional availability in both his work and his personal life, to which he reacted at times with renewed distancing, as if the increase in vulnerability also opened him to more intense feelings of pain and pleasure about which he was ambivalent and tentatively hopeful.

When Anna and Catherine eventually had a chance to talk about what had precipitated the crisis, it seemed that it had been a simple remark made by Anna, similar to the observation that Sarah eventually made to Catherine. When Catherine's response to Anna turned explosive and assaulting, Anna did not have the resources at the time to stand her ground. She felt—more than she was conscious—that her move toward maturity was destructive of her significant relationships. Following protocol, she had become defensive and withdrawn. Her small step toward growth had precipitated such a cataclysm that it did not seem worth the cost to proceed.

Paul also had settled into a comfortable and repetitive role with Anna. He had, in fact, built his supervision practice to relieve himself of the strain he felt seeing clients. The therapists he worked with, although struggling and unaware of their own entrenched protocols, were typically adapted enough not to disturb him too much. Anna, for example, found his attention and attraction to her appealing, although she was not consciously aware of it. Paul had learned to operate with emotional distance in all areas of his life. He had figured out how not to bring into his own supervision any of the issues that might give his supervisor something with which to stir him affectively. So, when Anna began to use her supervision with Paul in a way that was intense, he had become removed and passively hostile toward her. Yet he had been moved by Catherine's encounter with Sarah, when Anna eventually relayed it, because it corresponded to his own pained hope for more vitality. He deeply, and unconsciously, regretted the loss of connection in his life and work.

Conclusion

The case just described illustrates, above all, that resolving a protocol-based impasse is never neat. The emotional threads that underlie our most primary relational templates are a part of our history that cannot be undone, even if we learn to live differently with them. Yet these are the very interactions we are drawn to again and again, because as McLaughlin (2005) notes, "We seek to test and find ourselves in the intimacy of the therapeutic relationship, to become known to and accepted by the other, in whose sum we may more fully assess ourselves" (p. 158).

Therein lies the paradox. The closeness that comes of human relating gets under our skin in a way that can be felt as a fantasy of perfect merger and love or as a nightmare of constricting sameness and hatred. At the same time, it is in this intimacy with others that we finally know what we are capable of with regard to living in the world. In their sum, we can then most fully assess our potential for life.

REFERENCES

Arlow, J. A. (1963). The supervisory situation. *The Journal of the American Psychoanalytic Association, 11,* 576-594.

Beebe, B., & Lachmann, F. (2000). *Infant research and adult treatment: Co-constructing interactions.* Hillsdale, NJ: The Analytic Press.

Berne, E. (1961). *Transactional analysis in psychotherapy: A systematic individual and social psychiatry.* New York: Grove Press.

Berne, E. (1970). *Sex in human loving.* New York: Simon & Schuster.

Berne, E (1975). *The structure and dynamics of organizations and groups.* New York: Grove Press. (Original work published 1963)

Berne, E. (1977a). *Intuition and ego states: The origins of transactional analysis* (P. McCormick, Ed.). San Francisco: TA Press.

Berne, E. (1977b). Intuition IV: Primal images and primal judgment. In E. Berne, *Intuition and ego states: The origins of transactional analysis* (P. McCormick, Ed.) (pp. 67-97). San Francisco: TA Press. (Original work published in 1955)

Bion, W. R. (1977). Elements of psycho-analysis. In W. R. Bion, *Seven servants: Four works* (pp. 1-110). New York: Jason Aronson. (Original work published 1963)

Bollas, C. (1999). *The mystery of things.* London: Routledge.

Caravella, M., & Marone, A. (2003). Acute psychotic states: A clinical interpretation. *Transactional Analysis Journal, 33,* 246-253.

Clarkson, P. (1992). *Transactional analysis psychotherapy: An integrated approach.* London: Tavistock/Routledge.

Cornell, W. F. (2003). Babies, brains, and bodies: Somatic foundations of the child. In C. Sills & H. Hargaden (Eds.), *Ego states* (Key concepts in transactional analysis: Contemporary views) (pp. 28-54). London: Worth Publishing.

Ekstein, R., & Wallerstein, R. S. (1958). *The teaching and learning of psychotherapy.* New York: Basic Books.

Erskine, R. G. (1997). Fourth-degree impasse. In R. G. Erskine, *Theories and methods of an integrative transactional analysis: A volume of selected articles* (pp. 147-148). San Francisco: TA Press. (Original work published 1978)

Friedlander, M. (Ed.) (1991a). Special issue on transference and transactions. *Transactional Analysis Journal, 21*(2).

Friedlander, M. (Ed.). (1991b). Special issue on transference and transactions. *Transactional Analysis Journal, 21*(3).

Goldstein, W. N. (1991). Clarification of projective identification. *American Journal of Psychiatry, 148,* 153-161.

Goulding, M. M., & Goulding, R. L. (1979). *Changing lives through redecision therapy.* New York: Brunner/Mazel.

Goulding, R. L., & Goulding, M. M. (1978). *The power is in the patient: A TA/gestalt approach to psychotherapy* (P. McCormick, Ed.). San Francisco: TA Press.

Greve, B. (1976). Protocol fantasy and early decision. *Transactional Analysis Journal, 6,* 220-223.

Hargaden, H. & Sills, C. (2002). *Transactional analysis: A relational perspective.* Hove, England: Brunner-Routledge.

Hinshelwood, R. D. (1994). *Clinical Klein: From theory to practice.* New York: Basic Books.

Hostie, R. (1984). Eric Berne in search of ego states. In E. Stern (Ed.), *TA: The state of the art: A European contribution.* Dordrecht: Foris Publications Holland.

Hoyt, M. F., & Goulding, R. L. (1989). Resolution of a transference-countertransference impasse using gestalt techniques in supervision. *Transactional Analysis Journal, 19,* 201-211.

Klein, M. (1946). Notes on some schizoid mechanisms. *International Journal of Psychoanalysis, 27,* 99-110.

Johnson, L. M. (1978). Imprinting: A variable in script analysis. *Transactional Analysis Journal, 8,* 110-115.

Lyons-Ruth, K. (1999). The two-person unconscious: Intersubjective dialogue, enactive relational representation, and the emergence of new forms of relational organization. *Psychoanalytic Inquiry, 19,* 576-617.

McLaughlin, J. T. (1994, 5 March). *Analytic impasse: The interplay of dyadic transferences.* Paper presented for the 41st Karen Horney Memorial Lecture Panel of the Karen Horney Psychoanalytic Institute and Center and the Association for the Advancement of Psychoanalysis, New York, New York.

McLaughlin, J. T. (2005). *The healer's bent: Solitude and dialogue in the clinical encounter* (W. F. Cornell, Ed.). Northvale, NJ: The Analytic Press.

Mellor, K. (1980). Impasses: A developmental and structural understanding. *Transactional Analysis Journal, 10,* 213-220.

Moiso, C. M. (1985). Ego states and transference. *Transactional Analysis Journal, 15,* 194-201.
Müller, U. (2000). Old roots revisited: Reassessing the architecture of transactional analysis. *Transactional Analysis Journal, 30,* 41-51.
Novellino, M. (1984). Self-analysis of countertransference in integrative transactional analysis. *Transactional Analysis Journal, 14,* 63-67.
Ogden, T. (1982). *Projective identification and psychotherapeutic technique.* New York: Jason Aronson.
Rosenfeld, H. (1995). *Impasse and interpretation: Therapeutic and anti-therapeutic factors in the psychoanalytic treatment of psychotic, borderline, and neurotic patients.* London: Tavistock/Routledge. (Original work published 1987)
Searles, H. (1955). The informational value of the supervisor's emotional experiences. *Psychiatry, 18,* 135-146.
Steere, D. (1985). Protocol. *Transactional Analysis Journal, 15,* 248-259.
Stern, D. N. (1985). *The interpersonal world of the infant: A view from psychoanalysis and developmental psychology.* New York: Basic Books.
Woods, K. (2003). The interface between Berne and Langs: Understanding unconscious communication. *Transactional Analysis Journal, 33,* 214-222.

The original version of this article was published as "Impasse e intimata nella coppia terapeutica o di counseling: l' influenza del protocollo [Impasse and intimacy in the therapeutic or consultative couple: The influence of protocol] in Rivista Italiana di Analisi Transazionale e Metodologie Psicoterapeutiche, *25(11), 35-60, 2005. It was republished in the* Transactional Analysis Journal, *Volume 36, Number 3, pp. 196-213, July 2006.*

The Intricate Intimacies of Psychotherapy and Questions of Self-Disclosure

William F. Cornell

The cancer scare now seemed to be over after several weeks of Ben and me anxiously awaiting the results of a series of tests. Many around Ben waited with him, proclaiming variations of "Oh, it's probably nothing.... Everything will be OK." These were intended as statements of comfort, but Ben experienced them as dismissive and placating. Other than his session with me, there seemed no place where Ben could express his feelings of anxiety, shock, and a bereft anticipation of leaving his young children fatherless. Ben talked for most of the session about his relief on receiving the positive results, feeling a bit foolish about his level of anxiety while awaiting the results but eager to stay more fully engaged in life. I was deeply relieved. I have a deep regard and affection for Ben, and the thought of losing him to cancer was horrifying to me. As I had imagined the possibility of his being ill, I had been wondering silently if I would be capable of seeing him through the treatment process.

As he prepared to leave the session, Ben said, "Well, we won't have to talk about cancer any more." I responded, "I think it is something that we will need to come back to for some time, as the possibility of being seriously ill or dying has stirred up many important things that we need to continue talking about." "I think we can let it go," said Ben. "And besides, I don't feel I have the right to keep hurting you."

Hurting me? I had no idea what Ben was talking about. I pointed out that he had every right to say things that might hurt me, that it was my responsibility to deal with whatever feelings our work and relationship might stir up in me, but I had no idea how he felt he had been hurting me during this period of the cancer scare. Ben explained, "Virtually every time I used the word 'cancer,' it was like a shadow came over your face. Sometimes you looked like you were going to cry. I don't want to cause you pain."

I was dumbstruck. His words made instant sense to me. He had seen something in my face that I was not even aware of feeling, let alone showing. I was deeply touched by his noticing and his expression of concern. "I have some idea what you may have been seeing, Ben, and it's important we come back to this next week."

For the next week, I struggled with what, if anything, to say to Ben about the meaning of what he had seen on my face. I was stunned and rather embarrassed that something had been evident to him but not to me. I knew, as soon as Ben spoke, that the sadness he was seeing was there; it was not a projection on Ben's part. My mother died at age 40 of cancer, when I was in my late adolescence, my brother and sister in early adolescence. Her young death left deep, unmanaged scars, and my father died 10 years later of an intentionally untreated cancer. I could not stand the thought that Ben, who was just discovering the pleasures and satisfactions of his life, could have his young life taken away by this disease, that his kids might lose their father so early in their lives. My admiration and affection for Ben deepened in response to his caring and honesty with me. I knew that if I spoke of my parents' deaths, I could probably not do so without crying. What would it mean to Ben—who had grown up with a determinedly depressive mother and a father who converted all affect into rage—to see his therapist in tears?

In the next session, I told Ben that what he had seen on my face was undoubtedly a deep sadness that came from my own life. I would talk with him about it if he wished to know and if it would support his therapy. I suggested he take a week to think it over. He replied immediately that he did not think it was "his place" to know something so personal. I assured Ben it was his place to know something of me if he so chose, especially about something that had entered our relationship unbidden and unplanned. The question I wanted him to consider was whether my speaking of myself would support his therapy.

McLaughlin (2005) stressed that "whether we are analyst or patient, our deepest hopes for what we may find the world to be, as well as our worst fears of what it will be, reflect our transference expectancies as shaped by our developmental past" (p. 187). More than half a century earlier in his remarkable, though long unpublished, clinical diaries, Ferenczi (1932/1988) noted that it is through the "unmasking of the so-called transference and countertransference as the hiding places of the most significant obstacles to the completion of all analyses, one comes to be almost convinced that no analysis can succeed as long as the false and alleged differences between the 'analytical situation' and ordinary life are not overcome" (p. 212). For both Ferenczi and McLaughlin, the inevitable humanness and vulnerability of the analyst were simultaneously potential sources of trouble, insight, impasse, and/or mutual influence and understanding.

Ferenczi (1932/1988) also observed a certain merging of psychic realities in the analytic couple that brings affective vitality to the analytic endeavor: "The emotions of the analyst combine with the ideas of the analysand, and the ideas of the analyst (representational images) with the emotions of the analysand; in this way the otherwise lifeless images become events, and the empty emotional tumult acquires an intellectual content (?) [sic]" (p. 14). As we see, Ferenczi followed this statement with a question mark in parentheses. What does this question mark mean? Did Ferenczi question his own perceptions? Is it a question of what does one do clinically with this observation once it has been made? Is it a question to the reader to take up? Ferenczi's awareness of his own emotional limits and entanglements with his patients led to his experimentation with mutual analysis and his open acknowledgement of his mistakes and misunderstandings with regard to his analysands (Aron & Harris, 1993; Ferenczi, 1932/1988; Thompson, 1964).

McLaughlin's (2005) response to his own awareness of what he called "hard spots" and "blind spots" interfering in the relations with his patients was to remove himself temporarily from the transference pressures to the privacy of his woodshop, his "transference sanctuary," where he entered into a period of reverie and self-analysis so that he could return to his patient in a more open state of mind and affect (pp. 114-116). He seldom reported the content of his private self-analysis to his analysands; he used it, instead, to bring himself back to the analytic work, the relationship, and the mutual transferences with a clearer sense of self that would enable a more open engagement.

Poland (2005), in a paper delivered in recognition of McLaughlin's contributions to psychoanalysis, mirrors Ferenczi's observations about the psychic impact of the patient on the therapist's being. He wryly observes, "Positions of subject and object flow subtly and interchangeably. No matter how it seems on the surface, below the surface traffic is always two-way" (p. 18). Poland outlines four areas of danger and vulnerability for the analyst:

1. Countertransferential fears provoked by the patient
2. Fears idiosyncratic to the analyst's character that emerge during the course of some analyses
3. Those fears and vulnerabilities intrinsic to the analytic process (object attachment and loss; resistance and relentless negativism on the part of the patient)
4. Those resulting from the human condition, from the analyst's vulnerability to the demands of reality and fate even when working best (p. 16)

Poland (2005) writes in a deeply personal and self-revealing fashion and concludes, in contrast to Ferenczi and in accord with McLaughlin:

A word about self-disclosure. The agonizing personal introspective strife in which I was engaged as part of this woman's analysis was my own task, not to be carried out by my burdening my patient with the details of my private inner work. . . . Nonetheless, it was important that I try to resolve my own issues in myself, using them to facilitate but not to complicate the patient's work. My aim was to unburden the patient's analysis, not to burden it with my private labors. The analyst's fear may be triggered or even caused by the patient; the analyst's task is to sort out private issues privately. (p. 20)

While I admire the clarity and integrity of Poland's position, I see the choices regarding self-disclosure as variable, dependent on context and the place in time in the evolution of the therapeutic relationship. With Ben, for instance, my questions were whether I would burden him with self-disclosure at this point in his work with me and what kind of disclosure might be most appropriate and therapeutic. These questions are complex, not readily answered by any single theoretical position (Aron, 1991, 1996; Bollas, 1989; Davies, 1994; Maroda, 1991; McLaughlin, 2005; Searles, 1959, 1979; Slavin & Kriegman, 1998; Stern, 2003, 2004).

Questions of analyst/therapist self-disclosure have been, and continue to be, controversial (Bonovitz, 2006; Eagle, 2003; Gediman, 2006; Greenberg, 1995; Hartman, 2006; Hoffman, 1998; Renik, 1993, 1999; Slochower, 2006). I considered several possibilities as to what, if any more, to say to Ben should he ask. I might acknowledge to him that the shadow he had seen on my face was cast by my own history and simply ask for his associations and fantasies. I wondered whether if I did not disclose anything further about myself, it would hold open the space for Ben's own experience, conflicts, and choices as to whether or not to explore this terrain further. Could further self-disclosure on my part foreclose Ben's experience of himself? I might say something like, "This is a frightening place I know something about from my own life, so I know something of its importance and am willing to stay there with you in this fear and anxiety." I thought that perhaps my telling something of my own life's losses and feelings toward those I have loved might offer a kind of model and permission for Ben to move into territory that has been forbidden and shameful. I considered telling him more about my feelings for him and his children without telling him anything about my own life. Each seemed like a valid choice.

Over the days between our sessions, I found myself thinking particularly about Aron's (1991) article on "The Patient's Experience of the Analyst's Subjectivity," and I reread it with Ben in mind. Aron describes the needs of children to reach into the inner worlds of their parents and of patients' desire to know something of the interior lives of their analysts. He proposes that this knowing of the other's interiority is an essential developmental achievement in the capacity to think psychologically. I realized that for Ben, his father's internal world was a black, forbidding, and forbidden box. It was not to be known. In kind, Ben's internal world was of no interest to his father. Any expression of Ben's feelings was subject to ridicule and assault (in adulthood as well as in childhood). Early in treatment, Ben had told me that as a child he planted a fruit tree in the yard every year on his birthday. On his fifteenth birthday, he stopped planting trees because "by the time the tree bore fruit, I would be an adult, and I knew that once I was an adult, nothing would taste sweet any more. There would only be bitterness." Ben learned to live a solitary and silent life. It was "not his place" to expect truly to know someone else or to expect to be known.

Much in my own life and development had taught me that those closest to me, in a kind of benign neglect, were most content when I managed myself by myself (Corrigan & Gordon, 1995; Shabad & Selinger, 1995; Winnicott, 1949/1975). Ben, too, had learned to take care of himself and expect little but trouble and judgment from others. From the very beginning of our work, I had felt an identification with Ben. Our fathers had both fought in World War II and had been profoundly scarred. My father came back deeply withdrawn and silent; Ben's father came back self-pitying and violent. As sons, we each grew up with fathers whose internal worlds were deeply disturbed and sealed off. We each lived much of our own internal lives in silence. I decided, should Ben ask me to say more, it was time to tell him something of my own life, to let him learn directly something of my own subjectivity.

The following week, Ben did ask me to speak of the meaning of the sadness he had seen on my face. I told him the story of my parents' deaths and the impact on me, of my fantasies of what might happen to his children should he die so young, and of my admiration for his taking the early warning signs seriously and immediately pursuing help. I did cry. Ben listened to me with tenderness and interest, and something shifted in the shame he has often felt in the face of his own sadness and vulnerability, which he had always seen as "weak." He did not experience me as weak as I spoke frankly with him. There, in that moment, it was my speech rather than that of the client, my openness and vulnerability that served both Ben and me.

Time passed, and this interchange faded into the background of our sessions. When invited to write a paper for a special issue of the *European Journal of Psychotherapy and Counselling* on "Relational Psychology in Europe," I thought immediately of the experience with Ben and decided to write about it. Early in our work, Ben had given me a couple of his published papers to read. He is very accomplished in his field but had great difficulty writing about his work. He asked me to read some of his papers both to understand more about what he does and to help him deal with his writing blocks. I found his work fascinating (although difficult to comprehend), and we were able to address his writing blocks quite productively. In a further step of self-disclosure, I decided to give Ben the first draft of this paper to read for his perspective and also for permission to publish something about him.

He was deeply moved by the paper, touched that the encounter between us had meant something to me as well as to him. Ben said, "I've always known you were a thoughtful therapist, but reading the paper has shown me something of how you think. I learned a lot." He gave me permission to publish this account of what had happened between us.

I could sense that something had shifted in Ben at least in part as a result of this exchange about the shadow over my face. Ben reestablished contact with his father after a couple of years of silence following a particularly nasty fight. His father's behavior had not changed, but Ben began to sense that his father was anxious inside, as well as gruff, belligerent, and argumentative. When his father had to be hospitalized for a serious illness, Ben called regularly, and his father was able to express appreciation for Ben's concern. Once he recovered and left the hospital, Ben's father returned to his usual mode, but Ben found himself more accepting of his father's way of being and pleased that he, Ben, had been able to offer his father something different that at least for a little while had been received.

Recently, Ben asked if my paper about our work had been accepted for publication. I told him that it had. He said he admired me for writing something so honest and personal and that he thought it signaled a change in my profession that it had been accepted. Ben had once been in psychoanalysis, which he described as "trying to talk to a stone wall in a dark room," so he thought it was strictly forbidden for a therapist to say anything personal about himself.

I asked how the experience I had written about has stayed with him. He said that it has had numerous effects on him. First of all, my sharing myself with him had made me "both more human and more professional" in his mind. My decision to share the draft of the paper with him was "sweet and respectful." Most important, he learned that "to show my vulnerability was OK, healthy, that it makes me feel closer." He said that, while I had encouraged his vulnerability on many occasions, he could not trust it, but when he saw mine, he could feel what had been only an idea before. "I had always been ashamed of my withdrawal. But reading the paper I could see that you understood it and that you withdraw sometimes, too, so that really made it OK."

A second vignette illustrates a very different experience of an unexpected self-awareness and unwanted vulnerability. Charlie and I had struggled for years. Unlike the growing closeness and affection I felt for Ben, my years of involvement with Charlie were marked by determination but also bounded by caution and wary self-protection. Charlie was nearing 50, had never married, had no friends at the start of treatment, and wandered from job to job working always "beneath his potential" and his academic training. Over the course of therapy, his job status improved and tentative friendships were in the making. But our relationship seemed forever at the edge of fraying and unraveling. Charlie constantly underscored my failure to really "get him." In my failures, I joined a multitude of others who never seemed to "get" Charlie. I would quietly steam, wondering if it ever occurred to Charlie that were he to "get" someone else's experience, he might have a few friends, maybe even a wife and family.

I was acutely aware of the painful developmental history of Charlie's life, with relentlessly self-involved parents who seemed to see him as a not very attractive piece of furniture that had been delivered, unwanted, to their living room. They just stepped around him. I knew what he felt he needed from me, and I despaired of my capacity (or willingness) to give it to him. I could barely stand how he treated me, or others, and there seemed no room to address this with him. I careened between feelings of irritation and urgent anxiety that he would never get a full life for himself and a sense of guilt that I was not more helpful. Regular consultation helped me manage my counter-transference and do technically competent work, but in some fundamental way I could not open myself to Charlie in a way that would truly allow me to "get" him with my being as well as with my head.

Gerson (2003) describes the transferential relationship as the medium through which unconscious desires can begin to emerge and be articulated, while constantly shadowed and intertwined with memories (and anticipations) of failure, the bedrock of deadly and deadening anxiety and defense. And yet, Gerson (2005) argues, "We constantly seek others as transformational objects to make something about ourselves more available to ourselves." Charlie and I were constantly deadlocked in the mutual interplay of our negative transferences with each other. In contrast to the hope reflected in Gerson's statement, Charlie and I were *less* available to each other—not more—as a result of our defensive interactions.

Charlie and I fell constantly into the shadows, the urgency of desire seemingly a source of irritation and frustration rather than being hopeful and enlivening. I recalled some old song about a mutual admiration society; Charlie and I had formed a mutual irritation society. Then one day, quite unexpectedly, a high school acquaintance, a woman in whom Charlie had had considerable adolescent interest, came back into the city for a funeral. She gave Charlie a call, and they met for lunch. In session, Charlie was uncharacteristically bereft and, also uncharacteristically, upset with himself, rather than being upset with the world and everyone in it. "What's wrong with me, Bill? She has a family, a marriage, not the greatest but not so bad. I might have had a life with her. What is it I do wrong? I must do something wrong. You must help me see what I'm doing." I was quiet. I listened. I could feel my wariness yielding, my chest opening. I was afraid to say much of anything, as though I would break this magical spell. Near tears by the end of the session, Charlie was standing to leave and he said, "She is here for a funeral. If it had been me who'd died, would she have come? Who would have known to tell her I died? If I died tomorrow, who would come from out of state to be at my funeral? No one. Who would there be to call? No one. If I died tomorrow, there would not be enough people who cared to be pallbearers for my casket." Then he left.

I stood there, barely able to breathe. I felt nauseous and thought I was going to collapse. What Charlie had just described about his fears for his own death was the reality of my father's death and funeral. After my mother died, my father had become so withdrawn, isolated, and increasingly bizarre that by the time he died 10 years later, there was no one in his life, no pallbearers for his casket, only his mother, brother, two sons, and a daughter to attend his funeral. I had to go to a real estate company where he had worked briefly, and very unsuccessfully, to ask the staff to be his pallbearers. I began to understand my urgency, my irritation, and my inability to be open to Charlie and my self-deadening in the face of his unsocialized behavior and his relentless despair.

The session haunted me the rest of the day. I had to will myself to attend to my other clients. I went home that night and turned to my personal "sanctuary of transference": music. Bob Dylan, Neil Young, Joan Baez, music that carried me back to my dad in bitter compassion. I cried, this time in private. I felt the collapse of my dad's life and the impact of his choices on me. I could feel how deeply, unbearably, and unconsciously I had merged Charlie with my father. I could feel the beginnings of a willingness, an openness, a capacity to undo the knots between us. I did not tell Charlie what had happened to me in the moment when he spoke of his imagined funeral with no pallbearers. Unlike with Ben, I had no impulse to be personal with Charlie. I recalled a time when I did share a personal experience with Charlie in an effort (rather desperate and unthought-out) to make a link with him and feel some identification. Charlie responded, "That's really irritating. I don't pay you to hear about your life. I pay you to listen to mine. Please keep your life to yourself. Or pay somebody else to listen to you." Unlike Ben, for Charlie, given his character and where we were in our developing relationship, such self-disclosure would have been an intrusion, a burden, to use Poland's phrase. At another time in the treatment, this might not be the case. But at that point, personal self-disclosure to Charlie would not have facilitated our work or his self-understanding. What was possible for me, however, as a result of my self-encounter and realizations, was to return to Charlie with openness, patience, and, for the first time, hope.

I have no doubt that he felt the difference, although he never spoke of it. He, too, was in a different place after his lunch with his high-school girlfriend. He began to question himself, and I was able to engage with those questions without pressure or irritation. The vulnerabilities and psychic conflicts centered on the tragic deaths of my young parents were within me and deeply affected my work with these two men but in quite different ways. With Ben—probably not coincidentally a father, like me, and self-blaming, like me—my own history of loss facilitated a deep regard and positive identification with him. With Charlie, my history and vulnerability unconsciously as evoked in his presence fostered a defensive identification and a relentless wariness. The decisions I made in the context of my work with these men were, therefore, quite different.

Over the past quarter century, various models of relationally based models of psychoanalysis and psychotherapy have gradually informed one another, although each had been evolving in relative separation from the others from the 1930s until the 1980s. Ferenczi may not have been the first psychoanalyst to notice that the patient was not the only troubled and vulnerable person in the analytic couple, but he was the first to try to work with it clinically and write about it publicly. His experiments with "mutual analysis" may have been brilliant failures, but his emotional honesty inspired many, some of whom emigrated to the United States and eventually offered an alternative to the more classical analytic position dominant there before and after World War II (Thompson, 1950; Rudnytsky, Bokay, & Giampieri-Deutsch, 1996). Ironically, several of the innovators in relationally oriented models struggled in relative isolation and solitude: Ferenczi in Budapest, Fairbairn in Edinburgh, Sullivan in Washington, DC, and McLaughlin in Pittsburgh. Others, like Klein and Winnicott in London and Greenberg and Mitchell in New York, had the advantage of major urban centers of psychoanalytic thinking and a group of like-minded colleagues, although, in reading their work, one can see that they, too, were not always met with open arms by their more classically oriented colleagues.

In the United Kingdom, so often isolated from Europe, a different mode of relational psychoanalysis—object relations—was developing. In the object relations mode, the trouble and vulnerability within the dyad was seen as centered in the client; disturbances within the analyst were seen as products of the affective and infective impact of the patient, through splitting, projection, and projective identification. In the United States in the 1930s, Sullivan was laboring mostly alone but coming to his own conclusions about the inevitability of mutual influence in the therapeutic dyad. His work, together with that of Clara Thompson, Erich Fromm, and Frieda Fromm-Reichman, among other European emègrès, evolved into the school of interpersonal psychoanalysis.

It took several decades after the war for these models to reshape psychoanalysis in the United States. Greenberg and Mitchell's (1983) *Object Relations in Psychoanalytic Theory* and Mitchell's (1988) *Relational Concepts in Psychoanalysis: An Integration* was the first major effort to integrate interpersonal and object relational models into American psychoanalysis, which gave birth to what is now known as "relational psychoanalysis." During that same period, McLaughlin was writing a series of important papers exploring the use of the analyst's countertransference and the mutuality of influence within the therapeutic dyad. These emerging models stressed the importance of the analyst's own subjectivity within the psychotherapeutic endeavor. From the perspective of classical, ego psychological, and object relational models of psychoanalysis, the desires, disturbances, and resistances under study are those within the patient. Within the relational sensibility (although there are many variations of this paradigm), it is understood that both therapist and client bring aspects of their unformulated, unconscious experience into the consulting room, that the unconscious pressures of the desired and the prohibited exist in both members of the dyad (Stern, 1997). Hence, at times, there will be the inevitable vulnerability of the analyst that may well affect the work with the patient but does not necessarily come from the patient.

How to make use of countertransference and the therapist's human vulnerability varies from model to model, practitioner to practitioner. The relational models share a rough consensus that the nature of unconscious experience and the work of analysis are not only the retrieval of rejected and disavowed drives and infantile attachment needs, but a process of unconscious unfolding and discovery of emerging possibilities. As can be seen from the perspectives of Ferenczi and McLaughlin, two analysts of relentless curiosity and experimentation who wrote with unusual candor, as well as from the clinical vignettes presented here, a therapist's willingness to experience and inhabit his or her own vulnerabilities can deepen the therapeutic endeavor and be of compelling benefit to clients.

REFERENCES

Aron, L. (1991). The patient's experience of the analyst's subjectivity. *Psychoanalytic Dialogues, 1,* 29-51.
Aron, L. (1996). *A meeting of minds.* Hillsdale, NJ: The Analytic Press.
Aron, L., & Harris, A. (Eds.). (1993). *The legacy of Sandor Ferenczi.* Hillsdale, NJ: The Analytic Press.
Bollas, C. (1989). *The forces of destiny.* London: Free Association Books.
Bonovitz, C. (2006). The illusion of certainty in self-disclosure: Commentary on paper by Helen K. Gediman. *Psychoanalytic Dialogues, 16,* 293-304.
Corrigan, E. G., & Gordon, P.-E. (1995). The mind as object. In E. G. Corrigan & P.-E. Gordon (Eds.), *The mind object: Precocity and pathology of self-sufficiency* (pp. 1-22). Northvale, NJ: Jason Aronson.
Davies, J. M. (1994). Love in the afternoon: A relational consideration of desire and dread in the countertransference. *Psychoanalytic Dialogues, 4,* 153-170.
Eagle, M. N. (2003). The postmodern turn in psychoanalysis: A critique. *Psychoanalytic Psychology, 20,* 411-424.
Ferenczi, S. (1988). *The clinical diary of Sandor Ferenczi* (J. Dupont, Ed.; M. Balint & N. Z. Jackson, Trans.). Cambridge, MA: Harvard University Press. (Original work published 1932)
Gediman, H. K. (2006). Facilitating analysis with implicit and explicit self-disclosures. *Psychoanalytic Dialogues, 16,* 241-262.
Gerson, S. (2003, 3 May). *The enlivening transference and the shadow of deadliness.* Paper presented to the Boston Psychoanalytic Society and Institute, Boston, MA.
Gerson, S. (2005, 6 November). *Ghosts from the stage to the consulting room: The family unconscious in classics of 20th century theatre.* Paper presented to the Western Pennsylvania Forum for Relational and Body-Centered Psychotherapies, Pittsburgh, PA.
Greenberg, J. (1995). Self-disclosure: Is it psychoanalytic? *Contemporary Psychoanalysis, 31,* 193-205.
Greenberg, J., & Mitchell, S. (1983). *Object relations in psychoanalytic theory.* Cambridge, MA: Harvard University Press.
Hartman, S. (2006). Disclosure, dis-closure, diss/clothes/sure: Commentary on paper by Helen K. Gediman. *Psychoanalytic Dialogues, 16,* 273-292.
Hoffman, I. Z. (1998). *Ritual and spontaneity in the psychoanalytic process: A dialectical constructivist view.* Hillsdale, NJ: The Analytic Press.
Maroda, K. (1991). *The power of countertransference.* Chichester: Wiley.
McLaughlin, J. T. (2005). *The healer's bent: Solitude and dialogue in the clinical encounter* (W. F. Cornell, Ed.). Hillsdale, NJ: The Analytic Press.
Mitchell, S. (1988). *Relational concepts in psychoanalysis: An integration.* Cambridge, MA: Harvard University Press.
Poland, W. (2005, 15 October). *The analyst's fears.* Paper presented at "Generativity: Honoring the Contributions of James T. McLaughlin" Conference, Pittsburgh, PA.
Renik, O. (1993). Analytic interaction: Conceptualizing technique in the light of the analyst's irreducible subjectivity. *Psychoanalytic Quarterly, 62,* 553-554.
Renik, O. (1999). Playing one's cards face up in analysis. *Psychoanalytic Quarterly, 68,* 521-539.
Rudnytsky, P. L., Bokay, A., & Giampieri-Deutsch, P. (Eds.). (1996). *Ferenczi's turn in psychoanalysis.* New York: New York University Press.
Searles, H. (1959). Oedipal love in the countertransference. *International Journal of Psycho-Analysis, 40,* 180-190.
Searles, H. (1979). *Countertransference and related subjects.* New York: International Universities Press.
Shabad, P., & Selinger, S. S. (1995). Bracing for disappointment and the counterphobic leap into the future. In E. G. Corrigan & P.-E. Gordon (Eds.), *The mind object: Precocity and pathology of self-sufficiency* (pp. 209-228). Northvale, NJ: Jason Aronson.
Slavin, M., & Kriegman, D. (1998). Why the analyst needs to change: Toward a theory of conflict, negotiation, and mutual influence in the therapeutic process. *Psychoanalytic Dialogues, 8,* 247-284.

Slochower, J. (2006). The psychoanalytic other: Commentary on paper by Helen K. Gediman. *Psychoanalytic Dialogues, 16,* 263-272.

Stern, D. B. (1997). *Unformulated experience: From dissociation to imagination in psychoanalysis.* Hillsdale, NJ: The Analytic Press.

Stern, D. B. (2003). The fusion of horizons: Dissociation, enactment, and understanding. *Psychoanalytic Dialogues, 13,* 843-873.

Stern, D. B. (2004). The eye that sees itself: Dissociation, enactment, and the achievement of conflict. *Contemporary Psychoanalysis, 14,* 197-237.

Thompson, C. M. (1950). *Psychoanalysis: Evolution and development.* New York: Thomas Nelson & Sons.

Thompson, C. M. (1964). *Interpersonal psychoanalysis: The selected papers of Clara M. Thompson* (M. R. Green, Ed.). New York: Basic Books.

Winnicott, D. W. (1975). Mind and its relation to the psyche-soma. In D. W. Winnicott, *Through paediatrics to psychoanalysis* (pp. 243-254). London: Karnac. (Original work published 1949)

The original version of this chapter was published in the European Journal of Psychotherapy and Counselling, *Volume 9, Number 1, pp. 51-61, March 2001.*

Section II:
Questions of Theory

Theory is a metasensual phenomenon. It allows one to see something not seen by other theories; to have an unconscious possibility should the clinical need arise. To declare oneself against other schools of thought is like someone stating that one is an eye person and does not like the ear or auditory sense data, or for someone to declare that they trust what they hear, but never trust what they smell.

Bollas, 2007, p. 82

Section II

Introduction

When it comes to the world of theory, I am simultaneously a hopeless addict and a die-hard skeptic. The chapters in this section reflect both sides of this coin. A theory can open our minds and senses; it can also direct and limit our range of attention, thinking, and intervention. I chose Christopher Bollas's quote on theory as the epigraph for this section because he stresses the clinical function of theory to create conscious and unconscious possibilities for how we listen to our clients. We do our clients a serious disservice when we fit them into our theories because we are overly invested in a singular theoretical frame of reference. The chapters in this section represent a constant curiosity, challenge, and evolution of theoretical perspectives.

My undergraduate education was at Reed College, a rather unique educational institution in the United States. At Reed, students study only original sources; no secondary sources or textbooks are used. Classes are taught as small seminars, driven by the premise that that is the best way to learn to think and that good thinking generates more questions than answers. Students are never given their grades so as to reduce the competitiveness of the classroom environment. There are no classes in the senior year, which is instead devoted to writing a thesis in order to develop library, research, and critical-thinking skills. On completion of the thesis, the student defends it orally with members of his or her department. Reed theses are easily the equivalent of a master's thesis, with some achieving the quality of a doctoral dissertation. It is a remarkable educational experience.

The faculty of the psychology department when I was there, while maintaining the seminar system, was comprised of zealous Skinnerian behaviorists. They were dedicated to recasting psychology into the mold of hard science, studying only what could be directly observed and empirically validated. There was one lone (and often lonely) clinical psychologist on the faculty, also the only woman in the department and one of only two in the whole college when I first got there. She was my advisor, an advocate of Carl Rogers and a fan of A. S. Neil and Summerhill. So while running rats, on the one hand, I studied Carl Rogers, on the other. Reading Rogers led me to phenomenology, and it was the phenomenologists at that time who were giving the behaviorists a run for their theoretical money.

My senior thesis was titled "A Phenomenological Study of Outcome in a Behavior Modification Program for Mother-Child Pairs," a decidedly scientific-sounding title. During the behavior modification program—which focused exclusively on parenting behaviors of the mothers (who had severely physically disabled children) with absolutely no inquiry into the mothers' thinking, beliefs, or internal experience in any regard—I administered before and after tests evaluating self-perception and self-worth. One of the scales I used was developed by R. D. Laing and his associates (Laing, Phillipson, & Lee, 1966) early in his career. My tests indicated that these mothers' sense of self-worth, self-esteem, and well-being improved even though they were never directly addressed in the program. My thesis also included an extensive review of the psychotherapy outcome research of the day. At my oral exam I was shocked to be informed by my board that they had no questions, but I had been given an A- as the thesis was extremely well written and the literature review exemplary. I was informed by my friendly faculty that I had, however, claimed to have measured internal experience, and internal experience is not observable or quantifiable, so the premise of my thesis was invalid and they saw nothing to discuss. It was an extraordinary, and rather hilarious, contradiction to the entire premise of education at Reed.

I left Reed to attend the phenomenological psychology program at Duquesne, the only such program in the United States at the time. I found myself again in a nest of zealous true believers dedicated to what they called "the Duquesne project." Anything not related to phenomenology and the cause of phenomenology was of no interest (or validity). After those two formative experiences, I made a commitment to myself that I would never invest in or identify myself with a single theoretical framework. In my mind, the function of theories is to raise questions, to foster thinking. When a theoretical model is posed as the answer, I turn the other way.

This section is devoted to questions of theory. All of the papers are drawn from the *Transactional Analysis Journal*. All are written on the premise of using one theory to question or extend another. Transactional analysis is at the base of each of these chapters, and its theoretical premises are held as objects of both respect and scrutiny.

Chapter 5 was written 20 years ago. It was my first major transactional analysis paper and one of which I remain quite proud. It has stood the test of time in its content, but more importantly to me, it has modeled a style of critical thinking about theory and practice that I think is essential in our work. In the 2 decades since I wrote this paper, script theories in transactional analysis—including those of some of the theorists I critique in the paper—have continued to evolve. Many of the questions and challenges I raised in 1988 have been explored and debated in the pages of the *Transactional Analysis Journal* in the years since, influenced by newer developmental and infancy models, attention to transference and countertransference dynamics, neurobiological understandings and speculations, constructivist theories, contemporary psychoanalytic perspectives, and relational paradigms. The continuing evolution of script theory and technique is one of the areas in which transactional analysis has sustained its vitality and creativity.

Chapter 6 is the outcome a years of vigorous discussion between Francis Bonds-White and me. For several years, Francis and I, as representatives of the International Transactional Analysis Association, co-led preconference institutes at the annual conferences of the American Group Psychotherapy Association, an analytically oriented group. The groups were stimulating and challenging, calling into question what it is that promotes psychological and emotional change. The paper is a bit strident in tone, but we both tend to be strident people, and we wanted to provoke reactions.

Chapters 7, 8, and 9 are a body of interconnected explorations of the implications of contemporary psychoanalysis for my understanding and practice of psychotherapy. The thinking in these papers has been influenced by many, but the work of Christopher Bollas and Jim McLaughlin are at the heart. I began subscribing to the journal *Psychoanalytic Dialogues* from its inception. While I am not always enamored of relational perspective and methods, I love the format of that journal, with the major papers all having discussant papers so that the dialogues actually happened within the pages of the journal. From that I learned a great deal about how to hold the tensions among differing ideas. Over the years I have met many of the primary authors from *Dialogues* and found many colleagues who do not need you to agree with them in order to be interested in what you have to say.

Chapter 10 is a gem I coauthored with Jenni Hine. Jenni and I taught and trained many transactional analysis therapists and counselors over 20 years of working together. This article was an effort to articulate a more comprehensive model for counseling practice, to challenge some of the limitations often imposed on the counseling field, and to reframe a perspective on the Child ego state.

Chapter 11 is based on a keynote speech I gave in Canterbury, England, for the Institute of Transactional Analysis in 2000. It was a lot of fun and seemed the perfect way to close this section.

REFERENCES

Bollas, C. (2007). *The Freudian moment.* London: Karnac.
Laing, R. D., Phillipson, H., & Lee, A. R. (1966). *Interpersonal perception: A theory and method of research.* London: Tavistock.

Life Script Theory: A Critical Review from a Developmental Perspective

William F. Cornell

> Great literature has always provided a balance to the lopsided preoccupation of psychological science with pathology.... In contrast to the reductionism of science, the model of great literature often enlists an interactionist, longitudinal perspective and seeks to illuminate the myriad forces at work within and without an individual. A novelist would never diminish his protagonist with a finite label. (Felsman & Vaillant, 1987, p. 303)

Shortly before his death, Eric Berne (1972), using the analogy of a piano player, wondered if he was actually playing the piano or if he was mostly sitting there while a piano roll determined the tune:

As for myself, I know not whether I am still run by a music roll or not. If I am, I wait with interest and anticipation—and without apprehension—for the next notes to unroll their melody, and for the harmony and discord after that. Where will I go next? In this case my life is meaningful because I am following the long and glorious tradition of my ancestors, passed on to me by my parents, music perhaps sweeter than I could compose myself. Certainly I know that there are large areas where I am free to improvise. It may even be that I am one of the few fortunate people on earth who has cast off the shackles entirely and who calls his own tune. In that case I am a brave improviser facing the world alone. (pp. 276-277)

This frank and poignant personal observation is filled with fascinating contradictions and implications. Berne's comments seem to reflect his own conflicts about personal autonomy versus the authority of life script, true individual creativity versus the expression of family tradition, and the satisfaction of personal freedom versus the aloneness of autonomy. The conflict between individual expression and family and societal pressure are apparent throughout Berne's writings.

However, Berne never resolved these conflicts, even though his theory of scripts evolved over time. I think these conflicts remain, undermining the clarity and coherence of script theory and our practice as transactional analysts today. Some 18 years after Berne's death, the music roll remains the binding image and dilemma in our efforts to conceptualize the nature of life script and to translate those conceptualizations into effective educational and clinical techniques.

What is the nature and function of life script? What are the clinical implications of the script model transactional analysis therapists present to themselves and their clients? Although transactional analysts pay careful attention to the "scripty" beliefs and behaviors of clients, do they give equal attention to their own beliefs about script, about the coherence and validity of transactional analysis script theory? Does script theory hold up under the scrutiny of developmental theories and research or other theoretical perspectives?

In this chapter, some key developmental perspectives are reviewed and summarized after which the ideas of major transactional analysis script theorists are examined in light of developmental theory and research. Finally, a conceptualization of the evolution and function of the life script process is offered.

An Overview of Selected Developmental Theories

Developmental theorists attempt to delineate human development as a definable and predictable sequence of "stages," with earlier stages providing a foundation for later evolution. Whether studying cognitive, affective, social, moral, linguistic, or behavioral development, simpler levels of functioning develop into more complex and highly organized forms of psychological organization and function.

Freud. Within the psychodynamic perspective, Sigmund Freud presented the first developmental theory. Although his work has had a pervasive and lasting impact on the clinical understanding of human development, his ideas eventually began to yield to current developmental research. Freud (1938/1949) stated unequivocally that "neuroses are only acquired during early childhood (up to the age of six), even though their symptoms may not make their appearance until much later. . . . The events of the first years are of paramount importance for . . . [a child's] whole subsequent life" (p. 83). Freud's (1917/1938) conceptualization of the oral, anal, oedipal, phallic, and genital stages of psychosexual development was the first formal effort to delineate the evolution of psychological and emotional maturation. Freud's ideas were the product of his psychoanalytic reconstruction of childhood from his clinical practice and theoretical assumptions. His emphasis, and a lasting emphasis in the psychodynamic literature, was on the clinical and pathological implications of "fixation" at any one stage.

Erikson. Erik Erikson (1963), in probably the best known and most widely accepted developmental schema, significantly altered Freud's model by shifting from a psychosexual focus, with its emphasis on libidinal cathexis, to a psychosocial orientation that attempts to incorporate societal and interpersonal influences in human evolution. Erikson's stages of development reach into adult life. His work opened the developmental perspective to a recognition of social, cultural, and historical forces that influence the developing child's construction of reality. There is a great vitality in his account of human development. For Erikson (1968), periods of developmental crisis are as likely opportunities for new growth as occasions of overadaptation and acquiescence.

My first introduction to current developmental research was *Adaptation to Life* by George Vaillant (1977). The book was simultaneously exciting and disturbing. Vaillant presented vivid case studies and substantial data that indicated that the evolution of an individual's psychological construction of reality was anything but linear and certainly not cemented to the dynamics of the nuclear family. This material raised major questions about the validity of transactional analysis script theory and was the beginning of a review of the developmental literature that has culminated in this paper. The brief overview of developmental theories presented here stresses those based on direct, longitudinal studies rather than on clinical theorizing about development derived from adult psychopathology and psychotherapy.

Chess and Thomas. The work of Stella Chess and Alexander Thomas involved long-term studies of normal children, "high-risk" children and families, and children with physical handicaps. Their work presents compelling evidence of the resilience and plasticity of the psyche:

> The deaf child, the blind child, the motorically handicapped child—each can find a developmental pathway consonant with his capacities and limitations, thanks to the plasticity of the brain. By the same token, the environmentally handicapped child is not inevitably doomed to an inferior and abnormal psychological course. Whether the handicap comes from social ideology, poverty, a pathological family environment, or stressful life experiences, the plastic potential of the brain offers the promise for positive and corrective change. This central human potential for plasticity and learning bears directly on a number of issues in developmental theory—the significance of early life experiences, continuity-discontinuity over time, and sequential patterning of developmental stages. (Thomas & Chess, 1980, p. 28)

Chess and Thomas (1984, p. 293) conclude without equivocation that simple, linear prediction from early childhood through later childhood, adolescence, and adulthood is not supported by research data. Furthermore, they challenge the reliability of a causal explanation based on clinical reconstruction of childhood from adult problems.

Instead, Chess and Thomas emphasize the importance of the individual child's temperament and capabilities and the "goodness of fit" or the "poorness of fit" with that child's family, social, and school environment. They (Chess & Thomas, 1984, 1986) describe psychological development as occurring in a "biosocial matrix," an ongoing, continuous, and dynamic interaction of the biological and the social. Their research demonstrates convincingly that significant change can occur at any time in the course of development: "The evolving child-environment interactional process was affected by many emerging unanticipated influences—changes in basic function, new talents, new environmental opportunities or stresses, changes in family structure or attitudes, and possible late emerging genetic factors" (Thomas & Chess, 1980, pp. 103-104).

Chess and Thomas emphasize the importance for future psychological health of the child's development of "task mastery" and "social competence." Using weaning and toilet training as examples, typical Freudian (and script) theory tends to emphasize the experience of loss and frustration. In contrast, Chess and Thomas view these developmental transitions as steps in social competence and task mastery, noting the potential for achievement and satisfaction as well as for loss or frustration.

Vaillant. Adaptation to Life by George Vaillant (1977) was also based on a longitudinal study. It summarized the Harvard Grant Study in which 95 Harvard University students were tested and interviewed intensively during college and then followed systematically for 30 years. Vaillant emphasized the evolution and function of ego defense mechanisms in relation to psychological and interpersonal health and psychopathology.

There is striking congruence between Vaillant's view of defense mechanisms as "adaptive styles" or "coping strategies" and the functional, adaptive intent of script decisions as described in transactional analysis theory. Unlike Freud, Vaillant (1977) emphasized not the intrapsychic meaning of defense mechanisms, but "discussing defenses as actual behaviors, affects, and ideas which serve defensive purposes" (p. 7).

However, Vaillant's account of defense mechanisms and their development is far richer and more complex than that evident in the writing of most script theorists. Vaillant disputed the Freudian emphasis on fixation and maintained that there are many corrective experiences in the course of an individual's development and many pathways to health throughout childhood and adult life. He observed that dysfunctional thinking and relating in adulthood is "rarely the fault of any one person or event, for in human development, it is the sustained emotional trauma, not the sudden insult, that does the most lasting damage to the human spirit. No single childhood factor accounted for happiness or unhappiness at fifty" (Vaillant, 1977, p. 197).

Like Chess and Thomas, Vaillant argued vigorously against linear, causal linkages between childhood experience and adult life. He concluded in his 1977 book that "successful careers and satisfying marriages were relatively independent of unhappy childhoods" (p. 300) and that "the life cycle is more than an invariant sequence of stages with simple predictable outcomes. The men's lives were full of surprises, and the Grant Study provides no prediction tables" (p. 373).

The most relevant of Vaillant's (1977) conclusions for the reconsideration of script theory are these: Reconstructed, retrospective explanations are fraught with distortions; isolated traumas in childhood rarely have significant impact in adulthood; adaptive (defensive) patterns change both in childhood and adulthood; psychological evolution is often discontinuous; those judged initially to have the "worst" childhoods did not always have the "worst" adult lives; and significant, close adult relationships (spouse, friends, psychotherapist) had major influences on improved quality of life. Thus, the Harvard Grant Study offers further evidence of the remarkable resilience, plasticity, and unpredictability of the human psyche.

It is also important to note the work of Robert Jay Lifton (1983a, 1983b) and Robert Coles (1986a, 1986b), both of whom, while not writing specifically from a developmental perspective, based their work on the direct observation of nonclinical populations. The work of both Lifton and Coles is rich with implications that can expand and enliven the concept of script. They have described the yearning of the human mind to find and give meaning to life, often in the face of severe deprivation or tragedy. In *The Political Life of Children,* Coles (1986b) observed:

And, very important, a boy demonstrates evidence of moral development, a capacity for ethical reflection, even though both at home and at school he has been given scant encouragement to regard either migrants or Indians with compassion. . . . Children ingeniously use every scrap of emotional life available to them in their "psychosexual development," and they do likewise as they try to figure out how (and for whom) the world works. (p. 41)

Additional Developmental Theorists. It is not possible in this chapter to adequately review all developmental theorists. Maslow (1954, 1962) studied primarily healthy, achieving individuals and delineated his developmental hierarchy of needs and a major theory of human motivation. Wilson (1972) provided an excellent summary of Maslow's work in the context of a critique of Freudian psychology. Piaget (1977) addressed the most basic question of "how do people know" through his direct studies of children's evolving patterns of cognition and other studies of forms of knowledge. His was an interactionist perspective—viewing the child as an active agent engaged with the environment in his or her own learning. More recently, Kagan (1984) extended the study of cognitive development. Kohlberg (1984) researched moral development in children and delineated six sequential stages of morality. Kegan (1982) suggested a developmental theory that is of particular significance in relation to transactional analysis script theory. He attempted to integrate a psychodynamic perspective with the work of Piaget and Kohlberg. Central to Kegan's perspective is the ongoing and increasingly complex "meaning making" in the child's endeavor to comprehend the world and give form to it. Gilligan (1982) challenged the pervasive influence of the masculine perspective in developmental theories stressing individuation and autonomy and argued persuasively for the recognition of the role of caring and relatedness in human development. Loevinger (1976) addressed ego development, defining the essence of ego function as the striving to master, to integrate, and to make sense of experience. Stern (1985), after years of direct observation of infants, characterized infant development as a creative, highly interactive process. Mahler, Pine, and Bergman (1975) described preoedipal development in the infant and toddler's relationship to the mother. In his most recent book, Pine (1985), in contrast to most developmental researchers, writes the following:

I find it impossible not to think in terms of the events of the months and years until, say, age three as a primary determinant of psychological functioning. . . . All have, I believe, not only their origins, but a substantial degree of their final form established in this period. (p. 4)

While the developmentalists have addressed the nature and problems of human growth from various perspectives, most would agree that it is an interactive, creative, ever-changing process. Most agree that parents are not the exclusive, or even primary, source for a child's construction of reality or coping mechanisms. Most would agree—especially those who have engaged in long-term longitudinal studies—that significant growth and change can occur at any time of life. As Chess and Thomas (1984) conclude:

As the field of developmental studies has matured, we now have to give up the illusion that once we know the young child's psychological history, subsequent personality and functioning are *ipso facto* predictable. On the other hand, we now have a much more optimistic vision of human development. (p. 293)

Summary and Critique of Major Script Theorists

Berne. Beginning with *Transactional Analysis in Psychotherapy,* Berne (1961) offered this description of the nature and function of script:

Games appear to be segments of larger, more complex sets of transactions called *scripts*. Scripts belong in the realm of transference phenomena, that is, they are derivatives, or more precisely, adaptations, of infantile reactions and experiences. But a script does not deal with a mere transference reaction or transference situation; it is an attempt to repeat in derivative form a whole transference drama, often split up into acts, exactly like the theatrical scripts which are intuitive artistic derivatives of these primal dramas of childhood. Operationally, a script is a complex set of transactions, by nature recurrent, but not necessarily recurring, since a complete performance may require a whole lifetime. (p. 116)

Since the dominant influence in social intercourse is the script, and since that is derived and adapted from a protocol based on early experiences of the individual with his parents, those experiences are the chief determinants of every engagement and of every choice of associates. This is a more general statement than the familiar transference theory which it brings to mind because it applies to any engagement whatsoever in any social situation whatsoever; that is, to any transaction or series of transactions which is not completely structured by external reality.

While every human being faces the world initially as the captive of his script, the great hope and value of the human race is that the Adult can be dissatisfied with such strivings when they are unworthy. (pp. 125-126)

Thus, from the beginning, script was cast in a highly deterministic mode. Script is a "household drama," with neurotic, psychotic, and psychopathic scripts viewed as "almost always tragic." Script is viewed as the projection and reenactment of an elaborate transference phenomenon.

Berne was certainly a strong advocate for the intelligence and dignity of the individual in psychotherapy. He seemed at times to be very confident of a person's capacity to change. Berne (1966) wrote in *Principles of Group Treatment,* "Every human being is born a prince or a princess: early experiences convince some that they are frogs, and the rest of the pathological development follows from this" (pp. 289-290). For Berne, transactional treatment "aims at getting well, or 'cure,' which means to cast off the frog skin and take up once more the interrupted development of the prince or princess" (p. 290). But how readily can a person cast off the frog skin and recreate a healthy life? Not easily, Berne implied; it was he who introduced the images of witches, ogres, and implanted script electrodes into the language of script theory, a language that suggests the individual is more a product than a producer of script.

Five years after *Principles,* Berne (1970) wrote in *Sex and Human Loving*:

Man is born free, but one of the first things he learns is to do as he is told, and he spends the rest of his life doing that. Thus his first enslavement is to his parents. He follows their instructions forevermore, retaining only in some cases the right to choose his own methods and consoling himself with the illusion of autonomy. . . . In order to break away from such script programs, he must stop and think. But he cannot think about his programming unless he first gives up the illusion of autonomy. He must realize that he has not been up to now the free agent he likes to imagine he is, but rather the puppet of some Destiny from generations ago. Few people have the courage or elasticity to turn around and stare down the monkeys on their backs, and the older they get, the stiffer their backs become. (p. 168)

Berne's personal optimism seemed to collapse under the weight of a deterministic sense of destiny; he even capitalized "destiny" and offered "The Psychology of Human Destiny" as the subtitle of *What Do You Say After You Say Hello?* For Berne, the process of individuation seemed a courageous exception rather than the natural, common process it is presented to be in the developmental literature.

Much of the literature on development referred to earlier did not exist when Berne was evolving script theory. However, the work of Erikson, Piaget, and Maslow did exist but does not seem to have influenced Berne's thinking about human development. Like many clinicians, Berne became possessed by the effort to understand psychopathology. He lost track of health. This is a criticism to be made of many clinically oriented theorists. As Felsman and Vaillant (1987) emphasized, "Clinical language rarely includes the process of healthy adaptation. What is healthy and going well is often overlooked and obscured in the shadow of illness" (p. 302).

By the time he wrote the material later compiled for *What Do You Say After You Say Hello?,* Berne (1972) had given the developing child more choice and authorship in his or her script, but it was still a tale dominated by family drama, parents, grandparents, and intergenerational transmissions. In *Hello,* script was defined as "a life plan based on a decision made in childhood, reinforced by the parents, justified by subsequent events, and culminating in a chosen alternative" (p. 446). One wonders about the children Berne described: Did they ever change their minds, did their parents ever change, did they have friends, neighborhood, a culture? There is little sense of excitement and no sense of serendipity in the world as Berne described it.

Berne (1972) wrote that "the first script programming takes place during the nursing period, in the form of short protocols which can later be worked into complicated dramas" (p. 83), for which Berne provided a lengthy, rather nasty list of "breast-fed titles."

Berne's image of the helpless, needy, dependent infant—forever attached to and programmed by mother and family through a literal or symbolic umbilicus—does not hold up in light of current research. Rather, it introduces a severe and inaccurate bias to the foundation for a theory of script formation. For example, according to Chess and Thomas (1984),

> two striking characteristics of the child's behavior in the first weeks of life are his interest in manipulatory-exploratory behavior and the active social exchange with his caretakers. . . . Along these lines, we have suggested that the primary adaptive goals of the neonate and young infant, for which he is biologically equipped, can be conceptualized as the development of social relations and the mastery of skills and tasks—i.e., social competence and task mastery. (p. 16)

The observations of Chess and Thomas are verified and extended by the research of Daniel Stern (1985). His conclusions are based on direct observation of infant behavior. He delineated numerous contradictions between psychoanalytic literature on the therapeutically "reconstructed clinical infant" and research on the actual "observed infant." Current developmental research strongly suggests that infants influence and shape their parents as much as their parents shape them. Perhaps even more important is awareness of the child's mastery and evolving competence, an idea central to developmental theory but seriously lacking in Berne's description of script formation. The forces of submission and compromise override the experience of mastery in Berne's writing.

Although Berne did not work specifically within a developmental frame of reference, he offered his most thorough account of psychological evolution in *Hello*. He portrayed, in essence, progressive acquiescence. Maturity, for Berne, brings the mortgage, literally and symbolically. He wrote, "During the periods of maturity, the dramatic nature of the script is brought into full flower. . . . In fact, all struggles in life are struggles to move around the [Drama] triangle in accordance with the demands of script" (Berne, 1972, pp. 186-187). What of the struggles between adults that result in individuation and autonomy? What of the struggles that result in the resolution of problems, in deeper understanding and attachment between people, and in sustained love and individual differentiation? If Berne's vision of maturity is accurate for most people, it seems Peter Pan and all perpetual children made logical and compelling choices.

Berne acknowledged the existence of winners but wrote little about them, and he thought even winners were the product of more affirming and more productive parental programming and permission. Sprietsma (1978), writing from a treatment perspective, took a closer look at the "winner's script" and offered a diagram and language that elaborated on the concept of a winner. Although he did not challenge the concept of a "winner's script" theoretically, Sprietsma offered a useful clinical approach.

Allen and Allen (1972) emphasized factors outside the family sphere that can be crucial variables in a child's evolving script. Based on clinical experience, the Allens delineated a developmental sequence of eight permissions that enhance a person's "readiness" to interact with an ever-widening world. Their article represented a significant widening of the world of script theory. Like most current developmental schemas, the Allens' permission sequence suggests a literal hierarchy of development. For example, their "last" permission is that of "finding life meaningful," although it seems clear that children are busy virtually from the start making life meaningful. It is the making that Allen and Allen (1987) emphasized in a later article.

Groder (as cited in Barnes, 1977, p. 20) repeated Berne's observation that there seems to be a self that is "script free" and noted that Berne was not very articulate on the subject. While suggesting that there can be healthy scripts or script-free health, Berne never fully explored the question, and it remains unanswered by subsequent script theorists.

In Berne's view, nearly all the force of the vectors in psychological development is from the parents (sometimes grandparents and other authority figures) toward the child. For Berne, the child may have some limited range of choice in the face of the forces that impinge on him or her, but the child is by and large restricted and formed by these forces. What Berne came to characterize as the very nature of script is often reflected in the psychological systems of severely dysfunctional families, but it is not the essential nature of script. Both the literature and clinical experience demonstrate that in severely dysfunctional families (especially those that isolate themselves from normal social interaction), a child's range of choice and expression may be drastically restricted. For example, a recent collection of articles on "resilient children" (Anthony & Cohler, 1987) vividly describes the debilitating impact of living with psychotic, neglectful, impoverished, or abusive parents. However, these articles also examine and describe the factors outside of the family and within the child's own style of coping that support resilience and health. These factors are not adequately addressed in Berne's theories of script.

In Berne's thinking there was an overwhelming sense of self-limiting adaptation and little sense of self-enhancing adaptation. There was even less sense of the child's ability to influence his or her parents and childhood environment. Although it is often striking in clinical work to note the tenacity with which people cling to patterns of "scripty" adaptation, this tenacity is not always motivated by some fearful or defiant resistance but often by the pride and satisfaction of mastery, of self-expression, of having solved a difficult life dilemma with some degree of success. There is virtually no accounting in Berne's writing for this experience of mastery and individuation in script formation or in the maintenance of styles of adaptation in adulthood.

Steiner. Claude Steiner, too, seems to suggest a preponderance of conflictual compromise in the formation of script. He presents the developing child as victim to negative family and social environments. However, Steiner does give far more importance than Berne did to the social, cultural, and economic forces that influence a child's developing sense of self, autonomy, and possibility. Although a strong and eloquent advocate of individual rights and dignity, his theory of script does little to challenge the deterministic and reductionistic underpinnings of Berne's approach. Steiner (1974, p. 19) even attributed Berne's death to the influence of a life script that called for an early death of a broken heart.

Steiner's (1974) definition of script is as follows:

The script is based on a decision made by the Adult in the young person who, with all of the information at their disposal at the time, decides that a certain position, expectations, and life course are a reasonable solution to the existential predicament in which she finds herself. Her predicament comes from the conflict between her own autonomous tendencies and the injunction received from her primary family group.

The most important influence or pressure impinging upon the youngster originates from the parental Child. . . . That is, the Child ego states of the parents of the person are the main determining factors in the formation of scripts. (p. 55)

Steiner (1971, 1974) developed the script matrix, an elegant clinical tool and a major contribution to transactional analysis. The matrix, along with the three stacked ego state circles and the drama triangle (Karpman, 1968), provides a central image in transactional analysis. As a therapeutic tool, it is clear and impactful. As a central element in theory, however, it is restrictive and deterministic; it places much too much power within the nuclear family, with the ego states of the parents drawn above the child and script messages literally descending on the child. Since its introduction, numerous variations on the script matrix have been presented in the transactional analysis literature, although there has been little challenge to its theoretical limitations.

For example, in the script matrix the central emphasis on the nuclear family does a disservice to our understanding of the range of factors that significantly influence human development. Even limiting the image of the script matrix to the nuclear family, it would be more accurately drawn as shown in Figure 1.

The concept of script and the images used to represent it need to include the active influence of the developing child on the environment. Both Berne's and Steiner's conceptualizations of script are embedded in oedipal theory and Freudian assumption, with little acknowledgement of the curiosity, spontaneity, and expressiveness of childhood. Neither children nor adults create psychological

```
    Mother            Youngster            Father
```

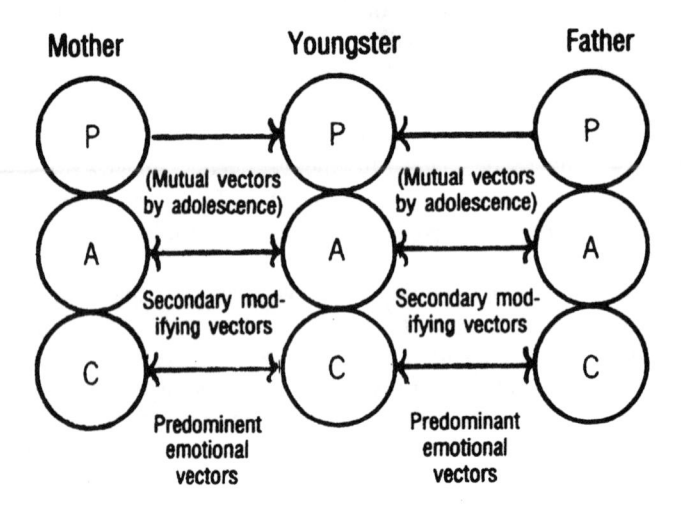

Figure 1
Mutual Vectors in Script Development

organization primarily around negative messages and experiences in childhood, as suggested by Berne and Steiner.

Levin. Within the transactional analysis literature, Levin has made a strong effort to present a developmental perspective. Ironically, however, of all the script theorists, Levin's accounting is the most deterministic. She writes the following:

> We record our entire personal history in our ego states. The way we were as children doesn't go away when we get older. It remains a dynamic part of us, motivating our current experiences. If we didn't get what we needed as children, we continue to seek it symbolically through dramatic scenes enacted in the here-and-now. The scenes are taken from our "script," our personal story or collections of early decisions and unmet needs, now long forgotten. We continue to use them to program our current experiences, even without being aware of them. Scripts represent our attempts to get needs met which were not met originally. When we play out our script as grown-ups, we act in ways which are symbolic of the original unsatisfactory childhood experience. Thus, script behavior is predetermined. We are controlled by yesterday, as if we were haunted by demons or hunted by witches. (Levin, 1985, pp. 29-30)

Levin (1985) describes infancy (birth to six months) as "Stage One: Being the Natural Child," and characterizes it as follows:

> The events of the first six months of our lives are crucial to all the rest of our development. The way we experience our existence for the rest of our lives is largely determined by the foundation we create while we are still helpless. Our first basic "set" or program is the building block upon which we support all our later developmental experiences and decisions. This is our basic position in life, our OKness, our right to be taking up space in the physical plane. It is our basic existential position. All the experiences from which we derive our first program are recorded in ego states which we call the Natural Child. They are on film and on file in each of us, a personal documentary of how we each arrive at our basic life position. (pp. 60-61)

This description of infancy and the establishment of a basic existential life position is not only in contradiction to the research on infant and child development, it is inconsistent with Berne's own conceptualization of the basic life position, which he saw as a phenomenon of later psychological development. Levin's emphasis on script as an effort to get "unmet" needs "met" and on needs as the primary focus of therapy distorts and severely limits our understanding of both pathological and healthy human development. A comprehensive theory of the evolution of self and script must attend to the influence of wants, desire, excitement, hopes, dreams, chance, and culture.

In *Cycles of Power,* Levin (1980) acknowledges that "repeating the stages of development implies that we naturally change, advance and mature even though we use the same pattern as before, building on the early skills in the same way that we build walking skills on the ability to crawl" (p. 7). At the same time, she presents "normal symptoms," which she suggests are indicative of unresolved issues at various developmental stages. Such clinical literalism is simply not supported by developmental research. In *Cycles of Power,* Levin's references are drawn almost exclusively from transactional analysis literature, virtually disregarding the vast clinical and research literature on development. This parochial approach, seen all too often in transactional analysis literature, does transactional analysis and TA clients a grave disservice.

Chess and Thomas concluded from their research that similar causes can lead to different symptoms, and similar symptoms can evolve or "be chosen" in response to different causes. Likewise, Stern (1985), in *The Interpersonal World of the Infant,* also addressed some of the clinical implications of data drawn from direct observation of infants rather than from interpretive reconstruction of infantile experience from psychotherapy with adults. Stern's (1985) central conclusion was that

the traditional clinical-developmental issues such as orality, dependence, autonomy, and trust, have been disengaged from any one specific point or phase of origin in developmental time. These issues are seen here as developmental lines—that is, issues for life, not phases of life. They do not undergo a sensitive period, a presumed phase of ascendency and predominance when relatively irreversible "fixations" could occur. It therefore can not [*sic*] be known in advance, on theoretical grounds, at what point in life a particular traditional clinical-developmental issue will receive its pathogenic origin. (p. 256)

The "theoretical infant," Stern concluded, does not exist. However, he did point out that the "clinical-developmental" literature may, in fact, offer useful therapeutic constructs or metaphors, even if these are not empirically valid. He also suggested that the "clinical-developmental" perspective (which would include much of transactional analysis script theory) may be more accurate for later phases of childhood, when symbolic functions play a more crucial role in psychosocial evolution.

The developmental literature indicates that the binding nature of psychological and emotional difficulty is the pervasiveness and the chronicity of the family dynamics, not a stage-specific problem. It also seems clear that even when family difficulties are chronic, the impact of the family can be significantly altered by the child's own attitudes toward the difficulties and by extra-familial experiences. For the clinician, the developmental literature suggests that the careful, continued attention to the effectiveness of a client's present-day functioning is more apt to facilitate self-enhancement than the therapeutic "redoing" of a specific developmental period.

Babcock and Keepers. Within the transactional analysis literature that incorporates a developmental perspective, *Raising Kids OK* by Dorothy Babcock and Terry Keepers (1976/1986) is consistent with current developmental theory and research and effective in its presentation of an active, evolutionary model of script formation. The process and importance of mastery, attachment, change, and individuation are well presented in Babcock and Keeper's book. Written primarily as a child-rearing manual for parents, it makes an important contribution to the transactional analysis literature. Babcock and Keepers present life script as an ongoing formative process usually not set until adolescence, describing it as the consolidation of family patterns, the child's "favorite" and "preferred" modes of managing, and cultural and historical influences. They emphasize the psychosocial perspective on human development and a stage-specific hierarchy. They also emphasize continued learning, relearning, and change, presuming a drive toward health and satisfaction. The child's experience of mastery in social relations and task competence, central for many developmental theories, is evident throughout Babcock and Keeper's presentation, and they acknowledge the impact of the baby and growing child on the parents.

The Gouldings. Robert and Mary Goulding made a major shift in script theory by demonstrating that script is the result of active decisions made in childhood rather than from injunctions imposed on (or implanted in) a developing child. They (Goulding & Goulding, 1978) observed:

> Although patients remembered remarkably similar early scenes and injunctions, each individual reacted uniquely. Our clients were not "scripted." Injunctions are not placed in people's heads like electrodes. Each child makes decisions in response to real or imagined injunctions, and thereby "scripts" her/himself. (p. 213)

The Gouldings' conceptualization of script emphasizes the "injunction-decision complex," an interactive process between the growing child and his or her parents in which the meaning the child attaches to parental injunctions and attributions is the binding force of the script.

For the Gouldings, script is flexible and changeable during its formation in childhood. The home environment is central in script formation, but the Gouldings acknowledge the influence of school, neighborhood, television, and world environments on the life decisions made during childhood. Their observations about the importance of the child's efforts to comprehend, adjust to, and influence his or her family and social environments are much more in keeping with the findings of developmental researchers. The Gouldings' approach to script in theory and technique challenges the determinism inherent in so much of script theory. Their treatment approach also brings humor, vitality, and action to script analysis and change. They seat the client in front of the piano, place his or her fingers on the keyboard, and encourage the audience to applaud. They train therapists to work within the client's construction of reality (past and present) and to allow for important script influences within and outside of the family.

The Gouldings' approach does, however, take on a reductionistic cast in their efforts to identify ten basic injunctions. I have heard countless transactional analysis clients and therapists speak of "having" a Don't Be injunction or a Don't Grow Up script, thereby missing both the subtleties and variations of an individual's childhood experience and meaning. It seems both more theoretically accurate and therapeutically useful to encourage clients to find their own words to express script conclusions, to articulate their own "meaning making." It is also crucial not to restrict the analysis of script to negative, restrictive decisions.

Erskine. In his article on "Script Cure," Richard Erskine (1980) offers a significantly different definition of script as "a life plan based on decisions made at any developmental stage which inhibit spontaneity and limit flexibility in problem-solving and in relating to people" (p. 102). He does not reduce script to childhood and the family. He presents script clearly as a mechanism of psychological defense, of coping, rather than as a debilitating, unconscious strategy for life. It directly mirrors the concerns of task mastery and social competence so central in much of the developmental literature. It is clear in the developmental literature, and in clinical practice, that a person relies on defense mechanisms, however limiting, to cope with trauma or life problems that cannot be adequately managed by current skills, knowledge, and environmental supports. For example, Thomas and Chess (1980) offered the following:

> Operationally, defense mechanisms can be defined as behavioral strategies with which individuals attempt to cope with stress or conflict which they cannot or will not master directly. This definition does not assume, as Freud did, that defense mechanisms are necessarily unconscious. (pp. 169-170)

These difficulties are not exclusive to childhood, nor are childhood coping mechanisms necessarily more compelling or permanent than those of later life.

Consistent with most script theorists, Erskine's definition stresses the pathological nature of script. Although he makes an important addition to the concept of script by clearly indicating that restrictive life script decisions can be made during any phase of life, Erskine does not address the individual's capacity to reopen and change those decisions in subsequent phases of life (in response to new and different life experience as well as therapeutic interventions). This is a theory of pathology, not one that adequately addresses the nature of human development and spirit. Kegan (1982) is critical of the psychotherapeutic/psychopathological attitude toward life. He calls psychotherapy "unnatural therapy" and urges therapists to remember the "natural therapy"—stressing that "theories are needed which are as powerful in their understanding of normal processes of development as they are in their understanding of disturbance" (p. 262).

Groder. Perhaps the most pointed and existential definition of script in the transactional analysis literature is provided by Martin Groder (as cited in Barnes, 1977):

> Each of us has the task each morning to recreate the universe from our central focus and this responsibility is unavoidable. Unfortunately, we tend to be habit-ridden and do the same lousy job every morning. This is what scripts are all about. (p. 19)

For Groder, the essence of script is the daily, unavoidable psychological construction and reconstruction of reality. Groder appears to agree with those authors already quoted: The script is habit-ridden, restrictive, self-limiting, and hence pathological. Interestingly, Alfred Adler (1956, p. 191), in his discussion of "the style of life," elegantly described the daily "pathology" of "being in script." He observed that once individuals settle into a style of life, they remove aspects of thinking, feeling, and relating from the "criticism of experience." The process of script formation and "meaning making" in life is not inherently pathological; "being in script" becomes dysfunctional when it involves hanging tenaciously on to certain beliefs about self and the world rather than allowing for the surprises and opportunities presented in actually living.

English. Fanita English is virtually alone among the major transactional analysis theorists in considering scripts to be valuable assets, another advantage humans have over other animals. She (English, 1977) states, without equivocation, that "our scripts enable us to blossom, rather than preventing us from doing so, even though they may contain certain 'conclusions' out of early childhood that can be dysfunctional or downright dangerous" (p. 288). English's conceptualization is strongly influenced by Piaget and particularly congruent with the ideas suggested by Kegan and Vaillant. As she says in "What Shall I Do Tomorrow? Reconceptualizing Transaction Analysis,"

> we all need a script. The child's need for a script reflects an inborn human need for structuring the time, space and relationships that are ahead of him, so that he can conceptualize boundaries against which to test his ongoing experience of reality. . . . By constructing the outline of a script, he can hold together his hopes, his fantasies, and his experiences. This becomes a basic structure out of which he can develop a perspective about his life. . . . During the script-structuring age period, the child experiences the intense excitement of being a living human being with ideas. (p. 290)

More than any other transactional analysis theorist, English captures the essence of meaning making, which is fundamental in much of the current developmental literature. However, consistent with many script theorists, English still places too much emphasis on childhood as the primary time for script formation and uses too literal an adaptation of developmental stages.

English (1977) does not ignore the dysfunctional, even pathological aspects of script; she contextualizes them:

> However many irrational elements there may be in script—including horrible devouring monsters, pitfalls, dangers, and even, in many cases, terrible endings for the unwary hero or heroine —there are also fairy elements of excitement, adventure, love, beautiful fantasy, and all kinds of magical tricks and prescriptions as to how calamity can be circumvented and how misfortune can be turned into good fortune. It is these latter aspects that offer clues as to how a person can fulfill himself through his script rather than in opposition to it and in fear.
>
> Even a script generated under the worst environmental circumstances contains within itself the Child's own genetic intuitions as to how he might fulfill his inner goals creatively, if certain malevolent fairies and cobwebs can be neutralized. Without a script, the Child ego state would be operating only out of a vacuum of time and space within which there would be no content from which to connect the past to the future, so he would be rootless, like a leaf in the wind. I suspect that certain cases of psychosis represent lack of script formation, as a result of which the individual has no background from which to experience the foreground and, therefore, he operates out of a condition of total disorganization. (p. 290)

There is tremendous power and vitality in English's conceptualizations. Her ideas are enlivening in the clinical context and more theoretically valid than most script theory. For her, script formation is *determining* rather than *determined,* formative rather than acquiescent, unpredictable and creative rather than reductionistic, focused on the future rather than embedded (mired) in the past. "Survival conclusions" for English are an aspect of script, not its primary purpose.

Conclusion

Transactional analysis as an approach to therapy stresses the dignity of people and their ability to change. This perspective is supported by developmental research, which has repeatedly demonstrated the enormous flexibility and resilience of the human psyche. Unfortunately, much of script theory as it has evolved is inconsistent with this perspective on human nature.

Although transactional analysis began as social psychiatry, it seems increasingly to have collapsed into a psychodynamic framework. The interpersonal is too often lost to an overemphasis on the intrapsychic.

It is not the intent here to remove the intrapsychic focus from script theory. The psychodynamic perspective brings a richness and depth to clinical understanding. It is one intent of this chapter to return the intrapsychic emphasis that permeates much of script theory to a place within a context of the interpersonal and cognitive/behavioral fields.

Script theory has become more restrictive than enlivening. Script analysis as it has evolved over the years is overly psychoanalytic in attitude and overly reductionistic in what it communicates to people about human development. In addition, the incorporation of developmental theory into script theory has too often been simplistic and inaccurate, placing primary emphasis on psychopathology rather than on psychological formation.

The richness, depth, and complexity of current developmental research and theory is not well represented in the transactional analysis literature, although it has a great deal to teach TA practitioners about the contexts in which people learn and change. Developmental studies of healthy individuals and longitudinal studies of human growth and psychological formation challenge some of the basic assumptions and attitudes underlying transactional analysis. Called particularly into question is the transactional analysis emphasis on the pervasive role of childhood and family-centered experiences in determining adult behavior.

Although life script is not inherently pathological, it may be hopelessly imbued with pathological meaning in transactional analysis theory and practice. Transactional analysts need to either significantly challenge and broaden the current conceptualization of script or to introduce a second, parallel term—such as psychological life plan—to describe healthy, functional aspects of meaning making in the ongoing psychological construction of reality. Perhaps it would be more inclusive to use a term such as "psychological life plan" to describe the ongoing evolution of healthy psychological development, with "life script" used to describe dysfunctional, pathological constructions.

By integrating the evidence from current developmental theory, life script could be more comprehensively defined as follows: Life script is the ongoing process of a self-defining and sometimes self-limiting psychological construction of reality. Script formation is the process by which the individual attempts to make sense of family and social environments, to establish meaning in life, and to predict and manage life's problems in the hope of realizing one's dreams and desires. Major script decisions can be made at any point in life. Times of crisis, during which a person experiences severe "self failure" or "environmental failure" or chronic "environmental failure" will likely foster more rigid, and therefore more dysfunctional, elements in an individual's script.

REFERENCES
Adler, A. (1956). *The individual psychology of Alfred Adler* (H.L. Ansbacher & R.R. Ansbacher, Eds.) New York: Basic Books.
Allen, J., & Allen, B. (1972). Scripts: The role of permission. *Transactional Analysis Journal, 2*(2), 72-74.
Allen, J., & Allen, B. (1987). To make/find meaning: Notes on the last permission. *Transactional Analysis Journal, 17,* 72-81.
Anthony, E. J., & Cohler, B.(Eds.). (1987). *The invulnerable child.* New York: Guilford Press.

Babcock, D., & Keepers, T. (1986). *Raising kids OK* (Rev. ed.). New York: Grove Press. (Original work published 1976)
Barnes, G. (Ed.). (1977). *Transactional analysis after Eric Berne: Teachings and practices of three TA schools.* New York: Harper's College Press.
Berne, E. (1961). *Transactional analysis in psychotherapy: A systematic individual and social psychiatry.* New York: Grove Press.
Berne, E. (1966). *Principles of group treatment.* New York: Oxford University Press.
Berne, E. (1970). *Sex in human loving.* New York: Pocket Books.
Berne, E. (1972). *What do you say after you say hello?: The psychology of human destiny.* New York: Grove Press.
Chess, S., & Thomas, A. (1984). *Origins and evaluation of behavior disorder: From infancy to early adult life.* New York: Brunner/Mazel.
Chess, S., & Thomas, A. (1986). *Temperament in clinical practice.* New York: Guilford Press.
Coles, R. (1986a). *The moral life of children.* Boston: The Atlantic Monthly Press.
Coles, R. (1986b). *The political life of children.* Boston: The Atlantic Monthly Press.
English, F. (1977). What shall I do tomorrow? In G. Barnes (Ed.), *Transactional analysis after Eric Berne: Teachings and practices of three TA schools* (pp. 287-350). New York: Harper's College Press.
Erikson, E. (1963). *Childhood and society* (2nd ed.). New York: Norton.
Erikson, E. (1968). *Identity: Youth and crisis.* New York: Norton.
Erskine, R. G. (1980). Script cure: Behavioral, intrapsychic, and physiological. *Transactional Analysis Journal, 10,* 102-106.
Felsman, J. K., & Vaillant, G. E. (1987). Resilient children as adults: A 40-year study. In E. J. Anthony & B. J. Cohler (Eds.), *The invulnerable child* (pp. 289-314). New York: Guilford Press.
Freud, S. (1938). *A general introduction to psychoanalysis* (J. Reviere, Trans.). New York: Garden City Publishing. (Original work published 1917)
Freud, S. (1949). *An outline of psychoanalysis* (J. Strachey, Trans.) New York: Norton. (Original work published 1938)
Gilligan, C. (1982). *In a different voice: Psychological theory and women's development.* Cambridge, MA: Harvard University Press.
Goulding, R. L., & Goulding, M. M. (1978). *The power is in the patient: A TA/Gestalt approach to psychotherapy* (P. McCormick, Ed.). San Francisco: TA Press.
Kagan, J. (1984). *The nature of the child.* New York: Basic Books.
Karpman, S. (1968). Fairy tales and script drama analysis. *Transactional Analysis Bulletin, 7*(26), 39-43.
Kegan, R. (1982). *The evolving self: Problem and process of human development.* Cambridge, MA: Harvard University Press.
Kohlberg, L. (1984). *The psychology of moral development: The nature and validity of moral stages.* San Francisco: Harper & Row.
Levin, P. (1980). *Cycles of power: A guidebook for the seven stages of life.* San Francisco: Trans Pubs.
Levin, P. (1985). *Becoming the way we are: A transactional guide to personal development.* Wenatchee, WA: Directed Media.
Lifton, R. J. (1983a). *The broken connection: On death and the continuity of life.* New York: Basic Books.
Lifton, R. J. (1983b). *The life of the self: Toward a new psychology.* New York: Basic Books.
Loevinger, J. (1976). *Ego development.* San Francisco: Jossey-Bass.
Mahler, M., Pine, F., & Bergman, A. (1975). *The psychological birth of the human infant: Symbiosis and individuation.* New York: Basic Books.
Maslow, A. (1954). *Motivation and personality.* New York: Harper & Row.
Maslow, A. (1962). *Toward a psychology of being.* Princeton, NJ: Van Nostrand.
Piaget, J. (1977). *Essential Piaget.* New York: Basic Books.
Pine, F. (1985). *Developmental theory and clinical process.* New Havan, CT: Yale University Press.
Sprietsma, L. (1978). A winner script apparatus. *Transactional Analysis Journal, 8,* 45-51.
Steiner, C. (1971). *Games alcoholics play: The analysis of life scripts.* New York: Grove Press.
Steiner, C. (1974). *Scripts people live: Transactional analysis of life scripts.* New York: Grove Press.
Stern, D. N. (1985). *The interpersonal world of the infant: A view from psychoanalysis and developmental psychology.* New York: Basic Books.
Thomas, A., & Chess, S. (1980). *The dynamics of psychological growth.* New York: Brunner/Mazel.
Vaillant, G. E. (1977). *Adaptation to life.* Boston: Little, Brown.
Wilson, C. (1972). *New pathways in psychology: Maslow and the post-Freudian revolution.* New York: Taplinger Publishing.

The original version of this article was published in the Transactional Analysis Journal, *Volume 18, Number 4, pp. 270-282, October 1988.*

Therapeutic Relatedness in Transactional Analysis: The Truth of Love or the Love of Truth

William F. Cornell and Frances Bonds-White

The past decade (the 1990s) has seen a shift in clinical theorizing among ego-oriented psychodynamic theories, transactional analysis among them. Interpretation and insight are no longer viewed as the primary means of therapeutic change. Therapists of many theoretical orientations now focus on the relational, transferential, and countertransferential components of the therapeutic process. The clinical literature is overflowing with relational models and language: mutuality, empathy, attunement, attachment, the holding environment, object relations, implicit relational knowing, intersubjectivity, reciprocity, emotional synchronicity, connectedness, the moment of meeting, and resonance. The relational zeitgeist has been further fueled by the popularity of such feminist-centered models as the relational model being developed at the Stone Center of Wellesley College and trauma-centered perspectives, both of which emphasize the active, maternal/corrective/relational role of the therapist. While the maternal/relational perspectives have done much to correct the unidirectional, paternalistic, authoritarian styles that dominated classical psychoanalytic and cognitive/behavioral orientations, we now see unquestioning applications of various relational models in contemporary transactional analysis that we think merit serious critique.

In "Analysis Terminable and Interminable," a deeply reflective clinical essay written by Freud (1937/1964) shortly before his death, he was still struggling with the nature of the therapeutic process. For Freud it was the love of the truth—the willingness to acknowledge psychic realities, to face oneself as honestly as possible—that was at the heart of the therapeutic process. We also see the commitment to therapy as a commitment to ruthless honesty on the part of both client and therapist. However, it seems that in many contemporary therapies, the relational field between therapist and client has been reversed from the love of truth to the truth of love, where the experience of being cared for and mirrored supersedes the experience of facing and understanding emotional and characterological realities. We suggest that in the long, often hard process of psychotherapy, it is ultimately the love (a facing) of the truth that is curative.

There has always been a tendency within transactional analysis psychotherapy to focus on personal change and management of emotions, rather than to struggle for a deeper understanding of the ambivalences of love and hate that motivate all human relationships. The central premise of this chapter is that if transactional analysis does not face and treat the darker, more conflictual aspects of people's functioning, we will be limited in what we offer clients and equally limited as to which clients we can effectively treat.

This chapter examines applications within transactional analysis of theories that emphasize empathy, attunement, and attachment as the primary tools in the therapeutic repertoire. We suggest that such an orientation can lead to enacting a subtle form of reparenting, which represents a considerable deviation from Berne's emphasis on personal responsibility, intrapsychic conflict, interpersonal manipulation, and the construction of one's life script. We find that the overuse of relational concepts in contemporary transactional analysis can result in an oversimplification of the therapeutic process, an overemphasis on the activity of the therapist, and a turning away from intrapsychic and interpersonal conflicts as crucial elements of psychotherapy.

The Parent Ego State and the Role of the Therapist

Since its origin, transactional analysis has placed great emphasis on the therapist's use, in one form or another, of his or her Parent ego states. Berne's delineation of the Parent ego state, both in structure and function, was an important correction for the classical psychoanalytic position of the neutral observer and the mechanistic operations of the behavioral models that he challenged during his lifetime. However, there has been a long-standing and problematic tendency in transactional analysis theory and technique to project the "bad stuff" out onto parental failure, environmental failure, and the larger social structure. This projective stance has been imbedded in transactional analysis language and theory from the beginning, as exemplified by Berne's (1972) notions of the "ogre father" and the "witch mother," Steiner's (1974) use of the term "Pig Parent," and the entire reparenting model of treatment (Schiff, 1977; Schiff et al., 1975). All too often the transactional analysis therapist is cast as a provider of the "good stuff" rather than as a clarifier of how the client maintains ineffective, other-destructive, and self-destructive patterns of defense. This bias in transactional analysis theory creates a consequent pressure on the therapist to move into a good parent/good object position vis-à-vis the client. When we help a client to "experience enough," to draw on a frequently advertised transactional analysis parenting slogan as an example, frequently all that we have accomplished is a temporary, mutually gratifying, narcissistic merger. When we envelope a client in empathic and attuned mirroring, we suggest that little is actually repaired and that nothing is changed in the client's psychological structure. By calming distress—the therapist's as well as the client's—we merely eliminate or postpone the struggles that are necessary for characterological change and psychological mastery. More problematically, we are in danger of promoting a nostalgically idealized infantile/maternal fantasy split off from the ongoing difficulties of actual life, not to mention the meaner side of human nature.

Berne's departure from the psychoanalysis of his day represented an effort at a radical critique of the traditional analysis of the individual psyche through free association, dream interpretation, and other classical techniques. He clearly created a transactional analysis, not a relational psychotherapy. Nowhere in his writings did he suggest that it was the internalization of the therapeutic relationship itself that cured the client. Rather, the task of the transactional analysis therapist is to facilitate the client's reflection on the ways, reasons, and beliefs in his or her style of relating so that the client has the choice to change how he or she relates. The therapist is a careful, honest observer of relationship patterns and beliefs, as we see in Berne's conceptualizations of games, rackets, and scripts. Berne watched, listened, thought about, described, interpreted, analyzed, and disrupted how people transacted with one another.

Ultimately, Berne maintained a one-person psychotherapy in that these interactions were analyzed in light of the social and psychological advantages the individual believed could be gained from the interactions. He offered an opportunity to see, think about, and alter how one thinks and behaves. His transactional analysis was intended to unsettle a client's familiar, defensive frame of reference through description, confrontation, interpretation, and humor. It seems quite clear that Berne's intent, consistent with a classical psychoanalytic position, was to alter the intrapsychic structure and function of the client through clarifying interventions, not through offering a corrective relationship.

Introspection, on the other hand, takes the cover off the black box, and lets the Adult of the person peer into his own mind to see how it works: how he puts sentences together, which directions his images come from, and what voices direct his behavior. (Berne, 1972, p. 273)

Thus we see that Berne's treatment group was not an empathic holding environment but an interpersonal study matrix. For example, in *Principles of Group Treatment*, he outlined eight therapeutic operations that "form the technique of transactional analysis" (Berne, 1966 p. 233). These included interrogation, specification, confrontation, explanation, illustration (humor and simile), confirmation, interpretation, and crystallization (pp. 233-247). These therapeutic operations are carefully described, illustrated, and clarified with warnings about how and when to use and not to use them. Note that empathy, holding, and attachment are not on this list. Rather, Berne's therapeutic interventions were designed to elicit self-observation and curiosity, to decontaminate and stabilize Adult ego state functioning.

Berne (1966) went on to describe "other types of interventions" (pp. 248-249) in which "the therapist may have to function deliberately as a Parent rather than as an Adult for a shorter or longer period, sometimes extending into years" (p. 248). These Parental interventions are support, reassurance, persuasion, and exhortation, which Berne suggested are most appropriate and necessary in the treatment of active schizophrenics.

Unfortunately, we see here a vagueness and confusion in Berne's use of terms, a confusion repeated over and over again in his writing and transactional analysis practice. His capitalization of Parent and Adult in this section suggests that he was describing a shift from the therapist having the Adult ego state in executive to having the Parent ego state in executive. We doubt that Berne intended that the therapist become a parental figure, but that, in fact, has become common transactional analysis practice.

For Berne (1972), the therapist sometimes made explicit use of his or her Parent ego state, as is clear in his description of the Parental functions of the transactional analyst in the use of permission, protection, and potency:

> Now we can speak with some assurance of the "three P's" of therapy, which determine the therapist's effectiveness. These are potency, permission, and protection. The therapist must give the Child permission to disobey Parental injunctions and provocations. In order to do that effectively, he must be and feel potent: not omnipotent, but potent enough to deal with the patient's Parent. Afterward he must feel potent enough, and the patient's Child must believe he is potent enough, to offer protection from Parental wrath.
>
> Here the transactions are: (1) Hook the Adult, or wait until it is active. (2) Form an alliance with the Adult. (3) State your plan and see if the Adult agrees with it. (4) If everything is clear, give the Child permission to disobey the Parent. This must be done clearly and in simple imperatives, with no ifs, ands, or buts. (5) Offer the Child protection from the consequences. (6) Reinforce this by telling the Adult that this is all right. (pp. 374-375)

Berne clearly focused on the identification and management of intrapsychic conflict. He described the therapist's use of the Adult ego state to enhance the client's Adult functioning on behalf of the conflicts within the Child ego state. He was not offering an empathic, corrective parenting experience. Berne was, in essence, saying to the client, "I am strong enough to stand up to and outside of the psychic forces operating inside of you. You can see that it is possible to tolerate the internal conflict that attends change. You can make choices of your own." Berne modeled containment, offering not so much a holding environment as a facilitating environment, to draw on the language of Bion and Winnicott. He offered a model of challenge, alignment with the Adult, and thoughtfully timed interventions to free the client to think and feel autonomously. He did not close the "as if" space of the therapeutic process by becoming a parental figure, but he did draw on the force of the parental attitudes of permission, protection, and potency to create a psychological space within which the client has the opportunity to develop autonomous functioning.

Mother/Infant Research: Clinical Implications

Even as we appreciate Berne and his therapeutic stance, we do not wish to ignore his limitations. It is clear that cognitive insight, interpretation, the analysis of transactions, blackboard diagrams, and wittily phrased observations are not always sufficient to reach those deeper levels of the psyche that sometimes fear and oppose psychological awareness and change. Along with other psychodynamic therapies, transactional analysis has begun looking at research on early human development in order to develop deeper understandings of preoedipal disorders. In fact, one of the strengths of approaches that emphasize empathy and attachment is the attention paid to preverbal formative experiences, since difficulties in the earliest months of life may underlie aspects of later script decisions.

Berne had little sense of the preverbal mother/infant relationship. In *What Do You Say After You Say Hello?* (1972), his discussion of prenatal and infant influences on script development consists of little more than clever lists of "breast-fed titles" and "bathroom scenes." He seems to have given little or no attention to Winnicott's (1958d, 1965) infant/mother observations, even though these were published during the time in which Berne was writing.

The mother/infant research that has taken place since Berne's death—including that of Mahler (1968), D. N. Stern (1985), Tronick (1998a), Lachmann and Beebe (1996), Emde (1988), Ainsworth (1969), and Main (1995), among others—has added rich dimensions to our understanding of the somatic and relational elements of script. This research has demonstrated the complexity of the infant's unfolding psyche, with its gradual and relentless integration of limbic, sensorimotor, and cognitive functioning (Bucci, 1997; Downing, 1997; Lichtenberg, 1989). Recent years have also seen the gradual application of infant research to adult psychotherapy. These clinical speculations are important, but it is equally important to understand that the adult therapeutic relationship is not a mirror or re-creation of the mother/infant relationship. Certainly aspects of the mother/infant experience will emerge in the therapeutic process with many clients, but so too will many other aspects and periods of psychic development. Green (2000) has written a compelling critique of the clinical applications of mother/infant research and offers a powerful reminder about the complexity of forces operating in adult psychotherapy.

An entire volume of the *Infant Mental Health Journal* (Tronick, 1998b) was devoted to a series of articles generated by the Change Process Study Group of Boston on the application of infant research to adult psychotherapy. These initial efforts are exciting, fascinating, and seriously flawed. In a critical discussion of the articles in that journal, Modell (1998) cautions:

> The analogy between adult and infant dyads breaks down at several points. One is that the adult therapeutic dyad, unlike the mother-infant dyad, is not a biologically determined process; second, in the adult therapeutic dyad both participants are encumbered with the weight of their affective memories of the past, whereas in the infant-mother dyad, the infant's past is just beginning. Therapeutic change in the adult entails a retranscription of affective memory; there is, especially in the cases of trauma, an implicit agenda—a transcendence and transformation of the past. This is not the infant's agenda. (pp. 342-343)

Overemphasis on the mother/infant relationship as the model for psychotherapy forces a regression in the therapeutic relationship and discounts the lived experience of the adult. Concerns over attunement, mirroring, or mutual regulation that have emerged from attention to the mother/infant relationship are one aspect of psychic development, but so are the infant's and child's capacities for motoric and cognitive competence, self-understanding, and individuation. Lichtenberg (1983, 1989; Lichtenberg, Lachmann, & Fosshage, 1992) presented a comprehensive application of infant research to developmental forces that span the human life and to adult psychotherapy. In a theory of motivation that is remarkably similar to Berne's conceptualization of human hungers, Lichtenberg (1989) described five motivational systems present at birth and operational throughout life. These include: (1) the psychic regulation of physiological requirements, (2) the attachment-affiliation system, (3) the exploratory-assertive system, (4) the withdrawal-aversive system, and (5) the sensual-sexual system.

Lichtenberg's motivational system involves, first, the infant/child's evolving capacities to use psychological capacities to respond to physiological needs and pressures. The attachment/affiliation system refers to the formation and maintenance of infant/parent bonds, extending the work of Bowlby and his followers, work now well known to most transactional analysis practitioners. The exploratory/assertive system refers to the capacity for aggression and moving out into the world, be it for self-protection or self-enhancing desires, while the withdrawal/aversive system describes the capacity to move away from the world for rest, privacy, or self-protection. Finally, the sensual/sexual system reflects the central, enduring importance of the body in relation to itself and others. Relational hungers are but one element in this motivational system, which emphasizes the infant's and young child's capacity for differentiation and competence as much as the need for relational attachment and contact.

We strongly suggest that any comprehensive model of psychotherapy must involve each of these motivational systems, being careful not to idealize one over another.

Bowlby and Winnicott: Achieving a Therapeutic Stance

The understanding of infant psychic processes came as a new awareness to ego psychologists and enabled them to work more systematically and effectively with early developmental disorders. However, the psychic life of infants has been explored by the Kleinians and the British Independent/Middle School for decades. Analysands of Ferenczi—namely Melanie Klein, who began lecturing in England in 1925, and Michael Balint, who migrated from Hungary to England in 1939—addressed the manner in which infants apprehend, perceive, and experience relationships with objects, both internal and external. Fairbairn (1952), Guntrip (1961), Winnicott (1958c, 1965), Balint (1969), Bion (1977), and Bollas (1987, 1989) have built on this work. Decades before direct infant observation research in the United States, these theorists saw the foundations of psychic structure and unconscious processes as rooted in the earliest months of life. They emphasized the crucible of the mother-infant relationship and posited curiosity as a basic drive and phantasy as a basic mechanism of all mental activity. Parallel with the work of these object relations theorists, Bowlby (1969) conducted research with infants and children that led to his theories on separation, attachment, loss, and the secure base.

In current transactional analysis practice, versions of Bowlby's emphasis on attachment patterns, Winnicott's holding environment, and Kohut's empathic attunement are replacing the original conceptualization of the Nurturing Parent. There is much to be appreciated about this addition to transactional analysis practice. However, in our reading of recent transactional analysis literature and through our participation in examination preparations and processes, we have grown concerned about the misunderstanding and fusion of disparate theories and techniques. Mixing the ideas of Bowlby (an ethnological model based on instinctual drives) with those of Kohut (a relational model developed to address American ego psychologists' disinclination to work with preoedipal conditions) and Winnicott (an observer of mother-child interactions) has occurred without also noting critical differences among these theoretical models. This theoretical "hash" creates an illusion of the convergence of ideas and clinical techniques. To those outside the transactional analysis community, this hash of ideas undermines the conceptual soundness of various efforts to deepen transactional analytic theory. To contribute to that deepening, and to the need for clarification, we concentrate here on the concepts and techniques that, in current discussions, are most frequently referenced: those of Bowlby, Winnicott, and Kohut.

As we examine the applications of Bowlby's work and attachment theory to adult psychotherapy (Bowlby, 1979; Gaines, 1997; Holmes, 1996; Karen, 1998), we find descriptions of a therapeutic relationship and process that are remarkably similar to Berne's. Attachment therapists use a concept of "internal working models" (Bowlby, 1979, pp. 117-118) that is virtually indistinguishable from the essence of Berne's script theory. In Bowlby's (pp. 145-149) description of the tasks of the therapist, he sounds quite like Berne. The "secure base" (pp. 145-146), a fundamental concept in Bowlby's model, is not an empathic immersion but a solid ground from which the client can explore himself or herself and the world. Bowlby invited the client to observe relational patterns and their underlying beliefs

> to help him consider how the situations into which he typically gets himself and his typical reactions to them, including what may be happening between himself and the therapist, may be understood in terms of real-life experiences he had with attachment figures during his childhood and adolescence (and perhaps may still be having) and of what his responses to them then were (and may still be). (p. 146)

In addition, attachment-based therapists now stress the client's development of the "reflexive self function" (Fonagy, Steele, Steele, Moran, & Higgitt, 1991; Holmes, 1996), which is again remarkably consistent with Berne's emphasis on capacities of the Adult ego state to observe the total person.

In Winnicott's object relations model, there is a progressive and ever-differentiating development that moves from absolute dependence to relative dependence to relative independence and finally to interdependence. This is paralleled by the development of interaction with the primary caretaker, which moves from merger with the object to relating to the object, to destroying the object, to the ability to use the object. In Winnicott's understanding of the role of the primary caretaker, there is first a phase of "primary maternal preoccupation" (Winnicott, 1958b, pp. 300-305), which begins during pregnancy and lasts for the first few weeks of the baby's life. Winnicott described the mother as being in a special state of consciousness, with her self- and bodily experience centered almost exclusively on the baby's somatic life. In his description of the holding function in the parenting of an infant, Winnicott presented a protective and provisional phase of parenting that is deeply anchored in the body. He described the function of the holding environment as bringing the world of reality to the infant in manageable doses. He saw the need for the holding function reemerging throughout life at transitional phases of childhood and adolescence and during times of severe loss, stress, and disorganization in adult life.

The holding function is, however, more complicated than the simple provision of safety and empathic responsiveness to the infant. Winnicott stressed that during infancy there are times when the parent not only holds onto the infant but also holds against the baby by surviving aggressive urges and ruthless demands. Central to Winnicott's thinking was the importance of the parent surviving the infant's aggression and hatred without undo punishment and retaliation. While parental failure is inevitable and a healthy force in development, retaliation is not. The security that develops through the parent's survival of the infant's aggression gradually enables the infant to be alone with well-being in the presence of another. Winnicott postulated that only in this secure aloneness could the true self emerge.

Winnicott (1971) saw parallels with these ideas in the treatment of difficult, regressive clients:
> The analyst, the analytic technique, and the analytic setting all come in as surviving or not surviving the patient's destructive attacks. . . . In psychoanalytic practice the positive changes that come about in this area can be profound. They do not depend on interpretive work. They depend on the analyst's survival of the attacks, which involves and includes the idea of the absence of a quality change to retaliation. (p. 91)

Slochower (1992) offered an excellent case discussion of this aspect of Winnicott's conceptualization of holding, which has far less to do with an attuned understanding of the client than it does with the containment of the therapist's own affect and her survival of her client's behavior.

The Winnicottian infant, rather like the Winnicottian client, is a complex creature, not simply the passive recipient of parental (or therapeutic) largesse. Aggression was defined by Winnicott as movement in the world, beginning with the infant's first kick. The Winnicottian infant, one remarkably similar to those we see in direct infant observation and research, is an active, ambivalent, and aggressive creature, moving away from as well as toward the parent. Winnicott's mother/infant observations and clinical writings are full of exquisite paradoxes. In an article on "Primitive Emotional Development," for example, he observed:

> I will just mention another reason why an infant is not satisfied with satisfaction. He feels fobbed off. He intended, one might say, to make a cannibalistic attack and he has been put off by an opiate, the feed. At best he can postpone the attack. (Winnicott, 1945/1958c, p. 154)

How often does a therapist offer, wittingly or unwittingly, empathy and comfort—the opiate, the feed—to ward off the ambivalence or aggressiveness of a client?

The Winnicottian infant becomes impatient with holding or feeding. There is a powerful developmental pressure for conflict and differentiation. The primary parental activities shift—often at the infant's initiative—from providing comfort and responses to physiological and affective states to facilitating and enjoying the baby's motor activity, independence, and competence. According to Winnicott, the infant's psyche then begins to dwell within his or her body, and the baby begins to differentiate self from other. The infant, in its developing motoric and ego capacity, presses on:

> The ego *initiates object-relating*. With good-enough mothering at the beginning the baby is not

subjected to instinctual gratification except in so far as there is ego-participation. In this respect it is not so much a question of giving the baby satisfaction as of letting the baby find and come to terms with the object (breast, bottle, milk, etc.) (Winnicott, 1965, pp. 59-60)

The Winnicottian infant (and client) is a restless, impatient, and demanding individual, much more interested in competence and differentiation than in perpetual contact and feeding. As clearly delineated in his classic article "Hate in the Countertransference" (Winnicott, 1947/1958a), the Winnicottian mother and therapist are not perpetually attuned and contactful creatures either. Winnicott stressed that unless the mother can tolerate her hate of the baby, she cannot tolerate the baby's hatred of her, and no true affect and no true self can emerge. Instead, the false self will exhibit sentimentality, and the true self will remain hidden.

Therapeutic Empathy: A Critique

The centrality of an empathic stance in psychotherapy has emerged largely from the work of Kohut and other self psychologists. In Moses's (1988) detailed examination of the role of empathy in psychotherapy, he pointed out that Kohut was cautious, if not downright skeptical, of the use of empathy early in his work, warning against a "sentimentalizing regression to subjectivity" (Kohut, as cited in Moses, 1988, p. 301) and empathy "when it is surrounded by an attitude of wanting to cure directly through the giving of loving understanding" (p. 307). By the end of his life, however, Kohut had come to see empathy and mirroring as curative agents, now warning against the consequences of empathic failure and arguing for a prolonged period of validating the client's reality. During this period it is the therapist's responsibility to demonstrate his or her understanding of how the client feels. This attitude casts the therapist/analyst into the role of the good selfobject, as presented in *The Theory and Practice of Self Psychology* (White & Weiner, 1986):

> The therapist ultimately has the task of trying to become the good self-object. . . . [The therapist] will have to empathically try to understand where the adult patient failed to receive the emotional oxygen he or she needed to develop a healthy self and . . . begin to fulfill this void. (p. 36)

This model views psychopathology as rooted in developmental deficits and deficiencies, which the therapist/analyst is then positioned to redress by filling voids and providing emotional nutrients.

Erskine and Trautmann are probably the most articulate representatives of this perspective within the contemporary transactional analysis literature.

> With my understanding that *life script and ego states are compensating attempts to manage relationship hunger and a loss of internal contact, the therapeutic focus can be placed on the relationship itself* (Erskine, 1980, 1988). From this perspective the purpose of analyzing ego states or a life script is not to erect a new, more useful structure, but rather to gather information about which relational needs were not met, how the individual coped, and even more importantly, how the satisfaction of today's relational needs can be achieved (Erskine & Trautmann, 1996). These therapeutic tasks are accomplished through contact-oriented, relationship focused methods:
> - *inquiry* into the client's phenomenological experience, transferential process, system of coping, and vulnerability;
> - *attunement* to the client's affect, rhythm, developmental level of functioning, and relational needs; and
> - *involvement* that acknowledges and values the client's uniqueness. (Erskine, 1997, p. 15)

This description of the central therapeutic task is now common in the practice of transactional analysis, whether it carries a reparenting, parenting, corrective parenting, empathic, or attachment label. If psychopathology is environmental in origin, the argument goes, then psychotherapy must be environmentally compensatory in its essential tasks. Storr (1988) reminded us that when Freud was asked what constituted health, he replied that it was the ability to love and work. Storr pointed out that human relationships are "a hub around which a person's life revolves, not necessarily the hub" (p. 15).

D. N. Stern (1985) wrote about empathy in the context of the parent-infant research:

> Seen in this light [intersubjectivist and self psychology], the parent-infant "system" and the therapist-patient "system" appear to have parallels.... I wish to inject some caution in drawing these analogies too closely, however. What is meant by the therapeutic use of empathy is enormously complex from our point of view. It involves an integration of features that include what we are calling core-intersubjective, and verbal relatedness as well as what Schafer (1968) has called "generative empathy" and what Basch (1983) has called "mature Empathy."... Attunement between mother and infant and empathy between therapist and patient are operating at different levels of complexity, in different realms, and ultimately for different purposes. (pp. 219-220)

Moses (1988) argued that "current theory and applications of empathic techniques, however, have become filled with illusions, fallacies and misapplications to the point that the concept is so overextended that it lacks any special meaning and its use has become quite unconstrained" (p. 578). He worried that empathy "has unconsciously and universally slipped into our clinical vocabulary with little scrutiny" (p. 579). Among the therapeutic liabilities that Moses discussed in connection with empathy is the risk that the treatment process and the therapist will be held hostage to the client's or the therapist's narcissistic wounds and vulnerabilities. The therapist may become preoccupied with the fear of being perceived as an uncaring or persecuting object. Perhaps there is also the fear of being perceived, by client or self, as a stupid object, an uncomprehending object, one that does not or will not understand. With the illusion of sufficient empathy, "The therapist does not have to confront the fear of not understanding the patient, or worse yet, let the patient know [that] he doesn't understand, [that] certain experiences are beyond comprehension" (p. 590). The mutual wish and subsequent pressure for therapeutic empathy and attunement may create a process in which the therapeutic understanding takes place more in the effort and mind of the therapist than in those of the client, something that we imagine would trouble Berne and that certainly troubles us.

Not knowing or understanding the other can create a rich, if somewhat anxious, space. Bollas (1989) challenged the American demand for knowing and understanding:

> In the United States of America, where many people sue at the drop of a hat, psychoanalysts might live in dread of a patient bringing a court action on the basis that his psychoanalyst doesn't know what he is doing. After all, other mental health professionals, armed with their diagnostic manual—the DSM III—can practice with certainty. To me this not knowing is an accomplishment. (p. 62)

For Bollas, as for Winnicott, empathic failure, rather than inevitably creating or recreating a narcissistic wound, can offer creative space and opportunity. Bollas is far more invested in the creation of differentiated and imaginative space than of confluent contact and attuned relatedness.

Stark's work (1999) entered the contemporary debate about relational processes in psychotherapy by delineating three central and enduring modes of therapeutic action and interaction. She did not privilege one mode over another or valorize one at the expense of others. She defined the therapeutic purposes of different aspects of therapeutic relatedness, suggesting that a comprehensive psychotherapy requires differing modes of relatedness over the course of treatment. Stark defined the first mode as providing knowledge through insight and interpretation, a model based on intrapsychic, structural conflict as in the classical psychoanalysis in which Berne had his beginnings. The second therapeutic mode is rooted in the models of developmental/structural deprivation and deficit. In this mode the primary therapeutic action is the therapist's provision of a corrective relational experience, which is what we see emphasized in current transactional analysis approaches centered on attunement and attachment. As summarized by Stark, the second mode stresses: "(1) the therapist's actual participation as a new good object, (2) the therapist's actual gratification of need, and, more generally, (3) the therapist's provision of a corrective (emotional) experience for the patient" (p. 28). The third mode of therapeutic action is one of authenticity and intersubjectivity—therapeutic encounters between two real people in the here and now that manifest and alter archaic beliefs and behaviors.

In Stark's delineation of these modes, the deficit model (mode 2) emphasizes the absence of good in the client's life, while the object relations/intersubjectivist perspective of mode 3 examines the presence of bad in the client's motivations and functioning. In the third mode,

> the therapist participates authentically in a real relationship with the patient—the intention being both to enhance the patient's understanding of her relational dynamics and to deepen the level of their engagement. Accordingly, in the third mode, the intersubjectivist therapist might choose to focus the patient's attention on (1) the patient's impact on the therapist, (2) the therapist's impact on the patient, or (3) the here-and-now engagement (or lack thereof) between them. (p. 126)

Within this perspective, the therapist pays close attention to how the client—through actual interactions, projections, and fantasized distortions—creates and maintains bad objects and ineffective or destructive relationships.

Berne's own style, and that typified by classical transactional analysis practitioners, was certainly rooted in the model Stark characterized as mode 1. We suggest that the transactional analysis models based in reparenting, attachment, and attunement models are examples of mode 2. We are not arguing for a distant, neutral therapeutic stance or for one that is constantly interpretive and confrontive (Cornell, 1994, 1997, 2000); rather, we are saying that while empathy, attunement, or attachment are perhaps necessary conditions for therapeutic change, they are not sufficient for enduring psychological change. Our concern is that when empathy and/or attachment are conceptualized as curative agents, a serious disequilibrium is introduced into the therapeutic process. Transactional analysis clinical theory has grown significantly past Berne's original style, but we strongly suggest that there was much in Berne's original model that continues to be of value. We further suggest that for transactional analysis to be an effective and comprehensive psychotherapy, it must include a process of mutually achieved relatedness in addition to the therapist's provisory relationship. We are arguing for the articulation within the transactional analysis literature of an understanding of the importance of a more complex and conflictual therapeutic space.

Inquiry, Disturbance, and Creativity

Bollas (1989) sees the therapist and a balanced therapeutic process serving the dual functions of soothing and disturbing the client. He delineates two fundamental, ongoing tasks in working within the transference relationship: elaborating and deconstructing. Elaboration has to do with states of mutual reverie in which the therapist enters the client's field of transferential desire so as to open the unconscious communication between therapist and client to new possibilities of self-expression and relational wishes. The therapist's quiet receptivity, inactivity, and frequent silence are crucial here. The therapist's silence allows the client an intrapsychic, associative freedom for self-discovery and a constructive solitude in the presence of the other. With the deconstructive function, the therapist serves as a disturbing force within the client's interpersonal field, presenting interpretations, queries, and disruptions in much the same way that Berne worked. Renik (1996) offers a similar perspective:

> What the patient wants—and, best case, gets—from the analyst is a perspective different from the patient's own. It is to be hoped that the analyst's perspective is a particularly wise one, but that cannot, and need not, be assumed. Ultimately, an analyst's expertise and appropriate authority do not rest on the premise that the analyst's view of the patient's conflicts is necessarily *more valid* than the patient's own, but rather on the fact that the analyst can provide an *alternative* perspective, a new way of constructing reality, that the patient can put to use—or not—according to the merit the patient finds in it. (p. 508)

D. B. Stern (1998) contrasts empathy with the therapeutic function of "inquiry" as described by Sullivan:

> Tolerance of uncertainty and ambiguity are built into the clinical practice of detailed inquiry (Sullivan, 1954). The aim of psychoanalysis carried out according to these precepts is not necessarily to know what the patient does not know, but rather to specify *that* the patient does not know, and where and when this not knowing takes place. The psychoanalyst who depends on inquiry is not responsible for knowing the patient before the patient does. (pp. 602-603)

Stern's thinking is similar to ours and to the model we want to offer as an alternative to or expansion of concepts of attunement and attachment. He acknowledges that the therapist's questions may well emerge at times from the therapist's empathic imaginings of the client's experience, but he argues that the therapist's task is to identify the client's gaps in experience, not to fill them. Filling the gaps in experience is the client's responsibility and choice. Stern's perspective is one in which the therapist "wishes to stimulate the patient's curiosity about experiences the patient never formulated" (p. 601). The formulation becomes the client's, not the therapist's, much as Berne would say that the decisions are the client's, not the therapist's.

In *The Empathic Imagination,* Margulies (1989) cast the therapeutic uses of wonder and empathy in terms not of relationship and attunement but of self-discovery.

I am interested here in the challenges of perceiving freshly and in particular of opportunities for the self to conceive of the self anew; in other words, the therapeutic activity of creativity to the image of self, the opening of new possibilities of self-perception. (p. 10)

In Margulies's use of empathy, he sought to engage in a creative rather than compensatory process with clients. Empathy, in Margulies's model, is a means of wonder, challenge, questioning, enlivening—at times a clash of worldviews, rather different from a goal of matching and entering the client's lived perspective. The therapist's curiosity about the meaning the client has made of his or her lived experience can awaken the client's curiosity and lead to an examination of and reflection on underlying basic assumptions.

Conclusion

We have drawn here on the work of Margulies, D. B. Stern, Stark, and Bollas, among others, to offer transactional analysis therapists an expanded framework for considering the therapeutic relationship and the central tasks and activity of the therapist. We find that these perspectives are consistent with the stance originally proposed by Berne, although with a depth of affective understanding and involvement that Berne did not accomplish in his lifetime.

It seems crucial to us that transactional analysts draw on original sources to gain a thorough understanding of human development. The writings of Winnicott, Bowlby, Kohut, and others is often significantly more complex than is reflected in transactional analysis training and practices. The work of Winnicott and Bowlby—supplemented by the newer research of D. N. Stern, Emde, and others who are observing real children interacting with parents—is beginning to teach us the norms of human development. This knowledge can help therapists identify deviations from those norms when they are exhibited by clients. This is crucial to understanding childhood decisions and script formations and provides a reference point for the therapist's curiosity about what leads to these deprivations and deviations in a particular individual and how they are defensively maintained in adult life. We further suggest that it is the therapist's and client's mutual curiosity and exploration of an individual's experience that is ultimately curative rather than the alleviation of the psychic pain that developed because of these experiences.

Pain, ambiguity, paradox, and conflict are inevitable in life. They are necessary in a deeply searching psychotherapy and, most importantly, can become vitalizing resources in living one's life. After a half century of writing about psychoanalysis and the nature of human beings, Freud was still wondering about the heart of the therapeutic process. For him, ultimately, it was the love of truth—the willingness and capacity to acknowledge reality about the self—that was essential in the therapeutic endeavor. Berne offered us a model of precise self-scrutiny, transaction by transaction. The parenting, attunement, and attachment models in transactional analysis suggest that it is the truth of love that is at the heart of psychotherapy. These theorists suggest it is the client's internalization of the therapist's love, understanding, and corrective provision that allows the client to leave the office and create a different life. While we would not disparage the experience of therapeutic empathy and attachment as an important element in the facilitation of the therapeutic process, we are warning against romanticizing and idealizing its curative power. We suggest that it is the gradual development of the client's capacities for curiosity, self-scrutiny, differentiation, and relational conflict within the therapeutic relationship that is carried outside the office as the basis for structural and interpersonal change.

REFERENCES

Ainsworth, M. D. S. (1969). Object relations, dependency and attachment: A theoretical review of the infant-mother relationship. *Child Development, 40,* 969-1025.
Balint, M. (1969). *The basic fault: Therapeutic aspects of regression.* London: Tavistock.
Berne, E. (1966). *Principles of group treatment.* New York: Oxford University Press.
Berne, E. (1972). *What do you say after you say hello?: The psychology of human destiny.* New York: Grove Press.
Bion, W. R. (1977). *Seven servants.* New York: Jason Aronson.
Bollas, C. (1987). *The shadow of the object: Psychoanalysis of the unthought known.* New York: Columbia University Press.
Bollas, C. (1989). *Forces of destiny.* Northvale, NJ: Jason Aronson.
Bowlby, J. (1969). *Attachment. Volume I of Attachment and loss.* New York: Basic Books.
Bowlby, J. (1979). *The making and breaking of affectional bonds.* London: Tavistock.
Bucci, W. (1997). *Psychoanalysis and cognitive science.* New York: Guilford Press.
Cornell, W. F. (1994). Shame: Binding affect, ego state contamination, and relational repair. *Transactional Analysis Journal, 24,* 139-146.
Cornell, W. F. (1997). If Reich had met Winnicott: Body and gesture. *Energy & Character, 28*(2), 50-60.
Cornell, W. F. (2000). Transference, desire and vulnerability in body-centered psychotherapy. *Energy & Character, 30*(2), 29-37.
Downing, G. (1997). *Korper und Wort in der Psychotherapie* [The body and the work in psychotherapy]. Munchen: Koselverlag.
Emde, R. (1988). Development terminable and interminable I: Innate and motivational factors in infancy. *International Journal of Psycho-Analysis, 69,* 23-42.
Erskine, R. G. (1997). The therapeutic relationship: Integrating motivation and personality theories. In R. G. Erskine, *Theories and methods of an integrative transactional analysis: A volume of selected articles* (pp. 7-19). San Francisco: TA Press.
Fairbairn, W. R. D. (1952). *Psychoanalytic studies of the personality.* London: Routledge & Kegan Paul.
Fonagy, P., Steele, M., Steele, H., Moran, G. S., & Higgitt, A. C. (1991). The capacity for understanding mental states: The reflective self in parent and child and its significance for security of attachment. *Infant Mental Health Journal, 12,* 201-218.
Freud, S. (1964). Analysis terminable and interminable. In J. Strachey (Ed. &Trans.), *The standard edition of the complete psychological works of Sigmund Freud* (Vol. 23, pp. 209-253). London: Hogarth Press. (Original work published 1937)
Gaines, R. (1997). Detachment and continuity: The two tasks of mourning. *Contemporary Psychoanalysis, 33,* 549-570.
Green, A. (2000). Science and science fiction in infant research. In J. Sandler, A-M. Sandler, & R. Davies (Eds.), *Clinical and observational research in psychoanalysis: Roots of a controversy* (pp. 41-72). Madison, CT: International Universities Press.
Guntrip, H. (1961). *Personality structure and human interaction.* New York: International Universities Press.
Holmes, J. (1996). *Attachment, intimacy, autonomy: Using attachment theory in adult psychotherapy.* Northvale, NJ: Jason Aronson.
Karen, R. (1998). *Becoming attached: First relationships and how they shape our capacity to love.* New York: Oxford University Press.
Lachmann, F., & Beebe, B. (1996). Three principles of salience in the organization of the patient-analyst interaction. *Psychoanalytic Psychology, 13*(1), 1-22.
Lichtenberg, J. D. (1983). *Psychoanalysis and infant research.* Hillsdale, NJ: The Analytic Press.
Lichtenberg, J. D. (1989). *Psychoanalysis and motivation.* Hillsdale, NJ: The Analytic Press.
Lichtenberg, J., Lachmann, F., & Fosshage, J. (1992). *Self and motivational systems.* Hillsdale, NJ: The Analytic Press.
Mahler, M. (1968). *On symbiosis and the vicissitudes of individuation.* New York: International Universities Press.
Main, M. (1995). Recent studies in attachment: Overview, with selected implications for clinical work. In S. Goldberg, R. Muir, & J. Kerr (Eds.), *Attachment theory: Social, developmental, and clinical perspectives* (pp. 407-474). Hillsdale, NJ: The Analytic Press.
Margulies, A. (1989). *The empathic imagination.* New York: Norton.
Modell, A. H. (1998). Review of infant mental health papers. *Infant Mental Health Journal, 19,* 341-345.
Moses, I. (1988). The misuse of empathy in psychoanalysis. *Contemporary Psychoanalysis, 24*(4), 577-594.
Renik, O. (1996). The perils of neutrality. *Psychoanalytic Quarterly, 65,* 495-517.
Schiff, J. (1977). One hundred children generate a lot of TA: History, development, and activities of the Schiff family. In G. Barnes (Ed.), *Transactional analysis after Eric Berne: Teachings and practices of three TA schools* (pp. 53-76). New York: Harper's College Press.
Schiff, J. L., with Schiff, A. W., Mellor, K., Schiff, E., Schiff, S., Richman, D., Fishman, J., Wolz, L., Fishman, C., & Momb, D. (1975). *Cathexis reader: Transactional analysis treatment of psychosis.* New York: Harper & Row.
Slochower, J. (1992). A hateful borderline patient and the holding environment. *Contemporary Psychoanalysis, 28*(1), 72-88.

Stark, M. (1999). *Modes of therapeutic interaction*. Northvale, NJ: Jason Aronson.
Steiner, C. (1974). *Scripts people live: Transactional analysis of life scripts*. New York: Grove Press.
Stern, D. B. (1998). Not misusing empathy. *Contemporary Psychoanalysis, 24*(4), 598-611.
Stern, D. N. (1985). *The interpersonal world of the infant: A view from psychoanalysis and developmental psychology*. New York: Basic Books.
Storr, A. (1988). *Solitude: A return to the self*. New York: The Free Press.
Tronick, E. (1998a). Dyadically expanded states of consciousness and the process of therapeutic change. *Infant Mental Health Journal, 19*(3), 290-299.
Tronick, E. (Ed.). (1998b). Special issue. *Infant Mental Health Journal, 19*.
White, M., & Weiner, M. (1986). *The theory and practice of self psychology*. New York: Brunner/Mazel.
Winnicott, D. W. (1958a). Hate in the countertransference. In D. W. Winnicott, *Through paediatrics to psycho-analysis* (pp. 194-203). London: Tavistock. (Original work published 1947)
Winnicott, D. W. (1958b). Primary material preoccupation. In D. W. Winnicott, *Through paediatrics to psycho-analysis* (pp. 300-305). London: Tavistock. (Original work published 1956)
Winnicott, D. W. (1958c). Primitive emotional development. In D. W. Winnicott, *Through paediatrics to psycho-analysis* (pp. 145-156). London: Tavistock. (Original work published 1945)
Winnicott, D. W. (1958d). *Through paediatrics to psycho-analysis*. London: Tavistock.
Winnicott, D. W. (1965). *The maturational processes and the facilitating environment: Studies in the theory of emotional development*. New York: International Universities Press.
Winnicott, D. W. (1971). *Playing and reality*. London: Tavistock.

The original version of this article was published in the Transactional Analysis Journal, *Volume 31, Number 1, pp. 71-83, January 2001.*

In the Terrain of the Unconscious: The Evolution of a Transactional Analysis Therapist

William F. Cornell

> Rather than regarding the unconscious as an impersonal set of nonsubjective functions and as a "seething cauldron" that impulsively and psychopathically seeks to irrupt, we might more empathically consider it to be a preternatural, personal subjectivity in its own right . . . and regard this unconscious subject as a conjoined twin, an alter ego, to the ego. . . . I suggest that the unconscious comprises not "objects" but phantoms as well as "presences" or "intelligences." (Grotstein, 2004, p. 103)

Psychoanalysis, in all of its many forms of execution, is unified by its efforts at systematic exploration of the interface between conscious and unconscious realms of experience. It is in this attention to the unconscious modes of organization and expression that psychoanalysis is most clearly distinguished from transactional analysis. Berne's earliest writings reflected a clear respect for the power of unconscious organization and motivation, an interest that seemed to fade in his later writing and recommendations for practice in transactional analysis. However, today we are seeing a return of interest in developing a coherent theory and practice of unconscious communication among many contemporary transactional analysis practitioners.

This chapter was inspired in part by the opening speech offered by Emmanuel Ghent (2002) at the conference given for the inauguration of the International Association for Relational Psychoanalysis and Psychotherapy (IARPP). Ghent was critical of the increasingly facile and superficial applications of the concept of relational "as it becomes clear that the term is being used to signify something like human contact or connection." He went on to emphasize that the field of relational phenomena in psychotherapy "is not confined to interhuman relations" (p. 4). He urged the audience to acquire "a new appreciation for the complexity and compass of the relational," including relations to one's self and self-organization, fantasy, perceptions, actions, cognition and memory, the interpersonal, and social relations, "not to mention the highly complex relations that exist between these different levels" (p. 5).

As I listened to Ghent, I found myself looking back over the course of my own personal therapies as well as the evolution of my professional training and experience. I realized that each phase of my personal and professional development offered a different sort of relationship to unconscious experience. The unconscious is not a singular phenomenon, and work within unconscious processes requires a multiplicity of relationships with oneself and others. My capacity as a psychotherapist to understand and relate to the varied manifestations of the unconscious has grown more complex as my work has matured. I offer this chapter as a contribution to the return of systematic attention to the realms of unconscious experience in transactional analysis. It is a theoretical exploration presented in a semiautobiographical discussion of my professional development as it was originally evoked by listening to Ghent.

The Bernean Unconscious

In his writings about intuition, collected together after his death, Berne (1949/1977a) defined intuition as "knowledge based on experience and acquired by means of preverbal unconscious or preconscious functions through sensory contact with the subject" (p. 4). Here he seems not to be utilizing a psychodynamic description of the unconscious so much as a just-below-awareness notion of the unconscious, a version of Freud's conceptualization of preconscious experience.

In a subsequent article in which he continued to explore "intuitive" functions, "Primal Images and Primal Judgment," Berne (1955/1977b) came the closest to a psychodynamic account of the unconscious:

> A primal image is the image of an infantile object relationship; that is, of the use of the function of an erogenous zone for social expression. A primal judgment is the understanding (correct or incorrect) of the potentialities of the object relationship represented in the image.... Primal images are presymbolic representations of interpersonal transactions, whose study leads directly to certain important areas of psychopathology. (p. 67)

This statement, originally published in 1955, could have been written by a British object relations or Kleinian theorist. It foreshadows the intersubjective and relational models that were yet to emerge within the psychoanalytic tradition.

I trained in transactional analysis in the early 1970s. Transactional analysis was then an exquisitely American psychotherapy, one of action and will power. As Berne (1966) put it succinctly in *Principles of Group Treatment*, "Transactional analysis is an actionist form of treatment, where psychoanalysis is to a much greater extent a contemplative one. The transactional analyst says, 'Get better first, and we can analyze later' " (p. 303). In those days, there was nothing that could not be fixed. There was not a patient who could not be cured, preferably quickly. It was the American way: Control it, fix it, and if it does not go our way, bomb it. (This was the era of the Vietnam war; not much has changed in the United States in this regard as we see now in Afghanistan and Iraq.) Woundedness equaled victimhood equaled a game. Fix it; redecide it; reparent it, reorganize it. Put the Adult ego state in charge. The therapist intervened with contracts and clarity, powered by the therapist's permission, protection, and potency, so as to liberate a "free" Child.

Transactional analysis as I first learned it was a psychotherapy of the ego (states), by the ego, and for the ego. The language of gestalt therapy, with such notions as "out of awareness," had infiltrated transactional analysis, but "out of awareness" is not quite the same as "unconscious." Berne's writings on intuition were not a part of our training in the 1970s. The transactional analysis I learned was a world of contracts, games, confrontation, and cognitive/behavioral change, one that was refreshingly clear, direct, and often effective.

Looking back on that training and my style of doing therapy then, I can now see that there was an implicit model of unconscious wishes and conflicts expelled from consciousness as unacceptable and unbearable in the childhood environment. A sense of unconscious process was contained in Berne's descriptions of intrapsychic conflict between the Adapted Child ego state and the idealized Free Child and in the formation of script, but a theoretical language acknowledging the unconscious disappeared from Berne's writings (Müller, 2002). There was no explicit theory of the unconscious.

By the time *Transactional Analysis in Psychotherapy* was published by Berne in 1961—when he was working hard to set himself apart from psychoanalysis—the flavor of the unconscious was disappearing from his writing. The "archeopsyche," a term potentially broad enough to contain an elaboration of the unconscious, was defined as the "archaic" psychic organ (p. 3) containing the "relics of childhood [that] survive into later life as complete ego states" (p. 17). A look through the indexes of Berne's books show no reference to "unconscious," although the word does crop up here and there in his texts. Berne and most of his transactional analysis colleagues were busy differentiating themselves from psychoanalysts. In a footnote to the section of *Principles of Group Treatment* that delineated the differences between transactional analysis and psychoanalysis, Berne (1966) made it clear that "this discussion is based on twelve years of psychoanalytic training with the New York and San Francisco Psychoanalytic Institutes. The writer, however, is not a member of any Psychoanalytic Society" (p. 292). He distinguished transactional analysis from psychoanalysis this way:

"Structurally, transactional analysis speaks of Parent, Adult, and Child, which are more personal than the superego, ego, and id spoken of in psychoanalysis. The former represent psychological, historical, and behavioral realities" (p. 295).

Berne's emphasis on "reality" swept away the less "realistic," more unconsciously informed subtleties of the "primal image." He firmly rooted transactional analysis within the ego psychology traditions of 1950s American psychoanalysis, banning the unconscious from transactional analysis theory, assigning it—with growing disdain—to the realm of old-fashioned, inefficient theorizing (Berne, 1971).

Yet Berne wrote of ulterior transactions, covert communication, the psychological level of communication, protocol, palimpsest, the group canon, and the group imago—terms that each seem to evoke something of the nature of the unconscious. In *Principles of Group Treatment,* Berne's descriptions of group dynamics are rife with allusions to unconscious processes, although he carefully eschewed that language. He wrote, for example, of the "private structure" of the individual within the group as "the most decisive structural aspect for the outcome of the individual's therapy" (Berne, 1966, p. 135). His description of the "private structure" "smells" a good deal like an unconscious structure, as does much of Berne's later terminology about script. But there was no explicit theory of the unconscious articulated in his writings.

One of Berne's enduring contributions to the evolution of psychotherapy was his effort to clarify and humanize therapeutic operations. I would emphasize that work with the unconscious is not at odds with a humanistic model, although much of Berne's original training in psychoanalysis was. I do believe that, had Berne lived longer, a reconceptualization of the unconscious would have emerged in his thinking as he struggled with the persistent, intransigent clinical problems he had begun to address in the writings collected posthumously in *What Do You Say After You Say Hello?* (Berne, 1972).

The Characterological Unconscious

At the same time that I was doing my transactional analysis training, I was also being trained in Radix body education, because I was looking for an approach to supplement what I found to be the overly cognitive approach of TA. Radix, as conceived by its founder, Charles Kelley (1974, 1978), was a neo-Reichian therapy model that took the political position that it was an educational model not a therapeutic model in an effort to distinguish itself from the psychoanalytic and psychiatric traditions in which Reich's work was grounded. Radix was also an attempt to develop a model that erased attention to the unconscious. We worked with body process, body structure, and emotional release, not with the unconscious and not with transference, as we were explicitly told.

Reich's (1949) model itself, however, was one of the unconscious, a model of the intrapsychic conflict between the ego in conflict with the more primary (and, for Reich, healthier) realms of emotional/somatic needs and desires. In his approach, the unconscious resided in the defense itself. The unconscious was a graveyard of repressed, disowned, discarded psychic wounds and defenses. Reich's psychotherapy centered on the analysis of resistance through the confrontation and change of characterological and body armor. Therapy worked to bring these patterns and the meaning of the unconscious defenses into conscious awareness. The goal was to make the defenses conscious and the patient would then be free: insight from the body to the mind.

For Reich, and my own young and eager therapeutic vision, the body held the possibility of paradise, freedom, and unbridled wisdom. For Reich, and my emerging clinical understanding, character was the expression of a contracted, defensive body. Character was a thick, stubborn, and unmoving structure of defense, confining mind and body so as to avoid life, movement, fluidity, vitality, and sexuality.

For me as a young psychotherapist, these were compelling models: the unconscious of intrapsychic conflict and character defenses. My relationship to the unconscious was to be that of a confronter and uncoverer, an ally of the conscious mind and the vibrant body, bringing light into the darkness of the defenses. This made me feel good, worthwhile, and competent. I was earning my keep, and

I was carrying out familiar tasks consistent with my own characterological defenses, that is, looking for things that were broken or hurting and setting out to fix them. Therapy was primarily a corrective and reparative process, and I was the corrector and repairer.

Some clients got significantly better through this combination of transactional analysis and neo-Reichian therapies. TA and Radix, each in different ways, valued movement and activity. We expected something to happen; the therapist was an agent of change (Cassius, 1975, 1980; Cornell, 1975, 1980). Many, including myself, accomplished some changes but were left unsatisfied, unmoved in some sense, and working too hard at being and staying well. I had not yet the age or experience to begin to see how a favorite (often ardently defended) clinical theory could function as an enactment of the therapist's script, a theoretically sanctioned structure for countertransference acting out. This was, in part, what I was doing as a TA/Radix psychotherapist.

The Transferential Unconscious

As my sophistication as a body psychotherapist grew, my understanding of the body's relationship to the unconscious (and thus of my relationship to the bodily unconscious) changed profoundly. I began to realize that in addition to the resistant unconscious that Reich delineated so clearly in his character theory, character was also a form of unconscious communication. There is a realm of unlanguaged, precognitive, somatic organization that functions below conscious awareness. There is a level of somatic organization that brings desire and vitality, as well as anxiety and defense, to daily experience. This is a level of bodily experience and desire that can enrich and enliven the therapeutic field and that can function as an ally to therapeutic process.

I began to open myself to the impact of various clients' character styles. How was it that in the 9 o'clock session certain thoughts and feelings seemed obvious and interesting, while at 10 o'clock my capacity to think seemed to disappear (did I need more coffee?) and only certain states of affect seemed possible? I began to see (and feel) that character was not simply constraining my clients but also informing me. I began to play with what I observed and experienced. Often when clients who mystified (or irritated) me left the office, I would "try them on for size," sitting as they sat, moving as they moved, re-creating their tones of voice and facial expressions. I began to have supervisees not only talk about their clients but become them, moving into their way of being in supervisory sessions.

Slowly, slowly, slowly, I began to develop different relationships with my clients' characterological forms. I began to understand the dance of character as a means of relating—sometimes limiting and deforming, always informing, and hopefully reforming. My understanding of character was acquiring new meaning as a rich field of unconscious communication.

I was also learning at that time from my fatherhood. I found myself pounded into a multiplicity of shapes and functions by my three very different sons, each of whom needed a very different kind of father. This father was only one man, but he needed to provide a multiplicity of psychic services in the lives of his sons. I carried out these diverse fatherly services with varying degrees of competence and satisfaction. I began to recognize that my clients, too, needed a breathtakingly diverse range of "services" from me, some of which made me very uncomfortable. Each client's character shaped, in many unspoken and unconscious ways, the interpersonal field between him or her and me. Each client's character style pushed me around during the hour, shaping, showing me something essential without a word being spoken (or, often, in contradiction to the words being spoken). It became clear that there is the potential for a vitalizing form of unconscious communication in the midst of the deadening function of character structure.

I realized that while the treatment contracts we negotiated Adult to Adult were useful and necessary, there was a good deal more action going on beneath the surface of conscious awareness within the transferential relationship. While Berne sometimes cast game and script theory as transferential acting out, his writing did not speak to the heart of what I was trying to understand. The labeling and analyzing of games and script placed me as a therapist at a distance from my clients. I knew I needed to enter, rather than merely observe, the transferential field (Cornell, 2000a, 2004). The transactional analysis literature and training of that time was not particularly useful to me in this process. I found echoes of this level of unconscious relatedness in Berne's concept of the protocol as the unconscious, relational infrastructure of subsequent, preconscious script decisions (Berne, 1961, 1963; Cornell & Landaiche, 2005), but this was one of many of his early ideas that he failed to elaborate in his later work.

I turned to a psychoanalytic supervisor, entered psychoanalytic therapy, and renewed my reading of psychoanalytic texts to address the issues that were emerging in my clinical work. While I had many disputes with analytic theory—and especially with analytic technique—I found that the contemporary analytic literature conveyed a rich landscape of therapeutic interiority and bodily relatedness. In particular, I discovered Winnicott (1965, 1971), Bollas (1989, 1992), and McLaughlin (1987, 1988, 1989, 1991, 2005). In reading Winnicott, I found his concept of the infant's gestures to the mother and began to reconceive of character as the interruption of nonverbal communication between infant and caretakers (Cornell, 1997, 2000b). I discovered in McLaughlin's writings an account of nonverbal, bodily expression, not in the standard psychoanalytic rendering of the patient's regressive, infantile behavior, but as "the primacy and durability of this early mode of psychomotor thought" (McLaughlin, 1989, p. 112). The idea of psychomotor thought was a phrase that could make a body therapist's heart sing. In McLaughlin's writing, I found an American psychoanalyst (of Berne's era and training) whose thinking extended Winnicott's (without seeming to know of Winnicott):

> The nonverbal gestural, postural, and mimetic components comprise the first communications between infant and caregiver, building out of the bodily and visual involvements between the pair and providing the necessary substrate for the more slowly organizing verbal capacities. The earliest memories of each of us are richly registered in these nonverbal modes, which continue throughout life to extend their own range and refinement even as they are eventually overridden by the emergingly dominant verbal mode that they support. (p. 112)

I remember my excitement, a kind of thrill of recognition, in reading about Bollas's (1989) concept of the personal "idiom" (pp. 9-10) as a sense of self that is like a vision-in-waiting, seeking new objects over the course of life to use as a living medium to help materialize this emergent self. The analyst is unconsciously pounded into one sort of shape or another, one shape after another, to be used to discover and manifest yet-unknown but relentlessly determined aspects of one's being. Bollas (1992) writes of being a character. He writes eloquently and persuasively of the "intelligence of form" captured by an individual's character. I had been trained to see character and form as stupid, overformed, and underinforming. In contrast, Bollas describes character as a form of creative intelligence.

I was beginning to acquire a new stance and attitude toward character. I had been trained in transactional analysis and Radix to confront, redecide, and repair characterological, script-based patterns. I was beginning to understand that often I, as well as the client, needed to stand in the field of the person's character style, to feel its full impact. I offer a brief case vignette to illustrate.

Seen from a characterological perspective, Tim is schizoid/paranoid—schizoid on a good day, paranoid on a bad day. He is a bright and fascinating guy and has lived alone his entire adult life. I have grown very fond of him. He did not speak much for the first year of therapy, often remaining silent through an entire session. This tended to make me rather anxious, but mostly I sat with him in reasonable comfort in the midst of his silence. It did not seem to be a silence of hostility or withholding, but one of bewilderment and distrust of what to do in the company of another human being. Sometimes, to disrupt the silence, I talked to him about whatever was on my mind. This could include anything from what I was going to make for dinner that night to what I was imagining might be going on in his mind. Somehow, through this process, he came to trust my interest in him and could even sense that I quite liked him.

Several years into our work, Tim missed a session. We had experienced a severe ice storm, and almost none of my clients made it to their sessions that day. He did not like missing sessions. Even during his silent phase he always kept his appointments. We had not been able to schedule a make-up session, so this was his last session before I was leaving on an international trip of 2 weeks. He came in very angry and said, "I don't know why I'm here. I don't know why I keep coming back. I don't know why I'm here." I replied, "You often don't know why you're here." He continued, "Well, you know, a couple of weeks ago we had a session that was so . . . it was so . . . intimate. I can't remember a fucking thing we talked about, but I remember how it felt. It was so important, and I left and I was just excited. I cannot remember what we talked about."

There was a long pause and then he continued, "That's how it is for me. I'm either in the loop, or I'm out of the loop. Right now, I'm out of the loop, and I don't have any idea why I'm here, and I think maybe this will be our last session. I'm not sure I'll keep my appointment when you get back. I'm just out of the loop. I just don't have anything to talk about." There was a long silence. I said, "You absolutely do not have to talk about anything. We can sit here and feel what it's like when you're out of the loop. It's about as unpleasant for me as it is for you. Let's see what happens."

He responded angrily. "You don't get it, do you? You really don't have any idea that I don't trust anybody—nobody—not even you. For as long as I've seen you, I haven't trusted you. If you think I trust you, you are a fool." He went on for a while in this fashion. I eventually said, "You know, it's difficult for me right now to sense anything other than how scared you are. You are so frightened. I am not aware of anything else right now other than fear." He looked stunned, "I don't feel afraid." I replied, "It's really fascinating that you can make statements like, 'I don't trust anybody' and 'If you think I trust you, you're a fool,' that you can make that statement and not know you are afraid. That's remarkable." He said, "You think I'm afraid?" "Well, let's try it the other way around," I replied, "and I say to you I don't trust anybody. Just imagine for a minute what I might be feeling to say something like that." He replied, "You're scared. It seems obvious when you say it. But I don't know that I'm scared when I say it. I don't feel scared." There was a long, silent pause. "I'm beginning to think I'm more insane that I realized." "Yes, you can be quite insane when you're around other people. Living alone you're quite sane, but when you walk into my office, then you can become quite insane, out of the loop. No feelings, no thoughts, no memory of what just happened between us a couple of weeks ago. We missed a session, now I'm leaving, everything becomes meaningless. It terrifies you. You break the loop."

I did not act to fix anything, to repair the container or take the edge off of the struggle. I named it. I entered it with him. This is his insanity, not as a pathological diagnosis but as an acknowledgment of how deeply frightened and troubled he is. There is a quality of madness in being able to make a statement like the one he made in that session and not know that one is scared. There is a place for what he calls his insanity between us. We can come to know it. In fact, we must come to know it. We can live it together while he decides if and how he may want to change it.

In his speech to the IARPP conference, Ghent (2002) challenged his relational colleagues to question the direction of their work. He said that he dreaded the day when patients would start complaining to their therapists, "You're not meeting my relational needs." Several people in the audience exclaimed, "It's already happening." Ghent went on to argue that in relational treatment the therapist is not busy providing a relationship but is examining the patterns of the patient's relationships, and not only with the therapist in the here and now, but throughout his or her history, with himself or herself, to internal fantasies, and to the person's social structure. There is a rich range of relations to be explored. If the therapist becomes caught up in needing to provide the relationship, then the relationship is not being examined and the field of unconscious communication is cordoned off from exploration.

Aron (1996) argues forcefully that the model of the analyst's subjectivity and the dyadic interplay of intersubjectivity hold a theoretical advantage over the models of transference and countertransference, emphasizing that "the terms subjectivity and intersubjectivity do not imply the pathological . . . and these terms do imply a continuous, ongoing flow of influence, in contrast to countertransference, which implies an occasional or intermittent event" (p. 73). I would argue that we need both the models of the transferential and intersubjective. I think we still need an understanding of transference and countertransference dynamics for two reasons. The first is that we do need to acknowledge psychopathology—our clients' and our own. I cannot speak for every psychotherapist, but I spent nearly 20 years of my adult life in psychotherapy and psychoanalysis out of concern for the impact of my psychopathology/countertransference on my intimates and my clients. The second reason is that I think there are profound, unconscious psychodynamics within the therapeutic couple that are not of mutual influence or cocreation but that are the products of our own histories, our own character structures. The concepts of subjectivity and intersubjectivity expand our understanding of the processes within the analytic dyad but should not replace the concepts of transference and countertransference. In this way, my style is more in keeping with writers like James McLaughlin and Christopher Bollas. I think we can best understand and address this negation of the other's differentness and subjectivity through our attention to character structure and the impact/enactment (in contrast to interplay) of the individual psychic universes of transference and countertransference.

Bollas and McLaughlin have been pivotal writers for me in my understanding of work within the transferential/countertransferential matrix. Both, in their own way, have fashioned models of therapeutic attention that are quite in keeping with what Freud originally proposed—models with a profound regard for unconscious communication—and that are quite distinct from the object relations and self psychology models. Bollas's and McLaughlin's conceptualizations of the relational unconscious have been liberating for me. I have read their work with pleasure, excitement, and a kind of love. I have loved witnessing their minds at work, their unfolding and examining of experiences. For these two analysts, each in different ways, the therapist's countertransference is a rich field of data emerging from the therapist's willingness to be moved, infected, affected, and informed by a matrix of unconscious communication and disturbance.

Phases of the therapy, or moments in any given session, can contain states of unfolding and mutual reverie: therapist and client, analyst and patient engaged at the edge of the as-yet-unknown. The analyst is open to the impact of familiar patterns and to the nonsensical and unfamiliar—ideas, images, shifts in mood, fantasies, dullness, anxieties seemingly showing up in the analyst's mind unbidden. Therapist and client are both involved in a kind of side-by-side reverie. As Bollas described it, each is engaged in a process of self-analysis in one another's presence, each informed by the other's presence.

I want to emphasize here that, at least in my reading and understanding of these two analysts, Bollas and McLaughlin are not talking of "intersubjectivity" or the "coconstruction" of experience and meaning in the ways often taken up in contemporary psychoanalytic and transactional analytic literature. I understand these authors to be saying that therapist and client do not dwell together in intersubjective states. When periods of intersubjectivity—that is, of the intermingling of unconscious experience—emerge during the treatment process, these periods are to be observed with separate minds. I think there is something subtle but crucially different in their account of unconscious communication and the analyst's use of self. Analyst and patient are not seen as constantly creating something between them. Therapist and client remain apart from while engaged with one another as separate subjectivities, often in uncertainty and struggle (McLaughlin, 1988, p. 373). For example, McLaughlin (1995) wrote:

> It is this private self that provides inner stability and nourishment. Yet it is also the hiding place for those most unwanted and troublesome aspects of what we fear we are and wish we were not. It is this aggregate that we zealously protect, keep mostly hidden, and cling to as our essence. It is what we bring to the other when we engage in the analytic dyad. (pp. 434-435)

The therapist is opening his or her conscious and unconscious experience to the impingement and influence of the patient's unconscious. Something about the patient is uncovered/discovered through the therapist's unconscious experience. The therapist is in-formed, something takes shape and substance in the analyst's mind (which is hopefully more open to what is emerging than the client's might be at that moment) and is returned as in-formation to the client. Bollas and McLaughlin articulate models of therapeutic relatedness that allow for uncertainty, dissonance, self-inquiry, and mutual exploration of unconscious meanings as separate but intimate parties.

The Psychotherapist's Multiple Relations to Unconscious Processes: A Case Illustration

Actual clinical work does not evolve in a neat sequence of conscious contracts and decisions gradually unfolding into ever deepening layers of unconscious work. We move constantly back and forth among various foci of attention and layers of experience, conscious and unconscious. This is illustrated in an example from a case consultation that shows the emergence of the various tasks and the multiplicity of interventions that may confront the therapist.

Sid came in for his weekly consultation unusually distressed and feeling an urgent need to discuss a client, Pat, whom he had mentioned occasionally but had never discussed in detail because things seemed to be moving along well enough. Recently, however, things had begun to sour, and the work was at a crisis point, with Pat threatening to quit treatment and Sid guiltily wishing she would.

Pat had entered therapy with Sid after moving to an unfamiliar city when her husband took a new position. She had hoped that the move would be good for both of them. She had been in therapy, unsuccessfully she reported, where she lived before. Familiar patterns of behavior that she had hoped would diminish with the move were returning anew, so she decided to enter therapy again. Two graduate degrees and a 15-year marriage to a successful, wealthy physician did not seem to add much stability to her life or sense of self. Pat's initial presenting problem was being unable to find a job that she wanted to take, but her attention quickly shifted to her chronic overuse of recreational drugs —marijuana, LSD, cocaine occasionally, and speed (her favorite). She and her husband had settled into their familiar, cooperative distance with each other, and Pat filled the gap with drugs. She reported that she found her husband, "like most things, intermittently interesting," but she found drugs to be a much more reliable companion.

It was not surprising that Pat's attitude toward therapy (and her therapist) rapidly mirrored her attitude toward most things interpersonal as she presented a kind of challenging, cynical disengagement. Sid, embarrassed by his rather frequent judgmental and irritated reactions to her, kept his feelings to himself and got busy trying to make himself useful to Pat. He initially established contracts with Pat to limit her drug use and set career goals for her life in this new city. Concerned about the persistence of her drug use and suspecting an underlying depression, Sid suggested meeting twice a week, to which Pat agreed. She developed a way of working with Sid that was overtly cooperative, on the one hand, and persistently noncompliant, on the other. Sid's irritation grew, and he sought consultation for the first time.

As the consultant, I underscored Pat's passive-aggressive behavior, interpreting her persistent drug use as hostile acting out against both her physician husband and her therapist. I pointed out that previous efforts at symptom-centered, behavior-control therapies had not accomplished much of anything and suggested that Sid begin working within the negative transference.

Sid experienced the consultation as clarifying but found himself largely unable to comply with the advice he was given. As he attempted to shift the frame of the work, Pat often experienced his new actions in relation to her (which often took the form of less overt activity) as offensive or disinterested. She would skip the next session when the previous one upset her. Sid soon discovered that in trying to work with Pat in the transference, he also had to work with his own countertransference, which included feelings he did not like in himself and that he could not find a way to express without sounding judgmental (which, of course, he was).

Reviewing his notes in preparation for further consultation, Sid realized that part of his irritation with Pat was that she had not been consistently paying the portion of his fee not covered by insurance. While a relatively small sum, Sid saw this as an aspect of her passive-aggressive behavior and transference acting out. In preparing to address it, he went back over his records and discovered that he had not been paying attention to the number of sessions they had met in the year. They had run over the number allotted by the insurance policy. Sid was extremely nervous about bringing up for discussion what was suddenly a more complex brew of issues and decisions.

Pat was indeed upset by the news and blamed Sid for not paying better attention. She saw his lapse as a further sign of his general lack of attention and concern for her. She suggested it was time to terminate, saying, "Maybe I'll have better luck with someone else." Sid pointed out that she was quite capable of affording his fee without insurance and that they needed to understand what was happening between them. He suggested they not make a decision at that time, but both think it over.

"This is about more than money, so let's not rush to a decision when we're both rather upset," said Sid. "We can talk about it in the next session—assuming you show up, that is." Pat became enraged at his comment, labeling it as hostile. Sid defended his comment as a "playful prediction of the future," based on her past behavior when she was upset with him.

Pat kept her next session but called in advance to cancel the one that was to follow the one she was keeping, leaving a message that she was starting a temporary job and would probably not be able to see him twice a week while she was working. At the start of the session, Sid—now wishing he had consulted more consistently about Pat—ventured a transference interpretation: "I wonder if your keeping this session while canceling the next is a way of simultaneously confounding my ill-considered prediction from our last session while still expressing your upset with me by canceling a later session." Pat denied his interpretation vehemently and attacked back, "I'm damned if I do and damned if I don't with you. If I disagree with you or get upset in here, I'm being passive-aggressive. If I cut back on drugs, that's nice but it's not enough cuz I'm still using. I finally get a job, and you accuse me of resisting therapy. I try to tell you how and why I think you're not really interested in me, and you tell me I'm resistant to treatment, to self-examination or some such fucking nonsense. I try to talk to you and I get psychoanalytic psychobabble in return. And then, to top it all off, I'm not supposed to get upset. I'm supposed to be grateful, I guess. There's no winning with you. You are not really interested in me—that's what all this means to me."

Pat then went on to tell Sid that in her distress, she had looked him up on the Internet. She had found several men in the area phone book by his name, but none were psychologists, so "Now I'm wondering if you're a legitimate therapist." Pat went on to stress that she did not feel safe with Sid and did not feel he was truly interested in her well-being. As further evidence, she pointed out that in the last session when she talked of suicidal feelings, he was cleaning his glasses. Sid acknowledged that he remembered that point in the session and explained that he had felt she was attempting to manipulate him with a suicide threat, and he was determined not to overreact. This did not reassure Pat, and she responded, "I don't want to talk about us any more. It's going nowhere."

Pat began to talk about her brother, who had died in a car accident 2 years earlier. She suspected he was drunk, although there was no evidence of that in the police report. She went on to talk about her guilt over her own drug use—a great deal of speed at that time—which kept her distant from her brother. She wondered if she had been more available to him if he would still be alive. She cried softly, a rare event in her sessions.

Sid listened but found himself preoccupied with the earlier portion of the session. He was relieved that Pat had gone on to talk about something substantial but felt bewildered by the impact of his transference interpretation. Now he wanted to quit. He hoped, privately, she would quit. He began to speculate to himself that she had more pronounced borderline tendencies than he had previously understood. He endured the session and her attacks, offering sympathy for her level of distress. "I am sorry that I've hurt you," he reassured Pat, "and I can see that I will need to do some things to repair our relationship. I think it is terribly important that we continue working together, still twice a week if possible. I'll look at my appointment schedule and suggest some alternative times that may fit your new work schedule." Pat left the session feeling better. Sid sought further consultation.

In the consultation, Sid related the sequence of events and asked for my advice regarding "what I need to do to repair the relationship." I suggested that the relationship was actually in great shape and not in need of repair but in need of "attention," as Pat had been stridently suggesting. To Sid's surprise, I was quite accepting of both his negative feelings toward Pat and the sequence of what Sid had experienced as embarrassing, nearly unforgivable, errors. I was reminded of a beautiful statement by Eigen (1998):

> The analyst must become an expert or artist adept at living through collapse of analysis. He studies processes that undo themselves. Little by little he learns something of what working with destructive processes entail. His growth in capacity to live through and work with destruction signals the patient that such capacity is possible. If the analyst can survive therapy, perhaps the patient can as well. (p. 67)

I suggested that the treatment contract needed to be refocused from Pat's behavior outside of the session (drug use, career, etc.) to her experience and Sid's within the session. The task was not for Sid to repair the relationship but for both of them to take up what was happening in a process of mutual self-examination. I asked Sid to think about what was evoked in him such that he could not respond to the fear that seemed to underlie her angry behavior. I focused on Pat's repeated efforts to communicate to him her experience of the consequences of disinterest: Sid's with her and Pat's with her husband, her brother, and herself. From the consultant's point of view (often an easier one when removed from the heat of the immediate encounters), Pat's talking about her brother's death was not a shift away from talking about her relationship with Sid but an unconscious effort to communicate and further illustrate her worry about the profound effects of disinterest.

Sid began to see, with some excitement, the complex levels of communication—mostly unconscious—that Pat had been bringing to her work with him. He felt himself shift in the consultant's office from embarrassment and avoidance to interest and nervous excitement. Various hypotheses began to take shape for Sid. He wondered if Pat's repeated confrontations of his "disinterest" were, perhaps, projections from a childhood of parental disinterest; he imagined childhood script decisions she might have made to reverse the field of parental disinterest and become the disinterested party herself by getting involved with drugs, distancing her husband, remaining uncommitted to a career, refusing to have children, and so on. He felt a surge of closeness to her as he recognized how terribly frightened she was—for whatever reasons—of her own interest and desire for the interest of others. He could begin to imagine their mutual anger as an effort to demand more of each other rather than to end the relationship. He began to recollect his frequent childhood efforts to stave off his mother's depression and his father's demands. The field of unconscious relatedness began to open up for Sid, and with it the possibilities of understanding and reengagement with Pat.

The Emergent Unconscious

Bollas (1999), in *The Mystery of Things,* challenges an implication of the object relations model, suggesting another possibility for unconscious communication between analyst and patient:

Left to itself, object relations theory will always return self to other through the here and now transference interpretation, enclosing the self in the cozy if solipsistic world of infant and mother; the Freudian action breaks this tie, sending the self into an uncertain and anxiously open-ended future. (p. 68)

Work within the transferential matrix can involve entering the field of desire—uncertain, unstable, precarious desires. It can be an opening—an emergence—into an unknown, yet-to-be-known future rather than an inevitable enactment of failed and broken relationships from the past.

Stolorow and Atwood (1992), in their discussion of the realms of the unconscious, describe what they call "the unvalidated unconscious," experiences that "could not be articulated because they never evoked the requisite validating responsiveness from the surround" (p. 33). This is a region of the emergent unconscious, of one's as-yet-unknown potential. This is a realm of unconscious experience that is not based in the repression or denial of impulse and need; it simply never had the recognition to help it come to life. Often, as character defenses soften and the capacity for unconscious communication becomes richer, client and therapist enter the realms of the unvalidated, emergent unconscious: fragile, wordless, tentative realms of desire and fantasy. This is the world of the yet-to-be-known.

At the same IARPP conference at which Ghent spoke, Ruth Stein (2002), in a panel discussion about Mitchell's (2002) *Can Love Last?*, introduced the concept of "unsanctioned passions," which can emerge when the deep realms of a person's psyche are activated in a long-standing psychotherapeutic or other intimate relationship. It is only in our most passionate and intimate relationships that I think these unsanctioned passions emerge. I think this happens—if we are lucky, determined, and intimate—in the later stages of psychotherapy. When client and therapist (or lovers or friends) can sustain a lively field of unconscious communication, a space opens up in which client and therapist can experience the full force of what Bollas (1992) calls the "psychic genera" (pp. 66-100). The rich potential of unconscious experience in these realms is in no way regressed or defensive (although it may have been deeply defended) but very much alive, passionate, and often transgressive. It is disturbing to sustain a therapeutic space within which we can undo both what has been historically forbidden and what was sanctioned as the accepted alternative to the forbidden so as to allow for the emergence of the unsanctioned, the radically new. The unsanctioned unconscious is a realm of mutual uncertainty, mutual vulnerability, and mutual differentiation and freedom within the therapeutic relationship.

Conclusion: Love of the Work

In bringing this chapter to a close, I want to return to Eigen's (1998) words:

We incessantly impact on each other, sending emotional ripples throughout our beings. One of our tasks is to help build equipment to process emotional impacts, to be able to live through what we create together. To some extent, a psychoanalyst must be a connoisseur of impacts. Shocks have different tastes. Some we get used to. But there will always be enough new shocks to broaden and shift what it is possible to experience. (p. 17)

Throughout our lives we are confronted by shocks we do not anticipate and cannot process alone. Therapist and client work together to develop the capacity for deeper experience and the expression of a self larger and more complex than that contained within the script system originally developed to ward off or manage the shocks of our childhood environments.

Knoblauch (2000) coined the term "resonant minding" (pp. 95-97) to capture this experience. Minding captures the sense of the process, stressing it over the location of an event. An essential aspect of my understanding of working within the interpersonal unconscious is that the therapist is busy "minding" the shop, constantly curious, wondering, a kind of auxiliary dreamer. Hopefully, when the patient goes flat, something will pop up in the therapist—something stays alive. I think of this aliveness as in the therapist, in the therapist's process of minding, rather than in the relationship. Something needs to stay alive and curious within me in the midst of the myriad ambiguities, dead spots, and anxieties that may fill many of the hours spent struggling together in sessions. If I stay alive, the work will stay alive. The therapist's curiosity, intensity of wondering and experience, creates the opportunity and space for unconscious communication.

During the seminar of the British Clinical Transactional Analysis Symposium in February 2002, to which this paper was also a contribution, Christopher Bollas (2002) touched on something very important and too rarely addressed: the privilege and the pleasure of doing this work. It is my hope that I communicate this pleasure in a myriad of ways to my clients. I love what I do, and that is true even in the depths of the most difficult, conflicted phases of the work. There is a profound shift in unconscious experience when client and therapist move into territories that have been historically drenched in punishment, shame, loss, prohibition, anxiety, or hatred, and discover in the midst of it all, the vivid pleasure of the work itself.

Clearly, I have learned a great deal from the authors I have quoted here; my work has deepened and matured from reading and knowing them. I no longer seek to "fix" my clients. I have learned to welcome unconscious experience in its many guises, to live with it with my clients, so as to learn together through the richness and unpredictability of the terrain of the unconscious. I think of my own recently concluded personal psychotherapy, my third long-term therapeutic relationship. It was a psychoanalysis. That experience fills the background of this chapter. As I prepared to terminate my personal psychoanalysis, I realized that I had not internalized my therapist as a new, good object, nor had I internalized our relationship per se. What I had internalized was a way of working, of reflecting, of being with myself in the presence of an attentive and ultimately beloved other.

REFERENCES

Aron, L. (1996). *A meeting of minds: Mutuality in psychoanalysis.* Hillsdale, NJ: The Analytic Press.
Berne, E. (1961). *Transactional analysis in psychotherapy: A systematic individual and social psychiatry.* New York: Grove Press.
Berne, E. (1963). *The structure and dynamics of organizations and groups.* New York: Grove Press.
Berne, E. (1966). *Principles of group treatment.* New York: Oxford University Press.
Berne, E. (1971). Away from a theory of the impact of interpersonal interaction on non-verbal participation. *Transactional Analysis Journal, 1*(1), 6-13.

Berne, E. (1972). *What do you say after you say hello?: The psychology of human destiny.* New York: Grove Press.
Berne, E. (1977a). The nature of intuition. In E. Berne, *Intuition and ego states: The origins of transactional analysis* (P. McCormick, Ed.) (pp. 1-31). San Francisco: TA Press. (Original work published 1949)
Berne, E. (1977b). Primal images and primal judgment. In E. Berne, *Intuition and ego states: The origins of transactional analysis* (P. McCormick, Ed.) (pp. 67-97). San Francisco: TA Press. (Original work published 1955)
Bollas, C. (1989). *The shadow of the object: Psychoanalysis of the unthought known.* New York: Columbia University Press.
Bollas, C. (1992). *Being a character: Psychoanalysis and self experience.* New York: Hill & Wang.
Bollas, C. (1999). *The mystery of things.* London: Routledge.
Bollas, C. (2002, 23 February). *Forms of the unconscious.* Presentation at the Advanced Clinical Symposium of the Clinical Practice Subcommittee of the Institute for Transactional Analysis, London.
Cassius, J. (1975). *Bodyscripts: Collected papers on physical aspects of transactional analysis.* Limited circulation manuscript.
Cassius, J. (1980). Bodyscript release: How to use bioenergetics and transactional analysis. In J. Cassius (Ed.), *Horizons in bioenergetics: New dimensions in mind/body psychotherapy* (pp. 212-244). Memphis, TN: Promethean Publications.
Cornell, W. F. (1975). Wake up "sleepy": Reichian techniques and script intervention. *Transactional Analysis Journal, 5,* 144-147.
Cornell, W. F. (1980). Structure and function in Radix body education and script change. In J. Cassius (Ed.), *Horizons in bioenergetics: New dimensions in mind/body psychotherapy* (pp. 88-99). Memphis, TN: Promethean Publication.
Cornell. W. F. (1997). If Reich had met Winnicott: Body and gesture. *Energy & Character, 28,* 50-60.
Cornell, W. F. (2000a, 8 November). *Entering the gestural field: Bringing somatic and subsymbolic processes into the psychoanalytic frame.* Paper presented to the Pittsburgh Psychoanalytic Society and Institute, Pittsburgh, Pennsylvania.
Cornell, W. F. (2000b). Transference, desire and vulnerability in body-centered psychotherapy. *Energy & Character, 30,* 29-37.
Cornell, W. F. (2004). The interrupted gesture: The body in relationship. In G. Marlock & H. Weiss (Eds.), *Bodypsychotherapie in theorie and practise* [Body psychotherapy in theory and practice]. Frankfurt: Hogrefe.
Cornell, W. F., & Landaiche, N. M., III. (2005). Impasse e intimata nella coppia terapeutica o di counseling: l'influenza del protocollo [Impasse and intimacy in the therapeutic or consultative couple: The influence of protocol]. *Rivista Italiana di Analisi Transazionale e Metodologie Psicoterapeutiche, 11,* 35-60.
Eigen, M. (1998). *The psychoanalytic mystic.* Binghampton, NY: ESF Publishers.
Ghent, E. (2002). *Relations* [Unpublished manuscript]. Introduction to the First Conference of the International Association of Relational Psychoanalysis and Psychotherapy, New York, 18 January.
Grotstein, J. (2004). "The light militia of the lower sky": The deeper nature of dreaming and phantasying. *Psychoanalytic Dialogues, 14,* 99-118.
Kelley, C.R. (1974). *Education in feeling and purpose.* Santa Monica, CA: The Radix Institute.
Kelley, C.R. (1978). *Orgonomy, bioenergetics and radix: The Reichian movement today.* Santa Monica, CA: The Radix Institute.
Knoblauch, S. (2000). *The musical edge of therapeutic dialogue.* Hillsdale, NJ: The Analytic Press.
McLaughlin, J. T. (1987). The play of transference: Some reflections on enactment in the psychoanalytic situation. *Journal of the American Psychoanalytic Association, 35,* 557-582.
McLaughlin, J. T. (1988). The analyst's insights. *Psychoanalytic Quarterly, 57,* 370-389.
McLaughlin, J. T. (1989). The relevance of infant observational research for the analytic understanding of adult patients' nonverbal behaviors. In S. Downing & A. Rothstein (Eds.), *The significance of infant observational research for clinical work with children, adolescents, and adults* (pp. 109-122). Madison, CT: International Universities Press.
McLaughlin, J. T. (1991). Clinical and theoretical aspects of enactment. *Journal of the American Psychoanalytic Association, 39,* 595-614.
McLaughlin, J. T. (1995). Touching limits in the analytic dyad. *Psychoanalytic Quarterly, 64,* 433-465.
McLaughlin, J. T. (2005). *The healer's bent: Solitude and dialogue in the clinical encounter* (W. F. Cornell, Ed.). Hillsdale, NJ: The Analytic Press.
Mitchell, S. (2002). *Can love last?: The fate of romance over time.* New York: Norton.
Müller, U. (2002). What Eric Berne meant by "unconscious": Aspects of depth psychology in transactional analysis. *Transactional Analysis Journal, 32,* 107-115.
Reich, W. (1949). *Character analysis* (3rd ed. rev.) (T. P. Wolfe, Trans.). New York: Orgone Institute Press.
Stein, R. (2002). *Can love last?* [Unpublished manuscript]. Panel discussion at the First Conference of the International Association for Relational Psychoanalysis and Psychotherapy, New York, 20 January.
Stolorow, R., & Atwwod, G. (1992). *Contexts of being: The intersubjective foundations of psychological life.* Hillsdale, NJ: The Analytic Press.
Winnicott, D. W. (1965). *The maturational processes and the facilitating environment: Studies in the theory of emotional development.* Madison, CT: International Universities Press.
Winnicott, D. W. (1971). *Playing and reality.* London: Tavistock.

The original version of this chapter was published in the Transactional Analysis Journal, *Volume 35, Number 2, pp. 119-131, April 2005. The original article was an elaboration of a paper presented at the Institute of Transactional Analysis Advanced Clinical Symposium, "Working with Unconscious Process," in London, 23 February 2002. The author expresses his gratitude to Mort Johan, Jim McLaughlin, and Christopher Bollas for their enduring influence on his thinking and his life.*

What Do You Say If You Don't Say "Unconscious"?: Dilemmas Created for Transactional Analysts by Berne's Shift Away from the Language of Unconscious Experience

William F. Cornell

> Our inner world, the place of psychic reality, is inevitably less coherent than our representations of it; a moving medley of part thoughts, incomplete visualizations, fragments of dialogue, recollections, unremembered active presences, sexual states, anticipations, urges, unknown yet present needs, vague intentions, ephemeral mental lucidities, unlived partial actions: one could go on and on. (Bollas, 1992, p. 47)

For reasons never directly articulated, between the publication of *Principles of Group Treatment* (Berne, 1966) and writing *What Do You Say After You Say Hello?* (Berne, 1972) in the years immediately following, Eric Berne dropped the word "unconscious" from his personal lexicon. In the glossary of *Principles,* the book in which he most fully articulated his values and philosophy of treatment, Berne (1966) defined script as "an unconscious life plan. In some cases it may be preconscious or conscious" (p. 368). In *What Do You Say After You Say Hello?* (Berne, 1972), published posthumously, script is defined as "a life plan based on a decision made in early childhood, reinforced by the parents, justified by subsequent events, and culminating in a chosen alternative" (p. 446). The phrase "life plan" remains, but "unconscious" is gone, with the new definition now referring to early childhood "decisions."

How did the word "unconscious" come to be taken out of Berne's writing in his final years? Why did he seem to shift to a decisional model of script and interpersonal dynamics? He did not speak to this change of terminology overtly in a clearly articulated theoretical fashion, but this change of language certainly suggests a significant alteration in his thinking. I say "overtly" because there is much in *Hello* that still suggests that many aspects of psychological motivation and organization are not conscious. For example, Berne opened the chapter, "How Is the Script Possible?" with the metaphor of Jeder at the piano. However, the piano is a player piano, and Jeder's fingers only appear to be responsible for the music. The tune emerging from the piano is actually controlled by the piano roll. Berne wrote that Jeder

> is under the illusion that the music is his own, and has for his witness his body, slowly wearing out from hour after hour and day after day of pumping. Sometimes, during the pauses, he rises up to take a bow or a boo from his friends and relatives, who also believe that he is playing his own tune. (Berne, 1972, p. 244)

If this is not a metaphor for unconscious motivation, I don't know what is! It may also have been a parable for Berne's feelings about his own life, his experience of slowly wearing out as he sat with his endless roll of paper, writing away in the study behind his house.

Perspectives from Members of the Original San Francisco Social Psychiatry Seminars

In his preface to *Hello*, Berne thanked the Teaching Members of ITAA and the members of the San Francisco Social Psychiatry Seminars for their contributions to the development of transactional analysis and to his thinking. To better understand the context for the changes in Berne's thinking, I decided to write to all those still alive who were members of the San Francisco Social Psychiatry Seminars between 1966 and Berne's death in 1970. I asked them why they thought Berne removed "unconscious" from his definition of script and why he described *Hello*, in the midst of writing it, as his most difficult book to write. The responses I received were fascinating and quite consistent. In this chapter I excerpt their comments and then discuss the relevance of unconscious experience in contemporary transactional analysis. My hope is to offer a perspective that addresses the pitfalls that Berne attempted to avoid by not using the Freudian concept of the unconscious.

Fanita English, Pat Crossman, Steve Karpman, Marty Groder, Len Campos, and Claude Steiner each responded to my inquiry about the erasure of "unconscious" in Berne's later writing. First and foremost, each emphasized Berne's growing rejection of psychoanalysis and disavowal of his analytic background in his efforts to create the new theory of transactional analysis.

Fanita English (personal communication, 19 October 2006) wrote most bluntly:

Berne was very conflicted about psychoanalysis and psychoanalysts. Several times I heard him say, "I am a better Freudian than the analysts" (and he was extremely well read). He came to hate the psychoanalysts. . . . A big blow to his (narcissistic) ego was the lack of recognition by psychoanalysts of *The Mind in Action* [Berne, 1947]. Instead of stroking and admiring his major contribution to clarifying psychoanalysis for unsophisticated readers, he was criticized for making it too simplistic! . . . TA was a definite nose-thumbing to THEM. . . . The central question is about Berne, and the use of the concept of unconscious should be seen in the context of the almost pathological anger/dislike/hatred/suspicion he (especially his Child) progressively developed about psychoanalysts and psychoanalysis (and I must say some deservedly—they all looked down their noses at him and TA). Berne's Adult knew darn well that there is an Unconscious—he tried to get around it. . . . Berne never denied that archaic processes and memories affect us in the now!

Pat Crossman (personal communication, 31 October 2006) similarly observed:

I met Eric Berne in the fall of 1964, and I left the seminar in 1969. In 1964 Eric was "small time." In 1969 he was "big time" and famous. And this is what killed him. He was like Sisyphus, always rolling the stone up the mountain but never quite making it. But what happens if he makes it! *Games People Play* [1964] was a runaway best seller and Eric was on top. That spoils the game. Eric became depressed and very unhappy and some of his disciples were less than kind. I remember in 1967 Jack Dusay and Claude Steiner standing up stating that there was no such thing as the "unconscious." I remember Eric commenting quietly, "Then what about the defenses?"

Steve Karpman (personal communication, 26 September 2006) wrote that Berne

was finishing up the complete separation of himself and TA from the psychoanalytic world, and a brand new identity for him and us without strings attached. . . . He would never allow us to use analytic words in the seminar."

Karpman (2006) has written of Berne that "he often smiled while saying, 'We're [transactional analysts] driving a brand new Mercedes while the psychoanalysts back east are still driving a Model T Ford.'. . . Freud was propped up as the 'straw man' whom we eagerly overthrew" (p. 286). Karpman went on to say, "Once I got kicked out of the seminar for twice using the passive, non-transactional word 'identification' " (p. 289). In his article, Karpman describes the rebellious and revolutionary atmosphere of the late 1960s and his own struggle to try (unsuccessfully) to integrate his psychoanalytic training with his new learning from transactional analysis. Like Berne, he decided to leave psychoanalysis behind in favor of the efficacy of transactional analysis.

Marty Groder (personal communication, 27 September 2006) wrote to me in his inimitable style:

As Eric's thinking imbued the ego states with increasing internal as well as social/transactional reality, the point of ascribing important issues like script to this theoretical black hole of the "unconscious" was becoming moot. TA became increasingly a decisional theory. . . . The EGO as a schmuck trapped in the orbit of the black hole of unconsciousness was ejected to the outer rim of the galaxy. . . . Also, by then he was isolated (by choice, in part) from all of his peers who could have validated and enriched his thinking. He had only us, his disciples, a limited, if intoxicating, source of sustenance.

We can clearly see this shift in tone in Berne's own writings during the last few years of his life. All his early work reflected a deep regard for the power of unconscious motivations balanced by an optimism regarding the strength of the ego and the impact of healthy social transactions and relations. With *Games People Play,* Berne (1964) set out to write a best seller and to set himself apart from the psychoanalysts. It does seem, however, that Berne's conflict was more with the psychoanalysts themselves than with psychoanalysis proper. In *Principles of Group Treatment,* written two years after *Games,* Berne offered a detailed, thoughtful, respectful differentiation of transactional analysis from psychoanalysis. But by the time of *Hello* and his last published talk, "Away from a Theory of the Impact of Interpersonal Interaction on Non-Verbal Participation" (Berne, 1971), his attitude toward psychoanalysis had become overtly bitter and mocking.

Bitterness, however, does not support the development of sound theory, and I would suggest that the evolution of transactional analysis theory has suffered for many years as a result of Berne's final bitterness and the inability of his colleagues at the time to critique his thinking and its limits. And yet, in the midst of his bitterness, Berne was also making important theoretical challenges and offering substantial alternatives to the psychoanalysis of his day (which, I must underscore, is not the psychoanalysis of our day).

Len Campos (personal communication, 26 September 2006), in his e-mail response to my query, wrote, "I think Berne dropped psychoanalytic metaphors such as 'the unconscious' because the newer metaphors of TA were more conducive to changing people's lives."

Claude Steiner (personal communication, 12 October 2006) wrote that Berne's

definitive statement on the matter was that unconscious was a PA [psychoanalytic] concept that should be used carefully and conscientiously (as should other PA concepts such as masochism or transference) in the fully psychoanalytic meaning—namely "dynamically repressed unconscious"—rather than all the obvious biological processes that are indeed out of awareness, but not unconscious in the PA sense. Scripts were also not unconscious in the PA sense but merely often (but not always) out of awareness.

Jack Dusay did not respond to my e-mail inquiry, but he did write a fascinating article in 1971, shortly after Berne's death, about Berne's studies on intuition. In it Dusay addressed some aspects of Berne's shift away from psychoanalysis. Given his place in the original seminar, I thought it important to quote Dusay here. In his discussion of two landmark papers of Berne's from 1957—"The Ego Image" (1957/1977a) and "Ego States in Psychotherapy" (1957/1977b)—containing the cowpoke story in which Berne first differentiated the Adult and Child ego states, Dusay (1971) commented:

Berne felt that the conscious and the unconscious, the ego and the id were involved, but *this was not directly important*. What was observed directly and was most obvious to both the patient and the observer, was the existence of two different *conscious* ego-states: one of an adult, and the other of a child. . . . This is where Berne parted ways with classical psychoanalysis. Although he did not reject psychoanalytic theory, he saw it was not directly useful for these new considerations. . . . His evolving system was concerned with the conscious derivatives of the primal images and primal judgments which had their conscious representation in what he called the Child ego-state. (p. 40)

Berne's Critique of the Freudian Conceptualization of the Unconscious

I used the phrase "unconscious experience" in my title rather than the more familiar phrase "the unconscious." Originally, when titling this paper, I used "the unconscious" quite automatically. However, as I began to write the paper itself, I realized that I needed to change the title, that what

I had written rather automatically (unconsciously?) did not reflect what I actually wanted to convey. The concept of the unconscious—the dynamically repressed unconscious of Freud's theories—is what Berne challenged in classical Freudian theory.

I think Berne's was an important theoretical challenge. Hie personal psychoanalysts were Paul Federn and Erik Erikson, both representatives of the ego psychology model of psychoanalysis, the model in which Berne was also trained. This view stresses the ascendancy of ego function over the ravages of the superego and the irrational, primitive, regressive impulses of the id. Superego, ego, and id were seen as functions within the mind, and the unconscious conveyed a sense of a place within the mind, a kind of dumping ground and holding tank for repressed and forbidden impulses. In classical Freudian theory, the unconscious was understood as the location of regression, irrationality, infantile transference fantasies, and psychopathology. This, I would suggest, is the model of the unconscious that Berne, quite rightly, wished to challenge.

Berne argued that script, defenses, and the Child ego state are not inherently irrational or pathological. He offered us a model of functional adaptation and creativity in addition to awareness of psychological defenses and psychopathology. He concluded that Freud's model of the unconscious was not useful in psychotherapy, that it was more obfuscating than clarifying. But Berne's theoretical challenge became contaminated by his personal bitterness. If a word, a concept, such as "unconscious" is officially derided and dropped from our professional lexicon, then how can we continue to think about it?

As Berne (1972) moved away from notions of the unconscious in his later work, he described intrapsychic experience this way:

> The Child expresses his wishes in visual images; but what he does about them, the final display through the final common pathway, is determined by auditory images, or voices in the head, the result of a mental dialogue. This dialogue between Parent, Adult, and Child is not "unconscious," but preconscious, which means that it can easily be brought into consciousness. Then it is found that it consists of sides taken from real life, things which were once actually said out loud. The therapeutic rule is a simple derivative of this. Since the final common pathway of the patient's behavior is determined by voices in the head, this can be changed by getting another voice into his head, that of the therapist. (pp. 368-369)

In this quote we see described a mode of psychotherapy with which we, as transactional analysts, are very familiar, one that deeply influenced the transactional analysts who were most closely affiliated with him at the time.

The next major transactional analysis book after Berne's death was Steiner's (1974) *Scripts People Live,* in which he defined script as

> based on a decision made by the Adult in the young person who, with all of the information at their disposal at the time, decides that a certain position, expectations, and life course are a reasonable solution to the existential position in which she finds herself. (p. 55)

Goulding and Goulding (1978), in another major text of that era, argued similarly: "Our clients were not 'scripted.' Injunctions are not placed in peoples' heads like electrodes. Each child makes decisions in response to real or imagined injunctions, and thereby 'scripts' her/himself' (p. 213). The Gouldings' work was a synthesis of transactional analysis with gestalt methodologies, and it was strongly influenced by gestalt theory, which also rejected Freudian theories of the unconscious. Central to redecision therapy is the client's return in the Child ego state to the remembered "scene" of the original decision so as to redecide from the current Child ego state. The decisional models of transactional analysis always seem to convey a sense of consciousness and intentionality in script formation. While it is clear that some aspects of script formation are consciously made and/or consciously remembered, I would argue that this is not always the case, and I contend that Berne did not mean to suggest that either.

Berne's Error

Thus we find, I think, that Berne's important correction to the classical psychoanalytic and ego psychological theories of his day was marred by his personal invective against psychoanalysts, which created a rigidity in his thinking that was passed on to the next generation of transactional analysts.

In taking the positions he did in his later writing, Berne was both right and wrong. He was, I think, right in that much of racket, game, and script behavior is preconscious and can be brought into consciousness (although I do not know that it is as "easy" as Berne suggested it was). Rackets, games, and much of script are defensive in nature, grounded in some childhood experience of threat and an effort to manage threats to the well-being of oneself and others; this level of experience is often preconscious. Where I differ with Berne, and where I think we need a theory of unconscious experience, is that not all of our internal experience is carried in dialogue or was learned from what was said. All that motivates people is not so obvious and observable as Berne came to emphasize in his later thinking.

Much of the internal structure and experience of the Child ego state is incorporated from what was done during our early relationships and family patterns (Cornell, 2003). There is a level of organization in the Child ego state that is learned at a body level and lived, experienced, and expressed not in the words of an internal dialogue, but in somatic organization, in unconscious fantasies and wishes, and through the styles of our contemporary relationships. This I understand as unconscious experience. It is not adequately described as "preconscious." These days, transactional analysts often refer to things in the head that are "out of awareness," which I think is a kind of linguistic gymnastics to avoid the "bad" word "unconscious." I do not think that preconscious or out of awareness captures the depth and compelling force of unconscious psychological organization. I want to strongly emphasize that because something is unconscious, it is not necessarily primitive, regressive, or pathological. Unconscious processes are foundational, fundamental, and unworded in our internal experience, an inherent and compelling means by which we "know" ourselves in the world of others, the "unthought known" described by Bollas (1987). This is the realm of experience, of affective and somatic organization, that Berne explored in his original concepts of intuition and protocol, which were decidedly modes of unconscious perception and organization.

The Richness and Vitality of Unconscious Modes

Cornell and Landaiche (2005) described the nonpathological aspect of unconscious processes through their elaboration of Berne's concept of script protocol:

Protocol-based behavior is not a game-like, ulterior form of communication, but a deeply compelling implicit (wordless) memory of primary relational patterns, lived through the immediacy of bodily experience. Protocols function as ongoing, unconscious templates for making judgments about the significant figures and encounters in our lives. Yet protocols are not necessarily pathological; they embody an innate human capacity for making unconscious sense of life with others. They only become problematic when they interfere with the ability to generate new bodily and relational possibilities. (p. 19)

Protocol is not a set of adaptive or defensive decisions, like a script. Protocol is not remembered in a narrative fashion but felt/lived in the immediacy of one's body.... We are suggesting that with his concept of protocol Berne was trying to capture the sense of the most fundamental, nonverbal aspects of what it means to relate to someone. (p. 21)

In my reading of Berne, something fundamental was lost in the richness of most of his thinking when he was overtaken by his need to distinguish himself from psychoanalysts. Also, in my reading of Berne, I see the "can-do" attitude of Americans, driven to accomplish, control, come out on top. Of course, "can do" is rather easily internalized as "must do," thus shifting from Adult to Parent ego states. I think transactional analysis has too often incorporated a must-do Parental attitude toward "curing" (fixing) clients. Clients do not come to therapists, counselors, and consultants only to "get fixed"; they also come to deepen self-understanding, to discover and explore unexpressed aspects of self-development, and to unfold more complex meanings and understanding of the self, what is sometimes called the "emergent unconscious" (Cornell, 2005). This work is enriched with a theory of unconscious experience and desire.

The understanding of the nature and function of unconscious experience in contemporary theory and research is very different from that described by Freud and classical psychoanalytic theory. In contemporary psychoanalytic thinking, the unconscious is no longer seen simply as the psychic trash bin of repressed impulses and childhood trauma but as a core of unformulated experience (Stern, 1997/2003) and unsanctioned or unacknowledged desire and potential (Bollas, 1989, 1992; Eigen, 1998; McLaughlin, 2005; Mitchell, 1993). Infant research and its various models of implicit relational knowing (Beebe, Knoblauch, Rustin, & Sorter, 2005; Fivas-Depeursinge & Corboz-Warnery, 1999; Holmes, 1996; Karen, 1998; Lyons-Ruth, 1998, 1999) present another perspective on unconscious organization and experience, one quite consistent with Berne's foreshadowing in his concept of protocol.

Contemporary cognitive and neuroscience research is also replete with models of the centrality (and health) of unconscious processes and "implicit," or "procedural," knowing (Anderson, Reznik, & Glassman, 2005; Bucci, 1997; Hassin, Uleman, & Bargh, 2005; LeDoux, 2002; Schacter, 1992, 1996; Schore, 2003; Siegel, 1999). This research and these theories emphasize that unconscious processes are not only reflections of infant and early childhood experiences but are a part of our ongoing, lifelong development. Like Freud, I do think that split-off aspects of childhood trauma and disturbance (as well as those of adult life) can be disavowed and so deeply spilt from consciousness that they become a repressed, dynamic component of unconscious experience. These split-off aspects of experience foster defenses and psychological/relational disturbances, the origins of which are not easily brought to conscious awareness. But I would argue that unconscious experience is richer and more complex than that conceptualized by Freud.

It is outside the scope of this chapter to attempt to delineate the rich implications of these models of unconscious experience. Suffice it to say, for the moment, that these new models offer understandings on unconscious, nonconscious processes that are very different from those developed by Freud and challenged by Berne. Now we need to challenge Berne and keep our theory and practice, our understanding of the meaning of unconscious, open, refreshed, and renewed.

Conclusion

I suggest that unconscious experience is a fact of the human mind and life. Our work as human relations professionals is impoverished if we ignore or deny it. In making this argument, I do not in any way wish to dismiss our attention to the conscious experiences and memories of our clients. Many conscious experiences and memories fill our consulting rooms, our own lives, and the lives of our clients with suffering, anxiety, hope, pleasure, love, and fury—all the passions and meanings of life. But all passion and meaning is not conscious.

So, the task for us now as transactional analysts is to think anew about the nature of unconscious experience, motivation, and organization and its place in the theory and practice of transactional analysis. We can do this without having to create yet another school of transactional analysis. I do not think we need a "relational" TA or a "psychoanalytic" TA or a "constructivist" TA to think about the incorporation of new understandings of the role of unconscious experience in our psychological and emotional functioning. I also want to emphasize that to incorporate an understanding of unconscious processes into transactional analysis theory and methodology, we do not have to become psychoanalysts or mimic their techniques.

REFERENCES

Anderson, S. M., Reznik, I., & Glassman, N. S. (2005). The unconscious relational self. In R. R. Hassin, J. S. Uleman, & J. A. Barch (Eds.), *The new unconscious* (pp. 421-481). New York: Oxford University Press.

Beebe, B., Knoblauch, S., Rustin, J., & Sorter, D. (2005). *Forms of intersubjectivity in infant research and adult treatment*. New York: Other Press.

Berne, E. (1947). *The mind in action*. New York: Simon & Schuster.

Berne, E. (1964). *Games people play: The psychology of human relationships*. New York: Grove Press.

Berne, E. (1966). *Principles of group treatment*. New York: Oxford University Press.

Berne, E. (1971). Away from a theory of the impact of interpersonal interaction on non-verbal participation. *Transactional Analysis Journal, 1*(1), 6-13.

Berne, E. (1972). *What do you say after you say hello?: The psychology of human destiny.* New York: Grove Press.
Berne, E. (1977a). The ego image. In E. Berne, *Intuition and ego states: The origins of transactional analysis* (P. McCormick, Ed.) (pp. 99-120). San Francisco, CA: TA Press. (Original work published 1957)
Berne, E. (1977b). Ego states in psychotherapy. In E. Berne, *Intuition and ego states: The origins of transactional analysis* (P. McCormick, Ed.) (pp. 121-144). San Francisco: TA Press. (Original work published 1957)
Bollas, C. (1987). *The shadow of the object: Psychoanalysis of the unthought known.* New York: Columbia University Press.
Bollas, C. (1989). *Forces of destiny: Psychoanalysis and human idiom.* Northvale, NJ: Jason Aronson.
Bollas, C. (1992). *Being a character: Psychoanalysis and self experience.* New York: Hill & Wang.
Bremner, G., & Slater, A. (Eds.). (2004). *Theories of infant development.* Malden, MA: Blackwell Publishing.
Bucci, W. (1997). *Psychoanalysis and cognitive science: A multiple code theory.* New York: Guilford Press.
Cornell, W. F. (2003). Babies, brains, and bodies: Somatic foundations of the child ego state. In C. Sills & H. Hargaden (Eds.), *Ego states* (Key concepts in transactional analysis: Contemporary views) (pp. 28-54). London: Worth Publishing.
Cornell, W. F. (2005). In the terrain of the unconscious: The evolution of a transactional analysis therapist. *Transactional Analysis Journal, 35,* 119-131.
Cornell, W. F., & Landaiche, N. M., III. (2005). Impasse e intimata nella coppia terapeutica o di counseling: l'influenza del protocollo [Impasse and intimacy in the therapeutic or consultative couple: The influence of protocol]. *Rivista Italiana di Analisi Transazionale e Metodologie Psicoterapeutiche, 11,* 35-60.
Dusay, J. (1971). Eric Berne's studies of intuition 1949-1962. *Transactional Analysis Journal. 1*(1), 34-44.
Eigen, M. (1998). *The psychoanalytic mystic.* Binghampton, NY: ESF Publications.
Fivas-Depeursinge, E., & Corboz-Warnery, A. (1999). *The primary triangle: A developmental systems view of mothers, fathers, and infants.* New York: Basic Books.
Goulding, R. L., & Goulding, M. M. (1978). *The power is in the patient: A TA/gestalt approach to psychotherapy* (P. McCormick, Ed.). San Francisco: TA Press.
Hassin, R. R., Uleman, J. S., & Bargh, J. A. (Eds.). (2005). *The new unconscious.* New York: Oxford University Press.
Holmes, J. (1996). *Attachment, intimacy, autonomy: Using attachment theory in adult psychotherapy.* Northvale, NJ: Jason Aronson.
Karen, R. (1998). *Becoming attached: First relationships and how they shape our capacity to love.* New York: Oxford University Press.
Karpman, S. (2006). Lost in translation: Neo-Bernean or neo-Freudian? *Transactional Analysis Journal, 36,* 284-302.
LeDoux, J. (2002). *Synaptic self: How our brains become who we are.* New York: Viking Press.
Lyons-Ruth, K. (1998). Implicit relational knowing: Its role in development and psychoanalytic treatment. *Infant Mental Health Journal, 19,* 282-291.
Lyons-Ruth, K. (1999). The two-person unconscious: Intersubjective dialogue, enactive relational representation, and the emergence of new forms of relational organization. *Psychoanalytic Inquiry, 19,* 576-617.
McLaughlin, J. T. (2005). *The healer's bent: Solitude and dialogue in the clinical encounter* (W. F. Cornell, Ed.). Hillsdale, NJ: The Analytic Press.
Mitchell, S. A. (1993). *Hope and dread in psychoanalysis.* New York: Basic Books.
Schacter, D. L. (1992). Understanding implicit memory: A cognitive neuroscience approach. *American Psychologist, 47*(4), 559-569.
Schacter, D. L. (1996). *Searching for memory: The brain, the mind, and the past.* New York: Basic Books.
Schore, A. N. (2003). *Affect regulation and the repair of the self.* New York: Norton.
Siegel, D. J. (1999). *The developing mind: How relationships and the brain interact to shape who we are.* New York: Guilford Press.
Steiner. C. (1974). *Scripts people live: Transactional analysis of life scripts.* New York: Grove Press.
Stern, D. B. (2003). *Unformulated experience: From dissociation to imagination in psychoanalysis.* Hillsdale, NJ: The Analytic Press. (Original work published 1997)

This article was originally presented as the keynote address, entitled "Cosa dici se non vuoi dire 'inconscio,' " on 8 December 2006 during the 7th National Meeting of the Società Italiana di Analisi Transazionale (SIAT) on "The Relevance of the Unconscious for Transactional Analysis Today," in Rome, Italy. It was later published in the Transactional Analysis Journal, Volume 38, Number 2, pp. 93-100, April 2008.

9

Nonconscious Processes and Self-Development: Key Concepts from Eric Berne and Christopher Bollas

William F. Cornell and N. Michel Landaiche, III

Expediency was one of Eric Berne's guiding principles. He strove to be efficiently and quickly helpful. He likewise developed his theory of human functioning and his practice of helping in a relatively short period of time (from 1957 to 1970). His contribution—transactional analysis (TA)—has been remarkably successful around the world in providing an efficient framework for professionals in a wide variety of organizational, educational, and clinical settings. However, given the quickness with which Berne worked out his theory and approach to practice, he understandably left gaps in a full understanding of human personality and interaction.

In those gaps, differing schools of thought soon emerged, including the classical, redecision, and Cathexis schools (Barnes, 1977). More recently, integrative approaches to transactional analysis have been offered by Clarkson (1992) and Erskine (1998). There is also a growing interest in what is known as relational transactional analysis (Cornell & Hargaden, 2005; Hargaden & Sills, 2002). There is even a method of transactional psychoanalysis (Novellino, 2005). Increasingly, transactional analysis practitioners have recognized the need to expand their understanding of human behavior and their practice methods in order to help clients and groups who are not responsive to traditional TA approaches. This parallels a similar trend in psychoanalytic circles whereby Klein's followers built on classical Freudian ideas in order to treat the psychotic patients Freud considered unanalyzable. Kleinian innovations have, in turn, been extended and modified by analysts from the British Independent tradition, by followers of Lacan in France, and by analysts affiliated with the American relational schools.

We believe that some of these contemporary psychoanalytic ideas can contribute significantly to an expansion of traditional transactional analysis. But we also think that traditional transactional analysis concepts can then be used to clarify those psychoanalytic ideas by translating them into more ordinary language and by emphasizing their practical use in people's lives. In this Bernean spirit, we will explore some of Berne's (1949/1977c, 1952/1977b, 1953/1977a, 1955/1977d, 1962/1977e, 1963, 1968, 1972) underdeveloped ideas related to nonconscious processes and the development of the self. Those ideas correspond to contemporary psychoanalytic thinking, particularly the early work of analyst Christopher Bollas (1987, 1989). We will then link Bollas's analytic concepts back to the practice of transactional analysis. In this way, we hope to remain true to Berne's vision while encouraging ourselves and our transactional analysis colleagues, as a community of professionals, to continue learning and growing.

A Conversation between Transactional Analysis and Psychoanalysis

Our thinking for this chapter was inspired by an invitation from the Societa' Italiana di Metodologie Psicoterapeutiche e Analisi Transazionale to present a 3-day workshop comparing the ideas of

Eric Berne with those of Christopher Bollas. One of us (WFC) was an expert in transactional analysis, body psychotherapy, and psychodynamic psychotherapy. The other (NML) knew little of transactional analysis but was trained as a counselor, psychotherapist, and organizational consultant with a background in object relations and group analytic theories. The workshop attendees engaged our different yet complementary backgrounds in a way that helped us to appreciate the meaningfulness of what we presented for their work in diverse fields as well as for their personal lives.

Eric Berne and Christopher Bollas also came from different yet complementary backgrounds. Both trained as psychoanalysts, although a generation apart in very different psychoanalytic cultures. Both were rebellious thinkers among their psychoanalytic colleagues. Berne (1910-1970) was trained in classical psychoanalysis and the American paradigm of ego psychology, which extolled the functions and capacities of the ego. That model infused Berne's thinking as he developed transactional analysis. He saw the ego (especially in its Adult state) as the road to health and autonomy. He also sought to make patterns of communication and beliefs about self and others conscious, with decisions made ideally under the guidance of the Adult ego state. More than a generation later, Bollas (1943-) was trained in London in British object relations theories, with particular emphasis on the Independent, Winnicottian tradition. Bollas's primary attention has been to patterns of unconscious communication and experiencing. Yet in contrast to Berne, Bollas has not conceived of the ego as ideally in charge but rather as relentlessly—and with great effort—swimming upstream against the forces of early object relations.

In spite of these contrasts, Berne and Bollas each sought to engage the intelligence and generative potential of their patients. Each worked to counter the sometimes authoritarian and rigid frameworks of their contemporaries. The freedom and essential hopefulness of their thinking also offer us an opportunity for dialogue today about what it means to be human and how to make the best use of our lives.

Nonconscious Processes: Internal and Interpersonal

When we encounter our clients and students, we must make sense of more than they put into words. They "speak" to us with gestures, body language, facial expressions, states of feeling, and unique ways of being. Whether we work individually or in groups, we must process enormous quantities of experiential data about which we and our clients/students may not be fully aware. As we work, we must also account for our own feelings, bodily reactions, intuitive cognitions, and interpersonal interactions, about which we may also be unaware. In short, a great deal of human relations work involves processes that are nonconscious.

Generally, the term "nonconscious" refers to physiological and psychological organization and learning that operate outside of conscious awareness. Nonconscious levels of mental and somatic functioning contain, among other things, the undigested remnants of past experiences, many of which may be haunted by loss, helplessness, rage, shame, or trauma. This is similar to the classical psychoanalytic idea of the dynamic Unconscious, a place within the mind often characterized (and caricatured) as the trash bin of childhood—the dark repository of repressed, split-off, rejected aspects of a "primitive" self and unwanted, unassimilated aspects of childhood. Yet, although the realm of nonconscious experience may well contain elements of developmental history and trauma, our minds and bodies also constantly inform, shape, and enrich our lives in nonconscious, fully healthy ways. We learn to do things such as walk, dance, drive, play sports, cook, care for children, and engage in conversation so that ultimately we do them without much conscious thought. In fact, we successfully live large parts of our lives without being fully aware of everything we are sensing, organizing, or doing.

Mancia (2004/2007) describes this nonconscious aspect of life in terms of implicit memory, which he says "extends the concept of the unconscious and considers a possible non-repressive origin, linked to a child's earliest preverbal and presymbolic experiences that cannot be recalled but nevertheless influence the person's affective, cognitive and sexual life even as an adult" (p. 7). He explains:

Implicit memory... stores experiences that are not conscious and cannot be described verbally. Here various forms of learning are filed, such as priming (meaning a person's ability to identify an object visually or [auditorily] as a result of having already been exposed to it, possibly not consciously but only subliminally); *procedural memory,* which keeps track of motor and cognitive skills such as the movements needed for certain sports, or to play musical instruments, and the memory of numerous everyday things we do automatically without even being conscious of how; [and] *emotional and affective memory,* where the brain stores its recollections of emotions arousing from affective experiences of the child's earliest relations with the environment, and particularly with the mother. (p. 32)

Indeed, without awareness, our bodies receive and process an extraordinary amount of environmental stimuli and accomplish highly complex activities (cardiopulmonary, digestive, motoric, visual, auditory, fight/flight, and immunological, to name a few). We could never process so much input or sustain so many activities with full intention and awareness. As a result, most of what we live occurs nonconsciously.

Usually, when professionals talk about consciousness and unconsciousness, they are referring to cognitive/emotional processes within the individual. But for this chapter, we want to emphasize that nonconscious processes are also interpersonal. Berne recognized that human beings are continually engaged in interactions and communications that are not always fully conscious. All of us pick up, are influenced by, and utilize nonverbal signals from one another without always knowing that we are doing so. Our physiological states of arousal and mood are sensitively regulated by the dynamics of our interpersonal fields. We often choose friends, lovers, and enemies on the basis of gut reactions, attractions, and intuitions that operate outside awareness. Naturally, such nonconscious processes also operate in professional relationships and in our transactions with clients and students, as we will discuss in greater detail later.

Thus, to avoid some of the connotations and misunderstandings often associated with the term "unconscious," we will speak here of "nonconscious processes." We want to address more than just a place in the mind; we want to consider an active, interpersonal dynamic that is central to human relations work.

Berne's Emphasis on Intuition

Early in his career as a psychiatrist, Berne (1949/1977c) had the job of assessing the psychological health of young men to determine their fitness for U.S. military service. These assessments had to be performed quickly, and Berne noticed that he began jumping to rapid conclusions about the men based on minimal interaction. When he later attempted to verify his conclusions, he found that many of his spontaneous insights turned out to be accurate. He became curious about how he could know something about a patient without receiving much overt information and without knowing how he came to his conclusions. This led him to wonder more broadly about how people know what they know.

Berne organized his thinking on this topic in a paper he delivered on 18 October 1947 to the annual joint meeting of the San Francisco and Los Angeles Psychoanalytic Societies. In that paper, he drew on the work of Edward J. Kempf, an early twentieth-century physician and psychoanalyst. Berne (1949/1977c) wrote:

E. J. Kempf... somewhat like Darwin, speaks of understanding emotional states in others by "reflex imitation through similar brief muscle tensions," and states that by this token "in a certain sense we think with our muscles." This method of judgment may be called "intuition through subjective experience." (p. 3)

Berne was challenging the usual notion of knowing as a purely mental process. When he highlighted phrases such as "reflex imitation" and "think[ing] with our muscles," he was acknowledging that we learn and know things in our bodies. He could well have been describing what we speak of today as "somatic resonance" or even "countertransference." In a paper published 6 years later, however, Berne (1955/1977d) emphasized that he was not confusing intuition with empathy, as some readers had assumed:

By intuition, [I am referring] to a spontaneous diagnostic process whose end products spontaneously come into awareness if resistances are lifted. In the case of empathy . . . [it] has a connotation of identification. Intuition, as the writer sees it, has essentially nothing to do with such adult forms of identification. It has to do with the automatic processing of sensory perceptions. (pp. 94-95)

In choosing the ordinary word "intuition," as opposed to coining something more technical, Berne (1949/1977c) sought to elucidate what he saw as an ordinary human capacity for processing sensory perceptions:

Intuition is knowledge based on experience and acquired through sensory contact with the subject [the other], without the "intuiter" being able to formulate to himself or others exactly how he came to his conclusions. . . . It is knowledge . . . acquired by means of preverbal unconscious or preconscious functions. (p. 4)

Not only is the individual unaware of how he knows something; he may not even know what it is that he knows, but behaves or reacts in a specific way as if . . . his actions or reactions were based on something that he knew. (p. 5)

Berne was alluding here to the fact that complex cognitive processing and decision making can occur outside awareness. He considered intuition to be "an archaeopsychic phenomenon" (Berne, 1962/1977e, p. 161). This nonconscious aspect of living would, of course, eventually form the basis for his concepts of protocol and script. But in his early writings, Berne did not consider intuitive, nonconscious decision making to be necessarily problematic. Nor did he seem to believe that it was even essential to make those processes conscious: "To understand intuition, it seems necessary to avoid the belief that in order to know something the individual must be able to put into words what he knows and how he knows it" (Berne, 1949/1977c, p. 28).

By characterizing these nonconscious cognitive processes as normal and likely pervasive, Berne was challenging the belief that we are consciously in charge of our lives. He was thus laying the groundwork for his analysis of transactions, in which such nonconscious processes can sometimes be understood to be operating at odds with the lives we seek to live with intention.

The Concept of Protocol

Berne began his professional career deeply influenced by psychoanalysis. He had hoped, early on, that he might eventually become a psychoanalyst himself. But as a rebel in a time that was highly intolerant of nonconformity, Berne ended up rejected by his psychoanalytic colleagues. Some of his later repudiation of psychoanalysis seems to have been a hurt and angry reaction to this treatment by his peers. But some of Berne's criticism of psychoanalysis was similar to that being voiced by other psychiatrists and psychologists of his era, part of an emerging cultural and professional challenge to psychoanalytic dogma. For these reasons, Berne strove to differentiate transactional analysis from psychoanalysis. In his final book, *What Do You Say After You Say Hello?* (1972), he eliminated nearly all references to the unconscious, arguably the most central premise of psychoanalytic theory.

Before that last book, however, Berne's writings were permeated with references to unconscious organization and motivation within individuals and groups. To address this discrepancy between Berne's earlier and later legacies, a 2-day conference entitled "Attualità dell'Inconscio" ["The Relevance of the Unconscious Today"] was convened in Rome in 2006 to reevaluate the idea of "the unconscious" and its utility for contemporary transactional analysts. (Selected papers from that conference along with other contributions on the topic appeared in a special edition of the *Transactional Analysis Journal* [Cornell & Tosi, 2008].)

Berne drew on the idea of unconscious organization when he created his concept of "protocol," an idea that he never developed as fully as he did his theory of script. In Berne's (1963) thinking, protocol was the largely unconscious pattern that shaped an individual's later script:

Each person has an unconscious life plan [or script], formulated in his earliest years. . . . *The original set of experiences which forms the pattern for the plan is called the protocol.* . . . In later years he strives to bring about as close as possible a reproduction of the original protocol situation, either to live it through again if it was enjoyable, or to try to re-experience it in a more benevolent form if it was unpleasant. (pp. 218-219, italics added)

The original drama, the protocol, is usually completed in the early years of childhood, often by the age of 5, occasionally earlier.... A protocol... is of such a crude nature that it is quite unsuitable as a program for grown-up relationships. It becomes largely forgotten (unconscious) and is replaced by a more civilized version, the script proper. (p. 228)

In an earlier paper (Cornell & Landaiche, 2005), we summarized protocol as follows:

Protocol-based behavior is... a deeply compelling implicit (wordless) memory of primary relational patterns, lived through the immediacy of bodily experience. Protocols function as ongoing, unconscious templates for making judgments about the significant figures and encounters in our lives. Yet protocols are not necessarily pathological; they embody an innate human capacity for making unconscious sense of life with others. They only become problematic when they interfere with the ability to generate new bodily and relational possibilities. (p. 19)

Fast (2006), although not describing protocol, nonetheless illuminates the concept when she writes, "These familial impressions ... [are] patterns established in the activities of family life, the 'stereotype plates' that might persist to govern a person's life even in adulthood: patterns of loving and hating, of fears and desires, of interpersonal relationships and action" (p. 278).

In essence, the protocol is a latent level of somatic and relational organization that operates outside conscious awareness and precedes the formation of script. Protocol is more than implicit memory, however. It is not just a record of the past. Rather, protocol is the result of the child's active effort to make meaning and sense of things, both bodily and preverbally.

Protocol shares some characteristics with Berne's conception of intuition. Both operate outside awareness, and both exemplify the human capacity to make complex, nonconscious sense of things. However, Berne used the two concepts differently. Whereas his use of the term "intuition" fits the standard meaning of the word, he adapted the term "protocol" to reference a form of patterning that is not commonly recognized. He spoke of protocol in order to indicate that we not only organize our experiences outside awareness, but those organizations also compel the decisions we make about living.

Berne wrote about protocol as forming in the early years of life. That emphasis on the impact of early development is shared by most psychologists, psychotherapists, and psychoanalysts. Indeed, Bollas, in his early work, wrote of the mother-infant relationship as establishing the basis for later relationship patterns. We will explicate some of his ideas later in this chapter. However, we also want to point out that nonconscious processes, intuition, and protocol are not just part of developmental history or simply archaic forms of knowing. Rather, they remain an integral aspect of every human being throughout life. Moreover, we establish new protocols as we experience and organize new things in life. Learning a new physical activity, for example, can change our experience of moving through the other areas of our lives. Learning a new way of relating can likewise reshape our nonconscious sense of what it means to be in the world with others.

The Unthought Known

As we began reading Berne and Bollas alongside one another, we had the sense of their texts and ideas dialoguing back and forth. We were struck by the number of parallels in their work, especially the way Berne's theory of intuition and his writings on how to listen clinically fit with Bollas's theories of unconscious communication and reception. As we noted earlier, Bollas has been a radical thinker in his own time. But he came of age when psychoanalysis had already begun to lose its power in psychiatry, and he thus had room to think more freely. That freedom has likely been a factor accounting for Bollas's relatively greater success in challenging psychoanalytic orthodoxy while retaining the respect of his analytic peers.

Indeed, whereas Berne wrote as if he had to promote and defend his ideas against a more dominant and pervasive theory of human functioning, Bollas writes as if others might find his ideas stimulating. He seems less encumbered than Berne in that respect. In fact, many of Bollas's concepts are more poetic than scientific. He chooses words or terms not for their efficiency, as Berne did, but to stir our imaginations.

Take, for example, Bollas's (1987) frequently referenced idea of "the unthought known" (pp. 277-283), which he elaborated in his first book. This phrase seems almost paradoxical; its terms nearly cancel each other out. In that way, Bollas captures some of the elusive, paradoxical quality of human mental activity. What we know may not yet exist in thought. What we repress, dissociate, or unthink may yet continue as a potent form of nonconscious knowledge. Bollas is introducing us to the strange realm of the human mind and body.

And yet Bollas's ideas are commonsensical as well. In his use of "the unthought known," he is suggesting that every individual has a bodily capacity to sense and organize countless impressions of the world and to use that knowing to make nonconscious decisions about life. This bodily way of knowing is available for use by the individual but is not consciously thought in the form of words, images, or symbols. This conception of nonconscious experiencing and knowing differs from the Freudian unconscious in that it is not just a product of repression, defense, or pathology. The unthought known is a normal, lifelong function for human beings. Bollas's concept also encompasses much of what Berne meant by intuition and protocol.

Moreover, these nonconscious processes apply to more than just individual behavior and psychology. Groups, families, and organizations also operate with patterns and assumptions that are known without anyone actually giving them conscious thought. Berne (1963) wrote about the primal power of the "group canon," which included the group's not always explicit governing constitution, its laws, and the resulting group culture (p. 147). He also wrote about the "group imago" as an individual and collective picture of what the "group is or should be like" (p. 321); he suggested that this imago could be "conscious, preconscious, or unconscious" (p. 321). He even discussed how protocol can affect an individual's group imago, although he was quick to add that there is not always a one-to-one correlation between the group imago and protocol (p. 241).

Anyone who has ever consulted in organizations knows the distinct feel that every organization develops: an atmosphere, a set of unspoken rules, a prevailing belief about what it means to survive as a group in the world. This, too, suggests the workings of protocol and the unthought known. And as members of organizations, communities, and families, we pick up these things intuitively from those around us, whether we become aware of doing so or not.

Formative Intersubjective Experiences

Part of Berne's radicalism as a psychoanalytically trained psychiatrist was his emphasis on interpersonal transactions at a time when the prevailing psychiatric view—so heavily dominated by psychoanalytic thinking—emphasized individual intrapsychic mental processes. Berne believed we need to attend to what happens to people as they relate to one another. He further saw that changing these relationship patterns can contribute significantly to improved psychological health. This has been a foundational insight of transactional analysis.

Berne's thinking in this regard was influenced by object relations theory, particularly the work of Melanie Klein (Harley, 2006). Berne was receptive to the Kleinian way of thinking at a time when Klein's ideas were not widely accepted in psychoanalytic circles, especially in the United States where Berne worked. This same object relations tradition also strongly influenced Bollas's work, although his teachers and mentors had already begun to form a distinct, independent tradition within the British psychoanalytic community. In his writing, Bollas especially shows his indebtedness to Winnicott.

Object relations theorists see the primal interaction between mother and infant as foundational to the growing child's psychology. But this image of the mother and child is not invoked primarily to explain psychopathology. Rather, the interaction within the mother-infant dyad is paradigmatic of the human process of growth and maturation. Yes, elements of the history of that primary relationship remain with us and impact us, but more importantly, that same process of maturing within asymmetric relationships occurs throughout life. It characterizes the forward movement of maturation and growth that we also attempt to facilitate as consultants, teachers, counselors, and psychotherapists. Just as Berne believed, nonconscious, intersubjective experiences play a fundamental role in how we continue growing as people.

Berne's Intuitive Function

Berne (1949/1977c) conceived of what he called "the intuitive function" (p. 30) as more than just an intrapsychic process. He saw it as an essential component in an interpersonal process, "part of a series of perceptive processes which work above and below the level of consciousness in an apparently integrated fashion, with shifting emphasis according to special conditions" (p. 30). Many of those "special conditions" pertain to ever-changing relational dynamics. Berne noted how human beings are exquisitely sensitive to one another, as if each of us is continually assessing one another—a fundamental psychological orientation that occurs outside awareness.

It is apparent ... that there are cognitive processes which function below the level of consciousness. In fact, human beings, when they are in full possession of their faculties, behave at all times as though they were continually and quickly making very subtle judgments about their fellowmen without being aware that they are doing so; or if they are aware of what they are doing, without being aware of *how* they do it. (Berne, 1952/1977b, p. 35)

Berne (1955/1977d) contended that "the normal adult, like the infant, understands some fundamental—that is, dynamically predominant—aspects of each person he meets" (p. 84). He linked this keen interpersonal sensitivity directly to the work of human relations professionals, which he often framed in terms of psychiatric or clinical roles:

The term "intuitive individual" as used here ... [refers] to the clinician who deliberately uses his intuitive faculties when desirable in his diagnostic and therapeutic work. Descriptively, such a clinician is curious, mentally alert, interested, and receptive of latent and manifest communications from his patients. (Berne, 1962/1977e, pp. 159-160)

Beyond that level of perception and assessment, Berne (1953/1977a) also observed the nonconscious communicative process in which we are also continually engaged: "In the case of interpersonal relationships ... intended, precise, formal, rational, verbal communications are of less value than inadvertent, ambiguous, informal, nonrational, nonverbal communications" (p. 57). He went on to say, "Interpersonal communication generally refers ... [to] communication which influences the development of the relationship between the autonomous portions of the personalities concerned" (pp. 58-59).

This attitude toward nonconscious communication is admittedly at odds with Berne's theory of games, for which transactional analysis is best known and which emphasizes the split-off, defensive, and manipulative intent of covert communications. In game theory, that which is covert is not simply nonconscious or hidden, it is hidden with an ulterior motive. Yet as the aforementioned passages indicate, Berne also appreciated other kinds of "ambiguous, informal, nonrational, nonverbal communications." Although he did not develop these concepts further, he was talking about the exchanges that occur as a normal part of human relations work. Moreover, in contrast to the usual idea of communication as a transfer of information, Berne was describing communication as an active process that "influences the development of the relationship." This development occurs between the "autonomous portions of the personalities," which are those self-aspects that exist independently and are not bound by problematic script roles. In other words, we convey and exchange nonconsciously our energy, passions, ideas, and idiosyncrasies in order to grow in relation to others.

The Shadow of the Object

One of the unfortunate aspects of object relations theory is its use of the word "object," which sounds impersonal, even inanimate. It is left over from a legacy within psychoanalysis of attempting to sound scientific and emotionally unentangled. One could just as easily substitute the word "other." Yet "object" is the word we are left to deal with, even in the work of someone who writes as vividly as Bollas.

For example, one of Bollas's (1987) more evocative phrases, borrowed from Freud, is "the shadow of the object." We can translate this as "the shadow of the other" or, more precisely, "the shadow of the significant other." This phrase is used to indicate that the individual's ego, or sense of self, always forms and functions in the shadow of the significant others who came before her or him (i.e., parents, grandparents, and so on). The word "shadow" suggests a trace or imprint, the felt sense and presence of our parents and their palpable early influence on us, an influence that precedes and in some cases supercedes specific messages received later from them. We are shadowed by the lives they lived and by their inadvertent legacies.

In choosing the word "shadow," Bollas (1987) is also suggesting an area of darkness within the ego that is hard to see or decipher. That shadowed area is structured, like protocol, and that structure and its history can likewise be difficult to trace.

Bollas (1987) notes, "The object can cast its shadow without a child being able to process this relation through mental representations or language" (p. 3). We experience our caregivers, teachers, and mentors in ways that may never be fully conscious or that may never be put into words. Bollas is indirectly asking that we also consider the profound, unworded impact that we, as professionals, can have on those who come to us for help in learning and growing.

The Mother's Idiom of Care

As described earlier, Bollas (1987) suggests that we are haunted by the shadows of our predecessors. He thus points to an imponderable situation. We may feel the weight or impression of the past, yet never know it in detail. That level of mystery, he implies, is part of the human condition.

On the other hand, Bollas is also suggesting a way out of that area of opacity. He believes it is at least possible to imagine the specificity with which we have each been imprinted. More importantly, he conceives of the care we have received from important others to have been structured like a language, yet a "language" or idiom that was not necessarily put into words and that was in some sense unique or idiosyncratic to those important others. Bollas (1987) invokes the complex interaction between the infant's emerging self and the mother's more developed sense of self:

We know that because of the considerable prematurity of human birth the infant depends on the mother for survival. . . . She both sustains the baby's life and transmits to the infant, through her own particular idiom of mothering, an aesthetic of being that becomes a feature of the infant's self. The mother's way of holding the infant, of responding to his gestures, of selecting objects, and of perceiving the infant's internal needs, constitute her contribution to the infant-mother culture. . . . The language of this relation is the idiom of gesture, gaze, and intersubjective utterance. (p. 13)

Bollas (1989) further writes, "Human idiom is the defining essence of each person" (p. 212). By using the term "idiom," he alludes to each individual's unique nucleus, a kernel that, under favorable circumstances, will grow and articulate itself. Each person's idiom thus unfolds in time. It also refers to our human capacity to speak with a voice that is our own and to create symbols or ways of being that speak uniquely of us as individuals. An idiom, therefore, reveals our "aesthetic of being"—how we respond to our preferences, displeasures, and erotic inclinations in life.

Yet Bollas uses the term "aesthetic" to convey more than just our bodily response to the world or to works of art. He is also talking about the sensuous ways we organize those experiences and, in effect, create new works. An aesthetic sense is more than just one of pleasure; it acknowledges more than what might be considered attractive. After all, we create works of art, in part, to make sense of a world that can be extremely difficult and painful, too. A sense of the terrible informs the ancient concepts of truth and beauty. We seek the aesthetic to rediscover meaning and a sense of satisfactory organization. Bollas is trying to describe how individuals carry their experiential, aesthetic organizations in their bodies, sometimes in an effort to repeat those experiences and sometimes in an effort to convey or communicate them to another. The aesthetic also implies the possibility of finding satisfaction and meaning in our own work as professionals and in our own processes of becoming.

Bollas considers the mother's idiom—her aesthetic or unique mode of expression—to be the source of a paradigmatic imprint on the developing child, an imprint not unlike Berne's idea of protocol in that the imprint is not just passively received but also shaped by the child's unique way of receiving and organizing it. Analogously, the idiom of any important person (e.g., a counselor, teacher, or mentor) will leave a unique, idiosyncratic impression on those whose growth and maturing he or she facilitates. Yet that impression will also be shaped, in turn, by the uniqueness of those growing and maturing individuals.

The Transformational Object

Words like "imprint" and "impression," however, do not quite capture what Bollas believes can be the far more fundamental transformation achieved through our key relationships. He refers to that more radical potential when he writes, "The mother's idiom of care and the infant's experience of this handling is . . . the most profound occasion when the nature of the self is formed and transformed by the environment" (Bollas, 1987, p. 32). More succinctly, "As the infant's 'other' self, the mother transforms the baby's internal and external environment" (p. 13).

This facilitating, transformative function of the mother—offered in service to the infant's development—is the basis for Bollas's (1987) concept of the "transformational object" (pp. 13-2). The mother is the paradigmatic object or other through whom self-transformation takes place. Yet formative relationships of this kind can occur for any of us across the life span, not just in infancy. So, although the transformational object is described in terms of the mother's role, Bollas means that object (or other) to be any person who performs a similar facilitative function in service of another's growth and maturation. That is, a transformational object is a significant other who engages with a child, student, patient, or client such that the engagement leads to fundamental change and growth. Bollas (1987) even says that "**the mother is less significant and identifiable as an object than as a process** that is identified with cumulative internal and external transformations" (p. 14).

How does this transformative process occur? Bollas derives his idea from object relations theory, in which the mother or significant other takes in, at a bodily level, the unworded, nonconscious experiences of the child, client, or student. We are not describing anything mysterious here. Berne had already discussed this in terms of the intuitive function. As human beings working with other human beings, we simply pick up more information about other people than we can consciously process and usually more than they consciously intend to communicate. And in the arena of human relations work, we are especially receptive to the experiential aspects that our students and clients find problematic. In the same way that a mother or father learns to detect the signs of a child's distress, we come to know what is troubling our students and clients. And in the same way that a parent may not have an immediate solution for a child's upset, we often have to sit with our client's or student's distress for a period of time before we can think of what to say or do.

That receptivity is only an initial step in a transformative process. In and of itself, receptivity (like empathy) is not sufficient for change. The human relations professional must find a way to feed back the experience so that the client or student can take it in and use it to do productive psychological work and to make useful changes in her or his life. The transformation, therefore, first takes place in the body of the mother or significant other, and not always consciously. What began as confusion or upset is transformed into something that can be lived within and perhaps thought about. It is the communication of that attitude toward the problem—an attitude lived nonconsciously in the body—that then allows the child, student, or client to experience a change in her or his body as well. The transformational object is thus an embodied process. Moreover, it is a process we experience as operating on our behalf. And when that internalized process brings us relief from confusion or upset, we may recognize the transformational object first as our own experience of gratitude toward those significant, transformational others—our parents, teachers, and mentors.

In addition to designating an actual person, the transformational object is also an internalization of a transformative interpersonal encounter. It is an often unconscious memory of past maturational experiences. It can even be a nonconscious recognition that through such interactions one can significantly change internal states of affect and cognition. We then sometimes instinctively seek such significant, transformational others to further our growth and development. As Bollas (1987) writes,

"In adult life... the [transformational] object is pursued in order to surrender to it as a medium that alters the self" (p. 14).

Bollas is speaking here of the desire that we have to achieve a fuller sense of self over the course of a lifetime and the recognition we have, often outside awareness, that we need others to help us with the difficult and sometimes painful experiences that come with maturing. So although Bollas evokes the maternal image as one of transformation, it is still an interpersonal process of growth that occurs throughout life and one for which we all will require subsequent transformational others.

Countertransference Readiness

The ongoing potential for transformation or maturation is what makes human relations work possible, difficult, and ultimately so rewarding. In light of this role we play as professionals, Bollas (1987) introduces the idea of "countertransference readiness" (pp. 201-202).

"Countertransference" is a term used in multiple, sometimes contradictory ways within the field of psychodynamic psychotherapy. For the purposes of this chapter, we use Bollas's sense of it as a form of nonverbal communication that occurs between the therapist and the client. Countertransference in this context refers to the professional's moment of receiving, bodily, the client's or student's way of being. We have discussed this receptivity in terms of problem areas or distress, but, of course, we also pick up our clients' and students' unique ways of being, their idioms, as Bollas would say. We learn through our intuitive function what it feels like to live in their bodies, how they experience their areas of difficulty, and how they embody their potential for creative change.

"Countertransference," as Bollas uses the term, refers to the professional's emotional, somatic, and freely associative resonance with the unworded, unthought known that the client or student relives in the therapeutic, consultative, or educative setting. These experiences of being with a client or student constitute important information about that individual's sense of self and way of relating to others. It is vital information in our work as human relations professionals. As Bollas (1987) writes, "By cultivating a freely-roused emotional sensibility, the analyst welcomes news from within himself that is reported through his own intuitions, feelings, passing images, phantasies and imagined interpretive interventions.... To find the patient we must look for him within ourselves" (pp. 201-202).

We can think of this process of finding the client or student within ourselves as a form of nonconscious communication. Part of that communicative process is instinctive, as Berne noted. Part of it is also nonconsciously intentional on the part of our clients and students, deriving from what Bollas sees as the universal desire to be known in a manner that permits our transformation. As such, the client or student may in effect be saying, without necessarily knowing, "This is how it is to be me." And with that declaration comes the implied plea to be taken in and accepted.

Countertransference readiness describes the willingness of the professional to take in and attend to that form of communication. It is the willingness to be receptive to the client's or student's nonverbal, emotional, somatic, and free-associative states of being. This receptivity also occurs in the midst of the ongoing therapeutic contract and work with conscious content. Yet opening in this additional way pushes the professional into a particular form, which in turn begins to shape the relationship. "This is what it's like to be in this body. And this is what it's like to be *engaged* with this body." As professionals, we use such nonconscious communication to begin bending ourselves to the task of working with our unique clients and students.

This interactive countertransferential process can be illustrated with a simple case example. A client, whom I (WFC) will call Hank, had worked hard in therapy and had made considerable progress. Yet he remained unfulfilled in a way we could not name. For weeks we explored his script, revisited childhood memories, discussed ongoing family dynamics—looking for a new insight to free him to be bolder and to take more risks, especially professionally. This was familiar ground, a familiar way for us to think together. It had once been productive, but it now felt stale. After a session in which I felt particularly frustrated, I asked myself, "If I don't keep looking in these familiar places, where might my mind go?" My first thought was of an ongoing joke between us. We often chuckled about how, in spite of his having a male life partner and being prominent in his local gay community, I kept forgetting that he was a man who was emotionally and sexually drawn to other men. What registered as an outward fact did not register as an internal, lived reality. I often related to him as an image of a "straight" man.

Then a sequence began to unfold in my mind: Why do I forget Hank is gay? He did not always recognize himself as such. As a young man, he had many close friends; his life seemed as limitless as theirs. He described his early years as a great time, not at all traumatic. But as his friends grew, they began to marry, and he did not. They begin to inhabit lives and senses of self that were congruent with heterosexuality, marriages, families, and professional roles. Hank could pass as normative and straight on the outside, but he had no growing sense of self to fill that image. He moved away, went to graduate school, lived alone, and felt increasingly different on the inside from others. His horizons shrank. Not knowing what it meant for him to be gay, he lived much of his adult life alone. He expected little. A low-level depression set in, almost imperceptibly. Even when he became happily partnered, he held himself back, in love and in work, out of a habit of neglecting his living, aspiring interiority.

As this sequence of associations unfolded, I could suddenly name the loneliness I had always felt, the sense of loss that shadowed his adult life, that palpable unfamiliarity of being in his own body. I realized that those early adult years were the ones we needed to revisit, not his childhood or family. For although I had been open all along to these feelings—open and ready for my countertransference to Hank—I had not noticed their quiet, disheartening persistence. I too had gone along with the outward image. When I described my reverie to Hank, he expressed puzzlement and began inexplicably crying. Yet in later sessions, he was better able to open to his own thoughts, memories, and dreaming. Together we began fostering the development of his more complex adult self, a process that had been arrested when his life choices and self-understanding diverged from those of his closest friends. What facilitated that stage of our work were the countertransference experiences I also carried: an agreement to forget by focusing on the surface of things, the nagging sense of being unfulfilled, frustration at trying "the same old thing," a sudden insight into the loneliness and loss.

This way of thinking about countertransference is less traditional than Berne's view. He saw it simply as the professional's unexamined script responses to the client or student. Yet in his final *Hello* book (Berne, 1972), when he talked about "how to listen" (pp. 321-322), Berne suggested an attitude of receptivity that is quite similar to Bollas's:

The listener . . . must free his mind of outside preoccupations. . . . [and] must put aside all Parental prejudices and feelings, including the need to "help." . . . [He] must put aside all preconceptions about his patients in general and about the particular patient he is listening to. . . . [The listener's] Adult listens to the content of what the patient says, while his Child-Professor listens to the way [the patient] says it. In telephone language, his Adult listens to the information, and his Child listens to the noise. In radio language, his Adult listens to the program, and his Child listens to how the machine is working. Thus, he is both a listener and a repairman. (p. 322)

To some extent, listening without preconceptions is impossible given the way our human minds work, that is, our minds seek familiar patterns and quickly move to categorize what we experience. Nearly everything we encounter can be filtered through the protocols we have previously established. But Berne directs us to listen freely and without prejudice because we are also capable of questioning our preconceptions. We can bracket what we already know in order to discover a more valid pattern of meaning. Bollas also considers it an accomplishment not to know, not to be too certain, but rather to leave room for what actually transpires between the client/student and professional, to leave space for curiosity, for bodily as well as mental responses, for intuition and feeling in addition to thought. Berne, likewise, had moments when he was confident that we can tolerate uncertainty and not knowing long enough to understand reality more clearly.

Berne was also describing how, as professionals, we listen with more than our ears or eyes. We listen to more than words. We listen with our full bodies. We permit ourselves to be emotionally responsive to what we receive in order to understand nonconscious internal and interpersonal processes. By talking about the different roles of our Adult and Child ego states, he was also talking about how we use different aspects of ourselves and so allow ourselves to function in multiple ways to help the growth of our students and clients.

The Multiple Functions of the Analyst/Professional

Bollas contends that each person who seeks help does so with a desire for change and with the fervent hope that the person he or she has engaged can be the means to that change. When we are in the role of student or client, we begin that relationship by conveying some sense of who we are. For no matter how we may try to hide, we immediately begin to communicate something of how we relate to ourselves, to others, and to the world. Moreover, no matter how reticent we may behave on the outside, we rather aggressively begin to shape the other person into the person we hope and believe will be the agent of the change we seek. This shaping of the therapist occurred in the case just described when Hank effectively conveyed both his stoic neglect of self-development and his pressing lack of fulfillment. Bollas (1989) writes about this as the patient using the analyst: "When an analyst is used to express a paradigm derived from an object relation, he is coerced into an object relation script and given a certain sustained identity as an object" (p. 17).

This closely matches Berne's observation of how clients and students reenact their scripts and recruit others to play roles in those scripts. Bollas would agree that sometimes the template or protocol that guides our quest for change may work against our aspirations. For both Bollas and Berne, one goal of a therapeutic, consultative, or educative relationship would be greater awareness of the way our lives may be problematically governed by script or nonconscious processes. This potential for the subtle reenactment of script exists alongside the striving for greater access to our Adult ego state, or observing ego, in order to make more satisfying choices in our lives.

Yet the kind of coercive or aggressive use of the analyst or professional that Bollas describes is not always problematic in the way that Berne saw it. Bollas, after all, is writing from within the Winnicottian tradition, which sees aggression as a healthy impulse, especially when such aggressive use of the significant other is not destructive but leads to maturing. Bollas operates from the assumption that human relations work entails a certain ruthless engagement. Depending on the needs of a student or client, the professional will be provoked nonconsciously into a particular kind of interaction. Again, this is frequently the client's or student's way of nonconsciously striving to grow by leading us into the kind of interaction that will matter to him or her. Bollas describes this as a process of eliciting certain elements in our personality. Yet he adds, "When ... an element is elicited in [us] to be used by the patient and then abandoned (with no aim to set [us] up as part of the logic) ... it is more likely to be a true self movement" (Bollas, 1989, p. 17).

In this passage, Bollas is offering a diagnostic guideline. He acknowledges that some relationships or script patterns have a repetitive, nonproductive quality. In such cases, the professional is likely to feel more than just utilized by the student or client. Rather, the professional is likely to feel trapped in a particular role, forced into an unyielding logic, which is emphasized in script theory. In contrast, Bollas suggests that self-aspects or elements can be provoked or elicited in us that, although possibly uncomfortable or unfamiliar, do not have that same immobilizing, repetitive quality. He is alluding to the more fluid process of healthy play in children whereby an activity is taken up out of a sheer sense of exploration, curiosity, or impulse, and then, when that particular form of play has run its course, is just as easily abandoned for some other generative activity. In fact, Bollas claims that through such a process of active, experimental engagement with a significant other, less than optimal relational protocols can be experientially modified.

In the case of Hank, I (WFC) had the sense of being inducted into a process of looking "in the same old places," part of my client's long-time habit of not taking seriously his internal world as an adult. But I also felt free enough to think outside that pattern. This induction and flexibility worked together to give me a unique insight into Hank's life in a way I could never have achieved by purely intellectual or verbal means.

So, when Bollas (1989) writes about "the psychoanalyst's multiple function" (pp. 93-113), he proposes that each client uses the analyst or therapist to achieve a particular experience of self for the ultimate purpose of growing. And since every client or student is trying to express a unique personality or idiom, the professional will end up being used in multiple, idiosyncratic ways. Not only will different individuals evoke different uses, but the same individual may experiment over time with different uses. This process of being used in service of growth is highly dynamic.

Parents may experience the different ways of being that their different children evoke in them or that an individual child has evoked over time as he or she has grown. Teachers, consultants, and therapists have likely also noticed the ways in which they are pushed, stretched, and shaped by the differing needs of their students and clients. Cornell (1988) has described this process of mutual influence in which the growing child has as much influence on the parents' scripts as the parents have on the child's developing script.

As professionals, our openness to such use—our countertransference readiness—creates the conditions by which we can learn our client's or student's personal idiom. Making ourselves available as whole persons to meet the developmental needs of clients and students, we offer the opportunity for transformative experiences.

Bollas is not, however, suggesting that we simply abandon personal boundaries or individual separateness. Excessive flexibility is as problematic for growth as excessive rigidity. Rather, successful parenting, teaching, and mentoring embody a vigorous process of give and take, a tension, sometimes an intense struggle. Moreover, this dynamic is not simply one of balancing the needs of two individuals. The roles in parenting and professional relationships are not as symmetrical as they might be in, say, an adult couple. The parent or professional will certainly have her or his own unique needs and ways of being, as will the child, student, or client. But the parenting and professional relationship exists in service to the aspirations for growth of the child, student, or client. In fact, all parties sacrifice something of their personal preferences to move toward the hope of such maturation.

Growth and Self-Formation

In the writings of both Berne and Bollas, there is an ongoing tension between the power of the past —with its constraining childhood experiences and relationships—and the forward-moving, generative forces of the human body and mind. For example, Berne argued, on the one hand, that we are all born "OK," that the Child ego state is the psychological center of vitality and creativity, and that we are driven by physis (or aspirations) to seek the best in ourselves and our lives. On the other hand, his clinical model is dominated by ideas about rackets, games, and problematic scripts—all constructions of psychopathology that reference the oppressive power of the past, the negative impact of parents, and the limiting and long-lingering effects of childhood challenges and beliefs.

We see a similar tension in Bollas's writing. In his first book, *The Shadow of the Object* (Bollas, 1987), he emphasizes the mother-infant relationship as foundational in the human psyche and all future relationships. Even its title, "The Shadow of the Object," suggests how we are constrained and haunted by history or fate. However, in his second book, *Forces of Destiny*, Bollas (1989) contrasts that sense of being fated with a sense of moving toward a desired destiny in a hopeful future. In that book, he articulates the generative force of unconscious desires and motivations. He describes an insistence within the unconscious that is not just about repression but that seeks to move forward productively in life.

Interestingly, Berne's (1972) subtitle for *Hello* is "The Psychology of Human Destiny," but he uses the word "destiny" sometimes to mean "fated," exactly the opposite of what Bollas means by destiny as an urgent sense of purpose and promise. Yet Berne's (1972) definition reveals more hopeful aspects as well: "The forces of human destiny are foursome and fearsome: demonic parental programming . . . ; constructive parental programming, aided by the thrust of life called Phusis [physis] long ago; external forces, still called Fate; and independent aspirations" (p. 56).

Although Berne (1972) would consider some of these more productive aspects of destiny—which we discuss in the following section—still, a sense of fatedness pervades his conception of script:

Each person decides in early childhood how he will live and how he will die, and that plan, which he carries in his head wherever he goes, is called his script. . . . A script is an ongoing life plan ... the psychological force which propels the person toward his destiny, regardless of whether he fights it or says it is his own free will. (pp. 31-32)

Physis and the Arrow of Aspiration

In his writing, Berne often comes across with a sense of humor that is skeptical, sometimes bordering on the sarcastic. Certainly, that humor and skepticism can be refreshing and enlivening. Some of his sarcasm has enough edge to wake us up to the stalled lives we may be living. But sometimes it seems bitter, a frantic defense against a gloomy view of human life, a view that developed, perhaps, as a result of being hurt. Indeed, one can catch glimpses of Berne's more tender side and, with it, his more hopeful view of life.

In describing this, we are not criticizing Berne. Rather, we are discussing the quality of his idiom. People responded in various ways to him. But for those who felt he changed their lives, his clear thinking, humor, and aggression were curative, transformational factors.

In working with his clients, Berne often focused on elements from the past and parental injunctions that had pressed on and influenced the growing child's and eventually the adult's sense of what it meant to live in the world. Yet he contrasted this more problem-focused concept of script with what he called "physis," a "force of Nature, which eternally strives to make things grow and to make growing things more perfect" (Berne, 1968, p. 89). Berne saw this force of life as one that survives even the most imprisoning scripts.

"Physis" is a Greek theological, philosophical, and scientific term that Berne (1968) borrowed and defined as "the growth force of nature, which makes organisms evolve into higher forms, embryos develop into adults, sick people get better, and healthy people strive to attain their ideals" (pp. 369-370).

Although Berne himself made little of this idea, or its implications for human relations work, Clarkson (1992) took its essentially hopeful view of life as key to her approach to transactional analysis: "*Physis* is nature, coming from the deepest biological roots of the human being and striving towards the greatest realisation of the good" (p. 12).

Berne and Clarkson seem nearly utopian in these passages. We may wonder how their conceptions square with the fact of death, with nonliving forces in nature, with organisms that do not evolve into higher forms but die out, with embryos that are not able to survive to adulthood, with sickness, and with failure. Berne, for one, would have been the last to deny these aspects of life. However, he seems to be asking us to recognize that while we are alive, while life persists, it has at its core a wellspring of potential and willfulness.

In choosing a term such as "physis," Berne was acknowledging a reserve of energy that is available to every living being. It is a source of liveliness, an eternal striving, that exists without our necessarily being aware of it, because it exists in every cell and for every form of life. By implication, Berne is urging us, as professionals, to recognize this nonconscious potential in each client or student who comes to us, no matter how stuck or collapsed. Physis is, for each of us, a powerful ally for our development and growth.

Although Berne's concept of script typically refers to transactional patterns that are defensive or that do not serve the individual well, he sometimes wrote about script in a way that suggested that it represents the child's effort to articulate a unique plan for life. In that sense, script can serve the individual's aspirations and hopes for living.

Berne conveyed the thrust of such hopes by incorporating an "aspiration arrow" into the script matrix (see Berne, 1972, p. 128). Clarkson (1992) believed that "the aspiration arrow represents the dynamic force of *Physis*" (p. 13). As she elaborated,

> Berne postulates that the autonomous aspiration of individual human beings rises from the depths of the somatic Child (oldest ego state) and transcends the limit-inducing downward pressures of the script which is shaped in the matrix of love and death in our earliest relationships. (p. 12)

The aspiration arrow, driven by physis, moves in the direction of optimal maturing or self-development. We are driven to move, in life, toward our truest, heartfelt desires. In an atypically elegiac mode, Berne (1972) acknowledged:

All men and women have their secret gardens, whose gates they guard against the profane invasion of the vulgar crowd. These are visual pictures of what they would do if they could do as they pleased. The lucky ones find the right time, place, and person, and get to do it, while the rest must wander wistfully outside their own walls. (p. 130)

By combining his concept of physis (as a force to be reckoned with), with his concept of aspiration (as a longing to be safeguarded), Berne was describing the vulnerability that can attend our efforts to live openly with integrity. In our work as professionals, it is important to respect the protective measures people take to guard their "secret gardens," just as we might say Berne attempted to guard his own with sarcasm. At the same time, something at the core, some force and vision, wants to be freed, wants to find its best expression in the world.

When we facilitate maturational processes, we must analyze not only the defensive scripts but also those scripts that have been created out of a sense of purpose and aspiration. As Berne (1972) rather sweetly put it, "The object of script analysis is to . . . open the garden of their aspirations to the world" (p. 131).

The Destiny Drive

Bollas (1989) describes something similar to the ideas of physis and aspiration in his discussion of destiny. He conceives of the "destiny drive" as the urge within each person to articulate and elaborate his or her unique personality, or idiom, through interactions with significant individuals. Given the urgency of this drive, each individual strives to become his or her own true being through experiences with others that release this potential. Bollas describes such formative interactions in terms of the transformational object.

As such, Bollas's destiny drive is an instinct for life, similar to Berne's physis. Bollas (1989) also lists "heredity, biology, and environment [as] factors contributing to one's destiny" (p. 33), which is strikingly similar to Berne's (1972) mention of "parental programming," "the thrust of life," and "external forces" (p. 56).

Berne's (1972) fourth force of destiny—"independent aspirations" (p. 56)—is also recognized by Bollas (1989): "A sense of destiny . . . would be a feeling that the person is fulfilling some of the terms of his inner idiom through familial, social, cultural, and intellectual objects" (p. 34).

Whereas Berne did little with his ideas about physis and aspiration, Bollas (1989) devotes full chapters to his conception of destiny as a drive and weaves this attitude toward life's potential into all areas of his work. For Bollas, fortune comes not just to "the lucky ones," as Berne would have it, but as a result of active, determined seeking.

Toward a Truer Self

Bollas conceives of our sense of destiny as driving each of us toward our unique idiomatic expression or fulfillment of a true self. Borrowing the idea of the "true self" from Winnicott, Bollas (1989) writes, "Infants, at birth, are in possession of a personality potential that is in part genetically sponsored and . . . this true self, over the course of a lifetime, seeks to express and elaborate this potential through formations of being and relating" (p. 11).

According to Bollas, we each start out our lives with this inherited potential. Yet the "true self" also refers to the *expression* of that potential, which we have discussed in terms of "idiom." A true self is both a possibility and an actuality. Actualizing our true idiom contrasts significantly with expressions or behaviors that are false or adapted, that betray our desire to become most urgently our potential selves. In fact, living falsely can lead to psychological and emotional pain that may show itself in various symptoms. For each of us, when our unique thrust toward life is thwarted, we live something like a death, something that is less than our full capacity for life, which is what happened for Hank, as described earlier.

Just as Berne was inclined to analyze problematic, scripty transactions, the psychoanalytic tradition has also tended to analyze and interpret psychopathological formations, typically seen as unconscious. But Bollas is describing a different nonconscious process, one that is not problematic or growth inhibiting. For although he admits that our drive toward destiny will largely operate outside conscious awareness, Bollas (1989) wants us to recognize that this difference has implications for professional practice: "We cannot analyze the evolution of the true self. We can facilitate it. We can experience its momentary use of our self" (p. 18).

Berne was able to identify script patterns in his patients because human beings, as learning creatures, tend to repeat what they have learned in the past, even if what they learned is not serving them well. Some certainty, even if painful, can seem better than an uncertain future of possibilities. Bollas is saying, however, that the process of living toward aspirations or a sense of destiny is not inherently repetitive; it is open to creative and novel solutions. So we cannot analyze or identify this evolutionary process because it literally has not yet come into being. And being truly alive and evolving, it will never settle into a pattern or script that can be analyzed, even if we have an image or plan for getting there.

Yet Bollas sees a role for the professional in terms of facilitating that evolution of the self. In particular, he sees us facilitating it through allowing our nonconscious selves to be engaged and used as transformational objects in service to the persistent hopes, however secret and fearful, that our clients and students inevitably bring with them.

Our Commitments to Reality

In highlighting this tension—which Berne and Bollas both embody—between despair and hopefulness about the human condition, we want to emphasize the crucial role such attitudes play in our approach to human relations work.

People come to us for help because they feel constrained by what they have already learned. Such limits can show up as depression, anxiety, overfunctioning, marital conflict, substance abuse, or any of the other symptoms from which our students and clients suffer. Behind every symptom is a sense of despair and a belief that life cannot be any better. Even manic beliefs about magical cures belie an underlying sense of impasse and failure. As professionals, we certainly do not want to meet those difficulties with facile solutions or naïve beliefs about the painlessness of life. Those only feed the sense of despair. Yet neither do we want to meet our clients and students with our own underlying sense of hopelessness or pessimism about being unable to work through life's struggles. It is important that we form an alliance with what Berne saw as each person's core OKness or physis and with what Bollas conceived as the emergence of the true self.

Berne (1968) suggested that, as human beings, we each must make a commitment to seeing life more realistically, with its struggles as well as its potential for growth:

> One of the most important things in life is to understand reality and to keep changing our images to correspond to it, for it is our images which determine our actions and feelings, and the more accurate they are the easier it will be for us to attain happiness and stay happy in an ever-changing world where happiness depends in large part on other people. (p. 46)

Maturation, in other words, is the process of coming to terms with the facts of our lives—in our minds and bodies—in the same way that we begin learning as babies to live with our experiences of hunger, fear, anger, other people, separation, and the world. Yet maturation is not just a process for babies and children. We mature for the whole of our lives to the extent that we want to learn more about the world and ourselves in it. And to help us get there, we often need a parent, friend, teacher, mentor, consultant, or therapist.

In this framework for human relations work, our professional role is to be present in the fullness of our nonconscious beings to this emergence into life and to allow ourselves to be engaged and used viscerally on the sometimes difficult path that attends any developmental challenge. Maturing is the lifelong process for which transformational others are often essential. Let it be our privilege to serve in that capacity. And let it also be our fortune to find those with whom we can each transform toward our own truer, fuller selves.

REFERENCES

Barnes, G. (Ed.). (1977). *Transactional analysis after Eric Berne: Teachings and practices of three TA schools.* New York: Harper's College Press.

Berne, E. (1963). *The structure and dynamics of organizations and groups.* New York: Grove Press.
Berne, E. (1968). *A layman's guide to psychiatry and psychoanalysis* (3rd ed.). New York: Simon & Schuster. (Original work published 1947 as *The mind in action*)
Berne, E. (1972). *What do you say after you say hello? The psychology of human destiny.* New York: Grove Press.
Berne, E. (1977a). Concerning the nature of communication. In E. Berne, *Intuition and ego states: The origins of transactional analysis* (P. McCormick, Ed.) (pp. 49-65). San Francisco, CA: TA Press. (Original work published 1953)
Berne, E. (1977b). Concerning the nature of diagnosis. In E. Berne, *Intuition and ego states: The origins of transactional analysis* (P. McCormick, Ed.) (pp. 33-48). San Francisco, CA: TA Press. (Original work published 1952)
Berne, E. (1977c). The nature of intuition. In E. Berne, *Intuition and ego states: The origins of transactional analysis* (P. McCormick, Ed.) (pp. 1-31). San Francisco, CA: TA Press. (Original work published 1949)
Berne, E. (1977d). Primal images and primal judgment. In E. Berne, *Intuition and ego states: The origins of transactional analysis* (P. McCormick, Ed.) (pp. 67-97). San Francisco, CA: TA Press. (Original work published 1955)
Berne, E. (1977e). The psychodynamics of intuition. In E. Berne, *Intuition and ego states: The origins of transactional analysis* (P. McCormick, Ed.) (pp. 159-166). San Francisco, CA: TA Press. (Original work published 1962)
Bollas, C. (1987). *The shadow of the object: Psychoanalysis of the unthought known.* New York: Columbia University Press.
Bollas, C. (1989). *Forces of destiny: Psychoanalysis and human idiom.* Northvale, NJ: Jason Aronson.
Clarkson, P. (1992). *Transactional analysis psychotherapy: An integrated approach.* London: Tavistock/Routledge.
Cornell, W. F. (1988). Life script theory: A critical review from a developmental perspective. *Transactional Analysis Journal, 18,* 270-282.
Cornell, W. F., & Hargaden, H. (Eds.). (2005). *From transactions to relations: The emergence of a relational tradition in transactional analysis.* London: Haddon Press.
Cornell, W. F., & Landaiche, N. M., III (2005). Impasse e intimata nella coppia terapeutica o di counseling: l'influenza del protocollo [Impasse and intimacy in the therapeutic or consultative couple: The influence of protocol]. *Rivista Italiana di Analisi Transazionale e Metodologie Psicoterapeutiche, 11,* 35-60.
Cornell, W. F., & Tosi, M. T. (2008). The relevance of the unconscious in transactional analysis today [Theme issue]. *Transactional Analysis Journal, 38*(2).
Erskine, R. G. (1998). *Theories and methods of an integrative transactional analysis: A volume of selected articles.* San Francisco: TA Press.
Fast, I. (2006). A body-centered mind: Freud's more radical idea. *Contemporary Psychoanalysis, 42,* 273-295.
Hargaden, H., & Sills, C. (2002). *Transactional analysis: A relational perspective.* Hove, England: Brunner/Routledge.
Harley, K. (2006). A lost connection: Existential positions and Melanie Klein's infant development. *Transactional Analysis Journal, 36,* 252-269.
Mancia, M. (2007). *Feeling the words: Neuropsychoanalytic understanding of memory and the unconscious* (J. Baggott, Trans.). London: Routledge. (Original work published 2004)
Novellino, M. (2005). Transactional psychoanalysis: Epistemological foundations. *Transactional Analysis Journal, 35,* 157-172.

The original version of this article was published in both English and Italian ("Processi non-consci e sviluppo del Sé: Concetti chiave di Eric Berne e Christopher Bollas") in Rivista Italiana di Analisi Transazionale e Metodologie Psicoterapeutiche, *17(54), 33-51, June 2008. It was subsequently published in the* Transactional Analysis Journal, *Volume 38, Number 3, July 2008.*

10

Cognitive and Social Functions of Emotions: A Model for Transactional Analysis Counselor Training

William F. Cornell and Jenni Hine

Traditionally in transactional analysis training, the informal but broad-reaching golden rule differentiating clinical transactional analysis from counseling has been that counselors do not work with intrapsychic dynamics; that is, they are not to intervene within the Child ego state. Counselors are to be trained to identify psychopathology but not to work directly with it. In fact, training in clinical transactional analysis, with its emphasis on diagnosis, psychopathology, and intrapsychic intervention, is not necessarily appropriate professional preparation for work that is focused on personal health and growth as encountered in counseling situations and as a result of normal maturation over the life span. On the other hand, nonclinical applications of transactional analysis often emphasize social-control contracts and interventions, which can create a limited focus on symptom management that is too divorced from the emotional vitality or the emotional damage sustained in and through the Child ego state.

This chapter suggests that emotions can be both regressive and progressive and that they are a fundamental and healthy source of motivation, energy, and meaning. Emotions are understood here as somatic and precognitive sources of desire and information that can help to focus and energize patterns of activity and contact. In our view, a crucial aspect of transactional analysis counseling contracts is forming a working alliance with the progressive aspects of emotional functioning. It is our premise that, while the form of their interventions will differ, both clinicians and counselors need a clear theoretical understanding of the role of emotions in human development, health, and relatedness.

This chapter is a contribution to the evolution of the counseling field in that it describes a training program designed to help counselors and other nonclinically oriented professionals to develop understanding, literacy, and technical skills in working with human emotions. We describe the primary emotions, emotional work in transactional analysis, and the functionality of emotions in cognitive and social processes, particularly in the context of counseling, with reference to some physiological aspects of affect as well as analytic, transactional analysis, and Reichian affect theories. Basic techniques and styles for working with affect are related to specific developmental goals of the counseling process.

A Transactional Analysis Counseling Perspective

The lines of professional demarcation among psychologically, socially, and educationally based theories and methodologies within mental health care have often been blurred. Formal training in transactional analysis is rather unique in that a separation between clinical and nonclinical practices has been maintained from the outset. This has been done in recognition of the fact that the tools of transactional analysis lend themselves to so many different therapeutic, developmental, and educational purposes.

Much effort has been made by the International Transactional Analysis Association (ITAA) and the European Association for Transactional Analysis (EATA) to refine, recognize, and credential the field of transactional analysis counseling. Its frame of reference is now established in the following definition, approved by the Training and Certification Council (T&C Council) (McNamara, Hine, & Lammers, 1995):

Transactional Analysis Counseling is a professional activity within a contractual relationship. The counseling process enables clients or client systems to develop awareness, options and skills for problem management and personal development in daily life through the enhancement of their strengths and resources. Its aim is to increase autonomy in relation to their social, professional and cultural environment.

The field of counseling is chosen by professionals who work in the socio/psychological and cultural fields of practice, for example, social welfare, health care, pastoral work, prevention, mediation, process facilitation, multicultural work, and humanitarian activities. (p. 2)

Mutual literacy between clinical and nonclinical theory and practice has not, however, often been achieved. Both clinical and nonclinical transactional analysis practitioners carry a specialized viewpoint. Like parents, counselors and psychotherapists carry the culture in which they "grew up" and trained, and they may transmit this culture (what Berne identified as the group canon) to their "offspring" (i.e., clients or patients) outside the awareness of both parties. Clinically trained psychotherapists may carry a picture of human functioning that is primarily oriented toward identifying psychopathology, while counselors trained in personal growth and social problems may carry a "too rational" picture of human functioning, ignoring or rationalizing the emotional substrate.

This difference in professional culture can lead to ideological depreciation of each other's work. Counseling and more socially/cognitively oriented methods of treatment are often viewed as a tolerated underclass in health care rather than as a recognized speciality and a valued profession, a practice to which transactional analysis has not been immune. This has led to competition and territoriality between two much-needed professions. Counseling is and needs to be a separate profession with distinct skills and goals, even though in some areas of the world members of the same profession can do both counseling and psychotherapy.

The huge transformation and fragmentation of society that has occurred in recent years—brought about largely by globalization and technology—requires that both individuals and society as a whole have the capacity to update their Parent and understand their Child and the Child of others in the midst of rapid cultural, social, and occupational changes. This is a vast task that requires more effort than can be supplied by clinicians alone; it can only be successfully carried out by a plentiful supply of well-trained and respected nonclinical specialists. When this does not occur, often society falls back on old remedies, such as the renouncement of personal autonomy in favor of domination by rigid external and internal controlling Parent emitted by church, state, or military structures, thus leaving people vulnerable to sects and dogmatic movements (see English, 1996).

Counseling Goals and Emotional Process

Through our counselor training program, we have identified the following skills that counselors need to develop to facilitate clients' expression and management of emotions:

1. The capacity to observe and differentiate emotions in the client and within the group
2. The means to attend to feelings observed in here-and-now dynamics as an aid to reaching a stated goal
3. The skill to check out with the client or the group what emotions are being experienced, without inviting or evoking regression or shifts into direct Child ego state expression
4. Sufficient emotional understanding to appreciate the significance of emotional states as signs of vitality, desire, and need that may require external recognition and support
5. Sufficient emotional understanding to identify those emotional states that may signal regressive pressures or defensive patterns that may require containment and possibly clinical interventions to supplement the counseling process

6. The capacity to be comfortable with, and empathically receptive to, the expression of emotion or conflict without losing Adult cathexis because of the practitioner's own anxieties
7. The capacity to direct and focus emotional experience and energy toward greater interpersonal impact and inner strength, greater success in reaching a chosen goal, and in groups, a more informed and empathic group process in the resolution of affect and conflict

History of Emotional Work and the Child Ego State in Transactional Analysis

In spite of his great interest in and skill at identifying and working with carefully differentiated ego states, Eric Berne had a lifelong ambivalence about working directly with states of affect. In Berne's view, emotions—especially intense emotions—were seen as indicators of regression or pathology and thus as something to be analyzed and managed through the Adult ego state.

There was always something contradictory in Berne's approach. He wrote that the Child ego state was the source of vitality and creativity, but he seemed always a bit afraid of the Child and tended to analyze it rather than work or ally with the Child. In fact, Berne's view of classical transactional analysis was similar to the frame of reference for nonclinical transactional analysis counseling set forth by the T&C Council and described earlier in this chapter. He said that clinical psychotherapy was to be done in psychoanalysis through work with the unconscious, mainly through interpretation and confrontation, but that in transactional analysis one should reach the Child through the Adult ego state.

The early 1970s saw a rapid and intense development of transactional analysis, especially with regard to theory and techniques for working with the Child ego state. While working from different perspectives, the writing and training of Bob and Mary Goulding, Richard Erskine, Fanita English, and Bill Cornell, among others, initiated a rather radical revision of direct therapeutic work with the Child.

The integration by Goulding and Goulding (1978) of gestalt theory and technique in their redecision therapy model introduced a new generation of transactional analysis psychotherapists to avenues of direct intervention with the Child ego state.

Erskine's 1975 article described the technical and theoretical division of various aspects of psychological functioning among different psychotherapeutic modalities, and he argued that transactional analysis offered the potential for being a truly comprehensive model for psychotherapy. He offered the diagram shown in Figure 1.

Erskine proposed that transactional analysis, with ego states as its central concept, had the theoretical structure to support therapeutic interventions in all three domains. For the effects of therapy to

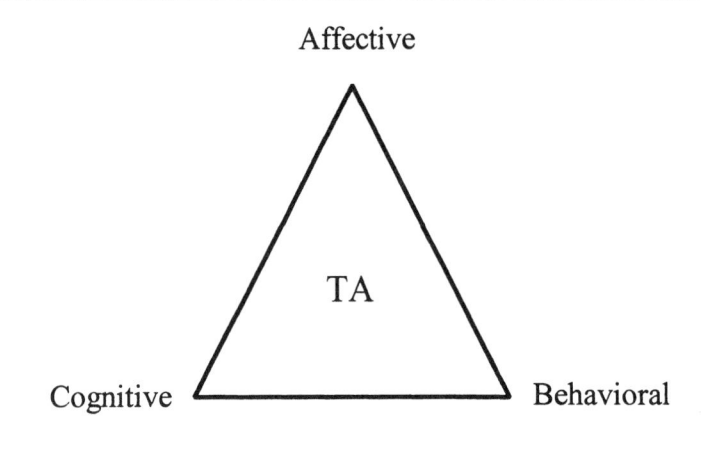

Figure 1
The Integrative Model (Erskine, 1975, p. 164)

be complete and lasting, the therapist must work with the client's thinking, behavior, and affect and over time to use contracts involving all three modes of psychological functioning.

During this same period, English (1971, 1972a) published her work on rackets and real feelings and the nature of the Child ego state (1972b). In her view, the Adult in the Child (A_1), which she nicknamed "Spunky," sustains the intuitive, creative movement of the child toward the world, while P_1 was characterized as "Spooky" because it was haunted by negative parental influences. C_1 was primitive and nicknamed "Sleepy" because it contained the depressed part of the Child and was pulled regressively toward nonlife. This latter view reflected English's affinity for psychoanalytic theory, including speculation about mortido, or the death drive.

In an article titled "Wake Up 'Sleepy': Reichian Techniques and Script Intervention," Cornell (1975) proposed that many transactional analysis views of the Child ego state were culturally contaminated and that it was an error to characterize C_1 as regressive or depressive. He suggested that the regressive or depressive aspects of C_1 reflected the weight of script injunctions and the inhibitions they provoke. He argued that the fundamental nature of C_1 is somatic, that is to say, it reflects the body and emotional impulses in an uninhibited manner. He insisted that the Child ego state was not pathological or regressive in function, but that pathology in the Child was due to failures in the environment and unmet needs, which can create pathological beliefs and behaviors in the Child.

These authors and trainers, among others in the early 1970s, suggested important innovations in transactional analysis theory that led to experimentation with technique. In this process, transactional analysis shifted from a modality dominated by social control and analytic technique to one that emphasized direct work with patterns of emotion and Child ego state experience.

The Innovations of Reich: Drive, Affect, and Society

Reich's theoretical and therapeutic innovations in psychoanalysis during the 1920s and 1930s were radical, and his underlying theory about human nature influenced many later theorists. The transactional analysis theory and philosophical values that Berne developed are consistent with Reich's, and the latter's writings influenced many second-generation transactional analysis theorists and practitioners.

As a student of Freud, Reich's work (1933/1970, 1932/1974) was founded on and framed by Freud's theory of drives. However, in contrast to Freud, who emphasized the chaotic and destructive aspects of drives and emotions, Reich, like Berne, thought that the essence of human nature was a drive toward life. Reich viewed psychopathology as the result of societal and familial denial and distortion of basic drives and sexuality. The "No" that patients felt toward their own bodies and needs was the internalization of the incapacity of parents and society to welcome and respond to children's intensity, vitality, and vulnerability. Throughout his career, Reich studied and wrote about the quality of the mother/infant relationship, parental support, and family life.

Of particular relevance to the counseling field, Reich was a pioneer in the development of educational and social approaches to mental health. Early in his career he had great faith in the potential impact of social and political interventions. He believed that if society's response to people's needs was adequate, most of them would grow up reasonably healthy and not need the difficult and expensive interventions of psychoanalysis and psychotherapy. Reich was therefore active in providing a wide range of services to promote family, mental, and sexual education and health.

The second theme in Reich's work that is especially relevant to understanding emotional work in transactional analysis counseling is his theory of character and body armor. Reich described layers of defenses—destructive webs of anxiety and resignation—that distort core impulses and can harden into rigid characterological and muscular armor. Viewed from a transactional analysis perspective, Reich's diagram (see Figure 2 for one version) provides a developmental and functional description of the evolution of the Child ego state.

The Core and Armor

At the core of the human personality and at the foundation of the infant's early development are

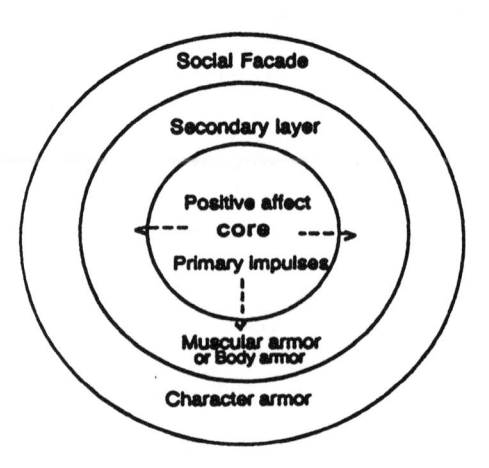

Figure 2
Layering of the Personality Structure

the somatic and affective drives, primary impulses and needs (including aggressive impulses and narcissistic drives) that are essential to living and growing and that are life enhancing and life preserving in their primary nature. These primary/core impulses are pleasurable and exciting states of affect and desire that compel the infant out toward the world.

In contrast, somatic and psychological pathology develop when the young child's drives are systematically frustrated, ignored, or punished. In the face of chronic constraint and inhibition, the primary impulses are increasingly split into what Reich called the basic antithesis of vegetative life; the result is the secondary, defensive layer of personality structure, which he referred to as body armor. This layer is charged with negative affects expressed through destructive impulses and fantasies that are increasingly contained by somatic and characterological rigidities (armoring).

The final capitulation of the child to a self-negating environment is the development of the character armor or resistances, which constitute patterns of interpersonal rigidity. If the defensive functions of the secondary and tertiary layers rigidify, the individual's life comes to be dominated by chronic states of anxiety, resignation, or rage. Reich observed that all too often, his patients had come to identify far more deeply with their defensive structures and consequent affects (i.e., rackets [Erskine & Zalcman, 1979]) than with their primary drives and wishes.

The broad sweep of Reich's fundamental concepts is remarkably parallel to the basic tenets of transactional analysis. Berne cast transactional analysis as a social psychiatry. Wishing to make transactional analysis a means of personal understanding and change available to people from all walks of life, he wrote not only of the psychology of the individual and the family, but of groups, organizations, and cultures. Reich, in even more aggressive fashion, cast his clinical insights into a broad framework of social and political commentary, demanding sweeping social and educational change. What Reich called "the Core," Berne referred to as "the Natural Child," and we, in turn, label "the somatic Child." One can readily see the transactional analysis concepts of rackets, games, and script mirrored in Reich's descriptions of the chronically defensive emotions of the secondary, negative layer of personality structure and the social façade.

Thus, we have found that familiarity with Reich's basic model of emotional expression and constriction, in combination with Berne's theories, provides counselors with a rich understanding of both the vital and defensive functions of emotions.

Functions of Emotions

In an attempt to inform contemporary psychoanalytic theory of the implications of current neuroscience research, Pally (1998) observed:

> What neuroscience emphasises is that emotion and the expression of emotion are involved in all important human endeavors, even those not previously considered emotional such as rational decision-making. . . . Emotion facilitates adaptive behaviours, contributes to adaptive problem-solving and organizes important social relationships. (p. 360)

In other words, in a sufficiently healthy personality structure, emotions are a basic source of information and motivation. Emotional reactions to situations are prerational signals that something important is happening that requires attention and activity.

In training transactional analysis counselors, we believe it is essential to offer trainees a model of healthy emotional functioning to underscore the centrality of emotions in healthy cognitive functioning and social behavior. In our view, one of Berne's most important transformations of psychoanalytic theory was his recasting of Freud's concept of the drive into a theory of human hungers (Berne, 1972), thereby simultaneously humanizing and socializing a central analytic tenet. In his description of structure, stimulation, and recognition hungers, Berne provided a basic theory of the functions and transactional meaning of emotions.

Transactional analysis provides a fine structure and language for describing emotional constriction and dysfunction. An emotional system becomes unhealthy when the range and expression of emotions is limited by parental prohibitions and childhood script decisions. In transactional analysis, a racket is understood as a habitual bad feeling that often repeats itself and tends to dominate and restrict emotional experience and communication. The individual no longer has a full range of emotional contact internally or externally. The interpersonal consequences are described in terms of games, which are the habitual use of particular behavior patterns maintaining archaic and defensive beliefs and emotional patterns.

While discussing the functions of the primary emotions in detail is beyond the scope of this chapter, in training counselors we outline the healthful and communicative expression of each primary affect, underscoring that emotional awareness is essential to clear cognitive functioning and effective communication. In our counselor training program, separate days are devoted to discussing theory and technique in working with primary emotional states, including anger, fear, sadness, joy, shame, depression, and sexuality.

Technical Implications for Transactional Analysis Counseling

To work only with social and cognitive functions during the counseling process would be to risk reinforcing in our clients limited self-experience and expression divorced from the richness and vitality of an emotional grounding. A degree of symptom understanding and control can be accomplished when work is limited to a cognitive/behavioral level of intervention, but transactional analysis has long emphasized the integration of thinking, feelings, and behavior in the development of intimate and autonomous functioning. While counselors work primarily with a client's thinking and behavior, this does not mean that emotions should be excluded from the counseling process. The question is how to work with emotions in counseling so as to enable "clients or client systems to develop awareness, options and skills for problem management and personal development" (McNamara et al., 1995, p. 2), thus facilitating the client's innate maturational processes and vitality.

In transactional analysis counseling, we work directly with and through the Adult ego state. Counselors do not intervene directly within Parent or Child ego state functioning but seek to facilitate contractual change of all three ego states through the Adult. In addressing emotional issues and processes, the transactional analysis counselor seeks:

1. To change Adult ego state functioning on behalf of the Child
2. To strengthen the alliance between Adult and Child
3. To facilitate connections between thinking and feeling
4. To identify obstacles to and generate options for deepening emotional contact and understanding

within relationships
5. To use the Adult to reframe the Parent so that it is considerate of the needs of one's own Child and the Child in others
6. To enable the Parent to put more emphasis on limiting and controlling negative social, environmental, and cultural pressures than on controlling and oppressing its own Child in order to win the approval of "oppressors"
7. To decrease cognitively the negative Parental demands, judgments, and drivers that so often motivate a person's behavior and ways of relating so as to free up the client's ability to experience emotionally and somatically based self-enhancing hopes and desires

In the following sections we outline several counseling techniques used to support and deepen emotional awareness and contact in counseling settings.

Identifying Progressive and Constructive Aspects of Emotions
Anger is a frequently misunderstood and pathologized emotion. Healthy anger and aggression create movement toward the environment and, when necessary, against the environment so as to force an unresponsive or threatening world to respond adequately. Our training perspective draws strongly from the writings of Winnicott (1984) and Whitaker (Whitaker & Malone, 1954). Winnicott (1984) saw great hope in aggressive behavior; he wrote that angry and delinquent behavior in children is a reflection of sufficient hope and determination to create enough of a nuisance so as to force someone in the environment to do something effective. Whitaker and Malone (1954), in a similar fashion, argued that an infant's or child's impulses to be angry are not an effort to destroy the object or the parents but to have an impact on them, to elicit or force a response. Whitaker and Malone observed:

Such aggression in infants aims initially not at the destruction of the object, but at securing a relationship with that object necessary for the satisfaction of a need in the infant, usually hunger. Only in the later development of the child when the problem of ambivalence arises does aggression take on a specifically hostile quality.... This primitive outgoing effort at need satisfaction provides the core of healthy aggression. (pp. 132-133)

Violence and hatred are seen as defensive distortions of the aggressive function, the gradual and ultimate outcome of chronic and severe environmental frustration, unresponsiveness, and/or intrusion. Counselors often need education and a process by which they can examine their own attitudes of judgment, fear, or anger about angry clients. The counselor's task in working with anger is to be empathic, responsive, respectful, and interactive in the face of issues that frustrate, irritate, or enrage an individual so as to assist the client in becoming more effective at soliciting or demanding environmental responses while avoiding harm to others.

Fear and anxiety may emerge when aggression fails or one's structure (psychological or environmental), safety, or the known and familiar is lost. Fear is the experience of disintegration, a falling apart of the inside or the outside. Counselors are frequently faced with people and families in transition or crisis due, for example, to illness, death, rape, domestic violence, accidents, divorce, and/or unemployment. All of these involve the loss of a known and expected structure and can result in panic, anxiety, fear, and/or loss of control.

The counselor's first task with a frightened client is to create an environment that is sufficiently safe and resonant so that the person can calm down and put words to what is going on inside. The counselor often needs to initiate contact without being too parental or directive. In a counseling relationship that is actively responsive, empathic, and containing, the counselor provides the client with someone to whom to attach as well as a chance to experience the loss of structure as a new experience rather than as a cause for defensive reactions of withdrawal, disconnection, or attack.

Sadness and grief are the primary emotions that usually arise in response to loss of another. Loss, despair, self-criticism, solitude, or depression may follow the loss of a loved one, a loved place, lost meaning, or a loss of personal capacity. Sadness and grief are both an experience of loss and an expression of attachment and desire. Thus attachment theory and theories of separation and autonomy are central aspects of training.

Primary goals of the counselor working with sadness and grief include enabling the client to experience the loss, achieve separation, and rebuild self-respect and identity. Self-respect and attachment are antidotes to self-criticism, guilt, and despair because they help the mourning person to avoid moving into persistent Victim sadness in the form of a racket.

Accompanying a person through deep sadness, grief, or despair can be a profoundly difficult and unsettling experience for mental health professionals. Counselors often feel intense pressure to provide the client with comfort for or relief from the pain and to minimize the depth of the experience, rather than accompanying the person and helping him or her learn from the experience of separation and loss. Counselors often need the opportunity to examine their own experiences and beliefs about loss in order to understand the progressive forces of loss, love, and attachment.

Love and joy present opportunities and problems of their own. Love and joy, like fear, involve a loss of self—a loss of limits and boundaries in the midst of being in intense contact with bodily sensations, the external world, or another person. And like fear, love and joy can evoke anxiety, avoidance, and defensiveness. The feeling of joy, with all its variations, from tenderness to orgasm, brings us more intensely and successfully in contact with people, the world, and our environment.

When the counseling environment is too rational, protective, parental, or task oriented, the experience of any or all of these emotions may be inadvertently stifled. Counseling can be much more than a crisis-relieving or problem-solving operation; although these tasks are essential elements in the counseling contract, they are not necessarily sufficient. Counselors need permission and the skill to inquire about areas of life that are endearing, satisfying, and exciting as well as those that are problematic so as to support the inborn striving for vitality, life, and health.

While it is not the counselor's task to heighten the transference, a transference relationship often develops. Clients' wishes for love, pleasure, and intimacy often emerge, sometimes for the first time, in the counseling relationship. Therefore, counselors need sufficient training in transference and countertransference to identify the emergence of these longings in a positive and supportive way. The counseling relationship needs to be a safe holding environment within which these spontaneous and often childlike longings can emerge and be acknowledged, one within which the client can find support for expressing such longings in his or her daily life and relationships.

Facilitating the Interrupted Gesture

Much of what shapes the developing infant and child is nonverbal and preverbal; thus, much of how the Child ego state becomes manifest is through nonverbal cues. That is, signals of significance, distress, and desire are provided through the body.

Taking this into account, in an effort to develop a comprehensive model of therapy—one that synthesizes transactional analysis, relational, and somatic theories of psychotherapy—Cornell (1997) uses the image of the "interrupted gesture," which was inspired by Winnicott's writings about the child's spontaneous gesture. In his exploration of the developmental relationship between the mind and the psyche-soma and his understanding of the evolution of the true and false selves, Winnicott (1965) wrote:

> Periodically the infant's gesture gives expression to a spontaneous impulse; the source of the gesture is the True Self, and the gesture indicates the existence of a potential True Self. We need to examine the way the mother meets this infantile omnipotence revealed in a gesture (or a sensori-motor grouping). I have here linked the idea of a True Self with the spontaneous gesture. (p. 145)

The development of the true self experience—the Natural Child in transactional analysis terms—is fostered by the parents' capacities to notice and facilitate their infant's spontaneous gestures.

The origin of an interruption to one of these gestures can vary from inattention and unresponsiveness in the caretaking environment to outright humiliation and punishment. These interruptions may carry parental injunctions at both emotional and behavioral levels and create conflict and impasses between Parent and Child, leading, at times, to the exclusion of C_1. These injunctions may require a psychotherapy environment for resolution.

However, within the counseling context, a new "facilitating environment" can be established in which these interruptions are noticed and attended to, thus allowing excluded and often vital aspects of the client's personality to emerge and develop. Attention to the process of interruption typically involves noticing inhibited or inhibiting nonverbal communication, for example, "I noticed that you were speaking in a forceful voice, and then suddenly your voice dropped. I wonder what it would be like if you continued in the stronger voice." Active attention on the part of the counselor to expressions in the eyes, tone of voice, posture, and movements of the shoulders, arms, and hands, as further examples, can bring the muted vitalities and impulses of the somatic Child into conscious awareness, fostering greater self-experience and range of emotional choice. Examples of this might include saying, "You seem to have a hard time looking at me as you talk about this"; "Your body looks increasingly tense; I wonder what that's like"; "You look like you're working very hard to hold yourself together"; "It looked for a moment like you were getting excited. What happened to your excitement?"; "I hear the force in your voice. What's that like for you?"; or "You say you agree, but it doesn't look like you agree." When these interrupted gestures are noticed and responded to, the client has an opportunity to experiment with new possibilities and to gain in self-respect and self-expression. Counselors also need training in identifying patterns of defense that may emerge in the face of new psychological or interpersonal possibilities so as to assess whether counseling interventions will be sufficient or whether referral for psychotherapy may be required.

Modeling by the Counselor

In parallel fashion, the counselor's conscious awareness and use of his or her own nonverbal behavior enhances the vitality of sessions. It is a particularly important form of modeling and permission to see and feel the counselor demonstrating variations in nonverbal communication through tone of voice, eye contact, active movement, and posture. Sameness in the counselor's way of being in the session deadens the potential for affect in the room and subtly promotes passivity and overadaptation rather than involvement and differentiation.

Alliance with Life-Enhancing Goals and Drives

Since clients commonly seek counseling during periods of life crisis or developmental transition, they often look for a responsive and supportive environment, often with the covert hope for protection and nurturance. However, contracts that are overly nurturing are likely to evoke dependency and regressive affect. While a counselor should not be distant or strictly rational, the counselor should be trained to identify and facilitate the progressive intent of emotional states. Consciously aligning himself or herself with the client's drives toward a more desired life, the counselor needs to see how the client's primary impulses can be both strengthened through cognitive and social strategies (so as to move through defensive reactions) and sustained in the face of environmental frustrations. If new options and experiences do not begin to dissolve somatic and character defenses, then the counselor may need to refer the client for psychotherapy.

Descriptive Interventions

It is essential in any change process that there be a way to make the covert overt, that is, for expanding conscious awareness. In a clinical setting, this goal is typically accomplished through confrontation and interpretation. Descriptive intervention is the counseling equivalent, one designed to bring together the awareness of cognitive, behavioral, and emotional aspects of experience and interaction. Within the counseling perspective, descriptive interventions seek to enliven the counselor/client interchange, to acknowledge and amplify consistently the client's affective experience, and to engage the Adult in simultaneous cognitive and emotional awareness. Nonjudgmental, descriptive interventions facilitate an increasing awareness and alliance between Adult and Child functioning.

Empathic Inquiry

In contradistinction to Reich's highly confrontive approach, the psychoanalytic interpretive mode, and the often confrontive and directive interventions of transactional analysis, the goals of counseling are better served through a dialogue of "sustained empathic inquiry" (Stolorow, Brandchaft, & Atwood, 1987). Stolorow, Atwood, and Brandchaft (1994) characterize this style of inquiry as conveying "an attitude that consistently seeks to comprehend the meaning of a patient's expressions from a perspective within, rather than outside, the patient's own subjective frame of reference" (p. 44). This process differs from styles of active listening or Rogerian reflective listening in that it does not simply communicate the therapist's understanding; rather, it questions in an empathic way so as to support the development of self-reflection, particularly regarding the more problematic areas of a client's life.

Although empathic inquiry was developed as a modification of psychoanalytic technique, we find it valuable in the counseling process. Through this attitude, the counselor can offer and teach a process of empathic, rather than critical, inquiry and curiosity. Such an attitude significantly enhances awareness and integration of emotion and cognition. The central question becomes, "How is it that this happens this way?" or "What is this like for you and those around you?" rather than "Why do you do this?" or "I would suggest. . . ."

Contract and Style

The heart of the counseling contract is facilitating the client's self-awareness and innate maturational forces. The contract is carried out through both content and style. It is a delicate balance to respond actively and intentionally to feelings within a professional contract that emphasizes social and cognitive skill development so as to strengthen self-awareness and autonomous functioning. An overly empathic or nurturing style can promote a fusion of experience and dependency rather than promote differentiation and mutual problem solving. An overly cognitive style can promote a pseudo-Adult style of functioning and adaptation, one that manages the vitality and vulnerability of the Child ego state rather than relating to it. The counselor seeks to facilitate simultaneous thinking and feeling. Like a good parent, the effective counselor finds ways to communicate interest and concern without becoming overly directive, defining, or comforting.

Differentiation and Conflict

While attending to emotions in the ways already described, the counselor needs also to create opportunities for differentiation and conflict: "What I'm going to say is quite different from what you just said"; "You don't seem to agree with me. What's your thinking?"; "I hear how you understand the situation, but for me it's rather different"; "When you talk of your struggles, you often describe yourself as sad. I wonder if you are aware of sometimes feeling angry?"; or "What's it like for you when our thinking or experience is different?" This style of observation and inquiry supports differentiation and independence without avoiding affect. It demonstrates a relationship within which there can be respectful and cooperative conflict.

Conclusion

While we have long felt the need for the differentiation and expansion of counselor training within transactional analysis, the urgency of this process has been clearly revealed during transactional analysis certification examinations. Some clinical exam board members have contested the right of counselors to address emotionality in their work on the grounds that this belongs to the field of clinical psychotherapy. This chapter is designed to increase mutual knowledge and literacy among different transactional analysis professional specializations and to highlight the care with which affective understanding needs to be integrated into the cognitive and behavioral interventions in all fields of practice. In addition, our hope is to demonstrate how essential it is to teach this effectively. This chapter is slanted toward the training of counselors, but it also has much validity with regard to work in organizational and educational settings. Finally, it could also be useful in the preparation of examiners for transactional analysis exams in all fields of practice.

REFERENCES

Berne, E. (1972). *What do you say after you say hello?: The psychology of human destiny.* New York: Grove Press.
Cornell, W. (1975). Wake up "sleepy": Reichian techniques and script intervention. *Transactional Analysis Journal, 5,* 144-147.
Cornell, W. (1997). If Reich had met Winnicott: Body and gesture. *Energy & Character, 28*(2), 50-60.
English, F. (1971). The substitution factor: Rackets and real feelings, Part I. *Transactional Analysis Journal, 1*(4), 27-32.
English, F. (1972a). Rackets and real feelings, Part II. *Transactional Analysis Journal, 2*(1), 23-25.
English, F. (1972b). Sleepy, spunky and spooky: A revised second-order structural diagram and script matrix. *Transactional Analysis Journal, 2*(2), 64-67.
English, F. (1996). The lure of fundamentalism. *Transactional Analysis Journal, 26,* 23-30.
Erskine, R. (1975). The ABC's of effective psychotherapy. *Transactional Analysis Journal, 5,* 163-165.
Erskine, R. G., & Zalcman, M. J. (1979). The racket system: A model for racket analysis. *Transactional Analysis Journal, 9,* 51-59.
Goulding, R. L., & Goulding, M. M. (1978). *The power is in the patient: A TA/gestalt approach to psychotherapy* (P. McCormick, Ed.). San Francisco: TA Press.
McNamara, J., Hine, J., & Lammers, W. (1995, December). Counseling definition. ITAA Counseling Task Force, *EATA Telegram No. 10.* Aix en Provence: European Association for Transactional Analysis.
Pally, R. (1998). Emotional processing: The mind-body connection. *International Journal of Psychoanalysis, 79*(349), 349-362.
Reich, W. (1970). *The mass psychology of fascism.* New York: Farrar, Straus & Giroux. (Original work published 1933)
Reich, W. (1974). *The sexual revolution: Toward a self-regulating character structure.* New York: Farrar, Straus & Giroux. (Original work published 1932)
Stolorow, R., Atwood, G. E., & Brandchaft, B. (Eds.). (1994). *The intersubjective perspective.* Northvale, NJ: Jason Aronson.
Stolorow, R. D., Brandchaft, B., & Atwood, G. E. (1987). *Psychoanalytic treatment: An intersubjective approach.* Hillsdale, NJ: The Analytic Press.
Whitaker, C., & Malone, T. (1954). *The roots of psychotherapy.* New York: Brunner/Mazel.
Winnicott, D. W. (1965). *The maturational processes and the facilitating environment: Studies in the theory of emotional development.* Madison, CT: International Universities Press.
Winnicott, D. W. (1984). *Deprivation and delinquency* (C. Winnicott, R. Shepherd, & M. Davis, Eds.). London: Tavistock.

The original version of this article was published in the Transactional Analysis Journal, *Volume 29, Number 3, pp. 175-185, July 1999.*

If Berne Met Winnicott:
Transactional Analysis and Relational Analysis

William F. Cornell

As I was getting ready for this trip, my son Caleb asked, "Dad, why are you going back to England already?" I managed to keep a straight face as I replied, "For the English breakfast." Now the theme of this conference is "Embracing Diversity," and my first encounter with the English breakfast was certainly an experience in embracing diversity. Eggs, overcooked bacon, sausages that seemed filled with sawdust, toast, plum tomatoes from a tin, and baked beans. I still remember looking at that plate and asking myself (I was too polite to ask anyone else), "WHO thought of this? How did this come to be? There has to be a story here." Perhaps most important of all was the question, "WHY are they still doing this?" I have since come to embrace the diversity of foodstuffs on that English breakfast plate and am, in fact, very fond of that particular meal. But I want to take that breakfast, and my shocked reaction to my first encounter with it, as a metaphor for the nature of theory and the questions we need to ask of our theories: Who thought of this? What is the story of our theory? Why do we still think and do things this way?

The stimulus for this speech was my serving on the boards of numerous teaching and supervising examinations at the Major International Transactional Analysis Conference (MITAC) in Zürich in 1998. Board members and examinees came from all over the world, with tremendous diversity in national, racial, ethnic, and professional backgrounds. This diversity was exciting, but the discussions in the exams themselves were unnervingly similar. The descriptions of therapeutic theory, clinical work, and supervisory intervention were relentlessly nice—all about empathy, holding environments, and attachment processes. This was not exciting. I heard watered-down versions of the language of Winnicott, Bowlby, and Kohut far more often than the language and concepts of Berne. I wondered how often and how deeply examinees had read these authors in the original, but it seemed I was alone in my discomfort. I finished those exams with the thought that our organization is now teaching doctrine rather than theory and thinking.

This led me to articulate a set of questions about theory: What is the nature and function of theory? Why do we need it? How do we use it and misuse it? How do we change it?

Eric Berne and Donald Winnicott were psychoanalytic contemporaries, both rebellious and creative forces in the evolution of psychodynamic psychotherapy. For both men, their creative work was born out of argument with their psychoanalytic colleagues and the dominant analytic culture/canon of their time. Berne's rebellion was much more overt than Winnicott's, and ultimately he abandoned his identity as a psychoanalyst to create the new discipline of transactional analysis. Winnicott, exercising the traditional English tact with great patience and skill, maintained his identity as a psychoanalyst (he called the group to which he belonged the "middle" or "Independent" school) and was content to argue quietly with Melanie Klein and to gradually nudge the psychoanalytic frame.

Berne's argument was with classical psychoanalysis and ego psychology as it was practiced in the 1940s and 1950s in the United States, which was quite different from how it was practiced in Britain at that time. He disliked the arrogant, distant, highly interpretive approach that dominated American psychoanalysis and psychiatry. As a result, among his many creative additions to psychodynamic theory and technique were the concepts of differing states of the ego, different ego functions, here-and-now analysis of transactions, mutual effort in the treatment relationship, and the client's responsibility to think and change.

For Winnicott (1958), the essence of the unconscious was not that it was denied and buried by repression but that it had not yet been discovered or given form; his was an emergent unconscious. Winnicott's central and enduring arguments were with Melanie Klein and her followers. For example, he challenged Klein's (1957/1975) insistence on the innate nature of the death instinct and the inherent destructiveness of the infant as well as her conceptualization of intrapsychic processes within the infant's mind. He also resisted her highly active and interpretive stance in the analytic process. Winnicott made major contributions to object relations theory, to patterns of infant care, and to the understanding of the therapeutic process as creating a psychological and relational space that freed the client to wonder, explore, and play.

Both Berne and Winnicott were deeply devoted to reframing psychoanalytic principles in colloquial language so as to be accessible to a broad public and immediately useful to people in their everyday lives. Both men developed language and notions that have been absorbed not only into the psychotherapeutic lexicon, but also into common language. Both wrote with directness and clarity.

Unfortunately, Berne seemed to have been driven too much by his need for recognition and approval. Feeling spurned by his psychoanalytic colleagues, Berne intentionally set out to write a best seller that would bring him fame, fortune, and revenge. He did write clearly, most evident in *Transactional Analysis in Psychotherapy* (1961) and *Principles of Group Treatment* (1966), but too often he tended to confuse clarity with simplicity as evident in *Games People Play* (1964) and *Sex in Human Loving* (1970). The result is that oversimplification has too often been an enduring legacy in the transactional analytic tradition.

Winnicott, during his 40 years of practice as a psychoanalyst, wrote more than 600 papers. While many were formal, theoretical papers designed for psychoanalytic journals, the majority were actually talks written for a broad spectrum of professional and lay audiences, a reflection of his dedication to communicating something about human nature, the creative spirit, and the centrality of early infant care. For his part, Winnicott, in his desire for clarity, did not fall into the trap of oversimplifying his thinking. To the contrary, he sustained clarity and complexity in his writing. While his papers from the 1930s and 1940s were carefully, diplomatically crafted, in the 1950s and 1960s his thinking became increasingly his own, growing in depth, richness, and complexity.

Berne set out for fame and fortune, founding an organization to carry on his work and optimistically naming it the "International Transactional Analysis Association" at a time when virtually all of its members were from California and could meet together comfortably in one small room. In contrast, Winnicott avoided the spotlight, writing and speaking quietly and actively resisting the creation of a movement/theory founded in his name or according to his "principles." He was deeply resistant to the creation of doctrine, seeing true theory as creative and ever-evolving efforts to comprehend and describe reality. He once wrote a joint letter to Anna Freud and Melanie Klein suggesting that their "rigid thinking" tended to create either iconoclasts or claustrophobes (Winnicott as cited in Rodman, 1987, p. 92). He subsequently wrote to Klein challenging her creation of "Kleinians" and arguing that "I personally think that it is very important that your work should be restated by people discovering in their own way and presenting what they discover in their own language" (p. 34).

My emphasis here is on two of the lessons I think we can learn from Winnicott: one about the dangers of idealizing and narcissistically identifying with our theories and the second about the nature of the therapeutic process.

In 1998 I attended a conference in Washington, D.C., celebrating "Freud at the Millennium." It was a controversial but fascinating conference, in part because many of the speakers were not psychoanalysts. One of the best talks, however, was by Judith Chused (1998), a psychoanalyst and training analyst in the Washington area. I seldom agree with what she writes, but I was very taken by this particular talk, entitled, "Why Theory?" Chused spoke first of her early years as a clinician, when she consciously turned away from the application of theory in her clinical work, rejecting it as paternalistic and authoritarian. She was determined to see each patient anew, as a unique being, casting herself as an empathic "good object" who would compensate for the traumas of the bad objects in the client's history. The results, she said, were not as she had imagined. She discovered that in her devotion to being a "good object" in her clients' lives, she was depriving them of the opportunity to see for themselves how they created and maintained their "bad objects" and sometimes became "bad objects" themselves.

Chused went on to talk about the consequences of therapists becoming narcissistically identified with their trainers and their theories. She reminded her audience that there are scores of articles in dozens of professional journals that describe the difficulties of treating narcissistic and borderline patients and of the mistreatment of these clients by their therapists. She said that she, too, like many of her analytic colleagues, had at times struggled with difficult clients. But she never felt that any of them wished to truly hurt her. She paused before going on to say that she has never been as mistreated by her clients as she had been by some of her colleagues in their fierce determination to protect their theories and egos from challenge.

Chused then discussed the dynamics that so often force clinicians to become profoundly identified with their theories, in the process turning theory into doctrine. She suggested that in perhaps no other profession are we given responsibility for other peoples' lives and well-being so many years before we are actually experienced and competent to assume that responsibility. Therapists cling to their identifications with teachers, training analysts, and theories to protect themselves and to ward off anxiety and chaos. Of course, as transactional analysts this brings to mind Berne's recognition of the resistive power of structure hunger.

In considering the nature of the therapeutic process, I see a fundamental flaw in Berne's theory and techniques, one that is too often perpetuated in contemporary transactional analysis. I am referring to the overuse of the Parent ego state and parental functions within the context of the therapeutic relationship. This is a flaw that I think can be largely corrected with some lessons from Winnicott.

The problem, as I see it, began with an aspect of Berne's theory that is one of his most important and creative: the delineation of a distinct Parent ego state. By delineating the Parent ego state, in both structure and function, Berne offered an important correction to the classical psychoanalytic position of the neutral observer and to the mechanistic operations of cognitive/behavioral models. The active, intentional use of the Parent ego state in therapy—especially as manifested in the therapist's use of permission, protection, and potency—was a major technical innovation. However, it resulted in variations of transactional analysis that have created an overreliance on the parental functions of the therapist.

In my early training in the 1970s, the Parent ego state was used in highly confrontational therapeutic styles and in the use of reparenting and corrective parenting structures. More recently, it has been the nurturing, provisional functions of the Parent that have been emphasized, increasingly theorized and articulated in terms of providing a holding environment, attachment, attunement, and/or empathy. Once upon a time we were supposed to confront our clients into health. Now, apparently, we are supposed to empathize them into well-being. Chused and Winnicott would both caution us that it is not so easy.

There has been a long-standing and seriously problematic tendency in transactional analysis theory and technique to project the "bad stuff" out onto parental failures, environmental failures, and the social structure. All too often now the transactional analysis therapist is cast as some sort of provider of the "good stuff" rather than as a clarifier of how the client maintains ineffective, other-destructive, and self-destructive patterns of defense. This bias in transactional analysis theory creates pressure on the therapist to move into a good parent/good object position vis-à-vis the client. If we help a client "experience enough," to use a popular example that surely qualifies as an idealized fantasy, what have we actually accomplished? If we envelope our clients with empathy and narcissistic mirroring, is something actually repaired, is something different in the client's psychological structure and functioning? We are in serious danger of creating a profession that is some kind of saccharine idealization of an infantile/maternal fantasy completely split off from the ongoing difficulties of actual life, not to mention the meaner side of human nature. Winnicott wrote rather pointedly that the infant is never satisfied with satisfaction, but rather tends to feel "fobbed off" by parental efforts to be overly satisfying. The infant is, in fact, more dedicated to unsatisfied and aggressive interests.

I heard many references to mother/infant research during examinations and at presentations at the Zürich MITAC. Daniel Stern (1985, 1995), who has apparently written the new "bible," was quoted everywhere, although not necessarily accurately. However, Stern's work is flawed, and his understanding of adult psychotherapy is seriously lacking. Certainly, studies of mother/infant relationships have transformed our understanding of infant and child development, but we make a mistake when we use the mother/infant relationship as the model for the psychotherapeutic relationship. They are not equivalent.

As Frances Bonds-White and I (Cornell & Bonds-White, 2001) have emphasized, Berne created a transactional analysis, not a relational analysis. He watched, listened, thought about, described, interpreted, analyzed, and disrupted how people transacted with one another. Ultimately, he maintained a one-person psychotherapy in that the events or patterns between two people were referred back to what goes on inside the client's mind so as to deepen the client's self-awareness and capacity to make new choices. Berne did not offer people new, kinder, gentler relationships; he offered an opportunity to see, think about, and alter how one thinks and behaves. Empathy, holding, and attachment were not among Berne's (1966) eight therapeutic operations (pp. 233-247). His transactional analysis was intended to unsettle a client's familiar, defensive frame of reference through description, confrontation, interpretation, and humor. Berne's treatment group was not an empathic holding environment; it was an interpersonal study matrix.

The most substantial effort Berne made to articulate a theory of relationships was in his description of time structuring: withdrawal, rituals, pastimes, activities, games, and intimacy (Berne, 1970, pp. 69-71). However, his last writings were permeated with pessimism and darkness. Perhaps his own unresolved issues around closeness and intimacy prevented him from developing a more complete therapy of relatedness and therapeutic intimacy.

In 1980, Laura Cowles-Boyd and Harry Boyd made an important—and much underappreciated—contribution to the application of time structure. They introduced play as the intermediate way of relating between the defensive, repetitive nature of games and the authentic and unpredictable nature of intimacy. In their emphasis on play, Cowles-Boyd and Boyd (perhaps inadvertently) mirrored one of Winnicott's central concepts. In fact, I consider Winnicott's ideas about play to be among his most important contributions to psychotherapy and a wonderful alternative to the corrective parenting style of therapy so often found in transactional analysis today.

Berne himself had supreme confidence in the strength of the Adult ego state. However, many have found this predisposition to the Adult insufficient to create and sustain lasting therapeutic change. Perhaps it is this lack that has led so many transactional analysts to rely on the overutilization of the Parent ego state, that is, the provision of the "good" therapeutic object. From my vantage point, I suggest that the Parent ego state provides a background of safety and concern, but it is not the therapeutic foreground. From a transactional analysis perspective, I have come to understand what Winnicott conceptualized as play as the ongoing intrapsychic and interpersonal interaction/exploration between the Adult and Child ego states of therapist and client. In contrast to many of my transactional analysis colleagues, I see the Child ego state as alive and well throughout the life span, a formative and vitalizing state of the ego rather than an archaic or traumatic splinter that needs to be integrated into the Adult.

In Winnicott's thinking, play was crucial to emotional development and to the creative and ongoing unfolding of life's learning. Play forms a bridge between the inner and the outer world, my world and yours, subjective and objective. In "Playing: A Theoretical Statement," Winnicott (1971/1982) wrote:

> Psychotherapy takes place in the overlap of two areas of playing, that of the patient and that of the therapist. Psychotherapy has to do with two people playing together. The corollary of this

is that where playing is not possible then the work done by the therapist is directed towards bringing the patient from a state of not being able to play into a state of being able to play. (p. 38)

> Play is immensely exciting. . . . The thing about playing is always the precariousness of the interplay of personal psychic reality and the experience of control of actual objects. This is the precariousness of magic itself, the magic that arises in intimacy, in a relationship that is being found to be reliable. (p. 47)

"A relationship that is being found to be reliable." This reliability creates space, the opportunity and possibility to question, to wonder, to play, to discover, to fight, to hate, and to love. In terms of reliability and relatedness, *how* the therapist is, the space he or she creates, is more important than anything that the therapist *does*. I suggest that when we as transactional analysis therapists move into the attitude (if not the actual behavior) of the Parent ego state, when we function from a parental position—confronting, reparenting, soothing, comforting, nurturing, attuning, empathizing, supporting—we close the playground, deaden the play space, subtly thwart the aggressive, the creative, and the individuating forces of our clients.

Play. Curiosity. Wonder. Diversity. Differentness. Differentiation. I have learned a great deal from reading Winnicott over the years. I have also learned a great deal from working with Christopher Bollas, a leading representative of the contemporary British Independent school. Bollas (1989) reminds us that our clients pay us to think and feel differently from them, not to think and feel like them or for them. Some of our clients in some phases of treatment will need an empathic, mirroring, holding style of relatedness as part of the therapeutic foundation, but I seriously question whether empathy and "good" object provision in its various forms are curative. We need to be careful not to undercut the responsibility, activity, and initiative—the hostility, for that matter—of our clients.

I recall a teaching seminar with Bollas in which he referred to self psychology as a 12-step program for the wounded American ego and described the overuse of empathy as the postponement of psychotherapy. In Bollas's view, not knowing the experience of another is inevitable and tolerating not knowing is a developmental accomplishment. Winnicott reminds us that parents must fail their children in order for them to grow and to come to discover and know themselves. A relationship that is found to be reliable is not one that is endlessly pseudoparental, empathic, attuned, or attached. Such relationships may be narcissistically gratifying and protective of the therapist, but they are also likely to "fob off" our clients. A relationship that is found to be reliable is one that stays put, stays interested, and stays invested in the face of differentness and conflict, be it theoretical difference, cultural difference, gender difference, or the inevitable and enlivening differences between therapist and client.

I encourage us all to keep the therapeutic playground open and the therapeutic relationship alive with playful and intimate possibilities.

REFERENCES

Berne, E. (1961). *Transactional analysis in psychotherapy: A systematic individual and social psychiatry*. New York: Grove Press.
Berne, E. (1964). *Games people play: The psychology of human relationships*. New York: Grove Press.
Berne, E. (1966). *Principles of group treatment*. New York: Oxford University Press.
Berne, E. (1970). *Sex in human loving*. New York: Simon & Schuster.
Bollas, C. (1989). *Forces of destiny: Psychoanalysis and the human idiom*. London: Free Association Books.
Chused, J. (1998, October). *Why theory?* Paper presented at the Freud at the Millennium: A Conference on the Occasion of the Library of Congress Freud Exhibit, Washington, D.C. (Sponsored by the International Institute of Object Relations).
Cornell, W. F., & Bonds-White, F. (2001). Therapeutic relatedness in transactional analysis: The truth of love or the love of truth. *Transactional Analysis Journal, 31,* 71-83.
Cowles-Boyd, L., & Boyd, H. S. (1980). Play as a time structure. *Transactional Analysis Journal, 10,* 5-7.
Klein, M. (1975). *Envy and gratitude*. New York: Dell Publishing. (Original work published 1957)
Rodman, F. R. (Ed.). (1987). *The spontaneous gesture: Selected letters of D. W. Winnicott*. Cambridge, MA: Harvard University Press.
Stern, D. N. (1985). *The interpersonal world of the infant: A view from psychoanalysis and developmental psychology*. New York: Basic Books.

Stern, D. N. (1995). *The motherhood constellation: A unified view of parent-infant psychotherapy.* New York: Basic Books.
Winnicott, D. W. (1958). *Collected papers: Through paediatrics to psychoanalysis.* London: Tavistock Publications.
Winnicott, D. W. (1982). Playing: A theoretical statement. In D. W. Winnicott, *Playing and reality* (pp. 38-52). New York: Tavistock/Methuen. (Original work published 1971)

The original version of this chapter was presented as the keynote speech at the Institute for Transactional Analysis Conference in Canterbury, England, on 6 April 2000. It was later published in the Transactional Analysis Journal, *Volume 30, Number 4, pp. 270-275, October 2000.*

Section III:
The Body in Psychotherapy

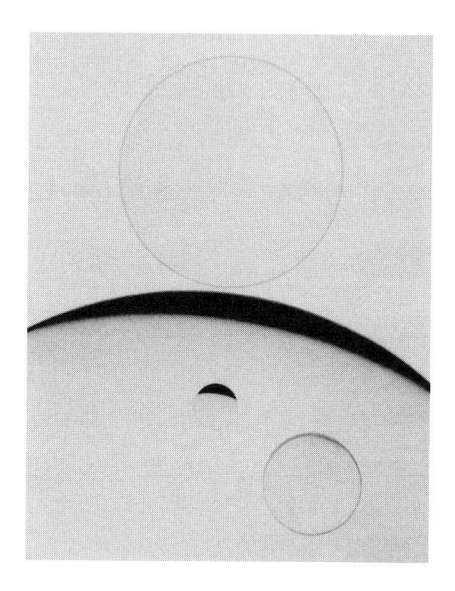

The ego... acquires a certain rigidity, a chronic, automatically functioning mode of reaction, that which is called "character." It is as if the affective personality put on an armor, a rigid shell on which the knocks of the outer world, as well as the inner demands, rebound. This armor makes the individual less sensitive to unpleasure but it also reduces his libidinal and aggressive motility, and, with that, his capacity for pleasure and achievement.

Reich, 1949, p. 342

Section III

Introduction

If there has been a foremost theme running throughout the course of my writing and development as a psychotherapist, it has been the body. In no other arena of my work has there been more questioning or more change.

I became enamored with the body in psychotherapy after reading Wilhelm Reich while still an adolescent. His work has been of singular importance to me, even though I have come to question much of it as I have become a more experienced and mature therapist.

I trained in Radix, a neo-Reichian modality, at the same time that I did my clinical training in transactional analysis. My transactional analysis trainer, Lois Johnson, was in my Radix training group, and we often took workshops together. The Radix model is based on intense characterological and bodily confrontation in the service of eliciting emotional discharge (catharsis). Some transactional analysts at that time, trained in similar ways, used cathartic body interventions to promote regression. It was a style of therapeutic work that had been very beneficial for me, but I became increasingly concerned about its efficacy (safety even) with some of my clients. I attempted to raise questions among my Reichian peers, but most Reichians were zealots and dismissed my questions, explaining my clients' difficulties as manifestations of characterological defenses.

Then one day, in the early 1980s, I walked into my waiting room to get a woman with whom I had been doing Radix work for several years. She had come seeking body therapy because she had a long history of childhood sexual and physical abuse. As I approached her, she drew back her fist and smashed me in the face, screaming, "I can't leave you, but what you are doing is destroying me." She was right, as we had both witnessed her becoming increasing disorganized and abreactive while we continued to work in our familiar, dramatic Reichian mode.

After that experience, I began to talk with all of my clients, about whom I had been quietly worrying, raising questions about what we were doing. The client who punched me was not alone in her experience. Several of these clients, all women, were therapists, and we decided to start reading. There was little on trauma at that point, but we began to recognize in the literature on posttraumatic stress disorder (PTSD) with Vietnam veterans what we were seeing in our work. That began a serious investigation of the trauma literature, experimentation with different ways of working with the body, and the writing of a series of articles on trauma, dissociation, and working differently with the body (Cornell, 1995, 1997, 2000; Cornell & Olio, 1991, 1992; Olio & Cornell, 1994). The article that ends this section, "Consequences of Childhood Bodily Abuse," coauthored with Karen Olio, was written at the start of this period of self-questioning. In it we introduced the concept of working at an affective edge, in which therapist and client stay at an edge of somatic/affective experience that maintains Adult ego state function and here-and-now awareness so as to facilitate integration of affect rather than trigger catharsis, regression, and/or dissociation. Major changes in both my theoretical understanding of somatically focused psychotherapy and my style of working with the body have been ongoing for over 20 years now since that punch in my face.

I described earlier in this book some of the factors in the evolution of my writing. Nothing has been more difficult to figure out than how to write about working at a body level, how to use the written word to evoke and communicate a process that is not experienced in words. I think my description of my experience of a tango lesson in Chapter 15 and the description of a single session in Chapter 14 come as close as I have been able to in doing this.

This section opens with a dialogue, Chapter 12, between Mick Landaiche and me on "Why Body Psychotherapy?" I had been preparing to give a talk to a psychoanalytic group about working with the body, and I was more than a little nervous about it. What could I say that was useful and comprehensible to an audience with a radically different frame of reference? Mick and I were driving somewhere in miserable weather, and I was more than a little nervous about the weather as well as thinking about the talk. Mick decided to ask me about why the body has been such a persistent focus of interest in my work, thinking that if nothing else it might lesson my anxiety about the driving conditions. He wrote as we talked. Without any plan as such, we realized when it was written up that it was a very straightforward, pragmatic discussion about body psychotherapy.

Chapters 13 and 14 are efforts to bring body-centered theory into the transactional analysis frame of reference, with particular attention to script and script protocol. I think these two chapters speak to an important, underdeveloped area of transactional analysis theory and technique and are closely linked to other chapters in this book addressing script protocol and nonconscious processes.

Chapter 15 was originally a discussant paper to a presentation by Lew Aron, one of the founders of the relational model of psychoanalysis. I was challenging some of the tenets and assumptions of relational thinking, emphasizing the self-organizing functions of the body, which are often quite nonrelational. Lew is an enthusiast but not a zealot, and a lively, respectful conversation ensued.

It gives me particular pleasure to be able to reprint "Body-Centered Psychotherapy" in this volume of papers. I was invited by Sharon and Robert Massey to write this as a chapter for the book they were editing entitled, *Comprehensive Handbook of Psychotherapy: Volume 3 Interpersonal/Humanistic/Existential* (Massey & Massey, 2002). Written in a more formal, academic style than I am typically accustomed to, it nevertheless affords a succinct overview of body-centered therapy, illustrated with several case examples.

REFERENCES

Cornell, W. F. (1995). A plea for a measure of ambiguity. *Readings: A Journal of Reviews and Commentary in Mental Health, 10*, 4-10.

Cornell, W. F. (1997). Touch and boundaries in transactional analysis: Ethical and transferential considerations. *Transactional Analysis Journal, 27*, 30-37.

Cornell, W. F. (2000). Transference, desire and vulnerability in body-centered psychotherapy. *Energy & Character, 30*(2), 29-37.

Cornell, W. F., & Olio, K. A. (1991). Integrating affect in treatment with adult survivors of physical and sexual abuse. *American Journal of Orthopsychiatry, 61*, 59-69.

Cornell, W. F., & Olio, K. A. (1992). Consequences of childhood bodily abuse: A clinical model for affective interventions. *Transactional Analysis Journal, 22*, 131-143.

Massey, R. F., & Massey, S. D. (Eds.). (2002). *Comprehensive handbook of psychotherapy: Volume 3 Interpersonal/humanistic/existential* (F. Kaslow, Series Ed.) (pp. 587-613). New York: Wiley.

Olio, K. A., & Cornell, W. F. (1994). Making meaning not monsters: Reflections on the delayed memory controversy. *Journal of Child Sexual Abuse, 3*, 77-94.

Reich, W. (1949). *Character analysis* (3rd ed. rev.) (T. P. Wolfe, Trans.). New York: Orgone Institute Press.

Why Body Psychotherapy?: A Conversation

William F. Cornell and N. Michel Landaiche, III

Mick Landaiche: *Your work as a psychotherapist has been influenced by several, fairly divergent schools of thought, right?*

Bill Cornell: Yes—I studied phenomenological psychology in graduate school, which has a strong philosophical base. After that I started my training in transactional analysis. I had been reading Reich and Berne in college and during graduate school. I thought of Berne as a phenomenological psychoanalyst. Lois Johnson was my clinical transactional analysis trainer. She and I trained together in the Radix, neo-Reichian program, back in the days when it was thought that trainers and trainees could intelligently handle more than one role in their relationship with each other. I wrote my first article for the *Transactional Analysis Journal* in 1975 trying to link Reichian theory of character armor with Fanita English's model of the second-order structure of the Child ego state. I've written a lot over the years on the relationship between transactional analysis and body-centered theories and trained in several forms of bodywork, which is central to my practice today. In the past 10 years I've been influenced mostly by contemporary psychoanalysts—by being in personal therapy, supervision, and training with them. I regularly read the work of contemporary psychoanalytic writers and have gotten to know a number of them personally. This has had an enormous influence on my practice. But I don't think of myself as practicing psychoanalytically.

ML: *Yet when I talk with you about your work and read your papers, something unifies your practice and what you teach.*

BC: That's my experience, too. I don't think of myself as practicing eclectically.

ML: *But isn't it hard to describe your approach in a systematic or integrative way?*

BC: (Laughs) That's not something I have a problem with. So much of how we practice operates outside conscious awareness.

ML: *That doesn't mean it isn't highly organized.*

BC: That's exactly why I think working with the body is so important. So much of our psychological organization, our experience of wholeness, comes from our physical sense of being in the world.

ML: *I have a lot of questions about what it means to work with the body. I have only worked as a talk therapist, but I am very oriented to the body—to visceral experiences, to bodily reactions and shifts in myself and in my clients. I think of mental representations as emerging from bodily, emotional experiences. I think of our bodies as the primary way we relate to one another, especially to our most important others. Yet I don't consider myself a body psychotherapist.*

BC: I'm not sure I would agree. The way you talk about your work is exactly the way contemporary body psychotherapists are thinking and writing.

ML: *But I don't touch my clients as part of my work. If the term "body psychotherapy" has any meaning, distinct from "psychotherapy," direct contact with the body has to be part of the work, or at least an option. I don't think it's enough just to consider the body or to reference it.*

BC: I guess that's true. Body therapists are trained to use their eyes as much as their ears, and hands are understood as an extension of the eyes—another means of gathering information. Most body psychotherapists are trained to do something, usually with their hands, although interventions are by no means always hands on. We may suggest things for clients to try in their own bodies through movement or self-sensing or suggest shifting awareness to different areas of the body. There is probably more learning through doing in body therapies than traditional, more cognitively based approaches.

ML: *There's something directive going on, something active, which I think differs from standard "talk" therapies.*

BC: I would agree. There is a risk in body therapies of the therapist leading and doing too much.

ML: *I also see body psychotherapy as supporting a larger psychotherapeutic effort.*

BC: What do you mean?

ML: *Well, people come to us for help. We provide that help in the form of psychotherapy, and one technique might be direct body contact or awareness.*

BC: That's right. I think about what each of my clients needs, since I can work in a variety of ways, depending on those needs. To me it's all psychotherapy, whether I'm talking, or working with my hands, or asking for associations to a dream. I don't always work directly with the body, even if I'm pretty much always thinking or feeling in terms of the body. I'm a psychotherapist, first and foremost.

ML: *So how would you define psychotherapy? That would seem essential to eventually defining body psychotherapy.*

BC: It's hard to define psychotherapy concisely. I think the purpose is to expand people's capacities to relate differently to themselves and to others, to have more access to unconscious levels of experience and organization, and to experience internal, conflicting mental and emotional states. The point of psychotherapy is to deepen our capacities for sexual and aggressive urges, understanding sexuality and our somatic experience as creative, generative functions. Interpersonally, psychotherapy is meant to develop more of a capacity for entering another person's experience more fully and deeply without losing track of oneself, to encourage engagement in relationships that serve some kind of passionate function or meaning, and to foster relationships that can embrace and support differences and conflict.

ML: *And so body psychotherapy works toward those outcomes with a focus on body processes?*

BC: Any meaningful psychotherapy, I believe, has the combination of outcomes that I mentioned, both personal and interpersonal. Body psychotherapy adds a component of paying more systematic attention to bodily process and experiences as part of a person's primary psychological organization. It's a conscious awareness of our bodies as important sources of self-experience and self-understanding.

ML: *It sounds like a pretty essential part of getting to know ourselves. But aren't there times when body psychotherapy isn't helpful?*

BC: For starters, over the years I've come to the conclusion that body psychotherapy isn't a good idea if the therapist isn't already trained well in psychotherapy—and I don't just mean trained in bodywork. I mean trained in working directly with the body in support of psychotherapeutic aims. There are also plenty of times when a focus on the body isn't most useful for a particular client at a particular period in therapy—although I think even then it is always relevant for the therapist to be thinking of what is happening in the client's body.

ML: *What do you mean?*

BC: Take, for example, a client who is talking about an early life experience, perhaps one that is disturbing. I'm not likely to interrupt to ask him what he's aware of in his body or to suggest he do something with his body. That would probably interfere with his process and the way he's coming to articulate or understand something about himself, maybe even to understand what it means to be talking to me. At the same time, I will be paying attention to how his body moves or doesn't move as he's talking, how he is breathing. I will be looking for clues in his story for the ways he may have physically experienced that early time in his life and may be reexperiencing it as he speaks to me. This gives me a much richer picture of what it is like for him to live in his particular body. I can use that as a guide to understanding his experience—where he gets blocked, where he wants to grow.

ML: *That sounds a lot like what I do.*

BC: Right. Any therapist can think in this way without having to be a body psychotherapist. But in terms of hands-on work or being directive about body awareness, even for someone with that kind of training there are still times when I make a decision not to do bodywork when I think it won't be helpful. Some of it is a matter of timing. I don't work rigidly.

ML: *Say more about that.*

BC: In working with clients with bodily trauma, I am not likely to initiate touch or in any way "act upon" their bodies. These are bodies that have already been acted upon, often suddenly, intrusively, without explanation or consideration of impact. Thus, contact with me as the therapist can be too overwhelming and can generate more stimulation than the person can take in or make sense of. In those cases, simple, directed exercises, rather than touch, can help raise awareness in a more controlled way and can help the person activate a capacity to take initiative, which is often what a person loses when traumatized. It is important in working with trauma at a body level that the client has the opportunity to initiate action or direct physical contact, to be in charge of what happens with and to his or her body. The goal is for the person's body to gradually become a resource again, rather than a threat.

ML: *That's got to be a tough call, though. I think of clients who seem pretty together on the surface —and who in fact have lots going for them—and yet they have vulnerable spots that we stumble into without any warning.*

BC: I always proceed slowly before doing any bodywork. And even then I want to make sure we can still talk to one another—that the bodywork doesn't become a substitute for verbal communication or a way to avoid the difficulties we have relating to one another. I've too often seen therapists intervene with a body technique or touch to release emotions or relieve stress within the therapeutic relationship rather than explore it. I tend to introduce the possibility of direct work with the body as something I'm considering long before I actually do it. There is a dialogue that proceeds body-level interventions and a dialogue that follows it, which is very different from how I was originally trained.

ML: *For what other reasons might you not do bodywork as part of psychotherapy?*

BC: This may sound paradoxical, but I don't do hands-on work with clients who are primarily seeking physical comfort and nurturance. And I say this knowing how important touch is in our lives. But I think this kind of touching can be at cross-purposes with the psychotherapy.

ML: *Why is that?*

BC: Because when clients get that kind of comfort from their therapist, it reduces the need and capacity for self-exploration. It changes the treatment relationship from one that is challenging and exploring to one that is nurturing and calming—which may be healing in some ways, but it's not about learning. For clients who ask for bodywork because they want to be touched in a nurturing way, I suggest that they work with a good massage therapist or someone who does bodywork with a different purpose in mind. It's not a question of nurturing touch being bad. It's just that it's not a primary function of the psychotherapy contract. The primary function of touch in psychotherapy, certainly in body-centered psychotherapy, is to be instructive to the client's and therapist's understanding of what is happening in the body and what it means. Touch can be comforting or corrective, but that is not its primary function.

ML: *Are there other client situations in which you don't use bodywork or even directed exercises?*

BC: I don't do direct, hands-on work with someone who is actively psychotic, that is, with someone who is having a hard time differentiating between internal states of mind and external events and stimuli. I don't think bodywork is helpful for someone who doesn't have a clear understanding of the function of touch from a psychotherapeutic perspective. I see touch in psychotherapy as being primarily structuring, informative, enlivening, and activating. Touch has the capacity to evoke things about one's experience of self and others. But if a client sees the touch as meant to be calming or controlling or sexually arousing—anything that makes our relationship rigid and that shuts down exploration—then I think touch isn't helpful without careful discussions of meanings and expectations. The meanings and impact of touch cannot be taken for granted. We cannot assume that our intentions as therapists, whenever we are directive or take initiative, match the experience of our clients.

ML: *What about directed exercises, where you aren't touching the client?*

BC: Those can be helpful in many instances, but I don't think those kinds of suggestions for physical activity or sensory awareness are useful if they do not follow the client's immediate bodily experience, that is, if the exercises don't elaborate that emerging experience in some way. Some body-centered therapists—as I did too often in the past—tend to rely on their repertoire of body-centered activities, which essentially conform the client's body to those activities rather than the other way around. Ironically, the body becomes essentially disembodied with this kind of practice, because it comes out of the mental repertoire of the therapist; it becomes routinized, rather than emerging from the client's growing awareness of somatic impulses. I think when we rely too heavily on certain body-focused activities we bypass the client's emerging sense of self. We are then working against the psychotherapeutic process.

ML: *In those cases, it sounds as if the therapist may be anxious about what is emerging and may be falling back on familiar "techniques" as a way of managing the intensity.*

BC: Yes, and that's not any different than what we may do as talk therapists when things get too intense. Body-centered work at its best is carefully attentive, subtle, and follows the client's process in the here and now. Reich vividly described the therapist's attention to the client's patterns of breathing, movement, and interpersonal relating that brought the person and the process either more to life or to become more defended/deadened. For Reich, the therapist worked attentively at the border of the enlivening and deadening processes that emerged in each session.

ML: *That reminds me of something the analyst Betty Joseph (1993) wrote: "One cannot help patients break out of the old methods of operating . . . except by following minute movements of emergence and retreat, experiencing and avoiding" (p. 96).*

BC: Indeed! Reich could have written that himself. Joseph addresses the tension between enlivening and deadening. It's constant, inevitable in psychotherapy. The therapist, whether working at a body level or not, needs to attend to both emergence and retreat, to use Joseph's language. Treatment modalities tend to split, favoring attention to one side of the coin or the other. Humanistic models tend to emphasize the support of emergence while often distracting from or avoiding the depth and power of retreat. Some analytic and many neo-Reichian models tend to emphasize the identification and interpretation of retreat/defense while minimizing the potentials of emergence, what Berne called "physis" (which Berne himself tended to ignore). When we know how to look and notice, we can literally see and experience the patterns, the struggles, between emergence and retreat in the bodies of both client and therapist.

ML: *Well, as a talk therapist, I ask this next question with some trepidation: Do you think there are psychotherapeutic outcomes that cannot be achieved without body psychotherapy?*

BC: I think it's partly an issue of efficiency. When a goal of psychotherapy is to facilitate a person's experience of being physically active in the world, with his or her body as an active and useful component of self-experience and self-understanding, then direct interventions with the body are the most efficient way of getting there. Traditional modes of psychotherapy—what you're calling "talk" therapy—aren't effective at promoting true sensorimotor learning or reorganization. If the body gets any attention at all in traditional psychotherapy, it's more an observed body than a working body.

ML: *The latter being a more direct experience compared to the observed body, which is more conceptual, one step removed?*

BC: Exactly. A working body, not just a working mind. The advantage of body psychotherapy—of working directly with the body as well as the mind—is that you develop a sense of self as having an exploratory body as well as an exploratory mind, an organizing body as well as an organizing mind. There is a tendency in transactional analysis for practitioners to think that working with the body means working with or within the Child ego state. I think that healthy Adult ego state functioning includes a connection to the body, awareness of the meanings of somatic reactions and patterns, and the capacity to *move* and *act* as well as to think. Working with the body is a primary means of working with the Adult ego state.

ML: *Can you give an example?*

BC: Take relationships—we can learn a lot by talking about them. Yet there is another level, deeply held in the body, that often doesn't shift with just talking. This is what Berne referred to as the tissue level of the psyche and the protocol level of script formation. Words—even someone else's understanding those words—often aren't enough to reach us deeply. But when we are able to use our bodies to press into one another, to move away from each other, when we are able to use our arms to reach, to connect, to push away, to stop—it evokes a whole other kind of organization that is profound. It gives us a whole new access to our sense of self with others.

ML: *The conceptual becomes embodied.*

BC: That's right. We can talk about being inhibited, or reaching, or grasping—but when we do those things with our actual hands, arms, and bodies, we access another kind of learning, one that operates at the sensorimotor level because it happens in the body. Sensory-somatic experience facilitates understanding at the cognitive and affective levels, too.

In good psychotherapy, as things change, people become more conscious of their different impulses. If they are living in an environment (outside the therapeutic setting) that welcomes those impulses, learning to act on them may happen quickly. But that kind of welcoming is not a fact of most people's lives. Too often, the people around them and their day-to-day environments support the status quo much more than change. Exploration and change are often met with opposition, disapproval, and shame. So if those kinds of active experiences can be had with the body therapist, the changes are internalized more quickly, more deeply because they are now part of the body's process, not just ideas.

ML: *What might that look like?*

BC: I worked with a woman who knew what she didn't want but not what she wanted. Talking about it was getting us nowhere. But when we worked directly with her bodily experience of not wanting—people talk of wanting as if it comes from the mind instead of the body—that force in her body, the force of not wanting, changed from her idea of it being something negative, a defect or defense, to the felt sense of a positive activity. Her not wanting was active. And once she could experience that, she could begin to expand that active sense into areas of more obvious wanting. But it had to come from a direct experience in her body. It didn't work for her as just an idea.

ML: *That brings to mind my own experience with tango dancing, which isn't framed as a psychotherapeutic activity, but which has still pushed into and against so many areas of vulnerability for me: relationships, especially with women, belonging as an individual in a community, having a sense of my own center and grounding, letting others publicly see what moves me erotically (and how I move erotically)—all of these were just ideas I didn't know how to address in standard talk therapy. But the discipline of the dancing provided me with a way to move through many painful experiences productively. I've seen a spillover in other areas of my life—at work, in my community. I had to have this sense of myself in my body in order to move past some of my psychological barriers.*

BC: Yes, that's it exactly, and all without paying the fees of a psychotherapist! When I teach about sensorimotor learning, I like to use the example of learning how to ski through my body. When I tried to learn skiing by remembering techniques in my mind, it was impossible. I was inept. When I learned by imitating someone's moving body, I "got" it.

ML: *What you've described gives me a sense of the limits of my own practice as a talk therapist. There are a number of things I will not be able to help my clients achieve if I just work with words.*

BC: Not to minimize what you do offer, but yes, I'd have to say that's true. That is partly what has kept me continually opening and refining the way I practice.

ML: *I know there are a lot of bodywork trainings out there, not all of them supporting body psychotherapy as you've defined it here. How would you evaluate a training program that would give me at the least the beginning of the kinds of skills you've defined here?*

BC: This is an important question. I am very leery of body therapy training programs that are technique centered or named after the trainer. For that matter, when I see any training program named after the leader or that only uses the theories of one or two people, I figure it's more of a religion, so I run the other way. More seriously though, technique-centered trainings (and there are a lot of them) overly focus the therapist on having to do something and do not pay enough attention to the internal experience of the client and dynamics between the client and therapist. I think every body therapist needs to have a clear theoretical frame of reference, a theory about why one might use touch in psychotherapy, along with the developmental aspects of touch, the functions of touch, and of physical contact over a lifetime. With that, I think the therapist needs direct experience with the different forms and functions of touch.

ML: *What you're describing sounds so basic.*

BC: It is. Body psychotherapy doesn't require a lot of complicated maneuvers. Those can be useful, but they first have to be grounded in a solid sense of how people function psychophysiologically and how they might respond to the use of touch in a manner that facilitates psychotherapy. For example, just sticking with the basic practice of touch, how can the therapist learn to match different styles of touch and contact to clients' different developmental needs, all with the goal of promoting self-awareness through touch?

ML: *I guess it's similar to learning how different clients make use of our asking questions or making statements—so much depends on where each person is psychologically or developmentally.*

BC: The therapist also has to learn the difference between touching and being touched. When a therapist is initiating touch, he or she is also being touched. There are times when the client is the one who needs to initiate or define the touching, not the therapist. Touch is a two-way process.

ML: *Similar to the way we think of transference and countertransference?*

BC: Touch is part of a complex, relational process. So a therapist's training would include recognizing the unconscious components of touch, the discrepancies between conscious intention and unconscious motivation, the client's reception of and not-always-conscious attribution of meaning to the touch.

ML: *It sounds like you're saying the therapist needs a psychodynamic understanding of the work, in which touch is just one component.*

BC: That is what I'm saying, in the sense that I think a psychodynamic orientation is the best way we have of working with very complex human processes. A body-centered therapist must have a strong grounding in character theory and some working understanding of unconscious processes. A body therapist has to have a theory of the mind as well as a theory of the body. I would also want a therapist to be exposed to multiple modalities of touch, to different theoretical frames of reference. Otherwise, it's too easy to get locked into one set of ideas and set of techniques.

ML: *That last requirement seems a bit much for a beginning body psychotherapist.*

BC: Perhaps. But I also think that we need to set expectations for what mature practice will look like and what we will need in terms of continuing education. It's not enough just to get a two-year certificate.

ML: *It's one of the hardest things to convey about practicing as a psychotherapist—the way we have to keep learning. Bill, thanks so much for taking this time to talk.*

REFERENCE

Joseph, B. (1993). Toward the experiencing of psychic pain. In M. Feldman & E. B. Spillus (Eds.), *Psychic equilibrium and psychic change: Selected papers of Betty Joseph* (pp. 88-97). London: Routledge.

The original version of this chapter was published in the Transactional Analysis Journal, *Volume 37, Number 4, pp. 256-262, October 2007.*

Babies, Brains, and Bodies: Somatic Foundations of the Child Ego State

William F. Cornell

> Babies were never like pathological adults.... If pathology is not infantile, then patients cannot be thought of as babies. Pathology develops in an individual who has been experiencing the world longer than the infant has.... Thinking that pathology is a linear outcome of an infantile/child experience is, as Kagan (1998) put it, a seductive idea but one that is incorrect. Adults are not infants, and pathology is not infantile—it is "adultile." (Tronick, 2001, p. 189)

Babies and brains have been getting a good deal of attention in the laboratory over the past few decades. Contemporary neurophysiological research and studies of infant/parent interaction are leading to radical revisions of theories of psychic development with equally radical implications regarding the nature of the psychotherapeutic process with adults.

In this chapter I hope to convey some of the clinical and theoretical implications of such research for Eric Berne's model of the Child ego state, which is at the heart of the clinical practice of transactional analysis. Although Berne developed his theory of ego states as an extension of the work of Federn (1952) and the brain research carried out by Penfield (1952), the clinical corollaries Berne based on Penfield's speculations no longer hold up. Taking this into account and drawing on my understanding of current research and my experience as both a transactional analyst and a body-centered psychotherapist, I will suggest a significant revision of what transactional analysis therapists have come to think of as the Child ego state.

Most clinical writing in the transactional analysis literature emphasizes the historical, fixated, and regressive nature of Child ego state functions. Parallel to this emphasis on the nature of the Child ego state are the models (or metaphors) of the therapeutic relationship, common among transactional analysts, as some sort of parenting, corrective, or compensatory relationship intended to be responsive to the traumas and environmental failures of childhood. In this chapter, I hope to demonstrate the limits and errors of conceiving of the Child ego state as a fixated repository of childhood experiences and as the infrastructure for characterological games and defensive scripts. I will also challenge the corrective/compensatory models of therapeutic relationships that seem to be an outgrowth of an out-of-date conceptualization of the Child ego state.

I do not deny regressive aspects of some Child ego state patterns, but in my view there are also powerful progressive and exploratory functions to those aspects of the human psyche that we transactional analysts have come to label "the Child ego state." I have come to think that it is a fundamental error to conceptualize the Child ego state as a repository of historical experience. I now understand that the level of mental organization transactional analysts call "the Child ego state" forms subconsciously and unconsciously within a matrix of emotionally and somatically based motivational forces that are organized and reorganized throughout the course of one's life. I suggest that what we have come to call "the Child ego state" involves subsymbolic (Bucci, 1997a, 1997b, 2001) neural, emotional, and sensorimotor processes that are crucial forms of psychic development and organization.

These processes are perhaps not best conceptualized as states of the ego or even as functions of the ego but are better understood within some of the more recently emergent language in the transactional analysis literature, such as activation states (Hine, 1997, personal communication 18 October 2001) or states of mind (Allen, 2000).

I want to emphasize at the start of this chapter that baby and brain research is unfolding at an extraordinarily rapid rate (Emde, 1999; Fonagy, 1999, 2001; Lachmann, 2001; Lyons-Ruth, 1998, 1999; Panksepp, 1993, 2001; Tronick, 1998, 2001). While I am not an expert in either field, I have been reading in both for many years as a fascinated clinician, drawing on a now rather distant academic background. The clinical implications are exciting, but since clinicians are in the earliest stages of digesting this work, its generalizability to psychotherapy with adults is not at all clear. Green (2000), among others, offers an especially compelling critique of the too-literal applications of mother/infant research. Similarly, Panksepp (2001), a psychobiological researcher with decades of experience, cautions, "Despite remarkable advances in neuroscience and psychology during the past few decades, our attempts to relate core psychological processes to neural processes remains rudimentary" (p. 139). Therefore, this chapter is speculative in intent, falling far short of a definitive statement. With these caveats in mind, I offer the following musings about babies, brains, and bodies in order to raise important questions and thus contribute to the evolution of ego state theory in transactional analysis.

The Roots of Transactional Analysis in Ego Psychology

Berne's own training in the late 1940s and early 1950s was in psychoanalysis, which was then dominated in the United States by models of ego psychology, a departure from the drive theories of classical Freudian analysis. In fact, Paul Federn and Erik Erikson, Berne's two training analysts, were among the leading theoreticians of the ego psychology movement at that time.

In the glossary of terms in Berne's (1947) first book, *The Mind in Action,* which he wrote when he still identified with psychoanalysis, Berne defined ego this way:

[It is] that part of the mind which is in contact with the outside world on the one hand and with the Id and the Superego on the other. It attempts to keep thoughts, judgments, interpretations, and behavior practical and efficient in accordance with the Reality Principle. Here we have used the word somewhat inexactly as almost synonymous with the conscious part of the mind. (p. 303)

In the body of the text itself, writing in his typically more informal fashion, Berne characterizes the ego as "a system which in some mysterious way can look at itself" (p. 66). When *The Mind in Action* was revised in 1968, with Berne now famous for creating transactional analysis, sections on TA were included, and Berne added a definition of ego states to the glossary. However, his definitions and descriptions of the ego in both glossary and text remained unchanged. In contrast, Freud's own understanding of the ego and its functions was complex and changed over the course of his writings (Laplanche & Pontalis, 1973, pp. 130-143). The understanding of the ego as "an agency of adaptation which differentiates itself from the id on contact with external reality" (p.130) was brought to the United States before and after World War II by immigrant analysts. The ego psychology school of psychoanalysis became dominant in the United States through the middle of the twentieth century.

In leaving psychoanalysis to create transactional analysis, Berne sought to create a metapsychology and a therapeutic process that were more interpersonal and phenomenological than the dominant analytic models of his day. Nevertheless, his new model was based squarely within the tenets of ego psychology. Reviewing Berne's theory of the ego and ego states, Rath (1993) concluded that "ego psychology represents the basis of the theory of personality structure and dynamics in transactional analysis" (p. 209). Today this grounding in ego psychology seems taken for granted by transactional analysts, even as they graft on subsequent (and often contradictory) psychoanalytic models, such as self psychology, object relations, and attachment theories.

The Problematic Child Ego State

The tenets of ego psychology served much of Berne's efforts quite well, but he ran into trouble with the limits of this model as he attempted to delineate what he first called "the archeopsyche," and subsequently described as "the Child ego state." The Child ego state, as conceptualized by Berne, has been the problem child of transactional analysis theory from the beginning. Berne himself never resolved his understanding of the Child ego state, and his writings about the Child are full of contradictions.

Berne's varying descriptions of the archeopsyche and the Child ego state created a theoretical hash that has profoundly affected clinical assumptions and techniques ever since Berne's original writings. The concept of a psychic organ suggests a capacity of the mind with a sense of the potential for action, whereas the concept of an ego state suggests a structure within the mind with a sense of fixation. Although Berne tended to use the terms "archeopsyche" and "Child" almost interchangeably, I think that the archeopsyche conceived as a "psychic organ" is a more inclusive concept that can incorporate some of the aspects of mental development that I will discuss in this chapter. In fact, with his idea of the Child, Berne hypothesized a supposed state of the ego that was founded in realms of experience that I suggest are far more accurately described as both pre-ego and sub-ego, that is, preceding the developmental capacities for ego organization and underlying the functions of the ego throughout the course of life.

Berne's conceptualization of ego states evolved during the writing of a series of early papers in the late 1950s, which were collected together after his death and published as *Intuition and Ego States* (Berne, 1977). However, even then, before he had articulated the transactional analysis model, his efforts to distinguish between the archeopsyche as a mental capacity and the Child ego state as a more clearly bounded mental/emotional structure were already in trouble. The Child ego state was presented as a sort of homunculus of the past, seated in the brain: "The Child in the individual is potentially capable of contributing to his personality exactly what a happy actual child is capable of contributing to family life" (p. 149). Later, in *Transactional Analysis in Psychotherapy,* Berne (1961) put it this way:

> When a previously buried archaic ego state is revived in its full vividness in the waking state, it is then permanently at the disposal of the patient and the therapist for detailed examination. Not only do "abreaction" and "working through" take place, but the ego state can be treated like an actual child. It can be nurtured carefully, even tenderly, until it unfolds like a flower, revealing all the complexities of its internal structure. (p. 226)

This version of the Child ego state seems to suggest a sort of resident child in the adult client's psyche and a visiting child in the psychotherapist's office. The clinical consequences of Berne's creation of direct parallels between the Child ego state and childhood and his reification of the Child ego state as a virtual little being in the brain have been theoretically rather troublesome, to put it mildly.

Confusion about the nature of the Child ego state is intensified in Berne's more colloquial style of writing within the texts themselves. For example, in 1972 Berne wrote:

> Each person carries within a little boy or little girl, who feels, thinks, acts, talks, and responds just the way he or she did when he or she was a child of a certain age. This ego state is called the Child. The Child is not regarded as "childish" or "immature," which are Parental words, but as childlike, meaning like a child at a certain age, and the important factor here is the age, which may be anywhere between two and five years in ordinary circumstances. It is important for the individual to understand his Child, not only because it is going to be with him all his life, but also because it is the most valuable part of his personality. (p. 12)

Here we have conceptual confusion and a reification of the Child ego state as an actual childlike presence and as childhood remnants within the adult psyche, remnants that can be both fixated (on a bad day?) and precious (on a good day?). Also, we have in this formulation the crucial, formative years of the Child ego state identified as two to five, when the developing youngster is becoming motorically and linguistically autonomous and does, indeed, have the beginnings of true ego functions. Significantly, however, much of Berne's writing seems to ignore the significance of the years from birth to two, which are emerging in current brain and infant research as crucial to psychological development as well as to the psychotherapeutic process.

In contrast to some of his more informal, colloquial writings, the formal definitions of the Child ego state Berne presented in his books were more consistent. "[The] Child ego state is a set of feelings, attitudes and behavior patterns which are relics of the individual's own childhood," stood as the original definition provided in *Transactional Analysis in Psychotherapy* (Berne, 1961, p. 77). In *Principles of Group Treatment* (Berne, 1966), he defined the Child ego state as "an ego state which is an archaic relic from an early significant period of life" (p. 362). And in *What Do You Say After You Say Hello?* (Berne, 1972), he wrote that the Child is "an archaic ego state. The Adapted Child follows Parental directives. The Natural Child is autonomous" (p. 442). (One wonders how an ego state can be simultaneously archaic and autonomous.)

Many transactional analysis clinicians have emphasized the archaic, fixated, defensive functions of the Child. Rath (1993) extended this perspective as follows:

The archeopsychic or Child ego state (colloquially called Child) is defined by the set of inadequate (pathological) states of the ego displayed in thoughts, feelings, and behaviors, which manifest themselves in the here-and-now during the development of the elements stored in the archeopsyche and which are, from the phenomenological point of view, regressive elements and psychic reactions of earlier stages (of development). (p. 210)

Erskine (1988), in a similar fashion, has argued:

The archaic state of the ego is the result of developmental arrest which occurred when critical early childhood needs for contact were not met. The child's defenses against the discomfort of unmet needs became egotized—fixated; the experience cannot be fully integrated into the Adult ego state until these defense mechanisms are dissolved. (p. 17)

According to this view, the archeopsyche/Child is viewed as a kind of storage container for archaic psychopathology, seemingly more of a container for weeds than the tenderly unfolding flowers sometimes suggested by Berne.

Clarkson and her colleagues at the Metanoia Institute (Clarkson & Fish, 1988; Clarkson & Gilbert, 1988) struggled perhaps the most mightily among transactional analysis practitioners with the theoretical dilemmas created by Berne's writings about the Child. Clarkson (1992) wrote:

Ego states were initially conceived of as vividly available temporal recordings of past events with the concomitant meaning and feelings which are maintained in potential existence within the personality (Berne, 1980/1961: 19). However, he distinguishes from this multitude of Child ego states: (1) Child as archaic ego states and (2) Child as fixated ego states. . . . Child ego states might be better referred to as "historical ego states" since a person's vivid experiences of today will be stored in natural psychological epochs, archaic by tomorrow. (pp. 44-45)

Although in this conceptualization the Child is still understood as a phenomenological repository of the experiences of history consistent with Berne's basic definitions and his emphasis on childhood, we also see some effort to resolve the question of how the Child can be viewed both as fixated, adapted, and autonomous in function and expression.

Transactional analysis theoreticians and clinicians have been aware of this quandary for a long time now, but it has yet to be resolved satisfactorily. Some have challenged the conceptualization of the Child as an archaic, fixated ego state. Schiff and her colleagues (Schiff et al., 1975), for example, viewed the Child this way: "The Child ego state is the source of all energy and is in control of cathexis. . . . Psychopathology can be thought of as the development of adaptations which control the Child as opposed to the Child controlling the adaptations" (p. 26).

Goulding and Goulding (1979) argued, "Some TA therapists believe that the Child ego state stops developing at an early age. We see the Child as ever growing and ever developing, as the sum total of the experiences he has had and is having in the present. . . . The Child develops. We have stressed that the *Child* does the work. The Child both experiences and copies, and then incorporates" (p. 20).

Blackstone (1993) extended the argument for the activity and changeability of the Child ego state and presented a model of the intrapsychic dynamics of the Child, drawing on object relations theories.

I am not arguing that it is mistaken to include historical and fixated elements within the definition of the Child ego state. Rather, I suggest that an emphasis on these elements does not sufficiently account for the nature of the Child ego state and that continued reliance on Berne's definitions maintains a serious limitation in theory and a significant bias in clinical work.

Implicit and Explicit Knowing

Our earliest means of learning and mental organization occur at the level of subsymbolic, sensorimotor, and affective experience that cannot be accurately described as states or functions of the ego. These realms of organization developmentally precede the capacities of the ego and underlie/accompany/inform/shape/color the nature of the Child, Adult, and Parent ego states throughout the course of life. Seen from the perspective of current neurophysiological and memory research, the psychological states of organization that transactional analysis calls "the Child ego state" does not develop until the middle of the second year of life. An immense amount of enduring learning is occurring in those first 18 months of life and throughout the life span through avenues other than the functions of the ego.

Brain and memory researchers (McClelland, 1998; Milner, Squire, & Kandel, 1998), while often using different terminologies, are converging on a quite consistent differentiation of implicit (procedural) and explicit (declarative) memory processes. Implicit memory precedes the evolution of explicit memory, which requires cortical functions that develop later. Implicit memory is not replaced by explicit memory but continues to operate in parallel with explicit memory, providing the unthought realms of knowing. Siegel (2001) summarizes contemporary research this way:

> The process of memory and those of development are closely aligned. For the first year of life, the infant has available an "implicit" form of memory that includes emotional, behavioral, perceptual, and perhaps bodily (somatosensory) forms of memory.... When implicit memories are activated, they do not have an internal sensation that something is being recalled. They merely influence our emotions, behaviors, or perceptions directly, in the here and now, without our awareness of their connection to some experience from the past.
>
> By the middle of the second year, children begin to develop a second form of memory, "explicit" memory (Bauer, 1996). Explicit memory includes two major forms: factual (semantic) and autobiographical ("episodic") (Tulving, Kapur, Craik, Moscovitch, & Houle, 1994). For both types of explicit memory, recollection is associated with an internal sensation of "I am recalling something now." (p. 74)

The felt sense of implicit memory is captured in Bollas's (1987) now famous phrase, the "unthought known." Implicit knowledge is formed and sustained through somatic activity and emotional experience. As summarized by Pally (2000), implicit memory is understood as memory for aspects of experience, historical and current, that are not processed consciously, that is, patterns of learning and experience that influence functioning but are not experienced as conscious remembering. Kihlstrom (1990) and Izard (1993) define a broader range of forms of implicit cognitions, which includes perception, memory, and learning. These realms of implicit experience and learning are also taken up and extended within models of both research and clinical practice by Bucci (1997a, 1997b) as subsymbolic processes, Ogden (1989) as the autistic-contiguous mode, Mitrani (1996) as unmentalized experience, Tronick (1998) and Lyons-Ruth (1998, 1999) as implicit relational knowing, Sharar-Levy (2001) as emotive motor memory clusters, and La Barre (2000) as nonverbal behavior.

Berne's writings about the Child ego state and script theory were primarily rooted in explicit memory, although what he defined as the script protocol is more reflective of implicit memory. Current transactional analysis perspectives based in attachment and empathic attunement models reach back into realms of implicit memory, although these have little to say about the infant's sensory, affective, and motor organization (i.e., the baby in relation to his or her own body, outside of relational experiences). In articles on the implications of neurodevelopmental research for transactional analysis, Allen (1999, 2000) also discussed the relevance of implicit and explicit memory for transactional analysis theory:

> Implicit memory develops earlier than explicit memory. It is nonverbal and nonsymbolic, but it is not less rich or more primitive. It is not replaced by explicit knowledge. It involves how we

feel and is a major element in relationships. Complicated music is understood implicitly. (Allen, 2000, p. 262)

It is important to note that implicit, nonverbal, subsymbolic experiences are not limited to the first year of life. They are constant elements in the psychic organization of experience, coexisting side by side with explicit and declarative realms of experience in the here and now. Life that can be languaged is not necessarily healthier, richer, or more mature; it simply has a different kind of psychic organization. Healthy functioning requires both implicit and explicit knowing, subsymbolic/nonverbal and symbolic levels of organization. A complete psychotherapy must work within both levels of mental organization. While it is certainly a primary therapeutic task to foster the development of the capacity for symbolic and verbal representation, it is not necessarily true that sensate and subsymbolic experience is in some way regressed and pathological or will be improved by the achievement of symbolic or languaged knowing. Just consider how societies build museums and concert halls for the work of those who are able to carry us through sensation, sight, and sound into unthought and unlanguaged realms of experience.

In actual life and in psychotherapy, the realms of implicit knowing and subsymbolic experience can simultaneously contain elements of past, present, and future. I offer a case example to illustrate. Ben, an accomplished physicist, began individual therapy as an adjunct to marital therapy. Both he and his wife had engaged in extramarital relationships at the time their youngest child entered college. While the marital crisis had precipitated therapy, Ben's attention quickly turned to the pervasive deadness in all aspects of his life. The brief but intense sexual liaison with a new partner had startled him with an experience of his own vitality and passion. "Most of the time," Ben said, "I'm so dead to the world, lost in my head, that I could fall off the edge of the world and not notice."

Therapy proved extremely difficult. Sessions were filled with bitter and deadening complaints about himself, his marriage, his work, his colleagues, me, the therapy. "Just what was it that I am paying you for?" was the disdainful question that ended most sessions. My efforts at observation, confrontation, or empathic elaboration were typically met with some version of "I think we already know that one. Perhaps you could come up with something new the next time we meet." His impatience and disdain colored everything. He saw no purpose in talking about his parents or his history, as he "knew all of that already." I found it increasingly difficult to speak. I did not know what to speak about as our talking seemed useless. I wondered to myself how it was that I found myself so often speechless in the presence of a man I both liked and admired, whom I was also quite certain felt considerable regard and affection toward me.

Then one evening I ran into Ben and his wife at a baroque concert. He opened the next session with, "I feel a bit silly saying this, but I was watching you during the concert. You never sat still. It was like you were dancing in your seat. What was going on in you?" Rather hesitantly I replied, "I can't listen to that music and sit still. I don't think that music was written to settle people down. I think it was written to inspire people, to move them. It moves me, and I move when I'm moved." Then Ben asked, "What goes on inside of you when you listen to music?" "I think I'm supposed to ask you that sort of question," I parried. "I asked you first," Ben persisted. I told him, describing body sensations, dancing in my seat, humming aloud, feeling a range of emotions, imagining what the original rooms and audiences looked like, wishing at moments I had a sort of belief in a god that seemed to inspire that sort of music, anger at my parents for never letting me learn to play an instrument, wondering if the performers traveled with their lovers or if some of them slept with each other. "What," I then asked Ben, "goes on inside of you?" "I analyze the structure of the music and try to see the notes on the page. Quite a contrast, huh? It's what I do with every aspect of my life. I analyze it and kill it."

"Kill it." Suddenly the session was filled with memories, sensations, and images of Ben's childhood: the deadness of his parents; his inability to somehow move them; his desperate and ultimately bitter wish to somehow touch and inspire his parents (and then his wife); the atmosphere created by his mother's depression and bitterness, which was ever present and always unspoken; and his father's constant withdrawal and solitude, including images of HIS father sitting alone at the breakfast table to start his day and finishing alone in the garden reading the newspaper. Ben felt how he himself was killing off so much of his life—killing his own vitality—that the deadness of which he so often complained was of his own making. Like his parents, Ben was a "killer." He now knew why he was in therapy.

This example illustrates both the regressive and progressive aspects of the Child ego state. Rarely in psychotherapy do we create new patterns of emotional and relational processes for the future without first circuiting back, if even briefly, into memories of the past (perhaps a powerful factor in why it has been so easy to equate the Child ego state with actual childhood and psychopathology). As we wrestle in psychotherapy with wishes for a future different from the past, the possibilities of the future seem inextricably bound up and blinded by the strictures of the past. Dropping into the realm of sensory experience that our discussion of the baroque concert opened up for him threw Ben back in time into a wealth of visceral/sensate/visual memories and threw him forward into a realm of unthought desires that had long seemed unthinkable, foolish, and impossible. Would I suggest that this conversation and the subsequent therapy brought him out of a Child ego state into an Adult ego state (an integrated or integrating Adult, as is often suggested in current transactional analysis theory)? I would not. Rather, I think these experiences strengthened his Adult ego state, deepening his self-reflective capacities. I would also suggest that these experiences strengthened his Child ego state functions in the here and now, providing an intensification and enrichment of his sensate and emotional capacities. I see these somatic experiences as inherent to the nature of the Child ego state, not simply as remnants of childhood but as current and constant accompaniments of other aspects of psychic and interpersonal functioning.

Emotion and the Brain

I have come to understand the Child ego state in procedural rather than structural and historical terms, which is to say, as a coherent and enduring system of organization and motivation. This system has deep, often compelling, historical roots, but it is a system that lives and changes in the present. The complexities and apparent contradictions of the simultaneously old and current elements in our emotional reactions are examined by Levenson (1999), who asked, "Is the human emotion system a masterpiece of design or the ultimate kludge?" (p. 482). He answered this way:

This conundrum results from the fact that of all of the building blocks that make up human beings, some of the evolutionarily oldest as well as some of the newest, are found in the emotion system. This confluence of old and new makes an extremely complex system, one that often serves us extremely well as we navigate the stresses, challenges and opportunities of life, but at other times bedevils and plagues us, even undermining our health. (p. 482)

The implications of this two-system design of the brain, as discussed in such pivotal books as Lichtenberg (1989), Schore (1994), LeDoux (1996), Bucci (1997a), Damasio (1999), and Pally (2000), as well as in countless articles in professional journals, have profoundly deepened and altered my understanding of the nature of the psychotherapeutic project in general and, as I attempt to address in this chapter, of the Child ego state in particular.

Berne developed a theory and therapy of primarily the conscious mind, with ego states as manifestations of different levels and kinds of consciousness. Like most ego psychologists of his era, he viewed emotions and affect with ambivalence, suspicious of their disruptive, regressive, irrational qualities. But things have changed since then! Levenson (1999), for example, offered a contrasting perspective that is rich in its clinical implications:

Emotion appears to function as a master choreographer, the ultimate *organizer* of disparate response systems. Emotion orchestrates the action of multiple response systems so that they act in a unified way in the service of solving problems. This view of emotion as an organizer stands in stark contrast to the oft-expressed view of emotion as a *disorganizer* or *disrupter*. In this latter view, emotion is the enemy of purposeful behavior and rational thought. (p. 495)

Likewise, Emde (1999) challenged the long-held biases of classical psychoanalysts and ego psychologists about affect and emotion to emphasize that "affective processes enhance developmental change in an everyday sense, not just at times of transition, and they are linked to cognitive processes" (p. 323).

Panksepp (2001) pushed this perspective on the organizing and motivating functions of emotions even further, concluding in language that is uncannily familiar to transactional analysts:

Because emotionality is remarkably ancient in brain evolution, there is every reason to believe that the underlying brain systems served as a foundation for the emergence of basic social and cognitive abilities. The basic emotion systems of the brain imbue environmental events with values (i.e., "valence tagging"), and deficiencies in emotions may lead to psychiatric problems characterized by distinct cognitive and social idiosyncrasies. In developing infants such processes may be psychologically decisive. Infants may fundamentally project their emotions into the world, and initially assimilate cognitive structures only in highly affective ways. . . . The rich interpretation of emotions and cognitions establishes the major psychic scripts for each child's life. (p. 141)

How do we reconcile these views of the role of emotion and affect in the organization of the brain and the motivation of behavior with the ego state model of transactional analysis? This is not an easy task as the ego state model now stands. Clearly, the researchers just cited see emotion as rooted in the very earliest stages of life, but this is quite different from seeing it as fixated or archaic. They suggest that emotions and affective states shape and inform cognition throughout the life span. Does Berne's (1961) definition of the Adult ego state as "characterized by an autonomous set of feelings, attitudes and behavior patterns which are adapted to current reality" (p. 76) or the subsequent theoretical elaborations of an integrated or integrating Adult ego state adequately embrace the models of emotion and cognition that these researchers describe? I think not. I see the Child ego state as a matrix of emotionally, somatically based organizing and motivating systems. Grounded in sensorimotor and implicit, procedural forms of knowledge, the Child provides systems of organization and motivation quite distinct from Adult and Parent states of the ego.

Movement and Sensorimotor Organization

One thing that babies and brains have in common is that they are firmly and permanently attached to a body, although the actions and organization of this body receive remarkably little attention in clinical theorizing. As one of the consistent voices on behalf of considering the body in theory (not to mention the consulting room), Boadella (1997) reminded psychotherapists, "Every patient brings to the session not only his problems but also his body: he can never leave it behind, even if he forgets it's his (as in depersonalization); or treats it as a mechanical object (as in the schizoid process); or as a source of threat (as in hypochondria)" (p. 33).

Significantly, the psychological and relational significance of sensorimotor organization and activity is now receiving attention in the body-centered literature (Boadella, 1997; Downing, 1996; Frank, 2001; Marcher, 1996; Rothschild, 2000). Within the transactional analysis literature, there have been a few writers who have touched on the sensorimotor realms (Ligabue, 1991; Steere, 1981, 1985; Waldekranz-Piselli, 1999). Downing speaks to the rather obvious but often overlooked fact that for the infant, the body is the means, the vehicle, to all that is outside. Seen from a developmental perspective, the inattention in clinical theory to sensorimotor processes is a curious oversight, one that reflects a long history of bias against and blindness about the body within psychology and psychoanalysis, many philosophical traditions, and countless religions. This position associates the brain with the mind while setting the body and mind in opposition.

Researchers Thelen and Fogel (1989) threw down a conceptual gauntlet:

Developmentalists, like other psychologists, have been concerned primarily with the formation of the complex symbolic and affective processes of the "life of the mind" and have paid less attention to the translation of ideas into movement—a "life of the limbs." Infants, however, are born with much movement and few ideas and, for the first year or so, lack symbolic and verbal mediating mechanisms between their mental state and the expressions of their bodies and limbs. At this stage of the life cycle, then, the link between the developing mind and the developing limbs may be especially direct. We see this formulation in no way competing with theories that focus more directly on mental structures but rather as a complement and supplement to understanding the development of cognition. (p. 23)

A substantial body of research has been developed within the general rubric of "dynamic motor theory," which suggests that many psychological phenomena presumed to arise from brain processes may actually develop more fundamentally from the activities of the muscles and limbs (Fischer & Hogan, 1989), that is, that the movements of the body organize and reorganize the brain.

Fischer and Hogan (1989) described the unfolding of levels of cognitive development linked to the sequencing of sensorimotor competencies. In the first weeks of life, the infant has a limited repertoire of reflex movements—such as turning his or her head to orient toward the mother's face—that come quickly under voluntary control. By 10 to 11 weeks babies have the capacity to carry out a limited but flexible sensorimotor sequence of action, such as following a ball with his or her gaze while opening a hand and extending an arm in the direction of the moving ball (in contrast to a singular movement of one part of the body). Sensorimotor activities quickly reach more complex layers of activities, or "mappings," and by the end of the first year have become flexible systems of sensorimotor competencies, such as "complex systems of sensorimotor actions: infant moves a rattle in different ways to see different parts of it" (p. 280). Not until sometime between 18 to 24 months are young children able to translate complex sensorimotor systems into representational systems (i.e., a child can pretend a doll is walking, walk the doll, and say, "Doll walk"). As Boadella (1997) observed, "The movement vocabulary of the child, during the first year and a half, is the foundation of his communicative rapport with the world: he interacts by means of motoric and vocal signs long before there is the capacity for semantic use of language" (p. 33). Call (1984) referred to this process as the "grammar of experience," by which he suggested that the development of language is grounded in the sensorimotor organization of the infant and toddler in relation to caregivers and the physical world.

Downing (1996), drawing on the work of Winnicott, Stern, Mahler, and others in particularly creative ways, writes with clarity and specificity about the importance of sensorimotor organization in the patterns of infant/parent interactions and its significance for adult psychotherapy. He stresses the importance of the infant's development of "affectmotor schemas" and "affectmotor beliefs" that are an elaboration and integration of the infant's sensorimotor development within the relational and affective patterns with caregivers. These patterns are not encoded in language but in literal affective and motoric experiences, that is, the somatic infrastructure. Downing conceptualizes these affectmotor schemas as forming prelinguistic, sensorimotor belief systems for connectedness, differentiation, and bodily effectiveness. He hypothesizes "that certain physical parent-infant bodily interactions . . . leave a trace. . . . This trace can be understood as a shaping, an influencing, of the infant's motor representational world. . . . The vestige of these early motor beliefs will later affect adult behavior and awareness." (p. 150). He stresses the importance of the parent-infant relationship fostering for the infant a sense of embodied agency, that "the infant's ability to impinge upon the other must equally be unfolded" and that the infant "must build up a motoric representation of the other as engagable, and of himself as able to engage" (Downing, 1997, p. 169).

Attention to the sensorimotor regions of the brain and realms of mental organization remind us in an important way that the infant is developing a relationship not only to an other(s) but also, equally importantly, to his or her own body and sense of selfhood. Infants spend many waking hours alone with themselves, discovering the pleasures of their bodies (Lichtenberg, 1989, p. 234) in relation to the body itself and the inanimate world as well as the interpersonal world. This becomes even more pronounced when the child begins walking and the world opens up dramatically. As Call (1984) described it, "For the first time the child experiences what must be something like a kinesthetic art gallery. The world changes as the child moves in the world" (p. 19). Thus, as the research of Thelan and her colleagues also demonstrates, while the brain and its neural activities can direct the movements of the body, the movements of the body and the acquisition of new sensorimotor patterns change the brain and its neural pathways as well.

All of this underscores the tremendous amount of learning and organization that occurs during infancy and throughout childhood and adult life, learning that is outside of the purview of the traditional definitions of the ego and most definitions of the Child ego state. The body brings the world to life not only for the developing baby and the growing child but also for adults and their psychotherapists. Shapiro (1996), as an example, has attempted to bring awareness of the body—both the client's and the therapist's—into the consulting room and the therapeutic process. She has criticized other psychoanalytic theorists who attempt to include a sense of somatic experience within the therapeutic process as having tended "to view these experiences as more primitive and pathological than verbally symbolized experience" (p. 299). Shapiro described the range of bodily experiences that are present in the therapist's office (whether they are attended to or not) as "a complex experience which includes the whole range of somatosensory phenomena: our breath, pulse, posture, muscle strength, fatigue, clarity and speed of thought, sense of boundedness, our skin, mucous membranes, bodily tension, facial expression, taste, smell, pulse, vitality" (p. 298); these have the potential to enliven the therapeutic process and its participants, to have an "interanimating and interpenetrating" experience of somatic and verbal interplay. In this regard, Waldekranz-Piselli (1999) made a major contribution to transactional analysis clinical technique by elaborating—within TA theory—an accounting of sensate and affectmotor explorations and the client's being "active in the process of discovering his or her being and living his or her own body as well as how this affects relating to others" (p. 46).

Sensorimotor processes clearly provide a means of knowing and relating to "reality" from the there and then as well as in the here and now. These are not patterns that are simply "remnants" from childhood, although they begin in childhood. They are means of exploring, knowing, and shaping the world throughout one's life. As Thelan and Fogel (1989) wryly observed, "The motor system is capable of generating novel form, as even an aging psychologist can learn to tap dance or to ski or to play a musical instrument" (p. 28). I recall the first time I stood at the age of 45 at the top of a black diamond ski slope, which a friend of mine (an expert skier) had decided I was ready to maneuver. I was terrified, and as I tried to follow his instructions, I fell repeatedly. Finally, my friend told me to simply follow him and "Do whatever I do." No words, no thinking, just doing, physically imitating his movements, developing a sense of how to use my body—my sensorimotor systems, to use Thelan and Fogel's language—generating novel forms and new possibilities. I made it to the bottom of the slope without falling, acquiring in the process substantial new skills in the life of my limbs. Skiing, like so many aspects of life involving the body, improves by doing it rather than talking about it.

Subsymbolic Experience

We are just beginning to develop terms and concepts that adequately convey the nature of prelinguistic, subcognitive experience. As transactional analysts have extended and deepened the reach of their clinical work, they have come increasingly to work within these realms of subsymbolic experience. Many transactional analysis theorists have desperately stretched the conceptualization of the Child ego state to address these arenas of developmental and clinical experience, as we see in the common notations of P_0, A_0, C_0. Taken from Berne's effort to establish a standard nomenclature for the transactional analysis literature, these zero-based ego states were meant by Berne (1969) to signify "at birth" (p. 111). The notation was taken up by Schiff and her colleagues (Schiff et al., 1975) to try to reflect the very earliest stages of motivation and organization within the ego state model. This notation was extended and formalized within Mellor's account of third-degree impasses, which "relate to primal protocols (Berne, 1972); that is, they originate during very young experiences, perhaps even pre-natal" (Mellor, 1980, p. 214). As transactional analysis theorists have attempted to describe these earliest, precognitive realms of experience, the concept of the third-degree impasse has taken an important place in the literature (Clarkson, 1992; Cox, 1999; Giuli, 1985; Levin-Landheer, 1982; Waldekranz-Piselli, 1999). Waldekranz-Piselli accounts for the P_0, A_0, C_0 levels of organization purely in terms of sensate levels of experience, reflective of the development of affectmotor schemas in a way that is more consistent with direct body experience than with ego function. I find this extension of an ego state model more obfuscating than clarifying and think we find far more accurate and clinically viable models outside of conceptualizations of the ego. Here I have found the work of Bucci most useful.

Bucci (1997a, 1997b, 2001), through her explication of subsymbolic processes, has made an especially important contribution from cognitive psychology to clinical theorizing and research within the realms of sensorimotor learning, implicit knowledge, and psychotherapy with adults. Subsymbolic processes refer to those means of mental organization and learning that are not dependent on language. This perspective has much to offer transactional analysis. According to Bucci (2001),

> subsymbolic processing accounts for highly developed skills in athletics and the arts and sciences and is central to knowledge of one's body and to emotional experience.... Balanchine communicated to his dancers primarily through these modalities. His communication was intentional, conscious, systematic and complex—within the motoric mode.... He did not resort to motoric or sensory modalities because verbal representations were repressed, but because the information existed only in a form that could not be captured in words.... We should emphasize that the prefix "sub" here denotes the subsymbolic as *underlying* symbolic representation, not as an inferior or primitive processing mode. (pp. 48-49)

Bucci (1997b) effectively evokes a sense of the body that is deeply familiar within the experience of doing body-centered psychotherapy:

> These sensory experiences occur in consonance with somatic and visceral experiences of pleasure and pain, as well as organized motoric actions involving the mouth, hands, and the whole body—kicking, crying, sucking, rooting and shaping one's body to another's.... These direct and integrate emotional life long before language is acquired. (p. 161)

We kick, cry, suck, experience pain and pleasure, shape one's body to another's (with any luck at all) throughout the course of life. These are not simply manifestations of infancy or archaic remnants of childhood but also of intimacy, play, eroticism, fighting, sexuality, and nurturing throughout the full life span. In these subsymbolic realms, the therapeutic process becomes a kind of exploratory, psychosomatic partnership (quite different and distinct from a corrective, pseudo-parent/child relationship) that can be often wordless but rich in meaning nonetheless.

A clinical example further illustrates the organizing and reorganizing potential of sensorimotor and subsymbolic activity. Abby was one of four siblings, two sons and two daughters, born to ambitious, upper-middle-class parents. The family prided itself on its social and political accomplishments, and the children were pressured to be outgoing, independent, socially competent, and academically accomplished. Abby, both as a child and as an adult, felt she often fell short of the mark. Her therapy tended to focus on professional concerns and self-doubts and the stresses of being a professional woman while raising very active children. In discussing struggles with colleagues or family members, Abby was intensely self-critical, rarely feeling or expressing anger or disappointment toward those around her. She was able to express anger and disappointment toward me, although with considerable apprehension and difficulty. The issues she raised with me were substantial and brought up in a way that enhanced the work rather than disrupting or distancing from it. Sessions were productive, and yet no underlying theme seemed to emerge. Abby remained uncertain as to why she was "really" in therapy and whether she could justify the time and expense.

During one session, she mentioned in passing that she had become preoccupied with a photograph she had seen in a magazine, one that both fascinated and disturbed her. She thought several times of bringing it up with me but hesitated, feeling embarrassed and uncertain of what to say about it. She finally decided to draw it, hoping she could then discover its meaning. After drawing, redrawing, and reworking the image several times, she asked to bring the drawing to a session.

The image was of three football players walking off the field, hunched over, soaked in rain and covered with mud. The figures were somewhat obscured in the rain and mist, their faces hidden by their helmets. The figures communicated both menace and fatigue. The men were physically close, touching each other, clearly part of a team. The drawing was finely rendered and quite moving as a drawing in and of itself.

As Abby began to associate to the picture, she thought of her father: his pride in his body and his athleticism, his preference for his sons over his daughters, his bullying and narcissistic authority and self-righteousness. All of this was familiar material from her previous therapy, Abby reported, and she expressed bewilderment at not being able to get through to whatever it was that made the image so compelling for her. I suggested that rather than drawing the image or talking about it, she become it physically, literally taking it on with her body.

A series of sessions ensued in which she worked standing up, mimicking each of the figures, gradually entering the posture of each, walking and moving in the way she imagined they would move. Each session would begin with her discussing whatever events of the week she wanted me to know about or that she needed to think through, and then she would stand up, put the picture on the floor, and begin to do some part of the picture. We spoke very little. I stood near her, offering no interpretations, simply asking her to relate what she experienced if she was so inclined. She did a lot and said very little, occasionally commenting on sensations in her body, on what she was feeling, on what she sensed the men in the picture might be feeling. No new memories or insights emerged, but she did begin having a new sense of her body. She began to notice a different sense of herself between sessions, feeling more substantial in herself with her thoughts and feelings. She realized she felt angry more often. She was moving into a way of being that had captivated her in the photograph, one that had been denied to her as a daughter in the family. Language and insight followed and were informed and enriched by her bodily activity and exploration.

As diverse strands of research about babies and brains come together with clinical theory, we are beginning to recognize the force of subsymbolic and sensorimotor processes that create formative and enduring "states of mind," to use Allen's (2000, p. 261) phrase. In the first of these strands, contemporary neurophysiological and brain scan research is demonstrating with increasing clarity the mutually influencing interactions of the subcortical, limbic functions with cortical (symbolic/verbal) functions (Bucci, 1997a; Hadley, 1989; LeDoux, 1996; Schore, 2001; Siegel, 2001). We now know that two distinct, concurrent, and lifelong modes of experience—the symbolic and the subsymbolic, the cognitive and the somatic—constantly shape psychic life. Both symbolic and subsymbolic realms of psychic experience are open to influence and alteration at any stage of life.

In a second crucial strand of research, more than 2 decades of direct observation of infants have dramatically altered our understanding of the nature of infancy, the infant/parent dyad, and the social construction of the human brain. From birth, human beings begin to form nonlinguistic schemas of an affective and sensorimotor world; these function as subcortical, precognitive templates that influence and are influenced by all subsequent cognitive and relational development. We are seeing the beginnings of a coherent theory of the somatic, affective, and nonverbal foundation of human functioning, as exemplified by Lichtenberg's (1989) description of the perceptual-affective-action mode, which operates without verbal representation or symbolic formation, and by Bucci's accounting of subsymbolic processing.

Evolving Concepts in Transactional Analysis

It is clear that current infant and neurophysiological research reflects a range of neural developments that cannot be adequately captured in Berne's model of ego states. We shall never see an ego state light up in a positron-emission tomography (PET) scan in a particular area of the brain. Clarkson (1992) addressed the limits of theories of ego states in transactional analysis by introducing the language of states of self. Hargaden and Sills (2001, 2002) have extended the conceptualization of self states within the Child ego state to address the more unconscious aspects of human functioning while retaining the basic model of the Child ego state. Rath (1993) attempted to broaden the conceptualization of ego states by utilizing the idea of self-organizing systems. In a related fashion, Gilbert (1996) developed the idea of ego state networks, drawing on research models of schemas and generalized representations.

Hine (1997) carried the model of neural networks farther, synthesizing neurophysiological and infant research to offer hypotheses as to the development and differentiation of ego states and describing the bridging between implicit and explicit knowing. Drawing on the work of Churchland (1995), Edelman (1992), Nelson and Gruendel (1981), and Stern (1985), among others, Hine (1997) offered a theory of ego state development and organization based largely on implicit memory and learning. She emphasized the concept of generalized representations of experience, concluding that "this fundamental neural process builds up into coherent networks of representations functioning as wholes, inter-linking each other with increasing mental complexity. Ego states appear to be an evolved example of this impressively powerful process of structuralization" (p. 278). She observed:

> Ego states exhibit several characteristics of GR [generalized representation] systems.... Ego states become comparatively stable and coherent systems, as do GRs.... In ego states the mental activity can be broad and can include thinking, feeling, and behaving. This is similar to the make up of a "generalized experience" as described by Moscovitch (1994).... In ego state systems the ego states have their own characteristic styles and give their own meaning to internal sensations and external perceptions. (p. 283)

Hine went on to suggest that the differing forms of mental activity characterized for each ego state reflects "the way each ego state system forms and how the perceptions that give rise to each system are processed and organized" (p. 284). From this perspective, she has sustained a model of discrete and differentiated systems of mental activity and organization.

Allen (2000), while not directly proposing a change of terminology, suggested a change of language that points a way out of the theoretical dilemma we have inherited from Berne. Drawing on contemporary brain research, Allen writes:

> *States of mind as precursors of full ego states:* How is the activation of widely distributed neural circuits regulated? This function seems to be performed by what has been termed a "state of mind," the total pattern of activation in the brain at a given time. It brings together several different neural networks, any one of which can become the dominant energy and information-processing unit of the moment.... Over time, these cohesive states become more and more easily activated and coalesce into self-states. As Post and Weiss (1997) concluded, "Neurons which fire together survive together and wire together" (p. 930).... In transactional analysis, we label the manifestations of such neural network activations "ego states." (p. 261)

Hine's and Allen's descriptions of systems of neural network activation speak more accurately at a theoretical level to the understanding of dynamic mental processes that is emerging in contemporary research than does our more familiar theory of ego states as psychic structures within the mind. Allen's (2000) reference to states of mind rather than states of ego opens up the frame of reference in accounting for the growth and change of somatic, emotional, cognitive, and behavioral organization. He seems to suggest that when schemas of neural organization reach the point at which "they also include socially shared and communicable language" (p. 262), they may then be conceptualized as ego states rather than states of mind.

Allen's perspective also mirrors one common to body-centered therapists, many of whom are trained to differentiate evidence of differing states of mental organization that are usually defined as "visceral/affective," "sensorimotor," and "cognitive." From a developmental perspective, the visceral/affective systems of the limbic regions dominate the earliest stages of neurophysiological and interpersonal organization, facilitated and extended by sensorimotor development and capped by the cognitive processes of the cerebral cortex. Each system is necessary for healthy functioning. While the visceral/affective and sensorimotor systems dominate early infant development, they do not then become remnants and repositories of the past but remain vital systems of mental organization coexisting with cognitive systems throughout one's life. These same subsymbolic systems are active (and hopefully utilized) in the ongoing psychotherapeutic process of linking thinking and feeling, past and present, in the midst of trying to create meaning and effectiveness in one's life.

It may well be that the most direct (and theoretically sound) means of change within the subsymbolic and affectmotor realms of experience involve systematic attention to various forms of nonverbal experience and communication, including such means of intervention as direct work with the body, increased focus on sensory awareness, attention to the interplay of transference/countertransference, and exploration of unconscious fantasy. It seems increasingly clear that when we are working within these foundational realms of mental organization, we are dealing with process not structure. While these processes (implicit, procedural, unconscious means of knowing) have definite coherence, they do not have the fixity of those states of mind we could call "self" or "ego." We are dealing with how things happen, in addition to the more familiar questions of what happened and who did what. In these realms of the therapeutic process, it is the activity and experience of seeking, moving, and exploring that create the therapeutic edge and the means of change.

Clinical Implications

Transactional analysis psychotherapy is alive, well, and growing. When we look at psychotherapy from the perspective of somatic processes and brain development, the field of the therapeutic process opens widely, far beyond the scope of the models of the therapeutic relationship most common in transactional analysis today. The models and metaphors of parental, patriarchal, or maternal presences have powerful draws for therapist and client alike. After all, if a client is unable to soothe himself, who better to provide that service than the therapist? If the client is unable to understand herself, who better to provide that understanding than the therapist? Winer (1994) has challenged this parental model and its many variations in psychotherapy:

It is too comfortable for therapist and patient to view themselves as parent and child, even seductive we might say. We all long for a wise and protective authority. The patient invests her therapist with that power and the therapist finds security in identifying with his patient's idealization of him. (p. 64)

Tronick (2001) has sought to deepen the understanding of the process of psychotherapy through the insights gained from infant studies. He has suggested the model of "dyadically expanded states of consciousness" through which "the collaboration of two individuals (two brains) is successful [and] each fulfills the fundamental system principle of increasing their coherence and complexity" (p. 193). He is cautious about simple applications of the infant/parent research that tends to turn psychotherapy into some form of parent-child relationship. I quote Tronick at length here, as his perspective raises crucial questions about our understanding of the Child ego state and our approaches as transactional analysts to the therapeutic process:

The adult was a "being" who once had infant capacities but who no longer has (or no longer only has) infant, toddler, or child capacities. . . . It is with these fundamentally and qualitatively different capacities that adults experience, even re-experience (interpret), their experiences. . . . We must not apply models of mother-infant/child interaction to the therapeutic situation in a simple-minded, noncritical fashion. Infants are not patients. Mothers are not therapists. . . . It seems to me we can learn a great deal about both by comparing and contrasting them to each other. Nonetheless, we should not confuse and confabulate mothers and infants, patients and therapists. (pp. 189-190)

Bonds-White and I (Cornell & Bonds-White, 2001) examined the clinical implications of the subtle and not-so-subtle models of mother/infant and parent/child relationships that are so common in transactional analysis psychotherapy. We have suggested thinking more in terms of relatedness rather than relationship to provide a conceptualization that shifts away from parent/child metaphors. We emphasize the establishment of a therapeutic space (in contrast to relationship) that allows the client to reflect, wonder, explore, and move. Seen from a body-centered perspective, psychotherapy is a means through which the client discovers personal agency. In working systematically with implicit knowing, bodily activity, and sensate/motoric organization, therapy can help bring the body into the mind of the client. It is my hope as a therapist to promote a kind of bodily learning and agency that will remain in the body of the client, an implicit somatic knowing that will remain with a client outside of the office and our relationship.

What happens to our images of ourselves as psychotherapists if we cast psychotherapy into the broad fields of activity and desire, beyond those of parenting, nurturing, and understanding? Psychotherapy becomes a field of uncertainty and potentiality, play and exploration, action and aggression, desire and imagination. Knoblach (1996), a psychoanalyst and jazz musician, captures the flavor of somatic and interpersonal enlivening in his article title, "The Play and Interplay of Passionate Experience: Multiple Organizations of Desire." I think that the conceptualization of the roles of play and desire within the therapeutic process point a way out of the long-standing binds and blind spots of transactional analysis theory, a theory that has become imbued with variations of parenting and corrective models of therapeutic activity. "Play and interplay" conveys the sense of mutual exploration, motoric activation, and the unconscious matrix of transference and countertransference within the therapeutic process. Play and interplay offer a therapeutic model more consistent with the emerging discoveries from research with babies and brains, rooting those babies and brains in active, moving bodies as well as within minds and ego structures.

There is a rich, emerging literature on the place of desire and passion in psychotherapy (Benjamin, 1995; Billow, 2000; Cornell, 2000, 2004; Davies, 1994, 1998; Dimen, 1999, 2001; Eigen, 1996, 1998; Knoblauch, 1996; Mann, 1997; Winer, 1994) that has many implications for the issues raised in this chapter. This literature goes beyond the scope of this essay but warrant the attention of those seeking to extend their thinking about the nature and purpose of psychotherapy.

Play and the creation of potential space were certainly crucial to Winnicott's (1971) understanding of both child development and the therapeutic process. Play is a complex and multifaceted phenomena. Among the contemporary brain researchers, Panksepp has worked extensively with studies of brain development in older children and has undertaken numerous studies of the role of play. Panksepp (2001) has stressed that "young children tend to be very active a good deal of the time" and that "all children need daily doses of rough and tumble (R&T) activities, for this may help to optimize brain development" (p. 146). Panksepp (1993) outlined the importance of play as follows:

> Human play has been divided into a large number of categories, including exploratory/sensorimotor play, relational/functional play, constructive play, dramatic/symbolic play, games-with-rules play, and rough and tumble play. Probably this last form, roughhousing play, is presently easiest to study in animal models, but . . . it has received the least attention in human research. This is understandable, for roughhousing is boisterous and often viewed as disruptive and potentially dangerous by adults. Of course kids love it (it brings them "joy"), and animals readily learn instrumental responses to indulge in it (Normansell & Panksepp, 1990). (p. 151)

In subsequent writing on the long-term psychobiological consequences of infant emotions, Panksepp (2001) names four primary and enduring emotional systems: seeking, play, lust, and care. Most psychotherapeutic models (certainly transactional analysis) have the care component nailed down thoroughly. My readings of the baby and brain research strongly suggest that we, as psychotherapists, are long overdue in adding much more systematic attention to seeking, play, and lust. I think we need a more rough-and-tumble approach to the psychotherapy of adults, bringing the full range of possibilities of two adult bodies and minds to bear upon the psychotherapeutic project.

Conclusion

Am I suggesting that we throw out the concept of the Child ego state? No, definitely not. There are certainly aspects of ego function—archaic, fixated, and defensively organized—that are very much as Berne described them in his accounts of the Child ego state and as we often see reflected in the transactional analysis literature. I would agree that these states are indeed aspects of ego function. I am, however, arguing that as transactional analysis has significantly extended its clinical reach, we have run into serious theoretical trouble as a result of the limits of ego state theory, especially in our conceptualization of the Child.

I am suggesting that the Child ego state emerges from a matrix of implicit, affective, and motoric systems of subsymbolic (pre-ego) organization and motivation. These are states of mind or neural organization that precede ego development and are the unconscious and preconscious realms of mental organization. The Child ego state reflect means of functioning in reality that may sometimes contain historically rooted distortions and defenses but at the same time involve a wealth of affective and procedural forms of knowing that enrich daily life and relatedness. We must articulate a theory of process as well as structure. I think that we are now seeking to evolve a clinical theory of the unconscious, procedural, somatic states of motivation and organization that come alive in the process of in-depth psychotherapy.

Consistent with the implications of contemporary research with babies and brains, we must begin to reconceptualize that level of bodily and emotional organization from that of Child ego states to that of fundamental and ongoing processes of neural activation, organization, and change. We can then conceptualize transactional analysis psychotherapy as a means and place for the activation of desires, the exploration of possibilities, and an enlivened, rough-and-tumble relatedness.

REFERENCES

Allen, J. (1999). Biology and transactional analysis: Integration of a neglected area. *Transactional Analysis Journal, 29*, 250-259.

Allen, J. (2000). Biology and transactional analysis II: A status report on neurodevelopment. *Transactional Analysis Journal, 31*, 260-269.

Bauer, P. J. (1996). What do infants recall? Memory for specific events by one-to-two-year-olds. *American Psychologist, 51*, 29-41.

Benjamin, J. (1995). *Like subjects, love objects: Essays on recognition and sexual difference.* New Haven: Yale University Press.

Berne, E. (1947). *The mind in action.* New York: Simon & Schuster.

Berne, E. (1961). *Transactional analysis in psychotherapy: A systematic individual and social psychiatry.* New York: Grove Press.

Berne, E. (1966). *Principles of group treatment.* New York: Oxford University Press.

Berne, E. (1968). *A layman's guide to psychiatry and psychoanalysis* (3rd ed.). New York: Simon & Schuster. (Original work published 1947 as *The mind in action*)

Berne, E. (1969). Standard nomenclature. *Transactional Analysis Bulletin, 8*, 111-112.

Berne, E. (1972). *What do you say after you say hello?: The psychology of human destiny.* New York: Grove Press.

Berne, E. (1977). *Intuition and ego states* (P. McCormick, Ed.). New York: Harper & Row.

Billow, R. M. (2000). From countertransference to "passion." *Psychoanalytic Quarterly, 69*, 93-119.

Blackstone, P. (1993). The dynamic child: Integration of second-order structure, object relations, and self psychology. *Transactional Analysis Journal, 23*, 216-234.

Boadella, D. (1997). Embodiment in the therapeutic relationship: Main speech at the first congress of the world council of psychotherapy, Vienna, 1-5 July 1996. *International Journal of Psychotherapy, 2*, 31-43.

Bollas, C. (1987). *The shadow of the object: Psychoanalysis of the unthought known.* New York: Columbia University Press.

Bucci, W. (1997a). *Psychoanalysis and cognitive science: A multiple code theory.* New York: Guilford Press.

Bucci, W. (1997b). Symptoms and symbols: A multiple code theory of somatization. *Psychoanalytic Inquiry, 17*, 151-172.

Bucci, W. (2001). Pathways of emotional communication. *Psychoanalytic Inquiry, 21*, 40-70.

Call, J. D. (1984). From early patterns of communication to the grammar of experience and syntax in infancy. In J. D. Call, E. Galenson, & R. L. Tyson (Eds.), *Frontiers of infant psychiatry, Vol. 2* (pp. 15-28). New York: Basic Books.

Churchland, P. M. (1995). *The engine of reason, the seat of the soul: A philosophical journey.* Cambridge, MA: MIT Press.

Clarkson, P. (1992). *Transactional analysis psychotherapy.* London: Routledge.

Clarkson, P., & Fish, S. (1988). Rechilding: Creating a new past in the present as a support for the future. *Transactional Analysis Journal, 18*, 51-59.

Clarkson, P., & Gilbert, M. (1988). Berne's original model of ego states: Theoretical considerations. *Transactional Analysis Journal, 18*, 20-29.

Cornell, W. (2000). Transference, desire, and vulnerability in body-centered psychotherapy. *Energy & Character, 30*, 29-37.

Cornell, W. F. (2004). The interrupted gesture: The body in relationship. In G. Marlock & H. Weiss (Eds.), *Bodypsychotherapie in theorie und practise* [Body psychotherapy in theory and practice]. Frankfurt: Hogrefe.

Cornell, W. F., & Bonds-White, F. (2001). Therapeutic relatedness in transactional analysis: The truth of love or the love of truth. *Transactional Analysis Journal, 31*, 71-83.

Cox, M. (1999). The relationship between ego state structure and function: A diagrammatic formulation. *Transactional Analysis Journal, 29*, 49-58.

Damasio, A. R. (1999). *The feeling of what happens: Body and emotion in the making of consciousness.* New York: Harcourt Brace.

Davies, J. M. (1994). Love in the afternoon: A relational reconsideration of desire and dread in the countertransference. *Psychoanalytic Dialogues, 4*, 153-170.

Davies, J. M. (1998). Between the disclosure and foreclosure of erotic transference-countertransference: Can psychoanalysis find a place for adult sexuality? *Psychoanalytic Dialogues, 8*, 747-766.

Dimen, M. (1999). Between lust and libido: Sex, psychoanalysis, and the moment before. *Psychoanalytic Dialogues, 9*, 415-440.

Dimen, M. (2001). Perversion is us? Eight notes. *Psychoanalytic Dialogues, 11*, 825-860.

Downing, G. (1997). *Korper und Wort der Psychotherapie* [The body and the word in psychotherapy]. Munich: Kosel Verlag.

Edelman, G. M. (1992). *Bright air, brilliant fire: On the matter of the mind*. New York: Basic Books.
Eigen, M. (1996). *Psychic deadness*. Northvale, NJ: Jason Aronson.
Eigen, M. (1998). *The psychoanalytic mystic*. Binghamton, NY: ESF Publishers.
Emde, R. (1999). Moving ahead: Integrating influences of affective processes for development and psychoanalysis. *International Journal of Psycho-Analysis, 80*, 317-339.
Erskine, R. (1988). Ego structure, intrapsychic function, and defense mechanisms: A commentary on Eric Berne's original theoretical concepts. *Transactional Analysis Journal,18*, 15-19.
Federn, P. (1952). *Ego psychology and the psychoses*. New York: Basic Books.
Fischer, K. W., & Hogan, A. E. (1989). The big picture for infant development: Levels and variations. In J. J. Lockman & N. L. Hazen (Eds.), *Action in social context: Perspectives on early development* (pp. 275-305). New York: Plenum Press.
Fonagy, P. (1999). Points of contact and divergence between psychoanalytic and attachment theories: Is psychoanalytic theory truly different? *Psychoanalytic Inquiry,19*, 448-480.
Fonagy, P. (2001). *Attachment theory and psychoanalysis*. New York: Other Press.
Frank, R. (2001). *Body of awareness*. New York: Gestalt Institute Press.
Gilbert, M. (1996). Ego states and ego state networks. Paper presented at the International Transactional Analysis Conference, Amsterdam, Netherlands.
Giuli, M. (1985). Neurophysiological and behavioral aspects of the P_0, A_0, C_0 structures of the personality. *Transactional Analysis Journal, 15*, 260-262.
Goulding, M. M., & Goulding, R. L. (1979). *Changing lives through redecision therapy*. New York: Brunner/Mazel.
Green, A. (2000). Science and science fiction in infant research. In J. Sandler, A-M. Sandler, & R. Davies (Eds.), *Clinical and observational psychoanalytic research: Roots of a controversy* (pp. 41-72). Madison, CT: International Universities Press.
Hadley, J. L. (1989). The neurobiology of motivational systems. In J. D. Lichtenberg, *Psychoanalysis and motivation* (pp. 337-372). Hillsdale, NJ: The Analytic Press.
Hargaden, H., & Sills, C. (2001). Deconfusion of the child ego state: A relational perspective. *Transactional Analysis Journal, 31*, 55-70.
Hargaden, H., & Sills, C. (2002). *Transactional analysis: A relational perspective*. London: Routledge.
Hine, J. (1997). Mind structure and ego states. *Transactional Analysis Journal, 27*, 278-289.
Izard, C.E. (1993). Four systems for emotion activation: Cognition and noncognitive processes. *Psychological Review, 100*, 68-90.
Kihlstrom, J. F. (1990). The psychological unconscious. In L. A. Pervin (Ed.), *Handbook of personality: Theory and research* (pp. 445-464). New York: Guilford Press.
Knoblauch, S. H. (1996). The play and interplay of passionate experience. *Gender and Psychoanalysis, 1*, 323-344.
La Barre, F. (2000). *On moving and being moved: Nonverbal behavior in clinical practice*. Hillsdale, NJ: The Analytic Press.
Lachmann, F. (2001). Some contributions of empirical infant research to adult psychoanalysis: What have we learned? How can we apply it? *Psychoanalytic Dialogues, 11*, 167-187.
Laplanche, J. & Pontalis, J.-B. (1973). *The language of psychoanalysis*. New York: Norton.
LeDoux, J. (1996). *The emotional brain*. New York: Simon & Schuster.
Levenson, R. W. (1999). The intrapersonal functions of emotions. *Cognition and Emotion, 13*, 481-504.
Levin-Landheer, P. (1982). The cycle of development. *Transactional Analysis Journal, 12*, 129-139.
Lichtenberg, J. D. (1989). *Psychoanalysis and motivation*. Hillsdale, NJ: The Analytic Press.
Ligabue, S. (1991). The somatic component of script in early development. *Transactional Analysis Journal, 21*, 21-29.
Lyons-Ruth, K. (1998). Implicit relational knowing: Its role in development and psychoanalytic treatment. *Infant Mental Health Journal, 19*, 282-289.
Lyons-Ruth, K. (1999). The two person unconscious: Intersubjective dialogue, enactive relational representation and the emergence of new forms of relational organization. *Psychoanalytic Inquiry, 19*, 576-617.
Mann, D. (1997). *Psychotherapy: An erotic relationship*. London: Routledge.
Marcher, L. (1996). Waking the body ego, part 1: Core concepts and principles; part 2: Psychomotor development and character structure. In I. Macnaughton (Ed.), *Embodying the mind & minding the body* (pp. 94-137). North Vancouver, BC: Integral Press.
McClelland, J. L. (1998). Complementary learning systems in the brain: A connectionist approach to explicit and implicit cognition and memory. *Annals of the New York Academy of Sciences, 843*, 153-178.
Mellor, K. (1980). Impasses: A developmental and structural understanding. *Transactional Analysis Journal, 10*, 213-221.
Milner, B., Squire, L. R., & Kandel, E. R. (1998). Cognitive neuroscience and the study of memory. *Neuron, 20*, 445-468.
Mitrani, J. L. (1996). *A framework for the imaginary: Clinical explorations in primitive states of being*. Northvale, NJ: Jason Aronson.
Nelson, K., & Gruendel, J. (1981). Generalized event representations: The basic building blocks of cognitive development. In M. E. Lamb & A. L. Browns (Eds.), *Advances in developmental psychology* (Vol. 1). Hillsdale, NJ: Lawrence Erlbaum Associates.
Ogden, T. H. (1989). *The primitive edge of experience*. Northvale, NJ: Jason Aronson
Pally, R. (2000). *The mind-brain relationship*. London: Karnac.
Panksepp, J. (1993). Rough-and-tumble play: A fundamental brain process. In K. MacDonald (Ed.), *Parent-child play: Descriptions and implications* (pp. 147-184). Albany, NY: State University of New York Press.

Panksepp, J. (2001). The long-term psychobiological consequences of infant emotions: Prescriptions for the twenty-first century. *Infant Mental Health Journal, 22*, 132-173.
Penfield, W. (1952). Memory mechanisms. *Archives of Neurology and Psychiatry, 67*, 178-198.
Rath, I. (1993). Developing a coherent map of transactional analysis theories. *Transactional Analysis Journal, 23*, 201-215.
Rothschild, B. (2000). *The body remembers: The psychophysiology of trauma and trauma treatment.* New York: Norton.
Schiff, J. L., with Schiff, A. W., Mellor, K., Schiff, E., Schiff, S., Richman, D., Fishman, J., Wolz, L., Fishman, C., & Momb, D. (1975). *Cathexis reader: Transactional analysis treatment of psychosis.* New York: Harper & Row.
Schore, A. N. (1994). *Affect regulation and the origin of the self.* Hillsdale, NJ: Lawrence Erlbaum Associates.
Schore, A. (2001). Contributions from the decade of the brain to infant health: An overview. *Infant Mental Health Journal, 22*, 1-6.
Shapiro, S. A. (1996). The embodied analyst in the Victorian consulting room. *Gender and Psychoanalysis, 1*, 297-322.
Sharar-Levy, Y. (2001). The function of the human motor system in processes of storing and retrieving preverbal, primal experience. *Psychoanalytic Inquiry, 21*, 378-393.
Siegel. D. J. (2001). Toward an interpersonal neurobiology of the developing mind: Attachment relationships, "mindsight," and neural integration. *Infant Mental Health Journal, 22*, 67-94.
Steere, D. (1981). Body movement in ego states. *Transactional Analysis Journal, 11*, 335-345.
Steere, D. (1985). Protocol. *Transactional Analysis Journal, 15*, 248-259.
Stern, D. N. (1985). *The interpersonal world of the infant: A view from psychoanalysis and developmental psychology.* New York: Basic Books.
Thelan, E., & Fogel, A. (1989). Toward an action-based theory of infant development. In J. J. Lockman & N. L. Hazen (Eds.), *Action in social context: Perspectives on early development* (pp. 23-63). New York: Plenum Press.
Tronick, E. (1998). Dyadically expended states of consciousness and the process of therapeutic change. *Infant Mental Health Journal, 19*, 290-299.
Tronick, E. (2001). Emotional connections and dyadic consciousness in infant-mother and patient-therapist interactions: Commentary on paper by Frank M. Lachmann. *Psychoanalytic Dialogues, 11*, 187-194.
Waldekranz-Piselli, K.C. (1999). What do we do before we say hello? The body as the stage setting for the script. *Transactional Analysis Journal, 29*, 31-48.
Winer, R. (1994). *Close encounters: A relational view of the therapeutic process.* Northvale, NJ: Jason Aronson.
Winnicott. D. W. (1971). *Playing and reality.* London: Tavistock Publications.

The original version of this chapter was published in Ego States *(Key Concepts in Transactional Analysis: Contemporary Views) (pp. 28-54) edited by Charlotte Sills and Helena Hargaden, London: Worth Publishing, 2003. It is republished here with permission. The author wishes to thank Jenni Hine, TSTA, Gianpiero Petriglieri, MD, Suzanne Robinson, MSW, and Robin Fryer, MSW, for their careful and critical readings of an earlier version of this manuscript.*

14

"My Body Is Unhappy": Somatic Foundations of Script and Script Protocol

William F. Cornell

Protocol is a kernel of nonverbal, somatic experience that may be touched or triggered in intimate relationships. Such moments are often impregnated with both hope and dread. When the experience of a therapeutic relationship evokes protocol, the Child ego state is deeply opened, and the transference dynamics that may be played out become more anxiety provoking and more difficult to tolerate, understand, and resolve for both client and practitioner. (Cornell & Landaiche, 2006, p. 204)

It had been a year since I last consulted with Lara and Emily. The previous year Lara had asked that I meet with her regarding her client, Emily, with whom she had been working quite productively for 3 years addressing Emily's eating disorder, body shame, and sexual anxieties. Emily was a successful young attorney, then involved in her first serious relationship. She was "fed up" (so to speak) with her constant preoccupation with her eating and weight and fearful that her bodily shame and preoccupations would ruin this loving relationship. The therapeutic work to this point had enabled Emily to value herself and be able to stand outside her "issues" enough to pursue this relationship. But as this man became more important to her, her body anxieties came flooding back. Lara, deeply saddened by Emily's struggle, became trapped in a cycle of reassurance, while Emily's sense of self-worth seemed to collapse into series of images of a fat, undesirable body. They were at a point of impasse and decided to seek consultation. Emily felt it important to have the point of view of a male therapist; Lara agreed and was particularly interested in a body-centered perspective.

We agreed on a rather unusual structure for the consultation: Lara and Emily would discuss their experience of their work together and of the current point of impasse with me listening; I would then do a therapeutic session with Emily with Lara watching and probably participating; then the three of us would discuss the work together. Listening to the opening conversation between Lara and Emily, two things were immediately apparent: First, there was a deep affection and intimacy between the two; second, Emily's experience/accounting of her body was almost exclusively in visual terms (i.e. how she saw herself and imagined others saw her). This visual frame of reference unconsciously directed both Emily's and Lara's attention to the surfaces of her being. Emily's use of a visual frame of reference was so dominant and familiar that it had become "invisible"—that is, unnoticeable to Lara and Emily—which I thought was contributing to the impasse in the therapy. Emily experienced herself only as a visual object, constantly subject to scrutiny. This experience was so familiar and compelling that it was re-created within the therapeutic couple, even though the intentions of their lookings were benign.

As I myself have so often experienced in seeking consultation at points of impasse, the consultant (or peer group) is an outside force, not so intimately subjected to the states of being and relatedness induced within the therapeutic relationship and thus more able to see, feel and imagine things anew. What seemed so familiar to Emily and Lara seemed sad and limiting to me. In keeping with our contract for body-centered exploration, I wondered what it would be like for Emily to use her eyes actively and aggressively in response to those around her.

Eyes became the focus of this first consultation. I worked with Emily to use her own eyes rather than lose herself in the actual or imagined gaze of others. We experimented with her using her eyes to repel unwanted expressions from others, to make demands on others, and most importantly, to hold Lara's eyes with her eyes. These experiments were a relief and a source of excitement for Emily. As the body-centered work came to an end, the three of us then spoke of the meaning of these somatic experiments, both in Emily's literal use of her eyes in relation to those around her and as a kind of metaphor for shifting from passive/receptive reactions to emotionally significant people to active/aggressive engagements.

A year later, Emily's relationship was deepening, the work with her eyes continued to foster a sense of independence and mastery, and eating was not at the center of her concerns. But gradually, as her years-long vigilance about food waned, Emily had put on a few pounds. While virtually invisible to anyone else—except, not coincidentally, her mother and her maternal grandfather—Emily's perceptions of herself became graphically distorted, and she once again saw herself held and judged disgusting in the eyes of others. She abruptly cancelled a beach vacation with her boyfriend. She knew this time that her reactions were entirely irrational but was unable to contain them. Lara, for her part, was bewildered and feeling ferociously protective in ways she knew might not be productive. They decided to have another in-person consultation.

As we began the new session, Emily told me that in her mind, everyone could see the extra weight, that people stared, joked about her behind her back, found her disgusting. "I know it's not true, but that is how it feels, and it feels entirely real." She was deeply upset with herself for this setback. She felt it started when she went to lunch with her maternal grandfather, and he commented constantly on how FAT everyone around them was. She was certain (and very likely correct) that he had noticed her weight gain and was indirectly commenting on it. Her mother (now in her sixties and bulimic for at least 40 years) had immediately noticed the weight gain and told Emily that her boyfriend would soon leave her. As I listened, I wondered (but did not say) if the deepening intimacy with her lover might also have triggered a step back into the safety and familiarity of a script-based focus on weight and undesirability. Her mother was convinced that Emily's father had abandoned them because he found his wife too fat and that her weight was the fatal cause of the ending of every relationship she had ever had. Emily described the experience of her sense of her body changing and being invaded again by the gazes of others. She felt helpless, unable to hold on to her gains from her therapy. She became convinced that Lara was just saying nice things to make her feel better.

Then she said to me, "My body is unhappy when it is fat." I responded with, "You mean that you feel happier with your body when it is thinner. You are unhappy with your body when you put on weight, and you imagine everyone else is, too." "No," she insisted, "my body is happier when it is thin, not me. My body is unhappy when it weighs too much. My body knows when it puts on weight." "My god," I thought to myself, "what an extraordinary statement." I suddenly found myself imagining this body of Emily's literally absorbing the anxiety and disgust of her mother's body toward itself and toward Emily's body when one, the other, or both were "too fat." I imagined Emily's young body literally an unhappy body in the grip of another's/mother's unhappy body in a symbiotic fusion, the sensations merged, the sensation of literally making her mother's body unhappy, the sensations of disgust. Only thinness brought some possibility of relief, acceptance, and fleeting happiness. I imagined the literal, unspoken, flesh-to-flesh transactions that must have impinged on Emily's body from birth. A phrase kept flashing through my mind, "The *weight* of the gaze of others." I felt that weight in my own body as well as a sadness and fierce protectiveness toward Emily. I could identify with Lara's wish to ward off the mother, reassure Emily of her worth and attractiveness, argue with her Parent ego state, and protect her.

I asked Emily to close her eyes and bring our conversation into her body. How was she sensing/feeling our discussion in her body? Could she put words to the experience of her body? "I feel heavy ... heavy like fat and heavy like sad ... weighted down," were Emily's first words. She continued,

"The eyes of the others are always so heavy." I repeated her words, slightly amplifying their intensity. I suggested she begin to *feel* the eyes of others surrounding her, intruding, judging, shaming, weighing her down. I asked that she feel how it is to be noticed for her exterior, the surface and size of her body. "What is it that people see and know (or think they know) about you when they see your size and surface?" I asked her quietly, several times over. "What is it about you that is not seen? What is it that is of no interest to these eyes at the surface?" I did not want Emily to speak in response to my questions but to be with the questions in her body. I asked Emily to feel the weight of the eyes on her body.

As time passed, I asked her to both describe and show what was happening in her body. "I'm being crushed. It crushes me." "Show me the crushing," I urged. Her body began to collapse, I moved behind her, and Lara moved in front to take my place. As her body began to collapse against me, Emily suddenly said, "I want to crush them!" She opened her eyes, looked at Lara, took Lara's hands, and began to press her back forcefully into my chest. She pushed long and hard until I finally gave way. Then she pulled herself forward into Lara's arms, crying. Gradually, Emily opened her eyes, locking them on Lara's, challenging her mother in a torrent of words, and speaking of Lara's importance to her with the force of both gaze and voice growing.

In time, she shifted her gaze from Lara to include me and began to reflect on the experience of her body. We spoke of the literalness of her body being happy rather than she herself being happy, of her sense of herself being so concretely tied to her bodily perceptions and sensations. Emily asked how this was possible and what to do about it. I described to her my fantasy that the "happy/unhappy body" was originally that of her mother, not her, but as her mother could literally not tell herself apart from her daughter, it all felt like one and the same. How could her body as a baby or a growing girl be happy when enveloped, nearly possessed, by her mother's profound anxiety and unhappiness with her own body? I wondered aloud about the confusion Emily may have felt in the midst of these crazy, destructive projections on her mother's part that were also ferociously loving and protective in their intent. Her mother seemed (and seems) to have had no sense of self separate from the external appearance of her own body, so how could she have helped Emily develop that separation?

Emily needed to develop a new relationship to her "unhappy" body and to explore the conflict between these two felt, sensate aspects of her self experience (Stern, 2004; Wood & Petriglieri, 2005). She needed to find ways to bring her "unhappy" body to her boyfriend, to Lara, and eventually to others who enjoy and value her so as to experience others' bodies that were happy to be with her, whatever the state and shape of her body. She knew this in her mind, but her body quite literally did not "know" this and needed very much to learn it.

Twenty Years Ago

Consistent with the implications of contemporary research with babies and brains, we must begin to reconceptualize that level of bodily and emotional organization from that of Child ego states to that of fundamental and ongoing processes of neural activation, organization, and change. We can then conceptualize transactional analysis psychotherapy as a means and place for the activation of desires, the exploration of possibilities, and an enlivened, rough and tumble relatedness. (Cornell, 2003, p. 51)

Before taking up a detailed discussion of the second session with Emily and Lara as an exploration of the nature of script and possibilities of script intervention, I want to take a theoretical interlude that can help inform the case discussion.

It has been 20 years since I wrote "Life Script Theory: A Critical Review from a Developmental Perspective" (Cornell, 1988), an article I look back on with real satisfaction. It turned out it was the first in a series I have written challenging some of the basic tenets of transactional analysis theory and practice. At the time I was troubled by several aspects of script theory and its clinical applications: Were the developmental stages as clear-cut as we were taught them? Was developmental arrest as permanent and causal in script formation as our theories suggested? Were script-related childhood events so readily available to recall? Was most script decisional? Was script inherently defensive or pathological? Were there just 10 or 12 script injunctions or exactly 5 miniscript drivers? Did what we were teaching hold up to contemporary developmental research? In my article I strongly argued that creativity, meaning making, and mutuality of influence were inherent in the process of script formation and enactment. I concluded:

> Script theory has become more restrictive than enlivening. Script analysis as it has evolved over the years is overly psychoanalytic in attitude and overly reductionistic in what it communicates to people about human development. In addition, the incorporation of developmental theory into script theory has been too often simplistic and inaccurate, placing primary emphasis on psychopathology rather than psychological formation. (p. 281)

I smile now as I read the bit about script theory being "overly psychoanalytic in attitude," as I was then not at all a fan of psychoanalysis and am now often accused by some of my TA colleagues of trying to turn transactional analysis back into psychoanalysis. The aspects of psychoanalysis I was quarreling with in the late 1980s were essentially the same as those Berne was arguing against in the 1950s and 1960s. Ironically, right at the time I was writing my script critique article, I was discovering the work of Winnicott, Bollas, and McLaughlin, psychoanalysts who were not the least bit reductionist in their thinking. Their work opened new vistas for me, and my interest in contemporary analytic work has grown ever since. During this same period, I discovered the work of Stephen Mitchell, and in 1991 *Psychoanalytic Dialogues* started publication, introducing me to the emerging relational theories of contemporary psychoanalysis.

At the time I was writing my 1988 critique, I was quite nervous about whether I was accurately representing the developmental researchers and theorists whose work I only knew through their writing. I sent each of them the first draft of the article to check on the accuracy of my understanding. To my surprise, almost all wrote back thoughtfully and with significant interest. I was particularly touched by a letter from Stella Chess, handwritten from her hospital bed after hip surgery. She wrote that she was delighted to know that "TA was still around"; she said that she and Alexander Thomas (Chess & Thomas, 1984) had been quite enthusiastic about transactional analysis but thought it had died out. She went on to say how much it meant to her as a researcher to see their work understood and applied clinically, that they often felt their work had little impact on the actual practice of psychotherapy, and that practitioners did not read research.

That experience began my practice of circulating early drafts of my papers to authors whose work I reference in major ways, especially those outside of my personally known circle of colleagues. That process has constantly informed and pushed my learning, introduced me to new colleagues among diverse disciplines, and let people outside the TA community know that transactional analysis is still very much alive.

Since writing the 1988 article, my understanding of script and how to work therapeutically with script-based processes has continued to evolve. My attention has been particularly drawn to third-degree script (what Berne called "tissue level") and to script protocol. This interest has grown, in part, out of my enduring interest in the somatic component of psychological and emotional experience. But the driving motivation for my exploration of the body (in theory and practice) is the fact that most of my clients have had very difficult lives, so the issues brought into treatment are anchored at a somatic, "tissue" level and simply are not affected in any enduring way by the traditional transactional analysis means of cognitive/interpretive interventions.

At the point when I was writing the critique of script theory, my clinical work was carried out in two parallel modes—one based in the cognitive/behavioral/interpersonal model of transactional analysis and the other grounded in a neo-Reichian, body-centered cathartic model. I was not happy with either the process or the results. Windows of new understanding began to open as I read people like Bollas and Winnicott, the relationalists, and the mother-infant researchers. Through supervision with Bollas and Stan Perelman, a Jungian analyst in Pittsburgh, I began to learn how to work more effectively with affective and unconscious states through the transference/countertransference matrix. I became more effective in working with states of both intrapsychic and interpersonal conflict, and the therapy became more intimate. My work with script emphasized conscious and unconscious efforts at meaning making and psychological structure more than those oriented toward fixation and defense.

But my body-centered work, stuck in the Reichian model of muscular armor and emotional discharge, evolved more slowly. Reading Winnicott gave me new insights into the gestural/communicative meanings of nonverbal behavior (Cornell, 1997). Body-centered theorists were beginning to speak of three realms of mental/somatic organization—the cognitive, sensorimotor, and visceral (affective/limbic)—that needed to be integrated in somatically based psychotherapy. This was my first real break from the cathartic model, and my work began to change. However, the door of my thinking about the body and somatic processes blew wide open when I read a series of articles and a book by Wilma Bucci (1997a, 1997b, 2001, 2002) elaborating her research into the interface of cognitive science and psychoanalytic theory utilizing what she calls "a multiple code theory of symbolic and subsymbolic processing" (1997b, p. 153). It is her work that I wish to elaborate here and then use in my discussion of the case consultations with Lara and Emily. After that I will apply it to my current understanding of script theory and the therapeutic process.

Applying Bucci's Multiple Code Theory to Script and Script Protocol
We are not accustomed to thinking of nonsymbolic processes, including somatic and sensory processes, that cannot be verbalized or even symbolized and that may operate outside of intentional control, as systemic and organized thought. It changes our understanding of pathology and treatment when we are able to make this shift. (Bucci, 2008, p. 58)

The "multiple codes" of Bucci's model are three major interacting and interdependent systems of mental and emotional representation and processing: symbolic verbal, symbolic nonverbal, and subsymbolic. These systems are fundamental and lifelong, although the verbal symbolic is the last to come "online" in psychological development.

The symbolic verbal is the dominant realm of most human relations work, be it psychotherapy, counseling, psychoanalysis, or organizational consultation. It is the mode of experience and communication most readily available in language and relatively open to reflection. This is the mode in which script decisions and Type I impasses are organized, recognized, and can be communicated. Memories in this mode are available for conscious, narrative recall.

The symbolic nonverbal is the realm of psychological organization that is both known and shown through nonverbal behavior and nonverbalized processing, likely experienced and/or expressed in visual, auditory, motoric, or tactile modalities. Although lacking words, the nonverbal symbolic generates reflective meaning that can be brought into words. Bucci suggests that this is the mode currently theorized in psychoanalysis as transference/countertransference enactments, that is, experience that is shown first as a way of becoming known and may then be available for languaged reflection. I suggest that this is the mode that Berne characterized as ulterior communication—that level of script that is more accurately characterized as the introjects of the unspoken parental patterns and expectations and the core of Type II impasses.

The subsymbolic mode includes affective, sensory, somatic, and motoric modes of mental processing that are not experienced in language, although they may be brought into language to some degree. As described by Bucci (2001), subsymbolic processing is

experientially immediate and familiar to us in the actions and decisions of everyday life—from aiming a piece of paper at a wastebasket or entering a line of moving traffic to feeling that the rain is coming, knowing when the pasta is *almost* done and must be drained to be "al dente," and responding to facial expressions or gestures. Subsymbolic processing accounts for highly developed skills in athletics and the arts and sciences and is central to knowledge of one's body and to emotional experience.

While subsymbolic functions maybe highly developed and organized and may occur within attentional focus, the special nature of the computation is such that it cannot be expressed fully in words.

We should emphasize that the prefix "sub" here denotes the subsymbolic as *underlying* symbolic representation, not as an inferior or primitive mode. (p. 48)

Bucci draws on the writing of Bollas to illustrate the emergence of subsymbolic processing as an essential part of the therapist's own process of discovery and understanding within the therapeutic process. She quotes Bollas's (1987) self-description: "I know I am in the process of experiencing something, but I do not as yet know what it is, and I may have to sustain this not knowing for quite some time" (p. 203); she also uses his now-famous phrase the "unthought known" to illustrate subsymbolic processing. She (Bucci, 2008) goes on to distinguish subsymbolic knowing from the standard conceptualizations of the unconscious:

> This experience occurs on a level that has been characterized as unconscious; the analyst knows, however, that he is "in the process of experiencing something"; the state that Bollas describes is not unconscious but involves consciousness—knowing and thinking—of a specific sort. (p. 58)

From the perspective of script theory, I see the subsymbolic modes being the dominant form of organization and processing for Type III impasses and what Berne considered the underlying somatic/relational protocol out of which script evolves.

While thinking about the therapeutic process from a psychoanalytic perspective, Bucci (2008) challenges certain aspects of psychoanalytic (and without knowing it, transactional analysis as well) biases:

> Whereas Freud's deep and generative insight concerning the multiplicity of the human psychical apparatus remains valid, the psychoanalytic premise of lower or more primitive systems—unconscious, nonverbal, irrational—being replaced by more advanced ones needs to be revised in the light of current scientific knowledge. We now recognize that diverse and complex systems exist, function, and develop side by side, within and outside of awareness, in mature, well-functioning adults throughout life. . . . The goal of treatment is better formulated as the integration, or reintegration, of systems where this has been impaired, rather than as replacement of one system by another. (p. 53)

The access to and interaction of all three modes (which Bucci [2008, p. 54] calls "the referential process") is essential to psychological health and functioning. From Bucci's perspective, it is the interference or dissociations within the referential process that underlie psychopathology, and the goal of psychotherapy and psychoanalysis is to reestablish and strengthen the referential capacities among these three modes of experience and expression. When our childhood and developmental environments (and I would include here our adult life environments as well) are reasonably predictable, relevant, and responsive, these three domains of experience are more likely to remain accessible to one another, open to new stimuli, and fluid in response to the environment and within the intrapsychic referential process (see Figure 1).

There is an uncanny mirroring of fundamental aspects of transactional analysis theory in Bucci's model (see Figure 2).

I see in it the three levels of games and script described by Berne: social/verbal symbolic, psychological/nonverbal symbolic, and "tissue" or somatic/subsymbolic. I also see the three types or levels of impasse. It is important to recognize that no one mode of experience/organization is seen as "healthier" than the others; that is, one is not privileged over the others, although they often are in theoretical models and clinical practice. All three modes are valid, essential, and lifelong means of experiencing, learning, and organizing. Health has to do with the capacity to utilize all three modes, to shift among them consciously and unconsciously so that each can inform the other (i.e., the referential process). Therapy can be understood as a process to facilitate and reinforce an openness and awareness of all three modes. Bucci (2008) further elaborates a model of emotion schemas (pp. 57-61) quite consistent with those described in the recent transactional analysis literature (Allen, 1999, 2000; Gildebrand, 2003; Hine, 1997)

The beauty of Bucci's work for me is that it is independent of any particular theoretical frame of reference, as she sees this process being carried out (although not always intentionally) in a variety of therapeutic modalities. I have found it enormously clarifying in my thinking about both transactional analysis and body-centered psychotherapy, as well in relation to the blind spots and limits of psychoanalytic thinking and technique.

Subsymbolic
- Analogic, not categorical
- Continuous processing – not based on discrete entities
- Nature of processing varies with modality
- May be dominant in sensory systems, smell, taste, and touch (texture)
- May be dominant in visceral and motoric (muscular) modalities

Verbal Symbolic
- Discrete entities
- Refer to other entities
- Can be combined to generate infinite variety of new entities
- Processing is amodal, abstract

Nonverbal Symbolic
- Discrete entities
- Refer to other entities
- Can be combined to generate infinite variety of new entities
- Nature of processing varies with modality
- May be dominant in visual, auditory, motoric, and touch (spatial) modalities

Referential Links

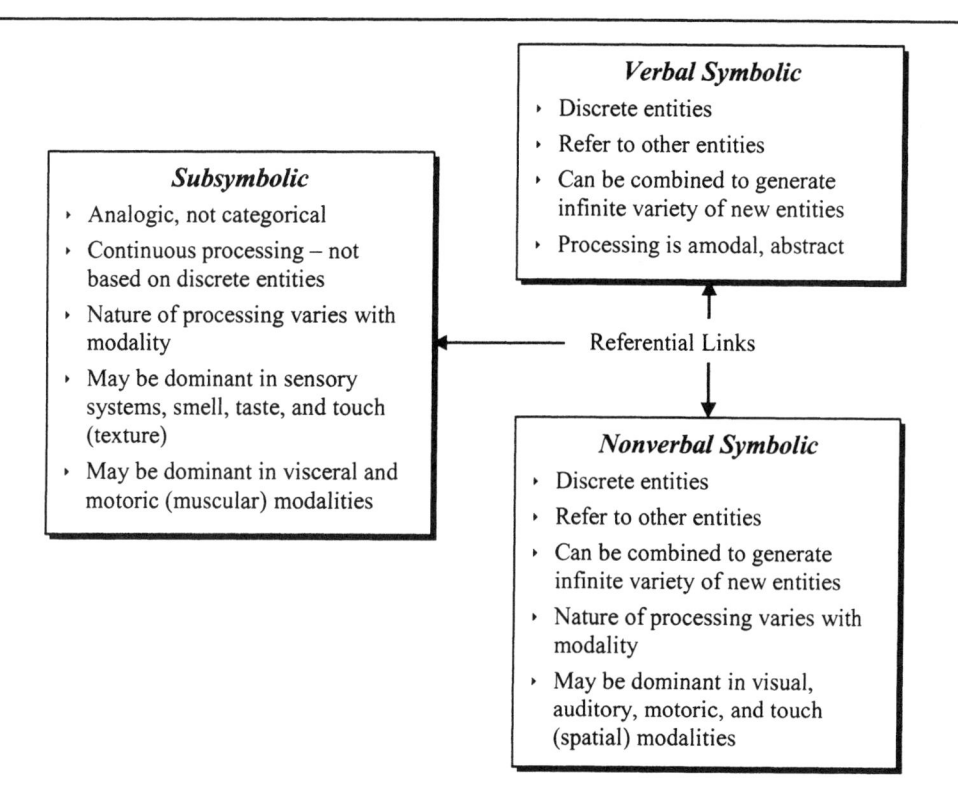

Figure 1
Components of the Multiple Code System (adapted from Bucci, 2008, p. 54)

WORDS
VERBAL SYMBOLIC

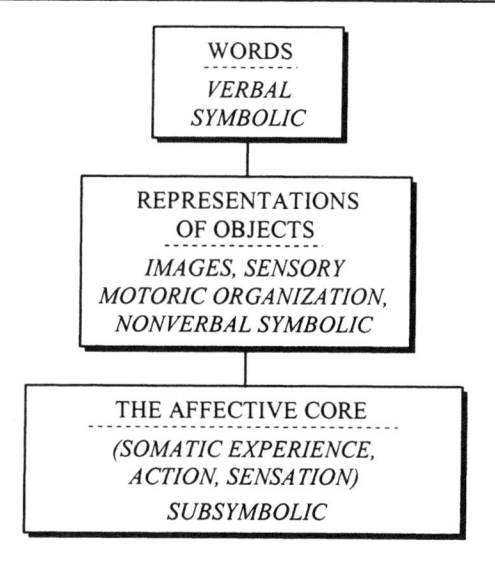

REPRESENTATIONS OF OBJECTS
IMAGES, SENSORY MOTORIC ORGANIZATION, NONVERBAL SYMBOLIC

THE AFFECTIVE CORE
(SOMATIC EXPERIENCE, ACTION, SENSATION)
SUBSYMBOLIC

Figure 2
Contents of the Emotion Schemas (adapted from Bucci, 2008, p. 59)

While there is an obvious kinship between subsymbolic realms and those levels of experience now described in terms of implicit/procedural memory and knowledge, there is an important corrective balance in Bucci's conceptualization of the subsymbolic and its centrality in human experience. In the clinical field, the model of implicit memory is best known and most often applied within the context of mother-infant research and the notion of implicit relational knowing (Lyons-Ruth, 1998). Bucci's model offers a vital correction in noting that not all subsymbolic or implicit knowing is relational and relationally based. The subsymbolic also includes vast arenas of somatic- and self-learning, organization, and expression that are not interpersonal but fundamentally intrapsychic and sensorimotoric (Cornell, 2007). The subsymbolic shapes, experientially and often unconsciously, explicit memory and the verbal symbolic. It is the sensorisomatic container within which much of our symbolic and verbal capacities develop. Alan Fogel (2004), a developmental researcher and theorist, offers a succinct synthesis of perspectives on implicit memory:

Implicit memory is primarily *regulatory,* automatized, and unconscious (Bargh & Chartrand, 1999). Implicit memories do most of the work of mediating between perception and action, as when stimuli are unconsciously evaluated, approached or avoided. Implicit memories are operating all the time and account for the organization and regulation of most of our adaptive behavior. (p. 207)

Regulatory implicit memories, then, seem to be composites of repeated early experiences rather than accurate records of single incidents (Epstein, 1991; Stern, 1985). These generalizations create an unconscious predisposition to act or feel in particular ways in particular situations.... They are unconscious and, under ordinary conditions, unable to be explicitly accessed. (p. 209)

Psychotherapy and psychoanalysis are, of course, interpersonal processes designed to enhance both self-cohesion and interpersonal capacities. Fogel has expanded the concepts of implicit and explicit memory to include that which he calls "participatory memory," a concept I see as very relevant to our thinking about script, script protocol, and the case material I present in this chapter. Fogel (2004) suggests, "There is a third type of memory, participatory memory, that forms a bridge between implicit (unconscious) and explicit (conscious) experience and may be one of the primary pathways for integrating infancy experiences into the autobiographical self" (p. 207). He argues further:

Participatory memories are lived reenactments of personally significant experiences that have not yet become organized into a verbal or conceptual narrative.... When experiencing a participatory memory, one is not thinking about the past. One is directly involved in a past as if it were occurring in the present. (pp. 209-210)

I wrote in the introduction to Section I of this book about Jim McLaughlin's confrontation of me when he said, "The closer something is to your heart, the quieter you become"; he was describing this level of memory, known at some level and at the same time unknown and not understood—an essential element in my script protocol. When I took Jim's comment to my analyst, it gradually became clear that I had, as a very young child, kept much of my love and enthusiasm quiet, profoundly so, as I was living with parents and grandparents who were endlessly sad and depressed. I loved them, needed them, and to be too happy, too exuberant, too visible, seemed like a sin. What Jim observed and commented on so succinctly was my script protocol—participatory memory in action. Clearly, my theoretical wonderings are not separate from my personal questions, one often compelling and informing the other:

Protocol is not a set of adaptive or defensive decisions like a script. It is not remembered in a narrative fashion but felt/lived in the immediacy of one's body. Protocol is the literal embodiment of the repetitive, often affectively intense, patterns of relatedness preceding the infant's capacity for ego function. (Cornell & Landaiche, 2006, p. 204)

And now we can return to the case.

Case Discussion: Script Protocol in Action

As maternal love is the first field of sexual foreplay, the hysterical mother conveys to her infant's body an anguished desire, as her energetic touches bear the trace of disgust and frustration, carrying to the infant's body communication about sexual ambivalence, "rolfed," as it were, into the infant's body knowledge, part of the self's unthought known. (Bollas, 2000, p. 48)

Thirty years later, verbally and nonverbally, Emily's mother is still communicating the same, affect-laden messages to her daughter and her daughter's body. As I reviewed my notes in preparation for writing this chapter, I asked myself what it was about this single consultation that came to mind as I imagined the issues I wished to address here. Why did this particular session stay in my mind in such a compelling fashion? I realized that there was something very moving in the stark contrast between the closeness of Lara and Emily and their dedication to her well-being and the malignant, incessant intrusion of Emily's mother, both unconsciously in Emily's being and in her actual, present-day interactions with her mother.

I thought of the passage from Bollas that I have used as the epigraph to this section of the book. Whose body is Emily actually experiencing? Who is in treatment: Emily, her mother, her maternal grandfather, the dyad of Emily and Lara, perhaps all of them? As I thought about my own therapy, pressing against the silences around my heart, whose hearts were being experienced?

I think now of a young man, about to be married and hoping soon to become a father, who recently came to me for therapy. The son (product, he might say) of a brutal, certainly narcissistic, if not psychotic, father, he said to me with breathtaking clarity in the first session, "I spent my life defying my father's will. Now I'm about to be married, I want to be a father myself, and all I can find is my father's mind in my mind. I feel like I am in his body. I have to have my own mind before I get married. I'm scared, and I don't understand this." At the tissue level of script, script protocol, unconscious enactment, participatory memory—frame it as you will—there was no clear distinction of self and other, mind and body for this young man.

To return to Emily and Lara, in keeping with work at the level of script protocol, I did not base my interventions on behavior change, behavioral permissions, support, cognitive interpretation, or empathic interventions. My interventions were fundamentally somatic and experiential, sensing and feeling our conversation and the eyes of others in Emily's body—the subsymbolic. Her experience was first expressed in sensation and movement, within the subsymbolic. In my mind were notions of hysterical Rolfings, enigmatic signifiers, and maternal narcissistic possession. These notions helped open my body to Emily's bodily struggles and to find a way to bring that struggle alive in the room within her body and among the three of us, in what Fogel (2004) would call "a participatory memory" (p. 207).

The focus in my first consultation with Lara and Emily was on the somatic level working directly with her eyes. The work was quite useful and self-sustaining until strained and ultimately overwhelmed by the deepening erotic intimacy with her boyfriend (my interpretation) and the encounters with her mother and grandfather. Emily could not sustain her ownership of her body. As we all do so often, Lara sought to relieve Emily's suffering, and I think we have all experienced the limits of those interventions. When the impasse is rooted at the "tissue" level, client and therapist must typically enter the suffering and live it together in order to experience an understanding in the mode in which the problem is being held and enacted. Emily captured this level of reality when she said, "I know it isn't true, but that is how it feels, and it feels entirely real."

When Emily said, "My body is unhappy," I initially heard this statement as a script belief. I redefined what she meant by saying, "You are unhappy with your body." But Emily meant what she said in the way she said it—this was a description of experience at the level of protocol (the subsymbolic). I realized then that a different level of intervention and involvement would be needed. I slowed myself down, shifted my attention into myself, noticed the ideas, fantasies, images, and body sensations that came up in me as I stayed with her statement: "My body is unhappy." Bits and pieces of things I have read came to mind, as did a few of my own clients. As I mentioned earlier, the phrase "the weight of the gaze" kept floating through my mind. I began to feel a continuity with what happened in my first session with Emily and Lara a year earlier and what was happening now, that is, a shift from Emily's experience of her own eyes to the impact of the eyes of others, real and imagined. As I often do, I was trying to experience in my own body what Emily was describing in hers, and I began to sense a place to start: the sense of being weighted down.

We shifted to the subsymbolic level of experince as I asked Emily to bring our conversation into her body, to feel our conversation in her body; I was, in essence, inviting her to think with and through her body rather than to think about it. This was a grounding in the subsymbolic, a grounding for an evolving referential process of connecting to other modes of experience. "Show me the crushing" is a very different intervention from "tell me about the crushing feeling"; the former anchored the work in her body and body movement. We reached an understanding in her body, through her somatic experience, rather than through her (or my) cognition.

Emily's spontaneous rush of words against her mother and her physical move toward Lara, unleashed by the expression of aggression in her body, began the shift from the sensate/somatic subsymbolic experience to that of the nonverbal symbolic and then to the verbal symbolic. She was then able spontaneously to include me in the dialogue with Lara, and the three of us could begin to reflect on the meaning of what had happened as well as look to the future.

It is a testimony to the quality of the work and the level of trust between Emily and Lara that we were able to cover so much ground in a single session. It is probably no coincidence that the presence of a third person—especially a male—helped to open the physical, sexual space between Emily and Lara for action and exploration (but that is probably the topic of another paper). Emily will need, repeatedly, to bring her body physically (subsymbolically) to her boyfriend and Lara; she will also need to bring her body experience verbally (symbolically) to those who can support and delight in her separation from her mother and her reclamation of her body and sexuality.

My encouragement to Emily at the end of the consultation—to begin to bring her "unhappy body" to her boyfriend, to Lara, and eventually to others—was not intended as support or permission. It was an instruction for the continuity of her therapy, the undertaking of a complex, difficult challenging of her experience of her body in relation to others.

When somatic/relational experience is located at a protocol level, there is often no clear distinction between self and (m)other. I opened this subsection with a quote from Bollas in which he describes the mother's bodily/sexual experience being "rolfed" into the infant's body knowledge. Emily's mother could not (and still does not) make the distinction between her own body and that of her daughter, between self and other. Mother's body is incorporated into Emily's body in a psychosomatic fusion/confusion of selves. Elmendorf (2007) captures this confusion at the level of protocol:

> If the mother is stirred by her infant in a way that she herself cannot contain, instead of offering back to the infant a metabolized version of the infant's experience, she may induce in the infant her own reactive affect. In such cases, the infant is faced with the *mother's* experience rather than the mother's reflection of the baby's experience. (p. 82)

Emily had little experience at a body level that others' perceptions were different from her mother's, that others' bodies would receive her body differently from how she was perceived/received by her mother's body. For her, something new needs to be known at a body level as well as at a cognitive level. Verbal permission, empathy, or support would have been rendered useless by the depth and pervasiveness of the "reality" of her somatic/relational protocol. Over and over, in the face of anxiety, shame, and doubt, Emily will need slowly to experience her body evoking responses in the eyes and touch of others in ways that are different from those that she has forever known through her mother.

At the level of protocol, it is extremely hard to tell who is having what experience, to whom a feeling or fantasy belongs. In this terrain, I have learned the most from the writings of Green (1986), Bollas (1999, 2000), Laplanche (1995, 1997, 1999), McLaughlin (2005), and Stein (1998a, 1998b, 2007). It was the work of these authors that came to my mind when Emily insisted that it was her body, not her, that was unhappy with its weight. It was the work of these authors that helped me comprehend the impregnation of Emily's body by that of her mother. Stein (2007) summarizes a central point of Laplanche's perspective, that of the enigmatic signifier:

> The enigmatic signifier... is a perplexing and impenetrable communication that is overloaded with significance, not only for the child who is its receiver, but for the adult who is transmitting it as well.... These messages introduce themselves into the infant's world through the most innocent and mundane gestures.... Such messages implant themselves as foreign bodies, haunting questions, in the child's psyche. (pp. 179-80)
>
> Obviously, the Laplanchian notion of a mother who normatively and regularly mystifies her child is quite different from the view in which the mother coconstructs a mutual choreography with it.... Such a picture is far from a "harmonious mix-up" (Balint) or attunement-disruption-attunement moments (Stern). (p. 182)

We might think of Emily's therapy and her relationship with Lara as being a fundamental reclamation project that involves extracting her body and sexuality from that of her mother.

Conclusion

In preparing for this essay, I thought about Emily, my own therapy, the young man about to be married, and others. How does it happen that for some, one's heart, one's mind, one's body, one's sexuality is not one's own? There are, to be sure, important things to be learned from the infant/parent research, attachment theorists, and models of implicit/procedural memory. These are avenues of study that have fundamentally altered our understanding of our work. And yet, in my experience at least, there is something more irrational, more compelling, more anguished at the foundation of the human psyche, at what we in transactional analysis would think of as the level of script protocol. There is something essential within the realms of the sexual, erotic, unconscious experience that are absent in theoretical models based on systems of memory and patterns of attachment. These models, while informative, are a bit too far removed clinically from the disturbances that we often live with in our intimate relationships and self-conflicts. It is no accident that the level of protocol, participatory memory, and enactment occurs often during periods of the most intense personal growth, the most intimate stages of psychotherapy, or the deepening of our intimate relationships.

I have often remarked that it was an aspect of Berne's genius that he conceived a therapeutic system that could be applied in many realms of therapy, counseling, education, and living, a system flexible enough to utilize cognitive, behavioral, and interpersonal interventions. His system continues to test itself, to evolve, and to extend its reach and efficacy. Work at the somatic level significantly extends our effectiveness in working with the nonverbal, foundational levels of psychic organization. It is my hope that the presentation and discussion of the session with Emily and Lara will illustrate the meaning of subsymbolic organization and ways of thinking about and working with the somatic realms of script protocol.

REFERENCES

Allen, J. R. (1999). Biology and transactional analysis: Integration of a neglected area. *Transactional Analysis Journal, 29*, 250-259.

Allen, J. R. (2000). Biology and transactional analysis II: A status report on neurodevelopment. *Transactional Analysis Journal, 30*, 260-269.

Bollas, C. (1987). *The shadow of the object: The shadow of the unthought known.* New York: Columbia University Press.

Bollas, C. (1999). *The mystery of things.* London: Routledge.

Bollas, C. (2000). *Hysteria.* London: Routledge.

Bucci, W. (1997a). *Psychoanalysis and cognitive science: A multiple code theory.* New York: Guilford Press.

Bucci, W. (1997b). Symptoms and symbols: A multiple code theory of somatization. *Psychoanalytic Inquiry, 17*, 151-172.

Bucci, W. (2001). Pathways of emotional communication. *Psychoanalytic Inquiry, 21*, 40-70.

Bucci, W. (2002). The referential process, consciousness, and the sense of self. *Psychoanalytic Inquiry, 22*, 766-793.

Bucci. W. (2008). The role of bodily experience in emotional organization. In F. S. Anderson (Ed.), *Bodies in treatment: The unspoken dimension* (pp. 51-76). New York: The Analytic Press.

Chess, S., & Thomas, A. (1984). *Origins and evaluation of behavior disorder: From infancy to early adult life.* New York: Brunner/Mazel.

Cornell, W. F. (1988). Life script theory: A critical review from a developmental perspective. *Transactional Analysis Journal, 18*, 270-282.

Cornell, W. F. (1997). If Reich had met Winnicott: Body and gesture. *Energy & Character, 28*(2), 50-60.

Cornell, W. F. (2003). Babies, brains, and bodies: Somatic foundations of the Child ego state. In C. Sills & H. Hargaden (Eds.), *Ego states* (Key concepts in transactional analysis: Contemporary views) (pp. 28-54). London: Worth Publishing.

Cornell, W. F. (2007). Self in action: The bodily basis of self-organization. In F. S. Anderson (Ed.), *Bodies in treatment: The unspoken dimension* (pp. 29-50). New York: The Analytic Press.

Cornell, W. F., & Landaiche, N. M., III (2006). Impasse and intimacy: Applying Berne's concept of script protocol. *Transactional Analysis Journal, 36,* 196-213.

Elmendorf, D. M. (2007). Containment and the use of skin. In J. P. Muller & J. G. Tillman (Eds.), *The embodied subject: Minding the body in psychoanalysis* (pp. 81-92). Lanham, MD: Jason Aronson.

Fogel, A. (2004). Remembering infancy: Accessing our earliest experiences. In G. Bremmer & A. Slater (Eds.), *Theories of infant development* (pp. 204-230). Oxford: Blackwell Publishing.

Gildebrand, K. (2003). An introduction to the brain and the early development of the Child ego state. In C. Sills & H. Hargaden (Eds.), *Ego states* (Key concepts in transactional analysis: Contemporary views) (pp. 1-27). London: Worth Publishing.

Green, A. (1986). *On private madness.* London: Karnac Books.

Hine. J. (1997). Mind structure and ego states. *Transactional Analysis Journal, 27,* 278-289.

Laplanche, J. (1995). Seduction, persecution, revelation. *The International Journal of Psycho-Analysis, 76,* 663-682.

Laplanche, J. (1997). The theory of seduction and the problem of the other. *The International Journal of Psycho-Analysis, 78,* 653-666.

Laplanche, J. (1999). *Essays on otherness.* London: Routledge.

Lyons-Ruth, K. (1998). Implicit relational knowing: Its role in development and psychoanalytic treatment. *Infant Mental Health Journal, 19,* 282-289.

McLaughlin, J. M. (2005). *The healer's bent: Solitude and dialogue in the clinical encounter* (W. F. Cornell, Ed.). New York: The Analytic Press.

Stein, R. (1998a). The poignant, the excessive and the enigmatic in sexuality. *The International Journal of Psycho-Analysis, 79,* 259-268.

Stein, R. (1998b). The enigmatic dimension of sexual experience: The "otherness" of sexuality and primal seduction. *Psychoanalytic Quarterly, 67,* 594-625.

Stein, R. (2007). Moments in Laplanche's theory of sexuality. *Studies in Gender and Sexuality, 8,* 177-200.

Stern, D. B. (2004). The eye sees itself: Dissociation, enactment, and the achievement of conflict. *Contemporary Psychoanalysis, 40,* 197-238.

Wood, J. D., & Petriglieri, G. (2005). Transcending polarization: Beyond binary thinking. *Transactional Analysis Journal, 35,* 31-39.

Solitude, Self, and Subjectivity: Discussant Paper to Lewis Aron's "Relational Psychoanalysis: The Evolution of a Tradition"

William F. Cornell

The relational and object relational models have had a deep influence on my work over the past 20 years. It has not always been an easy process. My chosen models of psychotherapy—transactional analysis and neo-Reichian body therapy—were both born out of schisms with classical psychoanalysis. Wilhelm Reich was expelled from the International Psycho-Analytic Association (IPA) in 1934 during the conference in which he was to present what was probably his most heartfelt paper. Eric Berne, an analysand of both Paul Federn and Erik Erikson, was removed from the San Francisco Psychoanalytic Institute for his efforts to present a more interpersonal and humanistic approach to therapy, one that he came to call "transactional analysis." Both men and their followers turned their theoretical backs on psychoanalysis for decades. I was often a lonely voice advocating a psychoanalytic sensibility and, in particular, attention to unconscious processes, within the transactional analysis and body-centered communities.

As Lew (2004) has so well summarized, the 1960s and 1970s saw the beginnings of enormous changes in psychoanalysis as the field opened up gradually to nonmedical practitioners and as it leaned/lurched toward an interpersonal and humanistic bent. The New York University (NYU) postdoctoral program was evolving, here in Pittsburgh. Jim McLaughlin was beginning to publish a series of quietly revolutionary papers, others were challenging orthodoxy, and all sorts of interesting things were gaining ground in the Independent and Kleinian schools in England.

On the West Coast, here in the United States, Eric Berne was forging his own humanized brand of psychodynamic psychotherapy, which he called "transactional analysis," also in reaction against the classical psychoanalysis and ego psychology of the day. Transactional analysis as a model had cut itself off from psychoanalysis and analytic perspectives for decades following Berne's death in 1970.

Originally, having read Freud, Jung, and Reich with great adolescent enthusiasm, I had wanted to become a psychoanalyst. However, I was quite taken aback by the orthodoxy, arrogance, and exclusiveness of the actual psychoanalytic training and clinical practice that I encountered. I decided to pursue training in transactional analysis instead of psychoanalysis. Thirty-five years ago, as the two-track system was developing at the NYU postdoctoral program—differentiating between a classical training model and an interpersonal/humanistic track—I was deciding to pursue training in transactional analysis. I was drawn to transactional analysis for two primary reasons. First, I was deeply involved in reading Wilhelm Reich, fascinated by the body, and quite sure that the transactional analysis community would be open to my interest in working with the body, whereas the analytic community would not. Second, Berne sought to develop a language and therapy process that drew clients directly into their treatment in a mutually defined working alliance, which appealed to my working-class roots.

Early in my transactional analysis training, I was quite taken by a central concept of Berne's—his notion of the human hungers. This was Berne's transformation of drive theory. He identified three fundamental "hungers" that motivated, organized, and disorganized human beings throughout their life span: structure hunger, stimulation hunger, and recognition hunger. For Berne, these hungers lived among themselves within the human psyche in a constant, rather competitive dialectical tension. I was keenly drawn to this idea of hunger—an active force, a force of activity, not just to relieve itself of its tensions on a field of objects but to seeks things, people, stimulation, and so on, and take them in.

In this essay I want to bring a body-centered sensibility to the relational field. I invite you all to hold a kind of dialectical tension among models of psychoanalysis and psychotherapy in general and, in particular, between solitude and subjectivity, between mind and body. Maintaining a dialectical process is not easy. We all tend to find comfort in a "track," a camp, a faith, a model, an organization.

In *A Meeting of Minds,* Lew Aron (1996) emphasizes as a central difference between the classical and relational viewpoints that "a relational view, by contrast, emphasizes that mind itself is a relational construct and can be studied only in the relational context of interaction with other 'minds' " (p. x). In this sentence, we see how hard it can be to think without splitting—the phrase "by contrast" creates a kind of split, rather than holding a dialogical tension. When I read that sentence, I hopped to the other side of the split—"Well, that's simply not true, that's a gross overgeneralization. The mind doesn't always, only develop in relation to others...." Now, of course, what Lew is arguing with is the classical Freudian model of human interaction as a sort of ping pong match between two parallel intrapsychic processes; this is the classical drive theory in which there is no real "other" as the object of the drives. The relational sensibility seeks to describe and emphasize the process between two people, a crucial corrective to the classical perspective.

To my mind, however, what the relational perspective too often overlooks is the fact that we as infants, children, and adults spend enormous amounts of time alone, in a solitary relationship with our own thoughts, affect states, reveries, and bodies. A huge amount of learning, psychic growth, organization, and disorganization happen through our bodily experience, sometimes alone, sometimes in relation to others. But the fact is that much of our learning and development has little or nothing to do with our interactions and relationships with others. Thus, I want to talk briefly here about the solitary side of human development and the therapeutic endeavor.

In his welcoming speech to the first conference of the International Association of Relational Psychoanalysis and Psychotherapy (IARPP), Emmanuel Ghent (2002) issued a kind of cautionary statement to the group of nearly 1,500 present:

> I want to emphasize, to remind you, that relational is not confined to interhuman relations, although [interhuman relations] play an enormously important part in matters having to do with psychotherapeusis. Also troubling to me is that in tending to limit the scope of the term relational to relations between people, we exclude all manner of other relations from consideration. We must not neglect the role of emergent self-organization.

Lew Aron (2004) asks us, "Why has it taken so long for us to recognize that we must develop a conception of the other not only as object but also as a separate subject? As separate psychic subject? As separate center of experience?" There are, of course, multiple factors, multiple answers, to this question. One factor is that the concept of "object" is rooted in Freud's drive theory and a nineteenth-century understanding of the mind. Freud's work was utterly radical at that time, but to have made the conceptual leap to "subject" rather than "object" would have been a leap beyond the pale. Furthermore, Freud had a way of marginalizing those who took a more relational and directly interactional approach to psychoanalysis. For decades, psychoanalysis was stuck with "object" as the anointed word. After his death, many brilliant minds on two continents struggled to deconstruct and reshape the understanding of the object and object relations, gradually coming to articulate a sense of subjectivity.

I would suggest that a crucial factor in the length of time it has taken for psychoanalysis to develop a theory of subjectivity has been its inattention to the formative forces of the body. Lew Aron and

Frances Sommer Anderson (1998) initiated a corrective step toward a reconsideration of bodily experience in editing a collection of clinical essays entitled *Relational Perspectives on the Body*. In his introduction to the book, Lew observes:

> If we keep in mind the distinction that I have made between an emphasis on the body as the source of the drives [as in classical theory] and an emphasis on the child's experience of the body as the foundation for the self, then we may judge these two somatic strategies quite distinctly and independently.... We are still left with the psychological experience of the body as fundamental to psychoanalysis. (p. xxi-xxii)

In my view, the experience of the body is central, not only for in childhood but over the entire life span; it is foundational to one's sense of self and agency.

The side of the dialectic that I would invite you to hold in mind (and body) is the centrality of the body in the formation of the psyche, of self-organization, of healthy solitude, of separate subjectivities. Seen from a body-centered perspective, human development swings constantly, throughout the course of life, between the body and the self in relation to others and the body and the self in relation to itself—that is, the realm of sensation, sensorimotor organization, and movement. These are the realms that underlie what Greenspan (1989) refers to as the capacity for agency, Bucci (1997) articulates as subsymbolic processes, Lichtenberg (1989) includes as the motivational needs of exploration and sensual enjoyment, Berne (1972) described as stimulation hunger, Ogden (1989) captures in his descriptions of the autistic/contiguous mode, and Panksepp's (1998) research into the motivational structures that he calls "lust, seeking, and rough-and-tumble play."

Seen from a developmental perspective, the frequent inattention in clinical theory to sensorimotor processes is a curious, and I suggest costly, oversight. The research model of dynamic motor theory developed by Thelan and Smith (1994) includes careful and systematic attention to body movement and sensorimotor organization as crucial underpinnings of cognitive and emotional development. Thelen and Fogel (1989), for example, emphasize that

> developmentalists, like other psychologists, have been concerned primarily with the formation of the complex symbolic and affective processes of the "life of the mind" and have paid less attention to the translation of ideas into movement—a "life of the limbs." Infants, however, are born with much movement and few ideas and, for the first year or so, lack symbolic and verbal mediating mechanisms between their mental state and the expressions of their bodies and limbs. At this stage of the life cycle, then, the link between the developing mind and the developing limbs may be especially direct. (p. 23)

The "life of the limbs" precedes and underscores the "life of the mind." The life of the limbs is never fully replaced by the life of the mind. They remain in constant dialogue, often in a dialectal tension.

I worry that in our swing from the classical, too often patriarchal, models of psychoanalysis to the relational, more feminist/maternal models, so deeply informed by object relations theories and studies of mother/infant/attachment processes that the analytic and therapeutic experience is seen too much through the filter of infancy and the maternal realm. The development of body and self start there, but they do not stop there. The therapeutic process and relationship is far more complex than a later-in-life redo of mom and baby. As the body of the baby moves from horizontal dependency on caregivers and the primary experience of the body in relation to others, the developmental process of the body itself in its sensorimotor organization shifts fundamentally away from the body in relation to mother to that of the body in relation to itself—sensorimotor competence, self-organization, agency. Throughout the life span, we swing back and forth between the body's organization in relation to others and in relation to itself.

Rather than a case illustration, I thought I would offer you a brief illustration of an adult's body flung between a struggle with itself and the experience of relatedness through the body from my own recent excursion into learning the tango. These are my notes from my first tango lesson (with danced demonstration):

- We learn to walk, forward and backward, forward and backward, alone, eyes open, eyes closed, without music, with music. The lesson structures are much like what I do so routinely in my

- body workshops; this gives me a new appreciation for peoples' vulnerabilities in these "simple" exercises.
- The tango, ideally, has a leader and a follower, although the follower doesn't exactly follow. The follower maintains a resistance, a tension—an active sense of personal space, a sense of autonomy, maintained throughout the dance.
- Miquel has a fine eye, a very fine eye. He watches intently, but he poses his observations and interventions in tentative language: "I don't really know, but I notice . . ."; "I'm not sure what this means in your body, but try this. . . "; "This may do nothing at all, but see what happens if you go like this. . . ." It is like a series of Winnicottian interpositions, interpositions rather than interpretations.
- Over and over again, I could not follow the verbal instructions. Miguel would have me put my hands on his body while he did what he was trying to teach me, and I could feel it in his body, in his muscles, his movement, and then begin to find it in my own.
- Walking alone, walking as a pair, leading, following, eyes open, eyes closed, no touch, then touch, listen to the music with your body, feel the music in your body, let your body absorb it, react with it.
- The leader in the couple is to communicate a clear and unambiguous intention with his body (RIGHT! It'll be a few years' practice on that one). The challenge for me was to stop anticipating and leading with my mind. "Your energy in your legs is into the floor, your energy in your chest is into the air and into the body of your partner. LEAD with your masculine chest!" How do I lead with my chest? How do I push the other around the floor?! "My mother wouldn't like this!" I protest to Miguel. To lean into the other. It feels so much like my early skiing lessons, to learn through my body, to lean down the mountain. It's not possible, I know I'm going to die.
- The whole experience was a gentle, but relentless, rather unyielding exposure of my body, then of our bodies as a couple, the body of the couple. I felt a deep awkwardness in the face of my ineptness, to learn something so different, feeling so inept, then the moments of excitement when my body would "get it," only to lose it again very quickly.

Here, in these notes, I hope you can hear and feel the dialectical tensions between body and self, organization and disorganization, excitement and shame, self and other. As we are more able to see and articulate the role of the body in psychic and interpersonal development, to grasp the interaction of soma, solitude, self, and subjectivity, the better we will be able to stabilize the developmental trajectory of intersubjectivity.

I wanted to speak primarily here about the role of the body in the development of self and subjectivity. But I also want to say a few words about the relationship between models of transference and countertransference and about intersubjectivity. Lew Aron (1996) argues forcefully that the model of the analyst's subjectivity and the dyadic interplay of intersubjectivity hold a theoretical advantage over the models of transference and countertransference, emphasizing that "the terms subjectivity and intersubjectivity do not imply the pathological . . . and these terms do imply a continuous, ongoing flow of influence, in contrast to countertransference, which implies an occasional or intermittent event" (p. 73).

I would argue that we need both models. I think we still need the understanding of transference and countertransference for two reasons. The first is that we need to acknowledge psychopathology —our clients' and our own. I cannot speak for everyone in the room, but I spent nearly 20 years of my adult life in psychotherapy and psychoanalysis out of concern for the impact of my psychopathology/countertransference on my intimates and my clients. The second reason is that I think there are profound, unconscious psychodynamics within the therapeutic couple that are not so much a cocreation of two subjectivities in the here and now as they are the products and projections of individual histories and character structures. The concepts of mutuality and intersubjectivity expand our understanding of the processes within the analytic dyad but should not replace the concepts of transference and countertransference. In this way, my style is more in keeping with writers like Jim McLaughlin, Christopher Bollas, and Jessica Benjamin. Lew summarizes Benjamin's understanding of intersubjectivity in this way: "Intersubjectivity is a developmental trajectory, in which recognition is inconsistently maintained. Intersubjectivity refers to a dialectic process where subjects recognize each other as separate centers of subjective experience, but also continually negate the other as separate subjects" (Aron, 1996, p. 67).

I think we can best understand and address that negation through our attention to the interpersonal impact of character structures one upon another in the enactment of the individual psychic universes of transference and countertransference.

REFERENCES

Aron, L. (1996). *A meeting of minds: Mutuality in psychoanalysis*. Hillsdale, NJ: The Analytic Press.
Aron, L. (2004, 2 April). *Relational psychoanalysis: The emergence of a tradition*. Paper presented to the Pittsburgh Psychoanalytic Society and Institute, Pittsburgh, Pennsylvania.
Aron, L., & Anderson, F. S. (1998). *Relational perspectives on the body*. Hillsdale, NJ: The Analytic Press.
Berne, E. (1972). *What do you say after you say hello?: The psychology of human destiny*. New York: Grove Press.
Bucci, W. (1997). *Psychoanalysis and cognitive science: A multiple code theory*. New York: Guilford Press.
Ghent, E. (2002, 18 January). *Relations*. Unpublished manuscript of introductory speech to the First Conference of the International Association of Relational Psychoanalysis and Psychotherapy, New York.
Greenspan, S. I. (1989). *The development of the ego*. Madison, CT: International Universities Press.
Lichtenberg, J. D. (1989). *Psychoanalysis and motivation*. Hillsdale, NJ: The Analytic Press.
Ogden, T. H. (1989). *The primitive edge of experience*. Northvale, NJ: Jason Aronson.
Panksepp, J. (1998). *Affective neuroscience: The foundations of human and animal emotions*. New York: Oxford University Press.
Thelan, E., & Fogel, A. (1989). Toward an action-based theory of infant development. In J. J. Lockman & N. L. Hazen (Eds.), *Action in social context: Perspectives on early development* (pp. 23-63). New York: Plenum Press.
Thelan, E., & Smith, L. B. (1994). *A dynamic systems approach to the development of cognition and action*. Cambridge, MA: MIT Press.

The original version of this chapter was a paper presented to the Pittsburgh Psychoanalytic Society and Institute on 2 April 2004.

16

Body-Centered Psychotherapy

William F. Cornell

The central organizing premise of the body-centered psychotherapies is that psyche and soma are indivisible in healthy cognitive and emotional functioning and that direct attention to cognitive, emotional, and bodily experience must be actively included within the therapeutic project. The perspective underlying the body-centered therapeutic modalities goes beyond a philosophical challenge to the traditional, enculturated Cartesian split between mind and body to posit as a central therapeutic principle that somatic processes—such as sensate experience, sensorimotor development, muscular movement and structure—all constitute forms of mental organization and function that underlie subsequent cognitive development and are essential to health and vitality. Any condition, concern, or symptom that brings a client into therapy will be explored simultaneously within cognitive, emotional, and bodily terms in a body-centered treatment approach. Diagnosis and treatment proceed from an understanding of the interactive influences of these different realms of mental and somatic experiencing. The integration of mental and bodily activity is promoted throughout the clinical process and is seen as an essential goal within this therapeutic perspective (M. Ludwig, personal communication, 5 April 2000).

In an overview of contemporary body-centered psychotherapies, Boadella (1997a) described the extension of the field of therapeutic attention and intervention in the body-centered modalities to include work with movement, breathing, body image, emotional expression, channels of contact, touch, and language. Perhaps more than any other characteristic, direct work with the actual movement and activity of the body within the therapeutic session distinguishes body psychotherapy from other psychotherapeutic modalities. Boadella observed:

Neuro-physiologically we know how dependent perception is on motility, and research into the body image shows a similar dependency. The movements of the body are a source of vitality affect, but are also intrinsic to the expression, or repression, of all other affects. The movement vocabulary of the child, during the first year and a half, is the foundation of his communicative rapport with the world: he interacts by means of motoric and vocal signs long before there is the capacity for the semantic use of language. (p. 33)

Boadella further emphasized, "All dimensions [of somatic processes] I have described are relational. Breath is relational, touch is communicative, movement is interactive, emotionality is contact-oriented, object relations become body-subject relatedness" (p. 39).

While the body-centered modalities originally developed within the psychoanalytic tradition (Boadella, 1973; Downing, 1997; Reich, 1949; Totton, 1998), these approaches have a philosophical and attitudinal base that has much in common with the humanistic and existential traditions (Downing, 1997; Johnson & Grand, 1998; Smith, 1977a, 1985). Body-centered psychotherapies tend to be non-normative, often challenging social and cultural norms in support of the deepening and intensification of individual desire and interpersonal contact. The overarching therapeutic goals are not focused so much on symptom relief as on the opening up of emotional experience and motoric freedom to develop a liveliness and gracefulness of the body.

History and Evolution of Body Psychotherapy

The development of body-centered psychotherapies has paralleled and sometimes interacted with the development of psychodynamic models of psychotherapy. Body-centered psychotherapies also have their own distinct history (Boadella, 1990). These therapies have rarely experienced acceptance within the more traditional fields of psychotherapy and have only recently emerged to the point of forming their own professional organizations in Europe and the United States. If the history of body psychotherapy were viewed as a family tree, virtually all of the roots would eventually wind back to Georg Groddeck, Sandor Ferenczi, and Wilhelm Reich (Boadella, 1990; Downing, 1997). During the 1920s and early 1930s, in Austria and Germany, an explosion of creativity and controversy in analytic theory and technique—led by Groddeck, Ferenczi, and Reich—formed the basis of virtually all of the body-centered psychotherapies being practiced today. The work of these analysts, who endeavored to enter somatic domains so as to extend modes of psychological treatment, were relegated to the shadows of psychoanalytic history. Their work evolved as a separate therapeutic modality, often practiced at the fringes of more conventional psychotherapies.

A medical pioneer who never became a member of Freud's inner circle, Groddeck (1977) practiced primarily as a physician rather than as a psychoanalyst; his work was based in a residential sanitarium that offered a combination of dietary, psychoanalytic, and somatic treatments. Before discovering Freud's work, Groddeck worked directly with the body through massage and other physical manipulations. Later, he continued to work directly with the body while incorporating psychoanalytic techniques. Looking back on his career, Groddeck wrote:

> The only achievement I can claim for myself with some justification is the introduction of a knowledge of the unconscious into the treatment of all patients, and particularly those who suffer from organic illnesses. . . . In treatment I rely on my head and on my hands. (p. 1)

Groddeck wrote frequently of the unconscious influences on both psychosomatic and organic illnesses, utilizing a style of deep massage and other somatic treatments (e.g., baths, exercise) while drawing on dream analysis, free association, and analytic interpretations. He speculated on the importance of the preoedipal, preverbal mother/infant relationship but did not carry these ideas into therapeutic work with adults.

Groddeck served as a mentor and friend to Ferenczi, whose work—unlike that of Groddeck and Reich—is undergoing a renaissance in contemporary psychoanalysis and psychotherapy (Aron & Harris, 1993; Haynal, 1989; Rachman, 1997). In his early analytic work, Ferenczi encouraged patients to actively suppress bodily activity, which at that time he viewed as an evasion of the analytic process; he wanted to see what analytic material would emerge if the body were stilled. In the second phase of his work, after reading and meeting Groddeck (Downing, 1997), Ferenczi began to experiment with encouraging movement. He came to see bodily activity as a form of expression rather than as an avoidance of communication and understanding. In the final stages of his work with severely disturbed patients, Ferenczi used a wide variety of physical and verbal techniques to enter as directly as possible into states of early affect and memory. Ferenczi (1955) wanted to reach "back to phases of development in which, since the organ of thought was not yet completely developed, physical memories alone were registered" (p. 122). He had come to see the necessity of working through the body and the transference/countertransference relationship to access the preverbal, infantile substratum of affective and relational experience.

Ferenczi was originally one of Freud's "favorite sons" and a member of Freud's inner circle, but he became thoroughly discredited by Freud and his cohort, with his later work actively suppressed by his colleagues. Groddeck influenced Ferenczi, and Ferenczi subsequently influenced Reich (Boadella, 1990; Downing, 1997). All three seemed to make the more proper Viennese analysts, including Freud himself, quite nervous. Haynal (1989), in his historical discussion of the Freud/Ferenczi controversies, speculated that "probably, the most unbearable thing for Freud was the knowledge that Ferenczi had entered the 'ordeal' of severely regressed patients. This could hardly have failed to revive memories of his own early experiences of the Breuer period" (p. 31). Haynal was referring to the years when Freud and Breuer worked together to understand and treat hysterics, a period of time that gave birth to psychoanalysis but proved less than successful for their patients and rather traumatic for the two men. Emery (1995) commented on the Dionysian (i.e., uninhibited) attitude inherent in Ferenczi's life and work, in contrast to Freud's attitudes of a more Apollonian perspective of reserve, intellect, and discipline. There was, indeed, a Dionysian intensity in the character and work of Ferenczi, Groddeck, and Reich. All three touched their patients, and all three experimented with technique and wrote frankly and eloquently about their treatment failures. Ferenczi and Reich both actively pressured their colleagues to speak and write more openly about technique. Ferenczi's challenges to theory and technique were mired in controversy and misrepresentation for half a century and only now are undergoing revival and reconsideration.

Reich (1961) emerged as the ultimate theorist of the psychology of libidinous drives, writing more systematically than any other psychoanalyst about the nature of drives and about the body in conflict with itself. Groddeck and Ferenczi were primarily clinicians, each quite willing to push the boundaries of technique for the welfare of their patients, particularly those patients whom other physicians and psychoanalysts had found difficult to treat. Their writings were more clinically than theoretically focused. It was Reich who undertook the development of a comprehensive theory of direct work with the body and the drives.

Once Freud had turned away from his experiments with physical, hypnotic, and cathartic interventions with his patients, he consistently privileged cognitive processes over those of the body. Freud's writings on technique after the beginning of the twentieth century came to form the canon of psychoanalytic methodology. He consistently warned against patients' persistent defensive and regressive movements into forms of "acting out," that is, avoiding the "psychical sphere" and yielding to instinctual impulses by entering the "motoric sphere" (Freud, 1912/1958d, p. 153). Freud (1911/1958a) argued, "Restraint upon motor discharge (upon action), which then became necessary, was provided by means of the process of *thinking,* which was developed from the presentation of ideas"(p. 221). Wittingly or unwittingly, Freud had reentered the Cartesian split of mind and body.

This was a splitting that Reich directly opposed, both theoretically and technically. He argued that therapeutic technique needed to enter directly into vegetative and motoric realms to create lasting change in psychic structure and that work in the psychical sphere must be grounded in work within the motoric sphere. The body, in its expressions and actions, was always a part of Reich's therapeutic attention and intervention.

Fundamentally altering the classical psychoanalytic approach, Reich turned to face his patients as they lay on the couch. In addition to the free associative and interpretive techniques developed by Freud, Reich's verbal interventions were descriptive and confrontive of what he first termed "character resistances." These could include chronically and defensively held facial and postural expressions, attitudes, ambitions, values, self-ideals, repetitive affects, fantasies, and other habitual presentations of self and styles of relating. Reich (1949) emphasized:

> What is added in character analysis is merely that we isolate the character trait and confront the patient with it repeatedly until he begins to look at it objectively and to experience it like a painful symptom; thus, the character trait begins to be experienced as a foreign body which the patient wants to get rid of. (p. 50)

However, insight did not necessarily follow in the wake of Reich's (1961) characterological confrontations. He observed that his precise and rather aggressive confrontations often produced visible bodily and physiological reactions. These physiological reactions were conceptualized as a second line of defense, which Reich came to describe as muscular armor, in which the emotional and motoric patterns were literally turned against themselves in a "vegetative antithesis" (pp. 255-265) of the original intent of the drives. Long fascinated by the physiological relationship between pleasure and anxiety within sexual and emotional experiences, Reich believed that he had made a crucial discovery. He perceived himself to be leaving the psychoanalytic domain and renamed his work "vegetotherapy." In addition to the conventional work of free association and interpretation, Reich began to work directly with patients' bodies so as to intensify physical and emotional expression. He thereby laid the foundation for the evolution of body-centered forms of psychotherapy.

The central clinical question for Reich (1949) was not what or why, but how, thus stressing process over content:

> What is specific of the character resistance is not *what* the patient says or does, but *how* he talks and acts, not what he gives away in a dream, but *how* he censors, distorts, etc. The character resistance remains the same in one and the same patient no matter what the material is against which it is directed. (p. 47)

Reich sought to bring the patient into the subtle and immediate experience of bodily process:

> We can learn much from this phenomenon [of inner emptiness and deadening] if we can make the patient relive the *transition* from the alive to the dead condition as vividly as possible, and if we pay the closest attention to the swings from one condition to the other during treatment. (pp. 325-326)

For Reich, the very essence of character analytic technique at both interpersonal and somatic levels was the delicate and carefully attended experience of shifting in the present moment between vitality and deadness, between the motility and the constrictions of the body. The how of the body underlay the content of the patient's what and why of session material. Reich focused his attention on the patterns of somatic expression, including breathing, posture, eye contact, patterns of muscular movement and inhibition, changes in skin color and temperature, and the quality of the voice in speaking (in addition to the content of what was being said). Totton (1998) provides a comprehensive exploration of Reich's theories and therapeutic style during this period of his work, all within the context of a discussion of the place of the body in psychoanalysis and psychotherapy.

The body emerged as central in Reich's clinical work not only through his work with resistance, but also through his attention to sexuality. From the 1920s on, sexuality was an enduring theme in his clinical writings (Reich, 1961, 1971, 1980), his research efforts (Reich, 1982, 1983), and his sociopolitical activities (Reich, 1974). Many of his earliest writings as a psychoanalyst explored the relationship between anxiety and sexuality, postulating that the inhibition of both sexuality and the capacity for intimacy underlay many of the interpersonal and somatic character defenses. Freeing up an individual's capacity for pleasure and sexual intimacy was a stated goal of therapy for Reich. He also worked in the social and political realms to support sex education and counseling. In 1929, with Freud's support, Reich founded the Socialist Society for Sex Consultation and Sexological Research, which operated six free clinics for workers in Vienna, programs that were subsequently expanded in Germany before he was forced to immigrate to Scandinavia. During his years in Norway (1934 to 1938), Reich undertook bioelectrical experiments with sexuality, foreshadowing the work of Masters and Johnson. While it is outside the parameters of this chapter to pursue Reich's work on sexuality in any greater detail, his efforts in his advocacy for healthy sexuality were radical and far reaching in their clinical and social implications.

As Reich left the psychoanalytic movement, he also left his wife, Annie, a fellow psychoanalyst. He became involved with Elsa Lindenberg, a well-known German dancer and movement specialist who had studied with Elsa Gindler and Rudolf Laban, both of whom had developed systems of body and movement training in Germany (Boadella, 1990). Their work influenced psychotherapy, physical therapy, and choreography in the 1930s, affecting the development of such diverse systems as Charlotte Selver's Sensory Awareness training in Europe and Kazuo Ohno's style of Buto dance in Japan. While Reich made little direct reference in his clinical writing to these body-movement specialists, clearly they exercised a strong influence on his shift to a deeply body-centered orientation. Laura Perls, too, studied with Elsa Gindler, bringing this emphasis on body movement into the therapeutic style she was developing with her husband, Fritz. Fritz Perls (Smith, 1977b) was a patient of Reich's during his characteranalytic period and, with Laura, drew heavily on this phase of Reich's work to develop what became known as gestalt therapy.

Reich fled the Nazi movement in Germany and Austria, immigrating first to Denmark and then to Norway, where he continued to develop vegetotherapy. Reich emphasized that the memories and transferential experiences emerging in therapy must be accompanied by appropriate affect. He sought to elicit intense emotional expression in the therapy session. Reich trained many therapists and psychoanalysts in techniques that now relied far less on verbal or interpersonal techniques than on working directly with the patient's muscular and movement patterns in a vigorous, hands-on style of therapeutic intervention. In this way Reich desired to bring body-level patterns of defense into conscious awareness. He used the patient's movements and emotional expression, combined with the therapist's direct physical intervention, to break through somatic defenses and to open up affective and cognitive awareness.

Reich immigrated to the United States in 1939. Theodore Wolfe—a physician and psychoanalyst who was married to Flanders Dunbar, the author of an influential textbook on psychosomatic medicine—sponsored Reich. Dunbar and Wolfe were interested in bringing Reich's psychosomatic theories to physicians and psychoanalysts in the United States. By this time Reich was deeply involved in his orgone theories and renamed his work "orgonomy." He came to believe that he had discovered a form of primordial energy, which he called "orgone," that was the substratum of both psychic and somatic experience. Reich came to conceptualize his therapeutic procedures as working directly with this energetic process and moving away from psychological and somatic explanations. This led to his discreditation and marginalization in mainstream psychiatry and psychoanalysis.

Reich did, however, train and influence a number of physicians and psychologists in the United States (Baker, 1967, Lowen, 1975; Sharaf, 1983). They, in turn, have developed therapeutic models of their own and gone on to educate a generation of body-centered therapists in such modalities as orgonomy (Baker, 1967), bioenergetics (Lowen, 1958, 1975), Radix body education (Kelley, 1974), biosynthesis (Boadella, 1987), and the work of Keleman (1986, 1989). These students of Reich drew heavily on Reich's emphasis on direct work with the body to elicit deep emotional expression, and they continue to have influence in North and South America and Europe. Each has viewed the body as the primary mechanism of both psychological organization and characterological defense.

There have been profound changes in the conceptualization of the body in contemporary models of body-centered psychotherapy (Cornell, 1997a, 2000; Downing, 1997, Johnson & Grand, 1998). Current theoretical models are rapidly incorporating the implications of research on the mother/infant dyad, trauma, and neurological processes. Models based in dance and movement (Caldwell, 1996), sensorimotor development (Macnaughton, 1996; Marcher & Bernhardt, 1996), trauma (Bernhardt, 1996; Levine, 1997), and bodywork (D. H. Johnson, 1995) have moved many body-centered psychotherapies beyond the Reichian perspective. Maul (1992) edited a collection of papers that provides a comprehensive overview of body-centered psychotherapies in Europe, while Caldwell's (1997) edited volume has done the same for many of the modalities currently practiced in the United States. Increasingly, attention is given to the relational and transferential aspects of somatic work (Cornell, 1997a, 2000), which emphasize the communicative intention of bodily activity. Seen from this perspective, all vital, intimate relationships at any age and developmental stage deeply influence the form, cohesion, and vitality of the body. A fundamental knowing of self and other forms first through the experience and use of all the senses of one's body in relation to that of another. Healthy development involves the integration of motoric and sensate processes within the context of a primary relationship, establishing subsymbolic, somatic schemas of the self in relation to one's own body, to cognitive and symbolic capacities, and to the desire for and experience of the other.

Efforts to integrate somatic experience into psychotherapeutic models are becoming increasingly evident. Smith (1985) and Kepner (1987) significantly extend the theory and techniques of gestalt therapy to more direct work with the body, placing bodily experience and activity at the heart of the therapeutic process. D. H. Johnson (1995), Krueger (1989), Brahler (1988), and Aron and Anderson (1998) have examined the centrality of bodily experience and activity within psychoanalytic and object relations perspectives. The experience of the body proves central in the theories of such contemporary French psychoanalytic theorists as McDougall (1989, 1995), Anzieu (1989), and Green (2000). The attitude toward the body within psychoanalytic perspectives in the United States has been far more ambivalent. From the perspective of the body-centered psychotherapies, the analytic attitude toward the body remains one step removed from the actualities of somatic processes; the body may be discussed, but it is rarely worked with directly through touch and sensorimotor activity.

Related Disciplines: Phenomenology and Bodywork

Phenomenological and Experiential Models. Attention to somatic and subsymbolic processes in psychological development and cognitive organization is now emerging in the theories and research of the cognitive sciences (Bermudez, Marcel, & Eilan, 1995; Bucci, 1997; Thelen & Smith, 1994; Varela, Thompson, & Rosch, 1991). For decades the body has been at the heart of the phenomenological perspective (Merleau-Ponty, 1964, 1967). From a phenomenological frame of reference, Gallagher drew on the work of Husserl and Merleau-Ponty to describe prenoetic consciousness. Gallagher (1995) suggested that "using Merleau-Ponty's model of embodied intentionality, we can develop an account of how the body, prior to or outside of cognitive experience, helps to constitute the meaning that comes to consciousness" (p. 233). He argued that "to the extent that some cognitive scientists persist in approaches that refuse to recognize the complications introduced by the various roles of the human body in cognition, they run the risk of creating abstract and disembodied paradigms" (p. 240). Bucci (1997) raised essentially the same argument with her psychoanalytic colleagues.

Within the phenomenological perspective, the body forms the structure of perception and experience. The body is fundamental, profoundly influencing consciousness while remaining largely out of conscious awareness. Phenomenologists emphasize the somatic realms of experience as preconscious. This offers a sharp contrast to the psychoanalytic conceptualization of the unconscious. For phenomenologists, bodily experiences precede and shape conscious thought and expression. For example, Merleau-Ponty (1962) observed:

> In this way the body expresses total existence, not because it is an external accompaniment to that existence, but because existence comes into its own body. This incarnate significance is the central phenomenon of which body and mind, sign and significance are abstract moments. (p. 166)

The body and its senses serve as the means and fabric of all subsequent organization and knowledge. As expressed by Kwant (1963):

> The body gives us a world . . . the world's structure depends on the structure of our body. The reason is not that the body causally influences the world, but that the body, precisely as body, gives meaning to the world. The body is intimately permeated with meanings. (p. 41)

Rooted in the phenomenological philosophies (M. Johnson, 1987; Kwant, 1963, 1969; Luijpen, 1960; Merleau-Ponty, 1962; O'Neil, 1989; Spiegelberg, 1972), a phenomenological psychology has emerged from within this philosophical tradition (Giorgi, Fischer, & von Eckartsberg, 1971; Spiegelberg, 1972; Valle & King, 1978). A phenomenological psychotherapy, as such, remains elusive, although phenomenology has had deep influences on psychotherapy and the existential/humanistic tradition (Boss, 1963; Binswanger, 1963; Frankl, 1967; Laing, 1960, 1961; R. May, 1966, 1969; Yalom, 1980). The mode of therapeutic inquiry within the phenomenological tradition reflects the effort to understand the world from within the lived experience of the client, in marked contrast to viewing the person from the outside in, as is more often characteristic of the classical psychoanalytic, cognitive, and behavioral traditions. The body offers the ground from which the therapy emerges, the ground of one's lived experience in the moment, but the body itself is not the field of therapeutic interventions as in the body-centered modalities.

The focus on the body's direct, lived experience provides a central organizing principle of the approaches characterized as experiential psychotherapies (Gendlin, 1962, 1981; Greenberg, Elliott, & Lietaer, 1994; Greenberg & Safran, 1987; Kepner, 1987; Sardello, 1971; Yontef, 1979). Extending the work of Gendlin (1962), Greenberg and Safran (1987) summarized the phenomenological/experiential perspective this way:

> Feeling in Gendlin's model is . . . a complex "bodily felt sense" that accompanies every meaningful act. It is this felt sense to which an individual attends when attempting to articulate the *meaning* of any concept or experience, whether or not it is emotionally toned. Therefore, *feeling is the bodily felt dimension of meaning*. It is the basic datum of our inwardly directed attention. It involves our preverbal, preconceptual, bodily sense of being in interaction with the environment, an internal sense of the felt meaning of things. (p. 47)

The experiential and gestalt-oriented modalities share a great deal in common with the body-centered traditions. These approaches highlight the facilitation of felt experience in the here and now so as to deepen and broaden the range of conscious awareness. They entail processes of discovering more than of uncovering and are thus distinguishable from psychoanalytic practices, which stress interpretation, verbalization, and uncovering. The phenomenological methods have evolved separate from the Reichian and neo-Reichian traditions, and the models have emerged with little influence on each other. The body-centered approaches bridge these two perspectives. Both the uncovering of unconscious, denied impulses and desires as well as the discovery and facilitation of novel experience and activity receive emphasis in body-centered psychotherapy.

Bodywork Modalities. The broad umbrella of bodywork or somatotherapies, distinct from body psychotherapy, refers to a second and separate tradition of work with the body. These are approaches for direct work with the body without accompanying psychological theories or systematic attention to the psychological impact of somatic intervention. Bodywork refers broadly to a loosely related spectrum of approaches to alleviating somatic malaise (e.g., deadness, depressiveness), chronic pain, and muscular tension. Bodywork practitioners seek to alter chronic postural and muscular patterns through teaching body awareness, altering movement patterns, and hands-on physical manipulation of the client's body. Many of the approaches characterized as bodywork—which include such methods as sensory awareness (Hanna, 1988, 1993), structural integration (D. Johnson, 1977; Rolf, 1989), the Feldenkrais method (Feldenkrais, 1950, 1981), and the Alexander technique (Alexander, 1918, 1923)—have typically been originated by people working outside of the psychological disciplines. D. H. Johnson (1995), editor of a book of essays by and interviews with many of the originators of bodywork methodologies, characterized the founders of these methods as follows:

> They worked quietly, wrote very little. Typically, they spent their lives outside of the vociferous worlds of university and research clinics. . . . These pioneers in embodiment are typically a feisty lot, unwilling to take at face value a poor medical diagnosis, a dull exercise class, ordinary states of consciousness. Rejecting the bleakness of conventional wisdom, they have chosen to survive outside the mainstream, like artists who often struggle to make a living by doing something other than their heart's work. (pp. ix, xi)

These disciplines have developed outside of academic structures and are taught and maintained by seeing, doing, practicing, and developing a kind of sensate, somatic knowledge based in accumulated and finely-tuned experience rather than knowledge of reading and quantitative research. Many of the originators had no academic or professional background for the work they developed. Ida Rolf (1989), a biochemist at the Rockefeller Institute, developed structural integration ("Rolfing"), a method of deep-tissue and fascial work to correct chronic postural distortions and inhibitions. Rolf first drew on her knowledge of yoga, osteopathy, and homeopathy to help the sister of a friend, a piano teacher who had lost the use of her hands after an accident and was unable to play the piano. Rolf systematized her discoveries into a model of postural realignment.

In a similar fashion, F. Matthais Alexander (1918, 1923), a Shakespearian actor, kept losing his voice. He watched himself speak in a mirror and gradually learned to see and feel the subtle, unconscious patterns of muscular movement and to identify chronic patterns of muscular misuse. He went on to develop a system of deep muscular release, known as the Alexander technique, to restore sensory perceptions and freedom of movement. This method is now used in many drama, dance, and music schools to correct subtle injuries and constrictions from the repetitive and expressive movements of the performing arts. The Alexander technique is utilized as a supplement to conventional psychotherapies to enhance bodily awareness.

Moshé Feldenkrais (1950, 1981), a nuclear physicist who became fascinated with Alexander's work, developed his own system of bodywork. He focused on the body in relation to gravity, with particular emphasis on habitual, unconscious patterns of movement and sensate function.

All of these and other related methods involve combinations of movements and exercises to enhance sensate/bodily awareness and direct hands-on intervention by the practitioner to facilitate somatic reorganization. Contemporary practitioners of bodywork are growing in awareness of the psychological and emotional implications of their work. So, too, body psychotherapists are increasingly acknowledging that many of the bodywork systems can enhance their skills in direct work with the body. Bodyworkers and body psychotherapists are working more and more collaboratively. The United States and European Associations for Body Psychotherapy are making concerted efforts to facilitate mutual dialogue and training among the diverse, although interrelated, disciplines of bodywork and body psychotherapy.

Touch in Psychotherapy

The intentional and systematic use of direct physical contact between therapist and client is fundamental to the body-centered psychotherapies. The use of touch in psychotherapy generates intense controversy and has contributed to the slow acceptance and sometimes the outright condemnation of body-centered techniques. A thorough discussion of the role of touch in psychotherapeutic change exceeds the confines of this chapter. A summary of theory, research, and clinical cautions is included here, since physical contact between therapist and client occur as standard procedures in the body-centered repertoire.

Traditionally, the taboo against touch between therapist and client is based on concerns about gratification and sexualization. Touch between therapist and client has been viewed as an intervention that places both parties at unnecessary risk of enactment of intimate, sexual, and/or aggressive impulses within the therapeutic dyad. A long-held, although now increasingly challenged, premise among psychodynamic theories implies that the gratification by the therapist of the client's needs and desires would short-circuit therapeutic motivation. Freud's (1912/1958d, 1913/1958c, 1914/1958e, 1915/1958b) insistence on the analyst as a detached, objective, anonymous, and nongratifying presence has long held sway in the psychotherapeutic superego, even among therapists who do not practice psychoanalysis. Freud's prohibitions echo and reinforce cultural prohibitions against touch and intimacy.

Casement (1982) insisted on the maintenance of Freud's rule of abstinence and prohibitions against touch. He argued that physical contact can become a collusive action by the therapist, confusing the symbolic and the literal and thereby collapsing the "as if" exploratory space necessary for the therapeutic process. McLaughlin (1995) questioned the prohibition against touch and offered a multilayered discussion of the meaning and impact of touch, in both literal and symbolic forms, within the therapeutic process:

> I much prefer to be available to respond to what I have found to be the turmoil around early relational struggles that, more often than sexual or seductive urgencies, drive such reachings-out for hand touch or holding. I find that this responsiveness facilitates, rather than hinders, the patient's analytic seeking.... The need, now satisfied, tends to subside as fuller verbal contact becomes possible between us. Where my responding has stirred some erotic feeling in my patient, it has remained analyzable. (p. 442)

Within the psychoanalytic tradition, exceptions to the taboo on touch have been made by some clinicians who saw justification for touch during periods of intense emotional distress or regression (Balint, 1968/1979; Fromm-Reichmann, 1950; Little, 1993; Pedder, 1976; Searles, 1965). However, any systematic discussion or empirical evaluation of the therapeutic role of touch has been nearly nonexistent in the psychoanalytic literature. A few psychoanalytic authors (Burton & Heller, 1964; Forer, 1969; McLaughlin, 1995, 2000; Mintz, 1969a, 1969b) have argued for the potential therapeutic value of occasional, nonerotic touch between therapist and patient. Mintz (1969a), for example, outlined four meanings and potential functions of touch in psychotherapy: providing direct libidinal gratification of the patient, offering touch as symbolic mothering, conveying a sense of being accepted, and conveying a sense of reality in the here and now. While cautioning strongly against the pressures or desires to gratify and be gratified, Mintz argued that the other meanings of touch can carry therapeutic value. Unfortunately, these challenges to the traditional cautions and taboos against touch in psychotherapy seem to disappear in the literature; rarely are these articles referenced or taken up for further discussion.

In a special issue of *Psychoanalytic Inquiry*, "On Touch in the Psychoanalytic Situation" (Ruderman, Shane, & Shane, 2000), psychoanalytic clinicians were invited to discuss their views on the use of physical contact, each using Casement's 1982 paper as the starting point. The articles were based entirely on the authors accumulated clinical experience and case examples. None offered any empirical studies, but the range of perspectives provided a stimulating clinical interchange.

The contributing authors, including Casement (2000) himself—who provided a reevaluation of his original paper and comments on each of the other authors—found reason to touch a patient under some circumstances. For example, Breckenridge (2000) concluded, "Using clinical examples I have tried to demonstrate that thoughtful, socially appropriate touching is no more inherently problematic than any other type of relational interaction in psychoanalysis" (pp. 19-20). For none of these authors, however, did touch become a standard part of the therapeutic repertoire. Holder (2000) summarized his views as follows:

> If, in conclusion, I come back to the title of my paper, "To Touch or Not to Touch: That Is the Question," I would, in general, come down on the side of "not to touch" because touching within a psychoanalytic setting involves so many imponderables and introduces so many parameters that it seems more prudent to refrain from it as much as possible and only resort to it in exceptional circumstances. To use it *actively* and *deliberately* as a technical tool seems to make the method of treatment into something that is different from psychoanalysis. (p. 63)

Casement (2000, p.166), too, while offering examples of touching certain patients under specific circumstances, questioned the use of touch as a deliberate or frequent technique.

Numerous ethical discussions of the use of touch in the contemporary psychotherapy literature include Smith (1985), Kepner (1987), Goodman and Teicher (1988), Holub and Lee (1990), Kertay and Reviere (1993), Epstein (1994), Cornell (1997b), Fagan (1998), Durana (1998), Smith, Clance, and Imes (1998), and Ruderman (2000). All of these discussions emphasized the importance of the clarity of therapeutic intent and the heightened responsibility of the therapist for examining the historical, interpersonal, and transferential implications of physical contact. Pope and Vasquez (1991) concluded:

> If the therapist is personally comfortable engaging in physical contact with a patient, maintains a theoretical orientation for which therapist-client contact is not antithetical, and has competence (education, training, and supervised experience) in the use of touch, then the decision of whether or not to make physical contact with a particular client must be based on a careful evaluation of the clinical needs of the client at that moment. When solidly based upon clinical needs and a clinical rationale, touch can be exceptionally caring, comforting, reassuring, or healing. When not justified by clinical need and therapeutic rationale, nonsexual touch can be experienced as intrusive, frightening, or demeaning. (pp. 105-106)

In a study of physical contact between male therapists and female clients, Geib (1998) outlined several criteria that guided a positive experience of physical contact as reported by the clients:

> The therapist provided an environment where the client felt that she, rather than the therapist, was in control; the therapist was clearly responding to the client's needs, rather than his own; the therapist encouraged open discussion of the contact, rather than avoiding the topic; and the therapist made sure that physical and emotional intimacy developed at the same pace, rather than being insensitive to the issue of timing. (p. 114)

Touch within the therapeutic relationship has also been challenged on the basis of casting such interactions as forms of countertransferential acting out and sexualization of the therapeutic relationship, resulting in the increased likelihood of boundary violations. Holroyd and Brodsky (1980) found that therapists (heterosexual male therapists with female patients) who admitted to having intercourse with patients were more likely to use nonerotic touching with opposite sex patients than did other therapists. In an earlier survey, Holroyd and Brodsky (1977) found that 80 percent of the therapists who acknowledged sexual involvement with a patient had become involved with more than one patient. Epstein (1994) indicated that the likelihood of touching being correlated with sexual contact is far more likely when weighted with other attitudes and activities involving personalizing, exploitive, and dishonest behaviors initiated by the therapist. This suggests that touch may be one form, among others, of acting out and exploitation on the part of the therapist, but this does not necessarily mean that touch, in itself, causes the acting out. If a therapist is not specifically trained in the use of physical contact and is not in ongoing supervision, the utilization of touch is of questionable clinical and ethical application.

Therapists within the humanistic tradition who advocate the use of touch in psychotherapy often frame these interventions primarily within the context of the therapist providing a corrective emotional experience of holding, nurturance, comfort, or soothing (Durana, 1998; Williams, 1992). Within the body-centered tradition, however, the use of physical contact provides a broad range of functions beyond that of comfort. These include the focusing and deepening of self-awareness and emotional experience, experimentation with patterns of contact and withdrawal, facilitation of sensorimotor organization and activation, sensate stimulation, provision of somatic structuring, and characterological confrontation. The case examples later in this chapter will illustrate direct intervention with touch designed to move through defenses and evoke new possibilities of bodily activity and experience, rather than to provide some form of comfort or nurturance.

Diagnostic Perspectives

Diagnosis is fundamental in the body-centered psychotherapies, but the diagnostic frameworks common in body psychotherapy have little in common with the symptom-cluster focus of the *Diagnostic and Statistical Manual of Mental Disorders* (*DSM-IV*) (American Psychiatric Association, 1994). Diagnostic concerns in body psychotherapy, like most psychotherapies, are centered, at least in part, on the alleviation of symptoms and self-generated and repetitive problems in living. Central to body-centered treatment is a focus on the change of character structure and motoric patterns. The presenting problems, identified symptoms, and initial concerns of the client represent conscious manifestations of underlying, unconscious characterological adaptations. Reich (1949) conceived of character as a narcissistic protective mechanism originally formed to manage infantile, instinctual conflict, particularly to minimize instinctual expressions that evoked disapproval of punishment by parents or other representatives of the social order.

Character constitutes a pervasive system of defenses involving habitual muscular and postural patterns, interpersonal/transferential configurations, and emotional and cognitive belief systems. The language of character types varies somewhat from one school of body psychotherapy to another, but most share a reasonably common understanding of the nature and function of character. They link character to efforts to manage severe developmental anxieties and environmental failures. Common diagnostic terms in the body-centered lexicon include schizoid, oral (depressive), psychopathic, masochistic, narcissistic, and hysteric.

Schizoid defenses are organized in the face of severe and chronic environmental rejection/hatred and represent a defensive effort to avoid the intense anxieties of psychic disintegration. Oral/depressive defenses are built in the face of severe and chronic deprivation of emotional and relational needs and typify a defensive effort to manage anxieties about abandonment. The psychopathic defenses (quite distinct from the antisocial or sociopathic personality disorders in the traditional clinical literature) are constructed in reaction to the experience of being overtaken/overwhelmed by parental needs, emotions, and demands and symbolize a defensive effort to maintain rigid control so as to manage the anxiety of being consumed or enslaved by others. The masochistic defenses are formed in the face of highly conditional patterns of parental affection and attention, love being subtly but pervasively transformed from a means of passionate attachment into patterns of loyalty and submission. Masochism denotes a defensive effort to contain or crush one's own instinctual impulses to manage the anxieties of parental judgment and shame. Narcissistic and hysterical defenses are developed in the face of parental rejection of the child's love, individuality, and autonomy, with the result that the child fears losing the self as a condition for a loving and secure relationship.

While the other character styles represent exaggerated, defensive efforts at self-control, the narcissistic and hysterical defenses are efforts to manage one's own anxieties about failure and loss of self/autonomy through acting out and control of others. Therapeutic efforts to treat characterological defenses than involve interventions designed to evoke and heighten awareness of characterological patterns at somatic, interpersonal, and cognitive levels so as to foster choice and change.

While no systematic research in body psychotherapy clearly demonstrates the effectiveness of these methods with particular diagnostic categories, a reading of the clinical literature, particularly numerous case studies, strongly suggests that certain client populations are more likely to become involved in the body-centered psychotherapies. Anecdotal information and case discussions in the body-centered literature suggest that such treatments are often sought by clients after completion of previous psychotherapy in an effort to deepen, extend, and consolidate the gains of verbally based psychotherapy. Body therapy may also be seen as a means to enter nonverbal and/or preverbal realms of experience that could not be sufficiently accessed in more traditional, language-dependent forms of psychotherapy.

The major problem areas (as defined in the *DSM-IV*) (American Psychiatric Association, 1994) likely to be treated using body-centered approaches include depressive disorders, anxiety disorders, somatoform disorders, problems of sexual desire and arousal, and the Axis II personality disorders. The adjustment disorders (the 309 codes) may be treated as well, but the symptoms of depressed mood, anxiety, and other acute disturbances of mood and well-being are more likely viewed as the tips of a characterological iceberg. To my knowledge, there have been no applications of the Global Assessment of Relational Functioning (GARF) Scale (Group for the Advancement of Psychiatry Committee on the Family, 1995; Kaslow, 1996) for assessment purposes within the body-centered literature. It would seem that this scale could be of particular value for pretreatment diagnosis and posttreatment evaluation of body-centered psychotherapies. Given the emphasis on characterological change, one would expect to see significant improvement on the GARF scale as a result of body-centered therapy, with its particular attention to altering character defenses so as to enhance the flexibility of relational boundaries, emotional awareness and expressiveness, and the capacity for intimacy and vulnerability.

Case Illustrations

Three case illustrations describe how body-centered psychotherapy unfolds and offer examples of active intervention with the body. The first case, Sarah, portrays the initial stages of a body-centered psychotherapy, including diagnosis, initial contracting and negotiation, and preliminary somatic intervention and exploration. The second case, Simon, provides an example of a body-centered intervention and its consequences in the midst of a more traditional, verbal psychotherapy. The third client, Jack, sought body-centered psychotherapy in an effort to "reclaim" his body from the sexual and emotional intrusions of his mother.

Sarah. Sarah was referred for body-centered psychotherapy by her previous, psychodynamic therapist. She had entered therapy originally to address issues of chronic dysthymia and anxiety. She reported these as part of her emotional experience since adolescence. Sarah said that it seemed appropriate that she was depressed and anxious during her adolescence, which was marked by repeated disruption and dislocation. She had managed both her depression and anxiety through the early years of her adult life by hard work, intense devotion to her career, and episodic drinking. She felt irritation with her emotions and her moods, which she described as leeching the quality out of her life. Sarah simply forged ahead, having little patience with herself. These coping mechanisms ran out of steam, however, when she quit work to become the full-time mother of a son and daughter, aged 4 and 6 when she first entered treatment. Both her depression and anxiety deepened significantly, interfering with her daily functioning and causing her to become unpredictably irritable and angry with her children. She sought psychotherapy and medication.

Sarah reported that her psychotherapy had been very useful, but after 3 years of productive work, the therapy seemed to reach an impasse. Sarah experienced a significant decrease in her depression and great improvement in self-esteem and in her relationships with her children. Her antidepressant medication significantly improved her sense of well-being, energy, and pleasure in daily life. Her anxiety, however, seemed largely unchanged. She had become dissatisfied with what now seemed like a dependency on her antidepressant and antianxiety medications. Her therapist suggested she try a different form of psychotherapy, one that would work more directly with her emotional patterns and her relationship with her body.

Before following the advice of her previous therapist to begin working with me, Sarah went off her antidepressant on an experimental basis. She found that her irritability quickly returned, that she had little desire to start her day, and that there was again little pleasure in her life. In this state of mind, she decided to contact me and do an initial (mutual) evaluation while still off her medication. She asked if I thought a return to her antidepressants would be wise and if it would interfere with the form of therapy she was seeking. I encouraged her to return to her psychiatrist and resume medication, assuring her that the medication would likely facilitate the therapy rather than interfere with it. Sarah resumed medication and entered body-centered psychotherapy.

Sarah was a bright, verbal, energetic, and tightly wound woman in her late thirties. It was clear that throughout her adult life, she had suffered from a dysthymic disorder (*DSM-IV,* 300.4) and a generalized anxiety disorder (*DSM-IV,* 300.02). The anxiety could be quite severe and debilitating at times but tended to be more episodic, whereas her dysthymia was chronic and more insidious. There was no evidence in her developmental history or current functioning of an Axis II personality disorder. Assessed on the GARF scale, Sarah rated a score of 80. Her ways of being and coping served the needs of her family well, so the overall functioning of the family relational units was quite effective, although marred by a tendency to be conflict avoidant. Her dissatisfactions were much more personal and intrapsychic. Viewed within the perspective of neo-Reichian diagnostic categories, Sarah was understood as a compensated oral, that is, someone who has compensated for her attachment and dependency needs with a defensive self-sufficiency so as to ward off underlying feelings of depression, loss, and anxiety.

Sarah traced the onset of her symptoms to her parents' sudden divorce during her adolescence. Her parents were too self-absorbed in their own transitions and worries to notice that Sarah was suffering. She cooperated with their self-absorption by maintaining a high functioning, "good soldier" attitude. She kept her sadness, loss, and worries to herself. Looking back, she could see symptoms of depression throughout her adult life, but she had successfully "stayed on top of them" through her activity level and professional success. Then her anxiety and depression "got the best of me," until her psychotherapy helped her get back on top again. In her initial session with me, Sarah reported that she had no patience with her anxiety. She hated it and wanted to be rid of it. She hoped the body therapy would help her somehow to dispose of the anxiety.

Our initial treatment contracts emerged in this initial session. Sarah asked that, for the time being, I not talk to her previous therapist. She felt that my perceptions would have more impact on her if they arose afresh and were not influenced by input from her previous therapist. I agreed. I suggested to her that she needed to learn about and learn from her anxiety, not get rid of it, further suggesting that her anxiety carried meaning that we needed to explore. Reluctantly, she agreed tentatively to adopt this exploratory attitude toward her anxiety. This suggestion on my part typifies a somatic intervention: to activate and explore rather than control or relieve.

We also discussed the use of physical contact as a part of our work together. I assured Sarah that the choice to use touch was entirely hers, since there would be options for attending to her body and working with body processes without the use of direct physical contact. She made reference to the importance of massage and chiropractic adjustments, forms of touch she found useful and safe. She said she imagined that being touched in a psychotherapeutic process would create some anxiety and vulnerability but felt it was necessary if she was going to gain more vitality in her life. We agreed to include touch among our means of working together, with the clear understanding that if she needed me to stop touching her for any reason, I would stop immediately. After stopping the physical contact we would discuss what happened, what felt wrong, and whether and how to continue. We agreed that any and all experiences involving touch could be discussed, including reactions, fantasies, and dreams that might emerge between sessions.

There was an immediate contradiction in the appearance/presentation of her body. Sarah is slender, wears makeup in an understated fashion, and gives careful attention to her appearance with a casual style of dress. She took active care of her body, getting regular massages and chiropractic and homeopathic treatments. Yet she rarely felt at ease in her body. Her casual appearance and careful care of her body belied a more pervasive sense of tension and conflict in her body. She carried a great deal of tension in her jaw, neck, and upper body, which she experienced as normal and from which she reported no particular discomfort. Her habitual patterns of muscular tension created a subtle but pervasive visual impression of a person who had to simultaneously hold herself up, back, and in.

At an initial, superficial level Sarah's body seemed quite at ease with being touched, but that changed quickly as I began to use my hands to provide support to her shoulders and neck. It was virtually impossible for Sarah to allow me to lift her head or support it with my hands. Her breathing became constricted, and her neck and shoulder muscles tensed. She tried to make herself relax. She felt embarrassed by her body's reactions, apologizing and reassuring me that she trusted me. She became immediately self-critical. I commented that her judgmental responses to her bodily reactions were like her judgments of her anxiety, that her judgments foreclosed the possibility of learning and exploring. Her inability to accept physical support of her neck and shoulders became the focus of attention. She reported that for days following the initial hands-on session she felt quietly, inexplicably sad. At the same time she felt hopeful that this style of work was "going to get through" to her. We continued to work with her neck and shoulders as a part of each session, in the midst of an ongoing verbal therapy process examining her patterns of closeness and affection with her children, husband, friends, and parents.

The work with her body consistently evoked anxiety and sadness, the latter of which she experienced as distinctly different from depression. She resisted her usual temptation to take Xanex to alleviate her anxiety. There were no particular memories, associations, or dreams connected to her sadness and anxiety, just states of affect that came over her. She was pleased that she could sometimes cry, and she became more tolerant of her anxiety. She continued to label her body reactions as "resistant," while I began to suggest other language for her body, for example, a "protective body," a "worried body," a "cautious body." I observed that her body seemed afraid of itself. That comment stuck with her. Sarah began to think of and experience her body as frightened rather than resistant—frightened of losing herself to her children's or husband's needs, frightened of not taking adequate care of her kids, frightened of becoming so depressed that she could not function, frightened that she would suddenly fall apart. Her sadness deepened; she would often cry quietly in session and at home afterward, although she did not know what she was crying about. Gradually, her body began to accept the support of my hands: "I feel like I can rest in your hands." She realized that she was constantly attending to her body, fixing it up, like mechanical maintenance, so that she would function properly. But there was no real kindness, rest, or support for her body; she managed her body more than cared for it.

As Sarah became more accepting of my physical support, she reported experiencing a tenderness in my hands and in my way of being with her. This reminded her of her father. I encouraged her to remember her father's tenderness and to talk about it as I held her head in my hands. She cried deeply, and we had a pivotal dialogue:

Sarah: Oh my god, I don't think I've rested since my Dad left us. I had to stay with Mom. I had to take care of her. I don't ever even rest in my husband's arms. Even when we make love, I don't rest. I don't let go. I always hold back. I loved my Dad, but I couldn't keep him. I lost him (deep crying). I'm not strong enough to feel this kind of pain.

Bill: I think you're afraid you're not strong enough to feel the depth of your affections.

Sarah: What did you say? I don't understand what you mean (long pause). I don't think I can tell the difference between pain and affection. They feel the same to me. I can't tell them apart.

Bill: Your affections became a source of pain, not comfort. You're terrified of your affections, terrified of losing someone else you love. It's unbearable. You learned young to hold yourself back. Don't reach out, don't hold on, don't let in.

These themes formed the heart of our work together. In a fashion typical of body-centered psychotherapy, the sessions wove back and forth between verbal explorations of Sarah's affectional patterns with her husband, children, and parents as well as with me during our ongoing explorations of her somatic patterns. Hands-on work formed a part of every session. As we shifted from verbal interaction to physical interaction, Sarah typically closed her eyes as I asked her a series of questions to help her focus on her body and find a starting point for the body-level work: "Where does your attention start to go in your body?" "Where is your body uncomfortable?" "What might that area of discomfort want?" "Is there a way you want to move?" "Is there something your body needs from me right now?" "Where/how would you like me to touch you?" These are but a few questions offered as examples of how a therapist and client can begin to orient to the body and bridge to direct body intervention. Through this style of somatic exploration, Sarah began to understand the habitual reactions of her body in relation to her sadness and anxiety. Her body became more able to contain these emotions, allowing her to have deeper experiences of these feelings, which gained meaning in the context of both her history and current life choices.

Increasingly, Sarah became aware of the somatic habits of holding her body up, back, and in, and she was more able to use her body as a means of approaching and engaging others. The body-centered interventions also provided a means by which she could explore her relationship with me. She examined and explored my physical and emotional support and her own difficulties in initiating contact, reaching out to me with her own arms and hands, noticing the wishes and desires in her body for physical contact. She lessened her caretaking ways of being with her children and found more playful means of involvement. She challenged the cooperative but passionless style of relating into which she and her husband had devolved over the years, and she spent more time outside of her home with a couple of close friends, intentionally deepening those relationships.

Simon. Simon was 31 when he entered psychotherapy. He was thin, almost emaciated in appearance. His therapy was paid for by his parents, who saw him as purposeless and depressed. Simon suffered from a schizoid personality disorder (*DSM-IV,* 301.20), with some paranoid ideation and significant indications of a depersonalization disorder (*DSM-IV,* 300.6). Within the diagnostic categorizations of a body-centered perspective, Simon would also be viewed as schizoid. On the GARF scale within his nuclear family, Simon would rate a score of 30. In his social life outside the home, Simon would rate a GARF score of 10.

Simon lived with his aging parents, becoming a kind of live-in, unpaid caretaker after failing at university and in his first and only love relationship. Now and then he took an occasional college course until he got bored or the schedule became inconvenient. He would at moments worry that he was totally inept at life and then declare indifference to life and its banalities. He had no friends. Simon could acknowledge that he was socially awkward and probably came across as at least shy if not strange. But he tended to explain away the aloneness of his life as mostly due to having to take care of his parents and the lack of privacy these living arrangements imposed on him. He occupied himself with science fiction novels and movies, computer games, and Internet fantasy chat rooms. His private fantasies, as he reported them in session, were dominated by chance encounters with someone who would take an interest in him and suddenly alter the course of his life.

Simon was curious about psychotherapy, seeking an interactive, psychodynamic therapy that he thought might help him understand himself better. He looked forward to having someone to talk with regularly, as he spent much of his time alone. He knew nothing of my orientation as a body-centered psychotherapist. Simon was happy to get out of the house for his sessions, content to lie on the couch talking of internal and external events, talking mostly to himself about himself and only vaguely aware of my presence. My questions, comments, and interpretations seemed to fall on deaf ears, as all possibility of change was cast into the future, after his parents' deaths.

One day I found myself saying out loud to Simon what I had often noted silently and rather sadly to myself, "Simon, you lie there like a corpse." Simon remained silent and unmoving. I continued, "I used to barely notice how you lie there. It was just how you are, but now this stillness has become disturbing to me. I can't ignore it. It makes me sad. I can't stand it. I wonder how the hell you stand it? How do you stand this, Simon?" After a time, he replied, "I don't know any other way of being. How do I make you sad? What do other people do when they lie here? Is there something I'm supposed to do?"

The fact of Simon's asking questions startled me. Rarely did he address me directly. He seemed content to accept silently whatever I might have to offer by way of linking or interpreting his dreams and fantasies. His rare questions to me sought intellectual explanations for his feelings and fantasies. Now, in response to my observation (outburst), Simon asked three very different questions, and in these questions there were clearly two of us in the room. These questions sought action, not insight, asking how rather than why. These were questions of the body, not the mind; they reminded me of Reich, who was far more interested in how a patient did something than why it was done. Simon's questions were about how to bring his body and his affect into the room. I commented on how different these questions were from his usual way of talking in sessions. Simon replied that it startled him and touched him to realize that I felt something for him. He now realized that I looked at him as well as listened to him. He said he structured his life so that he was rarely seen by anyone and he rarely saw anyone. He wondered what else I saw about him. I began to comment on what I noticed about his way of being in the room and his way of being with me. Most of my comments were purely descriptive, but at times I extended my observations with comments about how I felt or what I imagined was going on in him.

In contrast to Simon's usual practice of speaking aloud to himself, periods of silence began to develop. These were not his typical silences of mental reverie about events outside the office but quiet periods in which he attended to what was happening with him in the moment. In these silences, he struggled with new ways to talk to me. As I attended verbally to his body in the sessions, I began to encourage him to pay attention to his body as well. I inquired as to how he might begin to show me his experience through movement as well as tell me about it. He remained still.

Our work continued in this fashion for weeks. Then Simon dreamed that in a session he rolled to his side, and I came over to sit at his back, my hip and thigh against his spine. I immediately saw great significance to this dream because it brought his body and mine directly into the room and into relationship. The dream was the first signal that he wanted me to have something to do with him. I knew I needed to be cautious and not impose myself on Simon's dream. I decided to wait and see if and how Simon would take up the dream.

At first Simon was embarrassed by the dream, but it nevertheless struck him as very important. He could see that it was a sign of recognition of my support of him and perhaps a wish for more of my involvement. He reported that he was increasingly conscious of how little he noticed his body day to day, but that in his sessions with me, he was becoming aware of it. The dream returned as a topic of conversation for several weeks. He sometimes feared the dream image, which he worried was a kind of regressive cry for support from me when he already felt so inept at life. He worried that I would consider touching him to be silly or disgusting. He could make no sense of the particular body positions in the dream, that of my hip against his back.

One session Simon suddenly rolled to his side and asked me to move over and sit with him literally as in the dream. Although we had had no discussions about physical contact between us or about direct work with the body, I decided to do as Simon asked. I was confident that we were now sufficiently engaged with each other that should this move prove to be a mistake, it was a mistake from which we would learn. I sat with my hip against Simon's back. I waited to see what would happen, encouraging Simon to allow his body to react to this new situation in any way it needed. Gradually, Simon's body began to tremble and he began to cry softly. He said that he was stunned by the warmth of my body and touched by the strength he sensed in it. I encouraged him to take his time and accept anything that came up inside him as we sat together. He found himself thinking of his father's weak and withering body, which he found disgusting. In subsequent sessions he acknowledged that he had always seen his father as weak and disgusting. Simon felt as though his body had somehow absorbed the loneliness and weakness of his father's body, that he retreated to his head, where he had at least some sense of competence and even superiority.

Every few sessions Simon now asked me to sit with him, as I had in the dream. He felt it helped him separate his experience of his own body from that of his father's. He said that it was as though his body took permission to become stronger directly from the contact with my body. He entered into a kind of somatic partnership between his body and mine. He was more able to notice his body and talk about it with me. His body was becoming a source of meaning, and occasionally of excitement, to him. He began to feel that his body, as well as his way of life, could become different from his father's. From a body-centered perspective, these changes are understood as emerging from a gradual shift from a defensive overidentification with the mind as the self—typical of the schizoid personality—to an evolving sense of the self, increasingly organized within the body. Bodily activity and meaning begin to coexist with mental activity and meaning.

Simon's relentless fantasies of chance meetings with strangers were replaced by his sense of his ongoing contact with me. Transferential fantasies and wishes toward me became more frequent and open to reflection. Our attention in sessions weaved back and forth between his experience of being with me and his memories of his lifelong awkwardness and loneliness, his grief about his isolation, and his rage at his parents for their disinterest in and use of him. He began to consider social activities and a part-time job outside of his parents' home. He was able to address and gradually work through his rage at his parents while continuing to live at home and provide functional caretaking as they become increasing frail.

Jack. Jack was 40 when he sought body-centered psychotherapy after being in and out of psychotherapy for most of his adult life. He reported that his previous efforts at psychotherapy had always devolved into a morass of symbiotic dependency from which he could not extricate himself. He expressed the hope that a different form of therapy might help him mobilize himself and reclaim his body from his mother. Jack still lived in the same small town as his mother. He felt that she still possessed him psychologically and found her presence in the town constantly invasive in his daily life.

Jack presented a complicated mix of somatic and interpersonal defenses, not readily representing a single diagnostic category. Assessed within the *DSM-IV* diagnostic structure, Jack was seen as fluctuating back and forth (depending on his relational circumstances in the moment) between an avoidant personality disorder (*DSM-IV*, 301.82) and a dependent personality disorder (*DSM-IV*, 301.6), with the dependent side of his personality dominating previous therapeutic efforts. He also demonstrated significant signs of posttraumatic stress disorder (*DSM-IV*, 309.81). On the GARF scale, Jack rated a score of 45. Within the neo-Reichian characterological diagnostic structure, Jack was predominantly a hysterical character, with underlying features of shock trauma and oral collapse.

Jack was a single child with an absent father and a severely sadistic and narcissistic mother, who may have become psychotic during periods of severe stress. Jack's early childhood felt like a prison to him, trapped at home with a mother who loomed around him as endlessly needy, demanding, and viciously punitive when disappointed or frustrated. Jack experienced his mother as emotionally, physically, and sexually intrusive throughout his childhood. He took on the role of a husband substitute. Although there does not seem to have ever been actual sexual intercourse between Jack and his mother, Jack found himself to be the object of his mother's erotic desires. She frequently exposed her body to him. Bedtimes and bath times were particular points of extended, unwanted physical contact. Jack felt his mother's physical/sexual excitement. His efforts to establish private space for himself and his body evoked storms of rage. Not until adolescence was Jack finally able to set and enforce limits on his mother's access to his body.

As an adult, Jack was not able to sustain an intimate or sexual relationship. He was very successful at work but only able to sustain superficial relationships with coworkers, which did not lead to friendships outside of the office. His relationships with women typically began in bars, where he was drawn to women who appeared to him as shy and lonely. The relationships were short-lived, typically descending into patterns of mutual dependency and caretaking. There was little sexual activity. With each breakup, Jack would feel used and devastated, dropping into a prolonged period of social withdrawal.

Jack's treatment involved a combination of participation in an ongoing transactional analysis therapy group (Berne, 1966; Grimes, 1988) and individual body-centered psychotherapy. His work in the group was to examine his tendency to establish dependent relationships and to experiment with establishing differentiated relationships with other group members. His contract in the body psychotherapy was to make use of my body (in intentional contrast to his mother's making use of his body) to experience boundaries, develop a sense of bodily coherence, and learn to titrate levels of contact and consequent affect. Our work with the consequences of Jack's physical and sexual trauma is consistent with that described by Bernhardt (1996) in his account of the approach to "shock trauma" (p.158) at a body level:

> The cardinal principle in thinking about the somatic aspects of shock work is that the initial goal is not emotional release or understanding psychodynamic meaning, per se, but to help the client find a successful resolution of the neurological and psychomotor patterns that have been overwhelmed or given up during the shock situation. (p. 158)

The direct work with the body is designed to facilitate the client's development of such psychomotor resources as "the ability to stand, walk, run, push, hit, hold off, pull toward, move sideways, move away from" (p. 158).

In our work together, I followed Jack's lead, with my body available to his as a resource rather than as an intrusive presence. He could sit, stand, or lie down in session as he wished, feeling what was different from one position to another. He could be close to me, move far away, or sit against me as we talked. He could make use of my body literally to lean against me, push against me, pull me to him, and/or define and experience his body in relation to mine. When he came to sessions in a state of avoidant collapse, we worked with him sitting with his back against my chest. The intention was not to provide comfort but to give him the opportunity literally to feel through his body the structure, strength, and organizing activities of my body so as to imitate and internalize in his body what he sensed in mine. Baum, Keleman, and Cornell (1999) offer a discussion of direct bodywork with clients with traumatized, labile body and personality structures.

Research

Empirical, systematic research into the effectiveness of body-centered psychotherapy is extremely limited. Body-centered psychotherapy has developed clinically, as in the tradition of psychoanalysis (Green, 1996), relying on the model of individual case studies as the primary means of developing and advancing clinical theory and technique. Many body-centered practitioners are highly skeptical of academic models and the objectification of the scientific model, in spite of the fact that Reich (1982) himself engaged in scientific experimentation in the 1920s and 1930s and drew on the neurological and anthropological research of his day.

In a series of articles, Boadella (1991, 1992, 1997b) sought to place body psychotherapy in general and his own particular modality of biosynthesis within the scientific tradition and to gain recognition for body-centered modalities by the Swiss and European Associations for Psychotherapy. While Boadella's writings did not represent empirical studies of outcome effectiveness, they did place the evolution of body psychotherapy within the evolving models of psychotherapeutic and scientific research. He underscored the consistency between body-centered theories and contemporary developmental, infant-parent, and neurophysiological research.

J. May (2000) offers the most comprehensive overview and evaluation of the status of empirical research in body-oriented psychotherapy. He undertook a literature search for citations on body-oriented psychotherapies over the past 30 years, drawing on the American Psychological Association's PsychINFO abstract service, the journals *Bioenergetic Analysis* and *Energy & Character,* and other sources of literature on body-centered methods, all of which yielded a bibliography of 264 sources. Of these, May found only 26 articles reporting on 23 separate studies that involved some form of empirical outcome research, most of which he found to have significant methodological limits. Eighteen of these studies provided sufficient data for more careful review of outcome effectiveness. May set out the relevance of empirical research for body-centered treatment modalities, discussed the basic tasks of clinical research studies, and assessed the scientific characteristics of each of the studies he included in his report.

Where do we stand, then, regarding the effectiveness of body-oriented psychotherapy? Overall, 18 separate studies were reviewed. Of these, 13 could be interpreted as finding positive effects for body-oriented psychotherapy. Five showed no effects. Most studies reviewed here have significant methodological flaws that undercut to one degree or another confidence in their findings or their generalizability. It would be desirable to have additional studies with increased methodological sophistication. However, this review did not find them.

At the same time, this review uncovered no reason to believe that the literature in general is contaminated by systemic flaws biased in one direction only. I am inclined to accept the overall weight of the literature, which seems to lend considerable support to the notion that body-oriented psychotherapy is effective, at least with some clients under some conditions. There is considerable support for its effectiveness as a stand-alone treatment with both clinical and nonclinical populations. (p. 364)

Difficulties for research within the body-centered traditions have been complicated by the evolution of modalities within rather competitive frames of references that overly emphasize the differences among various approaches rather than the commonalities. The establishment of the European Association for Body Psychotherapy and the United States Association for Body Psychotherapy has begun to promote cooperative frames of reference and the founding of research committees. The current state of the art and science of body psychotherapy is, however, predominantly that of many theories presenting diverse and sometimes contradictory explanations as to which elements of the therapy are effective and crucial to change.

Clinical models are currently based on such theories as character analysis, confrontation of resistances, catharsis, reworking of intrapsychic and psychosomatic conflicts, deepening of sensory awareness, development of sensorimotor competencies, resolution of trauma, correction of developmental discontinuities or failures, and the working through of transference at a somatic level. It is imperative that these models be systematically examined through clinical observation, theoretical debate, and empirical research. Hypotheses about the causal agents of change in body-centered psychotherapy will need to be examined through systematic research in order for the field to advance and gain professional credibility.

Problems of meaningful clinical research are exacerbated by the complexity and multiplicity of foci and interventions in body-centered psychotherapies. These approaches do not lend themselves as neatly to quantitative research procedures as do the more time-limited, symptom-focused, singular-technique treatment strategies of the cognitive-behavioral models, which are well-suited to research protocols. Questions, challenges, and alternatives to traditional, quantitative research models are not unique to body-centered psychotherapists (Beutler, 1998; Borkovec & Castonguay, 1998; Edelson, 1994; Goldfield & Wolfe, 1998; Greenberg, 1994; Horowitz, 1994; Sandler, Sandler, & Davies, 2000; Spence, 1994). Safran and Muran (1994) outlined elements of research endeavors better suited to in-depth, long-term dynamic psychotherapies, of which body psychotherapy is certainly an example. They suggest attention be given to intensive analysis of change factors by multiple judges in individual cases (in contrast to the conventional case study), sensitivity to context in which interventions are administered, use of discovery-oriented and qualitative research, a focus on underlying mechanisms of the therapeutic process, identification of key change events (as is now routinely done in video research of infant-parent interactions), and development of models to identify regularities in the sequencing of recurrent patient states, patient activity patterns, and the patient-therapist interaction patterns that seem related to change.

In a discussion of problems of research in the effectiveness of the experiential therapies, Greenberg et al. (1994) argued that

emerging new genres of phenomenological and interpretive psychotherapy research are more consistent with basic assumptions of experiential therapists than are the traditional positivistic research methods (see Toukmanian & Rennie, 1992). These studies have begun to reveal a deeper set of processes and dimensions underlying the more observable client actions, contents, and impacts reviewed here. Rennie (1990, 1992), Angus and Rennie (1988, 1989), and Clark

(1990) have provided glimpses into the operation of some of these deep structures of experiential-humanistic therapy (and perhaps of other therapies as well).

Building on his elaborate analysis of clients' moment-by-moment experiences in therapy sessions, Rennie (1990, 1992) found that the center of client experience is *reflexivity,* or the turning of the client's awareness back on itself. According to Rennie, the central process of therapy consists in the client's alternation between immersion in action or experience and reflexive self-awareness. (p. 524)

These models of empirical, qualitative research offer more hope and relevance to the assessment and understanding of effective interventions in both experiential and body-centered modalities.

Conclusion

Grand (1998) characterized the core of the somatic psychotherapy perspective as one that considers that "the basis of our psychic life is the construction of bodily states, gestures, and ways of moving which have social and emotional meaning" (p. 172); he emphasized that "the shaping of bodily experience and the bodily structuring of emotion, feeling, and efficacy continue throughout the life span" (p. 172). With an 80-year history rooted in the often radical clinical explorations of Reich, Ferenczi, and Groddeck, the body-centered psychotherapies have developed outside of the mainstream of psychoanalytic, cognitive, and behavioral modalities. Nevertheless, body-centered modalities offer systematic approaches to the alleviation of chronic emotional, somatic, and characterological constrictions. These methods are focused not only on the alleviation of psychological and relational distress but also on the enhancement of vitality and intimacy.

Systematic, empirical research is severely limited within the field of body-centered psychotherapy. The research studies reported by J. May (2000) suggest the utility and effectiveness of body-centered approaches within the limited scopes of these research efforts. No studies to date indicate harmful outcome, although five demonstrated no measurable improvement. There are no systematic studies to test the various theoretical hypotheses regarding the causal factors promoting change in body-centered work. From a research point of view, there are far more questions than answers available in the body-centered literature to date.

Therapists need to be sensitive to the elements of risk in utilizing modalities that draw on techniques that often fall outside of cultural and professional norms. These include the use of touch, reliance on active and sometimes directive techniques, and training programs that may be strongly leader-identified and may operate outside of institutional settings and organizational controls. Therapists need to be aware of both the potential for idealization of and deference toward the therapist and the potential for undue anxiety that may be evoked by these methods. Clients may become concerned over the perceived lack of safety, lack of direction, disorientation and disruption, overstimulation, or the intrusiveness or pressure of these techniques. Active, experiential techniques may increase the possibility of transferential and/or countertransferential acting out. Ongoing supervision and consultation is thus recommended in the practice of body-centered psychotherapy.

Body-centered psychotherapy extends the reach of traditional psychotherapies. The former seem uniquely attuned and equipped to help clients address and correct preverbal developmental disruptions and traumatic intrusions on the body's cohesion and well-being. Body psychotherapists facilitate clients' explorations of interiority, with and without words, often not so much to alleviate symptoms or promote adaptation as to deepen and enrich the experience of oneself and one's life potential. Body psychotherapies seek not only to promote self-knowing but also a sense of agency in one's bodily presence in the world and in relation to others.

REFERENCES
Alexander, F. M. (1918). *Man's supreme inheritance.* New York: Dutton.
Alexander, F. M. (1923). *Constructive conscious control of the individual.* New York: Dutton.
American Psychiatric Association. (1994). *Diagnostic and statistical manual of mental disorders* (4th ed.). Washington, DC: Author.
Anzieu, D. (1989). *The skin ego.* New Haven: Yale University Press.

Aron, L., & Anderson, F. S. (Ed.). (1998). *Relational perspectives on the body*. Hillsdale, NJ: The Analytic Press.
Aron, L., & Harris, A. (1993). *The legacy of Sandor Ferenczi*. Hillsdale, NJ: The Analytic Press.
Baker, E. (1967). *Man in the trap*. New York: Collier Books.
Balint, M. (1979). *The basic fault: Therapeutic aspects of regression*. New York: Brunner/Mazel. (Original work published 1968)
Baum, S., Keleman, S., & Cornell, W. (1999). Clinical forum: The borderline personality and body psychotherapy. *The United States Association for Body Psychotherapy Newsletter, 4*, 8-22.
Bermudez, J. L., Marcel, A., & Eilan, N. (1995). *The body and the self*. Cambridge, MA: MIT Press.
Berne, E. (1966). *Principles of group treatment*. New York: Oxford University Press.
Bernhardt, P. (1996). Somatic approaches to traumatic shock (or post-traumatic stress). In I. Macnaughton (Ed.), *Embodying the mind & minding the body* (pp.150-171). North Vancouver, BC: Integral Press
Beutler, L. E. (1998). Identifying empirically supported treatments: What if we didn't? *Journal of Consulting and Clinical Psychology, 66*(1), 113-120.
Binswanger, L. (1963). *Being-in-the-world*. New York: Basic Books.
Boadella, D. (1973). *Wilhelm Reich: The evolution of his work*. Plymouth: Vision Press.
Boadella, D. (1987). *Lifestreams*. London: Routledge & Kegan Paul.
Boadella, D. (1990). Somatic psychotherapy: Its roots and traditions. *Energy & Character, 21*(1), 2-26.
Boadella, D. (1991). Organism and organization: The place of somatic psychotherapy in society. *Energy & Character, 22*, 1-58.
Boadella, D. (1992). Science, nature and biosynthesis. *Energy & Character, 23*, 1-73.
Boadella, D. (1997a). Embodiment in the therapeutic relationship. *International Journal of Psychotherapy, 2*(1), 33-44.
Boadella, D. (1997b). Psychotherapy, science, and levels of discourse. *Energy & Character, 28*(1), 13-20.
Borkovec, T. D., & Castonguay, L. G. (1998). What is the meaning of empirically supported therapy? *Journal of Consulting and Clinical Psychology, 66*(1), 136-142.
Boss, M. (1963). *Psychoanalysis and daseinanalysis*. New York: Basic Books.
Brahler, E. (Ed.). (1988). *Body experience*. Berlin: Springer-Verlag.
Breckenridge, K. (2000). Physical touch in psychoanalysis: A closet phenomenon?. *Psychoanalytic Inquiry, 20*(1), 2-20.
Bucci, W. (1997). *Psychoanalysis and cognitive science: A multiple code theory*. New York: Guilford Press.
Burton, A., & Heller, L. G. (1964). The touching of the body. *Psychoanalytic Review, 51*, 122-134.
Caldwell, C. (1996). *Getting our bodies back*. Boston: Shambhala.
Caldwell, C. (1997). *Getting in touch: The guide to new body-centered therapies*. Wheaton, IL: Quest Books.
Casement, P. J. (1982). Some pressures on the analyst for physical contact during the reliving of an early psychic trauma. *International Review of Psycho-Analysis, 9*, 279-286.
Casement, P. J. (2000). The issue of touch: A retrospective overview. *Psychoanalytic Inquiry, 20*(1), 160-184.
Cornell, W. F. (1997a). If Reich had met Winnicott: Body and gesture. *Energy & Character, 8*(1), 50-60.
Cornell, W. F. (1997b). Touch and boundaries in transactional analysis: Ethical and transferential considerations. *Transactional Analysis Journal, 27*, 30-37.
Cornell, W. F. (2000). Transference, desire and vulnerability in body-centered psychotherapy. *Energy & Character, 30*(2), 29-37.
Downing, G. (1997). *Korper und wort in der psychotherapie* [The body and the word in psychotherapy]. Munich: Kosel.
Durana, C. (1998). The use of touch in psychotherapy: Ethical and clinical guidelines. *Psychotherapy, 35*(2), 269-280.
Edelson, M. (1994). Can psychotherapy research answer this psychotherapist's questions? In P. F. Talley, H. H. Strupp, & S. F. Butler (Eds.), *Psychotherapy research and practice: Bridging the gap* (pp. 60-87). New York: Basic Books.
Emery, E. (1995). A note on Sandor Ferenczi and the Dionysian itinerary in psychoanalysis. *Psychoanalytic Review, 82*(2), 267-271.
Epstein, R. S. (1994). *Keeping boundaries*. Washington, DC: American Psychiatric Press.
Fagan, J. (1998). Thoughts on using touch in psychotherapy. In E. W. L. Smith, P. R. Clance, & S. Imes (Eds.), *Touch in psychotherapy: Theory, research, and practice* (pp. 145-152). New York: Guilford.
Feldenkrais, M. (1950). *The body and mature behavior*. New York: International Universities Press.
Feldenkrais, M. (1981). *The elusive obvious*. Cupertino, CA: Meta Publications.
Ferenczi, S. (1955). The principles of relaxation and neocatharsis. In S. Ferenczi, *Final contributions to the problems and methods of psychoanalysis* (pp. 108-125). New York: Basic Books.
Forer, B. R. (1969). The taboo against touching in psychotherapy. *Psychotherapy: Theory, Research and Practice, 6*(4), 229-240.
Frankl, V. E. (1967). *Psychotherapy and existentialism*. New York: Washington Square Press.
Freud, S. (1958a). Formulations on the two principles of mental functioning. In J. Strachey (Ed. & Trans.), *The standard edition of the complete psychological works of Sigmund Freud* (Vol. 12, pp. 218-226). London: Hogarth Press. (Original work published 1911)
Freud, S. (1958b). Observations on transference-love (Further recommendations on the technique of psycho-analysis III). In J. Strachey (Ed. & Trans.), *The standard edition of the complete psychological works of Sigmund Freud* (Vol. 12, pp. 157-171). London: Hogarth Press. (Original work published 1915)
Freud, S. (1958c). On beginning treatment (Further recommendations on the technique of psycho-analysis). In J. Strachey (Ed. & Trans.), *The standard edition of the complete psychological works of Sigmund Freud* (Vol. 12, pp. 121-144). London: Hogarth Press. (Original work published 1913)

Freud, S. (1958d). Recommendations to physicians practicing psycho-analysis. In J. Strachey (Ed. & Trans.), *The standard edition of the complete psychological works of Sigmund Freud* (Vol. 12, pp. 109-120). London: Hogarth Press. (Original work published 1912)
Freud, S. (1958e). Remembering, repeating and working through (Further recommendations on the technique of psycho-analysis II). In J. Strachey (Ed. & Trans.), *The standard edition of the complete psychological works of Sigmund Freud* (Vol. 12, pp. 145-156). London: Hogarth Press. (Original work published 1914)
Fromm-Reichmann, F. (1950). *Principles of intensive psychotherapy*. Chicago: University of Chicago Press.
Gallagher, S. (1995). Body schema and intentionality. In J. L. Bermudez, A. Marcel, & N. Eilan (Eds.), *The body and the self* (pp. 225-244). Cambridge, MA: MIT Press.
Geib, P. (1998). The experience of nonerotic physical contact in traditional psychotherapy. In E. W. L. Smith, P. R. Clance, & S. Imes (Eds.), *Touch in psychotherapy: Theory, research, and practice* (pp. 109-126). New York: Guilford Press.
Gendlin, E. T. (1962). *Experiencing and the creation of meaning*. New York: Free Press.
Gendlin, E. T. (1981). *Focusing*. New York: Bantam.
Giorgi, A., Fischer, W. F., & von Eckartsberg, R. (1971). *Phenomenological psychology* (Vol. I). Pittsburgh: Duquesne University Press.
Goldfield, M. R., & Wolfe, B. E. (1998). Toward a more clinically valid approach to therapy research. *Journal of Consulting and Clinical Psychology, 66*(1), 143-150.
Goodman, M., & Teicher, A. (1988). To touch or not to touch. *Psychotherapy, 25*(4), 492-500.
Grand, I. J. (1998). Psyche's body: Towards a somatic psychodynamics. In D. H. Johnson & I. J. Grand (Eds.), *The body in psychotherapy: Inquiries in somatic psychology* (pp. 171-193). Berkeley, CA: North Atlantic Books.
Green, A. (1996). What kind of research for psychoanalysis? *International Psychoanalysis: The Newsletter of the International Psychoanalytic Association, 5,* 10-14.
Green, A. (2000). *Chains of eros: The sexual in psychoanalysis*. London: Rebus Press.
Greenberg, J. (1994). Psychotherapy research: A clinician's view. In P. F. Talley, H. H. Strupp, & S. F. Butler (Eds.), *Psychotherapy research and practice: Bridging the gap* (pp. 1-18). New York: Basic Books.
Greenberg, L. S., Elliott, R., & Lietaer, G. (1994). Research on experiential psychotherapies. In A. E. Bergin & S. L. Garfield (Eds.), *Handbook of psychotherapy and behavior change* (4th ed.) (pp. 509-539). New York: Wiley.
Greenberg, L. S., & Safran, J. D. (1987). *Emotion in psychotherapy*. New York: Guilford Press.
Grimes, J. (1988). Transactional analysis in group work. In S. Long (Ed.), *Six group therapies* (pp. 49-113). New York: Plenum Press.
Groddeck, G. (1977). *The meaning of illness: Selected psychoanalytic writings*. New York: International Universities Press.
Group for the Advancement of Psychiatry Committee on the Family. (1995). Beyond DSM-IV: A model for the classification and diagnosis of relational disorders. *Psychiatric Services, 46,* 926-931.
Hanna, T. (1988). *Somatics*. Reading, MA: Perseus Books.
Hanna, T. (1993). *The body of life*. Rochester, VT: Healing Arts Press.
Haynal, A. (1989). *Controversies in psychoanalytic method: From Freud and Ferenczi to Michael Balint*. New York: New York University Press.
Holder, A. (2000). To touch or not to touch: That is the question. *Psychoanalytic Inquiry, 20*(1), 44-64.
Holroyd, C. J., & Brodsky, A. (1977). Psychologists' attitudes and practices regarding erotic and nonerotic physical contact with patients. *American Psychologist, 32,* 843-849.
Holroyd, C. J., & Brodsky, A. (1980). Does touching patients lead to sexual intercourse? *Professional Psychology, 11,* 807-811.
Holub, E. A., & Lee, S. S. (1990). Therapist's use of nonerotic physical contact: Ethical concerns. *Professional Psychology: Research and Practice, 21*(2), 115-117.
Horowitz, M. (1994). Psychotherapy research and the views of clinicians. In P. F. Talley, H. H. Strupp, & S. F. Butler (Eds.), *Psychotherapy research and practice: Bridging the gap* (pp. 196-205). New York: Basic Books.
Johnson, D. (1977). *The protean body*. New York: Harper Colophon Books.
Johnson, D. H. (Ed.). (1995). *Bone, breath, & gesture: Practices of embodiment*. Berkeley, CA: North Atlantic Books.
Johnson, D. H., & Grand, I. J. (1998). *The body in psychotherapy: Inquiries in somatic psychology*. Berkeley, CA: North Atlantic Books.
Johnson, M. (1987). *The body in the mind: The bodily basis of meaning, imagination, and reason*. Chicago: University of Chicago Press.
Kaslow, F. W. (Ed.). (1996). *Handbook of relational diagnosis and dysfunctional family patterns*. New York: Wiley.
Keleman, S. (1986). *Bonding: A somatic-emotional approach to transference*. Berkeley CA: Center Press.
Keleman, S. (1989). *Patterns of distress: Emotional insults and human form*. Berkeley CA: Center Press.
Kelley, C. R. (1974). *Education in feeling and purpose*. Santa Monica, CA: The Radix Institute.
Kepner, J. I. (1987). *Body process*. New York: Gestalt Institute of Cleveland Press.
Kertay, L., & Reviere, S. L. (1993). The use of touch in psychotherapy: Theoretical and ethical concerns. *Psychotherapy, 30,* 33-40.
Krueger, D. W. (1989). *Body self and psychological self*. New York: Brunner/Mazel.
Kwant, R. C. (1963). *The phenomenological philosophy of Merleau-Ponty*. Pittsburgh: Duquesne University Press.
Kwant, R. C. (1969). *Phenomenology of expression*. Pittsburgh: Duquesne University Press.
Laing, R. D. (1960). *The divided self*. London: Tavistock Publications.

Laing, R. D. (1961). *The self and others*. London: Tavistock Publications.
Levine, P. A. (1997). *Waking the tiger: Healing trauma*. Berkeley, CA: North Atlantic Books.
Little, M. (1993). *Transference neurosis and transference psychosis*. Northvale, NJ: Jason Aronson.
Lowen, A. (1958). *Physical dynamics of character structure*. New York: Grune & Stratton.
Lowen, A. (1975). *Bioenergetics*. New York: Coward, McCann & Geoghegan.
Luijpen, W. A. (1960). *Existential phenomenology*. Pittsburgh: Duquesne University Press.
Macnaughton, I. (Ed.). (1996). *Embodying the mind & minding the body*. North Vancouver, BC: Integral Press.
Marcher, L., & Bernhardt, P. (1996). The art of following structure. In I. Macnaughton (Ed.), *Embodying the mind & minding the body* (pp. 80-93). North Vancouver, BC: Integral Press.
Maul, B. (Ed.). (1992). *Body psychotherapy or the art of contact*. Berlin: Verlag Bernhard Maul.
May, J. (2000). A review of the empirical status of body-oriented psychotherapy. *Proceedings of the Second National Conference of the United States Body Psychotherapy Association* (pp. 348-388). Berkeley, CA: United States Body Psychotherapy Association.
May, R. (1966). *Psychology and the human dilemma*. Princeton, NJ: D. Van Nostrand.
May, R. (1969). *Love and will*. New York: Norton.
McDougall, J. (1989). *Theaters of the body*. New York: Norton.
McDougall, J. (1995). *The many faces of eros*. New York: Norton.
McLaughlin, J. T. (1995). Touching limits in the analytic dyad. *Psychoanalytic Quarterly, 64*, 433-465.
McLaughlin, J. T. (2000). The problem and place of physical contact in analytic work: Some reflections on handholding in the analytic situation. *Psychoanalytic Inquiry, 20*(1), 65-81.
Merleau-Ponty, M. (1962). *Phenomenology of perception*. London: Routledge and Kegan Paul.
Merleau-Ponty, M. (1964). *The primacy of perception*. Evanston, IL: Northwestern University Press.
Merleau-Ponty, M. (1967). *The structure of behavior*. Boston: Beacon Press.
Mintz, E. E. (1969a). On the rationale of touch in psychotherapy. *Psychotherapy, Research and Practice, 6*(4), 232-234.
Mintz, E. E. (1969b). Touch and the psychoanalytic tradition. *Psychoanalytic Review, 56*, 365-376.
O'Neil, J. (1989). *The communicative body*. Evanston, IL: Northwestern University Press.
Pedder, J. R. (1976). Attachment and new beginning: Some links between the work of Michael Balint and John Bowlby. *International Review of Psycho-Analysis, 3*, 491-497.
Pope, K., & Vasquez, M. (1991). *Ethics in psychotherapy and counseling*. San Francisco: Jossey-Bass.
Rachman, A. W. (1997). *Sandor Ferenczi: The psychotherapist of tenderness and passion*. Northvale, NJ: Jason Aronson.
Reich, W. (1949). *Character analysis* (3rd ed. rev.) (T. P. Wolfe, Trans.). New York: Orgone Institute Press.
Reich, W. (1961). *The function of the orgasm* (T. P. Wolfe, Trans.). New York: Farrar, Straus & Giroux.
Reich, W. (1971). *The invasion of compulsory sex-morality*. New York: Farrar, Straus & Giroux.
Reich, W. (1974). *The sexual revolution* (T. Pol, Trans.). New York: Farrar, Straus & Giroux.
Reich, W. (1980). *Genitality in the theory and therapy of neurosis* (P. Scmitz, Trans.). New York: Farrar, Straus & Giroux.
Reich, R. (1982). *The bioelectrical investigation of sexuality and anxiety* (M. Faber, Trans.). New York: Farrar, Straus & Giroux.
Reich, W. (1983). *Children of the future: On the prevention of sexual pathology*. New York: Farrar, Straus & Giroux.
Rolf, I. P. (1989). *Rolfing*. Rochester, VT: Healing Arts Press.
Ruderman, E. G. (2000). Intimate communications: The values and boundaries of touch in the psychoanalytic setting. *Psychoanalytic Inquiry, 20*(1), 108-123.
Ruderman, E. G., Shane, E., & Shane, M. (Eds.). (2000). On touch in the psychoanalytic situation. *Psychoanalytic Inquiry, 20*(1), 1.
Safran, J. D., & Muran, J. C. (1994). Toward a working alliance between research and practice. In P. F. Talley, H. H. Strupp, & S. F. Butler (Eds.), *Psychotherapy research and practice: Bridging the gap* (pp. 206-226). New York: Basic Books.
Sandler, J., Sandler, A-M., & Davies, R. (2000). *Clinical and observational psychoanalytic research: Roots of a controversy*. Madison, CT: International Universities Press.
Sardello, R. (1971). The role of direct experience in contemporary psychology—a critical review. In A. Giorgi, W. Fischer, & R. von Eckartsberg (Eds.), *Phenomenological psychology* (Vol. I, pp. 30-49). Pittsburgh: Duquesne University Press.
Searles, H. (1965). *Collected papers on schizophrenia*. New York: International Universities Press.
Sharaf, M. (1983). *Fury on earth: A biography of Wilhelm Reich*. New York: St. Martin's Press/Marek.
Smith, E. W. L. (Ed.). (1977a). *The growing edge of gestalt therapy*. Secaucus, NJ: The Citadel Press.
Smith, E. W. L. (1977b). The roots of gestalt therapy. In E. W. L. Smith (Ed.), *The growing edge of gestalt therapy* (pp. 3-36). Secaucus, NJ: The Citadel Press.
Smith, E. W. L. (1985). *The body in psychotherapy*. Jefferson, NC: McFarland.
Smith, E. W. L., Clance, P. R., & Imes, S. (1998). *Touch in psychotherapy: Theory, research, and practice*. New York: Guilford Press.
Spence, D. P. (1994). The failure to ask hard questions. In P. F. Talley, H. H. Strupp, & S. F. Butler (Eds.), *Psychotherapy research and practice: Bridging the gap* (pp. 19-38). New York: Basic Books.
Spiegelberg, H. (1972). *Phenomenology in psychology and psychiatry*. Evanston, IL: Northwestern University Press.
Thelen, E., & Smith, L. (1994). *A dynamic systems approach to the development of cognition and action*. Cambridge, MA: MIT Press.
Totton, N. (1998). *The water in the glass: Body and mind in psychoanalysis*. London: Rebus Press.

Valle, R. S., & King, M. (Eds.). (1978). *Existential-phenomenological alternatives for psychology.* New York: Oxford University Press.

Varela, F., Thompson, E., & Rosch, E. (1991). *The embodied mind: Cognitive science and human experience.* Cambridge, MA: MIT Press.

Williams, S. (1992). Withholding therapeutic touch. *Voices: The Art and Science of Psychotherapy, 28*(3), 58-61.

Yalom, I. D. (1980). *Existential psychotherapy.* New York: Basic Books.

Yontef, G. (1979). Gestalt therapy: Clinical phenomenology. *The Gestalt Journal, 2*(1), 27-45.

The original version of this chapter was published in the Comprehensive Handbook of Psychotherapy: Volume 3 Interpersonal/Humanistic/Existential *(pp. 587-613) edited by Robert F. Massey and Sharon D. Massey (F. Kaslow, Series Ed.), New York: Wiley, 2002. It is republished here with permission.*

17

Consequences of Childhood Bodily Abuse: A Clinical Model for Affective Interventions

William F. Cornell and Karen A. Olio

> One of the saddest lessons we have learned in all of our years of research on family violence is that human beings can absorb outrageous violence over long periods of time with barely a whimper and rarely a cry for help. (Gelles & Straus, 1988, p. 19)

The frequency of violence, coercion, and abuse in families and the sociocultural sanction of "intimate violence" (Gelles & Straus, 1988, p. 11) are described in disturbing detail in contemporary literature (Gelles & Straus, 1988; Gordon, 1988; Greven, 1991; Miller, 1983; Schechter, 1982; Straus, 1988). Partly as a result, psychotherapists are increasingly willing to acknowledge and treat the consequences of this violence. In addition, as the clinical literature reflects a deeper understanding of posttraumatic stress disorder (Figley, 1985; Horowitz, 1976; Ochberg, 1991; van der Kolk, 1987; Wilson, 1989), more attention has been focused on the psychological impact of wounds to the body as well as to those of the mind.

Every child copes to some degree with difficulties, disappointments, and dysfunctions in the family by making decisions about how to be and what to do both in the family and out in the world. However, when parents or other loving/authority figures violate children's bodies through physical and/or sexual abuse, these youngsters are overwhelmed by both emotions and physical sensations. Personal control is repeatedly taken away from these children as they are consumed by the feelings and needs of their abusers.

To deal with such abuse, survivors numb their bodies and disconnect from feelings related to the existence and/or meaning of their abuse (Lifton, 1979; Spiegel, 1986). As a result, disturbances of affect are almost universal among adults who were sexually or physically abused as children; they often experience lack of pleasure, diminished emotional awareness, emotional fragmentation, and depression in daily life. On the other hand, if the abuse is disclosed or triggered, often strong, sometimes uncontrollable affect emerges, which can be deeply disturbing and disorienting to both client and therapist (Blake-White & Kline, 1985; Gelinas, 1983; Swanson & Biaggio, 1985).

Currently, therapists are focusing more on integrating the affect and content of trauma into a coherent experience of personal history and ego identity (Lindberg & Distad, 1985; Rieker & Carmen, 1986; Wilson, 1989), keeping in mind that the impact of trauma on an individual is highly variable and reflects a multitude of factors, including the nature and severity of the abuse, how chronic it was, the victim's relationship to the abuser(s), the victim's developmental stage(s) at the time of the abuse, the patterns of coercive violence and/or affectionate seductive intrusion, and threats to life.

In spite of these variables, trauma also has consistent consequences that are often ignored or underestimated in the psychotherapeutic literature (Briere, 1989; Root, 1992; Terr, 1991; van der Kolk, 1987). Steele and Colrain (1990) described the experience of trauma as resulting in a "triad of helplessness, terror, and meaninglessness." Thus, the goal of working with affect in treating survivors "is to unfreeze this moment of ontological insecurity and to bring it into conscious awareness so that it can be reexperienced in a different way" (p. 13). Herman and Schatzow (1987) summarized this process as follows:

> The retrieval and validation of repressed memories has an important role in the recovery process. With the return of memory, the patient has an opportunity as an adult to integrate an experience that was beyond her capacity to endure as a child. The purpose of reliving the experience with full affect is not simply one of catharsis, but of reintegration. (p. 12)

Treatment approaches that focus on this reintegration of affect with adult victims of childhood abuse are demanding for both client and therapist. As Wilson (1989) explained, "Individuals suffering from post-traumatic stress disorder have . . . endured some of the most threatening and terrorizing experiences imaginable. . . . It typically presents the therapist with many challenges to their values and personal conceptions of a just and decent world" (p. 204). Such treatment requires a high level of engagement and consistency from the therapist as well as an understanding of the client's often pervasive patterns of denial and dissociation. In addition, effectively incorporating affective and body-centered techniques significantly facilitates such work.

This chapter presents a framework for describing the impact of childhood abuse on ego state development and functioning. It offers a treatment model for working with adult survivors at the "affective edge," where cognitive understanding and emotional/bodily awareness are both experienced without triggering defensive denial and dissociation. This approach emphasizes careful monitoring of the client's cognitive and emotional functioning both during and between therapeutic sessions.

Impact of Bodily Trauma on Ego State Development

Although childhood abuse does not lead to a single, differential profile of ego state function or script patterns, it does result in severe and lasting disruption of ego state boundaries and functions. The implications of this for treatment become clearer with an understanding of the types of damage done to the formation and subsequent functioning of each ego state.

Parent Ego State. Abusive families break the most fundamental parental contract: the provision of protection and security. The child's "illusion of invulnerability" (Lifton & Olson, 1976, p. 2) is shattered; he or she does not experience safety and continuity in the self or soothing and safety through his or her parents. The Parent ego state of an abuse victim typically reflects the contradictory task of preserving the self while often using attitudes and feelings incorporated from the abuser. Abuse survivors frequently struggle with thinking about and treating themselves and/or others as they were treated.

Victims of childhood violence may incorporate a Parent ego state that tolerates or even sanctions abuse, coercion, and violence, sometimes leading them to become abusive as adults (Burgess, Hartman, & McCormack, 1987; McCarthy, 1990; Schmitt & Kempe, 1975; van der Kolk, 1989). Rosenthal (1988) described this aggressive style of coping with abuse as "undoing" (p. 506), which reflects the child's identification with the aggressor and the incorporation of permission to act out "behaviors such as defiance, dishonesty, aggression toward peers, compulsivity" (p. 507). However, much research indicates that most abused children do not become abusive in turn but, rather, tend to severely inhibit their own aggressive and self-expressive functions (Bowlby, 1984; Gelles & Straus, 1988; Hunter & Kilstrom, 1979). Rosenthal (1988) described these self-inhibiting children as "indoing" (p. 506) individuals who are likely to be "depressed, apathetic, and overly compliant" having learned "to survive emotionally by internalizing . . . abuse and neglect in forms of damaged self-esteem and exaggerated inhibitions of aggression" (p. 507). These descriptions of depressive, self-inhibiting styles are consistent with observations in the recently completed report of the American Psychological Association's Task Force on Women and Depression (McGrath, Keita, Strickland, & Russo, 1990).

Adults who grew up in violent and/or incestuous homes may find it difficult to recognize patterns of abuse in current adult relationships as abnormal or dysfunctional. As van der Kolk (1989) observed, "People who are exposed early to violence or neglect come to expect it as a way of life. They see the chronic helplessness of their mothers and their fathers' alternating outbursts of affection and violence; they learn themselves that they have no control" (p. 395). Having endured as children without adequate protection or permission to stop or leave abusive relationships, adult survivors lack effective Parent ego state responses in the face of violence and coercion and are more likely to tolerate and absorb continued mistreatment.

Abusive families do not model honesty, kindness, respect, and responsibility. In children from such families, the Parent ego state functions of nurturance and structure are inhibited, and the pressure for control of self, others, and the environment is intensified. This dilemma in the Parent ego state is reflected in a woman's description of the consequences in her adult life of her childhood sexual abuse:

> I've been trained to shut up about it. Taught that it was nothing and at the same time that I have been scarred for life.... Lots of times I couldn't figure out what was the right thing to do: Am I standing up for myself or doing something harmful and neglectful to others?

Adult Ego State. Typically, the Adult ego state of a child in an abusive family forms in the shadow of the Parent ego state, rarely independent of it. The Parent often contaminates the Adult rather than the Adult functioning to inform and modify the Parent. Reality testing, interpersonal problem solving, and social skills—crucial elements in the formation of Adult ego state functioning—are lacking in abusive families. Such environments inhibit and distort the evolution of the Adult ego state, often resulting in patterns of ego state contamination and exclusion.

Even prior to instances of abuse, these families use denial as a dominant coping strategy. When abuse does occur, its existence is often denied, made invisible or inconsequential. If there is a response to the abuse, typically reality is distorted so as to justify the abuse as deserved, unintentional, or forgivable. In the face of trauma, instead of showing the appropriate responses necessary for fostering the development of Adult functioning, the responses in abusive families range from neglect and discounting to shaming and controlling.

Speaking and questioning—essential for the vitality and growth of the Adult ego state—are forbidden and often punished in abusive families. Silence, shame, and secrets are the typical enforcers in abusive relationships, resulting all too often in, as Gelles and Straus (1988) observed, "barely a whimper and rarely a cry for help" (p. 19).

Memory is another crucial element affecting the viability of the Adult ego state. Functioning in the present and planning for the future is most effective when access to past experience is available. The cumulative impact of an abusive family's patterns of blame and denial, along with the individual's self-protective attempts to limit such overwhelming experiences, often results in some degree of loss in both archaic and current memory (Olio, 1989). In addition to the loss of content, felt memory—that is, the emotional experience and meaning of the content—is lost. The Adult ego state then operates in spite of or in lieu of Child awareness rather than in service of the Child ego state.

It should be noted that it is not the trauma itself that is necessarily pathological in its consequences but the failure of the family and social environment to respond adequately—the failure to speak, to act, to acknowledge, to protect—that solidifies the damage and inhibits Adult ego state development.

Child Ego State. Although the effectiveness of each ego state is impaired by physical and sexual abuse, the damage to the Child ego state is likely to be the most severe. In the face of overstimulating, hostile, and intrusive experiences, the Child ego state becomes organized around safety rather than for curiosity, pleasure, or self-expression.

The use of dissociation typically causes a pervasive disconnection from bodily sensations and emotions that lead to a loss of sensations such as hunger, fatigue, and discomfort, as well as to emotional numbness. Adult survivors may experience an exclusion of the Child ego state and thus a disconnection from the emotional cues needed to motivate action on behalf of the self.

The self-protection required in the face of childhood abuse also fosters rigidity in Child ego state boundaries, which may suddenly rupture or disintegrate. For example, traumatic childhood experiences and feelings are not usually integrated into a coherent sense of personal history. Thus, flashbacks—such as memory fragments and/or intense affect triggered by external cues without conscious control or awareness—may suddenly intrude into current life, making Child ego state boundaries unpredictably labile. For adults with abusive histories, this sudden and unexpected loss of boundaries can serve as further evidence of the danger of feelings.

As a result of being taken over by the physical and emotional being of the abuser, the victim's feelings and sensations become a threat, something to be managed, rather than a source of vitality, pleasure, or contact. As Rosenthal (1988) observed, the "lack of animation defends the child from provoking the abusive parent" (p. 507), and when "the self—one's center of volition—is assaulted and razed, the child attempts to dismantle the inner initiatory self" (p. 508). A woman client described the experience of being endangered by her own feelings as follows:

> Traumatic has no meaning in our family. It was never safe to feel the trauma. Any expression of pain was regarded with suspicion and hostility, as melodrama rather than an authentic expression, or as a sign of weakness to be attacked and shamed.

Dissociation and Denial

The use of dissociation and denial are central in the effort to cope with and defend against traumatic experiences and their long-lasting consequences. Identifying and reducing the prevalence and strength of these defenses is at the heart of the therapeutic process with survivors of bodily abuse.

Dissociation. The healthy mind integrates consciousness, that is, awareness, affect, identity, and behavior. In dissociative states, one or more of these elements is split off from conscious experience, and with this separation, the mind disintegrates rather than integrates experience. Laughlin (1987) defined dissociation as "an ego defense or dynamism operating outside of and beyond conscious awareness through which affect and emotional significance is separated and detached (i.e., dissociated) from an idea, situation, object, or relationship" (p. 94). Dissociation may range from abrupt, momentary disruption of affective experience to a chronic impairment of identity and consciousness. One client described her experience of dissociation as follows:

> Sometimes it's like observing my life from outside of my body, other times I'm watching from inside with no experience of a body, only a head. For long periods of time I feel deadened, just going through the motions of life. Then, unexpectedly, I am flooded with feelings, often without any idea of what they are attached to. Sometimes I begin to tremble or cry while inside I feel calm and detached.

Dissociation protects the victim from overwhelming trauma and affect that cannot be integrated into consciousness or daily life. The profound and lasting consequences were vividly described by Lifton (1979):

> The dissociation becomes intra-psychic in the sense that feeling is severed from knowledge or awareness of what is happening. To say that emotion is lost while cognition is retained is more or less true, but it doesn't capture what the mind is experiencing. What is more basic is that the self is being severed from its own history, from the grounding in such psychic forms as compassion for others, communal involvement, and other primary values. . . . It is a disintegration in the sense of the coming apart of crucial components of the self. We can say that the dissociative disintegration characterizes the psychic numbing of the traumatic syndrome and it is at the heart of the experience. (p. 175)

When dissociation is used as a primary defense mechanism, the individual develops a diminished capacity for spontaneous affect, often a fragmented sense of identity, and ultimately a loss of personal history.

Denial. Denial refers to the defensive patterns by which a person does not acknowledge portions of reality, dismissing them from conscious awareness in order to maintain an intraspychic homeostasis. Laughlin (1987) defined denial as "a primitive and desperate unconscious method of coping with otherwise intolerable conflict, anxiety, and emotional distress or pain" (p. 57). As described by Rieker and Carmen (1986), "In its simplest form, the victim's feeling that 'this can't be happening to me' becomes 'this didn't happen to me' " (p. 365). The use of denial by adults abused as children covers the spectrum from denying the occurrence of the abuse to denying its importance and relevance to issues being addressed in therapy.

The patterns of denial evident in a client's current life originate in the family during childhood. Familial mechanisms of denial are not limited to abusive experiences but serve as a general, fundamental defense against threats to the family's frame of reference and symbiotic functioning. Abusive families have the uncanny ability to simultaneously justify dysfunctional and abusive behavior while denying its importance or consequence. Courtois (1988) concluded, "The family functions in such a way that its reality is distorted, the distortion is treated as reality" (p. 46).

For the child abuse victim, this denial becomes an important self-protective strategy. Because denial maintained systematically within the abusing family is often internalized by the abused child, the therapist must identify the patterns of denial and their origins within the family as well as examine how they are presently maintained intrapsychically by the client and interpersonally by both the client and the family.

Although patterns of denial may become evident early in therapy when abuse is initially considered, they continually reemerge as a means of self-protection in the face of additional memories or intensified affect. Abuse victims repeatedly discount their experiences, emerging memories, and feelings. Often they return to the explanations and excuses given by the family or search for alternative causes for their presenting problems. Typically abuse survivors locate the problem within themselves, reporting, for instance, "There's something the matter with me. I've made this up—I must be crazy." The therapist must repeatedly communicate that the problem is not the confusion or other symptoms the client experiences, but rather, the denial system learned within the family to discount the existence of the abuse or minimize its relevance.

Although patterns of denial are remarkably similar among abuse victims, the functions the denial serves are highly individualized. The idiosyncratic meaning, which necessitates a client's continued use of the defense, must be identified and specifically addressed to provide a foundation for safely dealing with traumatic memories. One of the most common functions of denial is to maintain the client's illusion of the family as loving and normal, or at least as no worse than other families. In other cases denial is used to maintain the illusion of a caring relationship with the abuser, leading to a need to protect that person. The child may have felt that the abuser was the only one who cared.

In combination, dissociation and denial form a more tenacious coping strategy than either defense used separately. One client described this as becoming "numb and dumb." Denial becomes more entrenched with the use of dissociation; it is easier to deny the existence or significance of an experience one does not feel. Those who do have memories of the abuse often refer to them without emotion, and the therapist may mistake this as an indication of resolution when actually it reflects the use of denial and dissociation.

The therapist and client should identify patterns of denial together before facilitating recall of abuse or using affective techniques. Such mutual effort confronts and clarifies Parent ego state contaminations and strengthens Adult ego state functions. When the client begins to disrupt patterns of denial and break the forced silence, profound vulnerability and terror usually results (Blake-White & Kline, 1985; Lister, 1982; Rieker & Carmen, 1986) and Child ego state boundaries become more fragile. As this affect becomes available, sessions become more emotionally charged, and the use of dissociation becomes more pronounced. It is the therapist's responsibility to recognize and monitor this dissociation. Early in treatment, clients are often unaware of when they have dissociated; the therapist must identify such moments and help clients recognize them so that ultimately clients can monitor themselves.

Although dissociation can grossly disrupt consciousness, it more frequently leads to a subtle, persistent disruption of consciousness or interpersonal contact. In extreme instances, the client may appear deadened, as though in shock, presenting violent and painful stories with no apparent affect. More typically, a client may present as if in suspended animation, making eye contact, for instance, but not showing expression or responsiveness in his or her eyes (looking but not seeing). In other cases, a client may respond reasonably or calmly in situations that should be upsetting.

Establishing an Affective Edge

Dissociation and denial substantially block self-awareness, resulting in a diminished capacity for appropriate emotional experience, expression, and action. This can be seen clearly in such theoretical models as E. W. L. Smith's (1985) concept of the "contact-satisfaction-withdrawal" (p. 29) cycle, a variation of Reich's (1961) work, which is central to most body-centered and affective treatment modalities.

This cycle begins with a want or need that results in physiological arousal that, if it becomes strong enough, will reach conscious awareness and be subjectively experienced as an emotion. These initial steps constitute the awareness phase of this cycle, reflecting an evolving internal experience that has not yet resulted in the expression of the experience.

When the experience of emotion is unimpeded, it leads to movement or action that, in turn, results in interaction with a person or the environment. When this interaction is successful, it produces some form of resolution or satisfaction of the original want. These three steps comprise the expressive phase of this cycle and, if completed, will be followed by the organism's withdrawal or rest until the cycle begins anew (Figure 1).

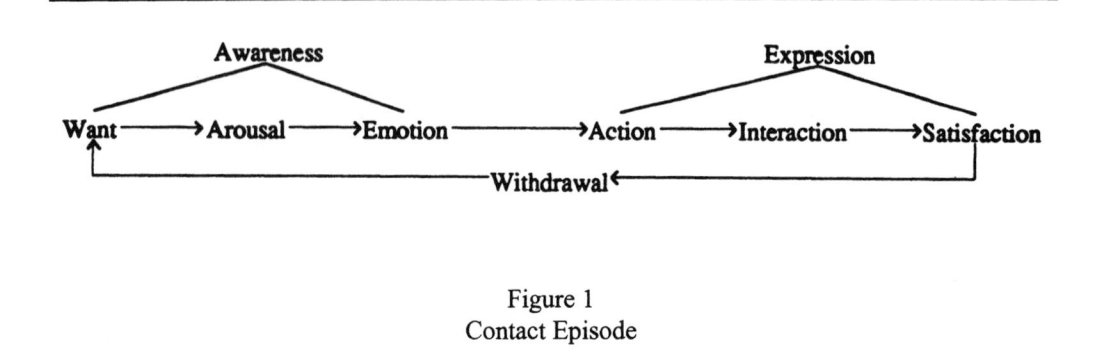

```
         Awareness                            Expression
Want ──→ Arousal ──→ Emotion ──→ Action ──→ Interaction ──→ Satisfaction
  ↑                                                              │
  └──────────────────── Withdrawal ←────────────────────────────┘
```

Figure 1
Contact Episode

Denial and dissociation disrupt awareness, resulting in an interruption in the first phase of the cycle. Because both awareness and expression are required for satisfaction and resolution, it is essential that the therapist help to establish and reinforce a foundation of consistent and reliable self-awareness in treatment with adult victims of childhood abuse. Only when survivors maintain a sense of self-connectedness while acknowledging the intensely emotional, traumatic memories does encouraging deeper expression of feeling result in integration and empowerment rather than renewed defense.

Many expressive, body-centered interventions and other cathartic techniques intensify and mobilize the expressive phase of the contact cycle. However, these techniques often trigger dissociative states with abuse victims because clients are prematurely overstimulated and/or encouraged to take action. Such techniques may appear to deepen affect and produce dramatic results in the session but often do not result in the client's sustained understanding of or connection to his or her experiences of abuse. Instead, the techniques are likely to cause a further splitting of Child and Adult functions. These experiences may be followed by memory loss of significant parts of the session, intense confusion, anxiety attacks, a disintegration of functioning, and often a reemergence and intensification of the client's defenses. Once this edge between what can be felt and what must be split off is exceeded and dissociative fragmentation or denial has reemerged, the client is no longer able to integrate the experience. At this point, the therapeutic opportunity is lost and trust in the therapist may be damaged.

Therefore, a central and ongoing emphasis in treatment with childhood abuse survivors must be to establish and maintain an affective edge of experience in which the client has moved out of denial sufficiently to allow a felt awareness of the abusive experiences or their consequences without reaching a level of intensity that triggers dissociation. Cole and Barney (1987) described this range between over-control (denial) and out-of-control (intrusive) phases as the "therapeutic window," which permits the safe reworking of traumatic material and results in the gradual integration of Child and Adult ego state functions.

When working with the affective edge, the therapist's stance and attitude are crucial for interrupting the client's denial. The therapist must maintain a sufficient level of emotional engagement in the therapeutic relationship to foster the client's felt awareness of internal experience and interpersonal contact. Without such engagement and responsiveness from the therapist, an affective edge is not likely to be achieved or sustained. Traditional attitudes of distance or therapeutic neutrality common in psychoanalytic, medical, psychiatric, and many cognitive approaches to psychotherapy are likely to harm rather than help victims of violence and bodily trauma by reinforcing patterns of denial (Lister, 1982; Wilson, 1989). Abuse survivors are extremely sensitive to any suggestion of disbelief or denial from the therapist. Even well-meaning comments such as, "Whether you were sexually abused or not, certainly we know you were emotionally abused," or "I don't have any reason to not believe you" are often experienced by the client as confirmation that the abuse did not really happen. An attitude of empathy, active engagement, and appropriate confrontation elicits and gradually alters the client's denial system and fosters the internalization of an attentive and responsive Parent ego state and an active Adult ego state.

By maintaining this affective edge while helping clients develop an increased capacity to tolerate traumatic memories with the associated feelings, the therapist temporarily becomes the living record of the therapy. When clients exceed this edge and their defenses are reactivated (e.g., "I must be making this up," "What did I say?" "I can't remember the last session," "It doesn't matter"), the therapist must hold the continuity of reality ("the evidence is . . .") and reflect appropriate affect ("This saddens me," "You look frightened"). In this way the therapist acts as a bridge to help the client reconnect to elements of his or her emotional experience that have been lost.

Use of Touch in the Therapeutic Process

It is not essential, of course, for a therapist to directly touch a client in order to attend to and alter bodily and emotional processes. However, we have found a unique power in the trained use of physical contact to facilitate the integration of traumatic memories and the associated affect in treatment with adult victims of childhood abuse.

There are various therapeutic approaches (Boadella, 1987; Lowen, 1975; Reich, 1961) that systematically utilize direct physical contact between therapist and client. Whereas a traditional psychotherapist uses verbal interventions (such as interpretation, empathic reflection, confrontation) to heighten a client's psychological awareness and understanding, a somatic therapist uses physical movement and touch to achieve similarly focused awareness on an emotional and body level. The somatic therapist (Reichian, neo-Reichian, bioenergetic) utilizes a psychodynamic perspective with particular emphasis on the formative influences of emotional and physical deprivation, upheaval, and trauma on how the person interprets and limits his or her experiences of life.

In a second group of body-centered approaches—those reflecting a physiological and movement orientation (Alexander, 1974; Feldenkrais, 1950, 1981)—touch is used to focus attention on and alter habitual, dysfunctional patterns of muscle tension and posture. Although they acknowledge the psychological aspects of chronic physical patterns, these approaches emphasize the use of touch to gently facilitate muscular change rather than to address intentionally psychological issues. Increasingly, body-centered therapists have respect for and a working knowledge of both perspectives (Gelb, 1981; Kepner, 1987; Kurtz & Prestera, 1976; E. W. L. Smith, 1985).

More conventional psychotherapies offer no systematic approach to the therapeutic use of touch between client and therapist. For example, the literature on integrating transactional analysis with touch and body-centered interventions is quite limited. What does exist could perhaps best be described as a grafting of techniques promoting regression and/or catharsis onto transactional analysis in order to intensify the cognitive or interpersonal strategies of TA. Unfortunately, most of these efforts are limited in their theoretical understanding.

Berne (1972), despite his intuitive awareness of body-script signals and their physiological components and his attention to physical cues in treatment, did not think that the use of touch or direct work with the body had a place in transactional analysis. He was emphatic that "transactional analysis as a therapeutic method is based on the assumption that words and gestures can have therapeutic effect without any bodily contact with the patient beyond a handshake" (p. 371). He did, however, suggest that when transactional analysts considered bodily contact desirable that they refer the patient to "a dance class, sensory-awareness group, or a 'permission class' " (p. 371) in which the leader should follow the primary therapist's prescriptions for bodily movement and contact.

Steiner (1974) took a markedly different position, considering touch as a "maneuver of great potency which . . . needs to be thoroughly explored and its therapeutic potential isolated from its harmful possibilities." He saw touch as "the most basic tissue transaction," which is "an essential ingredient when working with the tragic extreme of scripts" (pp. 275-276). Erskine and Moursund (1988, p. 43) further elaborated on the use of touch in transactional analysis treatment, describing "four major domains"—cognitive, behavioral, affective, and physical. In both the affective and physical domains, the use of touch or body-centered interventions may be appropriate.

When considering the specific uses of touch in transactional analysis treatment, one of the major foci has been on its nurturing and regressive functions. This view of touch as a contract between Nurturing Parent and Child, or between Child and Child, is also typical of permission work (Bellinger, 1974; Wyckoff, 1975) and similar to the regressive work characterizing Erskine and Moursund's (1988) affective domain. S. Smith (1990) further elaborated these nurturing and regressive functions by emphasizing the Parent-to-Child communication present when working with regressive elements in psychotherapy. Cornell (1975) offered a different view on physical contact in therapy by differentiating its use with Nurturing Parent-to-Child and Child-to-Child contracts from its use in the context of Adult-to-Adult contracts. With Adult-to-Adult contracts, informed and purposeful touch is designed to focus, inform, and heighten a client's self-awareness.

Although efforts at a theoretical reconciliation have been limited, numerous transactional analysts have described the use of specific body-centered techniques to supplement and deepen the more traditional cognitive and interpersonal focus of transactional analysis. For example, Steiner and his Radical Therapy colleagues (Issues in Radical Therapy Collective, 1973, 1974) were strongly influenced by the work of Wilhelm Reich (1961) and advocated the use of body-centered approaches as part of the therapeutic process. Steiner (1974) suggested the importance of establishing contact with one's physical responses through "centering" and "breathing" techniques in the treatment of "Joyless" scripts (pp. 287-291).

Numerous other authors (Cassius, 1975, 1980; Childs-Gowell & Kinnaman, 1978; Gowell, 1975; Johnson, 1980; Lenhardt, 1984) have described the use of neo-Reichian, bioenergetic, and sensory stimulation techniques in conjunction with transactional analysis. These interventions focus primarily on muscular rigidity used in the service of chronic emotional repression and inhibition and on breaking through this body armor to facilitate expression and catharsis. Although Erskine and Moursund (1988) did not indicate the sources of their approach to direct work with the body, "deep muscle massage and manipulation, pacing and leading breathing patterns, and encouraging or inhibiting movements" (p. 45) are used. More recently, Ligabue (1991) suggested that the use of body-centered interventions should be "less concerned with the cathartic experience that usually accompanies bodywork and more with exploring through the body the congruity between perceptions, feelings, actions, and an adequate temporal recollection of such [traumatic] experiences" (p. 27).

Regardless of the theoretical perspective with which the psychotherapist identifies, any use of touch must be mutually agreed to as one part of a broader treatment contract between client and therapist. Usually a client needs substantial time in therapy to establish a reliable, working alliance before he or she is open to the therapist's use of touch. Therapists should never use touch in the treatment of abuse victims simply as a matter of course or because that is their style of work. Throughout the course of treatment, it is the client's prerogative to say "No" to being touched by the therapist.

Choosing Therapeutic Interventions

It is crucial to make appropriate choices when determining which physical interventions to use in therapy with adult survivors of bodily abuse. Sinclair (1988) distinguished between difficulties created by tactile deprivation and those reflecting a history of negative touch (pp. 42-44); he also pointed out the practitioner's responsibility for monitoring the client's "acceptance of touch and sense of safety" (p. 60). E. W. L. Smith's (1985) differentiation of body-centered techniques into "soft," "hard," and "expressive" (p. 113) is helpful in considering the appropriate intervention for a given case.

Hard Techniques. E. W. L. Smith (1985) characterized hard techniques as those that are uncomfortable, at times even painful, but also often dramatic in their "releasing of blocked emotions and memory" (p. 125). These include bioenergetic stress and grounding techniques (Lowen & Lowen, 1977), vigorous large muscle movement (pushing, hitting, kicking), and the therapist's use of deep, insistent touch to mobilize the body or break through contracted musculature.

Expressive Techniques. The expressive techniques described by E. W. L. Smith (1985) involve "taking action, concrete musculoskeletal movement" (p. 135). These strategies, which include gestalt and psychodramatic techniques, frequently use symbolic or re-created interactions between therapist and client or among group members, often combining verbalization and intense physical activity to elicit emotional expression and corrective experiences.

These hard and expressive techniques, typical of the physical interventions referred to in the transactional analysis literature (Cassius, 1975; Childs-Gowell & Kinnaman, 1978; Erskine & Moursund, 1988), emphasize the expressive phase of the contact cycle. However, they are often counterproductive with victims of abuse because they may trigger anxiety, disorganization, and dissociation. Any use of such hard and expressive techniques should be undertaken with caution and only after patterns of denial and dissociation are significantly resolved.

Special caution is required with the use of interactive or psychodramatic techniques. Encouraging movement, sound, or words that facilitate the client's deepening internal experience of the abuse can be helpful. However, techniques that involve reenactment, in which the therapist in some form acts out the role of the original abuser, are ill-advised. Although these techniques can elicit memories and produce intense affect, with victims of abuse such interventions are likely to be intrusive and overstimulating, thus literally recreating the abuse experience and resulting in additional damage. Because of their histories, victims of abuse tend to disconnect from discomfort and often avoid potential conflicts with significant others; they are unlikely to refuse a therapist's direction and may minimize the impact of overstimulating and intrusive interventions. Thus it is crucial that the therapist accept responsibility for and monitor the intensity of the treatment.

Disruptions and distortions of contact between client and therapist have often been accounted for as the client's withdrawal, retroflection, projection, deflection, introjection, or attempts at confluence (Erskine & Moursund, 1988). With survivors of bodily abuse, there is an especially significant potential for disruption and distortion of contact as a result of the therapist's overpowering, overstimulating, or intrusive actions upon the client's body and personal boundaries.

Soft Techniques. The soft techniques E. W. L. Smith (1985) outlined—such as calling attention to posture, supportive touch, focused attention to sensations in specific areas of the body, deepened breathing, stretching, and eye contact—all enhance the awareness phase of the contact cycle and are useful in the treatment of abuse.

These techniques involve a level of direct physical contact designed to focus attention ("Notice how tightly you are holding your shoulders"), offer support ("See if you can let your neck relax and allow my hands to support your head"), provide containment ("It won't be too much, I'm here with you"), or facilitate movement ("Notice how much more movement and force there can be in your arms if you relax your back at this spot"). Unlike the hard and expressive techniques, this style of physical intervention is not intended to confront rigidity and armor, provoke an emotional response, or stimulate the client's body to some form of action. Rather, these interventions are intended to be educative and often help people develop a stronger sense of structure and substance at a body level. That is to say, soft body techniques heighten experience rather than change it.

Moss (1985), who stressed nonpainful, nonstressful bodywork in her model of feminist body psychotherapy, traced the softening of traditional Reichian techniques through a history of women therapists. Kepner's (1987) perspective is consistent with this softer approach as it advocates "not making something happen, but on discovering what does happen, and so taking into account the critical phenomenon of ownership, or its absence, and resistance" (p. 157). Such a view is consistent with the idea that the therapist should use the minimum necessary intervention to facilitate movement and awareness (Cornell, 1980). This level of physical intervention significantly assists clients in the re-owning of their bodies and experience.

Other Strategies

Various other therapeutic approaches that are not body centered are also effective strategies for emotional awareness and integration with victims of abuse. For example, self-awareness and emotional experience may be strengthened by the use of support or treatment groups (Cole, 1985; Courtois, 1988; Faria & Belohlavek, 1984) in conjunction with ongoing individual therapy. Because abuse survivors are well trained to keep secrets and to minimize the damage done to them, group sessions with other survivors can be powerful in helping to break patterns of silence and denial.

The use of trance in the context of ongoing therapy may also be a useful affective strategy (Brown & Fromm, 1986; Edelstein, 1981). Hypnotherapy can be an alternative to physical and body-centered interventions, facilitating both recall and affect. However, as with bodywork, trance must be carefully moderated so as not to overwhelm the client with intense or uncontrolled affect. Brown and Fromm (1986) warned:

Since most PTSD patients fear loss of control, the therapist's encouragement of emotional displays merely intensifies that fear and does not facilitate working through of the trauma.... The primary emphasis of the treatment should be *integration,* not emotional expression. (p. 273)

Because body-centered techniques, hypnosis, and collateral group treatment can trigger flashbacks and elicit intense affect, their use should be paced in a way that allows material to be assimilated in ongoing treatment. Frequent use of such techniques may be overwhelming, resulting in increased difficulties in daily functioning, the heightened use of denial and dissociation, and/or premature termination from therapy.

No single approach to affect is effective with all victims of abuse. Some clients find body-centered techniques extremely useful, whereas others cannot tolerate touch but can utilize hypnotherapy. No treatment strategy should be initiated unilaterally by the therapist, who must consistently model a respectful and responsive Parent ego state. Deciding which affective technique will be constructive and empowering for an individual client evolves from a collaborative discussion of the range of therapeutic options. The client's full Adult involvement and informed consent in treatment planning is essential.

Special Considerations and Cautions

When clients use both denial and dissociation, the therapeutic process of acknowledging and integrating the experience of trauma is fragmented. Holding on to this experience without dissociating or forgetting varies from moment to moment and from session to session. Resolution has not occurred if clients only acknowledge the trauma in the safety of the therapeutic relationship (Herman & Schatzow, 1987; Swanson & Biaggio, 1985; Tsai & Wagner, 1978). Victims of abuse may tolerate sharing details of the trauma with the therapist but experience a reemergence of denial and dissociation when they disclose these memories to others.

In addition, resolution of the abuse in an archaic context may not spontaneously generalize to present life. Almost universally, clients experience some areas in which their childhood victimization is subtly replayed in their current lives. Even when survivors are able to acknowledge their original traumas, until they are able to confront other forms of victimization in their current lives, the childhood abuse is not completely resolved. Standing up for themselves in current life gives abuse victims the experience of an option not available to them as children and diminishes the need to use denial and dissociation.

Throughout treatment with abuse survivors, it is incumbent on the therapist to inquire directly about the quality of a client's daily life experiences. The recurrence of some or all of the following coping mechanisms indicates the affective work is proceeding too rapidly or intensely:

1. Persistent escalation of feel over thinking
2. Persistent avoidance of involvement with (or reported detachment from) intimate partners and friends
3. Panic attacks, often accompanied by self-hatred
4. Inability to recall content from one session to the next
5. Recurrent splits in consciousness, that is, thinking about themselves and the therapeutic work without affect, or sudden disruptive bursts of affect with body numbing, detachment, or no conscious content
6. Frequent loss of contact with the therapist or self during the session
7. Self-destructive behaviors
8. Patterns of unresponsiveness to bodily needs (hunger, fatigue, temperature, physical comfort)

In work with abuse survivors, the therapist must develop a significant, responsive therapeutic relationship (Olio & Cornell, 1993) in order to provide a context within which a client may confront both childhood abuse and the character defenses necessary in a trauma-inducing family. This therapeutic relationship underlies all technique. The safety, responsiveness, and consistency of the relationship provide the Parent structure and values that are the foundation for all treatment; it is the glue in the effort to reconnect thinking, feeling, memory, and identity.

Conclusion

If the injunction is a demand made by a witch or giant whose features are distorted with rage, whose voice smashes through all the defenses of the child's mind, and whose hand is ever ready to strike humiliation and terror into his face and head, it requires enormous therapeutic power. (Berne, 1972, p. 116)

A distinctive pattern of damage occurs when a family's neglect and dysfunction are combined with violations of a child's bodily boundaries. This pattern of damage has implications for both transactional analysis theory and treatment protocols.

Denial and dissociation are primary coping mechanisms in managing the emotional and physical impact of bodily trauma, and a central therapeutic goal is the integration of affect and cognition, both within the therapeutic process and in current life relationships and activities.

We emphasize the therapist's active and emotional engagement with the client, using a Parent ego state that is consistent, carefully attentive, responsive, and highly respectful. We offer a model for the development and careful monitoring of an affective edge during treatment in which nonintrusive touch as well as nonphysical, affective techniques can be used effectively to facilitate the gradual integration of thinking and feeling. It is our hope that the therapeutic attitudes and interventions described here will facilitate the recall and integration of traumatic experiences from childhood into a broader and more cohesive self, allowing for a gradual deepening of physical and emotional awareness in adult life.

REFERENCES

Alexander, F. M. (1974). *The resurrection of the body*. New York: Delta (Dell Publishing).

Bellinger, L. (1974). *The keep on truckin' manual*. Watsonville, CA: Keep on Truckin' Publications.

Berne, E. (1972). *What do you say after you say hello?: The psychology of human destiny*. New York: Grove Press.

Blake-White, J., & Kline, C. M. (1985). Treating the dissociative process in adult victims of childhood incest. *Social Casework: Journal of Contemporary Social Work, 66*, 394-402.

Boadella, D. (1987). *Lifestreams: An introduction to biosynthesis*. New York: Routledge & Kegan Paul.

Bowlby, J. (1984). Violence in the family as a disorder of the attachment and caregiving systems. *American Journal of Psychoanalysis, 44*, 9-27.

Briere, J. (1989). *Therapy for adults molested as children: Beyond survival*. New York: Springer.

Brown, D. P., & Fromm, E. (1986). *Hypnotherapy and hypnoanalysis*. Hillsdale, NJ: Lawrence Erlbaum Associates.

Burgess, A. W., Hartman, C. R., & McCormack, A. (1987). Abused to abuser: Antecedents of socially deviant behaviors. *American Journal of Psychiatry, 144*, 1431-1436.

Cassius, J. (1975). *Bodyscripts: Collected papers on physical aspects of transactional analysis*. Memphis, TN: Author.

Cassius, J. (1980). Bodyscript release: How to use bioenergetics and transactional analysis. In J. Cassius (Ed.), *Horizons in bioenergetics: New dimensions in mind/body psychotherapy* (pp. 212-244). Memphis, TN: Promethean Publications.

Childs-Gowell, E., & Kinnaman, P. (1978). *Body-script blockbusting: A transactional approach to body awareness.* San Francisco: Transactional Pubs.

Cole, C. (1985). A group design for adult survivors of childhood incest. *Woman & Therapy, 4,* 71-82.

Cole, C., & Barney, E. (1987). Safeguards and the therapeutic window: A group treatment strategy for adult incest survivors. *American Journal of Orthopsychiatry, 57,* 601-609.

Cornell, W. (1975). Wake up "sleepy": Reichian techniques and script intervention. *Transactional Analysis Journal, 5,* 144-147.

Cornell, W. (1980). Structure and function in radix body education and script change. In J. Cassius (Ed.), *Horizons in bioenergetics: New dimensions in mind/body psychotherapy* (pp. 80-100). Memphis, TN: Promethean Publications.

Courtois, C. (1988). *Healing the incest wound: Adult survivors in therapy.* New York: Norton.

Edelstein, M. G. (1981). *Trauma, trance and transformation: A clinical guide to hypnotherapy.* New York: Brunner/Mazel.

Erskine, R. G., & Moursund, J. (1988). *Integrative psychotherapy in action.* Newbury Park, CA: Sage.

Faria, G., & Belohlavek, N. (1984). Treating female adult survivors of childhood incest. *Social Casework: Journal of Contemporary Social Work, 65,* 465-471.

Feldenkrais, M. (1950). *Body and mature behavior: A study of anxiety, sex, gravitation and learning.* New York: International Universities Press.

Feldenkrais, M. (1981). *The elusive obvious.* Cupertino, CA: Meta Publications.

Figley, C. (Ed.). (1985). *Trauma and its wake: Traumatic stress theory, research, and intervention* (Vol 1). New York: Brunner/Mazel

Gelb, M. (1981). *Body learning: An introduction to the Alexander technique.* New York: Delilah Books.

Gelinas, D. (1983). The persisting negative effects of incest. *Psychiatry, 46,* 312-332.

Gelles, R., & Straus, M. (1988). *Intimate violence: The definitive study of the causes and consequences of abuse in the American family.* New York: Simon & Schuster.

Gordon, L. (1988). *Heroes of their own lives: The politics and history of family violence.* New York: Penguin.

Gowell, E. C. (1975). Transactional analysis and the body: Sensory stimulation techniques. *Transactional Analysis Journal, 5,* 148-151.

Greven, P. (1991). *Spare the child: The religious roots of punishment and the psychological impact of physical abuse.* New York: Knopf.

Herman, J. L., & Schatzow, E. (1987). Recovery and verification of memories of childhood sexual trauma. *Psychoanalytic Psychology, 4,* 1-14.

Horowitz, M. (1976). *Stress response syndromes.* New York: Jason Aronson.

Hunter, R., & Kilstrom, N. (1979). Breaking the cycle in abusive families. *American Journal of Psychiatry, 136,* 1320-1322.

Issues in Radical Therapy Collective. (1973). *Wilhelm Reich and body politics. Part I.* Berkeley, CA: Author.

Issues in Radical Therapy Collective. (1974). *Wilhelm Reich and body politics. Part II.* Berkeley, CA: Author.

Johnson, L. (1980). Sexuality-vision-feeling. In J. Cassius (Ed.), *Horizons in bioenergetics: New dimensions in mind/body psychotherapy* (pp. 162-178). Memphis, TN: Promethean Publications.

Kepner, J. (1987). *Body process: A Gestalt approach to working with the body in psychotherapy.* New York: Gestalt Institute of Cleveland Press.

Kurtz, R., & Prestera, H. (1976). *The body reveals: An illustrated guide to the psychology of the body.* New York: Harper & Row.

Laughlin, H. (1987). *The ego and its defenses.* Northvale, NJ: Jason Aronson.

Lenhardt, V. (1984). Bioscripts. In E. Stern (Ed.), *TA the state of the art: A European contribution* (pp. 89-106). Dordrecht, Holland: Foris Publications.

Lifton, R. J. (1979). *The broken connections: On death and the continuity of life.* New York: Basic Books.

Lifton, R. J., & Olson, E. (1976). The human meaning of total disaster. *Psychiatry, 39,* 1-18.

Ligabue, S. (1991). The somatic component of the script in early development. *Transactional Analysis Journal, 21,* 21-30.

Lindberg, F., & Distad, L. (1985). Post-traumatic stress disorders in women who experienced childhood incest. *Child Abuse and Neglect, 9,* 329-334.

Lister, E. (1982). Forced silence: A neglected dimension of trauma. *American Journal of Psychiatry, 139,* 872-876.

Lowen, A. (1975). *Bioenergetics.* Northvale, NJ: Coward, McCann & Geoghegan.

Lowen, A., & Lowen, L. (1977). *The way to vibrant health: A manual of bioenergetic exercises.* New York: Harper & Row.

McCarthy, J. B. (1990). Abusive families and character formation. *American Journal of Psychoanalysis, 50,* 181-186.

McGrath, E., Keita, G. P., Strickland, B. R., & Russo, N. F. (1990). *Women and depression: Risk factors and treatment issues.* Washington, DC: American Psychological Association.

Miller, A. (1983). *For your own good: Hidden cruelty in child-rearing and the roots of violence.* New York: Farrar, Straus & Giroux.

Moss, L. (1985). Feminist body psychotherapy. In L. B. Rosewater & L. G. Walker (Eds.), *The handbook of feminist therapy* (pp. 80-90). New York: Springer Publishing.

Ochberg, F. (1991). Post-traumatic therapy. *Psychotherapy, 28,* 5-16.

Olio, K. A. (1989). Memory retrieval in the treatment of adult survivors of sexual abuse. *Transactional Analysis Journal, 19,* 93-100.

Olio, K. A., & Cornell, W. F. (1993). The therapeutic relationship as the foundation for treatment with adult survivors of sexual abuse. *Psychotherapy, 30*(3), 512-523.

Reich, W. (1961). *The function of the orgasm* (T. P. Wolfe, Trans.). New York: Farrar, Straus & Giroux.
Rieker, P., & Carmen, E. (1986). The victim-to-patient process: The disconfirmation and transformation of abuse. *American Journal of Orthopsychiatry, 56*, 360-370.
Root, M. P. P. (1992). Reconstructing the impact of trauma on personality. In L. S. Brown & M. Ballon (Eds.), *Personality and psychopathology: Feminist reappraisals* (pp. 229-265). New York: Guilford Press.
Rosenthal, K. (1988). The inanimate self in adult victims of child abuse and neglect. *Social Casework: Journal of Contemporary Social Work, 69*, 505-510.
Schechter, S. (1982). *Women and male violence: The visions and struggles of the battered women's movement*. Boston: South End Press.
Schmitt, B., & Kempe, H. (1975). Neglect and abuse of children. In V. Vaughan & R. McKay (Eds.), *Nelson textbook on pediatrics* (10th ed.) (pp. 107-111). Philadelphia: Saunders.
Sinclair, M. (1988). Acceptance of touch. *Massage Therapy Journal, Fall*, 41-63.
Smith, E. W. L. (1985). *The body in psychotherapy*. Jefferson, NC: McFarland & Co.
Smith, S. (1990). Regressive work as a therapeutic treatment. *Transactional Analysis Journal, 20*, 253-262.
Spiegel, D. (1986). Dissociating damage. *American Journal of Clinical Hypnosis, 29*, 123-131.
Steele, K., & Colrain, J. U. (1990). Abreactive work with sexual abuse survivors: Concepts and techniques. In M. Hunter (Ed.), *The sexually abused male: Application of treatment strategies* (Vol. 2, pp. 1-56). Lexington, MA: Lexington Books.
Steiner, C. M. (1974). *Scripts people live: Transactional analysis of life scripts*. New York: Grove Press.
Straus, M. (Ed.). (1988). *Abuse and victimization across the life span*. Baltimore, MD: Johns Hopkins University Press.
Swanson, L., & Biaggio, M. K. (1985). Therapeutic perspectives on father-daughter incest. *American Journal of Psychiatry, 142*, 667-674.
Terr, L. (1991). Childhood traumas: An outline and overview. *American Journal of Psychiatry, 148*, 10-20.
Tsai, M., & Wagner, N. (1978). Therapy groups for women sexually molested as children. *Archives of Sexual Behavior, 7*, 417-429.
van der Kolk, B. A. (1987). *Psychological trauma*. Washington, DC: American Psychiatric Press.
van der Kolk, B. A. (1989). The compulsion to repeat the trauma: Re-enactment, revictimization, and masochism. *Psychiatric Clinics of North America, 12*, 389-411.
Wilson, J. (1989). *Trauma, transformation and healing: An integrative approach to theory, research, and post-traumatic therapy*. New York: Brunner/Mazel.
Wyckoff, H. (1975). Permission. In C. Steiner (Ed.), *Readings in radical psychiatry* (pp. 106-121). New York: Grove Press.

The original version of this article was published in the Transactional Analysis Journal, *Volume 22, Number 3, pp. 131-143, July 1992.*

Section IV:
Supervision in Practice

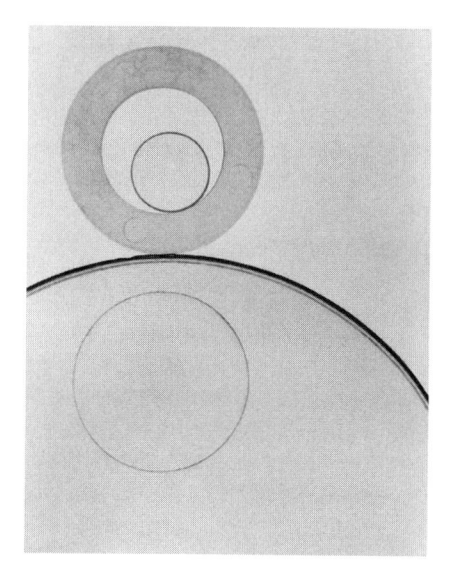

To think in the way I am proposing requires a therapeutic balancing act. . . . Trying to hold all my responses in mind, I negotiate between acceptance and rejection, attraction and repulsion, curiosity, disgust, and boredom—a sort of guarded neutrality. . . . Ultimately this congeries of shame, disgust, and excitement, which no neutrality of mine can ever excise from a patient's and analyst's psyche or from their culture, must itself be explored.

Dimen, 2003, p. 265

Section IV

Introduction

Transactional analysis is rather unique among the human relations, teaching, counseling, and psychotherapy professions in that it has a formal system of preparation for supervision and training. One does not become a supervisor in transactional analysis as a result of being around longer than anyone else and having accumulated a lot of experience (and hopefully then wisdom) in the field. In transactional analysis, supervision and training are seen as unique skill sets, different from the practice of the discipline itself. To become a supervisor or trainer in transactional analysis one must take a Training Endorsement Workshop that assesses a candidate's skill set and philosophy of training and supervision. A candidate's training and supervisory activities are themselves supervised and mentored by senior trainers. Finally, a candidate sits for three oral examinations by his or her peers over the course of a day. It is within this tradition that the chapters in this section were written. As the reader will notice, many of the chapters in Section V on ethics also touch on issues of supervision; these topics are closely intertwined and separating them into two sections was somewhat arbitrary. However, the chapters here focus more specifically on the theory and experience of supervision.

The section opens with a recent paper coauthored with Carole Shadbolt (the supervisee) and Robert Norton (the pseudonym of the client in the supervised case). I chose this article to lead off this section because it is based on where and why I started in transactional analysis—my reading while still in college of Berne's paper on supervising psychotherapists in a hospital in the presence of the patients who were being discussed, patients who in turn were invited to share their perspectives on the treatment. Chapter 18 is an unusually detailed case discussion of a supervisory session, including my actual notes to myself during the hour and discussions by both the therapist and the client.

Chapter 19 is an early paper coauthored with Marilyn Zalcman and one that I consider a bit of a classic, if I say so myself. Marilyn and I wrote this paper (and a subsequent one, "A Bilateral Model for Clinical Supervision" [Zalcman & Cornell, 1983]) out of concern that transactional analysis training had become too focused on technique, that is, on what to do rather than on how to think about why to make any particular intervention. We stressed the importance of supervisees learning to think theoretically, and not only from a transactional analysis model. We outlined what we consider to be the four essential areas of competence that need to be addressed in comprehensive supervision: theoretical and empirical knowledge, clinical skills and expertise, ethical and professional practices, and personal skills and development. Ultimately, this article formed the basis of the revision of the ITAA Training and Standards Manual.

Chapter 20 raises questions and offers a perspective (one not always welcomed) on dual relationships in transactional analysis, a subject that continues to generate important debates in transactional analysis and other mental health disciplines. I have long thought that when providing counseling, therapy, or consultation to clients in mental health settings it is important to make room for multiple roles. I think there is a multiplicity of role and function—transferential complexity, if you will—in all working and/or intimate relationships. I think it quite reasonable in working with clients who are also in my professional field that we expect ourselves to be able to recognize and manage multiple roles or functions. However, allowing for dual relationships places extra burdens on both parties. The therapist/supervisor needs to be especially attentive, responsive, self-reflective, and responsible.

I have no doubt that the strict rules in some associations against dual relationships protect the professional in the dyad, but I am not sure they serve the client all that well. Many will not agree with me, but I think open discussion and rigorous self-examination are the most essential elements of a responsive and ethical training and supervision structure.

REFERENCE

Dimen, M. (2003). *Sexuality, power, intimacy*. Hillsdale, NJ: The Analytic Press.

Zalcman, M. J., & Cornell, W. F. (1983). A bilateral model for clinical supervision. *Transactional Analysis Journal, 13*, 112-123.

18

Live and in Limbo: A Case Study of an In-Person Transactional Analysis Consultation

William F. Cornell, Carole Shadbolt, and Robert Norton

> Sitting here in Limbo
> Like a bird ain't got a song
> Yeah, I'm sitting here in Limbo
> And I know it won't be long
> 'Til I make my getaway, now.
> Meanwhile, they're putting up a resistance,
> But I know that my faith will lead me on.
> *Jimmy Cliff*

This is a case study of a single clinical consultation done "live" through direct observation of a therapy session followed by consultation and discussion with both therapist and client present. This mode of consultation is based on transactional analysis supervisory models first outlined by Eric Berne (1968/1977b) and John O'Hearne (1972).

For the purposes of this chapter, the authors have chosen to use the word "consultation," in contrast to "supervision" (the more common term in transactional analysis), to suggest a slightly different frame of reference for ongoing professional learning among peers. Supervision is, of course, a means by which we receive ongoing training and, in transactional analysis, prepare practitioners for examination and certification. "Supervision" implies a relationship between a senior professional and a less experienced practitioner. In the case presented here, the consultation occurred between two peers. The term "consultation," in contrast to "supervision," underscores a peer relationship, with both parties bringing their observations and skills to the process. Consultation also reflects the desirability of ongoing professional learning, questioning, and peer support.

Theoretical Grounding

Berne's (1968/1977b) article entitled "Staff-Patient Staff Conferences," published in 1968 in the *American Journal of Psychiatry* and written with his typical droll sense of humor, described a rather radical structure for involving patients directly in staff conferences in psychiatric hospitals. In it, he argued forcefully on behalf of recognition of the intelligence and integrity of patients. According to Berne, the purposes of psychiatric staff conferences included: (1) giving the patient the advantage of the best available professional opinions, (2) instructing the staff, (3) enhancing staff morale, (4) teaching participation and the free expression of opinions, and (5) stimulating thinking and the organization of thoughts (p. 153). The actual outcome, Berne wryly noted, given typically rigid hospital hierarchies, was often quite different from the stated intent.

In his own clinical and hospital practice, Berne (1968/1977b) "established the custom of having all staff conferences in the presence of the patients" (p. 155). The conference meetings were carefully structured to provide equal, respectful talk by staff and patients:

This makes the situation bilateral. The staff has the privilege of listening to how each patient expresses himself, and in return the patients are given the same courtesy. . . . The conference is absolutely "straight." When it ends the patients leave and so does the staff. There is no other staff conference or "post conference" conference. . . . Thus the staff is trained and expected to say everything worth saying while the patients are listening. An uneasy member who is holding back or is not talking "straight" is so informed, usually then and there. (p. 156)

Berne (1968/1977b) was explicit in his intentions that "the staff-patient staff conference first attacks the comfortable and well-established sociological roles of 'therapist' and 'patient' . . . [in which] everyone is treated as a 'person' with equal rights on his own merits" (p. 158). He found that the patients typically had much more ease and appreciation of this format than did the staff but that most therapists were able to adjust to this transparency of thought and observation and came to appreciate the process. Berne concluded that "experience shows that nearly all patients can call up just as much ego strength as therapists can if they are 'given permission' to do so, and the staff-patient staff conference is one way of giving that permission" (p. 164).

O'Hearne (1972) adapted Berne's structure for ongoing transactional analysis training and supervision. He, too, found patients more open to the experience than therapists but that gradually everyone became involved and learned. O'Hearne summarized the results in this way:

Advantages of the method for patients are:
1. Regression, including magical expectations, is minimized.
2. Objectivity regarding patients' troubles increased rapidly.
3. Patients quickly learn that therapists are people too; that none of them are infallible.

Advantages of the method for therapists in training are:
1. They stay awake.
2. Their learning is facilitated by less geographic and psychological distance from patients.
3. They learn that no therapist always has all the answers for all the questions.
4. They learn that patients are much tougher than they thought; that the therapists' words and theories are not magic. (pp. 183-184)

These were the models that brought me (WFC), the consultant/author in the case reported here, into transactional analysis as I witnessed the application of Berne's model in my first job in a residential treatment center for deeply disturbed children. At this center, every child and his or her parents were included in every treatment plan meeting. I was deeply impressed by the capacities of children, regardless of age or diagnosis, to speak thoughtfully about what was and was not working in their treatment and to be involved in the establishment of treatment goals and strategies. I decided to train in transactional analysis. Later, as a transactional analysis trainer and supervisor, I instituted a modification of Berne's staff-patient supervision groups; these were semiannual sessions in ongoing supervision groups called "Bring A Client Day." Each therapist brought a client, who attended the full day's session. Each client chose a therapist from the group (other than his or her own) with whom to do a piece of work; this work was observed by the supervisor, the client's own therapist, and the other therapists and clients in the group. The supervisory discussion then included the thoughts and observations of all participants. Therapists and clients alike were engaged in a process of mutual learning; clients reported that this process demystified therapy and demonstrated great results for the Adult ego state capacities of the clients as well as the therapists.

These models formed the basis of the in-person consultation session described in this chapter.

History of the Client

Robert and I (CS) have been meeting for a number of years. Initially, he came to me, then in his mid-forties, for support in completing a counseling and psychotherapy training because he was experiencing anxiety about being thrown out of the course. Robert questioned his ability to get through the demanding requirements of the course and felt that the tutors there did not really think he was up to standard. He was stalled in his written work for the training. He felt threatened, feeling himself to be bullied somewhat to express anger he did not feel during experiential exercises. He also felt goaded and then humiliated by another student, who reminded him of someone with whom he had gone to school.

Robert is married with no children. He founded his own business, which he still successfully manages today. His mother is alive and lives close by. His father, who died of lung cancer when Robert was in his thirties, had been an untreated, unconfronted alcoholic whose drinking ruined the family, reducing them to debt and ultimately to losing their long-time family home and contents to pay off creditors. Robert's mother used him as a confidant during his father's long deterioration, and his father used him as a banker.

Robert believes that his father's drinking and decline were the result of trauma that occurred during World War II and a humiliating redundancy (being laid off work) in the 1960s from which he never really recovered. Culturally speaking, Robert's extended family is a mixture of aristocracy and dysfunction. Mother came from a family of high achievers: politicians, doctors, and bankers of high social standing and wealth. His father's family equally distinguished themselves in a more pathological way: All were alcoholics, as Robert described them, and, quoting his maternal grandfather, "shysters and tricksters." They were, nevertheless, intelligent. Many had served in the army, and some had died on The Somme in World War I. Robert still loves his father very much, recalling his father's love of children and nature until life became more than he could handle and he retreated into alcoholism.

Robert's mother married his father against her family's wishes and counsel; they predicted disaster for the relationship. When their predictions came true, they were not forthcoming with support. She never reconciled with them. She was and remains a stoic woman of breeding, her values and instincts being of another era. She stayed with her husband through thick and thin, never complaining or criticizing him (except to her son), despite ruin, hardship, and social disgrace. Robert is the oldest of three and the parentified child, with a sister whom he rarely sees now and a younger brother whom he believes is well on the way to following in his father's footsteps.

Robert remembers his early childhood as blissfully happy. He felt himself to be an adored and adoring child. At age 6 this changed dramatically and forever when he was sent to boarding school in keeping with family tradition. From then on his childhood was a miserable and shaming routine of bullying and manipulation by both pupils and staff alike. He tells of the first incomprehensible days of being in the boarding school, shocked and stunned, feeling like a curtain was falling, a line was being drawn, something was lost forever, as he saw it. As Robert spoke about this gradually in our therapy sessions, he showed little emotion. I, on the other hand, found it almost unbearable to listen to him and contain my feelings. I was awash with outrage, anger, and incomprehension as he lapsed into what was to become a familiar pattern of passive silence. He seemed lost for words, stuck and in great need of an unnameable soothing. I would invariably—immediately or eventually—fill this silence.

Robert longed to leave the "hellhole" of boarding school or tell his mother of the harsh treatment and abusive environment, but somehow he felt he could never quite do so. As a young boy, he intuited that to reveal his suffering would be to let his family down and disappoint his parents. He remembers his mother's inexplicable tears as she saw him off at the train station after the holidays. The only way he felt he could manage this agonizing and puzzling parting was to take care of her and reassure her that he was alright, thus swallowing his own misery. Enduring misery in stoic, passive silence mirrored his mother and came to play out between us.

Surviving the boarding school experience by withdrawing in the early years, Robert gradually learned to secretly manipulate and cheat, on the one hand, and to make himself popular and respected by his affability and sense of fair play, on the other. He was traumatized by this long experience, from which he never escaped, but he left the school at 16 as head boy. In a scene straight out of *Tom Brown's Schooldays* (Hughes, 1857/2004), he relates coming across a "young 'un" being bullied by an older boy just as he had once been, and taking the bully on, much to the relief of the younger lad. This became his mission. He felt fulfilled when he could be the rescuer of those he saw as vulnerable, repeating the stance he took with his mother and would later take with his father and in countless subsequent relationships. Of course, this pattern was then enacted between us.

The school was made notorious in later years when one of Robert's school friends, now a grown man, spectacularly blew the whistle in a newspaper report on the alleged Spartan regime of ice-cold baths, rigorous exercise, and psychological and sexual abuse. That and subsequent prosecutions by others did much to unlock, make understandable, and exonerate the loathing and shame my client had for himself for his cheating and manipulative behaviors at the school. My client and his brutalized childhood can be found exquisitely described by Nick Duffell (2000) in his book about the English boarding school system, *The Making of Them*.

To meet Robert is to come face-to-face with the kind of person these boarding school systems sought to breed. To meet Robert is to come face-to-face with English charm, good manners, and passivity. He is one of the upper classes, an ex-public schoolboy, the so-called backbone and pride of England. He is courteous to a fault. I find it astonishing how he has not become or shown me, consciously or unconsciously, the shadow side of this dynamic. He has never revealed any hint of the "brute," and perhaps the gentle man he is defends against that; if so, I can understand why he clings doggedly, if unconsciously, to this defense, even as his awareness of and distress over his lack of aggression and sense of self keep him in treatment.

When we first met, Robert had been married for many years. He and his wife, despite trying for years to have a family, were childless. They had tried in vitro fertilization (IVF), did not want to adopt, and stopped trying to conceive when she was diagnosed with cervical cancer. Among the many losses in Robert's life, this is the one he finds most painful; he believes he has led an unfulfilled life as a result of it. His greatest wish was to have his own biological children, and because he has not, he sees himself as incomplete, emasculated, and a parent-in-longing. Sex is therefore disappointing, poignant, and anguished, usually ending for him in disappointment.

History of the Therapy

Given Robert's background and patterns of adaptation over the course of his life, a major but unsurprising feature of his marriage is that he has not managed to communicate his feelings of deep disappointment to his wife over almost anything he dislikes—especially their childlessness. At the same time, he remains gentlemanly, considerate, and pleasant at a social level. But this chronic festering situation repeats the passivity he displayed at school, with his mother and father, at the college, and in all his relationships. It is a central feature of his personality structure and has been a characteristic of our therapeutic relationship and the process between us. At the time of this writing, he still has not shared his feelings fully with his wife.

On paper, so to speak, the therapeutic task back then seemed clear enough—straightforward, you might be saying to yourself, as you read the details. Thoughts of transactional analysis decontamination, deconfusion, and impasse work (probably Type III) leading on to redecision may come to mind. Passivity and symbiosis and game roles might be another avenue to pursue. My transactional analyst's mind ran in the same directions. However, the lived-in experience of being with my client was far from straightforward. It was as if his passivity and way of being as just described was him, from the top of his head to the bottom of his feet and through the cells of his being.

Robert did successfully finish his counseling training, by which time in therapy he had begun a different therapeutic journey of meaning making in his life. We did much good work, but his seemingly all-encompassing passivity, as I have described it, was the thing that exercised, puzzled, and troubled me and was the factor that, despite all my skills, efforts, and our reenactments, did not shift significantly. This was the one aspect of our work that I repeatedly took to supervision. I knew that despite all our good work, this passivity was the central struggle of Robert's life, and unless resolved, or at least understood, he would not be fully free. Half free perhaps, a job well-enough done certainly, as far as it went. Robert, perhaps, would have settled for this, as he often spoke of leaving therapy. But by now I was in for the endgame. I wanted a more fully successful outcome for my now much-loved client. I resolved to do everything in my therapeutic power to assist him, whatever that took.

A major feature of our relationship was that Robert has continually sought ways of being polite and helpful to me. His courteous chivalry always defended against his openly expressing any hostile feelings toward me in sessions or outside, as surely as any knight in armor defended a damsel in distress. For my part, occasionally in the early days, much to my now considerable embarrassment, from time to time I found ways to accept his help (just as his mother had done?). There were always real reasons to do so, I reasoned, both therapeutically and externally. But I was not then the therapist I am now.

I give an example of the pull I felt to enlist his help. Shortly after I had identified this process of reenactment of white knight and distressed damsel between us followed by his almost invisible resentment, Robert and I were at the beginning of the session in my newly decorated and carpeted work room. As he sat across from me, I noticed a dark stain appearing under the door and starting to spread. My room was being very slowly flooded by the torrential downpour outside. My instinct was to ask for Robert's help to get the furniture out quickly and save the carpet. I did not do so, choosing instead to wait until the session was over to attend to the water. The slow-seeping water did not reach him and was not so serious, but my instinct to abandon the session and ask for his help was immensely strong. Previously, in our enactments, there had always been "real" reasons that would have compelled me to have asked for his assistance. He would have provided such assistance without question or hesitation, appearing happy to help, while growing quietly resentful.

Other reenactments of his past relationships as they played out between us emerged gradually. They were nearly imperceptible to me and had a bat-squeak (barely audible, subtle) quality of communication to them. Gradually, I learned to tune in to this shadow-like communication. We were eventually able to speak about and acknowledge both his wish to manipulate, cheat, and look after me as well as my impetus to accept his offerings and his disavowal of his true feelings. Later, he would subtly question the value of our sessions. We came to understand the meaning of his questioning the value of our work and periodically wanting to leave, only to change his mind later.

We also unraveled the curious erotic nature of the exchange of money as he paid for his sessions and what it symbolized. Each time Robert offered me his check in his usual gentlemanly manner, I had the emerging feeling of his reluctance to part with his money. For example, he held the check so that I had to reach out for it. On the one hand, it was as if at any moment he might think better of paying me and snatch it away, and, on the other, it was like being given a present that I did not deserve. It was an unconscious communication to me of his feelings of having to financially bale out and look after his father. For my part, afterward, I felt an unpleasant, grubby sensation of not deserving payment, of taking his money, of ripping him off somehow, of not having done my job. Perhaps, I sometimes wondered, this was how his father had felt?

In transactional analysis, the issue of money has been largely relegated to what we understand as the business contract, and its deeper relational meanings between therapist and client are not generally addressed. Transactional analysis is not alone in this. Dimen (1994) has written that in psychoanalysis, money is often an embarrassing, difficult topic. In recent years, there has been much more openness and willingness to debate and write about this seemingly taboo topic. Freud himself—rather reminiscent of Berne's straightforward, objective manner—advised that in the consulting room money should be dealt with in the same matter-of-fact manner as sex and ought to be approached with the client without shame by indicating the price at which the therapist values his or her time.

These days this objectivity seems less likely to be attempted, although the relational nature and meanings of the exchange of money are not always so easily dealt with. There is acknowledgment and debate about anxieties in both therapist and client that are brought to the surface. In the United Kingdom, there are often remnants of our once prominent, and now more subtle, class distinctions that can imbue money with multiple levels of meaning not directly related to the overtly stated contracts of the therapy. Anxiety for the therapist may concern such issues as how much to charge, whether to offer low fees, how to charge for missed sessions, and "working-for-love-and-not-money" moral contradictions, as well as transferential matters particular to the working couple. All are difficult to address without revealing an underbelly of dependency on the client by the therapist given the unsavory, ongoing nature of charging for therapy and the global impasse-like fact of acknowledging that this is how therapists make their living. So, while the therapist might wish to deal with money as a simple business and commercial transaction, what it arouses appears to be primitive passions. And struggles in the therapist about this issue, as with any other, are likely to be felt by the client, whether or not they are taken up directly.

For Dimen, the issue of money reaches beyond psychoanalysis. She draws on social psychology, feminism, anthropology, and class to illustrate the centrality and, in some respects, the impossibility of the issue of money and psychotherapy. Drawing from Marx, Dimen (1994) quotes, "In our culture, money has the same unconscious effect no matter in what trade it is used. By reducing everything to a common denominator, it robs everything and every person of individuality and thereby debases what it touches" (pp. 87-88). Love and money are not good bedfellows, and for the client, "the monthly bill rasps against the longing for love" (p. 91). It is easy to see how, in this paradoxical situation, love also brings forth its partner—hate—under the destructive and degrading leveler of needing to pay for attention. The issue of money seems likely, therefore, to expose a codependency in therapist and client and resonances in the relationship that find their psychological roots in love and hate.

Both Robert and I were no exception to these struggles, and we have managed to speak about them openly and mutually. Not that we have resolved the issue entirely, but being willing to struggle with the meanings for both of us has somehow moved the process along. Issues related to fees and finances have been among the areas in which Robert and I have been able to move from unspoken enactments to a verbal, reflective exploration.

In a similar vein, I was deeply, although often silently, aware that I was a female therapist in Robert's world, a world that he experienced as dominated by women. There came a time when I began to be aware of thinking about having a male figure present with us in sessions. I realized that from time to time, on the edge of my awareness, I was thinking in sessions of the need for a man. The missing absent father, perhaps? I would even imagine my male consultant, with whom I had recently begun working, sitting in the room with us. At first this was an unwelcome distraction, but as I gave attention to it, my fantasy or reverie gathered shape and had a deep longing attached to it. This male figure did not necessarily have to do with what I could not do or had not done. Rather, I increasingly felt we needed a male witness to the stuckness that Robert and I had begun to identify as him being in a type of "limbo" of agitated silence. This was a silence that I could not tolerate and that invariably I would fill.

I took about 2 years to act on this fantasy of a male witness/mentor in our work and to ask my client if it might be possible to include a male consultant in a session. By then, I had thought carefully about what I hoped to achieve from this unusual request and my motives in asking for it. First and foremost, I wanted the consultant to see us and what we were like together, to know what he saw. I was pretty sure it would be illuminating and possibly reparative for Robert. But as confident as I was in the process, it also felt rather risky. Would it upset the balance of our relationship, and if so, was that necessarily a bad thing? I feared that in front of my consultant, mistakes I might have made would be glaringly obvious and that my work would be revealed as damaging in the eyes of both Robert and my consultant. This could be potentially shaming. Also, what was I carrying and acting out in transferential terms with my consultant? Should not this be properly addressed in consultation, separate from the client? I hypothesized at one point that this was probably Robert's grief for his father, the father he had lost three times over—first when he was sent to boarding school, second when his father disappeared inside a whiskey bottle, and third when he actually died. I, like his mother, was at a loss to help my grieving son as he was protecting me from his fury and frustration. We both needed the "father."

My fantasy would not be denied. Finally, I discussed my process and idea with my client and then with my consultant. Both readily agreed, seemingly without the many questions with which I had wrestled. Even before the actual live session, which I had come to think of as consultation of our therapeutic relationship, the dynamic changed between Robert and me. Robert was moved that I had thought and bothered enough about what was going on between us, and it led to a new mutuality of contact between us and an opening up of nondefensive dialogue.

Live and in Limbo: A Case Study of an In-Person Transactional Analysis Consultation 223

The Consultant's Session Notes

What follows is a literal transcription of my (WFC) notes as consultant taken during the session. Quotes and descriptions of the interactions between Robert and Carole are in regular type; my thoughts, associations, fantasies, and interpretations are in brackets and italics.

Robert: Begins talking immediately. "Limbo . . . I've been in limbo all my adult life. . . . " [*What changed in his adult life?*]

Robert: Speaks of illness, both he and his wife having had cancer: "I'm trying to unravel this with Carole." [*Unravel—danger, come apart—openings, come closer*]

Robert: "I can't do it out there. I feel emotion in here with Carole. Not out there. [*"Can't do it" . . . sex . . . get it up out there . . . action, aggression*]

Robert: "I have a rich inner life. . . . My real life is dominated by women, only women, no men. . . . I let it go on and on." [*Limbo*]

Long period of silence.

Robert: (to Carole), "What happens now?" Silence. [*Limbo, waiting*]

Carole: "The final piece . . . an explosion? Touch? Bodywork perhaps . . . something now."

Robert: "I talk about leaving therapy." [*I let it go on & on . . . limbo*] "not disastrous—looking for intimacy."

Carole: (to consultant): "I've been much more open with Robert. There's more intimacy between us." [*Robert silent . . . hands moving constantly. Masochistic/enduring/limbo—agency/aggression*]

Robert: "I'm confused about leaving you and my wife. . . . If I talked to R [wife] about things I really feel, we might bust up . . . terrifying, I'm a coward—overly terrified, like being terrified of the dark. Talking about what I feel, but I foresee disaster, not intimacy." Close to tears. [*Limbo—unborn, "unblessed"—this is limbo, not purgatory. Purgatory is for sinners, limbo is for the unblessed, the place to wait forever*]

As I (WFC) am writing, Robert continues to speak—the cancers, bad luck, childlessness. Childlessness, the greatest loss of his life. [*GRIEF not an embryo inside, a malignancy growing inside*]

Robert: "Negative . . . so much negativity—it must be difficult" for you (to Carole), my lack of commitment, for my wife, too." [*Brutal*]

Robert: "Masculinity. . . . Bill is here. I emasculate myself—I have always held back on my masculinity. The only time I feel in charge is when I say, 'I'm leaving.' Then I can be decisive, on my own. But that's woolly, not steely." Gestures toward Carole with his hands.

Carole: "Do you want to move closer?" [*MOVE—Don't ask, move closer—"I am moving closer" definitive*] Carole takes Robert's hands.

Robert: "I feel vulnerable. . . . Biopsies, cancer, raw."

Carole: Moves to the floor, "Touch is encouraging."

Robert: "Yeah." [*How?*]

Robert: "I'm wondering how you're feeling?"

Carole: "Moved." [*Holding hands . . . still*]

Robert: "How did we get here? I regret that I didn't take initiative."

Carole: "Go ahead." [*Don't encourage . . . ask what gets in your way? . . . Nothing happens*]

Carole: "What happens to your wondering?"

Robert: "I drifted off. I'm sorry about that . . . drifting off." [*Apologize?! Limbo forgiveness? Hands immobile: "Go away!"*]

Robert: "I don't know what to do. . . . I get scared. Vulnerable with intimacy. . . . I want to be giving of myself—deep down I hold back. It's always that way with women."

Carole: "You're coming forward."

Robert: "How is this for you?" [*Robert disappears himself again. How is this for you?—SEX*]

Carole: "I have a sense of sexuality, closeness, intimacy . . . fine. . . . " [*Not fine—withholding real expression, withheld. Don't reassure. . . . What is his experience? Explore.*]

Carole: "Sexuality, passion—I want to talk about it."

Robert: "I feel sad. I'm neutralized." [*Neutered*]. Three women in my life, no sex with any of them."
Carole: "I named it. I regret putting words in your mouth."
Robert: "Neutral. [*Limbo, nowhere*] I'm neutralized, acted upon. [*Transference statement*] I'm neutral. I stay in Neutral." [*Limbo*]
Long period of silence.
Robert: "I want to speak to you (turning to the consultant). What do you think I should do? I pull back." Consultant does not respond. [*Intimacy, vitality, aliveness*]
The session ends.

The Consultant's Feedback

For me (WFC), as the consultant, the theme of a pained, limbo-like waiting came to embrace the central struggle of Robert's life and his therapist's often premature efforts to relieve both Robert's distress and his passivity in the face of it. To my mind, Robert's life had been one of repeated, tragic losses—losses that no one around him seemed able to help him grieve. I saw Robert's defensive reaction to these many losses and his inability to grieve and metabolize them as a deeply entrenched pattern of masochistic endurance and suffering. I thought that the defensive interplay between Robert and Carole was that of a mutually masochistic endurance, both trying to minimize or relieve the suffering while at the same time avoiding the potential for a much more passionate and intimate relationship between them.

Initially, I read through my process notes with Robert and Carole, pretty much as they are written here, in an impressionistic, evocative way. This is a common style of initial presentation for me as a consultant or supervisor, as I seek to model a freedom in the associative process of listening, feeling, and imagining that precedes a more analytic, rational level of reflection. I hoped that Robert and Carole would feel the sense of "limbo" as I had experienced it watching and listening to them. I wanted the consultative discussion to take place within the emotional/somatic atmosphere of "limbo."

In my technical feedback to Carole, I emphasized her subtle but frequent rescuing of Robert, her taking too much initiative, interrupting his silences and passivity with her own activity. I thought she both needed to tolerate her discomfort in the face of his inactivity and explore his experience during those periods so that his silence and immobility could become meaningful. His silence, inactivity, and threats of leaving therapy were, in fact, forms of activity and indirect expressions of aggression and power. I articulated more fully my understanding of the cumulative impact of the multiple losses of his life, the defensive function of his capacity for masochistic endurance, and the need for Robert and Carole as a therapeutic couple to enter into his grief.

I complimented Robert on his willingness to take this risk with his therapist by agreeing to work in front of a complete stranger in a rather unusual fashion. This, I thought, underscored his determination to bring more life to his life and a resilience that he and Carole needed to rely on more vigorously. It was clear to me as I spoke with Carole that Robert knew exactly what I was talking about and experienced some relief in having it articulated. I emphasized his deep ambivalence toward his own aggression and his fear that emotional honesty would lead to great catastrophe rather than to intimacy. I described the erotic connection I felt that Robert and Carole had with each other, a healthy and enlivening outcome of the work they have been able to do together.

The Therapist's Reflections

This single consultation session has been hugely influential in moving forward the process between Robert and me (CS) in our work. Hearing Bill's understanding that Robert's limbo state was in some way an expression of his power in the relational dynamic between us, I came to view the limbo experience and expression as a progressive rather than a regressive statement, one that was as informative as it was defensive in relational terms. As new understandings opened for me, I engaged in more reading to facilitate my work with Robert.

I replaced my treatment goal of "changing" the limbo experience to one of acknowledging Robert's limbo and of meaning making between us. Instead of seeking in the therapeutic contracts with Robert to change this central, core part of him, we would instead seek to make meaning of it and make a legitimate, rather than a shameful and pathological, space for his experience. This changed way of working increased the quality of contact and intimacy in our relationship and brought me to the realization that our stuckness had been, in fact, partly due to my determination to do whatever I could to help him "change." Not surprisingly, this fits with my own script story and what I had thought of (mistakenly, as it turns out) as a struggle I had overcome as a therapist and human being to need to be of use to people whom I regarded as in trouble. This represented the impasse between us, and as I acknowledged this to Robert, I was more able let go of the need and desire to do something. Our work became more mutual, real, and vital.

In "The Therapist's Fear of Doing Harm," Benjamin (2006) describes the process by which the therapist rather than the client needs to change. She argues that the therapeutic pair need to survive ruptures and mistakes between them. This is certainly true of my work with Robert. Bluntly, I could now see that I had probably been barking up entirely the wrong tree, and for a long time at that. I was probably still wanting Robert to allow me to help him. Somewhat guiltily, I faced the shame and acknowledged this to him. So now it was me in the hot seat, so to speak, and the process of accountability on my part, since it was not just a one-off moment, was both uncomfortable and entirely relevant to our work together.

More recently, having read an article elaborating Berne's concept of script protocol and its potential relationship to periods of therapeutic impasse (Cornell & Landaiche, 2006), I also began to wonder whether the limbo moments were a glimpse for Robert and for me of his protocol. I began to wonder if his passivity was a script-level adaptation to an underlying protocol of his experience of dependent, or close, relationships. I began to wonder if our stuckness was an impasse at the protocol level between us.

Protocol, as Cornell & Landaiche describe it, is a central, if neglected, concept in Berne's early transactional analysis theory. Berne himself described protocol as "a primal image . . . an impression made on the child's body, by a significant other's 'mode of relating' (Berne, 1955/1977a, p. 68). It is a cluster of sensations, organized outside awareness by the child, one that reflects his or her experience of another before the child has access to words or symbols" (Cornell & Landaiche, 2006, p. 202). What Berne described in the 1960s as protocol would be known today as "implicit relational knowing" (p. 203). This certainly began to make sense for me of the enduring nature of the limbo moments and of Roberts's experience, feeling it as he did in his body. "Protocol is a kernel of nonverbal somatic experience that may be touched or triggered in intimate relationships" (p. 203). The crucial point for me to have realized and affirmed in my work with Robert (and with a number of other clients) is, as Cornell and Landaiche put it, "the most salient aspect of protocol, as distinct from script, is that it cannot be cognitively changed, redecided or rescripted. Protocol can only be brought into awareness, understood, and lived within" (p. 204).

Over time, since the consultation, the stuckness Robert and I have experienced in the therapy has gradually evaporated. Our work has taken on a truth and trust that had not been present before. Now I truly could see how this therapy could have a successful outcome for Robert and for me, not so much in terms of the behavioral changes he might or might not make, but because in our relationship it was possible to talk about and discuss everything, even his disappointment with me and my shame that I could not really give him what he wanted. This has been a huge and intimate change in our working relationship.

One recent session in particular bears witness to this trust and change and captures the bodily nature and understanding of the protocol level of our work. I had begun to ask Robert to describe, if he could, his physical sensation as he again mentioned "limbo." Without words he slowly and deliberately moved his hands, moving from left hand to right and back again across his body, again and again as if he were passing an object from one side to the other. This repeated action produced an extreme, surprising, and rare expression of uncensored, authentic, spontaneous emotion. He was hugely distressed and disturbed, saying he felt himself to be "in between." He felt nauseous and wanted to vomit, which he actually did. This seemed a moment of antithesis to his accustomed passivity—a true catharsis and a physical response to what lay beneath his script.

I was stunned by the memory that then emerged. He remembered that shortly after his birth, so the story goes, his mother was still in the delivery room with her husband and baby Robert. They were visited by her own father and her mother-in-law. The latter pair was at loggerheads, as her father had always been against her marriage. I suspect Robert's mother may have been afraid of her father and her mother-in-law and what might occur. What she did was to hold Robert, newly born, aloft between the feuding pair. Whether they actually passed him like an object from one to another we do not know, and what he might have taken in of this atmosphere, of course, he did not remember cognitively. But he most definitely remembered it at a body level, and I was a witness to his distress. He experienced again how he had embodied this sense of himself being held in limbo, this time through the activity rather than the passivity of his body. Unable to move. Held in limbo. Live and in limbo.

Robert could now recognize at a deeper level how he had always felt in between, had been the placating rescuer to his alcoholic and weak father and weeping mother, had allowed and endured the beatings and abuse at boarding school as in almost all his other relationships. Although we were both shaken by the intensity of the emotion and his body awareness, it was a precious moment, long awaited by both of us. It was a kind of undoing, and definitely an explanation of the limbo as a glimpse of the protocol.

Robert's Reflections

The effect of asking for live consultation has been central to reshaping the work Carole and Robert have been doing together, as was the writing of this chapter, in which Robert has taken part. He has read it and his own contribution about the single session follows here.

I (RN) was excited before the session with my therapist and her consultant, mainly, I think, because there would be three of us: a father, a mother, and me. It would be an opportunity for me to be how I was not able to be with my natural parents. In my own family, I could not be clear or honest about my needs, and I felt caught in my family culture of passivity.

How much did a passive father who felt himself a failure affect me? How much did his decline in middle age, when I felt him to be particularly dependent on me, pull me down? I have often felt shame and a sense of worthlessness in spite of trying to do the right thing. The excitement before the session had something to do with the prospect of meeting an involved father who would be able to listen, guide, and encourage me as a man.

I got a great boost from feeling that this was being done for me, that my therapist cared and attended to me even to the extent of bringing a male figure into the process. And, as I am writing, I am also wondering if I might have felt a sense of inadequacy deep down: Wasn't she satisfied enough by having me in the room? Why was she inviting another man along? These questions give rise to my fears around sexuality and my ambivalence about my own potency. While I feel a great longing to express my physical and sexual self, and can imagine it, I also have doubts about my masculinity, preferring to keep myself to myself!

The experience has somehow focused my thoughts on masculinity around the consultant, my father, and myself. There is something that I am struggling with about me being or becoming a man as I want to be, and now that I am putting pen to paper, I sense that the session was a dynamic in this, before, during, and after.

I am asking myself how the state of limbo—which has been with me for so long—can be changed into my feeling more present and more alive in relationship, allowing myself more freedom of expression rather than my self-imposed compromise.

There is something about potency and challenge in relationships that I have never felt able to do. I think one of my hopes was that I would learn something about this from the male consultant. He should know about it!

The downside of the actual session was that I still ended up feeling in limbo, reasonably happy to experience as the one in the middle, the mediator—in between my therapist and her supervisor and, as with my parents, I was the junior, the "underling." Somehow I had a feeling of having to fit into a framework. Allied to this was the sense that my therapist was on display, and, of course, I did not want to let her down. So I am now aware that I was even more guarded than usual of putting my foot in it, which is perhaps exactly what I need to stop being so concerned about.

Looking Back at the Consultation

It was fascinating to read Robert's account of our meeting. Each of us experienced the consultation session with some commonalities of understanding and each with different points of emphasis and understanding. It seems clear from Carole's account of the continuing work she and Robert did that the consultation was useful (although falling short of the one-session cure of which we all dream), and the success of breaking the impasse is also clear in Robert's reflections. The transferential elements of the therapeutic relationship continue, although they are much more readily available for reflection since the consult. Robert's final paragraph speaks particularly to the ongoing transference issues that continue to be addressed in their work.

One particularly salient aspect of the in-person consultation in this instance is that of the consultant being male. More often than not, while the gender of the therapist (or genders of the therapeutic dyad) should not be ignored in the work, gender is not pivotal. And yet there are some treatments, or points in the treatment process, where gender is crucial. It was important here that the consultant was a man who could bring the interest and skill of a man into what for Robert was a seemingly endless series of enmeshments with women in primary relationships, someone who would offer a live contrast to his father's passivity and self-destructiveness. We ran the risk of undercutting Carole's authority if the gender dynamics were ignored or minimized. In Robert's words, "There is something about the potency and challenge in relationships that I have never felt able to do." The consultation presented an opportunity to enhance challenge and potency for all involved and demonstrated challenges that were enlivening rather than demeaning or controlling.

Robert's comments and the unfolding of the therapeutic work speak to another important aspect of supervision and consultation: breaking up the therapeutic dyad. While the therapeutic dyad offers rich potential for self-exploration, mutual discovery, and intimacy, there is the ever-present risk of the dyad slipping into solipsistic ruts. Consultation brings a third mind to the dyad. Transactional analysis was founded on group therapy. Berne's work was grounded in groups. Berne's preference was to work with clients, whenever possible, for periods in group and then individually. The group offers a very different milieu from individual therapy. In the letter that introduces new clients to my (WFC) practice, I state that I am involved in weekly consultation and ongoing professional seminars and that it is very likely that over the course of treatment I will bring the therapy to consultation. I want to signal to clients from the beginning that "we are not in this alone" and that healthy relationships make regular use of external resources. At points of deep conflict and impasse, I have taken clients for direct supervision as we have described here. I also often tell clients when I have received consultation and report back the results.

While in-person consultation can be revealing and productive, it can also be deeply unsettling to therapist and client alike. It is also not magic, which can be disappointing and lead to suffering the loss of magical expectations. The therapeutic dyad may well find new insight and working space, but the work will need to continue. One cannot readily tick off a list of characteristics that qualify or disqualify particular kinds of clients from participating in this style of supervision. Berne developed this approach with patients in psychiatric hospitals, and I (WFC) learned of Berne's model in a facility that worked with deeply disturbed children. It was always Berne's premise that, given the chance, even the most troubled people would make use of their Adult ego states. This would suggest that the contract for the consultation and the commitment to follow-through are the most crucial factors in the application of this process. It is a process that conveys respect to therapist and client alike for their willingness to engage in the examination of their working relationship in the presence and with the facilitation of another.

Conclusion

Robert's articulate description of his understanding of the single consultation session has led to further rich exploration between him and his therapist. Grief for his father and his father's lack of involvement as a man and father to him has resurfaced. His father's gentleness, but also his reticence to become truly engaged as a father with his son, have led Robert to make a deeper sense and meaning of his own sexuality and confusions about gender roles as they spring from his relationship with his father.

To return to O'Hearne's model and in assessing what happened in the consultation session and after, I (CS) believe all the points he made in his model to be relevant and correct. As can be read from his own account, Robert can certainly speak about his situation from an objective position. He has also learned from the work and changes in direction since the session that his therapist is a person and that I am not infallible. We have formed a more overt, effective, and aggressive working partnership. For my part, I most certainly have stayed awake and realized that I do not know all the answers and that Robert is a tough, equal, but different and mutual partner in this long journey of meaning making we are in.

REFERENCES

Benjamin, J. (2006, 9 October). *The analyst's fear of doing harm*. Paper presented at the London Voluntary Sector Resource Centre sponsored by Confer, London, England.

Berne, E. (1977a). Primal images and primal judgment. In E. Berne, *Intuition and ego states: The origins of transactional analysis* (P. McCormick, Ed.) (pp. 67-97). San Francisco: TA Press. (Original work published 1955)

Berne, E. (1977b). Staff-patient staff conferences. In M. James & Contributors, *Techniques in transactional analysis for psychotherapists and counselors* (pp. 153-165). Reading, MA: Addison-Wesley. (Original work published 1968)

Cornell, W. F., & Landaiche, N. M. (2006). Impasse and intimacy: Applying Berne's concept of script protocol. *Transactional Analysis Journal, 36*, 196-213.

Dimen, M. (1994). Money, love and hate: Contradiction and paradox in psychoanalysis. *Psychoanalytic Dialogues, 4*, 60-100.

Duffell, N. (2000). *The making of them: The British attitude to children and the boarding school system*. London: Lone Arrow Press.

Hughes, T. (2004). *Tom Brown's schooldays*. New York: Penguin. (Original work published 1857)

O'Hearne, J. (1972). The patient as collaborator. In M. James & Contributors, *Techniques in transactional analysis for psychotherapists and counselors* (pp. 176-186). Reading, MA: Addison-Wesley.

The original version of this chapter was published in the Transactional Analysis Journal, *Volume 37, Number 2, pp. 159-171, April 2007.*

Teaching Transactional Analysts to Think Theoretically

William F. Cornell and Marilyn J. Zalcman

Any system of psychotherapy is, to some extent, self-limiting and biased. The theory and techniques of each psychotherapy method have evolved within the cultural context of the times and often in reaction against the shortcomings of existing approaches. Within each theory of psychotherapy are embedded basic assumptions about the nature of human beings and the causes of behavior. These assumptions reflect the current understanding of human functioning from biological, psychological, philosophical, and, sometimes, socioeconomic perspectives. Whether or not these assumptions are recognized or articulated in a particular psychotherapy method, they significantly influence clinical observations, explanations, and the interventions used.

There is, furthermore, a tendency among clinicians to accept and communicate about theory as though it provides "real" explanations for why people do what they do. As Hess (1980) depicts the situation, "Often practitioners work with their assumptions and theories to the point where they become unnoticed, as unnoticed as the air we breathe. On too few occasions do we take the opportunity to scrutinize our values and theories" (p. 3). This lack of critical thinking about theory and its underlying assumptions is likely to reinforce the belief that what is proposed by the theory is "fact" rather than an effort to clarify experience and foster understanding. Although a therapist's use of a particular model of therapy may be skillful, failure to question the underlying assumptions and limitations of that model may result in the clinician circumscribing opportunities to learn from clinical experience. In turn, the clinician may inadvertently restrict the focus of therapy sessions, teaching clients to understand themselves from a perspective more limited than necessary. As an alternative to the use of theory as "reality" or orthodoxy, Chapanis (1961) identified several functions that theoretical models can serve for clinicians: They can be used to describe and understand complex phenomena, to learn complex skills, to identify new relationships among existing factors, to provide a framework for experimentation, and to have fun playing with how concepts and observations fit together.

The practice of psychotherapy can become a numbing routine of problem solving and emotional management with clients. In the face of the demands of a practice, clinicians may turn to training and supervision for technical answers and emotional support. In developing our approach to clinical supervision, we have sought to go beyond the immediate pressures of clinical practice and the biases of any one model to foster the kind of "noticing" that Hess encourages. In our view, teaching clinicians to use theory in all of the ways Chapanis cited is crucial for the training of competent psychotherapists and is all too frequently absent or insufficiently covered in both academic and private training programs. Learning to "think theoretically," to challenge assumptions, and to test out theory in clinical practice prepares clinicians for self-supervision, continuing growth, and creative contributions to the field.

This chapter presents our "Content Outline for Transactional Analysis Training and Supervision," which we have found valuable in planning for and teaching trainees to differentiate between theoretical, technical, ethical, and personal concerns in evaluating their work. Then, focusing specifically on the interaction between theoretical knowledge and clinical technique, we present the general goals and specific strategies that we have developed to counteract rigidity and orthodoxy in practice and to promote disciplined and creative thinking about theory and its clinical applications.

Content Outline for Transactional Analysis Training and Supervision

In our article, "A Bilateral Model for Clinical Supervision" (Zalcman & Cornell, 1983), we identified *therapist activities* as one of three dimensions of *therapist operations* that need to be monitored in a comprehensive supervision model. Whereas the *functional mode* refers to how a therapist intervenes and the *focus of attention* refers to the area that a therapist defines as most relevant to the therapeutic task, the *therapist activities* refer to the areas in which the therapist must develop effective functioning. Helping a clinician to differentiate and understand the range of therapeutic activities is often the first supervisory task once basic theory and technique have been learned.

We divide therapist activities into four basic categories: theoretical and empirical knowledge, clinical skills and expertise, ethical and professional practices, and personal skills and development. In Figure 1 we specify what we include in each of these four areas.

I. **THEORETICAL & EMPIRICAL KNOWLEDGE**
   A. TRANSACTIONAL ANALYSIS THEORY
   B. GROUP THEORY
   C. OTHER PSYCHOTHERAPY THEORIES
   D. MEDICAL/PSYCHIATRIC
   E. BEHAVIORAL SCIENCES
   F. SOCIAL SCIENCES
   G. NEUROSCIENCE AND MEMORY RESEARCH
   H. STUDIES OF MOTHER-INFANT/CHILD RELATIONS AND ATTACHMENT PATTERNS
   I. OTHER

II. **CLINICAL SKILLS & EXPERTISE**
   A. CLINICAL APPLICATION OF THEORY
   B. GROUP DYNAMICS
   C. INTERVENTION DECISIONS
   D. PREDICTION OF OUTCOMES
   E. DIRECTION OF TREATMENT
   F. SPECIALIZED TECHNIQUES
      1. Transactional analysis
      2. Others

III. **ETHICAL & PROFESSIONAL PRACTICES**
   A. ETHICS
   B. PERSONAL VALUES
   C. PROFESSIONAL BACKGROUND
      1. Privileges
      2. Responsibilities
      3. Capabilities
      4. Limitations
      5. Specialized training
   D. OTHER PROFESSIONS
      1. Privileges
      2. Responsibilities
      3. Capabilities
      4. Limitations
      5. Communication with
   E. DEVELOPING & MAINTAINING A PRACTICE
   F. CONTINUING EDUCATION

IV. **PERSONAL SKILLS & DEVELOPMENT**
   A. PERSONAL THERAPY ISSUES
   B. PRESENTATION OF SELF
   C. QUALITY OF RELATIONSHIPS
      1. Therapist-client
      2. Supervisory
      3. Peer
      4. Personal
   D. QUALITY OF LIFESTYLE
      1. Sources of strokes
      2. Balance and diversity
      3. Social activities

Figure 1
Content Outline for Transactional Analysis Training and Supervision

---

Theoretical and Empirical Knowledge. This includes not only transactional analysis theory or the theory of a particular TA school but also the theory and research findings from group literature, other psychotherapy methods, the medical/psychiatric field, behavioral sciences, social sciences, neuroscience and memory research, and studies of mother/infant relations and attachment patterns. Including information about all of these topics in ongoing training and supervision enables trainees to develop a broad base of knowledge and appreciation of the diversity of theories and research that may be applicable to therapy. Having developed the conceptual skills and facility of thinking in theoretical and empirical terms, therapists are more likely to be able to identify the strengths and limitations of a particular system of psychotherapy, to evaluate research findings, and to understand that any theory, no matter how useful in clinical work, is only one of many possible systems for understanding and helping to change human behavior. Without this broad base of knowledge and understanding, therapists may become overly invested in a given approach. Instead of considering the limitations of their approach, they may inaccurately identify themselves or their clients as failing.

Clinical Skills and Expertise. As an area of transactional analysis training and supervision, this involves much more than teaching specialized techniques for intervening with clients in therapy sessions, whether those techniques have been developed in transactional analysis or other modalities. Learning to apply theoretical concepts to specific clients and clinical situations, understanding and using group dynamics (whether with couples, families, or groups), making decisions about which interventions are most appropriate and most likely to be effective, predicting the outcomes of specific interventions or treatment strategies, and considering the direction of treatment or treatment planning (whether for a session or over time) are all necessary skills for transactional analysts. The ability to apply all of these skills to diverse client populations and clinical problems is what we define as "clinical expertise."

Ethical and Professional Practices. This involves the development of values, awareness, and abilities to practice therapy within the professional mental health community. In giving attention to this area, the following goals need to be accomplished: becoming cognizant of and adhering to the ethical codes of the ITAA and other professional groups; examining personal values and distinguishing them from what are appropriate expectations for clients; understanding the privileges, responsibilities, capabilities, and limitations of one's own profession as well as those of related professions; learning how to communicate with other professionals; learning practical approaches to developing and maintaining a practice; and developing an appreciation for and the practice of obtaining continuing education. Whether trainees have participated in formal academic programs and had experience in traditional mental health settings or not, the importance of discussing and monitoring this area should not be underestimated. Lack of attention to these aspects of functioning may have a significant impact on the effectiveness of a therapist. For example, therapists may not be sufficiently aware of the limitations of their preferred modality or may not be trained in effectively communicating with fellow professionals working in different modalities. Either could result in a therapist continuing to work with a client when referral would be more appropriate.

Personal Skills and Development. This is the area of training and supervision in which attention is given not only to unresolved therapeutic issues but also to the whole array of personal skills and situations that have an impact on an individual's functioning as a therapist. These may not involve therapeutic impasses per se, but instead may require simple instructions about doing things, learning skills, practicing, or making adjustments. "Presentation of Self" refers to the various personal habits, social skills, and level of comfort the trainee has that may affect his or her interactions with others. For example, a trainee having difficulty talking in front of groups may simply need to gain experience (i.e., to be given opportunities to practice and receive feedback). In examining the "Quality of Relationships," skills and comfort may need to be developed in relating to clients, supervisor, colleagues, and/or personal acquaintances. Attending to the "Quality of Lifestyle" includes consideration of the therapist's sources of strokes, balance and diversity of activities, and social activities. This is important not only for the therapist's well-being but also for the protection and autonomy of his or her clients. If a therapist's personal life is not sufficiently gratifying and well-rounded, clients may be relied on as the primary source of the therapist's stimulation and satisfaction, resulting in both the therapist and client becoming overinvolved and overdependent on each other.

In our opinion, all four areas of the content outline for transactional analysis training and supervision need to be given balanced attention instead of restricting teaching or supervision to one area or to a particular aspect of one area. Transactional analysts trained in programs that overemphasize a few of the content areas will not be sufficiently prepared to identify the possible sources of therapeutic problems and will be more likely to limit their range of observations, options, and explanations. In supervision that stresses clinical demonstrations and the specific techniques favored by the sponsoring trainer, clinical skills (Section II) will be the primary focus, with transactional analysis theory (Section I.A) being limited to the theory and concepts espoused by that particular trainer. When unresolved therapeutic issues are assumed to be the primary source of therapeutic error, personal therapy issues (Section IV.A) may become so heavily emphasized that other important considerations are ignored. In both instances, the breadth and depth of understanding fall short of the desirable goals. Competence as a transactional analyst requires knowledge of and investment in theoretical understanding, clinical mastery, ethical and professional conduct, and personal development. Limitations in one or more of these areas will result in more therapeutic errors and less likelihood that the therapist will be aware of the need for correction.

Goals and Strategies for Teaching Theoretical Thinking

When viewed within the framework of the content outline for transactional analysis training and supervision, we define the requirements for using theory effectively and flexibly as: (1) a proficiency in theoretical and empirical knowledge, (2) a repertoire of clinical skills, and (3) the facility for interrelating the two in actual practice. All too often one or more of these abilities is lacking, which hampers the effectiveness of therapists who seek transactional analysis training. Academically trained clinicians usually have a strong theoretical background but lack the clinical experience and acumen to apply their knowledge to specific clients and situations. Clinicians trained in nontraditional settings, although highly skilled in establishing therapeutic relationships and using clinical techniques, often do not understand why they use specific techniques or how to relate them to theory. Whether the imbalance is skewed in the direction of theory or clinical skills, as long as it exists, the trainee's ability to relate theory to clinical practice will most likely be impaired.

In examining our various approaches to teaching transactional analysts to integrate and interrelate theory and clinical skills, we have identified three primary goals:

1. To enhance the capacity for objectivity toward one's own work and the ability to conceptualize from multiple frames of reference
2. To support the development of a flexible therapeutic style that is both suited to the individual therapist and responsive to the varied needs of clients
3. To foster collegial relationships and self-supervision skills that will stimulate professional attitudes and learning that continue beyond the supervisory relationship

In the following discussion, we present some of the strategies we have developed to accomplish these goals.

Objectivity and the Ability to Conceptualize. In the broadest sense, we encourage trainees to identify and examine the ideas, assumptions, and beliefs that underlie their approach to therapy and their definitions of the tasks and responsibilities of therapists. The underlying matrix for their beliefs and assumptions is likely to reflect educational experiences and cultural biases, the influence of mentors and other significant teachers, their experiencing successful resolutions of personal conflicts and crises, and their individual script. This network of factors results, for many therapists, in a strong personal identification with the approach they practice. The importance of a positive belief system in facilitating change is well documented (Cousins, 1979; Frank, 1963; Lieberman, Yalom, & Miles, 1973; Simonton & Simonton, 1975). However, if unexamined, these beliefs can limit the objectivity and autonomy of the professional.

With a broader theoretical base, the therapist is less likely to develop an isolated, chauvinistic view of the method chosen as a primary frame of reference. Therefore, we encourage all trainees to have a working knowledge of at least one other theoretical model in addition to their primary framework. By "working knowledge" we mean an understanding of the theory in practice as well as academic knowledge of it. Our emphasis here is not on the acquisition of additional techniques but on the comprehension of different theoretical structures, which expands both intellectual and technical options. In our view, it is desirable, at any point in the treatment process, for the therapist to be aware of several choices for actual interventions and for theoretical explanations of their clinical decisions.

From our point of view, familiarity with diverse theoretical models improves a clinician's ability to assess the appropriateness of a specific modality for a particular client and to make appropriate referrals. This knowledge enhances clinical expertise and flexibility, thereby reducing the likelihood of encountering points of severe impasse. Those times when a therapist and client become "stuck" are frequent presenting problems in supervision. It has been our experience that often this stuckness is not so much a result of the client being entrenched in script or the therapist being caught in some unresolved, personal therapeutic issue as it is neither person knowing what else to do or how else to solve the problem.

In our approach to supervision, we do not begin by assuming that a therapeutic error on the part of a supervisee is evidence of personal treatment issues (i.e., that the supervisee is somehow "invested in" the mistake). A therapeutic error is not in and of itself evidence of the therapist's personal issues, nor does it require a therapeutic intervention from the supervisor to the supervisee. In the absence of relevant information and skill, pathological or script-bound behaviors on the part of the therapist may fill the gap. Only if a trainee's errors continue after he or she is offered options for understanding the clinical problem or for intervening with the client do we presume that personal issues need to be confronted. While we expect trainees to be involved and invested in their own personal therapy, we do not expect the therapist's personal treatment to result in competence as a therapist. We believe that the development of diverse theoretical knowledge and sound critical thinking will both reduce the potential influence of the therapist's script and enhance the therapist's desire for continued professional growth.

We have found that developing a historical context for the theory and practice of transactional analysis fosters an understanding that psychotherapy theory can be alive and evolving. Developing this historical perspective involves teaching about the intellectual climate and prevailing ideas that existed when the approach was first introduced, following the evolution of the theory and method, comparing it with other developing psychotherapies, and raising questions about the gaps that exist. In transactional analysis training, presenting a historical context usually means beginning with an overview of Berne's work and how he challenged the psychoanalytic approach dominant at the time. While founded in an understanding of psychodynamics, the transactional analysis approach—along with family-oriented, gestalt, existential, and behavioral therapies—questioned the efficacy of analytic technique and presented alternatives. Having established an understanding of the context in which transactional analysis started, we then take a particular concept of Berne's, cite his sources from other authors, and trace the development of the concept by Berne and other transactional analysis authors who have revised, expanded, or changed Berne's original ideas. Our transactional analysis reading list is organized chronologically to help give trainees an active sense of the development of TA theory and to underline the fact that theory and technique will continue to change as long as this system is alive. We want therapists to have the information, perspective, and freedom to come to their own appreciation and understanding of the concepts and tools that are central to their work.

Teaching therapists to distinguish between theoretical concepts and clinical techniques is especially important in moving from didactic presentations to clinical application. Most therapists have been trained to focus on the client and what needs to be done to facilitate change. The difference between theory (explanatory models for understanding the client) and clinical interventions (ways of getting information about clients or helping them to change) become blurred in day-to-day practice. And, when presenting cases for supervision, a clinician can easily shift so rapidly between labeling behaviors with theoretical concepts and describing actual behaviors of the client that the distinctions between theory, clinical techniques, and descriptions of the client become even more obscure. Zalcman (1981) has developed a schema for differentiating transactional analysis concepts from transactional analysis techniques, one that we have found useful for helping supervisees in organizing their thinking and presentations.

An additional strategy developed to relate the application of theoretical knowledge to clinical techniques has become known as "The Cards." Inspired by a supervision session with Lois Johnson in which she assigned each supervisee to track one aspect of the treatment process during peer-group supervision, Cornell developed a series of feedback cards that focus on various aspects of the treatment being supervised. The cards are distributed at random so that individual trainees never know exactly what they will be asked to observe and describe. The questions often challenge trainees to stretch their powers of observation and theoretical understanding and to apply transactional analysis theory and techniques to actual cases.

Examples of feedback cards focused on theoretical understanding:
1. Describe the symbiosis you image for this client as a child with his/her parents. What was allowed within the symbiosis and what was "against the rules"?
2. Describe the client's presenting problem in terms of ego state contamination or exclusion.
3. Present and support an argument that the client's current difficulty is not a result of script.
4. What basic script belief must change in order for the client's racket system to change?
5. What game behavior was evident in this piece of work? How do the games maintain symbiosis?
6. "Neurosis is a solution, not a problem." Relate this statement to the therapy you just observed.

Examples of feedback cards focused on clinical interventions:
1. How could you have used the group differently?
2. If this client were in an ongoing group with you, what might you anticipate happening in the next session? Why? What would you do?
3. Describe a temporary, functional symbiosis you might enter into with this client at this point in treatment.
4. How could the therapist have used his or her Parent ego state differently?
5. What was the single most effective intervention made by the therapist?
6. Offer three contracts for the client's consideration.

Examples of feedback cards focused on imaginative and playful responses:
1. If you had this client's mother in treatment, what might you consider for her first treatment contract?
2. Imagine and describe this client at 80 years of age.
3. Imagine and describe the therapist as a student giving his or her first oral presentation to his or her fifth-grade class.
4. Imagine and describe the client as a 5-year-old having a fight with his or her best friend.
5. Imagine and describe the therapist as an adolescent in the midst of his or her first serious romantic relationship.
6. If you had been the client here, how could you have outsmarted the therapist and maintained your script?

Utilizing feedback cards serves to keep everyone actively and thoughtful involved in the material presented for supervision and in the group process. In addition, immediate conceptualization is encouraged, lively debate frequently occurs, and trainees learn how much they have to offer one another.

Flexible Therapeutic Style. Training structures that are designed to provide direct experience with the thinking and working styles of a variety of professionals offer trainees the opportunity to explore, experiment, and gradually develop a unique therapeutic style of their own. We require individuals who are preparing for certified membership in the ITAA to have both didactic and supervisory experience with other Certified Transactional Analysts and Certified Teaching and Supervising Transactional Analysts in addition to their work with us. We find that this requirement enriches the learning experience for all involved while keeping the model of the "ideal" therapist open to change.

Exposure to a variety of therapeutic styles and approaches tends to offset overadaptation to the primary trainer, a negative aspect of the mentor model, which is often a primary vehicle for transactional analysis training and supervision. In the mentor model, the trainee essentially becomes an apprentice therapist studying under a master therapist. As described by Levinson and his colleagues (Levinson with Darrow, Klein, Levinson, & McKee, 1978, p. 97), the mentor serves as a teacher, sponsor, host and guide, exemplar, counselor, and facilitator of "realizing the Dream" (in this instance, becoming a transactional analyst). The trainee also has several roles in the relationship: client, supervisee, supervisor of other trainees, cotherapist, and sometimes even business partner. Training may be conducted in structured teaching programs, supervision sessions, or while doing cotherapy or engaging in a therapy practice together. The primary vehicle for training is clinical demonstration by the trainer with subsequent discussion. Often the focus is on the mentor's techniques and rationale for doing therapy (i.e., "Here's what I do and why I do it").

The positive features of using the mentor model are similar to those discussed by Levinson et. al. (1978). Having a mentor who initiates, instructs, and supports the novice therapist can contribute significantly to the ease with which the trainee "learns the ropes," establishes a place within the profession, and learns essential skills and values. However, when the majority of a therapist's training and supervision are obtained from the mentor, there are likely to be limitations, if not complications, in the development of professional knowledge and skills. Barnes (1977) pointed out the restrictions on autonomy that may ensue from too close an allegiance to a given transactional analysis "school" or trainer:

> Some individuals in TA make the assumption that their teacher or therapist has the truth, knows the way to right living, and uses only the correct methods. They do not see the diversity of TA approaches as something to be appreciated; they must choose one and then turn it into the way to conceptualize and do TA. (pp. 12-13)

Even if such an allegiance is not fostered in the mentor relationship, opportunities to observe a wide variety of therapeutic styles and conceptualizations of the therapeutic process are diminished. Furthermore, emphasis in this model is too easily focused on example and technique rather than on the critique of the theory and its clinical applications.

Along with exposure to diverse professional models outside of the primary supervisory relationship, we have found it extremely useful to create diversity within the supervisory structure itself. We give careful attention to the structure and procedures of ongoing supervision, utilizing a variety of supervisory formats. In the first year or so of the training and supervision process, we tend to provide a fairly predictable structure, one that is consistent with Erskine's (1982) description of the "skill development" phase in the beginning stage of training. Each supervisory session begins with a didactic presentation of a particular clinical issue and relevant theory (e.g., game identification, script intervention, racket analysis, group process, the initial interview, etc.); the remainder of the session is focused on applying the concepts to clinical work. For those trainees with little or no direct clinical experience, Cornell has developed forms to be written monthly that describe and assess both the group process and the functioning of individual clients in the context of their treatment contracts in relationship to the therapist and group members. These forms are turned in regularly to the supervisor for written responses or direct supervision.

Once basic theory and technique are mastered, we open up the range, structure, and strategies of supervision, intentionally keeping the structure and procedures of supervision group sessions unpredictable. The purpose and design of a given session need to be clear to the supervisor but do not need to be known in advance to the trainees (see Zalcman & Cornell, 1983, pp. 120-122). In any case, we do not believe that any supervisory or therapeutic routine accurately mirrors the diversity and complexity of therapeutic problems and puzzles that clients bring to us each week. If supervision falls into a predictable routine, trainees may mistake the routine for the treatment process itself. By introducing an element of unpredictability in the supervision process, we seek to challenge trainees to develop a flexible therapeutic style along with creative thinking. Exposed to unpredictability, trainees may be confronted with their expectations and rigidities regarding the role of the supervisor, the function of the group, or the task of the therapist.

Among the procedures we use are peer-group supervision (as familiar to most transactional analysis practitioners), audiotape review, role playing, videotape feedback, experimentation with different styles of group process, ongoing case consultation (to follow systematically the treatment of one client over an extended period of time), and the invitation of trainees' clients to attend and be treated

within the supervision group (a variation on Berne's [1968] staff-patient staff conference). At times, in peer-group work, therapists will draw cards at random that give instructions to approach the therapy in a particular way. Examples of instructions to therapists include:
1. Confront each discounting or redefining transaction initiated by the client during this work
2. Consistently respond to the client from your Child ego state
3. Consistently respond to what the client presents with parenting interventions
4. Relate the client's presenting problem to behavior that is observable in this group and develop an appropriate contract for change

Trainees, in role playing clients, may also receive instructions, unknown to the rest of the group, to present their problems in particular ways. For example:
1. Present your problem and then consistently escalate the feelings over thinking
2. Exclude your Child ego state
3. Blame your therapist for whatever is wrong
4. Present your problem and then consistently discount and minimize it

Along with adding excitement to supervision, these strategies ensure that supervisees will use aspects of their personalities they may underplay, experiment with techniques that seem risky or alien to their preferred style, and learn to evaluate their work in a variety of ways. Diversity in supervisory techniques and experiences in the supervision groups are more likely to elicit flexibility in trainees' thinking about and engaging in the therapeutic process.

Collegial Relationships and Self-Supervision Skills. In Berne's (1966, pp. 170-171) outline of clinical seminars and supervision, he presents two systems for discussing clinical issues: (1) the "European" system (a hierarchical presentation of comments from most junior to most senior member of the group), and (2) the "American" system (speaking when the spirit moves you). Berne clearly preferred the European system. He noted that the American system offers equal rights but often results in junior and less aggressive people keeping quiet. We, too, have found that the active involvement of all trainees is valuable in clinical discussion and, as described earlier, have developed structures that challenge and, when necessary, require trainees to actively participate in the evaluation of the clinical work being presented by themselves and others. While the focus of a particular supervision session for an individual trainee is contractual with the supervisor, that trainee is also expected to participate actively in the supervision of the others in the group. The purpose of engaging trainees in supervising one another is to encourage them to think out loud in theoretical terms about what they hear and observe in other people's work and to incorporate these evolving conceptual skills in treatment planning and their own self-evaluation. The longer-range purpose is to teach self-supervision skills and how to establish and work within a collegial atmosphere.

The third principle—the facility for interrelating knowledge and clinical skills in actual practice—is one of attitude. The attitude is based on the recognition that the supervisory relationship will end. Termination is successful when trainees leave excited about learning, are able to think critically (rather than judgmentally) about their work, and are able to relate to themselves and fellow clinicians with interest and respect. By fostering interactive, collegial relationships and self-supervision skills among trainees, we hope to ensure continued well-being and learning after formal supervision and certification are completed.

Conclusion

In our opinion, didactic teaching and clinical supervision in transactional analysis training need to be designed to maximize exposure to and practice with theoretical concepts, clinical interventions, and interrelating the two. The ability to use theory and techniques is not sufficient. If therapists are unable to correlate their theoretical framework with clinical interventions, they will not be likely to critically evaluate their own work, the methods they are using, or the theory they have adopted. They will not, in effect, be able to use theory in all of the ways Chapanis recommends, which were described earlier and which we endorse. It is the ability to interrelate a psychotherapy theory and its clinical applications that distinguishes a clinician from a technician.

In this chapter, we have focused on transactional analysis training and supervision in our presentation of frameworks and strategies for teaching clinicians to think theoretically. With some modifications, however, we think that this approach could be used for training therapists in other psychotherapy methods. The content outline for transactional analysis training and supervision, for example, could be revised by substituting for transactional analysis theory (Section I.A in Figure 1) and for specialized transactional analysis techniques (Section II.F.1) the particular psychotherapy method being taught. The specific content to be covered would vary in detail and emphasis depending on the psychotherapy method being taught, but the basic categories and principles for using the outline, as we have described them, would be applicable.

Likewise, both the goals and strategies for teaching theoretical thinking could be applied to teaching other psychotherapy methods. Engaging therapists in actively questioning their conceptual frameworks and correlating their ideas with their clinical observations will compensate greatly for the biases and limitations of any given psychotherapy method. And, it will result in more effective therapists who are more likely to continue their own learning and substantially contribute to the further development of psychotherapeutic theory and practice.

REFERENCES

Barnes, G. (1977). *Transactional analysis after Eric Berne: The teachings and practices of three TA schools.* New York: Harper's College Press.

Berne, E. (1966). *Principles of group treatment.* New York: Oxford University Press.

Berne, E. (1968). Staff-patient staff conferences. *American Journal of Psychiatry, 125,* 286-293.

Chapanis, A. (1961). Men, machines and models. *American Psychologist, 16,* 113-131.

Cousins, N. (1979). *Anatomy of an illness as perceived by the patient: Reflections on healing and regeneration.* New York: Norton.

Erskine, R. G. (1982). Supervision of psychotherapy: Models for professional development. *Transactional Analysis Journal, 12,* 314-321.

Frank, J. (1963). *Persuasion and healing.* New York: Schocken Books.

Hess, A. K. (Ed.) (1980). *Psychotherapy supervision: Theory, research and practice.* New York: Wiley.

Levinson, D. J., with Darrow, C. N., Klein, E. B., Levinson, M. H., & McKee, B. (1978). *The seasons of a man's life.* New York: Ballantine Books.

Lieberman, M. A., Yalom, I., & Miles, M. (1973). *Encounter groups: First facts.* New York: Basic Books.

Simonton, O. C., & Simonton, S. S. (1975) Belief systems and management of the emotional aspects of malignancy. *Journal of Transpersonal Psychology, 7,* 29-47.

Zalcman, M. J. (1981). *Clinical applications of TA theory: Concepts and techniques.* Unpublished document available through author.

Zalcman, M. J., & Cornell, W. F. (1983). A bilateral model for clinical supervision. *Transactional Analysis Journal, 13,* 112-123.

The original version of this chapter was published in the Transactional Analysis Journal, *Volume 14, Number 2, pp. 105-113, April 1984.*

Dual Relationships in Transactional Analysis: Training, Supervision, and Therapy

William F. Cornell

The psychotherapy and counseling professions are increasingly struggling with issues related to professional ethics and liability (American Psychological Association, 1992; Gutheil & Gabbard, 1993; Herlihy & Corey, 1992; Herlihy & Golden, 1990; Peterson, 1992; Pope & Vasquez, 1991; Roswell, 1988). In a field that is, by its very nature, often ambiguous, these issues can be especially troubling and difficult to define. In fact, there is today in the field of psychotherapy a growing tendency toward conservatism and rules and regulations. However, the International Transactional Analysis Association, which has in its membership many psychotherapy and counseling professionals, has sought intentionally in its Code of Ethics (International Transactional Analysis Association [ITAA], 2002) to avoid rules while still providing relevant and helpful guidelines and principles. Inherent in transactional analysis ethics and techniques are several important values: contractual treatment, individual responsibility, protection of the client and his/her developmental needs, and personal autonomy. In the ITAA Code of Ethics itself, items 6, 7, 8, and 11 most directly relate to training and supervisory relationships, although nowhere in the code are those relationships addressed specifically. In addition it should be noted that the ITAA code is written in terms of relationships with clients, and it is unclear whether trainees can be defined as clients.

When the overarching values of contractual treatment, individual responsibility, client protection, and personal autonomy are brought to bear on the mixture of training, supervision, therapy, and certification processes comprising professional development in transactional analysis, numerous ambiguities and contradictions emerge. For example, a Teaching (or Provisional Teaching) Member of the ITAA may provide overlapping services to trainees, including theoretical instruction, technical instruction, live demonstration, direct supervision, personal therapy, professional evaluation, examination preparation, and recommendation for examination.

It is possible in many psychotherapy models for a practitioner to be recognized or authorized to practice clinical work without having had personal psychotherapy. In contrast, transactional analysis has always valued personal therapy as part of the training process (Clarkson, 1992; Erskine, 1982; Goulding & Goulding, 1978).

There is a long tradition in transactional analysis of mixing therapeutic and training relationships, although in the transactional analysis literature there is no theoretical or practical consistency on the subject. Some trainers, who insist on differentiating elements of professional and personal development, discourage or even forbid overlapping or dual roles. However, the trend among transactional analysis practitioners is in the direction of separating the roles and responsibilities of training and/or supervision from those involved in doing personal therapy.

Personal Experience in Transactional Analysis Training

It has been impossible to prepare this chapter without reflecting on my own transactional analysis therapy and training. I began my transactional analysis training in the early 1970s with Lois Johnson, who was my supervisor, frequent therapist, and friend. At the same time, I was also training in neo-Reichian therapy through the Radix Institute, where Elaine Warburton was my primary supervisor and therapist. We, too, became friends. Lois was also in the Radix training program at the same time that I was and sometimes took sessions from Elaine. It is clear to me now—as it was then—that my relationships with Lois and Elaine re-created many of the dynamics within my family of origin. As the eldest son in my family, I was an overfunctioning pseudo-adult, my mother's confidante, my father's peer (and sometimes his father). I rarely had the chance to be a kid and did not depend on my parents. This was clear to me, to Lois, and to Elaine. Should we, therefore, have avoided our multiple-role relationships? I do not think so. My relationships with Lois and Elaine were far more functional, productive, and honest than were those with my parents. Much of the current literature on ethics and malpractice issues with respect to dual relationships suggests that the client and/or supervisee is victimized to some degree by such arrangements. I did not then, and do not now, feel victimized by Lois or Elaine. Those relationships, whatever their limits and problems, were coconstituted.

After completing my transactional analysis and Radix training, I began therapy with a psychologist in Pittsburgh, a professional relationship that lasted many years. At the start, I negotiated a contract that involved only a therapeutic relationship, a contract we maintained. There were many times when I brought to sessions elements of my professional activities or struggles with clients, but they were always addressed in the context of my ongoing therapy. Our work was singular in role and purpose.

Was that therapeutic relationship better or more ethical than the ones I had with Lois and Elaine? I do not think so. It was different in both its process and its function in my growth. It offered me a certain kind of depth and freedom in self-exploration. On the other hand, I never lost track of the contracted artificiality of my relationship with that therapist. There were times when the rigidity of our contract seemed absurd. One summer his house was damaged and much of his farmland was destroyed by tornadoes. He appeared in sessions frequently exhausted and obviously upset. He would talk a little about how he was feeling, and then we would go on with the "real work" of our therapeutic relationship. I wanted to go to his house and help clear his land, but I chose not to "contaminate" our relationship. In this and other incidents, I felt less than a real and whole man.

I think that what my later therapist and I accomplished in therapy over the years was more a reflection of his skill than a product of our having maintained a singular relationship. My earlier relationships with Lois and Elaine offered the depth and freedom of mucking through the complexities and ambiguities of relationships that reflected the realities and pains of everyday intimacy and friendship. Rarely in our interpersonal (or object) worlds do we carry but one meaning, purpose, or role with significant others. I will always cherish both the muddle and the honest struggle of my relationships with Lois and Elaine.

In later years, I was in individual (and sometimes group) supervision with psychoanalytically oriented therapists. This supervision added important perspectives to my work. It taught me to be patient, to be more cautious and more sensitive to the developmental vulnerabilities of my clients. I am also more respectful of the need to maintain a singular, consistent, long-term holding environment with many clients. I am more conservative in the sense of being less likely to engage in multiple tasks and roles with a client or supervisee.

However, even now I do not have any unquestioning or unquestionable rules against multiple relationships with clients and trainees. It is my personal bias that rules are to be avoided in addressing the issues of dual relationships in supervision and therapy. What I seek to provide in this chapter is a differentiation of the processes and roles in transactional analysis training and supervision, as well as questions and guidelines to assist trainers and trainees in assessing supervisory contracts and in making choices related to potential dual relationships.

An Overview of Dual Relationships in Supervision

In their book *Dual Relationships in Counseling,* Herlihy and Corey (1992) emphasized:
Dual relationships are rarely a clear-cut matter. Often, judgment calls and the careful application of ethical codes to specific situations are needed. Dual relationships are fraught with complexities

and ambiguities. They can be problematic along a number of dimensions: (1) they are pervasive, (2) they can be difficult to recognize, (3) they are sometimes unavoidable, (4) they can be very harmful but are not always harmful, and (5) they are the subject of conflicting advice from expert sources. (p. 7)

Herlihy and Corey went on to note that, in their opinion, "Some dual relationships are beneficial and . . . they are not always avoidable" (p. 9). They also pointed out that their opinions "are not universally shared" (p. 9).

In contrast, Pope and Vasquez (1991) stressed the risks inherent in dual relationships and expressed concern that acknowledging the potential benefits of dual relationships for a client can actually be a means of justifying inappropriate behavior or behavior that is more gratifying to the therapist than to the client. "They remind us that there is virtually no research evidence to support the hypothesis that dual relationships are a safe and effective means to produce therapeutic change" (Pope & Vasquez as cited in Herlihy & Corey, 1992, p. 10). Pope and Vasquez (1991) were unequivocal in their position:

> The supervisor, for example, must ensure that the supervisee is neither encouraged nor allowed to become the supervisor's therapy patient. Some forms of supervision may share common aspects with some forms of therapy. Sometimes supervisees, in the course of supervision, become aware of personal concerns, psychological problems, or behavioral difficulties that might benefit from therapy. If the supervisee decides to seek therapy for these matters, he or she should consult a separate therapist (one with whom the supervisee has no dual relationships). . . . [T]he client's welfare must be primary. The supervisor must ensure that no aspect of the training process unduly jeopardizes the client. (pp. 169-170)

Pope and Vasquez did not discuss the possibility that a joint supervisory/therapeutic relationship could, in some circumstances, help to ensure the client's welfare.

Wise, Lowery, and Silverglade (1989) also suggested that the most central role of supervision should be protecting the client's interests (as cited in Herlihy & Corey, 1992, p. 113) rather than the supervisee's. Cormier and Bernard (1982) concluded that, given this goal, a supervisor cannot provide the supervisee with ongoing, personal, intrapsychic attention. Whiston and Emerson (1989) observed that there are not many guidelines to help supervisors distinguish between the responsibilities inherent in supervision of trainees and the personal growth of these same individuals (as cited in Cormier & Bernard 1982, p. 112). Finally, Herlihy and Corey (1992) concluded:

> We think that it is a mistake for supervision to focus exclusively on client cases or problem-solving strategies regarding how to deal with clients. Thus, supervision can be useful in helping students become aware of personal limitations or unresolved problems that intrude into effective helping. However, there is a difference between helping students identify and clarify those concerns they need to explore versus converting supervision into an in-depth personal therapy session. (p. 115)

Whiston and Emerson (1989) distinguished between the supervisor's identifying a supervisee's therapeutic issues and directly undertaking to treat such issues. An initial level of intervention, consistent with supervisory responsibilities, is to clarify how a supervisee's personal problems may be interfering with professional effectiveness. To go beyond identification and clarification is to provide treatment, which they recommend be carried out by a separate therapist.

Lloyd (1992) expressed alarm that the growing concern over dual relationships has become too "emotionally charged" and "has now escalated to a central ethical problem to the extent that the 'dual relationship phobia' seems to have developed in counselor education" (p. 60). Lloyd questions, "Why should counselor educators, and counselors in general, be allowed to avoid the struggle of making responsible decisions by hiding behind a prohibition concerning multidimensional relationships?" (p. 61). He goes on to say:

> Counselor educators who do not want the responsibility of mediating tough decisions, and who are afraid that they might misuse the trust of the student, probably should avoid all situations where conflicting interests might exist. Some might question why these persons have entered

counselor education in the first place. Their timidity, however, should not be imposed on the rest of the profession under the guise of ethical standards. (p. 62)

For Clarkson and Gilbert (1991), even within a purely supervisory relationship, there are inevitably multiple roles. They delineated four elements of the training relationship: the working alliance (Adult-to-Adult contracts), the I-thou relationship (the "real" or core relationship), the transferential relationship, and the developmentally needed (corrective/reparative) relationship. Working from a psychodynamic and transactional analysis frame of reference, Clarkson and Gilbert clearly identified the therapeutic aspects of supervisory work.

Writing from an analytic and developmental perspective, Ekstein and Wallerstein (1972) saw the middle stage of supervision as marked by the eruption of personal conflicts, defensive posturing, and avoidance of issues, a phase during which the supervisor functions primarily as a teacher and counselor. Stoltenberg and Delworth (1987) similarly identified the second stage of supervision as characterized by "disruption, ambivalence, and instability" (p. 70). They recommended process interventions and stronger confrontation, noting that at this stage "the distinction between providing supervision and providing psychotherapy is most often an issue" (p. 91). They recommended referral to an appropriate professional for ongoing therapy if indicated (Ekstein & Wallerstein, 1972; Stoltenberg & Delworth, 1987).

Rubin (1989) stressed the "powerful intellectual and emotional processes that characterize the development of psychotherapists [and] the high levels of anxiety experienced by supervisees and supervisors as they engage in the process of teaching, learning, and treating" (p. 387). He presented illustrations of intense, difficult confrontations at critical moments in the supervisory process, moments at which the issues of a supervisee's clinical effectiveness and personal defenses merge, thus limiting competence and learning. As a supervisor, I frequently share the following observation by Rubin:

Intense anxiety may be associated not only with one's early practice but also with advanced instruction in psychotherapy. The tasks of the supervisor relate to clarification, support, confrontation, and teaching as they touch upon the core of the supervisee's fears in learning. The use of the supervisor's skills as psychotherapist—identifying difficulties, considering the appropriate timing and focus of an intervention, having the ability to tolerate and contain the anxieties encountered on both sides, and finding the means to communicate to the other—are of particular significance in the critical supervisory process. (p. 395)

Alonso and Rutan (1988) addressed the experiences of shame frequently evoked through the process of clinical supervision, stressing that "in order to become expert, the work must be exposed, 'dumb' questions must be asked, personal flaws will be illuminated" (p. 577). They thoughtfully and emphatically described the vulnerabilities of supervisees and the conflicting goals and loyalties of the supervisor. The parallels between supervisory and therapeutic processes are clear in their writing, and I found their article particularly meaningful.

Although much of the literature on supervision centers on graduate students and relatively inexperienced therapists, the personal vulnerabilities described by Alonso and Rutan are familiar to me. As a clinician with 35 years experience and a wide-ranging theoretical background, I continue to engage in weekly consultation. Experienced therapists do not typically raise issues of "what do I do now" in supervision. The issues are more subtle and personal, the distinction between supervision and therapy even more blurred.

Differentiating Between Supervision and Therapy Contracts

As a transactional analysis trainer, I have four primary supervisory goals (Cornell & Zalcman, 1984):

1. To establish theoretical and clinical competence in transactional analysis methodology
2. To enhance the supervisee's capacity for objectivity toward his or her own work and the ability to conceptualize from multiple theoretical frames of reference
3. To develop adequate diagnostic skills and a sufficiently flexible therapeutic style to meet the needs of a diverse client population

4. To foster collegial relationships and self-supervision skills that will stimulate self-esteem, professional values, and an attitude toward learning that will continue beyond the supervisory relationship

It has been my experience both as a transactional analysis trainee and a trainer that the various purposes and styles of psychotherapy training and supervision are not adequately differentiated. I have observed that some transactional analysis trainers exhibit a certain grandiosity and need to control such that they feel it essential to be involved in most, if not all, aspects of a trainee's development. I have also seen trainees (through idealization or positive transference) attribute to their trainers a level of potency and unique skill and understanding such that there is a real reluctance or resistance to engaging in supervision or treatment relationships with other trainers or therapists.

In my own work as a trainer, I have grown significantly more conscious of the implications of providing dual or multiple relationships for the personal and professional development of my trainees. As stated earlier, I have no rule against such relationships. To simply outlaw the dual relationships of supervisor/therapist does not adequately address the complex issues involved; rather, it imposes rigidity on a complicated and often ambiguous profession, reduces the choices and autonomy of the supervisee, and does not necessarily ensure the optimal welfare of a supervisee's clients. Supervision is not a unitary phenomenon; it is learning structure that can have several forms and a process that changes over time.

Kitchener (1988) wrote a seminal article on the problems of dual relationships. She identified three central factors in assessing and predicting the likelihood of harm being created by a dual relationship: (1) incompatibility of expectations, (2) divergence of obligations associated with the roles, and (3) the power and prestige of the professional [supervisor, in the context of this chapter] (p. 219). Kitchener and Harding (1990) observed, "Incompatibility of expectations and divergence of obligations may cause the professional to lose objectivity, divide loyalties, and neglect the wellbeing of the client. The power and prestige of the professional contains the potential for exploitation" (p. 147). They are cautious with regard to the dual relationship of supervisor and therapist. I have found this model particularly helpful in assessing the possibility of conflict and harm in supervisory and therapeutic activities and in negotiating clear contracts with trainees.

Psychotherapy for Psychotherapists

Psychotherapists who provide psychotherapy to other therapists often face complex clinical as well as ethical difficulties (Bridges, 1993; Burton, 1973; Kaslow, 1984; Sachs & Shapiro, 1976). The decision of a clinical supervisor to provide ongoing therapy to a supervisee adds to the potential for ethical conflicts. In fact, at times, clinical and ethical issues can be difficult to differentiate.

Alonso (1985) stressed that therapy—especially psychodynamic therapy—always includes a transferential relationship, which heightens periods of "regression in the service of emotional growth" (p. 17). In the supervision of psychotherapy, although there is still a transferential relationship, the emphasis is on progressive movement with "a concerted effort to shore up and strengthen the supervisee's healthiest defenses" (p. 17). It is in this conflict between regressive and progressive pressures that the potential for serious and sustained ethical conflict between dual-role expectations and obligations can emerge. Appropriate confrontive supervisory interventions may contradict or threaten a therapeutic (often the more regressive and dependent) relationship. Likewise, appropriate clinical choices in terms of the psychotherapist/client's personal therapy can create ethical dilemmas in terms of supervisory responsibilities.

Psychotherapists treating other therapists can easily overidentify with their therapist/clients, especially as countertransferential struggles emerge while seeing a therapist/client at times of crisis and dysfunction. Conflicts may be experienced between wanting to support and protect the therapist/client while simultaneously worrying about the quality of care being provided to the therapist/client's clients. A therapist/client may bring issues and emotional difficulties from clinical practice into personal therapy sessions and perhaps even present material that reflects poor clinical work. Where is the boundary in such cases between therapy and supervision? In addition, a therapist may struggle with (or avoid altogether) difficult negative transference and countertransference reactions out of fear that an angry therapist/client may communicate a critical attitude about the therapist/trainer to the professional community at large.

In psychotherapy supervision there is an overt contract about learning new therapeutic skills and incorporating the supervisory process into one's therapeutic style. Theory and technique are openly examined and discussed. The contract to learn about therapy is rarely overt in the psychotherapy of psychotherapists. When I provide treatment to therapist/clients, I am always aware that our way of working is likely to be incorporated in my clients' work with their clients. This is a subtle but not insignificant pressure in the work, and discussing these issues directly may not be relevant to the therapist/client's therapy. Bridges (1993) observed:

> Therapists cannot infer from their own treatment experiences what the valence of a particular intervention will be for their patients. The silent and sometimes unconscious power of the mentoring relationship between a therapist and a therapist's patient is remarkable. Often, the crucial learning about how to conduct psychotherapy that occurs in that special treatment relationship is not available for supervision, self-reflection, or scrutiny. (p. 42)

Supervisory Models and Structures

In my own clinical and supervisory work, my first concern is to recognize and validate the primary contract initiated by the client or supervisee. If a person approached me first for therapy and then later requested supervision and/or training, my first concern is to preserve the therapeutic relationship. Any subsequent decision is made within the context of how adding aspects to the relationship might diminish or damage therapy. Adding a supervisor element (especially if it is ongoing and simultaneous) to a therapeutic relationship significantly alters all three of Kitchener's (1988) factors: role expectations, obligations, and power. Such a change can be extremely problematic and needs to be carefully discussed. In my experience, the incompatibility is more likely to be too great (and therefore inadvisable) if the client is in the beginning stages of therapy (a phase that usually involves more regression and dependence) or is a novice therapist (which requires the supervisor to be especially alert to the needs of the supervisee's clients, even to the point of overriding the personal comfort and concerns of the supervisee).

If, on the other hand, my first contact with an individual is in a training or supervisory context and that person then approaches me for individual therapy, I must ask a different set of questions. Is there something unique that I can provide as my supervisee's therapist? If not, then what would be gained by developing a dual relationship? There is abundant information that the people who best survive the dysfunctional patterns in their family of origin are those who have significant relationships outside the family (Chess & Thomas, 1984; Dugan & Coles, 1989; Shengold, 1993). I am cautious not to duplicate the patterns of an isolated nuclear family in which a limited range of relationships or perhaps a single relationship forms the primary source of a person's self-esteem and opportunities for recognition and support. There is much to be gained by individuals having different and significant professional relationships, including greater individuation through access to differing perspectives and roles. In addition, when multiple professional relationships are available, the therapist or supervisor is not so likely to be overwhelmed by the centrality of his or her role in the trainee/client's life, and the trainee or client is less likely to become overly dependent on the influence, goodwill, and support of the supervisor/therapist.

In attempting to delineate the different functions and procedures in various supervisory models, I have found the work of Hess (1980) particularly useful. What follows reflects his work and my own elaboration of it. In identifying the procedures used to provide psychotherapy training and/or supervision, several models are evident in the counseling, therapy, and transactional analysis literature. I think a purposeful differentiation of these roles is useful in assessing potential problems and risks in dual roles within various supervisory relationships. Hess (1980) defined six approaches to professional development; I have added "ongoing clinical supervision" as a seventh. Each serves, I think, a specific function, and ideally all are included in an overall training program.

Lectures. A lecture usually involves one "acknowledged master" presenting material to a large group in a didactic format. The communication is typically one-sided with information flowing from the lecturer to the group. It is not even necessary with this format for the lecturer to be present as the increasing use of audiotapes and videotapes in training and education demonstrates. The purpose of a lecture is to provide new information and professional enrichment and to open up possibilities for new directions in one's professional development.

In transactional analysis, the lecture format is commonly used for the introductory TA 101 workshop, which trainers and therapists often encourage clients to attend. There seems to be little conflict of purpose, expectation, or responsibility to make this dual relationship questionable. For example, individuals in supervision with me often attend (by choice, not requirement) training workshops and lectures I present. The probability of incompatible expectations and power are more likely, however, at professional conferences when workshops and lectures overlap with social functions, organizational activities, and personal relationships.

Teaching. In a teaching format, the group is likely to be smaller than at a lecture, and it will often meet for more extended periods. The focus is still likely to be content centered and goal oriented, with the teacher in a superordinate position and class members in a subordinate position. The teacher evaluates and grades the performance of each student, increasing the likelihood of role conflicts in terms of expectations and the power differential in dual relationships.

Case Review. This typical supervisory format in agency and hospital situations is usually done on an individual or small-group basis. In an agency context, typically several staff members present cases to a senior staff member who functions as consultant and teacher. Rather than emphasizing the ongoing development of a personal supervisory relationship, the focus is more specifically client and problem centered. For the supervisee, case consultation may not provide the level of personal attention available in ongoing individual supervision, but Hess (1980) observed that this format can still be useful in solving immediate therapeutic problems, clarifying clinical decision making, providing a vehicle for mentoring, and learning through the presentations of colleagues and the accumulation of collective wisdom.

Hess (1980) pointed out that in a case conference, staff members may go through the motions, although they often consider these meetings a waste of time. Individual therapists risk exposure and judgment by both peers and senior staff, feelings related to technical competence and self-esteem can be intense, and power and authority issues are common. The authority, monitoring, and evaluative aspects of case reviews are incompatible with a simultaneous therapeutic relationship with a fellow staff member, although social relationships are common, and through them individuals may act out the subgroupings (group imagoes) of staff conferences.

Collegial/Peer Review. In this format, supervision is therapist centered rather than client centered. Often case consultation and personal support occur simultaneously rather than each being a separate function. In therapist-centered peer review, the primary focus is on providing support for the therapist in a way that allows colleagues to offer different viewpoints on the therapeutic process. Collegial-peer review encourages exploration of the therapist's thoughts, feelings, and attitudes.

Hess (1980) stated that this format works best when the participants are truly equal in role and status, with the dominant purpose being mutual support and growth. However, this format can be limited by its informality and unstated or shifting goals, and social relationships are common, thus making a therapeutic relationship between members of a peer-review group incompatible with the expectations and focus inherent in the peer emphasis.

Ongoing Clinical Supervision. Supervision may be carried out individually or in a small group. In such settings attention to the material is much more detailed and personal than in other formats (Dent, 1993; Kaslow & Friedman, 1984; Rubin, 1989; Shanfield, Matthews, & Hetherly, 1993). Dialogue, self-exposure, and conjoint problem solving are encouraged. There is a strong quality of mentoring in these relationships, and a deep trust and mutual regard evolves between the supervisor and the supervisee. In-depth personal supervision always evokes the atmosphere of a therapeutic relationship. However, the primary focus of attention for the supervisor is on the diagnosis, clinical understanding, adequate treatment, and protection of the supervisee's clients. The supervisor's responsibility is to establish an environment that supports the supervisee's skill acquisition, effectiveness, and self-esteem. In the context of this relationship, the supervisee routinely presents problems, not successes, and may frequently experience what Alonso and Rutan (1988) referred to as "the learning regression" (p. 578). The supervisee will likely experience feeling anxious, inadequate, confused, embarrassed, dependent, angry, and/or other unpleasant reactions. In this context, the supervisor carries primary responsibility for the well-being of the therapist as well as for that of the clients being discussed.

In clinical supervision, potential ambiguity and conflict over expectations, obligations, or power are likely. The implications of dual relationships resulting from social or therapeutic activities need to be carefully considered and openly discussed. It is my view that any business or sexual relationship is completely incompatible with a supervisory relationship.

Monitoring. This supervisory situation meets the legal, ethical, bureaucratic, or organizational requirements of an agency, a government body, a funding source, or a professional association. The goal in monitoring supervision is to maintain minimal acceptable standards of care and to meet regulatory requirements. The monitor is likely to be seen by the supervisee as an enforcer, a censor, or an external evaluator, and in this era of growing concern for liability, third-party reimbursements, and managed health care, the monitor style of supervision is seen with increasing frequency. This style of supervision does not serve the client or the therapist particularly well as it is designed primarily to meet the needs of an external body.

A therapist would need to be exceedingly insecure or sociopathic to enter into either a friendship or a therapeutic relationship with a monitor. Expectations, obligations, and power differentials are all incompatible with multiple relationships with a monitor.

Therapy. In this format, the supervisor essentially functions as the supervisee's therapist. As Hess (1980) described:

The therapist model may be the most common for supervisors to assume. This probably occurs by default because the supervisor may not have considered various other supervisory processes and models. Since the supervisor is a psychotherapist now involved in a helping interaction with another human, it is not surprising at all that supervision may become psychotherapy. (p. 23)

This is particularly common in the "parallel process" (Gediman & Wolkenfeld, 1980; Sachs & Shapiro, 1976; Wolkenfeld, 1990) model of clinical supervision, in which most therapeutic errors are presumed to be evidence of the therapist's individual psychopathology with the parallel being between the client's treatment issues and the therapist's personal difficulties and blind spots.

This model of supervision is sometimes relevant. It is not uncommon for supervisees to want to use their supervision as a vehicle for their personal therapy, centering it more on themselves and their own feelings and difficulties than on the problems and needs of their clients. The danger arises when the therapist's needs are not clearly identified as the overt focus of supervision and if a more client-centered supervisory structure is not also provided. Often transactional analysis trainees express anxiety or disappointment about seeking therapy from someone who is not versed in TA. These anxieties are not to be taken lightly, but they need to be explored rather than becoming the determining factor in developing a dual relationship.

It is common in transactional analysis group supervision for the supervisor to offer brief pieces of "demonstration therapy" with a supervisee as the client. Here the intent is usually to introduce and model a particular technique, and the supervisor's primary focus is thus in keeping with the ongoing training/supervisory contract. This is quite different from a supervision group collapsing into a treatment group for the therapists.

Conclusion

I do not think that either the supervisory process or the welfare of therapists and clients is best served by rigid rules or unquestioning prohibitions against dual training/therapeutic relationships. I question the contemporary trend to forbid multiple functions within professional relationships. I think that many intimate, long-term relationships (including those between parents and the children) involve evolving, overlapping, multiple functions and that these complexities need to be examined, rather than simply avoided, within our professional learning relationships.

I consider it the supervisor/trainer's ethical responsibility to delineate clearly the purpose and structure of a given supervisory task and then, given that task, to negotiate overtly a working relationship with the supervisee. When the possibility of a dual relationship is being considered, both supervisor and supervisee need to discuss openly the potential for dissonance and conflict in relation to factors such as role expectations, obligations, and power.

Contracts are a central organizing principle in our work as transactional analysts. When considering a dual relationship or multiple functions within a professional relationship, particular attention needs to be paid to the contracts involved. It is the responsibility of the professional member of the dyad to ensure the maintenance of the primary contract. If other secondary (or subsequent) functions interfere with the primary contract, the arrangement needs to be renegotiated so as to preserve the most fundamental function. The intentional and conscious engagement in multiple functions or dual relationships places an extra burden of responsibility for the monitoring of motivations and countertransference on the member of the dyad who is being paid for his or her services and expertise.

Both a supervisor and a supervisee have the right to seek consultation with a third party before solidifying a supervisory agreement when dual relationships are involved. If dual relationships do occur, it is advisable to asses on a regular basis the effectiveness of the agreements and to consider alternatives. If conflicts or recurrent difficulties emerge within the multiple functions, the participants will need to decide what the primary professional task is that needs to be preserved, with referral to other professionals for other needs and tasks. Ethical choices and behavior are best ensured by clear theory, flexible models, direct and informed decision making, and choices from among alternatives.

REFERENCES

Alonso, A. (1985). *The quiet profession: Supervisors of psychotherapy.* New York: Macmillan.
Alonso, A., & Rutan, J. S. (1988). Shame and guilt in psychotherapy supervision. *Psychotherapy, 25,* 576-581
American Psychological Association. (1992). Ethical principles of psychologists and code of conduct. *American Psychologist, 47,* 1597-1611.
Bridges, N. (1993). Clinical dilemmas: Therapists treating therapists. *American Journal of Orthopsychiatry, 63,* 34-44.
Burton, A. (1973). The psychotherapist as client. *American Journal of Psychoanalysis, 33,* 94-103.
Chess, S., & Thomas, A. (1984). *Origins and evolution of behavior disorders: From infancy to early adult life.* New York: Brunner/Mazel.
Clarkson, P. (1992) *Transactional analysis psychotherapy: An integrated approach.* London: Travistock/Routledge.
Clarkson, P., & Gilbert, M. (1991). The training of counselor trainers and supervisors. In W. Dryden & B. Thorne (Eds.), *Training and supervision for counseling in action* (pp. 141-169). London: Sage Publications.
Cormier, L. S., & Bernard, J. M. (1982). Ethical and legal responsibilities of clinical supervisors. *Personnel and Guidance Journal, 60,* 486-491.
Cornell, W. F., & Zalcman, M. J. (1984). Teaching transactional analysts to think theoretically. *Transactional Analysis Journal, 14,* 105-113.
Dent, M. (1993). *A mentor model of supervision.* Unpublished manuscript.
Dugan, T. F., & Coles, R. (Eds.). (1989). *The child in our times: Studies in the development of resiliency.* New York: Brunner/ Mazel.
Ekstein, R., & Wallerstein, R. S. (1972). *The teaching and learning of psychotherapy.* New York: Basic Books.
Erskine, R. G. (1982). Supervision of psychotherapy: Models for professional development. *Transactional Analysis Journal, 12,* 314-321.
Gediman, H. K., & Wolkenfeld, F. (1980). The parallelism phenomenon in psychoanalysis and supervision: Its reconsideration as a triadic system. *Psychoanalytic Quarterly, 49,* 234-255.
Goulding, R. L., & Goulding, M. M. (1978). *The power is in the patient: A TA/gestalt approach to psychotherapy.* San Francisco: TA Press.
Gutheil, T. G., & Gabbard, G. O. (1993). The concept of boundaries in clinical practice: Theoretical and risk-management dimensions. *American Journal of Psychiatry, 150,* 188-196.
Herlihy, B., & Corey, G. (1992). *Dual relationships in counseling.* Alexandria, VA: American Association for Counseling and Development.
Herlihy, B., & Golden, L. B. (1990). *Ethical standards casebook* (4th ed.). Alexandria, VA: American Association for Counseling and Development.

Hess, A. K. (1980). *Psychotherapy supervision: Theory, research and practice.* New York: Wiley.

International Transactional Analysis Association. (2002). ITAA code of ethics. Retrieved 25 April 2008 from http://www.itaa-net.org/itaa/EthicsManual/EthicsManualCh2.htm .

Kaslow, N. J. (Ed.). (1984). *Psychotherapy with psychotherapists.* New York: Haworth Press.

Kaslow, N. J., & Friedman, D. (1984). The interface of personal treatment and clinical training for psychotherapist trainees. In N. J. Kaslow (Ed.), *Psychotherapy with psychotherapists* (pp. 35-57). New York: Haworth Press.

Kitchener, K. S. (1988). Dual role relationships: What makes them so problematic? *Journal of Counseling and Development, 67,* 217-221.

Kitchener, K. S., & Harding, S. S. (1990) Dual role relationships. In B. Herlihy & L. B. Golden (Eds.)., *Ethical standards casebook* (pp. 146-154). Alexandria, VA: American Association for Counseling and Development.

Lloyd, A. P. (1992). Dual relationship problems in counselor education. In B. Herlihy & G. Corey (Eds.), *Dual relationships in counseling* (pp. 59-64). Alexandria, VA: American Association for Counseling and Development.

Peterson, M. R. (1992). *At personal risk: Boundary violations in professional-client relationships.* New York: Norton.

Pope, K. S., & Vasquez, M. J. T. (1991). *Ethics in psychotherapy and counseling: A practical guide for psychologists.* San Francisco: Jossey-Bass.

Roswell, V. A. (1988). Professional liability: Issues for behavior therapists in the 1980's and 1990's. *The Behavior Therapist, 11,* 163-171.

Rubin, S. S. (1989). At the border of supervision: Critical moments in psychotherapists' development. *American Journal of Psychotherapy, 43*(3), 387-397.

Sachs, D. M., & Shapiro, S. H. (1976). On parallel processes in therapy and teaching. *Psychoanalytic Quarterly, 45,* 394-415.

Shanfield, S. B., Matthews, K. L., & Hetherly, V. (1993). What do excellent psychotherapy supervisors do? *American Journal of Psychiatry, 150,* 1081-1084.

Shengold, L. (1993). *"The boy will come to nothing!": Freud's ego ideal and Freud as ego ideal.* New Haven: Yale University Press.

Stoltenberg, C. D., & Delworth, U. (1987). *Supervising counselors and therapists: A developmental approach.* San Francisco: Jossey-Bass.

Whiston, S. C., & Emerson, S. (1989). Ethical implications for supervisors in counseling of trainees. *Counselor Education and Supervision, 28,* 318-325.

Wise, P. S., Lowery, S., & Silverglade, D. (1989). Personal counseling for counselors in training: Guidelines for supervisors. *Counselor Education and Supervision, 28,* 326-336.

Wolkenfeld, F. (1990). The parallel process phenomenon revisited: Some additional thoughts about the supervisory process. In R. C. Lane (Ed.), *Psychoanalytic approaches to supervision* (pp. 95-112). New York: Brunner/Mazel.

The original version of this article was published in the Transactional Analysis Journal, *Volume 24, Number 1, pp. 21-29, January 1994.*

Section V:
Perspectives in Ethics

The challenge in professional ethics is to present risk taking in a way that is proportionate to the potential benefits and dangers. There is something between risk aversion and risk amplification that is an existentially more accurate representation of both how therapy works and what is relationally and psychologically healthy. Therapy models the interplay between trust and risk. . . . Risk taking is as unavoidable in therapy as it is in life.

Bond, 2006, p.84

Section V

Introduction

It is no accident—given that the chapters in this section were written most deeply from my heart—that in them I talk about my sons, my own father, and fatherhood. Nothing has been more satisfying to me than being a father. Stephanie and I were determined as parents to raise our children with the freedom to develop and keep their own minds. We gave them unusual degrees of independence and responsibility, and there were moments when we thought we might have gone a bit too far. But in the long run, things have turned out well. Seth, Noah, and Caleb are fine young men. They lives their lives each in his own way and with great intensity. Like their father, they are not always easy to get along with, and like their parents, they do not take social norms for granted. Their lives might be seen by some as rather at the edge of what could be considered normal or secure, especially since all three accept an element of risk in their lives. But more importantly, each, in his own way, lives a life of hard work, responsibility, and devotion to those he loves. In my mind and heart, this is the core of ethics.

These days ethical standards are all too often derived, moralistic lists of do's and don'ts. One of the things I admire about the International Transactional Analysis Association is its code of ethics, which consists of statements of principles based in an ethic of individual, mutual, and community responsibility.

It was never my intention in writing the chapters contained in this section to tell people what to do or think or to solicit agreement with my point of view. Rather, it has often been my intention to provoke the reader to self-reflection. Several of the chapters here are taken from columns and essays I have written as editor of the ITAA newsletter, *The Script,* and consequently, the tone in many of them is quite informal and personal.

Chapter 21 is one of my earliest papers from the *Transactional Analysis Journal,* one that brings back fond memories as it starts with the story of an unexpected encounter with Miriam Patchen, the widow of the poet Kenneth Patchen, whose work I dearly love.

Chapter 22 is much more recent and troubled, and yet it elaborates many of the same themes I touched on in that early paper.

Chapters 23 and 24 are very much linked, especially since they were both synthesized from columns I wrote for *The Script.* From my experience as a writer and editor within the transactional analysis communities worldwide, I write about what I think it means to be a member of a professional community—especially one that spans an extraordinary range of cultures, languages, and professional disciplines.

Chapter 25 addresses the ethics of physical contact between client and therapist, a rather central and enduring question for a body-centered psychotherapist and one that is discussed in several contexts within the pages of this book. This particular chapter considers the ethics of touch, research into the efficacy and safety of touch, and a model for thinking about touch in psychotherapy and counseling.

Chapter 26 mirrors some of the issues addressed in Chapter 20 on dual relationships. Here I examine a more disturbing set of experiences of intense transference and countertransference through the review of three books. I wrote this piece at a time when I was just seriously beginning to immerse myself in the psychoanalytic literature on transference and countertransference. It was like a new world opening up to me. I used the book review format numerous times during the early and mid-1990s, in part to sharpen my critical skills as a reader and to develop my own skills as a writer. It also worked better for me during that time because intense parenting responsibilities during that period left me little time to think or write in a more extended form. I really enjoyed writing these essays, which appeared in the *Transactional Analysis Journal.*

There is perhaps no ethical issue more personally, emotionally, clinically, and morally complex than suicide. Chapter 27 is an elaboration of an article on suicide that I wrote for the ITAA newsletter, *The Script,* from a deeply personal perspective. It is an effort to raise questions about the meaning of suicidal feelings and impulses and the challenges to therapists and counselors. There are no simple answers in this terrain.

The final chapter in this book was coauthored with my youngest son, Caleb, just 16 at the time it was written; it is accompanied by an essay recounting an experience with my eldest son, Seth. I knew when I begin thinking about this book that I wanted to conclude it with these deeply personal pieces from *The Script.* I still remember the pride I felt at what Caleb was able to write; my heart aches when I read it even now.

It seems essential to me to end this volume with a reminder that the work we do is fundamentally social and political in its implications. We have no right to do the work of influencing the course of peoples' lives if we detach ourselves from the political, cultural, and economic realities in which they struggle to develop and thrive. So many times I have sat with a client, his or her life in an anguished shambles, hearing his or her history and wondering to myself, had I lived that life, would I be functioning as well as the person turning to me for help?

REFERENCE

Bond, T. (2006). Intimacy, risk, and reciprocity in psychotherapy: Intricate ethical challenges. *Transactional Analysis Journal, 36,* 77-89.

Teaching People What Matters

William F. Cornell

During the 1983 ITAA Summer Conference in Oakland, California, I took a day off to visit Miriam Patchen, who lived in the San Francisco Bay Area. Miriam was the widow of Kenneth Patchen, a poet whom I have long admired. Patchen was a poet and a painter, whom Henry Miller (as cited in Morgan, 1977) described as the

"Man of Anger and Light," to whom it would give . . . supreme joy to destroy with his own hands all the tyrants and sadists of this earth together with the art, the institutions and all the machinery of everyday life which sustain and glorify them. (p. 33)

Kenneth and Miriam were devoted individualists and pacifists. At the time of my visit, Miriam and I had been corresponding for a few months but had never met. She stood in her front door and without so much as a hello, greeted me with the question, "Tell me something. How is it that a handsome and kind-hearted young man like yourself got caught up in such a foolish profession?" A lively and important discussion ensued.

Miriam challenged me to explain and justify how it was that I could support peoples' preoccupations with personal history and problems when there is so much trouble and violence in the world. "Why don't you," she asked, "simply tell people to do something useful?" I tried, with moderate success, to explain my understanding of the purpose of my work. I explained that my own work had a broader and more optimistic purpose than the traditional Freudian notions with which she was familiar. I described the work of Reich and Berne and their challenges to traditional psychotherapy. All too many people, I pointed out, are so consumed with physical or psychological survival or with "earning their keep" emotionally that they rarely contribute genuinely or freely to society. Psychotherapy can not only help people feel better about themselves but also to become more effective members of family and society. I also acknowledged that much of contemporary "humanistic" psychotherapy can foster a highly narcissistic view of the world.

Miriam's challenges mirrored the concerns of a number of theorists who have had a deep influence on my thinking and values, including Wilhelm Reich, Abraham Maslow, and Colin Wilson. The impact of arguing with Miriam, talking with her about her life with Patchen, and seeing Patchen's paintings stayed with me for days. She provoked a period of important reflection for me.

On returning home, I sent Miriam a copy of a letter I had written to my son Noah the morning he was born. Noah had almost died during his birth. I wrote to him, in part:

You're a powerful teacher, my boy. A teacher of what matters, what really matters. It's a fragile lesson, Noah, one that we all have to learn and relearn. I sat there this morning holding your mother, almost too frightened to hope. Watching you, looking at your mother, listening to you, talking to your mother, waiting. Waiting and remembering. Waiting and thinking. Thinking of the old and familiar quarrels I have with myself, that I have with your mother. That all mattered, suddenly and clearly, so much less. I knew what mattered. I sat there feeling how immense my love is for your mother and brother and how strong it could be for you. How much life, just life, matters. Thank you for fighting, for living, for reminding me of what matters. Sometimes I forget. Keep reminding me, please.

Noah's near-death forced a fundamental confrontation within me. Miriam's challenges 5 years later did the same. I realized, again, that my work, in its essence, is that of teaching and reminding people of what matters.

William Everson, a provocative poet and conscientious objector during World War II, in discussing "the poet as prophet," quoted R. G. Collingwood (as cited in Bartlett, 1980):

> The artist must prophesy not in the sense that he foretells things to come, but in the sense that he tells his audience, at the risk of their displeasure, the secrets of their own hearts. But what he has to utter is not, as the individualistic theory of art would have us think, his own secrets. As spokesman of his community, the secrets he must utter are theirs. The reason why they need him is that no community altogether knows its own heart; and by failing in this knowledge a community deceives itself on the one subject concerning which ignorance means death. For the evils which come from that ignorance the poet as prophet offers no remedy, because he has already given one. The remedy is the poem itself. Art is the community's medicine for the worst disease of the mind, the corruption of consciousness. (p. 186)

I have always turned to poets and artists to refine my perception, to refresh my spirit, and to remind me of my broader purpose. I have long believed that psychotherapists have much to learn from artists and their more open and passionate contact with the unconscious and the body. I also believe that when psychotherapists do their work well, we offer our communities the same sort of "medicine" described by Collingwood and Everson and offered by real artists.

On my waiting room wall hangs a quote from a poem, "History," written by Lew Welch (1968):

> Every 30 years or so, Elders arm Children
> with expensive weapons and send them away
> to kill other children similarly armed.
> Some do not return. Some return
> Maimed or terrified into madness.
> Many come back brutal.

In my office hangs a poetry broadside handwritten by Gary Snyder (1965) and sent to Reed College as his contribution to the Poet's Read-In Against the Vietnam War and addressed to President Johnson:

> Dear Mr. President,
> There is no bomb in Gilead.
> The Red Chinese are not the Red Indians:
> You could have saved the Sioux.
> Please stop them building roads
> in the North Cascades.
>
> There were great white birds
> in the tops of the banyon trees
> calling across the town,
> when I was in Saigon.
>
> Respectfully yours,
> Gary Snyder

These broadsides hang in my workspace not because I expect clients to agree with me but because I want them to know that I am a conscientious objector, that my values are an important part of who I am, and that my concerns go beyond the immediate pressures of the therapeutic situation. It is my belief that an active sense of purpose and values is an essential element in health and well-being.

In recent years, social scientists and psychotherapists have been willing to wrestle not only with the causes of violence, but with the development of methods to treat and counteract violence. Reich (1946), in such works as *The Mass Psychology of Fascism,* was a pioneer in the effort to understand the sources of power struggles and violence and to describe the interconnectedness of individual psychology with economic, moral, and political forces. Reich (1962) viewed the nuclear family as an "educational apparatus," which served the primarily political function of an ideological factory that created an individual who "from the moment of his first breath" was dependent on the existing social structure. Claude Steiner's (1974, pp. 110-114) concept of the stroke economy, his brilliant synthesis of Berne's and Reich's thinking, demonstrates that the "economic" forces within the family stroking environment are designed to support not only the social structure but the family structure as well. With the understanding of the stroke economy, transactional analysts have one of their single most powerful tools for confronting and changing dysfunctional, competitive, and controlling family and social structures.

In "The Death of Bill Evans," Clayton Eshleman (1983a) wrote:
> Can't see the wound for the scars,
> a small boy composed of scabs is staring into
> the corner of his anatomy—where walls and floor end
> he figures he ends, so he wears his end
> like glasses before his eyes,
> beckoned into the snow he will be beaten
> by children he thought were his friends,
> the implication of his hurt is so dark
> it will scab over to be rescabbed the next time,
> and he will not grow by any internal urge to mature
> but by scabbings until, grown big, he will be the size of an adult
> and his face will look like a pebbly gourd.
> He will stay inside the little house I have built for him, in which to stand up he must stoop. (p. 32)

We are also coming increasingly to understand the factors that foster physical and sexual violence within families. Frank Bolton, Jr. (1983, pp. 32-34), summarizes current research in high-risk families as demonstrating that several factors are crucial in influencing the likelihood of violence within families: the capacity and experience of bonding and attachment (bonding hopefully occurring at birth and attachment developing through the parent-infant relationship), the physical and environmental resources of the parents, the social resources of the parents, and the emotional resources of the family. Both the prevention and treatment (Gelles, 1974, 1979; Klaus & Kennell, 1976) of family violence are now far more effective than even a decade ago. Therapists and social scientists are increasingly interested and effective in organizing against child and spouse abuse and rape. This work matters.

Treating and counteracting violence matters. It is not, however, sufficient. If transactional analysts are to be significant agents of change, if we are to offer significant medicine to our communities and to the world community, we need to move beyond issues of individual survival and well-being. We need to engage ourselves and others in a broader sense of purpose. My personal understanding of my work as a psychotherapist—of what matters—is strongly shaped by the work of Reich and the existentialists. Colin Wilson (1972), in his book on Abraham Maslow's work, writes, "According to Maslow, mental health depends upon the will being fired by a sense of purpose... In Maslow's psychology, the central place is given to the sense of values, the human response to what is worthwhile" (p. 47). Reich opened each of his books with the statement, "Love, work and knowledge are the well-springs of life. They should also govern it." Reich (1971, pp. 26-32) did not consider therapy complete until a person was capable of truly loving another, not out of need but out of true desire for and interest in the other. Reich (1943a, 1943b, 1943c) wrote eloquently about true curiosity and questioning about life and about the naturalness and satisfaction of work. Both involve an active and satisfying movement beyond the self to a greater sense of giving and purpose in life.

This article began to take shape for me when I heard there was to be a special issue of the *Transactional Analysis Journal* centered on issues related to nuclear disarmament (Trautmann, 1984). When I consider the very real possibility of a nuclear disaster within the lifetime of my family, I often feel personally helpless and inconsequential. I also remember something that Carl Sagan said during the panel discussions that the ABC network televised after the movie, *The Day After*. He compared the current efforts to achieve nuclear disarmament with the enormous shift in social consciousness during the nineteenth century in outlawing slavery and during this century in changing racist and sexist prejudices. He pointed out that enormous social change is possible and has been achieved before, usually requiring two or three generations to complete. Sagan emphasized that such social change is initiated by individuals and that it has succeeded in the past in spite of enormous social and economic resistance.

Sagan's comments help me to maintain some perspective and hope. I believe it is our responsibility as change agents to contribute to this social and political change. I think that being an international organization with unique and potent understanding and expertise, we are in a position to make a significant contribution to that shift.

The people whom I quote here, along with Noah and Miriam Patchen, have been important in teaching and reminding me of what really matters and of the significance of individual choice. Victor Frankl (1967) wrote:

Man is not free from conditions, be they biological or psychological or sociological in nature. But he is, and always remains, free to take a stand toward these conditions: he always retains the freedom to choose his attitude toward them. Man is free to rise above the somatic and psychic determinants of his existence. (p. 3)

Clayton Eshleman (1983a) writes:

> What does a father feel picking the shrapnel
> out of his one hour old infant's thighs?
> I will try to say: he feels with the force of rock
>   against steel, his body twangs with a hatred
>   so vegetal it cannot yet get beyond his shoulders.
> In the grief and numbness mounting to his eyes
> a bayonet child is being conceived who shall wear for a head
> the shredded flag of no one's salvation. (pp. 106-107)

REFERENCES

Bartlett, L. (Ed.). (1980). *Earth poetry: Selected essays and interviews of William Everson, 1950-1977.* Berkeley, CA: Oyez.
Bolton, F. G., Jr. (1983). *When bonding fails: Clinical assessment of high-risk families.* Beverly Hills, CA: Sage Publications.
Eshleman, C. (1983a). Certification. In C. Eshleman, *Fracture* (pp. 105-107). Santa Barbara, CA: Black Sparrow Press.
Eshleman, C. (1983a). The death of Bill Evans. In C. Eshleman, *Fracture* (pp. 32-33). Santa Barbara, CA: Black Sparrow Press.
Frankl, V. (1967). *Psychotherapy and existentialism.* New York: Washington Square Press.
Gelles, R. J. (1974). *The violent home.* Beverly Hills, CA: Sage Publications
Gelles, R. J. (1979). *Family violence.* Beverly Hills, CA: Sage Publications
Klaus, M. H., & Kennel, J. H. (1976). *Maternal-infant bonding: The impact of early separation or loss on family development.* St. Louis, MO: C.V. Mosby.
Morgan, R. (Ed.). (1977). *Kenneth Patchen: A collection of essays.* New York: AMS Press.
Reich, W. (1943a). The biological miscalculation in the human struggle for freedom. *International Journal of Sex-Economy and Orgone Research, 2*(3), 97-121.
Reich, W. (1943b). Give responsibility to vitally necessary work. *International Journal of Sex-Economy and Orgone Research, 2*(3), 93-96.
Reich, W. (1943c). Work democracy versus politics. *International Journal of Sex-Economy, 2*(3), 122-157.
Reich, W. (1946). *The mass psychology of fascism.* New York: Orgone Institute Press.
Reich, W. (1962). *The sexual revolution: Toward a self-governing character structure.* New York: Farrar, Straus & Giroux.
Reich, W. (1971). *The murder of Christ: The emotional plague of mankind.* New York: Farrar, Straus & Giroux.
Snyder, G. (1965). *Dear Mr. President.* Holograph broadside. Portland, Oregon.
Steiner, C. (1974). *Scripts people live: Transactional analysis of life scripts.* New York: Grove Press.
Trautmann, R. (Ed.). (1984). Special issue: Nuclear disarmament. *Transactional Analysis Journal, 14*(4).
Welch, L. (1968). *Courses: No credit no blame no balm.* San Francisco, CA: Cranium Press.
Wilson, C. (1972). *New pathways in psychology: Maslow and the post-Freudian revolution.* New York: Taplinger Publishing.

The original version of this chapter was published in the Transactional Analysis Journal, *Volume 14, Number 4, pp. 240-245, October 1984.*

The Inevitability of Uncertainty, the Necessity of Doubt, and the Development of Trust

William F. Cornell

It was nearly a year ago that I came up with the title for this speech. I was under a tight deadline from the ASAM [the Turkish group that helped organize the 2006 World TA Conference in Istanbul], which was in the early stages of preparing the program and needed a title and descriptive paragraph fast. I came up with "The Inevitability of Uncertainty, the Necessity of Doubt, and the Development of Trust," probably under the influence of either too much coffee or too much wine—I can't recall which. A lot has transpired during the year since, both in my own life and in the world at large, so if I were to title this speech now, it would be "Trust and Distrust/Hope and Hatred."

I have come to Istanbul from Kosovo, where I was visiting my son Seth and daughter-in-law, Ghadah. Seth works for the Organization for Security and Cooperation in Europe (OSCE) at their headquarters in Pristina. It would seem, in spite of its name, that the OSCE is forced to spend much more of its resources providing security than promoting cooperation. In addition to staying in Pristina, we drove to Prizren, a predominantly Muslim community near Albania. Our route took us to Gracanice, a Serbian enclave and Roma (gypsy) village where Ghadah, a Sunni Muslim, worked for a foundation promoting education for Serbian and Roma children, and to Mitrovice, a Serbian-identified city near the Serbian border. On our journey we drove in a white, clearly marked OSCE vehicle, and the welcome—or lack thereof—was palpable as we moved from one area to another. We were welcomed in the Muslim, Kosovarian territories but not in the Serbian/Orthodox Christian communities. We passed war memorials guarded by United Nations (UN) tanks, the UN facilities surrounded by bomb walls and razor wire, and the Christian churches surrounded by walls and razor wire, often guarded by UN soldiers and tanks.

Kosovo is relatively stable at the moment, but the tension, distrust, and hatred simmers just below the surface. It was a stark reminder of the compelling need for us to learn to work more effectively with hatred and violence through political, social, economic, educational, and therapeutic means.

I left Kosovo filled with a father's pride and—given the continuing disintegration of Iraq, the renewed destruction of Lebanon, and the obvious tensions in Kosovo—a quiet despair. As I flew to Istanbul, the prime ministers of Serbia and Kosovo were meeting face-to-face for the first time since 1999, when NATO bombed Serbia to bring the ethnic cleansing of ethnic (Muslim) Albanians to an end. The talks ended in a stalemate.

My speech today will be more about hatred than hope, more about distrust than trust, for I believe if we do not learn to face our hatreds, there will be no true hope or trust. We are thrown into deep uncertainty and doubt at times of war and profound cultural conflicts, like those we are now facing throughout the world. We are thrown back to reexamining the nature of our cultural and social structures. It is probably no accident that the theme of last year's international transactional analysis conference in Edinburgh was "Freedom and Responsibility" and that this year's theme is "Trust and Uncertainty in the 21st Century." The April 2006 issue of the *Transactional Analysis Journal* is devoted to papers from last year's conference, and in my introductory editorial to that journal, I wrote that "these articles bring new meaning and spirit to Berne's vision of transactional analysis as a social psychiatry" (Cornell, 2006, p. 76). As we can see from this year's conference program, Berne's vision continues to inspire us.

Pearl Drego's (1996) article "Cultural Parent Oppression and Regeneration," published a decade ago in the *Transactional Analysis Journal*, is based on her treatment of and research into the oppression of women in India. In the article she observed that

> while the culture of the group requires analysis outside the individual, understanding the Cultural Parent involves introspection and self-awareness. The culture of a group is carried by individuals, and it is possible to become aware of it within the [individual] personality. (p. 59)

Drego's (1983, 1996, 2005) writings on the Cultural Parent build on Berne's (1963) work in *The Structure and Dynamics of Organizations and Groups*. She seeks to provide a means for examining and changing the impact of culture and cultural oppression on the individual's psychology. This morning I will be speaking to intercultural tensions and the necessity of understanding distrust and hatred in the movement toward intergroup and cultural change.

Earlier this year I watched the documentary film by Martin Scorcese (2005) on the beginnings of Bob Dylan's career. Dylan has been a hero of mine since I was a teenager, and Scorcese made a brilliant presentation of Dylan's early years. The film was, however, more than Dylan's story, as it wove his life into the cultural revolutions of the civil rights and antiwar movements of the 1960s. It was a time in the United States of turmoil, idealism, and hope. As the documentary came to an end, I wept. But mine were not tears of joy or appreciation. They were bitter tears, tears of rage and despair. What has happened to my country? How has my generation created the United States of 2006? How have we elected George W. Bush as president? How have those of my generation allowed these wars, cultural arrogance, unbridled hostility, religious ignorance, and prejudice? Scorsese captured the cultural and political landscape of the 1960s vividly. It was in this cultural spirit that transactional analysis was born. Eric Berne and his rabble-rousing colleagues were part of the heart of the 1960s in the San Francisco Bay Area. It was the era in which I grew up and with which I deeply identify.

At the beginning of this year, I went back into therapy after a very difficult 2005. The man I chose as my therapist is a forensic psychiatrist. I agreed to see him after hours at his office in the African-American center in the midst of one of Pittsburgh's now poorest neighborhoods, an area that was once a vibrant jazz and cultural center in the city. After several weeks, I was leaving a session and found the doors locked. It was late, dark, and I had no idea how to get out. Eventually, a man came up to me and said, "Do you want to get out?" I told him I did. "Well, I'll let you out," he said, "if you look at me." "What do you mean?" I asked. He replied, "You've been coming here for several weeks, and you've never looked at me. You act like I don't exist." I was stunned, filled with shame, and mumbled something like, "I'm sorry. I don't really know what you mean. I've been coming to see my therapist, so I'm rather preoccupied when I get here. I don't think I see anybody really." "Maybe, but you walk by me every night and you don't see me, never bother to say 'hello.'" So maybe, but you're a white guy, I'm black, and black people are used to white people looking past them. You're not going to look past me. Look me in the eye." I did. "My name is James, what's yours?" James asked. "Bill." "OK, Bill, next week you look me in the eye, say 'Hi James, how's it going?' and we'll start getting to know each other." Now we always greet each other and we are getting to know one another, even as I still arrive preoccupied and often leave even more so.

I have given that encounter with James a great deal of thought. At the end of last year, I sold my family home in the country and moved into the city into a predominantly poor, African-American neighborhood, one that is beginning to be revived. There is a great deal of tension in this neighborhood. There I do see my neighbors, but I don't know how (or if) to greet those who are black. I don't know the body language, the social protocol on the street. A few days after the confrontation from James, I was walking to my house and passed two African-American men in a deep, animated conversation. I stepped to the side as I passed them. One of the men turned around and approached me angrily, "We don't bite, you know. You stepped away from us like we scared you. We don't bite, mister." This time, though, I did not feel ashamed. I had consciously stepped aside so as not to intrude on their conversation, as I would with anyone. This time I felt some understanding of the man's reaction, and I was able to talk with him comfortably. And yet I knew, here again, was an experience of men accustomed to being avoided, even shunned (Lewin, 2000), so the man's assumption of my avoidance was not ungrounded. We had misread one another, with distrust and tension on both sides.

I tell these stories here because they are everyday examples of uncertainty, of cultural and racial distrust. In these instances we can see both the subtlety and the depth of cultural misunderstandings. I am trying to understand my own racism, my anxieties, my ways of insulating myself from unpleasantness and differentness, and I don't like this process very much.

I am accustomed to welcoming theoretical differences, challenges, and even conflict in my various roles as therapist, professional colleague, trainer, writer, and editor. In these familiar arenas, the experience of differentness and conflict is exciting and enjoyable. In my work as a psychotherapist, I know that conflict—even hatred—is meaningful.

For example, many of my clients have had exceedingly difficult lives, and they are in various ways rather difficult people. Often their work with me is their third or fourth effort at psychotherapy. They have little reason to be hopeful or trusting, little motivation to be pleasant or reasonable. When I sit with a client in the face of hatred or despair, I see a body that is scarred and battered. I can usually feel a link, and I can bring some comprehension to the hostility and distrust. Sometimes I am an effective partner in the face of deeply distressed affect. Sometimes I am not so effective, but together we eventually work things out. I feel a meaning to these disturbances and some confidence that our work will make a difference. But I find it incredibly difficult to feel hope or trust when I cast these issues onto a societal and political scale.

In my recent writing, I have argued for a theoretical and therapeutic attitude that is neither too certain of the therapist's knowing nor too comforting in what is provided to the client. It can be quite seductive and gratifying to the human relations professional to be seen as the good and understanding parent, the provider of the "secure base" (Bowlby, 1979; Kohlrieser, 2006). Secure base—it is nearly impossible for me to speak this term these days without thinking of the gross injustices carried out by the U.S. government in the name of Homeland Security, a seductive if empty and deceptive promise promulgated by George W. Bush and the current U.S. administration. As a psychotherapist, I can comprehend how so many Americans have been willing to sacrifice their thinking and autonomy, not to mention the rights and autonomy of other peoples, in exchange for the illusion of protection and security. But as a citizen of the United States, I am also frightened and appalled.

A psychologically secure base is a necessary foundation for our work, but I do not think it is a sufficient model for working with distrust, violence, and hatred. As professionals using transactional analysis to promote personal, group, and organizational change, we need to think very carefully when we imagine that we can offer our clients a secure base. What is it we think we are providing? What is it our clients imagine we are offering? I think the ideal of a secure base needs to be changed to that of a "vital base" within which we offer a challenging, experimental, often conflicted, and rather uncomfortable relationship through which both people must shift their familiar frames of reference. Whether the work is between individuals or groups, both parties must shift their frames of reference if trust of any substance is to develop.

I think that as a community, it has often been difficult for transactional analysis practitioners to face squarely the degrees of shame, hatred, and irrationality of which we are all capable. Berne (1972) warned us most bluntly when he wrote of the Little Fascist in each of us:

If the Little Fascist comes out openly, he is a cripple-kicker, a stomper, and a rapist, sometimes with some excuse or other such as toughness, objectivity, or some justification. But most people suppress these tendencies, pretend they are not there at all, excuse them if they show their colors, or overlay and disguise them with fear. [These] form the basis for third-degree or "tissue" games that draw blood. He who pretends these forces do not exist becomes their victim. His whole script may become a project to demonstrate that he is free of them. But since he is most likely not, this is a denial of himself. . . . The solution is not to say, as many do, "This has nothing to do with me" or "It's too frightening," but rather "What can I do about it and what can I do with it?" (pp. 269-270)

We can, perhaps, more easily make arrangements (games) within our dyadic relationships to avoid anxiety, hostility, and differentness, but within and between groups the experience of anxiety, unpredictability, hostility, and differentness is far harder to avoid (Schermer & Pines, 1994). It is probably no accident that Berne addressed the darker side of human relations more frequently and directly in his writings on groups. In *Principles of Group Treatment,* for example, Berne (1966) outlined the satisfaction in groups of the basic human hungers for stimulation, recognition, and structure, stressing that "people will pay almost any price to have time structured for them, as few are capable of structuring their own time autonomously for very long" (p. 230). He warned that a derivative of structure hunger is leadership hunger and that in turning oneself over to a leader, there is enormous compromise in one's willingness to think. Ultimately, all too often, the idealized leader then imposes restrictions or prohibitions on one's right to think for oneself.

It is no accident that it was after World War I that a deeply troubled Sigmund Freud (1921/1955) wrote "Group Psychology and Analysis of the Ego," in which he described the nature of group regression into what he called "mobs and hordes." A group's identification with the leader creates a sense of closeness and belonging. Freud warned of the idealized and dependent transferences to The Leader, the subsequent distortions of superego and ego functions, and the dynamics of such groups as the military, the church, and the state. His conclusions are mirrored in Berne's writings on groups. Neither Freud nor Berne was very optimistic by temperament—their writings were often infused with a deep pessimism and even cynicism—but both were, nonetheless, often idealistic in their visions for the work they founded.

Freud, for example, was deeply affected by the horrors and utter irrationality of World War I, and he determined that psychoanalysis had a responsibility to its communities. He initiated the creation of free clinics in every major city with a psychoanalytic institute, requiring that all practicing analysts devote at least one day per week to offering free treatment (Danto, 2005). Vienna, Berlin, Frankfurt, Budapest, Paris, and London all witnessed the creation of free psychoanalytic clinics that offered in-depth psychoanalysis, libraries, and mental hygiene classes, a profound expression of Freud's ideals and leadership. All of these clinics except those in London were closed down within a few years by the Nazis. Freud was one of the last Jewish analysts to flee Europe for safety elsewhere. I cannot imagine the despair he must have endured in the last year of his life in England as he witnessed, yet again, his idealism overrun by hatred and irrationality.

It might seem on the surface paradoxical that of the many Jewish psychoanalysts who fled the Nazis and established psychoanalysis in the United States, most turned their backs on the social and political aspects of psychoanalysis. They enshrined ego psychology in the United States, a model that returned to the psychology of the individual and emphasized the rational. Many became deeply conservative in their practice and hungry for the sanction and approval of authorities. Eric Fromm and Erik Erikson (one of Berne's analysts), among a very few, maintained the social and more radical perspective in psychoanalysis in the United States.

I try to imagine the profound despair of those emigrating analysts, fleeing for their lives, often leaving family behind to die. I can understand their inward turning and imagine the subtle cynicism underlying their return to, wish for, and idealization of the rational and the power of the ego.

It was within this socially cleansed psychoanalytic environment that Berne was trained, and it was this he challenged in creating transactional analysis as a social psychiatry, with groups at the heart of his work. In the October 2006 issue of the *TAJ,* Steve Karpman (2006) writes of the spirit of that time in the birth of transactional analysis. Here again, in Berne's work, we witnessed a reestablishment of an ideal, a rebirth of hope. Now nearly half a century later, we struggle with despair, surrounded by hostility and irrationality around the world. How do we hold our values and pursue our ideals, without idealization and without turning our therapeutic values into saccharine but hollow slogans?

I will talk here primarily about racism, but in so doing I ask you to be thinking about misogyny, homophobia, religious fundamentalism, ethnic and nationalistic superiority, and all forms of institutionalized hatred. Race, like culture, is a complex intermingling of psychological and social factors. It is not simply about the color of one's skin any more than culture is about one's country or ethnicity of origin. One's racial or ethnic identity includes such factors as physical characteristics, geographical location, family structure, income, history, and politics as well as economic, educational, and developmental opportunity. Donald Moss (2003) edited *HATING in the First Person Plural*, assembling the essays in that book by sending a group of psychotherapists three words—nigger, cunt, and faggot, among the ugliest words in the English language—and asking each author to write an essay on one of those words. It is a powerful collection of writings from which I learned a lot, a book that has helped me to think about and work more clearly with the multiple meanings and sources of bias and hatred. Alan Bass (2003), in an essay in *HATING*, speaks to my experience with James and in my new neighborhood as he observes:

> When racism is part of the everyday environment, there is a particular tendency to disavow its traumatic effects, while of course peremptorily re-creating a traumatic environment. And there can be the tendency on the part of an allegedly neutral observer . . . to disavow that all these dynamics are at work. (p. 41)

Maurice Apprey, an African-American psychoanalyst, examines the suffering of African-Americans in particular but writes with a voice that echoes among all populations that are oppressed, assaulted, marginalized, or held in contempt. He uses the image of "transgenerational haunting" (Apprey, 1996a, 1996b, 1998, 2003), by which he means the victim is host to the ghosts of the original aggressors, a haunting passed unconsciously from one generation to the next. He writes that an individual's "interior space is filled with shadows, ghosts, and silhouettes where past and present, inside and outside, are ill-defined . . . [and so] urgently strives [without conscious awareness] to repeat historical injury, choosing an inappropriate object to attack" (Apprey, 1998, p. 34).

Berne and Drego, in their writings on the deep influences of cultural and group character, repeatedly demonstrate the split—often a total contradiction—between the professed etiquette of the Cultural Parent ego state and the emotional and bodily realities of the character of the group. In *The Structure and Dynamics of Organizations and Groups,* Berne (1963) observed that "group character" provides the mechanisms for handling individual anxieties and patterns of emotional expression. Drego (1996) elaborated Berne's concept to include emotionally charged attitudes and deeply inscribed ways of feeling, sensing, expressing, loving, and relating. I would add hating to this list. In describing the dynamics of group cultures, Berne (1963) wrote:

> Character is more "primitive" than etiquette. Etiquette requires a restraint, and understanding and knowledge of social behavior. . . . Character is a more direct expression of instinctual life. The group character is chiefly an expression of that aspect of the personality which will later be called the Child. (pp. 151-152)

Drego refers to group character as the cultural shadow that envelops and contaminates the Child ego state. The term "character" has its origins in Greek, meaning "branded, cut into the skin"; character cuts deep. Apprey (2003) stresses, "Into this cut [character], as it were, may be inserted a world of lived experience where the oppressed has lost sight of the original enemy. Influenced by this absence, a people may attack its own, as in Black-on-Black crime" (p. 9). In transgenerational haunting, then, a contemporary generation is unwittingly possessed by an earlier generation. Such possession preserves history, but in a poisonous, unmetabolized version (p. 12).

For Apprey (2003), "In violent ethnonational conflicts, the pivotal issues are difference and identity" (p. 6), where the dread of differentness—the Other, in his language—is avoided at all costs so as to preserve identity (structure and recognition hungers, in Berne's terms). Transgenerational hauntings are drenched in histories of violence, injury, shame, powerlessness, and economic deprivation—the "brandings" of previous generations then carried in the group character (Gilligan, 2000). We must not underestimate the enduring and irrational force of intergenerational injury, hatred, and violence. Uncertainty and doubt inhabit the domain of the tensions between the familiar and the different, between Self and Other. Apprey is not speaking of self and other as we typically do in object relations theory, but of Self and THE OTHER, where the Other represents a threatening, alien identity or way of life. It is a differentness that cannot be explored or made a part of one's own life and identity, so it is rendered inferior, disgusting, evil, or dead. This is the domain of a fundamental experience of differentness in which the experience of "I'm Not OK, You're Not OK" is a very real tension that must be acknowledged. This tension is not to be bridged by some saccharine application of "I'm OK, You're OK" as an unthinking idealization of the human spirit.

In working with distrust, hatred, prejudice, and violence, we must look first at ourselves, honestly. All will not be pretty. If we cannot look honestly at ourselves and our professional and ethnic cultures, we will be of little value to those we wish to help. In working with prejudice and violence, shame and distrust, we need to look together with the person at both him or her as an individual and the history of that individual and also at the histories of the familial, racial, and ethnic groups to which the individual belongs. As therapists, teachers, trainers, and members of the remarkably international community of transactional analysts, we must face and make room for distrust and dissonance in our work. To develop real trust, we must first acknowledge and express distrust.

In his discussion of the Little Fascist, Berne stated that the answer to these vicious and hateful aspects of ourselves is first to acknowledge them and then ask, "What can I do about it and what can I do with it?" What can we do? In Drego's (1996) article on her work with Indian women, she stresses that

> to bring about a change, the oppressive Cultural Parent and its injunctions, myths, and reinforcements must be cleansed at the individual level as well as at the group level. Therapy with individuals needs to be supported by group discussions among mothers, group support systems among women, retraining programs for families, and new kinds of relationships between mothers and their children—in short, a form of cultural therapy similar to one Erikson (1963) described: "'group therapy' of a kind which would not aim at psychiatric improvement of the individual participant but at an improvement of the cultural relations of those assembled" (p. 127). (pp. 74-75)

This is transactional analysis as a true social psychiatry, with group work, education, and counseling at its very foundation.

Drego addresses the cultural oppression of the individual by families and groups. Apprey addresses intercultural conflict and violence. He brings his experiences from African-American communities to work in conflict resolution with various groups faced with ethnonational violence. He delineates a process necessitating the involvement of outside facilitators through which Self and Other, as individuals and groups, can begin to open up new opportunities.

The first stage of the work, as outlined by Apprey, is the acknowledgment of polarized views and the space for this polarization to be fully expressed. In the polarization phase, each side defines its own identity while demonizing the differentness of the Other. The second phase is one of differentiation within each of the polarized groups, which allows participants to see that even within the group with which they identify, there are a multiplicity of positions. The third phase involves the "crossing of mental borders" (p. 23) through which each side attempts to enter the Other's frame of reference through meaningful dialogue and "propelled by an ethic of responsibility" (p. 23; see also Bond, 2006; Kohlrieser, 2006). The Bush administration and the leaders of many of the regions currently engaged in armed conflict seem completely unwilling to engage in this process. As I said earlier, meaningful trust is possible only when both parties shift their frames of reference. The fourth and most crucial phase is the one within which the emerging ethics are grounded in joint projects of concrete and mutual benefit. There is little evidence on the world stage today of opposing groups undertaking these last two processes, which we have witnessed in our time in the work of the Truth and Reconciliation Commission in South Africa. The South African efforts have not eliminated poverty or erased racism, but they have allowed enough healing so that functional social structures based in nonviolence can begin to be established. Apprey outlines a process that I believe is consistent with our process of groupwork in transactional analysis, a process that conveys realistic ideas and ideals that can deepen and enrich our work with cultural and intergroup conflict, violence, and prejudice.

In our work—be it as therapists in individual or group treatment, teachers, trainers, or consultants—we must create the space and the opportunity for the realities of our individual and collective anxieties, shamings, and hatreds to be aired (Nitsun, 1996). We must not avert our gaze. In looking at ourselves and each other within the space of despair, shame, distrust, polarization, and hostility, we create a container, an environment in which interchange, understanding, and informed, quiet trust can gradually develop. This work takes time. It requires great determination and the willingness to remain engaged during periods of doubt, uncertainty, distrust, and polarization.

In conclusion, I turn to the words of two artists. More than any other members of our societies, I think it is our artists who are able to work within their cultural histories and traditions and at the same time stand outside the social and cultural norms in critical reflection and representation. I close with a brief quote from an essay by Adrienne Rich (1979) entitled "Women and Honor: Some Notes on Lying":

> An honorable human relationship—that is, one in which two people have the right to use the word "love"—is a process, delicate, violent, often terrifying to both persons involved, a process of refining the truths they can tell each other.
> It is important to do this because it breaks down human self-delusion and isolation.
> It is important to do this because in so doing we do justice to our own complexity.
> It is important to do this because we can count on so few to go that hard way with us. (p. 188)

And then there is Dylan (1963/1985), who wrote "With God on Our Side" in 1963:

> Oh my name it is nothin'
> My age it means less
> The country I come from
> Is called the Midwest
> I's taught and brought up there
> The laws to abide
> And the land that I live in
> Has God on its side.

Through the next six stanzas, Dylan outlines the wars of the United States, each carried out "with God on our side." The song ends this way:

> So now as I'm leavin'
> I'm weary as Hell
> The confusion I'm feelin'
> Ain't no tongue can tell
> The words fill my head
> And fall to the floor
> If God's on our side
> He'll stop the next war. (p. 93)

It has been more than 40 years since Dylan wrote those words. Dylan's God did not stop the next war, nor has anyone else's, but in the name of various gods, several wars have been started.

Thank you so much for giving me the opportunity to speak with you today.

Afterward: As I was leaving the conference, Diane Salters (2006) gave me a parting gift, a book, *A Human Being Died that Night* by Pumla Gobodo-Madikizela (2003). She is a clinical psychologist who served on South Africa's Truth and Reconciliation Commission's Human Rights Violations Committee. The book is Gobodo-Madikizela's complex and moving accounting of her interviews with Eugene de Kock, who is serving 212 years in prison for crimes against humanity in his capacity as the commanding officer of apartheid death squads. She describes the complicity of the Dutch Reformed Church in apartheid policies and the South African Army's killings of enemies of the State, a reminder of Freud's linkage of the group psychology of hordes, the State, and the Church. Soldiers were issued a special edition of the Bible, each of which was inscribed on the first page with a message in Afrikaans from State President P. W. Botha (as cited in Gobodo-Madikizela, 2003):

> This Bible is an important part of your calling to duty. When you are overwhelmed with doubt,

pain, or when you find yourself wavering, you must turn to this wonderful book for answers. ... You are now called to play your part in defending our country. It is my prayer that this Bible will be your comfort so that you can fulfill your duty, and South Africa and her people will forever be proud of you. Of all the weapons you carry, this is the greatest because it is the Weapon of God. (p. 53)

REFERENCES

Apprey, M. (1996a). Broken lines, public memory, absent memory: Jewish and African Americans coming to terms with racism. *Mind and Human Interaction, 7,* 139-149.

Apprey, M. (1996b). *Phenomenology of transgenerational haunting: Subjects in apposition, subjects on urgent/voluntary errands.* Ann Arbor, MI: UMI Research Collections.

Apprey, M. (1998). Reinventing the self in the face of received transgenerational hatred in the African American community. *Mind and Human Interaction, 9,* 30-37.

Apprey, M. (2003). Repairing history: Reworking transgenerational trauma. In D. Moss (Ed.), *HATING in the first person plural* (pp. 3-28). New York: Other Press.

Bass, A. (2003). Historical and unconscious trauma: Racism and psychoanalysis. In D. Moss (Ed.), *HATING in the first person plural* (pp. 29-44). New York: Other Press.

Berne, E. (1963). *The structure and dynamics of organizations and groups.* New York: Grove Press.

Berne, E. (1966). *Principles of group treatment.* New York: Oxford University Press.

Berne, E. (1972). *What do you say after you say hello?: The psychology of human destiny.* New York: Grove Press.

Bond, T. (2006). Intimacy, risk, and reciprocity in psychotherapy: Intricate ethical challenges. *Transactional Analysis Journal, 36,* 77-89.

Bowlby, J. (1979). *The making and breaking of affectional bonds.* London: Tavistock Publications.

Cornell, W. F. (2006). Letter from the editor. *Transactional Analysis Journal, 36,* 74-76.

Danto, E. A. (2005). *Freud's free clinics: Psychoanalysis and social justice, 1918-1938.* New York: Columbia University Press.

Drego, P. (1983). The cultural parent. *Transactional Analysis Journal, 13,* 224-227.

Drego, P. (1996). Cultural parent oppression and regeneration. *Transactional Analysis Journal, 26,* 58-77.

Drego, P. (2005). Acceptance speech on receiving the 2004 Eric Berne Memorial Award. *Transactional Analysis Journal, 35,* 7-30.

Dylan, B. (1985). With God on our side. In B. Dylan, *Lyrics: 1962-1985* (p. 93). New York: Alfred A. Knopf. (Original work published 1963)

Freud, S. (1955). Group psychology and the analysis of the ego. In J. Strachey (Ed. & Trans.), *The standard edition of the complete psychological works of Sigmund Freud* (Vol. 18, pp. 69-143). London: The Hogarth Press. (Original work published 1921)

Gilligan, J. (2000). *Violence: Reflections on our deadliest epidemic.* London: Jessica Kingsley Publishers.

Gobodo-Madikizela, P. (2003). *A human being died that night.* Claremont, South Africa: David Philip Publishers.

Karpman, S. (2006). Lost in translation: Neo-Bernean or neo-Freudian? *Transactional Analysis Journal, 36,* 284-302.

Kohlrieser, G. (2006). *Hostage at the table: How leaders can overcome conflict, influence others, and raise performance.* San Francisco: Jossey-Bass.

Lewin, M. (2000). "I'm not talking to you": Shunning as a form of violence. *Transactional Analysis Journal, 30,* 125-131.

Moss, D. (Ed.). (2003). *HATING in the first person plural.* New York: Other Press.

Nitsun, M. (1996). *The anti-group: Destructive forces in the group and their creative potential.* London: Routledge.

Rich, A. (1979). *On lies, secrets, and silence: Selected prose 1966-1978.* New York: Norton.

Salters, D. (2006). Simunye—sibaningi: We are one—we are many. *Transactional Analysis Journal, 36,* 152-158.

Schermer, V. L., & Pines, M. (1994). *Ring of fire: Primitive affects and object relations in group psychotherapy.* London: Routledge.

Scorsese, M. (Director). (2005). *No direction home: Bob Dylan* [Motion picture]. United States: Paramount Pictures.

The original version of this chapter was originally presented as a keynote speech on 27 July 2006 during the World TA Conference in Istanbul, Turkey. It was later published in the Transactional Analysis Journal, *Volume 37, Number 1, pp. 8-16, January 2007.*

A Community for Thinking

William F. Cornell

> Thinking is neither coerced nor coercive. It is exploratory, suggestive; it does not prove anything, or finally arrive anywhere. Thus, to say people are thoughtful or thought provoking suggests that they are open-minded, reflective, challenging—that they are more likely to question than to assert, inclined to listen to many sides, capable of making sensitive distinctions that hold differences in play rather than dividing in order to exclude, and desirous of persuading others rather than reducing them to silence by refuting them. (Minnich, 2003, p. 20)

I had the good fortune to attend the Freud at the Millennium Conference held in Washington, DC, in October, 1998, celebrating the opening of the Library of Congress exhibit on "Freud: Conflict and Culture." The conference, sponsored by the International Institute of Object Relations Therapy, was organized as an international symposium on science, art, culture, politics, and psychoanalysis. As a psychoanalytic conference, it was quite unique, with its strong emphasis on art, history, and politics. It was a rich and rare opportunity to reappreciate the radical genius of Freud and his followers and to reflect on the meaning of this profession in the life of culture as well as in the lives of individuals.

Among a number of outstanding speeches and papers, I found Judith Chused's paper, "Why Theory?" especially powerful. Chused is a member of the board of trustees of the Freud Archives at the Library of Congress and a training and supervising analyst with the Washington Psychoanalytic Institute. Her talk was eloquent, personal, and blunt—directly addressing some of the concerns I have often raised in our transactional analysis communities regarding colleagues rendering personal attacks against colleagues under the guise of (or instead of) challenging ideas.

Chused stressed the fact that the professions of psychoanalysis and psychotherapy are rather unique in that we as therapists are given responsibility for the well-being of clients years before we truly know what we are doing. The result is that we often become overly dependent on theory and technique as a way of managing both our own anxieties as well as the uncertainty and responsibility of the work. Chused described the tendency to embrace and rigidify ideas and techniques learned from training analysts and early supervisors or teachers, important early learnings imbued with the glow of positive transference and the relief of alleviating at least some of the anxiety inherent in the work. In contrast, Chused suggested that theory should serve as a creative process that brings meaning and coherence to one's work rather than as a source of authority and rules. In fact, she described, theories can be used defensively to hold clients at bay and to protect us from difficulties of our own making.

Chused referred to Freud's (1930) phrase "the narcissism of small differences," warning of the consequences when these differences are acted out destructively among colleagues in theory wars. She commented that she has often found attacks on theory by colleagues more disturbing than challenges from clients. The experience of conflict with a client and the mutual commitment found in the psychological working through of differences is a precious experience, one that is all too often absent in theory wars in which warring factions do not address their own psychological motivations and needs.

Theory building is a painstaking process for most of us, one that often occurs in the midst of struggling with uncertainty and failure. Chused offered a vivid description of the process by which psychoanalytic and psychological theories become both the "children" and the "protectors" of their authors, a powerful combination. Theories serve to make sense of experience and they protect their creators from uncertainty and narcissistic vulnerability. According to Chused, "The wish for certainty creates fury and blame when theories fail." The wish for certainty seems also to create fury and blame when colleagues suggest that one another's ideas are in some way flawed or failing.

There is a serious liability to our clients when we become so narcissistically identified with a particular theory or style of practice that clients are deprived of the opportunity to fully "use" and "shape" the therapist according to their unique needs, as Winnicott suggests is necessary for psychological individuation and growth. When this sort of narcissistic identification occurs within the therapist to his or her mentor or theory, there is a great likelihood that the therapist will shape the work and thus shape the client's experience. The client's permission and opportunity to shape the therapist and the working relationship are minimized.

The intensely creative process of mutual inquiry, challenge, and discovery are thus short-changed within the therapeutic process. I would make much the same observation in the professional, theoretical arena: that narcissistic identification with one's ideas and way of working thwarts creative dialogue and the opportunity to be unsettled, influenced, and shaped by the experiences of others.

Theory is about the capacity to imagine and think. A professional community is one in which colleagues join to question, imagine, learn, and think together. As an editor of two ITAA publications— *The Script* newsletter and the *Transactional Analysis Journal*—I think often about the functions of journals and newsletters within professional organizations. A recent essay by Elizabeth Minnich, "Teaching Thinking: Moral and Political Considerations," gave me new insights and a great boost of enthusiasm and purpose, which is what I hope to convey here. The ITAA and transactional analysis associations worldwide now sustain three primary functions for our community: training and examination/certification, conferences, and publications. My primary personal investment is in our publications.

As an educator, Minnich makes an important distinction between the learning involved in the acquisition of knowledge, on the one hand, and the development of the capacity to think, on the other. Needless to say, there is a rather essential link between the two: Our knowledge is more useful when we can think effectively about it rather than simply acquiring and retaining it (so often the primary focus of our educational systems), and we can think better when we have something of interest and value about which to think.

Addressing the function of knowledge in a learning community, Minnich (2003) stresses that
we teach knowledge, as we teach language and socialize our children, to conserve our world by preparing newcomers to join and continually revitalize it. . . . Knowledge gives us something we share that matters enough to have opinions about; opinions give us differing perspectives about the meanings as distinct from truth claims of knowledge. This is why, as teachers, we try both to convey knowledge and to encourage students to develop worthy opinions about it—to think about it, without submitting to it. (p. 21)

It is through our training, examination, and certification processes that transactional analysis organizations convey and assess the knowledge and skill bases of our members, establishing the core competencies essential for both our professional identities and for the service and protection of our clients. It is an essential function, the foundation really, of our professional organizations.

Conferences and publications provide different functions for our members—those of continuing education and revitalization of our community and the challenging and evolving of theory and technique among colleagues. Conferences and publications are essential vehicles for a learning community. Conferences provide us with times to socialize, to create and renew friendships, and to engage in face-to-face education and exchange of ideas. Conferences convey information and thinking among members, but ultimately they represent an ephemeral process. In contrast, our journals and newsletters provide the permanent record of our professional discourse, the lasting archives of our efforts to think together, to convey new thinking and possibilities that in time become incorporated into our body of technical knowledge and recognized theory. Our publications are a primary means of sustaining a community for professional learning and development.

I turn to Minnich and her way of evaluating "thinking papers" in contrast to "reports" of funds of knowledge. I found this part of her essay immensely stimulating and deeply instructive as a member of an editorial board. I think an essential aspect of serving on an editorial board is not simply evaluating manuscripts for content but also promoting thinking and mutual learning among authors and reviewers. I know how much I have learned as a writer, teacher, and therapist from serving as an editor and reviewer. In her essay, Minnich (2003, pp. 23-24) delineates ten criteria she uses to evaluate a paper as a thinking paper, which I have summarized here:

1. *Freedom of mind:* I want to see the activity of an individual mind, to see the effects of moments of confusion from which fresh insights arose.
2. *Inclusiveness:* A thinking paper also shows the effects of the author's having anticipated possible other perspectives (not just objections), taken them into account, and been enriched by them. It may then reach a conclusion, but it may simply leave the reader with a more complex picture.
3. *Rhetoric:* The work reaches out to speak with many people, engaging them through understanding of their languages, their ways of thinking, their knowledge, and their emotions.
4. *Beauty:* Sentences (even imperfect ones) flow, words and phrases are both apt and evocative.
5. *Play:* Throughout the paper I watch for markers that indicate that the writer was caught up in imaginative moments, not tied down to or locked within what he or she already knew.... Such play is not always fun: It can take us to scary places. But it also unclenches, releases.
6. *Emotion:* The author is present to the reader as a full person—one who cares, gets frustrated, feels anger, remembers hurt, becomes excited in ways that press thinking further and deeper.
7. *Originality:* These papers, when they are good, are never interchangeable in voice, logic, or language. They are the author's own work, recounting a story of an intellectual, emotional, imaginative experience.
8. *Reflexivity:* One can see the author thinking about his/her thinking as it unfolds.
9. *Revelation:* The author says, "Now I understand," or "A better question emerged," or "I recognized that...." There is a sense of illumination.
10. *Connections:* With and through all the other qualities, such papers track the often odd affiliations among ideas and feelings, other perspectives, audiences, and purposes. This is an independent mind, open and communicating in a way that respects and enjoys differences and wanders across and around them without anxious desire to reduce them to sameness.

With these words, Minnich has articulated a kind of gold standard for a learning community and for the process of writing and publishing.

REFERENCES

Freud, S. (1930). Civilization and its discontents. In J. Strachey (Ed. & Trans.), *The standard edition of the complete psychological works of Sigmund Freud* (Vol. 21, pp. 64-145). London: The Hogarth Press.

Minnich, E. K. (2003, September-October). Teaching thinking: Moral and political considerations. *Change, 35*(5), 18-24.

The material in this chapter is based on two previously published articles: "The Narcissism of Small Differences," The Script, Volume 28, Number 9, p. 2, December 1998, and "A Community for Thinking Together," The Script, Volume 34, Number 2, p. 2, March 2004.

On Learning, Knowing, and Telling: Reflections on Clinical Research and Writing

William F. Cornell

Standing in the Clinical Tradition

There has been long-standing tension in our profession between the two traditions of clinical observation and empirical research. Is psychology a hard science? Must psychotherapy be founded on or proven within models of empirical science? Or are psychology, psychotherapy, and the human relations disciplines really softer, social sciences? Or are they, in fact, more of an art form?

Freud began as a neurologist and initially tried to formulate psychoanalysis within the scientific/neurological traditions of his time. However, he abandoned this model in favor of a clinical model. Transactional analysis most certainly developed within a clinical tradition. There were no control groups, blind evaluations, or statistically valid, large outcome samples that fostered the development of new theory and technique. There was just one guy, a smart guy, Eric Berne, who was not satisfied with his own clinical work or that of many of his colleagues, so he thought he would try some things out, see what happened, and talk it all over with some respected cohorts. This is the heart of the clinical tradition. This is how transactional analysis was born, solidly in the clinical tradition.

Now transactional analysis, as with most contemporary forms of psychotherapy, is under pressure to prove itself through research. It remains to be seen to what extent the quality and effectiveness of transactional analysis—or any psychotherapy—is improved by research, but the pressure is there, and it is a substantial demand in the name of legitimization. The pressure is generated to some extent by our university colleagues, who seek to bridge the gap between research and practice. Many of these scholar/clinicians are doing wonderful work. But the most intense pressure comes from government bodies, regulating organizations, and insurance companies.

Like many practicing psychotherapists, I pay lip service to the relevance of research, but when I am honest with myself, I have to admit it is only lip service. I learn and practice within the clinical tradition.

I was initially trained in behaviorism by some excellent behavioral psychologists in the heyday of Skinnerian behaviorism. The behaviorists thought that they had finally created a scientific psychology. They studied overt, observable behavior through quantifiable methods. Better yet, they could study people (mostly college students earning extra credit or seeking to get on the professor's good side, but we could ignore the sample bias), rats, pigeons, or even elephants (a specialty at Reed College where I was a student). It was all more or less the same: one brain, one organism as good as the next. Behavior was behavior, after all. However, stuff that went on inside the mind could not be observed, could not be measured, and therefore was not in the realm of real science. So the behaviorists created a model for psychology that fit the model of the "hard," empirical sciences. Unfortunately, it did not fit the realities and complexities of people's lives and has not added much to the field of psychotherapy. Ironically, it was a behavioral psychologist who gave me Berne's (1961) book *Transactional Analysis in Psychotherapy*, warning me that he "didn't think much of the guy's psychoanalytic theories, but he sure knew how to observe behavior." I realized with Berne's book that it was possible to make sense of the outside and the inside of experience at the same time and left behaviorism for transactional analysis.

Behaviorism evolved into cognitive-behaviorism, which continues to evolve into more hyphenated models of behavioral-cognitive-affective interactions. Interestingly, these sound an awful lot like what we have been doing in transactional analysis for decades. Cognitive-behavioral models of psychotherapy are the ones most commonly researched because they fit the needs of researchers: They are symptom focused and short term. This does not mean they are more valid than other modalities, just easier to study. True, cognitive models for treating depression and anxiety are wonderful examples of research-friendly work that has helped to develop important therapeutic models and techniques. However, when we apply these models to more complex forms of emotional difficulty and/or to longer-term psychotherapy—the sorts of issues that most transactional analysis therapists work with on a regular basis—the more empirically based models run into trouble.

Aaron Beck (the founder of cognitive-behavior therapy), in his book *Cognitive Therapy of Personality Disorders* (Beck, Freeman, & Associates, 1990), provided a good example of what goes wrong. There are no broad, empirically based samples here, the book being based largely on uncontrolled observation of cognitively oriented clinicians working with personality-disordered clients. The results are not impressive. Beck and his colleagues address the enormous complexities of developing and carrying out an empirical research project with issues as complex as these. Nevertheless, they offer a cognitive model. The result is a book that is not very convincing from a clinical perspective, although cognitive work with personality disorders is probably reimbursed by insurance companies. I, for one, learned far more about working with personality disorders from my transactional analysis training and the psychoanalytic literature than I did from Beck's book.

With his opening statement in a book chapter published in 2000, the French psychoanalyst Andre Green (2000b) fires a provocative shot across the bow of the current zeitgeist for empirical research in clinical psychotherapy.

> The noble term "research" carries such an amount of prestige that it is to be expected that any reference to it might compel one to bow before it. Unfortunately, compared with the richness of the clinical experience of psychoanalysis, the findings of researchers look very meager. (p. 21)

Green (2000a) expresses dismay that "today, science is synonymous with the truth. If something is not validated by the scientific method, it is regarded as negligible" (p. 46). Green's arguments, intended to provoke and often bordering on the polemical, are contained in the book *Clinical and Observational Psychoanalytic Research: Roots of a Controversy* (Sandler, Sandler, & Davies, 2000). Now a title like that is not likely to send most psychotherapists racing off to their local bookstore to buy a copy. However, masked by the title, the bulk of this book is a fascinating and remarkably blunt debate between Green and Daniel Stern on the role of research in clinical psychotherapy. It will get you thinking.

Green writes as a psychoanalyst and for psychoanalysts in the clinical tradition, but his perspective speaks more broadly to the field of psychotherapy. For example, he wrote:

> Up till now, the great contributors to psychoanalytic theory (Freud, Abraham, Ferenczi, Rank, Melanie Klein, Bion, Winnicott, Lacan, Hartmann, etc.) have all enriched our knowledge with their work stemming from their single mind and from working through their own experience with their patients. On the other hand, there is no one single major discovery for psychoanalysis which has emerged from research. (p. 24)

He goes on to emphasize that the model of empirical science tends to discount or ignore entire fields of knowledge—history, religion, art, and institutions, among others—that are forms of knowledge in and of themselves and tremendously important in shaping the mind, consciously and unconsciously. As he says, they are often "completely absent from the minds of researchers" (p. 26).

Green's argument is primarily against the role and overvaluation of quantitative, empirical research. This is the science of hypothesis testing and empirical verification. In his rejoinder to Green, Stern (2000) emphasizes the place of scientific research that is hypothesis generating, arguing that "it is necessary to clarify that there are many modes of science. They cannot all be lumped together and dismissed as one" (p. 76). Anne Alvarez (2000) takes up the discussion of Green's and Stern's papers by stressing that social scientists and philosophers of science offer broad definitions of research that include "systematic qualitative research, naturalistic observational case studies, and the discoveries made in the clinical situation by the psychoanalyst" (p. 100). She urges the reader to read research and "take what seems to illuminate something for you, and forgive it for being only a partial truth" (p. 103).

Green (2000a) also tackles Stern's mother/infant research in less than flattering terms: "I find these ideas highly speculative, in no way less so than Freud's or Melanie Klein's most unproved hypotheses" (p. 54). Food for thought! The debate between Green and Stern is outside the scope of this chapter, but it is energizing to say the least. Given the influence of Stern's work in transactional analysis, this debate should be required reading for transactional analysis clinicians.

Personally, I think Green goes overboard in his assault on research, but he makes one think. I worry that he assumes that most clinicians engage in his level of disciplined thinking, which is a fundamental necessity and safeguard within the clinical tradition. However, having done clinical supervision for many years now, I know, sadly, that this is not the case. Many psychotherapists are poorly equipped or not inclined toward critical theoretical thinking. For example, I do not believe our transactional analysis training fosters the critical thinking that the clinical tradition requires. Without it, we need the safeguards of empirical research.

I do agree with Green's position that Stern's work, and that of many researchers, is highly speculative and biased in its own way. I also share Green's concern that the current emphasis in much of the psychotherapy literature on mother/infant research is transforming the psychotherapeutic relationship into a latter-day mother/infant redoux. This is in contrast to viewing the relationship between therapist and client as an exploratory one between two adults with far more mental and interpersonal equipment at their disposal than a baby has with its mother.

Process-Centered Research

I admit to a certain lack of excitement and unmistakable skepticism as to what most empirical research in psychotherapy has to date offered the practicing psychotherapist. When we moved to Pittsburgh so that I could start graduate school, we got a new dog, adding to the three we brought with us from Oregon. I named our new dog Empirical Validation in memory of the Reed Psychology Department and in honor of the graduate school zeitgeist. I often took the dogs to class with me and loved roaming the halls of the psychology department calling out for "Empirical Validation," only to have this sweet mutt come bounding through the corridors. Some of the faculty were amused. That dog was the most meaningful and gratifying empirical validation I found in my academic life.

"Empirically supported treatment" is a forceful buzz word in contemporary psychotherapy. The term came into fashion, I believe, through the 1995 publication of an American Psychological Association (APA) Task Force report on "Promotion and Dissemination of Psychological Procedures" (Task Force, 1995). A special issue of the *Journal of Consulting and Clinical Psychology* (Vol. 66, No. 1, 1998) was devoted to a discussion of the impact and limits of the report, in particular, and of the valorization of what is considered empirically supported treatment modalities. For those particularly interested in these issues, that issue offers a rich and varied discussion of the value and limitations of empirical research. The journal is well worth an afternoon's reading. Given the limited space here, I will quote only one of the discussants, Sol Garfield, who presents an eloquent critique of the standardized treatment procedures wedded to protocols and manuals that do not mirror the realities of actual psychotherapy and overlook the crucial variables of patient variability and therapist skill. Garfield (1998) wrote:

> I have emphasized patient and therapist variability because they are important factors in influencing psychotherapy outcome and in countering the emphasis currently placed on psychiatric diagnosis and type of psychotherapy. Providing periods of training in therapies that have empirical support for individuals who lack certain personal qualities of empathy and warmth as well

as skills in relating to and understanding others will not necessarily lead to positive outcomes. ... Instead of trying to reduce therapist variability in research on psychotherapy by adherence to training manuals, we psychologists should instead intensively study those therapists who consistently secure the best results and attempt to discover those therapist variables and therapy interactions that appear to be linked to superior outcomes. (p. 123)

To my mind, Garfield offers both clinical wisdom and a valid research model. I think that process-oriented research as presented in the Toukmanian and Rennie (1992) and Talley, Strupp, and Butler (1994) volumes as well as the clinical research of Wilma Bucci (1997, 2005, 2007) offer practicing psychotherapists, counselors, and trainers models of practical value.

Steven Weinberg (2001), a particle physicist, wrote an essay entitled "Can Science Explain Everything? Anything?" In it he wrestled with the nature of scientific explanation, scientific description, and the nature of "cause," arguing that clear descriptions of phenomena are often confused with explanations of causal forces. These are not equivalent. A strong theoretical description may help us understand something more clearly, but it does not necessarily explain or validate the phenomenon described. Weinberg stressed the difference of the nature of phenomena typically explored in physics in contrast to things studied in other disciplines:

Biologists, meteorologists, historians, and so on are concerned with the causes of individual events, such as the extinction of dinosaurs, the blizzard of 1998, the French Revolution, etc., while a physicist only becomes interested in an event, like the fogging of Becquerel's photographic plates that in 1897 were left in the vicinity of a salt of uranium, when the event reveals a regularity of nature, such as the instability of the uranium atom. Philip Kitcher has tried to revive the idea that the way to explain an event is by reference to its cause, but which of the infinite number of things that could affect an event should be regarded as its cause? (p. 47)

Psychotherapy is an enterprise of infinite variables—two (and sometimes more) people in a room, communicating with conscious and unconscious motivations, working in a context of the myriad of people outside the room (present and past) with expectations (overt and covert) of these two people who are trying to make sense of the client's emotional and relational patterns—and it is not easily or elegantly reduced to cause and effect. "Empirical support" can create as much illusion and false reassurance as it can certainty and validation. Weinberg (2001) continued:

Further, science can never explain any moral principle. There seems to be an unbridgeable gulf between "is" questions and "ought" questions. The moral postulates that tell us whether we should or should not do so cannot be deduced from our scientific knowledge. (p. 50)

Psychotherapists live in the gaps among "ises" and "oughts" and "maybes," between certainty and uncertainty, the realms of ambiguity and ambivalence. At the same time, the wish to see clearly, to know, and to understand are inherent in the role of the therapist, the trainer, and the teacher. The *Transactional Analysis Journal* has had what I suspect is a rather unusual privilege, that of having two former scientists as editors. Tony Tilney and Ted Novey, as scientists and therapists, convey a scientific attitude, an attitude toward investigation and exploration, that is richly relevant to the tasks of psychotherapy. Tony said that all the great innovators in psychology have been dedicated investigators but few have been good researchers. Berne was a great investigator. His work inspired many and has been taken up, examined, challenged, and reworked by three generations of transactional analysis practitioners. Our work now is not as Berne thought it or practiced it. This, too, is a form of investigating, understanding, and skill development that does not reflect the empirical research paradigms. However, it constitutes a valid form of discovery and verification.

On Clinical Presentations

For many years I published theoretical and technical articles with no case material beyond brief, illustrative vignettes. Presenting substantial case material had always felt to me like a violation of a client's personal privacy and the intimacy of the therapeutic relationship, more of an issue for me of privacy than confidentiality, per se. Reich himself published lengthy, brilliant case discussions on the treatment of schizophrenic, masochistic, hysteric, and impulsive character pathologies (the impulsive character being a thinly veiled autobiographical reflection on his own character). As I have sought to write to a broader clinical audience of diverse disciplines, I have been challenged to write detailed case presentations. In so doing, I have had to examine my reservations about the publication of case material.

Glen Gabbard's (2000) "Disguise or Consent: Problems and Recommendations Concerning the Publication and Presentation of Clinical Material" is a deeply thought-provoking article. Gabbard, a psychoanalyst at the Menninger Clinic, has written extensively on a broad range of ethical dilemmas in psychoanalysis and psychotherapy. While I do not always agree with him, his writing always causes me to think and challenge my own frame of reference. This particular article of Gabbard's has been especially evocative and instructive to me.

Gabbard and the other authors grapple with the competing and often conflicting goals of protecting a client's confidentiality while making use of case material in teaching and publishing. As I read Gabbard's article, I thought about my experience not only as an author but as a trainer, supervisor, supervisee, and client. How have I learned as a psychotherapist? How do I come to "know" something? There are multiple modes of learning. My clinical knowledge is shaped, enlivened, and limited by my experience as a client and trainee. My clinical work is informed, challenged, and constantly altered by my reading. I am a member of a peer study group that meets weekly, alternating month-long, detailed case presentations with reading and discussing contemporary literature.

Perhaps more than anything else, my work has been shaped by my ongoing supervision. I have always remained in individual consultation or therapy, always with a therapist who works from a different frame of reference than my own. I consulted with the same man for more than 10 years. It has deeply influenced how I work with people, how I bring myself to clients, what I expect of myself and my clients. All of this has required careful self-examination in the midst of presenting detailed case material presented in a way that protects the privacy of my clients. Currently, I am making arrangements for supervision with an analyst trained within the French traditions of psychoanalysis.

As a supervisor and trainer for many years now, I have been aware of the complex issues of ensuring client privacy and confidentiality while supporting therapists' clinical learning. I have been in practice in a relatively small city for 35 years now. I am well known not only as a therapist, but also as a trainer and supervisor. Probably one-third or more of my clients are themselves practicing psychotherapists. The assurance of confidentiality is an absolute necessity. Successful psychotherapy and psychotherapy supervision require a unique combination of privacy and openness, which are not always easy bedfellows. In the letter outlining the structure and limits of my practice, which I give clients at the start of their work with me, I state that I am in weekly consultation and may, on occasion, discuss our work with my supervisor. I present my cases for supervision in a way that carefully guards the identity of the client; it is the dynamic of the therapy not the facts of a client's life that are at the heart of supervision. My clients who are themselves therapists sometimes ask whom I see for consultation. This is information I share freely. Sometimes clients know him as a colleague and ask that I not discuss their therapy with him. I always respect that, agreeing that if I need consultation I will seek it with a colleague out of state.

Presenting case material for supervision is substantially different from presenting case material for publication. The supervisory relationship is, in and of itself, confidential, an additional layer of protection for the client. The supervision is focused on behalf of the client, to deepen an understanding of the client and to improve the work, while the publication of case material serves a different agenda. Supervision addresses the issues and competence of the therapist first and foremost. When my consultant confronts my enmeshment with a client in order to avoid conflict—"Bill, this is shitty psychotherapy. You know that. You know better than this. Stop it. Speak to what needs to be addressed." —he is talking about me, not my client. When he confronts my tendency to tolerate and absorb endless sessions of rage from a client, he may be addressing the client's motivations and conflicts, but he will be primarily addressing my script, my persistent countertransference, my characterological blind spots, my grandiosity. Nevertheless, clients can experience great vulnerability and/or anxious projection in the face of knowing that their work is being discussed with someone they do not know.

Presenting case material for publication or professional education, a primary mode within the clinical tradition, creates a complex web of issues. The most obvious difference is that this material goes into a permanent and public record, a very different context from private consultation. The selection of a particular client to discuss in professional writing can reflect a myriad of conscious and unconscious motivations. The fact is, case material in the professional literature tends to be self-serving.

We have had a long-standing tradition in transactional analysis supervision and certification examinations of using audio tapes of actual therapy sessions. Would an exam board sanction the presentation of a tape of a treatment failure to foster a frank discussion of what went wrong and to support the capacity for real clinical judgment and self-assessment? I think not. These days we prepare our trainees carefully to foster clinically sanitized tapes demonstrating textbook transactional analysis.

It is also rather rare to see a clinical article presented with case material that both supports and challenges the author's perspective. Case failures are rarely written up in the professional literature, although a number of recent psychoanalytic articles have presented some exceptionally frank and reflective discussions of therapeutic failures. In Gabbard's (2000) article, he noted that

many of us write in an effort to master complex and difficult counter-transference situations in our clinical work. Adverse consequences from published case material may in some cases reflect our own unanalyzed hostility towards the patient we choose to use as a clinical example. (p. 1076)

I would add to Gabbard's mention of unanalyzed hostility a brief list of the possibilities of unexamined overidentification, guilt and reparation, idealization, affection, narcissism, or self-aggrandizing exploitation as possible motivations for selecting a particular client for publication. The list could undoubtedly be longer. Decisions to publish work with a particular client are not casual decisions or decisions not without consequence.

Gabbard (2000) spoke eloquently to tensions between guarding "the privacy inherent in privileged communications" while allowing "free exchange of information for psychoanalysis to develop as a science" (p. 1072). He offered no simple solutions or cookbook recommendations, which is part of his eloquence. He outlined five strategies for dealing with these issues: (1) thickly disguising the patient's actual identity and external circumstance while preserving the scientific integrity and clinical veracity of the material; (2) sharing the material to be published with the patient and securing the patient's informed consent; (3) use of actual process records, transcript or session notes, of actual sessions with little or no identifying information about the patient; (4) use of composites of the clinical material drawn from several clients, organized around common clinical issues; and (5) use of a colleague as author, typically a consultant or supervisor, ensuring the complete anonymity of both therapist and patient. Each of these strategies has its limitations and liabilities, conscious and unconscious, ethical and clinical. Each needs to be carefully considered within the contexts of the clinical needs and vulnerabilities of the individual client, the motivations of the author, the context of the professional presentation or publication, and the intention of the article. Gabbard's essay is not only a thoughtful discussion of publication-related issues, it is also a thoughtful reflection on the nature of the therapeutic process and therapists' motivations.

Since originally writing the pieces on which this chapter is based, I discovered the research and writing of Judith Kantrowitz (1996, 2006) on the impact of patients on their therapists and on the risks and responsibilities of therapists writing about their patients. She offers no easy solutions, no lists of do's and don't's. She demonstrates what good close-to-the-subject, clinical research offers: thought-provoking questions rather than proscribed answers and conclusions. Anyone involved in training, supervision, or case writing will profit from studying her books.

REFERENCES

Alvarez, A. (2000). Discussion II. In J. Sandler, A-M. Sandler, & R. Davies (Eds.), *Clinical and observational psychoanalytic research: Roots of a controversy* (pp. 100-107). Madison, CT: International Universities Press.

Berne, E. (1961). *Transactional analysis in psychotherapy: A systematic individual and social psychiatry.* New York: Grove Press.

Beck, A. T., Freeman, A., & Associates. (1990). *Cognitive therapy of personality disorders.* New York: Guilford Press.

Bucci, W. (1997). *Psychoanalysis and cognitive science.* New York: Guilford Press.
Bucci, W. (2005). Basic concepts and methods of psychoanalytic process research. In E. Person, A. Cooper, & G. Gabbard (Eds.), *Textbook of psychoanalysis* (pp. 339-355). Washington, DC: American Psychiatric Press.
Bucci, W. (2007). Four domains of therapeutic discourse. *Psychoanalytic Inquiry, 27,* 617-639.
Gabbard, G. (2000). Disguise or consent?: Problems and recommendations concerning the publication and presentation of clinical material. *The Internationnal Journal of Psycho-Analysis, 81,* 1071-1086.
Garfield, S. L. (1998). Some comments on empirically supported treatments. *Journal of Consulting and Clinical Psychology, 66* (1), 121-125.
Green, A. (2000a). Science and science fiction in infant research. In J. Sandler, A-M. Sandler, & R. Davies (Eds.), *Clinical and observational psychoanalytic research: Roots of a controversy* (pp. 41-72). Madison, CT: International Universities Press.
Green, A. (2000b). What kind of research for psychoanalysis? In J. Sandler, A-M. Sandler, & R. Davies (Eds.), *Clinical and observational psychoanalytic research: Roots of a controversy* (pp. 21-26). Madison, CT: International Universities Press.
Kantrowitz, J. L. (1996). *The patient's impact on the analyst.* Hillsdale, NJ: The Analytic Press.
Kantrowitz, J. L. (2006). *Writing about patients: Responsibilities, risks, and ramifications.* New York: Other Press.
Sandler, J., Sandler, A-M., & Davies, R. (Eds). (2000). *Clinical and observational psychoanalytic research: Roots of a controversy* (Monograph No. 5). Madison, CT: International Universities Press.
Stern, D. N. (2000). The relevance of empirical infant research to psychoanalytic theory and practice. In J. Sandler, A-M. Sandler, & R. Davies (Eds.), *Clinical and observational psychoanalytic research: Roots of a controversy* (pp. 73-90). Madison, CT: International Universities Press.
Talley, P. F., Strupp, H. H., & Butler, S. F. (1994). *Psychotherapy research and practice: Bridging the gap.* New York: Basic Books.
Task Force on Promotion and Dissemination of Psychological Procedures. (1995). Training in and dissemination of empirically-validated treatments: Reports and recommendations. *The Clinical Psychologist, 48*(1), 3-23.
Toukmanian, S. G., & Rennie, D. L. (Eds.). (1992). *Psychotherapy process research: Paradigmatic and narrative approaches.* Newbury Park, CA: Sage.
Weinberg, S. (2001). Can science explain everything? Anything? *New York Review of Books, XLVIII*(9), 47-50.

This chapter is based on three previously published articles: "Standing Within the Clinical Tradition," The Script, Volume 31, Number 4, pp. 1, 2, May-June 2004; "Seeking Empirical Validation (Woof!)," The Script, Volume 31, Number 5, pp. 2, 3, July 2001; and "On Learning, Knowing, and Telling: Further Reflections on Clinical Research and Case Studies," The Script, Volume 31, Number 6, pp. 2, 3, August 2001.

Touch and Boundaries in Transactional Analysis: Ethical and Transferential Considerations

William F. Cornell

The use of direct body contact between therapist and client is common in contemporary transactional analysis, although that was not always the case (for a review of this issue in the transactional analysis literature, see Cornell & Olio, 1992, which is Chapter 17 in this volume). While the ITAA Code of Ethics (2002) requires "providing for physical safety appropriate to the form of activity involved, and obtaining informed consent for high-risk procedures," there is no ethical sanction of or prohibition against transactional analysis therapists touching their clients, nor is there any requirement for specific training or demonstration of competence in the use of body-centered interventions.

A similar stance was adopted by the American Counseling Association, which formed a Body Therapy Network (Goodstone, 1993). Physical contact techniques most often used in the practice of transactional analysis reflect some variation of corrective parenting, sensory stimulation, rebirthing, neo-Reichian work, or other body-centered techniques. The most explicit accounts of physical interventions involve the adjunctive use of bioenergetic theory and technique. Cassius (1975, 1980) attempted a thoughtful integration of transactional analysis and bioenergetic theory, especially with regard to the understanding of characterological structure; he took the use of touch for granted. In contrast, Childs-Gowell and Kinnaman (1978) presented the use of highly stimulating and intrusive techniques—calling them "a transactional approach to body awareness"—in a way that was crude in its understanding of bioenergetic and neo-Reichian work and offered virtually no regard for the possible impact of such interventions on a varied client population. The use of touch in transactional analysis is a technical choice, and yet, unfortunately, there is no theory of touch as such in the transactional analysis literature.

As the practice of psychotherapy, at least in the United States, becomes increasingly rule- and litigation-bound, using touch in the therapeutic process puts the therapist at risk: "Safety" and "boundary" issues become paramount, all too often overriding theoretical and clinical questions. I vividly recall a panel discussion entitled "The Seductive Boundary" at an American Group Psychotherapy Conference some years ago, during which a forensic psychiatrist stated bluntly that if a therapist is sued and had touched the client in session, regardless of whether or not touch was at issue in the lawsuit, the therapist would lose the case. During that same panel, a psychoanalyst stated without equivocation that there was no clinical rationale to justify a therapist touching a client and that the therapist's use of touch was typically countertransferential acting out.

There has been a long-standing and rather curious split between language-centered and body-centered therapeutic approaches in attitudes toward the use of physical contact with clients. In the Reichian and neo-Reichian traditions, the therapist's use of touch is taken for granted, and clients' "negative" reactions to direct physical contact tend to be viewed as resistant or defensive. Among approaches to psychotherapy that rely primarily or exclusively on talking for communication and therapeutic change, especially those with a psychoanalytic base, there is little or no theoretical attention paid to the therapeutic possibilities of physical contact between therapist and client. Beyond the question of a handshake in greeting or at the end of a session, the complex, potentially rich issues of touch in the therapy process are too often dismissed with the advice (or rule): "Don't."

Approaches to psychotherapy that are predominantly analytic or cognitive in orientation are typically asomatic: Cognitive and relational experiences are the primary focus of attention and mode of expression within the theory and the therapy. With remarkably few exceptions, Freud's discomfort with and prohibitions against touch have been incorporated as unquestioned doctrine. A recent, but by no means unusual, example can be found in the Scharffs' *Object Relations Therapy of Physical and Sexual Trauma* (Scharff & Scharff, 1994). The Scharffs stated explicitly that

> we focus on the direct impact to the body in family life. We look at the effects of domestic personal violence on the child.... We also look at impersonal violence to the body of the newborn, the child, the adolescent, and the adult in the form of sudden or massive body part destruction over which the child or adult has no control. (pp. 23-24)

But in discussing treatment, they take the position that "we do not use physical touch to express our intentions, but convey through our attitude of dedication to the therapeutic task that we are holding the patient in the mind" (p. 67). No ethical, clinical, or theoretical explanation is given for this position; the reader, and presumably the client, is to take this on faith.

In the vast bulk of the psychoanalytic literature—a literature that is immensely rich and stimulating in so many regards—the body and its place in the therapeutic process receive scant attention, even as the understanding of affect is becoming increasingly central in contemporary analytic theory (Ablon, Brown, Khantzian, & Mack, 1993; Krystal & Krystal, 1988; Shapiro & Emde, 1992). Even among those analytic theorists who write about the body and psychosomatic issues (Fast, 1992; Kramer & Akhtar, 1992; Krueger, 1989; McDougall, 1989; Stolorow & Atwood, 1991), the body and nonverbal expression are discussed largely as a presymbolic or traumatic means of communication; direct physical contact between therapist and client is not discussed or used. One is left with the impression that neither the client nor the therapist has a body in session, that the body should somehow be tucked quietly away until the therapeutic hour is over. Analytic theory worries that touch is gratifying, although anyone touched by a bioenergetic therapist or orgonomist is not likely to find the contact gratifying or comforting with any remote consistency. "Gratification" is rarely the intent of the physical interventions of a Reichian-oriented therapist.

Within the psychoanalytic tradition, those theorists who advocated and used direct physical contact with clients (e.g., Reich or Ferenczi) have either been largely marginalized and discredited or viewed as using limited and unusual interventions for highly disturbed and regressed clients (Dupont, 1988; Ferenczi, 1930; Goodman & Teicher, 1988; Little, 1990; Rachman, 1993). These provocative and often controversial cases are seen as exceptions that have little to do with the true work of psychoanalysis or psychodynamic psychotherapies. The potential lessons they suggest are ignored, apparently irrelevant for more "normal" clients. There is virtually no systematic, coherent exploration or questioning, ethically or clinically, about this issue in the psychoanalytic literature.

Within the psychodynamic/humanistic literature, Johnson (1985, 1987), Smith (1985), Kepner (1987), and Kertay and Reviere (1993) present careful clinical and ethical perspectives on incorporating direct body contact in ongoing psychotherapy. Transactional analysts will, I believe, find Johnson's work particularly instructive and readily incorporated into the transactional analysis framework.

Approaches to bodywork and many body therapies are too often arelational. Massage, Rolfing, and Feldenkrais work, among other somatic therapies, emphasize the client's experience of and relationship to his or her own body; the experience of relatedness with the therapist is secondary and sometimes even irrelevant to the work. The touch of the practitioner (teacher, worker) is a necessary and facilitating skill, not a means toward relationship. For example, Reich's work was based on drive theory—the notion of instinctual energy, libido, orgone, Radix; he paid little attention to the therapeutic relationship. Reich's primary attention was to the patient's "relationship" (expression, tolerance, resistance) to his or her own drives. Reichian and bioenergetic theory and technique pay close attention to body and character structure but, until recently, little to the relational and transferential aspects of therapy.

There are crucial, enduring ethical and clinical issues always present when touch is an aspect of psychotherapy. Kertay and Reviere (1993) stated:

> The matter of touch is so important and so pervasive that the question may not be whether or not therapists *should* touch their patients, but rather *how* touch is utilized and processed in therapy. Where there is agreement in the literature, it is clear that therapists who utilize touch must be clear about their own motivations and must take full responsibility for their own and their patient's responses to touch. To ensure the requisite awareness and responsibility, we recommend ongoing supervision or peer consultation for the therapist who utilizes touch as a significant part of the psychotherapeutic process. (p. 39)

Even when a client has specifically sought a body-centered psychotherapist or bodyworker, the therapist should not take the use of touch for granted. It is the central premise of this chapter that each time a therapist touches a client, history (bad and good), affect, and desire (often transferential) are simultaneously evoked. It is clear to me that the use of physical contact in psychotherapy requires something different—and often something more—of the therapist than is often required in cognitive and verbal modes of therapy.

Something of which I am constantly and keenly aware as a body-centered psychotherapist is that I am working against cultural (and often professional) norms. As a teenager, I was first drawn to Reich's work because he wrote with passion and encouraged the passions of his patients. He railed against normality, conformity, resignation. He paid a high price for his passionate intent throughout his career, from one political/cultural environment to another. In an interview discussing the evolution and principles of Bodynamic psychotherapy, Lisbeth Marcher, founder of this approach, said:

> The worst thing about character structure is it limits our ability to be in mutual connection with ourselves, with others and the world; it keeps us from being able to commit to life. Here I am a bit like Reich. I think Reich chose life. He did it at great cost to himself, but he still did everything he could to be alive. He did it in spite of his character. And his vision of character as *armor*, as something between us and life, still contains a core of truth for me. . . . At its core, therapy should be a radical process for each person who undertakes it. It should disturb our own individual status quo. . . . We are both very political, but he had to work against his culture, and I have had the luxury of being able to work with mine (Danish). Wars are the stupidest expression of character, of choosing power over life. Maybe we both learned something from being witness to that. (Bernhardt & Marcher, 1995, pp. 35-36)

In going against cultural norms as professionals and in evoking through touch the impact of cultural as well as familial restrictions in our clients, we create heightened vulnerabilities for them and for ourselves. We risk professional and cultural sanction. Body-centered psychotherapies are evocative, intimate, and rather precarious for client and therapist alike. Boadella (1991) presented a provocative history and discussion of issues concerning the professional vulnerabilities, competitiveness, and power/authority problems in the evolution of the somatic psychotherapies.

Ethical Fundamentals

One of the most fundamental safeguards in body-centered psychotherapy is that the use of physical contact can be called into question by either the client or the therapist at any point in the process. The client always has the right to say "no" to being touched. The therapist may have questions about the "no," but it is respected first and discussed (possibly interpreted or confronted) later. The use of physical contact is not resumed without the client's understanding and agreement.

Goodman and Teicher (1988) summarized the findings and conclusions of Gelb's 1982 research with a small sample of women clients who experienced nonerotic touch in the course of their psychotherapy. Gelb found positive outcome to be correlated with the following factors:

1) Patient and therapist discussed the "touch event," the boundaries of the relationship, and the actual or potential sexual feelings; 2) The patient felt in control of initiating and sustaining

contact; 3) Contact was not experienced as a demand or need satisfying for the therapist; 4) The overall expectations of the treatment were congruent with the patient's experience of the treatment; 5) The emotional and physical intimacy were congruent. (p. 496)

Beyond the permission to say "no," there needs to be an overt acknowledgment that there are unique vulnerabilities in working this way, a vulnerability to the work itself as well as to one's own personal issues. The therapist needs to say and demonstrate from the beginning that nonverbal experience can and needs to be talked about. The mind is not the body's enemy. The body is not the enemy of the mind. Language can deepen experience and contact rather than substitute for it or distract from it. Language is brought to the body, and the body is brought into language.

Touch, Relatedness, and Transference

In my frame of reference, it is an essential ethical and clinical safeguard that any psychotherapist or counselor using direct physical contact with clients is trained in and responsive to transference and countertransference issues. The use of touch will evoke, address, and hopefully help correct such historical experiences and distortions as:

- Deprivation and neglect
- Overstimulation, intrusion and bodily violation, or sexualization
- Parental narcissistic use of the child
- Deadening of vitality and use of the body as an instrument

These chronic historical distortions of body experience will emerge within both the bodily and the interpersonal processes in therapy, and the responsible therapist actively attends to both. The use of physical contact in psychotherapy inevitably intensifies a client's experience of the emotional relationship with the therapist. For most individuals this is both good and bad news; it involves the hope for acceptance and change paired with the dread of reexperiencing the failures and damage of earlier love and caretaking relationships. To actively engage our clients in the midst of their hopes and their dreads, we must attend directly to both interpersonal and body processes and open ourselves to emotional struggle and learning with our clients. It is a bit too easy for body-centered therapists to avoid the emotional demands and their own vulnerabilities in depth work by primarily attending to the body as though it were a thing (counterpulsation, character structure, muscular armor, anorgonia, underboundedness, etc.), thus subtly blaming the body and depersonalizing the work.

For example, a client with a pervasive developmental history of neglect and deprivation may present with a "pain structure" or schizoid character. The therapist will come to observe the various ways that such a client may have learned to live in spite of rather than through his or her body, often turning against the body and any experience of need. Clearly, there will be crucial work to be done at a body level, and the body will defend itself against itself in a variety of physiological and characterological ways. It is also likely that this client may openly or secretly wish for a relationship with the body therapist that is parental, attentive, nurturing, and enlivening. The body therapist's willingness and capacity for resonance and relatedness will be every bit as therapeutic as the body-level interventions. Each can enhance the other. The therapist's touch will likely simultaneously excite and threaten this client. Such a client will also likely project an attitude of disinterest or disgust onto the therapist. It will become a challenge and the responsibility of the therapist to remain emotionally engaged and responsive in the face of negative transference and countertransference reactions, in the midst of the client's withdrawal and avoidance.

In a different but common example, a client who was the object of a parent's narcissistic use may experience the therapist's touch and interventions as a demand and an intent more important than the client's own experience or needs. The work at a body level may become mechanical, a kind of performance—an effort/task done for the other (now the therapist rather than the parent) rather than an experience and expression of the self. Bodywork for these clients may be literally work—an endeavor to earn the therapist's attention, to preserve the relationship, to avoid criticism, to be a good client. Or, a complete reversal may emerge in which the therapist—his or her contact, effort, energy, and feelings—becomes an object for the client's use. There is no personal relationship as such but rather operations between useful instruments of need or desire. Both body and person (of either the client or the therapist) become depersonalized and objectified. Such attitudes and patterns may emerge within the transference relationship, but they are at greater risk of further reification when touch and body-centered techniques are used.

These relational/transferential reactions will and should emerge in any therapeutic process. In more conventional, language-based modalities, transference and deeper affect will most likely emerge slowly, subtly, and at a level of affect that can be gradually observed and more readily tolerated by both therapist and client. In body therapy these reactions can be evoked unexpectedly, often before there is a firm foundation of relationship and language and with more affective intensity than is common in conventional modalities. The therapist's use of touch will deepen the client's experience of bodily experience and relational needs. The client will need the therapist's emotional resonance and competence to allow the emergence and expression of the remembered and projected relational and bodily failures not only through emotional discharge, but in interpersonal contact. The transferential relationship, if permitted, will not only evoke the scars of the past but enable the wishes and desires of the future.

Touch and Boundaries: Contact and Differentiation

Boundaries are a big deal these days in the world of psychotherapy. Increasingly, the expectation (especially in the United States) is that therapy should be free of risk and disappointment. This attitude is encroaching subtly but profoundly on the practice of therapy and the expectations clients may bring to the work. "Watch out!" "Be careful." "Not too much now." "The world is a dangerous place." "If someone disappoints or hurts you, retaliate. It's your right as an American." Say no to drugs (unless prescribed by a physician—6 million on Prozac at last count). Our clients can't take too much. Say no to clients: "We can't touch; it's too confusing for you." "You can't know about me as a person or have multiple aspects to this relationship, it's probably too much for you." "Don't worry (or think or struggle); I'll keep you safe." Safety first.

Reich (1983) observed tellingly in his article "The Source of the Human 'No'," that it is in the experience of the mother's "no" to the infant, in her rejection, rigidity, coldness, anxiety, and detachment through her skin and touch, that the child begins to turn against his or her own body, sacrificing the capacity for physical and relational vitality long before the development of language. Reich articulated and confronted the social/cultural amplification and enforcement of these primary "no's." Often what brings a client to a body-centered psychotherapist is the accumulation of lifelong experiences of the unspoken/unspeakable "no's" that have deadened the person's vitality and capacity to say "yes" or "I want." What happens if we become so cautious in our approach to and contact with clients that we contribute more to deadening than to awareness and enlivening?

When we touch clients we often evoke their most fundamental and damaging experiences of physical and relational contact. And yet, through competent and informed touch, we have the opportunity to offer an experience at a body level of both contact and differentiation, of excitement and limits. The experience of touch is essential in the formation of bodily and interpersonal boundaries. Skin, the body's largest organ, best exemplifies the nature and function of boundaries: The skin is a semipermeable membrane that covers and protects, forming a barrier against the environment while at the same time allowing a deeply sensate experience of it. There seems to be a developmental sequence of a gradually expanding process of boundary formation and activity: skin contact and parental holding, muscular and bodily movement, evolving bodily independence and competence, interpersonal differentiation and relatedness. Healthy boundaries are firm but permeable and negotiable. Healthy boundaries are alive and relational, not constrictive and isolating (Boadella, 1986; Cornell & Olio, 1992; Greenspan, 1995).

Kepner (1987, p. 168), in his integration of gestalt theory and body-centered therapy, offered a succinct and elegant synopsis of the function of boundaries as rooted in body process: (1) the maintenance of difference, (2) the rejection of danger, (3) coping with obstacles, and (4) the selection and appropriation of assimilable novelty. Each of these boundary functions has physical and interpersonal dimensions. In the capacity to maintain difference, there is the bodily ability to feel (and thus know): "This is good for me, that is bad"; "I like this, I don't like that." It also comes to represent the interpersonal capacity to differentiate me from not-me, self from other. Warding off danger involves the body/person's capacity to act by either withdrawing or fighting, to say and enforce, "Stop, enough, no." The physical and physiological boundaries that evolve as a child copes with tolerating frustration and disappointment, overcoming obstacles, and regulating the pace and intensity of new sensations and activity lay the foundation for a growing sense of mastery, the body ego evolving into an interpersonal ego.

It is my opinion that most conventional and analytic psychotherapies play it too "safe" (rigid) with issues of touch in the therapeutic process. I fear that in the name of protecting clients, therapists all too readily infantilize them and deprive them of opportunities for contact, struggle, conflict, differentiation, and mastery through the body. If it is assumed that touching a client is always bad, unethical, sexually or countertransferentially motivated, or simply too risky, clients are not invited forward into contact at a body level. I fear then that the psychological ego, the ego of the mind, must again substitute or compensate for an impoverished, fragile, skin/body ego.

If, on the other hand, it is assumed that touch is good, if it is taken for granted, if the client must say "yes," and if any "no" represents defense and resistance, then we risk the unnecessary wounding of our clients. Clients—especially those with abusive, traumatic, or narcissistic histories—will too likely adapt to the therapist's expectations, thus deadening or dissociating from their own bodily experiences, which will at times be of "no" or "not now." Differentiation and boundedness may be sacrificed yet again for contact or to avoid conflict. It is through the therapist's consistent and informed attention to both bodily and interpersonal boundaries that we can facilitate an embodied exploration of both "yes" and "no."

Touch, Structure, Mastery, and Ego Development

The maturational relationship between the body ego and the psychological ego is evident in Kepner's (1987) and other gestalt theorists' discussions of boundaries and boundedness. Within the neo-Reichian literature, Boadella (1986) and Kelemann (1979, 1989) emphasized the formative processes in a child's development and in the therapeutic process. Marcher (Bernhardt & Marcher, 1995) and her Bodynamic colleagues emphasized "resourcing" and ego strength, through which the capacity develops to manage frustration and overcome obstacles in an embodied way without losing contact with one's needs or the environment. Winnicott (1965) insisted that parents must sometimes fail for children to mature, that a healthy child develops the capacity for an essential aloneness as well as for object relatedness. This is a realm of growing technical and theoretical understanding in the neo-Reichian therapies and transactional analysis theory.

In the early stages of body-centered psychotherapy with a client, the therapist's physical contact and relatedness serves a variety of primary functions: initiating, nurturing, supporting, holding, containing, deepening, focusing. Within the evolving realms of mastery and ego development, the therapist's use of physical contact and the therapeutic relationship itself will increasingly provide more of a facilitating process than a holding environment. In this phase of the work, the therapist is likely to do far less, instead creating a space—Winnicott's potential space—within which the client can do and be more. At both a bodily level and in the relational/transferential processes, this later phase is a likely time for the client to initiate, to reach out and sustain contact, to demand something different/more of himself or herself and the therapist. Body-level work will increasingly involve strengthening and supporting movement into the world without disruption to or loss of relatedness. Physical contact will be used to facilitate increasingly the client's capacity to organize and sustain emotional and interpersonal structure. The informed use of touch remains crucial. This phase of treatment can evoke a range of bodily and transferential issues: emotional abandonment during the separation/individuation phase; a parent's narcissistic withdrawal or withholding; the loneliness of the latency years; the rage and awkwardness of adolescence; and the all-too-common substitution of competence and pseudoindependence for contact, intimacy, and dependence. Transferential issues of loss and abandonment reemerge in the maturing therapeutic relationship because the excitement and anxiety of growing up and moving on is so often accompanied by a profound sense of loss, often endured in silence. If a body-centered therapist attends only or primarily to the physical and energetic processes of separation and maturation, the loss of relationship may again be unintentionally recreated and pass unnoticed.

Through the continued use of touch, the therapist can more clearly communicate empathy and continued involvement while directly supporting increasing autonomy and activity. The therapist communicates and demonstrates at a body level that relatedness and closeness do not have to be sacrificed for competence and autonomy.

Conclusion

It is my hope that this chapter will serve as a stimulus for self-reflection, discussion, and argument. As I come to its end, I feel as though I have written a very "American" paper, one filled with the issues and concerns (phobias?) of contemporary psychotherapy in the United States. Having the good fortune to work within an international community of therapists, I am aware that some of the issues raised here are seen quite differently in Europe and South America, where touch carries different meanings from those often attributed to it in the United States. There is, for instance, a pan-European organization for body-centered psychotherapists. An important discussion could ensue with regard to the meaning of touch, with the ethical and transferential/ countertransferential implications, in psychotherapy in various cultures.

This chapter is an effort to underscore the unique opportunities and vulnerabilities that accompany the use of touch in the therapeutic process. It is my hope that therapists assess the appropriateness of touch from a position of clinical, ethical, and transferential awareness rather than from one informed by theoretical doctrine alone. Particular attention is paid here to the heightening of transferential issues through the use of touch. This chapter presents a discussion of the impact of the therapist's use of physical contact on the client's evolving patterns of dependency, relatedness, interpersonal and emotional differentiation, and mastery.

REFERENCES

Ablon, S. L., Brown, D., Khantzian, E. J., & Mack, J. E. (1993). *Human feelings: Explorations in affect development and meaning.* Hillsdale, NJ: The Analytic Press.
Bernhardt, P., & Marcher, L. (1995). *The art of following structure: Exploring the roots of the bodynamic system.* Berkeley, CA: Unpublished manuscript.
Boadella, D. (1986). What is biosynthesis? *Energy & Character, 17*(2), 1-23.
Boadella, D. (1991). Organism and organisation: The place of somatic psychotherapy in society. *Energy & Character, 22,* 1-58.
Cassius, J. (1975). *Bodyscripts: Collected papers on physical aspects of transactional analysis.* Memphis, TN: Author.
Cassius, J. (Ed.). (1980). *Horizons in bioenergetics: New dimensions in mind/body psychotherapy.* Memphis, TN: Promethean Publications.
Childs-Gowell, E., & Kinnaman, P. (1978). *Bodyscript blockbusting: A transactional approach to body awareness.* San Francisco: Trans Pubs.
Cornell, W. F., & Olio, K. A. (1992). Consequences of childhood bodily abuse: A clinical model for affective interventions. *Transactional Analysis Journal, 22,* 131-143.
Dupont, J. (Ed.). (1988). *The clinical diary of Sandor Ferenczi* (M. Balint & N. Z. Jackson, Trans.). Cambridge, MA: Harvard University Press.
Fast, I. (1992). The embodied mind: Toward a relational perspective. *Psychoanalytic Dialogues, 2*(3), 389-410.
Ferenczi, S. (1930). The principle of relaxation and neocathexis. *International Journal of Psychoanalysis, 30,* 428-446.
Goodman, M., & Teicher, A. (1988). To touch or not to touch. *Psychotherapy, 25,* 492-500.
Goodstone, E. (1993, March). Defining body therapy. *The Advocate,* 12.
Greenspan, M. (1995, July/August). Out of bounds. *Common Boundary,* 51.
International Transactional Analysis Association. (2002). *The ITAA code of ethics.* San Francisco, CA: Author.
Johnson, S. M. (1985). *Characterological transformation: The hard work miracle.* New York: Norton.
Johnson, S. M. (1987). *Humanizing the narcissistic style.* New York: Norton.
Keleman, S. (1979). *Somatic reality.* Berkeley, CA: Center Press.
Keleman, S. (1989). *Patterns of distress: Emotional insults and human form.* Berkeley, CA: Center Press.
Kepner, J. I. (1987). *Body process: A gestalt approach to working with the body in psychotherapy.* New York: Gestalt Institute of Cleveland Press.

Kertay, L., & Reviere, S. L. (1993). The use of touch in psychotherapy: Theoretical and ethical considerations. *Psychotherapy, 30,* 32-40.
Kramer, S., & Akhter, S. (Eds.). (1992). *When the body speaks: Psychological meanings and kinetic clues.* Northvale, NJ: Jason Aronson.
Krueger, D. W. (1989). *Body self and psychological self: A developmental and clinical integration of disorders of the self.* New York: Brunner/Mazel.
Krystal, H., & Krystal, J. H. (1988). *Integration and self-healing: Affect, trauma, alexithymia.* Hillsdale, NJ: The Analytic Press.
Little, M. I. (1990). *Psychotic anxieties and containment: A personal record of an analysis with Winnicott.* Northvale, NJ: Jason Aronson.
McDougall, J. (1989). *Theaters of the body: A psychoanalytic approach to psychosomatic illness.* New York: Norton.
Rachman, A. (1993). Ferenczi and sexuality. In L. Aron & A. Harris (Eds.), *The legacy of Sandor Ferenczi* (pp. 81-100). Hillsdale, NJ: The Analytic Press.
Reich, W. (1983). *Children of the future.* New York: Farrar, Straus & Giroux.
Scharff, J. S., & Scharff, D. E. (1994). *Object relations therapy of physical and sexual trauma.* Northvale, NJ: Jason Aronson.
Shapiro, T., & Emde, R. N. (Ed.). (1992). *Affect: Psychoanalytic perspectives.* Madison, CT: International Universities Press.
Smith, E. (1985). *The body in psychotherapy.* Jefferson, NC: McFarland.
Stolorow, R. D., & Atwood, G. E. (1991). The mind and the body. *Psychoanalytic Dialogues, 1*(2), 181-195.
Winnicott, D. W. (1965). *The maturational processes and the facilitating environment: Studies in the theory of emotional development.* Madison, WI: International Universities Press.

The original version of this chapter was published in the Transactional Analysis Journal, *Volume 27, Number 1, pp. 30-37, January 1997.*

Boundaries or Barriers: Who Is Protecting Whom? A Personal Essay/Book Review

William F. Cornell

When Boundaries Betray Us: Beyond Illusions of What Is Ethical in Therapy and Life
 by Carter Heyward (HarperSanFrancisco, 1993)

The Power of Countertransference: Innovations in Analytic Technique
 by Karen Maroda (Wiley, 1991)

The Empathic Imagination
 by Alfred Margulies (Norton, 1989)

Heyward on *When Boundaries Betray Us*

A dear friend and fellow therapist sent me a review—"A Question of Boundaries," by Lorna Hochstein (1994)—of Carter Heyward's book *When Boundaries Betray Us*. Hochstein's review is a wise and thought-provoking discussion of some of the issues Heyward raises in her disturbing book. Hochstein comments, "*When Boundaries Betray Us* is not bedtime reading. I tried that once and was awake for hours" (p. 40).

Once I started reading Heyward's book, I could not put it down. I found myself sad, angry, shocked, disbelieving, questioning—my mind racing with several recently favorite books coming to mind, two of which I shall review and discuss here in the context of Heyward's story. Hochstein's primary focus in her discussion of *When Boundaries Betray Us* is on the issues of therapeutic boundaries and "neutrality." I plan to discuss Heyward's book here within the context of countertransference and the therapist's involvement and level of activity in the therapeutic relationship.

Carter Heyward, a lesbian, feminist Episcopal priest and theologian, has written her book in an extraordinarily personal way. I do not know that it could have been written in any other manner. She intends to disturb our profession, and she succeeds. I can easily imagine many readers dismissing this book: It is too emotional, her expectations were unreasonable, the author is just plain nuts, this is a nightmare illustration of unresolved transference, her recollections and attributions of intent to her therapist are distorted, it could not possibly have happened this way, and so on. Even if some or all of these disclaimers and judgments are to some extent true, the issues raised in this book cannot be ignored. Whatever distortions Heyward's story may contain, this book relates an anguished account of a client's depersonalization in the face of therapeutic "neutrality" and anonymity and the use of a therapist's power.

When Boundaries Betray Us is the story of the author's proposal for a post-therapy personal/professional relationship with her psychiatrist. Elizabeth Farro (the pseudonym for Heyward's psychiatrist) refused any post-treatment personal relationship. The issues of friendship and authenticity became the pivotal and ultimately destructive focus of Heyward's attempt at psychotherapy with Farro. In the aftermath of the collapse of the therapy, Heyward wrote this book to help heal herself and to insist that psychotherapists examine themselves and come to "understand how badly abusive we can be by withholding intimacy and authentic emotional connection from those who seek our help" (p. 10).

I often had to struggle to keep reading Heyward's book. The political/spiritual rhetoric, for me, often obscured rather than illuminated the issues and experiences at hand. Heyward resorts too frequently to the pervasive influence of patriarchal structures to explain her therapist's impasse and rigidity. I did not find this explanation in and of itself remotely adequate. I also had to struggle personally to accept her theological language, for example, "I experienced Elizabeth Farro as a woman hungry for the movement of the Sacred, longing to be touched and blessed by the Holy, yearning to embody a confidence in this Spirit" (p. 31). Such theopolitical language labels and obscures experience rather than examines it. Additionally, I am an atheist—an intense skeptic of things labeled "spiritual" (in contrast to "intense," "profound," "disorienting," "moral," "responsible," etc.). I question whether spiritual and religious issues belong in the psychotherapeutic process unless the client specifically seeks pastoral counseling or directly raises issues within a theological framework as a part of his or her own personal development.

In setting my personal biases aside, however, I was able to find Heyward's efforts and arguments with her therapist compelling. Farro seemed to enter theopolitical discussions with Heyward in some kind of technical effort to establish a working alliance and/or to mollify her client. The result was a confusing mixture of personal, transferential/countertransferential, moral and theological issues, which certainly at times suggested that theirs was more than a "merely" professional, therapeutic relationship.

The issue of friendship became the focus of a confusing, conflictual, and ultimately destructive therapeutic relationship. Heyward is frank about the transferential, romantic, and erotic components of her wish for a continuing post-therapy relationship with Farro. While this therapist was quite willing to discuss the transferential aspects of Heyward's feelings toward her, she seemed to refuse any substantial discussion of her own countertransferential reactions with her client. Heyward insisted on honesty and mutuality from her therapist. As Farro refused any personal involvement or, apparently, any personal self-disclosure, Heyward struggled to understand her therapist's position:

> I was unable to lay aside my desire for a friendship further down the road. "Friendship" was taking on a larger meaning, I believe, to both Elizabeth and me than the term ordinarily denotes. In relation to Elizabeth, friendship for me had to do with the trustworthiness of our relationship because it signaled the authenticity of a shared commitment to a mutually empowering process —by its very nature a process of relational openness and change. (p. 67)

It seems quite clear that Heyward gradually became reconciled to her therapist's refusal to have a post-therapy relationship. What she refused to give up on was her insistence that Farro be honest with her personally about her own feelings for Heyward and her reasons and feelings about not having a personal relationship. Heyward demanded authenticity at least within the therapy relationship. That does not appear to have happened. Instead, Farro appears to have attacked and pathologized her client and hidden herself behind a façade of professional rules and the professed attempt to "do no harm." Heyward quotes Farro as having made her argument in this way:

> It is important that I be clear with you and that you understand me. If we had met at a dinner party, we might be friends. Since we met here at the office, we will not be friends. Ours is a professional relationship. Is that clear? (p. 34)

If Heyward's rendering of the exchange is even reasonably accurate, Farro seems to fuse understanding with compliance. This therapist seems more interested that Heyward follow the rules than explore the meaning of Heyward's wishes or the feelings behind her own rigid position. Many months after the statement quoted above, Farro, according to Heyward, indicated that she did indeed want to be friends but could not because it entailed risk: "There is always a possibility that it would harm you, Carter. I would have to be 100% sure that it wouldn't and since we can't be 100% sure of anything, I couldn't risk that" (p. 79).

This is a ridiculous explanation. If psychotherapists held themselves to a standard of 100% certainty of no risk, we would be unable to involve anyone in any aspect of psychotherapy. Psychotherapy is fundamentally relational and as such is ambiguous, conflicted, and risky. I am reminded of a recent, rather intense discussion with a colleague about dual relationships and post-therapy personal relationships. Her position was essentially that "once a client, always a client" and of "doing no harm," being extremely careful to do nothing that had the potential, however remote, of hurting a client. Hers is a stance I see as certainly ethical and highly, perhaps overly, protective. I argued that it can be differently but equally ethical to take risks—possibly creating anxiety, disappointment, even harm for either the client or the therapist—and deal directly and honestly with the potentially negative outcomes of mutually chosen risks.

Farro seemed willing to join with her client in some unconventional ways, doing sessions seated on the floor with a candle burning between them, discussing theological and political as well as psychological issues. This way of joining appears to have been superficial. It seems that this psychiatrist, for reasons that remain unclear throughout the book, was not able or willing to enter into a true exploration of her relationship with Heyward at either a personal or transferential/countertransferential level. Instead, for a period of time, Farro pressed Heyward to look outside the therapy for explanations of the distress within the therapy. I think that was an example of an all-too-common error of a therapist's diverting attention away from the affective struggles within the therapy relationship. Heyward, in an all-too-common response, began to comply with her therapist's direction in an effort to preserve the relationship.

In the early stages of therapy, Heyward saw aspects of her own issues mirrored in the limits and vulnerabilities of her family in that, "like my parents and grandparents, I was shaped in part by a fear of loss, fear of intimacy, fear of sitting quietly with others or alone with myself" (p. 52). But then, in a disturbing fashion, the affective quality of Heyward's understanding and memories of her family began to change to include "remembering" examples of "abuse." Heyward's childhood was not innocuous, but the traumatic, conflicted aspects of her early years took on heightened significance, as if to explain her difficulties in therapy. She reflects on this phase of the therapy: *"In this moment, I slipped unawares into Elizabeth's therapeutic framework, and for the first time in therapy, I began to believe I really was in some way crazy for caring so much about this relationship"* (p. 87).

The point is not that there is nothing else for me to feel about, or learn from, these childhood brushes with violence. *The point is that the emotionally violent character of my relationship with Elizabeth somehow "attached" itself psychologically to each of these events—the molestation and the spankings—and, over a number of weeks in the spring of 1988, both events emerged as other and larger than they had been in my life.* (p. 92)

Gradually, Heyward was able to recognize that while the emerging memories were not exactly "false," neither were they "quite right" or "entirely true" (p. 97). She was able to bring her focus back to the difficulties in the here and now with Farro, renewing her demands and confrontations of her therapist. The difficulties were never resolved, and Heyward finally terminated her therapy.

As I entered Heyward's story, I kept thinking of one of the first things my consultant said to me (and the reason I chose to stay with him as my consultant): "A patient has only one responsibility in treatment, to ruthlessly pursue a relationship with you. The patient's work is to be ruthless in the pursuit of vitality and reality. It's your job to tolerate that ruthlessness and be yourself without retaliating when the work becomes difficult." Carter Heyward demonstrated that ruthlessness in the course of her aborted psychotherapy, in her self-examination after termination, and in her choosing to write this book.

The other books I will comment on in this chapter discuss how the therapists bring themselves as persons and as competent, appropriately bounded professionals to the therapeutic relationship and the therapeutic work. These books encourage risk, an endeavor rather out of favor in these days of increasing caution and conservatism in psychotherapy. Current trends and pressures are increasingly defining therapeutic boundaries as unilateral and impermeable, protective barriers more than boundaries. Healthy boundaries are permeable and changeable.

Maroda on *The Power of Countertransference*

Karen Maroda's *The Power of Countertransference* was given to me by my then psychotherapist, a classically trained psychoanalyst in his mid-seventies, as a way of opening up a discussion of our relationship with each other. One might say, of course, that I must have approached this book with my own transferential and idealized fantasies strongly at hand; I did indeed. My therapist also gave me a copy of a review he had written of this book for a psychoanalytic journal. The book I have read and reread; his review awaited completion of this commentary.

In her discussion of the "real" relationship in psychotherapy, Maroda quotes Thomas Szaz (as cited in Maroda, 1991): "In psychoanalytic *theory,* the concept of transference serves as an explanatory hypothesis; whereas in the psychoanalytic *situation,* it serves as a defense for the analyst" (p. 435). Maroda thoughtfully and bluntly confronts the artificial (and, therefore, destructive) barriers that psychotherapists place between themselves and their clients, the misuses of power, authority, theory, and professional anonymity. A few brief quotes best communicate her thinking and values:

> One of the most important tasks of analytic treatment is to accept limitations, loss, and human frailty, but this does not mean that the patient should accept responsibility for the therapist's limitations as well as his own. (p. 105)
>
> Many people believe that for the analytic therapist to admit her own pathology is dangerous. I believe that it is the need to preserve the mask of sanity that is dangerous. (p. 107)
>
> Granted, some patients do like to find fault with their therapists to deflect away from themselves, but the solution to this problem is certainly not for the therapist to engage in the same behavior. (p. 107)

Maroda does not by any means advocate a kind of wholesale self-disclosure on the part of the therapist. Her emphasis is on the honesty of the therapist's discussion of his or her own feelings and attitudes toward the patient and about himself or herself in relationship to the patient. Therapists need not talk about their lives outside the therapy, but they need to talk about their own psychological lives within the therapeutic relationship. This appears to be central in Heyward's demands of her therapist. Maroda suggests that therapists should not discuss their own affective and countertransferential reactions to relieve their own anxiety or aggressiveness, but at the client's request so as to facilitate reality, safety, and deepening affective understanding. For Maroda, "The point of disclosure is to rationally demonstrate affect, not to intellectualize. Therapist intellectualizations are usually met by the patient accusing the therapist of being lifeless, mechanical, overly intellectual or non-responsive" (p. 130).

A central and crucial concept in this book is that of "countertransference dominance" (p. 49), which emerges and distorts the therapeutic process when the therapist refuses to experience, identify, or acknowledge his or her own countertransference reactions and conflicts. Countertransference dominance will be acted out inevitably and destructively, perhaps taking "the form of keeping a non-therapeutic distance from the patient or refusing to merge with the patient out of fear of being out of control" (p.53). As I read Heyward's book, this concept came to mind; her experience seemed very much a description of an extended countertransference dominance that eroded and ultimately destroyed her psychotherapy.

Maroda concludes her discussion of countertransference dominance with a perspective that I imagine Carter Heyward longed to hear from her psychiatrist:

> If we are committed to facilitating deep, long-term analytic treatments that draw their strength from the curative aspects of regression, then it seems apparent that we would do well to pay more attention to the reality that this expereince will always be somewhat mutual. Once we accept the idea of mutual regression, then the impact of the therapist's current needs, as well as psychological history, become far more important than what has been mutually acknowledged to date. And the role of the patient as guide and mutual healer, rather than passive recipient of the therapist's wisdom, becomes crucial to the conduct of a successful treatment. (p. 65)

It is difficult for me to imagine these words being written by a male analyst. Part of the shock I felt at the attitude and behavior of Heyward's therapist is that she is a lesbian psychotherapist and professed feminist. For her part, Heyward drew on the work of the Stone Center (Jordan, Kaplan, Miller, Stiver, & Surrey, 1991) at Wellesley College and befriended Janet Surrey, an associate at the

Stone Center, in the midst of her struggle with Elizabeth Farro. I thought often of the Stone Center writings as I read Maroda's book. Although she does not appear to be familiar with their work and makes no direct reference to the feminist literature, Maroda does refer to Christopher Bollas (1987, 1989) and the intersubjectivist writers (Stolorow, Atwood, & Brandchaft, 1994; Stolorow, Brandchaft, & Atwood, 1987). At least in the writing of this book, she sticks strictly to the analytic literature on transference and countertransference, although she certainly confronts the traditionally male-dominated attitudes of authority, control, and objectivity and presents a powerfully feminist perspective within analytic theory. I imagine her concern is to articulate thoughtfully the theory and experience of mutual relatedness, quite separate from issues of masculine, feminine, or the politically correct.

Margulies on *The Empathic Imagination*

In *The Empathic Imagination*, Alfred Margulies approaches the process of analytic psychotherapy with an emphasis on the experience and conscious use of wonder, imagination, and paradox, drawing on "three disparate sources for understanding the mysterious journey to the interior of another: phenomenology, psychoanalysis and poetry" (p. 3). This book often reads as much like a literary essay as a psychoanalytic text. Margulies's thinking reflects a lively, uneasy, and unresolved tension between the analytic and the existential. For a psychoanalyst, he has a rare understanding of the phenomenological perspective: "The whole effort of phenomenology is to recover a naive contact with the world. How can one approximate the bare and subtle essences of things?" (p. 6). He goes on to write:

> The therapeutic truth was a dialectic, a creation of the relationship itself, a continuous coming into being of *possibilities* requiring further exploration. Even our hard won therapeutic facts had been transformed continuously.... It is my contention that the working methods of phenomenology and psychoanalysis are alike in their relationship to the creative process. They are methods that optimize the potential for novel perceptions and thoughts; they permit the surprise configurations of the new arising from the old.... This element of surprise is at the heart of both the phenomenological reduction and free association—they were methods devised as first steps in the process of discovering unthought-of possibilities. Such receptivity demands a capacity to tolerate uncertainty. (p. 12)

Quite separate from the issues raised by Heyward's book, *The Empathic Imagination* is an exceptional, reflective book, its writing vivid with imagination, emotion, and questioning. Like Maroda, Margulies never minimizes the experience or realities of his clients, and he does not shy away from intensity or uncertainty. His book demonstrates profound respect and curiosity, and I return to it often, sometimes to quiet myself, to remember why I do this work, and to renew my determination.

Nothing I have read about empathy in psychotherapy is better than what I found in this book. Just as Maroda is cautious and intentional in her use of countertransferential self-disclosure, Margulies is cautious and intentional in his use of empathic imagination. He draws from Buie's (1981) analysis of the four components of empathy: conceptual empathy, self-experiential empathy, imaginative imitation empathy, and resonant empathy (affective contagion) (Margulies, 1979, p. 17). He focuses on the experience of imaginative empathy as the heart of the creative process in psychotherapy. Margulies simultaneously encourages and cautions:

> Imaginative empathy . . . stresses the active, searching quality of entering the other's world: Imagination constructs a new world, one not immediately accessible to the observer.... When all is said and done, imaginative empathy remains imaginative. Empathy must be checked and rechecked against real experience if one is not to lose one's way and make a fiction of the other. ... There is to remain a constant vigilance to countertransference phenomena in the broadest sense. The therapist must strive for a position of tension between knowing and not-knowing. Empathy is not merely a resonating with the other, but an act of will and creativity. As Hazlitt (Bate, 1964, p. 262) put it, "The extremest resources of the imagination are called in to lay open the deepest movements of the heart." (p. 18)

It is at this juncture that Heyward, Maroda, and Margulies can be read as companion texts. For Margulies, the act of empathy inevitably creates disturbance, anxiety, confrontation, and collision between therapist and client, "both a cleft and a fusion within a larger world view" (p. 99). It would seem that neither Heyward's psychiatrist nor Heyward herself could tolerate the cleft or the fusion. In Margulies's view, it is not the task of the therapist to alleviate a client's suffering or to intellectually analyze and interpret it. The fundamental task is to enter the suffering, the conflicts, the paradoxes, to enter the feared and hidden places, creating new meaning and possibility.

Heyward's book is full of the poetry she wrote to, for, and about her therapist. It was a stanza of a poem called "Transference" that first brought Margulies's book to mind. In the poem, Heyward writes: "I am obsessed with you/ and with myself and utterly/ preoccupied with my obsession" (p. 42). In a letter from Beverly Harrison (Heyward's partner and lover) included in a response section at the end of the book, Harrison also refers to Heyward's "obsession" (p. 208) with her failed therapy and the writing of the book. Their mutual use of the term "obsession" (and there is certainly an obsessive quality both to Heyward's woundedness and her quest for reconciliation) reminded me of an extraordinary paragraph in Margulies's book. I quote here at length:

> World views and their inscapes are often dominated by a single preoccupation. It can be a symptom, a grief, another person, a physical illness, hunger, sexuality, addiction, revenge, a past event, a quest for stimulation and novelty, or even an affect. The preoccupation itself becomes larger than life and forms the gravitational center of the person's universe. Everything attains relevance and meaning with respect to the preoccupation; nothing escapes its sway. As it becomes more ensconced, the entire world comes within its compass. Clinically, we use such terms as addiction, compulsion, obsession—diseases of the mind. But to the one who endures, it is the hub of existence. (p. 100)

It is precisely at the point of obsession that a person's worldview demands entry and understanding. It is precisely at that point that we must tolerate uncertainty and often wrenchingly intense contact. It is precisely at that point that Margulies endeavors to stand with empathy and wonder, knowing conflict and paradox are inevitable and necessary. It is precisely at that point that Carter Heyward's psychiatrist appears to have fled and imposed rules in lieu of relatedness. For reasons unknown and unexplained, she would not enter and explore Heyward's increasingly obsessive and desparate demand for mutuality and honesty. As Heyward became more "ruthless" and unrelenting in her expectations and woundedness, her therapist became increasingly cold, distant, and ultimately hostile.

As I read *When Boundaries Betray Us,* I kept trying to figure out Farro's training and theoretical background. I kept wishing she had read *The Empathic Imagination,* that she knew how or had the courage to let go and "fall forward," as the poet David Whyte (1990, p. 44) described it. Instead, she stood outside her client's world and judged it. In so doing she left Heyward feeling increasingly crazy, implying that the difficulties lay exclusively in Heyward's past rather than within the current antitherapeutic relationship.

Heyward speaks eloquently to the heart of the matter as she relates a conversation with Janet Surrey about parallels between a past, conflicted friendship and her failed therapeutic relationship:

> I'll have to say that my relationships with both David and Elizabeth were, as Elizabeth suggested, chaotic, embodying the sort of psychospiritual raw material out of which real love is born, but not without struggle. For Elizabeth, this meant, primarily, danger; for me, it meant a powerfully creative relational opportunity—dangerous, but important. . . . It was not that any of us was bad, or sick, or wrong. It's just that, in our most creative, deeply mutual possibilities, we become dangerous people. We always do—dangerous to the professional and personal structures of patriarchy itself, dangerous to the structures of our own lives. (p. 167)

As psychotherapists we need to minimize the potential for doing harm, but ours is, at its heart, a dangerous and precarious profession. We can protect ourselves from the emotional demands and immediacy of our clients, from the raw and often primitive contact that is the foundation of true psychotherapy. We can hide behind self-righteous rules, "singular" relationships, intellectual and moral cowardice. This is the challenge Heyward offers our profession. Does psychotherapy become another institution, lining up behind the institutional church and institutionalized medicine?

Why did the writing of Maroda and Margulies come so forcefully to mind as I struggled with *When Boundaries Betray Us?* I think that Carter Heyward demanded two fundamental things of her psychotherapist: authenticity and empathic courage. What she seems to have received instead was pejorative blaming, deceit, rigid rules, and depersonalization. What Heyward asked of her therapist was not that she behave irresponsibly or that she abandon her own frame of reference, but that she honestly and empathically enter Carter's frame of reference and worldview—not that they be the same, but that they arrive at a mutual respect and an understanding of their differentnesses. It is impossible to read this book without having some aspect of one's professional and/or personal frame of reference disturbed. For this I give Carter Heyward my thanks.

REFERENCES

Bollas, C. (1987). *The shadow of the object: Psychoanalysis of the unthought known.* New York: Columbia University Press.

Bollas, C. (1989). *Forces of destiny: Psychoanalysis and human idiom.* London: Free Association Books.

Buie, D. H. (1981). Empathy: Its nature and limitations. The Journal of the American Psychoanalytical Association, 29, 281-307.

Hochstein, L. (1994). A question of boundaries. *Sojourner, 19*(9), 39-40.

Jordan, J. V., Kaplan, A. G., Miller, J. B., Stiver, I. P., & Surrey, J. L. (1991). *Women's growth in connection: Writings from the Stone Center.* New York: Guilford Press.

Stolorow, R. D., Atwood, G. E., & Brandchaft, B. (Eds.). (1994). *The intersubjective perspective.* Northvale, NJ: Jason Aronson.

Stolorow, R. D., Brandchaft, B., & Atwood, G. E. (1987). *Psychoanalytic treatment: An intersubjective approach.* Hillsdale, NJ: The Analytic Press.

Whyte, D. (1990). *Where many rivers meet.* Langley, WA: Many Rivers Press.

The original version of this chapter was published in the Transactional Analysis Journal, *Volume 25, Number 2, pp. 180-186, April 1995.*

Thinking about Suicide: Standing in the Face of Despair

by William F. Cornell

While I have learned much over the years about suicide from reading and discussions (often arguments) with colleagues, it has been from my clients that I have learned, and continue to learn, the most.

I was delighted to read Bob Drye's (2006) article entitled "The No-Suicide Decision: Then and Now." It was a wonderfully rich and informative piece, read and discussed by many and reprinted in the United Kingdom's *ITA News*. I was personally pleased with Bob's piece because his 1974 article on stroking the rebellious Child was a pivotal one for me in my transactional analysis training. It was the concept I used as the basis for the teaching portion of my Teaching Member exam (which I did entirely in the voice of Grover from Sesame Street). In his 2006 article, Bob reminded us of the history of the concept, its diagnostic function, and that the intervention represented an invitation for a decision rather than the establishment of a contract. Bob's article led to further reflection for me, as I have often questioned the ways in which the "no-suicide contract" has come to be used in transactional analysis training and practice.

Suicidal risk is an inevitable element in our human relations work. Few in our fields of practice escape confrontations with clients' loss of will to live or active desire to die. These issues force us to face the limits of our influence on others, our responsibilities in the face of such feelings and intentions in our clients, our own personal theologies and values, and countertransference reactions, not to mention ethical and legal requirements. It is a topic that must remain open to study, reflection, and discussion. I have thought back over my work with suicidal clients during the past few years as I prepared to write this piece, and two clients read earlier versions of this chapter and contributed their own thoughts.

In their introduction to *Essential Papers on Suicide* (Maltsberger & Goldblatt, 1996)—part of the wonderful New York University Press series of "Essential Papers" compilations—the editors wrote:

> Trainees are taught to tick off items in the DSM IV checklist for the major depressive syndromes, but they are not taught how to assess depressive anguish. Indeed, anguish is not even listed among the criteria for diagnosing depression in the standard nomenclature (American Psychiatric Association, 1994, p. 327). There we find "depressed mood" and "diminished interest or pleasure" mentioned, but nothing explicit to direct attention to the howling wind of depressive agony. (p. 1)

With the no-suicide intervention developed by Bob Drye with Bob and Mary Goulding (1973) and as redescribed by Drye (2006), we have an invaluable tool for immediate risk assessment and emergency intervention. It is a technique that has come to be used widely across psychiatric and mental health disciplines. Here I wish to expand on modes of thinking and intervention that speak to the meaning of suicidal thoughts and intentions and that offer clients alternatives to suicidal actions.

Edwin Shneidman (1996, 2001) devoted his career to research about and the treatment of suicide; he writes with clinical clarity and compassion, never pathologizing suicidal drives. His work was originally brought to my attention by a client who was trying to understand her suicidal feelings. Shneidman (1996, p. 25) lists clusters of frustrated psychological needs that often underlie suicidal ideation. He emphasizes five categories:

- Thwarted love, acceptance, and belonging related to frustrated needs for succorance and affiliation
- Fractured control, predictability, and arrangement related to frustrated needs for achievement, autonomy, order, and understanding
- Assaulted self-image and the avoidance of shame, defeat, humiliation, and disgrace related to frustrated needs for affiliation, dependence, and shame-avoidance
- Ruptured key relationships and the attendant grief and bereftness related to frustrated needs for affiliation and nurturance
- Excessive anger, rage, and hostility related to frustrated needs for dominance, aggression, and counteraction

It is interesting that in the midst of Shneidman's extensive reviews of the literature on suicide, I could find no reference to the use of no-suicide decisions, although I found his thinking very consistent with our values and practice in transactional analysis. He vividly describes the dark, self-reinforcing spiral of the suicidal mind, in which virtually all experience leads to the same conclusion: Death is the only or best alternative to an unendurable life. It is the closing off of the suicidal mind that Shneidman addresses with theoretical and technical clarity. He writes:

One of the first tasks of any aspiring helper or therapist with a highly suicidal person is to address the constriction [of thinking], to "widen the blinders," to let some light in so that the person can see new angles. And, as we will see, the therapist must gently disagree with the death-laden premises of the suicidal person. The suicidal person's thinking pattern has constricted; often it is dichotomous with only two possibilities: yes or no, life as I want it or death, my way or nothing. (Shneidman, 1996, pp. 60-61)

Shneidman goes on to illustrate how he creates a "lousy list" (called "lousy" because when a client is actively suicidal, it is a bit grandiose to expect him or her to feel enthusiastic about much of anything; the therapist needs to accept and tolerate the despair). The "lousy list" is a list—drawn up by the client and therapist together—of possible options in the face of the despair, and suicide remains one of the options on the "lousy list."

This idea raises the question of how to "gently disagree" with a client's suicidal ideation without becoming overly parental and controlling and while promoting thinking and exploration of new possibilities.

Script-level change can create periods of severe stress, guilt, and anxiety both intrapsychically and interpersonally. It is not uncommon for people in the midst of significant script change to find themselves with suicidal fantasies. I recall one woman, very bright and competent, who was on the verge of making immense life changes that went against the patterns of her past, familiar ways of doing what others expected. She faced the dismay and disapproval of her family and was suicidal. I said to her, "You are experiencing what a dear friend of mine once called 'deep psychic doodoo' " (which transactional analysis therapists are more likely to call "script change"). She greeted this with curiosity and humor, asking if it was a category in the *DSM-IV*. It is not, although perhaps it should be. I assured her that I was looking forward to learning more about this struggle in her. I told her that I had learned something important from a book by James Hillman (1976) called *Suicide and the Soul* (which was given to me years ago by another suicidal client), in which he suggested that suicidal fantasies often represent the urgent need to kill off one's life as one has been living it rather than ending life itself. Key to Hillman's perspective is the willingness (necessity, he would suggest) to experience the client's suffering together and out of that suffering and anguish to find meaning. The whole book is a reflection on the darker aspects of human experience. I assured her that both her anguish and her autonomy would be taken seriously in our work, even as she suffered the judgments of friends and family.

Another client, a man, had to drive across a bridge over a major river to get to my office. For several sessions he reported that as he drove over the bridge, he had the fantasy of stopping his car and jumping off the bridge. Initially, I responded by wondering if the confusion, guilt, and hope he experienced in coming to see me felt like too much as he got close to the office, so the bridge would be an end to his internal conflicts and confusion. We would take some of this up, usually briefly, in each session.

One day I responded—with rather obvious humor and affection—"Well, if you do decide to jump off the bridge, take a minute to call me on your cell phone so I won't think you're just stuck in traffic and I can make use of the time rather than sitting around waiting." "Don't they give you empathy classes in grad school?" he replied. "Yeah, but I skipped empathy and statistics—always thought they were overrated," I said. I would rather argue with him than empathize, I explained, just as he needed to stand up for himself in the picture rather than take himself out of the picture. My comment, as one might expect, moved our conversation into other directions, that is, into his fantasies (and mine) about how those around him would respond should he actually jump off the bridge. Would anyone care all that long? Would most people think he deserved to take his life?

At a subsequent session he told me that this time his fantasy was of driving the car off the bridge rather than just jumping. "What do you make of that?" he asked. I responded, "Maybe you're looking for a way to make a bigger splash," this being related to his fear that should he actually commit suicide, it would not have that much impact on his family. I told him my wise-ass comeback was a comment on his rather bizarre idea that somehow driving his car off a bridge might make a bigger impression on those around him than the life he has led and what he could do in the future.

Another man spoke frequently of his sense that it was "ethical" to commit suicide when he had made decisions and taken actions that caused others pain or harm. Once he asked me for my opinion about what he was saying. I clarified that he was asking me for my personal opinion and values and then told him, "No matter what the rationale, I think suicide is profoundly unethical and fundamentally selfish. If one causes pain or harm to others—and we all do at one time or another, unintentionally or intentionally—one has the responsibility to deal with the pain. I have worked with many people over the years who have had parents, spouses, or other loved ones commit suicide, and the consequences for the living are horrendous." My client had never considered this possibility, having always imagined his death as a relief to himself and others and never considering that it might, in fact, be viewed as hostile and/or tragic by those left behind.

One client told me that during 20 years of previous psychotherapies—not one of which had changed his suicidal ideation—he was always told, "Don't do it," which he translated into "Don't even think about it." He had not done it, obviously, but the feelings and fantasies persisted with disturbing regularity. He asked me to agree that no matter what else we spoke of in a given session, we would always take some time to talk about suicide. I agreed. Given the intensity of our focus, we also worked out a contract for between-session phone contact (something I rarely do) when he needed to touch base. He is one of the clients I asked to review my first draft of this chapter. He wrote back, "Many therapists are afraid to discuss an individual's desire to end his or her life, but those discussions make suicide less frightening and more objectionable."

A female client spoke frequently of her suicidal fantasies, insisting on her right to end her own life if she so chose. She was unmarried, had no children, and felt her life was her own with no obligations to anyone. I saw her life as more subtly suicidal, filled with self-destructive and self-inhibiting patterns. We discussed all of this openly, vigorously, sometimes contentiously. One day she asked why it was that with all of our conversations about suicide, I had never once made any reference to hospitalization. I explained that if I had her hospitalized, she would be held briefly, medicated, and sent home. I would have covered my ass, but I imagined she would feel even more defective, ashamed, and even more like committing suicide. I said bluntly, "You are an intelligent woman. You use that intelligence in some areas of your life, but certainly not all. I expect you to bring your intelligence to the issues that cause you to feel suicidal and to figuring out how to live the life you want to live." I perhaps failed to "gently" disagree with her suicidal ideation, as Shneidman recommends, but disagree I did. We were then able to engage actively in challenging her constricted thinking, working together to understand both its childhood roots and its current life consequences.

Shneidman draws on Karl Menninger's (1938) classic *Man Against Himself*, emphasizing the need for therapists to attend not only to direct, lethal acts of suicide but also to what he calls patterns of "subintentional" death (Shneidman, 1996, p. 63). He elaborates Menninger's categories of "chronic suicide" (asceticism, martyrdom, neurotic invalidism, alcoholism, smoking, etc.), "focal suicide" (self-mutilization, psychologically laden accidents, etc.), and "organic suicide" (exacerbation of psychological factors that promote organic disease).

Shneidman's books are rich in clinical understanding and techniques. I hope many of you will follow up on my comments by reading the books listed at the end. There is much more I could summarize here from *The Suicidal Mind*, but considering space limitations, I want to finish with a fascinating commentary Shneidman offers toward the end of the book. He is reflecting on the mass suicide among the Nazis (after their slaughter of millions) in contrast to the way the Japanese emperor chose to handle defeat. On 14 August 1945, in a rare radio broadcast (Shneidman mentions that most Japanese had never heard the voice of their emperor), Emperor Hirohito told his people, "It is according to the dictates of time and fate that we have resolved to pave the way for a good peace for all generations to come by enduring the unendurable and suffering what is unsufferable" (as cited in Shneidman, 1996, p. 161). Shneidman comments, "He ordered his people to live. Sometimes the most difficult thing in the world is to choose to endure life" (p. 161).

The previous text was originally published in the ITAA newsletter, *The Script*. I have decided to finish this chapter with a more personal perspective, written several years ago for the Forum, the ITAA Internet discussion list.

In my early years as a transactional analysis therapist, I used the "escape hatch" procedures—including no-suicide agreements—like a sacred ritual. I knew well from my own years as a heroin addict and several near-death experiences of the destructive tendencies that life circumstances can evoke in most of us. I was frightened by the depth of despair and rage that many clients experienced, so I found great comfort in the illusions of no-suicide and no-homicide "contracts." They gave me some sense of doing something. I work frequently with suicidal and homicidal clients and have learned many crucial and difficult lessons over the years. But my most important learning was much closer to home.

I learned a profound lesson about suicide as I faced my father's efforts at suicide. My father was a decent, distant, and very fragile man. Something happened to him (or he did something, I don't know which) during World War II from which he never recovered and about which he would never speak, although it was clear to me from early on that it was not easy for my dad to live a normal life.

When I was 19 and Dad was 41, my mother died of a medical error. My father never recovered from her death. Twice he called me, loaded gun in hand, to ask me to talk him out of pulling the trigger. I talked fast and hard. Finally, he called me (he was living in Arizona, I was in Pittsburgh) to tell me that he had been diagnosed with esophageal cancer (he was smoking and drinking heavily by then) and that he had refused treatment. He said he wanted the cancer to kill him.

I was furious. We had many arguments until I told him that I had lost all of the little respect I had for him, that I would no longer see him or talk to him, that he was welcome to die and he would die alone. My father told me then, "You do not have the right to ask me to live. You don't have that right. I don't have the strength you want me to have. I don't have it in me any more. You don't have to get up every morning and face my life. You do not live my life. I do. You face your life, and it's a very good life you've made. My life fell apart. I fell apart. I know you wish I were a stronger man than I am, but I'm not. I have to face my life every morning, and I don't want this life. I want to leave it, and you can't ask me to stay."

For many months I did not speak to him again, but his words never left me. "You do not have the right to ask me to live." I finally realized that I was horrified of his despair, of there being something like that inside of me, terrified that I did not have the strength to face his despair. I wrote a long letter and went to see him. It was not easy. We talked, cried, and argued. Gradually, I came to understand his decision and to support him.

Ironically, as his condition deteriorated (it could have been quite treatable), he collapsed and was hospitalized. His physicians tried to have him declared mentally incompetent to force treatment on him. I defended his rights and decision as competent. Other than pain-killing drugs, he received no other medical intervention. He died as he wished. He asked me to find some way to give meaning to his death through my work. Before he died, we planned his funeral (I delivered it, as he wanted no minister present) and chose the music—all songs by Joan Baez, whom he adored.

His funeral started with this poem, "Old Welch Poem" by Henry Treece, sung by Joan Baez:

> I take with me where I go
> A pen and a golden bowl;
> Poet and beggar step in my shoes,
> Or a prince in a purple shawl.
>
> I bring with me when I return
> To the house that father's hands made,
> A crooning bird on a crystal bough,
> And O, a sad sad word!

Through this experience with my Dad, I learned I could face despair. I learned lessons of love and that there are sometimes losses from which people do not recover. I learned something of my limits as a son and as a therapist. I did not need to ward it off with a no-suicide condition for entering therapy.

It is not easy to enter the disturbed and disturbing terrain of the profound despair, hopelessness, and fury that can lead a person to end life. I have come to believe that it is an individual's choice and right to continue or end his or her own life. I have also come to find that when I stand with a person facing that despair, most find a way, a meaning, to continue, to create a life worth living. This does not mean that I am a quiet onlooker in the struggle. It often means intensely personal encounters and conflicts.

I think these are deeply personal decisions. I certainly do not expect other therapists to necessarily agree with my position. Questions of suicide go right to the heart of our profession, to questions of personal autonomy, morality, and responsibility.

REFERENCES

Drye, R. C. (1974). Stroking the rebellious child: An aspect of managing resistance. *Transactional Analysis Journal, 4*(3), 23-26.
Drye, R. C. (2006). The no-suicide decision: Then and now. *The Script, 36*(6), 3, 4.
Drye, R. C., Goulding, R., & Goulding, M. (1973). No suicide decisions: Patient monitoring of risk. *American Journal of Psychiatry, 130,* 170-174.
Hillman, J. (1976). *Suicide and the soul.* Dallas, TX: Spring Publications.
Maltsberger, J. T., & Goldblatt, M. J. (Eds.). (1996). *Essential papers on suicide.* New York: New York University Press.
Menninger, K. (1938). *Man against himself.* New York: Harcourt, Brace and Co.
Shneidman, E. S. (1996). *The suicidal mind.* New York: Oxford University Press.
Shneidman, E. S. (2001). *Comprehending suicide: Landmarks in 20th century suicidology.* Washington, DC: American Psychological Association.

The original version of the first part of this chapter was published in The Script, *Volume 37, Number 2, pp. 1, 2, March 2007.*

Reflections on Violence

The Root of the Problem
by Caleb Cornell

For the past 3 years, I have attended a small private school in Pittsburgh, Pennsylvania. The school has a very liberal attitude as far as dress, school conduct, and curriculum are concerned. The other students tend to be, as I am, misfits in the world of public school. It was a welcome environment. It was a necessary environment as well. If I had not left my former public school, I might have caused one of the first of a recent rash of high school shootings.

When I first heard about the massacre at Columbine High School in Littleton, Colorado, on 20 April 1999, I was neither surprised nor shocked. Over the past 2 years, these tragedies have become commonplace. As the day of the shootings went on, more information about the "Trenchcoat Mafia" came to light. They were kids who were outsiders at Columbine High School. Not just outsiders, but misfits who were teased by the more "acceptable" majority of the students: the football players, the future military recruits, the religious children who had a perfectly normal life in which they were not only accepted, but embraced. The more I hear about how Dylan Klebold and Eric Harris listened to "goth" music and how they often cited lyrics from the industrial band KMFDM, the more disgusted I become at how our country reacts to this sort of thing. It was not the music that caused this or the lack of metal detectors at the school. And even though the Nazism that these kids were reportedly involved in more than likely played a part, the real problem lies deeper.

I think the root of Eric and Dylan's rage lay in how their peers reacted to them—the mocking and the teasing that they endured. Thirteen deaths were not caused because someone made fun of them once, but because they were psychologically tortured by other students every day. When you are forced to live in a society that rejects you in all forms, all the time, and never lets you forget that you are different, in your mind the only solution to these problems is to rid these people of their lives. You have an immeasurable amount of rage inside of you that, no matter what you do, cannot be suppressed.

Dylan and Eric were friends only with others who were in the same situation. I, on the other hand, in my former school, eventually had no friends at all. I was the only one there who held my views. I had books and other objects thrown at me while walking down the hall and was constantly insulted because of my appearance and outspoken views, not only by students but also by some faculty. "Satanist! Faggot! FREAK!!" I went through this every day for 2½ years. There was no one in the school to go to for help or guidance. During my freshman year, I begged my father daily not to make me go to school, but to no avail. I began experiencing violent stomach pains, often going home from school early. I used this to my advantage, faking sickness at least twice a week in order to go home.

I began having violent fantasies about walking through the halls with a duffel bag full of guns, shooting whomever I saw, as well as throwing grenades into classrooms. I have never been a violent person and doubt that I ever will be. I have been involved in only one fight, in which one punch was thrown, by the other person, of course. He was a kid much bigger than me, who had been taunting me for months, walking straight up to me in the hall and yelling things at me. I got sick of it and one day told him that he was nothing but a stupid redneck and that if what he wanted was to hit me, to just do it. That resulted in two scars on my face. He was suspended, but when he returned to school, the taunting got worse. I could find no solace. I felt that the entire world was against me, that I was the iconoclast to everything. When my feeling that violence was the only way out became all I thought about, I got scared.

The final straw of my last few days in public school was when I saw a much bigger kid brutally punch a much smaller kid for no reason other than to make his presence known. I was the only one willing to tell the principal and police who had done it. I was assured that no one would find out I had ratted. Wrong. The next day, people I had never met before came up to me asking why I had ratted him out. I was hit in the head with a book in the hall. I complained to my guidance counselor, who told me to continue with my day. I then found a note in my locker with "Die fag" written on it. That was it. I told my counselor that if he did not excuse me to leave, I would leave anyway. I did not return to school for weeks, and when I did, it was only for 3 days before transferring. I am sorry to say that by that point the only thing that prevented me from going on a shooting spree through the school was the lack of resources. I simply could not get any guns. Otherwise, I can guarantee I would have carried it out.

I am sure that Dylan and Eric went though almost the same thing I did. This has not been brought to the attention of the media in an adequate fashion. I do not hear the television reporters and magazines saying, "They shouldn't have been teased" or "We should have cared for their needs." This does not happen in public schools. The purpose of public schools is to teach you what they think you need to know and get you out. If you do not comply, they see this as a threat instead of a cry for help. Too often the misfits in high schools are ignored or passed off as meaningless problems. The faculty does not care about the welfare of a teen who wears all black and is not one of the popular, cooperative kids. That is where the problem lies: in the ignorance of the schools themselves. Schools should not wait until there is a violent act, whether extreme or not, to see warning signs. I read short biographies of the students who were killed in Littleton and was amazed to see that they were exactly the kind of kids who put me through hell. Football players. Adamant Christians. Patriots. The normal kids. The ones who belong. All we ever read in a newspaper or magazine or watch on the news is how horrible it is that "these wonderful kids have been taken from us." It is horrible, but never once will you ever read, "Why were Klebold and Harris treated like that? Why did everyone make fun of them? Why couldn't people accept them for who they were?"

This is why these shootings happen and will continue to happen. The one thing the media, the schools, and the government continue to overlook time after time is the ignorance of the severe cruelty that such "good kids" are capable of. Too many children today are prone to violence or cruelty, and not enough people are aware of it. For such things to stop occurring, the parents, teachers, and children of this country must realize that if you constantly barrage and torment someone who is different from you, you must be prepared to suffer the consequences of your actions.

Although resentment still lies within me (and probably always will), I know that violence will cause nothing but more blame put on those of us who are antisocial. People are not antisocial because they want to be. People are antisocial because of how society made them. No one should be shocked when these shootings happen. We should expect it. I do not like the fact that this is true, but there is no other reality now. Never should someone say, "Why did this happen? How could this have happened?" You can take the most peaceful, fun-loving kid, put him or her in a setting where he or she is hated and tormented, and see how he or she turns out. It is not the security systems of schools that need to change, but the environment. Acceptance of one another is the only way to avoid another Columbine.

A Father's Perspective
by William F. Cornell

Caleb is 16, our youngest son. As I was writing my column for *The Script,* the war in what is left of Yugoslavia was escalating. Caleb and I discussed the war, and in his school he was an outspoken, minority voice opposing military intervention in Kosovo. It was a Tuesday afternoon when Caleb tried to reach me by phone, so upset by the teasing and opposition he was getting from other students that he was afraid he would lose control and hurt someone. He wanted to talk to me to calm himself down. When he couldn't reach me, he left school rather than risk losing control. It was the Tuesday of the Columbine High School killings.

I asked Caleb to cowrite this article with me for *The Script* knowing that he identified strongly with the boys who carried out these killings as well as student shootings at other schools. Nothing that Caleb has written here surprised me, but I was not prepared for the impact of his written words. I was both stunned to read about his fury and anguish and touched to see the courage of his honesty and his capacity for self-reflection.

I could not read Caleb's essay without thinking of all three of our sons. Stephanie and I raised our kids to be independent and outspoken thinkers—providing them as best we were able with a broad range of life experiences, quite different from most of the other kids growing up in the rural and underdeveloped area where we live. We were active, progressive parents, but Stephanie and I, each in our own way, are rather shy. Our sons have mirrored our difficulties in peer relationships.

Caleb tends to meet the world like a full-force gale. He is frequently angry, outspoken, and disarmingly articulate. Caleb is also a tender and deeply compassionate young man of rather exceptional maturity. Peer relationships, however, have always been a struggle for him. He has tended to pair with older kids who graduate, leaving Caleb to start all over again. Now Caleb is lead singer and lyricist for a punk band and has established a more stable peer group, but he has suffered tremendously at the hands of kids his own age.

Caleb was 13 when things began to go seriously wrong at school. He was outspoken about racial, religious, and political issues, confronting bigotry and taking unpopular stands forcefully. Caleb became increasingly isolated. His grades dropped from nearly all As to Cs and Ds. In spite of frequent, often confrontational, meetings with school personnel, nothing really changed. My attention was focused on the school staff. As is so clear from Caleb's account, I consistently underestimated the impact of other students' behavior.

After the violent incidents at school that Caleb describes in his essay, he had been back 2 or 3 days when we had a conversation I will never forget. One of the first school shootings had just occurred, and Caleb told me that he had frequent fantasies of walking into school with a gun and killing kids. I asked him why he thought those kids killed and he did not. "We don't have any guns here. That's the only difference, Dad. Believe me, if we had guns in this house, there were days I've been so mad I would have taken one to school." I found another school for Caleb immediately, and since then I have witnessed the dramatic difference a competent and dedicated staff can make. Caleb's difficulties have not evaporated overnight, but he has found a place where he expects to be helped and taken seriously.

As I read Caleb's essay, I thought back to an earlier, nearly tragic, incident in Caleb's life. When he was 11, he was at an all-night camp-out in a friend's back yard. About 1 am the kids, boys and girls, were seated around a campfire. Two local police saw the fire, decided the kids must be drinking or doing drugs (not true), and swept in on them without warning from the dark. Caleb at that time had very long hair and an earring. One of the cops picked Caleb up from behind by his hair, clamping his wrists in handcuffs behind his back. Caleb fainted, falling face-first into the campfire. Miraculously his glasses stayed on, so his eyes were not damaged, but he was horribly burned on the face and neck. He ended up in the intensive care burn unit, where he received extraordinary medical and psychological care. After the accident, I wanted to sue the police and township government. Caleb refused, saying that it had been an accident and that a lawsuit would only create more trouble. Caleb asked instead that I meet with and confront the chief of police, show the photographs of his burned face to the assaultive police officer, and offer the police training on how to deal with adolescents. That is what we did. In contrast, to this day Caleb holds school officials accountable for what happened to him, seeing it as malicious and intentional, not accidental. He wants to sue the school district, which is not an easy thing to do, although we continue to consider it.

It has been difficult for me to write anything here but as a father. As I approached writing a companion piece to Caleb's, I kept wondering, what do I have to offer to my colleagues other than Caleb's honesty?

Just as we were completing the last issue of *The Script,* Robin and I received a brief statement from George Kohlrieser about the Columbine killings. A year earlier, Caleb had read George's article on conflict resolution in *The Script* theme issue domestic violence and said, "This guy really knows what he's talking about." I was deeply touched by George's comments on the Columbine tragedy and glad to publish it right away. I also showed it to Caleb, and this consolidated our decision to write something together for this issue.

As George has so often said, "People do not kill people—people kill objects." I agree, especially on a social and political scale. Over and over again our political leaders turn other leaders and peoples into objects, things, demons, so as to justify killing them. I think at a social and political level, people kill objects or demons, not people.

In my clinical experience, however, I see a somewhat different picture. I think people do kill other people, sometimes very intentionally; people kill particular people with particular intent. This is my understanding of what Caleb is describing about his own feelings and fantasies and his identification with Eric Harris and Dylan Klebold. I think people become capable of killing others when they have come to feel like objects or things themselves. I doubt that people want to kill, but they can be driven to choose it rather than not to choose it. I think it takes extraordinary, sustained neglect, humiliation, and cruelty to bring a person—adult or child—to the point that he or she can kill. Caleb offers us a vivid, personal description of this kind of marginalization and dehumanization and the helplessness, despair, and fury it can create within an individual. Caleb challenges us to ask the right kinds of questions, complicated and uncomfortable questions, about what happened in Littleton and other schools, about what kids need from their communities, about the centrality of peer relationships.

Three-fourths of adolescent deaths are caused by drug and alcohol abuse, suicide, and violence. These are social diseases. "The National Longitudinal Study of Adolescent Health" (*Journal of the American Medical Association,* 10 September 1997), a study of 12,000 teenagers in grades 7 through 12, demonstrated that the single most important variable in the psychological health of adolescents is the experience of positive emotional attachments to parents and teachers. A recent book, *Peer Power: Preadolescent Culture and Identity,* by Patricia and Peter Adler (Rutgers University Press, 1998) outlines in chilling detail the social evolution and psychological impact of peer groupings, reinforcing the relentless stratification in social groups at school and their place in preadolescent and adolescent identity formation.

Caleb has dreadlocks, wears a nose ring, and dresses in black, his clothing covered with punk and political patches. He is also white, very bright, and straight. He also has a father who could afford to take him out of public school and finance a private school education on very short notice. What of the kids who are poor, inarticulate, African American, Latino, gay? Orlando Peterson, a Harvard sociologist speaking to the *New York Times* on the Littleton massacre, challenged, "There is a disturbing double standard in the way we discuss the problems of different groups of people and in the way we label deviant behavior. If the terrorist act of white, middle-class teenagers creates an orgy of national soul-searching, then surely the next time a heinous crime is committed by underclass African American or Latino kids, we should engage in the same kind of national soul-searching."

Transactional analysis is practiced and taught worldwide. As practitioners of a methodology that reaches across national and cultural boundaries, we have a unique opportunity and responsibility to try to effect social as well as individual good. As theorists and therapists we must continue to push our theory and technique into the darker reaches of human nature. Caleb's essay speaks to these darker realms, the forces of hatred and ostracization, the potential for cruelty and murder.

It seems that the darker side of Berne's writings has rarely been taken up in any systematic way by subsequent transactional analysis theorists. Transactional analysis has been developed largely within the realms of psychological daylight, too deeply shaped by American demands for support, safety, protection, and happiness, the mental attitude of the white middle class that demands comfort, gratification, and homogeneity. Berne always seemed aware and wary of the uglier, more destructive aspects of human nature. Whether we examine adolescent violence or the unending outbreaks of social and political violence justified under the banners of nationalist, ethnic, or religious identity, we are faced with the destructive capacities of human nature and group behavior. The issues that Caleb addresses take us back to our roots as a social psychiatry, a group and community therapy.

The central, visual imago of transactional analysis theory are the stacked circles of ego states and the script matrix, images derived from notions of the individual ego and the nuclear family. Transactional analysis script theory needs to be extended to deal more systematically with group behavior, peer relationships, and latency and adolescent patterns of belonging and identity.

We need social and political as well as clinical intervention. In the United States, in most states, it is possible for a kid to purchase a gun before it is legal for him or her to buy beer or to vote. The lack of gun control in the United States is absurd and immoral. I recall the bullies of my grade school and high school years, the teasing and tormenting by the in-group of the outcasts, fist fights, a couple of suicides, our high school burned down by a guy from another town trying to kill a janitor. But fortunately, there were no handguns. Richard Reeves, writing a column in the *International Herald Tribune* (12 May 1999), also recalled the violence of his adolescence in Jersey City: "If a fight escalated, people went for the maximum available weaponry. Fists. Bottles. Rolling pins. Baseball bats. Knives. There was blood, broken bones, cracked heads. People were patched up, generally, and life went on. If there were guns, there was killing. Life did not go on. That was the difference. . . . The difference is guns. That is why those children died in Littleton. And why others will die. This is not complicated reasoning. It is an obvious fact."

If you live in the United States, please do not be silent or passive about the urgent need for serious, systematic, severely enforced gun control. Give money to gun control organizations. And wherever you live in the world, lobby for the government support of community-based mental health services in all neighborhoods and schools. Do not be passive or silent. Give time. Give money. Write letters. Write articles. Raise hell about the needs of our kids and the socially outcast.

At this moment, I am mostly keenly aware of the compassion, resilience, and decency that Caleb has maintained throughout an adolescence that has been far from easy. I deeply appreciate his willingness to write for *The Script*. I hope his comments will bring a little more insight and compassion toward kids who are driven toward violence and social marginalization.

Fierce in Reason and Compassion
by William F. Cornell

Just a few days ago, Robin Fryer and I were finalizing the copy for this issue of *The Script*. Then it was Tuesday, 11 September, the day of the terrorist attacks in New York and Washington, DC. Like everyone else here, I spent the day stunned, listening to the radio as I tried to listen to clients, trying to make some sense of their reactions and my own and most urgently trying to reach my sons and my friends.

Suddenly, the United States, like so many other nations in the world, was the tragic target of the hatred and violence bred by nationalistic, ethnic, and religious fanaticism. What we saw and experienced that day was a level of violence and destruction that is beyond comprehension.

I found it personally appalling that within 12 hours of the first plane crashing into the World Trade Center, US President George W. Bush was promising vengeance (thinly veiled in the language of justice) and making a declaration of war while in the next breath saying a prayer. He seemed oblivious to the way in which his fusion of vengeance and prayer was virtually identical to what we now suspect was the pretext of the terrorists. We can be pretty sure that the terrorists were praying to their own version of God, certain in their own moral goodness and superiority as they directed those planes to their targets.

In 1965 I graduated from high school in a small, upstate New York, working-class town. I was the brightest kid they had ever seen around there, the pride of the village. At that time the Vietnam War was escalating, and in the time-honored tradition of nationalistic fervor, American political and military leaders had relentlessly and successfully transformed the North Vietnamese people into monsters who were no longer truly human. This entitled us to slaughter them en masse, our ultimate God-sanctioned victory assured as we strove to save the world from Communist atheists. Upon graduation, I was immediately inducted into the service; although I refused to comply, I was inducted anyway and granted a student deferment, which I also refused. Instead, I sought conscientious objector status on political and ethical grounds, challenging the prevailing religious requirement. My lawsuit against the Selective Service went on for years; meanwhile, I went off to college. But I was no longer the pride of the village; the town turned against my family, and my parents and siblings were subjected to such hostility that within a year they decided to leave, never to return.

Thirty-five years later my oldest son, Seth, decided to backpack on his own through Cambodia and Vietnam. Several weeks into his trip, I received a middle-of-the-night panicked call from him in Hanoi; he said he was in trouble and needed money right away, reeling off a bank number where I should send cash. Then the phone went dead, and I had no idea how to get back in touch with him. I sent the money immediately, but Seth never picked it up. I called the US Embassy, but they could not trace him. Finally, desperate, I called back to the bank in Hanoi where the bank manager assured me they had the money but my son had not appeared. He offered to call all of the other banks in Hanoi to see if Seth had been to any of them. After doing so, he called me back to say there was no word on Seth but they would do what they could. I began to cry, "Why are you doing this for me?" I asked him through my tears. "Because I am a father, too," he replied. "But why would you help me after what my country did to your people? I can't believe you are so kind." I will never forget his answer: "We are a good people. We have always been good people. You did not make the war. We did not make the war. Our leaders made the war. We have no reason to hate you. I hope you find your boy. Our people will not hurt him; they will help him." Seth never did get the money I sent him, but he made his way virtually penniless from Hanoi to Hong Kong with the help of the people we were taught to fear and hate.

Within hours of the horrors in New York, Washington, DC, and Pittsburgh, I was receiving phone calls and emails of concern and condolence from ITAA friends and colleagues around the world. I know this is true for other ITAA members in the United States as well. These calls have been a powerful and soothing reminder that the ITAA can be, needs to be, a truly international community. Robin and I decided to postpone production of this issue briefly so that we could include some of these moving and thought-provoking messages.

It breaks my heart to see the forces of fear, hatred, and demonization swing into full force yet again. As American political reactions to this week's terrorist attacks unfold, it does not look as if we can rely on our nation's leaders to help people grapple with fear, hatred, tragedy, loss, unyielding anguish, and vulnerability. Wrapping ourselves in American flags—or any flag—or in the banners of fanaticism or vengeance will not reduce the tragedy or the vulnerabilities that stalk the peoples of this world. We need to wrap ourselves in tears and reason, not nationalistic diatribes. Former U.S. Senator Bob Kerrey, one of the few current American politicians who actually fought in the Vietnam War, said yesterday of the terrorists' action, "I condemn it morally, and I do think it was cowardly. But physically, it was the opposite of cowardly, and if you don't understand that, then you don't understand the intensity of the cause. . . . There is hatred out there against the United States, and yes, we have to deal with terrorism in a zero-tolerance fashion. But there is anger, too, and they ought to have a place for a hearing on that anger, in the International Court or wherever we give them a hearing" (*New York Times,* 15 September 2001, p. A16). We must bring our skills, our reason, our compassion, and our humanness to bear upon our lives together even—and perhaps most especially —at those moments when we most fear it to be futile and inadequate.

I do not know the name of that banker in Hanoi. I do know the name of my President. I hope that George W. Bush can find within himself the determined wisdom of that Vietnamese father. During the memorial service at the National Cathedral in Washington, DC, 3 days after the attacks, President Bush said, "This nation is peaceful, but fierce when stirred to anger." We need now a leadership and a people who are fierce in reason and compassion, not fierce in anger. I hope that Bush can realize, even in the midst of unfathomable tragedy, that people of every nation, every faith, every race, and every ethnic identity are good people. We cannot afford once more the facile "solution" and self-indulgent relief of revenge. We must find the will and the means to confront and ultimately to develop alternatives to cycles of vengeance, violence, and moral superiority. We must give the nations and peoples of the world time to come together in a fiercely reasoned way, to finally, finally not resort first to war but to find the means and resolve to isolate and punish criminals while helping people understand the depths and divisiveness of our mutual fears and demonizations.

My father, as did so many of his generation, fought in World War II. He came back broken by what he witnessed, never to recover. I grew up during the Vietnam War, which I was fortunately able to resist as a conscientious objector. The United States and Vietnam endured a vicious, fruitless war. The United States saw the return of tens of thousands of devastated soldiers; the death toll for the Vietnamese was never fully counted. My sons have grown up during the Afghan and Iraq wars, privileged enough not to have to be soldiers. We are again witnessing the horrendous consequences of a mindless and unnecessary war, the deaths and injuries of the "enemies" again uncounted.

All of this has deeply shaped my bearing as a psychotherapist. For his part, Freud had two sons who fought in World War I (over his objections). That war profoundly impacted Freud's thinking. I close here with a quote from his deeply personal essay "On Transcience":

[World War I] broke out and robbed the world of its beauties. It destroyed not only the beauty of the countrysides through which it passed and the works of art which it met on its path but it also shattered our pride in the achievements of our civilization, our admiration for many philosophers and artists, and our hopes of a final triumph over the differences between nations and races. It tarnished the lofty impartiality of our science, it revealed our instincts in all their nakedness and let loose the evil spirits within us which we thought had been tamed forever by centuries of continuous education by the noblest minds. It made our country small again and made the rest of the world far remote. It robbed us of very much that we had loved, and showed us how ephemeral were many things that we regarded as changeless. (Freud, 1916/1957, p. 307)

REFERENCE

Freud, S. (1957). On transience. In J. Strachey (Ed. & Trans.), *The standard edition of the complete psychological works of Sigmund Freud* (Vol. 14, pp. 303-310). London: The Hogarth Press. (Original work published 1916)

The original version of "The Root of the Problem" and "A Father's Perspective" was published in The Script, *Volume 29, Number 5, pp. 1, 7, July 1999. The original version of "Fierce in Reason and Compassion" was published in* The Script, *Volume 31, Number 6, p. 2, September-October 2001.*

Epilogue

Looking Back/Looking Ahead

The morning I began writing this epilogue, I received a phone call from the wife of my former analyst. He had been seriously ill for the past year, and she called to tell me that he had been admitted to hospice. She thought I would want to know and to come see him. I did, holding his hands, caressing and kissing him, thanking him, and saying good-bye. He died the following day.

Mort Johan was 86 and had maintained his practice until the age of 82. I was his last analytic patient. We had come to love each other dearly. Ours was not a romanticized love but the kind of love that is born of a willingness to face many hard places together.

I began working with Mort in 1991. He warned me then that he was 70 and was planning to retire at 80, which might not allow all the time we might want for the therapy. As we began to discuss how we would work, he told me that he had been classically trained and had always practiced in that mode, but he had come to have grave questions about that model. Over the course of his career, Mort became increasingly disenchanted with the stiff formality he had been originally trained to maintain as an analyst. It did not suit his natural warmth or love of life. He gently but persistently challenged the more dogmatic approaches to treatment, which too often constrained the fundamental humanness of the psychoanalytic relationship.

Mort had been asked to review Karen Maroda's (1991) *The Power of Countertransference*, which had just been published, and he told me that it had had a profound effect on him. By sheer coincidence, I had also just read and even reviewed Maroda's book (see Chapter 26 of this volume). That book gave Mort a frame of reference to use in remodeling his way of working. "I want to learn to practice differently—I want to get good at this damned job before I die," he told me. He also hoped, since I had already had a substantial amount of solid psychotherapy, that our work could be a kind of experimental laboratory. So began a therapeutic/analytic excursion that lasted 11 years. During our time together, I watched Mort quietly transform a mode of working that had been all too often distant and intellectual for him into a mutual exploration with his patients.

In 1995, the evening before Thanksgiving, I received a completely unexpected phone call from Rose, the woman who became my second mother in Portland, Oregon, after my own mother died while I was in college. Rose had been diagnosed with pancreatic cancer and was given a few weeks to live. I was bereft beyond anything I had ever known, even more than when my own parents died. Thanksgiving being a major American holiday, all of my friends and my analyst were out of town. I left Mort an anguished message. The evening he arrived back in town from his holiday, he called from the airport, telling me that he was driving directly to his office and for me to meet him there. I told him I was feeling a bit better at that point and it really wasn't necessary. He responded that he wasn't asking my opinion, that I was to come to his office, that I was not to go through this alone.

The next night, as I lay restlessly in bed, Mort called to say he imagined that sleep would be hard to find that week and perhaps hearing his voice at bedtime would make it a bit easier to rest. He suggested that I have a friend call each night at bedtime—not exactly standard analytic technique but reflective of the kind of engagement he was willing to make. Rose died 30 days later, on Christmas eve.

As Mort and I approached termination in 2002, he said that he would like to have a personal relationship of some sort when our work was done. I declined, saying that I wanted to experience a complete termination and all that it would evoke. I told him that I did, however, want to be with him if he became ill and when he was dying. Given the very premature deaths of my parents, I wanted to witness and accompany a man of his vitality into the end of his life. He agreed. While we often saw each other at professional meetings and he followed my writing with great interest, we kept our distance while still feeling all the affection and warmth between us.

Years passed, and one day Mort called suggesting we meet for lunch; he asked explicitly that I bring my partner, Mick, with me. Over lunch he told me that he had been diagnosed with an extremely rare, untreatable form of blood cancer that was asymptomatic but would gradually affect the lining around his brain. Mort and I started meeting regularly for casual, quietly intimate times together. As the illness began to ravage his brain, he spoke openly of his own parents' deaths, his determination to live as fully as possible until he could no longer do so, his bitterness that he and his second wife, Arlene, could no longer dance the salsa (one of his great pleasures), his dread of being stuck in some state of debilitation more dead than alive. His mind stayed fresh and full of humor for quite some time, and then the disease began to encroach, his short-term memory collapsing. He had brain surgery in the hopes of forestalling some of the deterioration. Mick and I saw him in intensive care and after his release from the hospital. It became clear that the course of the disease was not to be slowed, and Mort decided not to pursue further treatment. Fortunately, he was not doomed to a long period of debilitation.

I have had the good fortune in recent years to know and work with two psychoanalysts from Eric Berne's generation: Mort Johan and Jim McLaughlin. While I was working with Jim McLaughlin to edit his book (McLaughlin, 2005), I suddenly realized that all of his significant papers—those truly in his own voice—were written after he was 60. When I asked him about that, he mused in his subtly sardonic way, "Well, let's see. I was born an Irish Catholic. My father died when I was 6 weeks old. I was raised by a depressed, Catholic mother. I went to Catholic school. Then I went to medical school and became a psychiatrist. Then I went into the military. Then I became trained as a psychoanalyst with full orthodoxy. It's a miracle I found my own mind at any age!"

Mort and Jim were colleagues and friends, both trained as analysts during the same time period and within the frame of neo-Freudian orthodoxy. I witnessed both of these men in the later years of their lives confront their profession's conventions and create new ways of thinking and working. The gifts I received from them were many, but the most precious were their examples of ruthless self-scrutiny, relentless curiosity, and the capacity to change at any stage of life.

Even now, my thoughts drift back over the many colleagues I have had here in Pittsburgh and throughout the world in my community of the ITAA. These relationships have affected over 2 decades of wondering, learning, thinking, teaching, and writing the papers that have been collected in this volume. When I think of the next 20 years of the evolution of transactional analysis—which is now, itself, in its sixties as a theory and system of practice—my deepest wish is that we, as a community of professionals, do not ossify. I have a deep and abiding regard for Eric Berne, both in his rebellious creativity and his piercing intelligence. I hope that he would be proud of the work we are doing now as a global community. I also have a deep and abiding regard for the dignity and humanness of our model; it fosters respect and competence across the span of human relations work—counseling, psychotherapy, education, and organizational development. It was part of Berne's genius to create a model that had the flexibility to be applicable in many of the realms in which people live and learn.

I hope our work as transactional analysts stays alive through respectful discourse with other disciplines while avoiding the deadening and homogenization caused by governmental and third-party regulation. I remain deeply committed to the ITAA's continuing publication of journals and volumes of creative and challenging papers that will inform our community and reach beyond it. I hope in another 20 years that I may have another volume of papers to offer our community!

And so, with many thanks to the wonderful transactional analysis community, in honor of Eric Berne, and in loving memory of Jim and Mort, I say adieu for now.

REFERENCE

Maroda, K. J. (1991). *The power of countertransference: Innovations in analytic technique.* Chichester: Wiley.

McLaughlin, J. T. (2005). *The healer's bent: Solitude and dialogue in the clinical encounter* (W. F. Cornell, Ed.). Hillsdale, NJ: The Analytic Press.

Additional Publications by William F. Cornell

Books

Cornell, W. F., & Hargaden, H. (Eds.). (2005). *From transactions to relations: The emergence of a relational tradition in transactional analysis.* Oxfordshire: Haddon Press.

McLaughlin, J. T. (2005). *The healer's bent: Solitude and dialogue in the clinical encounter* (W. F. Cornell, Ed. & Intro.). Hillsdale, NJ: The Analytic Press.

Cornell, W. F. (In press). *The impassioned body: Somatic experience and meaning in psychotherapy.* Oxfordshire: Haddon Press.

Chapters

Cornell, W. F. (1980). Structure and function in radix body education and script change. In J. Cassius (Ed.), *Horizons in bioenergetics: New dimensions in mind/body psychotherapy* (pp. 88-97). Memphis, TN: Promethean Publications.

Cornell, W. F. (1988). Analise transactional como uma psicologia da saude—uma perspectiva pessoal [Transactional analysis as a psychology of health: A personal perspective]. In R. Shinyashiki (Ed.), *Os analistas transacionais hoje los analistas transacionales hoy* (pp. 33-39). Sao Paulo: Editora Gente.

Cornell, W. F. (2005). Deep in the shed: An analyst's mind at work [Editor's introduction]. In J. T. McLaughlin, *The healer's bent: Solitude and dialogue in the clinical encounter* (pp. 1-16). Hillsdale, NJ: The Analytic Press.

Cornell, W. F. (2008). Self in action: The bodily basis of self-organization. In F. S. Anderson (Ed.), *Bodies in treatment: The unspoken dimension* (pp. 29-49). New York: The Analytic Press.

Cornell, W. F. (2008). Loves and losses: Enactments in the disavowal of intimate desires. In D. Mann & V. Cunningham (Eds.), *The past in the present: Therapy enactments and the return of trauma* (pp. 82-101). London: Routledge.

Cornell. W. F. (In press). An eruption of erotic vitality between a male analyst and a male client. In B. Reis & R. Grossmark (Ed.), *Heterosexual masculinities.* New York: The Analytic Press.

Articles/Papers

Cornell, C., & Cornell, W. F. (2002). Quand des enfants tuent d'autres enfants [When kids kill other kids]. *Actualites en Analyse Transactionelle, 26*(103), 93-94.

Cornell. W. F. (1975). Wake up "sleepy": Reichian techniques and script intervention. *Transactional Analysis Journal, 5,* 144-147.

Cornell, W. F. (1991). Theorie du scenario et recherches sur le croissance [Theories of script: A critical review from a developmental perspective]. *Actualites en Analyse Transactionelle, 15*(58), 68-84.

Cornell, W. F. (1992). Review of *Confessions of a psychologist: Is physical touch therapeutic?*. *Transactional Analysis Journal, 22,* 189-191.

Cornell, W. F. (1992). Reflections on generative lives: A review of three books. *Transactional Analysis Journal, 22,* 243-247.

Cornell, W. F. (1992). Women and depression/silencing the self: A review. *Transactional Analysis Journal, 22,* 191-194.

Cornell, W. F. (1994). Shame: Binding affect, ego state contamination, and relational repair. *Transactional Analysis Journal, 24,* 139-146.
Cornell, W. F. (1995). A plea for a measure of ambiguity. *Readings: A Journal of Reviews and Commentary in Mental Health, 10*(2), 4-11.
Cornell, W. F. (1995). L'A.T. et les relations a doubles roles: Formation, supervision et therapie [Dual relationships in transactional analysis: Training, supervision, and therapy]. *Actualites en Analyse Transactionnelle, 19*(75), 119-130.
Cornell, W. F. (1996). Capitalism in the consulting room. *Readings: A Journal of Reviews and Commentary in Mental health, 11*(1), 12-17.
Cornell, W. F. (1997). La honte: Affect inhibiteur, contaminations, reparation relationnelle [Shame: Binding affect, ego state contaminations, and relational repair]. *Actualites en Analyse Transactionnelle, 21*(81), 6-14.
Cornell, W. F. (1997). If Reich had met Winnicott: Body and gesture. *Energy & Character, 28*(2), 50-60.
Cornell, W. F. (1999). Si Reich avait connu Winnicott: Le corps et les gestes [If Berne had met Winnicott: Body and gesture]. *Actualites en Analyse Transactionnelle, 23*(90), 44-52.
Cornell, W. F. (2000). Transference, desire, and vulnerability in body-centered psychotherapy. *Energy & Character, 30*(2), 29-37.
Cornell, W. F. (2001). There ain't no cure without sex: The provision of a "vital" base. *Transactional Analysis Journal, 31,* 233-239.
Cornell, W. F. (2003). Wenn sich Berne und Winnicott begegnen wurden [If Berne met Winnicott: Body and gesture]. *Zeitschrift fur Transaktionsanalyse, 20*(2), 112-123.
Cornell, W. F. (2003). The impassioned body: Erotic vitality and disturbance in psychotherapy. *British Gestalt Journal, 12,* 92-104.
Cornell, W. F. (2003). Entering the gestural field: The body in relation. *Energy & Character, 32,* 45-55.
Cornell, W. F. (In press). A stranger to desire. *Studies in Gender and Sexuality.*
Cornell, W. F., & Hine, J. (2000). Les emotions ont une function cognitive et sociale: Une perspective transactionnelle en champ guidance ou conseil [Cognitive and social functions of emotions: A model for transactional analysis counselor training]. *Actualites en Analyse Transactionelle, 24*(95), 85-96.
Cornell, W. F., & Landaiche, N. M., III. (2005). Impasse e intimita nella coppia terapeutica o di counseling: L'influenza del protocollo [Impasse and intimacy: Applying Berne's concept of script protocol]. *Rivista Italiana di Analisi Transazionale e Methodologie Psicoterapeutiche, 11,* 35-60.
Cornell, W. F., & Landaiche, N. M., III. (2006). Impasse et intimite dans couple de travail en therapie ou en conseil: L'influence du protocle [Impasse and intimacy: Applying Berne's concept of script protocol]. *Actualites en Analyse Transactionnelle, 30*(120), 11-44.
Cornell, W. F., & Landaiche, N.M., III. (2007). Engpass und intimitat im beratungs - und therapie-paar: Der einfluss des skriptentwurfs (protocol) [Impasse and intimacy: Applying Berne's concept of script protocol]. *Zeitschrift fur Transaktionsanalyse, 24*(2), 105-129 (Teil 1); *24*(3), 185-199 (Teil 2).
Cornell, W. F., & Olio, K. A. (1994). La dimension affective du traitement d'abus corporals subis dans l'enfance [Consequences of childhood bodily abuse: Affect, ego states, and therapeutic implications]. *Actualites en Analyse Transactionnelle, 18*(72), 179-192.
Olio, K. A., & Cornell, W. F. (1993). Therapeutic relationship as the foundation for treatment with adult survivors of sexual abuse. *Psychotherapy: Theory, Practice and Research, 30,* 512-523.
Olio, K. A., & Cornell, W. F. (1994). Making meaning not monsters: Reflections on the delayed memory controversy. *Journal of Child Sexual Abuse, 3*(3), 77-94.
Olio, K. A., & Cornell, W. F. (1998). The façade of scientific documentation: A case study of Richard Ofshe's analysis of the Paul Ingram case. *Psychology, Public Policy, and Law, 4,* 1182-1197.
Zalcman, M. J., & Cornell, W. F. (1983). A bilateral model for clinical supervision. *Transactional Analysis Journal, 13,* 112-123.

About the Author and Coauthors

William F. Cornell, M.A., Teaching and Supervising Transactional Analyst (psychotherapy), studied behavioral psychology at Reed College in Portland, Oregon, and phenomenological psychology at Duquesne University in Pittsburgh, Pennsylvania. He followed his graduate studies with training in transactional analysis and body-centered psychotherapy. Bill has published numerous journal articles and book chapters, many exploring the interface between transactional analysis, body-centered psychotherapy, and psychoanalytic modalities. He is editor of the ITAA newsletter, *The Script,* and a coeditor of the *Transactional Analysis Journal.* Bill edited and wrote the introduction to *The Healer's Bent: Solitude and Dialogue in the Clinical Encounter,* a collection of the psychoanalytic writings of James McLaughlin. With Helena Hargaden, he was a coeditor and author of *From Transactions to Relations: The Emergence of Relational Paradigms in Transactional Analysis.* He is also the author of the forthcoming book *The Impassioned Body.* Bill maintains an independent private practice of therapy, consultation, and training in Pittsburgh, Pennsylvania, U.S.A., and leads frequent training groups in Europe.

Frances Bonds-White, Ed.D., is the president of the International Association for Group Psychotherapy and Group Processes (IAGP) (2006-2009), a Teaching and Supervising Transactional Analyst (psychotherapy), and a Fellow of the American Group Psychotherapy Association. She has a private practice in psychology/psychotherapy in Philadelphia, Pennsylvania, U.S.A., and is known for her work with artists, musicians, and composers and for the excellence of her supervision in group psychotherapy.

Caleb Cornell is a bartender in Pittsburgh, Pennsylvania, U.S.A., and the lyricist and lead singer for the punk group Wrath Cobra.

Jenni Hine, Teaching and Supervising Transactional Analyst, EAP, now retired, was the main founder and leader of the Geneva Transactional Analysis Training Center after being a TA practitioner for 15 years. She has been on the ITAA Board of Trustees, the EATA Council, and served as vice president of the Suisse Romande TA Association. She specialized in both clinical and counseling TA and strongly supported the development of the counseling field in Switzerland and Europe as a whole. Jenny has written articles on TA counseling, game analysis, and ego state theory.

N. Michel Landaiche, III, Ph.D., is a psychotherapist for the student counseling center at Carnegie Mellon University, Pittsburgh, Pennsylvania, U.S.A.

Robert Norton (a pseudonym), a qualified counselor, lives and works in Oxfordshire, United Kingdom.

Karen Olio, M.A., M.Ed., LPC, is the author of numerous articles on the treatment of trauma and in independent practice in Norwalk, Connecticut, U.S.A.

Carole Shadbolt, M.Sc. (Psych), Teaching and Supervising Transactional Analyst (psychotherapy) lives and has an independent clinical and supervisory practice in Oxfordshire, United Kingdom. She has written a number of articles focusing on sexuality, diversity, and prejudice.

Marilyn Zalcman, M.S.W., Teaching and Supervising Transactional Analyst, lives and practices in McLean, Virginia, U.S.A.

About the International Transactional Analysis Association

Transactional analysis is a psychological and social theory with mutual contracting for growth and change. The International Transactional Analysis Association is a nonprofit organization established to stimulate the growth and development of creative and useful theory and applications of transactional analysis (TA) in psychotherapy, education, business, counseling, and other fields of human interaction.

Transactional analysis is a system of both theory and practice. The ITAA is the professional association for those persons who are certified as having demonstrated competence in treatment, counseling, teaching, or consulting using transactional analysis. The ITAA contracts with an administratively separate organization, the Transactional Analysis Certification Council, to oversee a rigorous certification process.

The ITAA is dedicated to facilitating international communication among people and groups who use transactional analysis. The ITAA works to build understanding, knowledge, and acceptance of transactional analysis and to provide theoreticians and practitioners with techniques of proven value for enriching life, a forum for evolving new transactional analysis theory and methods, and an ethical framework. The values of the ITAA are, in part, that "all individuals shall have the opportunity to live autonomous and socially responsible lives, that respect is given to the individuality and common humanity of all people, and that relationship shall be carried out without discrimination."

After many early years of growth and development, the organization is now committed to refining theory and practice. To stimulate original scientific contributions to the development of transactional analysis, the ITAA presents an annual Eric Berne Memorial Award.

There are four levels of membership in the ITAA:
- **Associate:** a general-interest, nonvoting membership
- **Student Member:** a voting-level membership for full-time college students
- **Regular Member:** a voting-level membership for professionals who have certification through another source or who are in the process of attaining competency-based certification in transactional analysis
- **Certified Member:** competency-based membership acquired after passage of written and oral exams; includes specialties in clinical, educational, organizational, and counseling areas
- **Teaching Member:** for those who have completed training and examination to become a Teaching and/or Supervising Transactional Analyst

Benefits of membership include:
- The quarterly *Transactional Analysis Journal*
- *The Script* newsletter nine times a year
- International conferences and designated (business) meeting discounts
- Many intangibles, such as international networking, committee involvement, group rates on insurance and travel programs, and much more

For information on membership and upcoming events, please contact:
International Transactional Analysis Association
2186 Rheem Dr., #B-1, Pleasanton, CA 94588-2775, U.S.A.
phone: 925-600-8110 * fax: 925-600-8112
E-mail: itaa@itaa-net.org • Web site: http://www.itaa-net.org

Index

abuse, 20, 112, 133, 199-211, 220, 226, 255, 281, 298
adaptation, 31, 54, 55, 57, 59, 63, 93, 123, 142, 194, 220, 225
Adapted Child, 79, 144
Adult ego state, 68, 70, 79, 98, 108, 116, 119, 128, 133, 138, 144, 147, 148, 201, 203-205, 218
affect, 9, 13, 14, 19, 23, 24, 26, 28, 30-33, 36, 37, 41, 46, 71, 72, 81, 91, 102, 105, 114, 116-119, 122, 123, 133, 147-149, 167, 168, 172, 176, 177, 179, 188, 190, 192, 199-205, 207-209, 226, 231, 259, 271, 276, 277, 279, 281, 286, 288, 303
affective edge, 133, 203-205, 209
aggression, 10, 69, 71, 108, 110, 120, 154, 168, 200, 220, 224, 291
ambivalence, 71, 116, 120, 147, 167, 224, 226, 241, 271
anger, 9, 10, 12, 14, 24, 35, 36, 87, 91, 112, 119, 120, 146, 151, 218, 219, 253, 267, 291, 300
anxiety, 10, 12, 14, 21, 27, 31-34, 40, 42, 44, 81, 88, 95, 112, 117, 118, 120, 121, 127, 159-161, 168, 178, 179, 185-189, 194, 202, 204, 207, 218, 221, 241, 245, 260, 265, 269, 279, 281, 285-287, 291
Aron, Lewis, 41, 42, 83, 134, 171, 172, 174, 175, 177, 180
assessment, 7, 11, 16, 20-22, 29, 103, 186, 194, 256, 273, 290
attachment, 41, 46, 58, 61, 66, 68-70, 72-76, 120, 121, 125, 127, 128, 142, 145, 169, 173, 185, 187, 209, 230, 255
attunement, 66, 69, 70, 72-75, 127, 145, 169
autistic, 145, 173
autonomy, 5, 12, 27, 53, 56-59, 61, 98, 115, 120, 174, 185, 186, 231, 232, 235, 238, 242, 259, 281, 291, 294
avoidance, 21, 28, 87, 121, 177, 209, 241, 259, 278, 291
awareness, 12, 21, 27-31, 34, 41, 43, 58, 68, 70, 79-81, 92-95, 98-101, 103, 106, 108, 112, 115, 119, 120, 122, 123, 128, 133, 135-138, 140, 145, 149, 150, 153, 164, 179-182, 185, 186, 193, 194, 199-210, 220, 222, 225, 226, 231, 258, 277, 279, 281
behavior, 6, 7, 16, 19, 20, 25, 29, 30, 32-34, 43, 44, 51, 58, 60, 64, 67, 71, 82, 85-87, 93, 94, 97, 101, 102, 117, 119, 120, 122, 129, 142, 144, 145, 147-149, 163, 166, 167, 169, 195-197, 203, 229, 231, 234, 236, 240, 246, 261, 268, 269, 286, 297-299
Berne, Eric, 4, 6, 7, 8, 10, 11, 16-18, 20, 23, 25, 27, 29-31, 53, 56-60, 66-70, 73-75, 78-82, 90-95, 97-112, 115-119, 125-128, 135, 138, 139, 141-145, 147, 148, 150, 152, 153, 155, 162-164, 169, 171, 172, 191, 205, 209, 215, 217, 218, 221, 225, 227, 233, 236, 253, 255, 258-262, 268, 271, 298, 303
biological, 55, 92, 110, 220, 229, 256
bodily experience, 30, 71, 81, 94, 101, 138, 139, 169, 172, 173, 176, 180, 194, 279
body, 4, 9, 13, 14, 28-31, 33, 46, 52, 69, 71, 80-82, 90, 94, 98, 102, 105-107, 109, 117, 118, 121, 122, 133-142, 145, 146, 148-154, 156-164, 166-183, 185-197, 199, 200, 202, 204-211, 225, 226, 245, 251, 254, 256, 258, 259, 267, 275-282
body psychotherapy, 98, 134-136, 138-140, 176, 177, 182, 183, 185, 186, 192, 193, 207, 209, 281
bodywork, 135-137, 139, 180-183, 192, 206-208, 223, 276, 278
Bollas, Christopher, 3, 32, 42, 51, 52, 70, 73-75, 82, 84, 87, 88, 90, 94, 95, 97, 98, 101-109, 111, 113, 129, 145, 162, 164, 167, 168, 174, 287
borderline personality, 195
Bowlby, John, 69, 70, 75, 125, 200
brain, 5, 12-14, 54, 99, 141-143, 145, 147-149, 152-155, 268, 303
brain research, 12, 141, 142, 153, 155
Bucci, Wilma, 69, 95, 141, 145, 147, 151, 152, 163-166, 173, 181, 271
canon, 16, 18, 80, 102, 115, 125, 178
caring, 40, 56, 184, 203, 285
catharsis, 133, 193, 200, 205, 206, 226
Cathexis, 54, 97, 116, 144, 158
change, 3, 5-7, 9, 10, 12, 13, 18-20, 23, 25-27, 31, 33, 34, 36, 43, 46, 52, 54-57, 61, 62, 64, 66-69, 71, 74, 79-81, 83, 90, 92, 101, 105, 106, 108, 118, 119, 122, 125, 126, 128, 133, 139, 140, 148, 149, 153, 154, 161, 163, 167, 178, 183, 185, 186, 189, 193, 194, 205, 207, 221, 225, 231-234, 236, 243, 255, 256, 258, 259, 262, 267, 275, 278, 284, 285, 291, 296, 303
character analysis, 178, 193
character defenses, 80, 87, 122, 179, 186, 209
character structure, 81, 84, 185, 256, 277, 278
Chess and Thomas, 54-56, 58, 61
Child ego state, 25, 30, 31, 52, 63, 68, 79, 93, 94, 109, 114-117, 119, 121, 123, 128, 135, 138, 141-145, 147, 148, 150, 152, 154, 155, 159, 169, 201, 203, 236, 261
cognition, 56, 78, 105, 123, 148, 149, 168, 181, 202

cognitive, 6, 7, 9, 12, 13, 23, 30, 31, 54, 56, 64, 66, 68, 69, 79, 80, 95, 98-100, 103, 114, 116, 119, 122, 123, 127, 139, 148, 149, 151-153, 162, 163, 167-169, 173, 176, 178, 180, 181, 185, 186, 193-195, 200, 205, 206, 269, 273, 276, 277
cognitive/behavioral, 6, 7, 64, 66, 79, 119, 127, 162
collaboration, 3, 16, 17, 21, 154
communication, 3, 25-27, 30, 74, 78, 80-84, 87, 88, 91, 92, 94, 98, 101, 103, 105, 106, 119, 122, 137, 142, 151, 153, 163, 167, 169, 176, 177, 206, 221, 230, 244, 275, 276
conflict, 10, 17, 18, 20, 24, 35, 46, 53, 59, 62, 66, 68, 71, 73, 75, 79, 80, 92, 112, 116, 121, 123, 129, 136, 161, 162, 178, 185, 187, 188, 202, 227, 242, 244-246, 259, 262, 265, 280, 288, 298
confrontation, 21, 67, 68, 79, 80, 116, 122, 128, 133, 146, 166, 185, 193, 205, 241, 254, 258, 287
conscious, 23, 26, 27, 30, 31, 33, 34, 51, 78, 80, 81, 84, 85, 90, 92, 95, 98-102, 104, 106, 112, 122, 135, 136, 139, 140, 142, 145, 147, 151, 162, 163, 166, 180-182, 185, 190, 194, 199, 201, 202, 204, 209, 242, 246, 261, 271, 273, 287
consciousness, 24, 30, 71, 79, 93-95, 99, 103, 147, 169, 181, 182, 202, 203, 209, 254, 256
contact, 3, 16, 17, 20, 21, 23, 24, 28, 29, 31, 43, 70, 72, 73, 78, 79, 100, 114, 119-122, 135-137, 140, 142, 144, 176, 179, 183-185, 187, 189-192, 195-197, 202-207, 209, 222, 225, 243, 251, 254, 275-281, 287, 288, 292
containing, 36, 79, 120, 280
contracts, 10, 16, 17, 19, 28, 79, 81, 84, 85, 114, 117, 122, 187, 206, 221, 225, 234, 235, 239, 241, 242, 246
Cornell, William F., 30, 66, 74, 78, 81, 82, 94, 97, 100, 101, 109, 116, 117, 121, 128, 135-140, 154, 155, 159, 161, 163, 166, 180, 184, 192, 206, 208, 209, 215, 225, 230, 235, 238, 241, 258, 275, 295
counseling, 7, 24, 52, 113-117, 119-124, 163, 169, 179, 215, 218, 220, 238, 239, 243, 246, 251, 262, 275, 284
countertransference, 24-27, 41, 44-46, 52, 81, 83-85, 106, 107, 109, 121, 140, 153, 155, 162, 163, 174, 177, 243, 246, 251, 272, 278, 283, 285-287, 290, 302, 303
couple, 5, 27-29, 31, 33, 36, 37, 41, 43, 45, 83, 84, 109, 159, 174, 189, 221, 224, 299
creativity, 9, 52, 53, 74, 75, 93, 109, 116, 162, 177, 287, 303
deadening, 28, 44, 81, 138, 146, 278-280, 303
decision, 9, 25, 32, 35, 37, 43, 57, 59, 62, 85, 86, 90, 93, 100, 119, 137, 184, 242-244, 246, 290, 293, 294, 298
deconfusion, 220
decontamination, 220
defenses, 13, 20, 34, 55, 80, 81, 87, 91, 93, 95, 122, 133, 144, 155, 179, 180, 185, 186, 191, 202, 204, 205, 209, 241

delusion, 263
denial, 20, 87, 117, 200-205, 207-209, 259
depression, 5, 9, 10, 12-14, 18, 20, 34, 85, 87, 107, 112, 119, 120, 146, 186-188, 199, 200, 269, 290
despair, 44, 112, 120, 121, 257-260, 263, 290, 291, 293, 294, 298
development, 6, 8-13, 17, 20-22, 24, 27, 28, 30, 42, 54-65, 68-71, 75-78, 91, 92, 94-97, 101, 103, 105, 107, 108, 110, 113-121, 123, 128, 133, 141, 143-146, 149, 150, 152-155, 162, 163, 172-181, 192, 193, 200, 201, 209, 215, 230-233, 235, 238, 241-244, 246, 254, 256, 257, 266-268, 271, 279-282, 284, 303
diagnosis, 17, 20, 23, 29, 83, 114, 176, 182, 185, 186, 218, 244, 270
dialectic, 173, 287
dialogue, 12, 32, 46, 90, 93, 94, 98, 123, 137, 168, 173, 183, 188, 222, 244, 262, 266, 303
disagreement, 17
disavowal, 91, 221
disruption, 36, 169, 186, 194, 200, 202, 203, 207, 280
dissociation, 133, 200-204, 207-209
drama triangle, 59
dream, 67, 136, 177, 179, 190, 191, 227
dyad, 27, 36, 45, 46, 69, 84, 102, 152, 167, 174, 180, 183, 216, 227, 246
dynamic motor theory, 173
dynamics, 6, 22-27, 31, 52, 54, 61, 74, 80, 83, 88, 90, 99, 103, 113-115, 127, 140, 142, 144, 159, 227, 230, 231, 239, 258, 260, 261
ego, 4, 23-25, 29-31, 45, 52, 55, 56, 59, 60, 63, 65-68, 70-72, 78-80, 91-94, 98, 104, 107-110, 113-117, 119, 121, 123, 125-129, 133, 135, 138, 141-145, 147, 148, 150-161, 166, 169-171, 194, 199-205, 208-210, 218, 227, 234, 236, 260, 261, 280, 299
ego function, 31, 56, 93, 155, 166
ego state, 25, 30, 31, 52, 59, 63, 67, 68, 70, 79, 93, 94, 98, 108-110, 114-117, 119, 121, 123, 127-129, 133, 135, 138, 141-145, 147, 148, 150-157, 159, 160, 169, 200, 201, 203-205, 208, 209, 218, 234, 236, 261
emotions, 9, 12, 14, 24, 41, 66, 99, 114, 115, 117-121, 123, 137, 145-148, 155, 185, 186, 189, 199, 201, 207, 267
empathy, 66, 68, 69, 71-77, 99, 100, 105, 125, 127-129, 168, 205, 270, 281, 287-289, 292
empirical, 16, 183, 184, 192-194, 215, 230-232, 268-271
empirical research, 192-194, 268-271
energy, 33, 103, 110, 114, 116, 144, 153, 169, 174, 180, 186, 192, 276, 278, 281
English, Fanita, 1, 63, 64, 91, 115-117, 135
enigmatic signifier, 168, 169
enlivening, 44, 46, 64, 110, 129, 137, 138, 155, 162, 224, 227, 278, 279

Index

Erikson, Erik, 54, 57, 93, 142, 171, 260, 262
Erskine, Richard, 24, 62, 72, 97, 116, 118, 144, 206, 207, 235, 238
ethics, 29, 34, 215, 230, 238, 239, 251, 262, 275, 281
experience, 3-5, 7-9, 11, 12, 14, 16, 18, 20, 21, 24-26, 28-36, 42-47, 51, 55, 56, 58-63, 66, 68-73, 75, 78, 79, 81, 84, 85, 87-91, 93-96, 98-101, 104-109, 112, 116, 117, 119-123, 125, 129, 133, 135-147, 149-164, 166-170, 172-182, 184-186, 188, 190-192, 194-208, 215, 218-220, 223-227, 229, 231-235, 238, 241-243, 245, 251, 252, 255, 259-262, 265-267, 269, 272, 276, 278, 279, 284, 286, 287, 291, 294, 298, 302
experimentation, 10, 28, 41, 46, 117, 133, 185, 192, 229, 235
exploration, 11, 18, 20, 21, 28, 75, 78, 83, 84, 108, 121, 128, 137, 139, 152, 154-156, 160-162, 168, 173, 179, 186, 189, 222, 227, 239, 244, 271, 276, 280, 285, 287, 291, 302
exploratory body, 138
facilitating environment, 68
Fairbairn, W. R. D., 45, 70
family, 5, 7, 8, 10, 11, 14, 15, 17, 20, 21, 31-33, 44, 46, 53-55, 57-59, 61, 62, 64, 94, 101, 106, 107, 117, 118, 143, 151, 152, 177, 186, 187, 189, 199, 201-203, 209, 219, 220, 226, 233, 239, 243, 253-256, 258, 260, 261, 276, 285, 291, 292, 299, 300
fantasy, 8, 21, 63, 67, 78, 87, 127, 128, 154, 161, 168, 189, 222, 291, 292
father, 10, 33, 34, 40-45, 81, 105, 146, 152, 160, 167, 188, 190, 191, 219-222, 226, 239, 251, 256, 293, 295, 297, 298, 300, 301, 303
fear, 9, 13, 32, 35, 42, 63, 68, 73, 83, 84, 87, 112, 119-121, 208, 224, 225, 243, 259, 280, 285, 286, 292, 300
feelings, 6, 9-11, 14, 24, 26, 29, 32, 35, 37, 40, 42, 44, 81, 83, 85, 86, 90, 98, 106, 107, 112, 115, 117, 119, 123, 144, 148, 152, 187, 189, 190, 199-203, 205, 206, 219-221, 236, 244, 245, 267, 277, 281, 284, 286, 290-292, 298
Ferenczi, Sandor, 70
Fischer, Constance, 16, 17, 18, 181
Fischer & Hogan, 149
Freud, 54, 55, 62, 66, 72, 75, 79, 84, 91, 93, 95, 97, 104, 117, 119, 126, 142, 164, 171, 172, 177-179, 183, 221, 260, 263, 265, 268-270, 276, 301
Freudian, 55, 56, 59, 87, 91-93, 97, 102, 142, 172, 253, 303
games, 6, 15, 20, 23, 30, 56, 67, 79, 81, 91, 92, 94, 95, 103, 109, 118, 119, 126, 128, 129, 141, 155, 164, 189, 234, 259, 260
Games People Play, 6, 15, 91, 92, 95, 126, 129
gay, 106, 107, 298
generalized representations, 152, 153
gestalt therapy, 79, 179, 180
gesture, 104, 121, 129, 169, 196

Goulding, Robert & Mary, 24, 25, 62, 93, 116, 144, 238, 290
grief, 120, 121, 191, 222, 224, 256, 288, 291
Groddeck, Georg, 177, 178, 194
group, 4, 6, 11, 18, 27, 28, 45, 52, 57, 59, 67, 69, 79, 80, 88, 90, 92, 95, 98, 102, 115, 116, 125, 126, 128, 129, 133, 144, 159, 172, 186, 191, 192, 205-208, 218, 227, 230, 231, 234-237, 239, 244, 245, 257-264, 272, 275, 297, 299
guilt, 44, 86, 121, 246, 273, 291, 292
hands-on, 137, 180, 182, 188, 189
holding environment, 66-68, 70, 71, 121, 127, 128, 239, 280
hunger, 7, 10, 72, 112, 120, 127, 172, 173, 201, 209, 260, 288
impasse, 23-29, 31, 32, 34-39, 41, 112, 150, 159, 164, 167, 186, 220, 221, 225, 227, 233, 284
incest, 209-211
infant, 29, 30, 33, 56, 58, 60, 61, 68-73, 82, 87, 95, 101-104, 109, 117, 118, 120, 121, 126, 128, 129, 141-143, 145, 148, 149, 152-158, 162, 166, 168-170, 173, 177, 180, 192, 193, 230, 255, 256, 270, 279
infant-parent, 192, 193
initial interview, 16, 17, 19, 21, 235
injunction, 59, 62, 209
interaction, 17, 23, 27, 30, 32, 33, 46, 55, 59, 71, 73, 88, 92, 95, 97, 99, 102, 104, 108, 122, 128, 141, 154, 164, 172, 174, 181, 184, 189, 193, 204, 230, 245
internalization, 24, 67, 75, 105, 117, 205
interpretation, 18, 31, 66-68, 73, 86, 87, 116, 122, 128, 138, 148, 167, 178, 182, 205
interrupt, 136
interrupted gesture, 121
intersubjective, 73, 79, 83, 84, 102-104
intimacy, 9, 14, 23, 24, 27, 28, 31-39, 121, 128, 129, 151, 159, 160, 167, 179, 183, 184, 186, 194, 216, 223-225, 227, 239, 252, 271, 278, 280, 284, 285
intrapsychic, 23-27, 55, 64-68, 73, 74, 79, 80, 93, 102, 103, 114, 126, 128, 144, 162, 164, 166, 172, 187, 193, 240
introjection, 207
intuition, 29, 30, 79, 92, 94, 99-102, 107, 143
Intuition and Ego States, 29, 143
Klein, Melanie, 26, 45, 70, 97, 102, 125, 126, 234, 269, 270
Kleinian, 26, 70, 79, 97, 102, 126, 171
language, 6, 8, 13, 20, 24, 28, 30, 57, 58, 66-68, 79, 80, 90, 97, 98, 104, 107, 119, 125, 126, 138, 142, 148, 149, 151-153, 163, 171, 174, 176, 185, 186, 188, 258, 266, 267, 275, 278, 279, 284, 299
libido, 276
life script, 8, 20, 53, 54, 59, 61, 62, 64, 67, 72, 169
masochism, 32, 92, 185
McLaughlin, James, 3, 4, 23, 36, 38, 41-43, 46, 52, 82, 84, 95, 162, 166, 168, 171, 178, 183, 303

meaning making, 63, 64, 162, 163, 220, 225
medication, 12-14, 186, 187
memory, 30, 34, 69, 78, 83, 94, 98, 99, 101, 105, 145, 153, 156-158, 166, 169, 177, 200, 201, 204, 209, 226, 230, 270, 303
mind, 5-12, 14, 23, 24, 28, 34, 36, 41-43, 46, 52, 56, 57, 67, 73, 80, 82, 84, 91, 93, 95, 98, 99, 102, 106, 107, 109, 121, 126-128, 137-140, 142, 143, 147, 148, 152-158, 160, 161, 167-170, 172-174, 176, 178, 181, 187, 190, 191, 195-199, 202, 209, 220, 221, 224, 227, 251, 254, 267-269, 271, 278, 280-283, 286, 288, 291, 293-295, 303
mind object, 46
Mitchell, Stephen, 45, 87, 95, 162
moral, 14, 54, 56, 221, 254, 266, 267, 271, 284, 288, 299, 301
mother, 7, 10, 11, 33, 40, 41, 44, 51, 56, 58, 67-73, 82, 87, 99, 101, 102, 104, 105, 109, 117, 121, 128, 142, 154, 160-162, 166-169, 173, 174, 177, 180, 186, 191, 219-222, 226, 230, 234, 253, 270, 293, 302, 303
mother-infant, 69, 70, 101, 102, 109, 154, 162, 166
motivation, 31, 56, 69, 78, 90, 95, 100, 114, 119, 140, 147, 148, 150, 155-157, 162, 183, 259
motoric, 69, 71, 99, 149, 151, 154, 155, 163, 176, 178, 180, 185
movement, 14, 27, 71, 80, 81, 102, 117, 120, 122, 126, 136, 138, 142, 148, 149, 167, 168, 173, 174, 176, 177, 179, 180, 182, 190, 204-208, 242, 255, 258, 279, 280, 284
muscles, 99, 149, 174, 188
muscular armor, 117, 163, 178, 278
mutuality, 17, 45, 66, 88, 162, 174, 222, 284, 288
narcissism, 265, 267, 273
narrative, 30, 31, 94, 163, 166
Natural Child, 60, 118, 121, 144
neglect, 13, 36, 42, 108, 172, 200, 201, 209-211, 242, 278, 298
neural network, 153
neurobiology, 158
neurotic, 57, 293
nonconscious, 95, 97-103, 105-108, 110-112
nonverbal, 27, 29, 31, 82, 94, 99, 103, 106, 121, 122, 145, 146, 152, 153, 159, 163, 164, 168, 169, 186, 225, 276, 278
nonverbal symbolic, 163, 164, 168
Nurturing Parent, 70, 206
object relations, 45, 46, 66, 70, 71, 74, 79, 84, 87, 98, 102, 103, 105, 126, 129, 142, 144, 172, 173, 176, 180, 261, 265, 276
objectivity, 7, 218, 221, 232, 241, 242, 259, 287
organization, 25, 29-31, 54, 60, 78, 81, 90, 94-96, 98, 100-102, 104, 125, 126, 135, 136, 139, 141, 143, 145-151, 153-157, 161, 163, 164, 166, 169, 172-174, 176, 180, 181, 185, 217, 256, 257, 281
paradox, 75, 287, 288
parallel process, 24-27, 31, 37

Parent ego state, 67, 68, 127-129, 160, 200, 201, 203, 205, 208, 209, 234, 261
passion, 95, 146, 155, 277
passivity, 122, 220, 224-227
permission, 18, 42, 43, 58, 64, 68, 79, 121, 122, 127, 168, 191, 200, 201, 206, 266, 278
phenomenology, 16, 51, 52, 181, 196-198, 287
physical abuse, 133, 210
physical contact, 28, 137, 140, 183-185, 187, 189-191, 195-197, 205-207, 251, 275-278, 280, 281
plasticity, 54, 55
play, 6, 10, 11, 15, 16, 21, 25, 30, 35, 60, 61, 81, 91, 92, 95, 98, 99, 103, 106, 108, 112, 126, 128, 129, 146, 150, 151, 154, 155, 172, 173, 182, 219, 265, 267, 280
Poland, Warren, 41, 42, 45
posttraumatic stress disorder, 133, 191, 199
potency, 68, 79, 206, 226, 227, 242
preconscious, 30, 79, 82, 90, 93, 94, 100, 102, 155, 181
preoedipal, 56, 68, 70, 177
primal image, 29, 79, 225
Principles of Group Treatment, 57, 67, 79, 80, 88, 90, 92, 95, 126, 129, 144, 260
procedural memory, 99, 166, 169
process, 3, 6-9, 14, 16, 17, 19, 21, 24-27, 29-31, 34, 37, 40, 41, 46, 54-57, 61-70, 72-75, 79-82, 84, 87-89, 98-100, 102-109, 111, 112, 114-117, 119, 120, 122, 123, 126, 127, 133, 136, 138-143, 145, 148-151, 153-158, 162-164, 168, 169, 171-173, 175-180, 183, 187, 188, 193, 194, 200, 202, 205, 206, 208-211, 217, 218, 220-222, 224-227, 233-236, 238-245, 259, 262, 263, 265-267, 270, 271, 273-277, 279-281, 284, 286, 287
process-centered research, 270
projection, 11, 26, 40, 45, 57, 207, 272
projective identification, 24, 26, 31, 45
protocol, 23, 27, 29-39, 57, 80, 82, 94, 95, 100-102, 104, 105, 108, 139, 145, 159, 162-164, 166-170, 225, 226, 258
psychoanalysis, 6, 23, 26, 41, 43, 45-47, 52, 67, 73-80, 83, 88, 91-93, 96-98, 100, 101, 103, 116, 117, 124-126, 129, 142, 148, 156-158, 162-164, 166, 169-175, 177-180, 183, 184, 192, 195-197, 209, 221, 222, 246, 260, 265, 268, 269, 272-274, 276, 281, 287
psychotherapy, 3-16, 19-24, 27, 40, 43, 45, 51, 52, 54, 56, 57, 61, 62, 65-67, 69, 70, 72-76, 78-80, 83, 87-89, 93, 98, 106, 115-117, 121-126, 128, 129, 133-140, 142-144, 146, 147, 149, 151, 154-157, 161-164, 166, 169, 171, 172, 174-187, 189, 191-198, 205-207, 209-211, 215, 218, 222, 229-231, 233, 236-238, 241-243, 245-247, 251-253, 256, 259, 265, 268-288, 302, 303
psychotic, 30-32, 57, 59, 97, 137, 167, 191
PTSD, 133, 208

racket, 94, 119, 121, 234, 235
reality, 29, 41, 44, 54, 56, 57, 62-64, 71, 72, 74, 75, 90, 92, 107, 112, 126, 129, 142, 155, 167, 183, 201-203, 205, 281, 285, 286, 296
recognition hunger, 172
redecision, 25, 30, 93, 97, 116, 220
reexperiencing, 136, 278
referential process, 164, 168, 169
reflection, 12, 28, 37, 56, 67, 75, 120, 123, 126, 163, 168, 191, 205, 224, 227, 239, 243, 251, 253, 263, 272, 273, 281, 290, 291, 297
Reich, Wilhelm, 16, 80, 81, 117, 118, 122, 131, 133, 135, 138, 171, 176, 177, 178, 179, 180, 185, 190, 192, 194, 204, 205, 206, 253-255, 271, 276, 277, 279
Reichian, 80, 81, 114, 117, 133, 138, 162, 163, 171, 180, 182, 187, 191, 205-207, 239, 275, 276, 280
rejection, 10, 91, 185, 279
relational, 10, 12, 13, 27-33, 36, 45, 46, 52, 66, 67, 69, 70, 72-76, 78, 79, 82-84, 94-97, 101, 103, 108, 121, 125, 126, 128, 140, 145, 147-149, 152, 155-158, 162, 164, 166, 168, 170-173, 175-177, 180, 183-187, 191, 194-196, 221, 224, 225, 271, 276, 277, 279-281, 284, 288
relational models, 45, 46, 66, 79, 171
relationship, 6, 9, 12, 14, 16-21, 23-25, 27-29, 31-38, 40-45, 56, 67, 69, 70, 72, 74-76, 78-81, 83, 86-89, 101-103, 106, 108, 109, 115, 117, 120, 121, 123, 126-129, 135, 137, 141, 149, 151, 154, 159-161, 169, 172-174, 177-180, 184, 185, 187, 189-191, 199, 203, 205, 208-210, 217, 219, 220, 222, 224-228, 232, 234-236, 239-247, 255, 259, 266, 270-272, 276-281, 283-288, 302
reparenting, 66, 67, 72, 74, 127, 129
repression, 87, 102, 109, 126, 176, 206
rescuer, 219, 226
resilience, 54, 55, 59, 64, 224, 299
resistance, 17, 21, 41, 59, 80, 174, 179, 217, 242, 256, 276, 280, 294
resonance, 66, 106, 278, 279
reverie, 41, 74, 84, 107, 190, 222
ritual, 46, 293
Rogers, Carl, 51
schizoid character, 278
script, 4, 6-9, 13-15, 20, 23-27, 29-34, 36-38, 52-65, 67, 69, 70, 72, 75, 79-82, 87-94, 100, 101, 103, 106-113, 117-119, 139, 145, 157-164, 166, 167, 169, 200, 205, 225, 226, 232-235, 251, 252, 259, 266, 267, 272, 291, 293, 294, 296-299, 301
script analysis, 62, 64, 111, 162
script decision, 25
script matrix, 59, 110, 299
script protocol, 23, 94, 145, 159, 162, 163, 166, 167, 169, 225
self, 5-7, 9-14, 18, 20-23, 26-28, 30, 31, 36, 37, 39-46, 51, 58, 59, 61, 63-65, 67-78, 82, 84-89, 94-98, 103-112, 118-124, 127-129, 133, 136-140, 142, 147, 151-153, 159, 161, 164, 166-174, 178, 180, 185-188, 191, 194-197, 200-204, 206, 208, 209, 215, 216, 220, 226, 227, 229, 230, 232, 236, 239, 242-245, 251, 255, 256, 258, 261-264, 272, 273, 278, 280-282, 284-288, 291-293, 297, 300, 303
self-disclosure, 40, 42, 43, 45, 46, 284, 286
self-reflection, 12, 28, 123, 243, 251, 281, 297
sensation, 145, 146, 160, 167, 173, 221, 225
sensorimotor, 30, 69, 138, 139, 141, 145, 148-153, 155, 163, 173, 176, 180, 185, 193
sensory, 29, 79, 100, 138, 139, 145, 147, 151, 153, 163, 179, 182, 193, 206, 275
separation, 10-12, 33, 45, 70, 91, 112, 114, 120, 121, 161, 168, 202, 256, 280, 281
sexual abuse, 20, 199, 201, 220
sexuality, 27, 80, 117, 119, 136, 151, 168-170, 179, 216, 223, 226, 288
shame, 9-11, 43, 88, 98, 119, 139, 159, 168, 174, 185, 201, 220, 221, 225, 226, 241, 246, 258, 259, 261-263, 291
skills, 10-12, 14, 20, 21, 27, 51, 58, 61, 62, 99, 114, 115, 119, 139, 150, 151, 163, 183, 215, 217, 220, 229-232, 235, 236, 241-243, 252, 271, 300
social psychiatry, 64, 88, 91, 118, 129, 260, 262, 273, 299
somatic, 30, 31, 69, 71, 80, 81, 94, 98, 101, 106, 110, 114, 117, 118, 121, 122, 133, 136, 138, 139, 141, 145, 147, 149-157, 159, 160, 162-164, 166-169, 173, 176, 177, 179-182, 185-187, 189, 191-196, 205, 224, 225, 256, 276, 277, 281
somatic experience, 31, 136, 139, 150, 159, 168, 180, 225
somatic knowing, 154
somatic organization, 81, 94
somatic processes, 154, 163, 180
somatic/relational, 164, 168
stages of development, 54, 61
Steiner, Claude, 17, 59, 60, 67, 91-93, 206, 255
Stern, Daniel N., 30, 56, 58, 61, 69, 73, 128, 149, 153, 166, 169, 269, 270
Stern, Donnel B., 42, 46, 74, 75, 95, 161
stimulation hunger, 172, 173
stress, 20, 62, 70, 71, 86, 133, 137, 182, 191, 199, 200, 207, 291
strokes, 18, 230, 231
structure hunger, 10, 127, 172, 260
subjective, 12, 99, 123, 128
subjectivity, 42, 45, 46, 78, 83, 84, 171, 172, 174
suffer the illness, 32
suicide, 86, 290-294, 298
supervision, 3, 6, 21, 24, 26, 27, 29, 31, 32, 36-38, 135, 162, 185, 194, 215-218, 220, 227, 229-247, 270, 272, 273, 277
symbiosis, 220, 234
temperament, 55
The Mind in Action, 91, 95, 142

therapeutic canon, 16, 18
therapeutic relationship, 9, 16, 18, 19, 21, 25, 31, 33, 37, 42, 67, 69, 70, 75, 88, 127, 129, 137, 141, 154, 159, 184, 205, 208-210, 220, 222, 227, 239, 240, 243-245, 271, 276, 280, 281, 283-286, 288
thinking, 3, 6, 12-14, 16, 21, 28, 30, 32, 34, 35, 37, 42, 45, 51, 52, 55, 57, 59, 63, 71, 75, 80, 82, 89-92, 94, 95, 97-100, 102, 107, 110, 117, 119, 123, 125, 126, 128, 134-136, 141, 150, 153-155, 162-164, 166, 169, 178, 190, 192, 200, 209, 217, 222, 229-237, 251-253, 255, 259, 260, 265-267, 269, 270, 285-287, 290-292, 297, 301, 303
third-degree, 150, 162
touch, 135, 137, 140, 146, 168, 174, 176, 180, 183-185, 187, 189, 194-198, 205-209, 215, 223, 241, 251, 275-282, 292, 300
transactional analysis, 3-10, 13, 15-17, 22-26, 30, 31, 52-56, 59-70, 72-82, 88, 91-98, 100, 102, 103, 110, 112-119, 121, 123-130, 133-135, 138, 140-145, 147, 148, 150-158, 161, 162, 164, 169-172, 191, 205-207, 209-211, 215-218, 220, 221, 225, 227-239, 241-247, 251, 252, 255-260, 262, 264-266, 268-271, 273, 275, 276, 280-282, 289-291, 293, 294, 298, 299, 303
Transactional Analysis in Psychotherapy, 56, 79, 88, 126, 129, 143, 144, 268, 273
Transactional Analysis Journal, 3, 4, 15, 25, 52, 64, 88, 95 , 100, 129, 135, 140, 156-158, 169, 216, 246, 251, 252, 255-258, 271, 281, 294
transactions, 6, 23, 27, 56, 57, 68, 79, 80, 92, 99, 100, 102, 111, 126, 160
transference, 7, 9, 24-27, 31, 41, 46, 52, 56, 57, 74, 80, 83-87, 92, 93, 121, 140, 153, 155, 159, 162, 163, 174, 177, 193, 195-197, 227, 242, 243, 251, 265, 273, 278, 279, 283, 286, 287
transformational object, 105, 111
trauma, 13, 21, 34, 55, 62, 66, 69, 95, 98, 133, 137, 180, 191-193, 199-202, 205, 208-211, 219, 276,
treatment, 3, 5, 7, 11, 13, 14, 16-27, 32-34, 36, 38-40, 42, 43, 45, 57, 58, 62, 67, 68, 71, 73, 79-81, 83-88, 90, 92, 95, 100, 115, 126, 128, 129, 137, 138, 144, 156-158, 162-164, 167, 169-171, 176-179, 184-187, 191-193, 200, 203-211, 215, 218-220, 225, 227, 230, 231, 233-238, 240, 242, 243, 245, 255, 258, 260, 263, 270, 271, 273, 276, 278, 280, 283, 285, 286, 290, 293, 294, 302, 303
treatment plan, 16, 218
trust, 27, 32, 36, 43, 61, 82, 83, 168, 204, 225, 240, 244, 257, 259, 262, 263
unconscious, 13, 25-32, 34, 36, 44, 46, 51, 62, 70, 74, 78-85, 87-96, 98, 100-102, 105, 109, 111, 116, 126, 136, 140, 152, 154-157, 162, 164, 166, 167, 169, 171, 174, 177, 181, 182, 185, 202, 221, 222, 243, 254, 271, 273
Vaillant, George, 20, 53, 54, 55, 57, 63
verbal, 29, 73, 82, 88, 92, 95, 103, 108, 137, 146, 148, 150-152, 163, 164, 166, 168, 173, 174, 177, 178, 180, 183, 186-189, 205, 222, 277
verbal symbolic, 163, 164, 166, 168
victim, 34, 59, 121, 200, 202, 203, 259, 261
violence, 120, 199-201, 205, 209-211, 253-257, 259, 261, 262, 276, 285, 295, 296, 298, 299, 301
vitality, 9, 37, 41, 52, 54, 62, 64, 80, 81, 94, 109, 114-117, 119, 121-123, 146, 176, 179, 180, 187, 194, 201, 202, 224, 278, 279, 285, 303
vulnerability, 11, 21, 26, 27, 37, 41, 43, 45, 46, 72, 88, 111, 117, 123, 139, 186, 187, 203, 266, 272, 278, 300
What Do You Say After You Say Hello?, 57, 69, 80, 90, 100, 144, 209
Winnicott, D. W., 42, 45, 68-73, 75, 82, 86, 98, 102, 108, 111, 120-121, 125, 126-129, 149, 155, 162-163, 174, 266, 269, 280
withdrawal, 43, 69, 120, 128, 146, 185, 191, 204, 207, 278, 280
working couple, 27, 28, 31, 221
working through, 177, 193, 208, 265, 269